SIAM AND THE WEST
1500–1700

SIAM AND THE WEST
1500–1700

BY

DIRK VAN DER CRUYSSE

TRANSLATED BY

MICHAEL SMITHIES

SILKWORM BOOKS

First published as *Louis XIV et le Siam*
Paris, Fayard, 1991

ISBN 974-7551-57-8

First published in 2002 by
Silkworm Books
104/5 Chiang Mai–Hot Road, M. 7, Chiang Mai 50200, Thailand
E-mail: silkworm@loxinfo.co.th

Set in 11.5 pt. Garamond by Silk Type
Printed by O. S. Printing House, Bangkok

01 02 03 04 05 5 4 3 2 1

"For us, Great King, overwhelmed by your blessings, charmed by your virtues, touched to the bottom of the heart by your goodness, caught by surprise at the sight of your profound wisdom and of all the miracles of your reign, our life seems too short, and the whole world too small, to publish what we think about it . . . The whole Orient will soon know, and all the centuries will come to learn, of the incomparable virtues of Louis the Great . . . "

First Siamese ambassador, Kosa Pan, to Louis XIV, Versailles, 14 January 1687

"Sire . . . posterity will count among the conquests of Louis the Great the kings of Siam and China bowing before the cross of Jesus Christ. With you one is not embarrassed to give unto Caesar what belongs to Caesar, and to God what belongs to God, since today in France God and Caesar have but the same interest."

Guy Tachard, S.J., Dedication to Louis XIV, *Second voyage au Royaume de Siam,* 1689

"There are few episodes in French history more remarkable than the events connected with the intercourse between the Court of Versailles and that of Siam in the reign of Louis XIV."

Sir John Bowring, *The Kingdom and People of Siam*, 1857, II, 69

To my sons Alexander and Christopher, who early on discovered Thailand, and endured me throughout my long intellectual journey to Siam

CONTENTS

ACKNOWLEDGEMENTS

The first edition of this book was the result of meetings, long discussions, and research in numerous archival collections and libraries. As I wrote it, I met everywhere more sympathy and assistance than I could reasonably hope to find. I shall not repeat here my debts to the numerous persons who helped me prepare that edition, though my gratitude remains undiminished.

For this revised English edition, I must thank the trustees of the Toyota Foundation and the French Culture Ministry for supporting the translation of the book, and Ms Trasvin Jittidecharak for being willing to undertake its publication.

Soon after this book first appeared in French, I made the acquaintance of Michael Smithies at a dinner at the Belgian embassy in Bangkok. Far from being vexed at my having called him a "gifted parodist" (he had just published a charming historical fiction, the personal memorials of Kosa Pan), he offered me his friendship. A recognized authority on the history of contacts between South-East Asia and the West, and a prolific author, he was willing to undertake the translation of this book. I would like to express my gratitude to him here, for I could not find a better nor a more gifted translator. The changes we have made to the original text are designed to bring it up to date and be more appropriate for an English-reading public.

PREFACE

WHEN THIS book was first published in 1991, we had to go back more than a century to encounter the most recent books in French devoted to the highly colourful history of relations between Louis XIV of France and Somdet Phra Narai of Siam. Little had been done in France since the two small publications which Etienne Gallois and Lucien Lanier produced in 1862 and 1883[1] devoted to the exchange of embassies between Louis XIV and Phra Narai.

We had to be grateful, though for the subsequent publication outside France of two key documents, the *Mémoire sur la vie de Constance Phaulkon* of Fr Claude de Bèze, and the *Voyage de Siam* of Fr Joachim Bouvet.[2] The exhibition organized at the Orangerie in Paris by the Musée Guimet for the third centenary of the first embassy to Siam and the recent republication of the original 1691 French edition of La Loubère's *Royaume de Siam* (not to mention two recent reprints of the English translation of 1693)[3] and two editions of the Siamese memoirs of Forbin,[4] indicate that the focus of attention is turning once again to this extraordinary episode, and gives rise to the hope that other contemporary texts dealing with Siam, published three hundred years ago or still unpublished, will see the light of day. Indeed, since this book was first published, Céberet's account of his mission of 1687–1688 has appeared in French,[5] Choisy's *Journal* has appeared in English for the first time and been republished in French,[6] and the present publisher has produced a volume incorporating Chaumont's account of his embassy, Choisy's reflections on it,[7] and a book giving François Martin's viewpoint on events in Siam as seen from Pondichéry.[8] The Siam Society has continued to support research into this period in its long-established *Journal of the Siam Society*, and has published a facsimile edition and translation of the Mabre-Cramoisy brochure of discourses given at Versailles by the Siamese ambassadors in 1686 and 1687[9] and a volume devoted to the enigmatic adventurer Phaulkon,[10] a key player in the events of 1685–1688. Most recently an important text by de La Touche, presumed lost, has been published, giving an eye-witness account of the attack on the French in Mergui in 1688.[11] Another eye-witness account of the siege of Bangkok, by Vollant des Verquains, now unobtainable in French, is due to appear in English translation shortly.[12]

The images of ambassadors from Versailles in wigs and lace ruffles mounted on elephants crossing rice fields, and of Siamese mandarins prostrate before the throne of Louis XIV, sum up a chapter of diplomatic and cultural history. At the end of the seventeenth century, the West began to discover exotic cultures thanks to the accounts of travellers and missionaries. The court of Louis XIV, imbued with its own excellence and intolerant of other modes of behaviour and thought, was little adapted to discoveries of this nature.

It was by chance that the original French edition of the present work appeared exactly three hundred years after Simon de La Loubère's two-volumed *Royaume de Siam*, the most important book devoted to Siam to appear to that date. La Loubère wrote that "it would not be just to contemn every thing, that resembles not what we do now see in the Court of France,"[13] and it is in this spirit that *Siam and the West 1500–1700* has been conceived. But it goes without saying that the subject poses specific problems. Let us consider some.

First of all, a confession. One can be a specialist in the seventeenth century devoted to the literature and cultures of the age, without limiting oneself to the geographic and historic parameters normally imposed. Thirty years of travel and sometimes lengthy stays in Asia, a study of Buddhism, readings and reflections on the nature of relationships between East and West preceded this book. It was not by chance that I was keen to explore the ground between the Catholic Louis XIV, who revoked the Edict of Nantes giving freedom of worship to Protestants, and the serenely Buddhist Siam of Somdet Phra Narai, considered as a *dharmachakravartin* or "monarch who causes the turning of the [Buddhist] Wheel of Law."

It is impossible to explain Franco-Siamese relations without considering the other European nations who preceded the French in Siam: the Portuguese, the Dutch, and the English. Since I come from a Dutch-speaking milieu and have spent some months in Brazil, I was able to read the numerous documents in Portuguese and Dutch relating to the exchanges between Europe and Siam before 1662, when the first group of French arrived, and their comments thereafter.

The first four chapters of this book are devoted to the pre-French period in Siamese-European relations. One cannot understand the problems the French missionaries encountered without knowing something of the history of the *Estado da Índia*, the relations between Portugal and Siam in the sixteenth century, and the *Padroado*. Likewise, one needs to understand the aggressive presence in Siam of the VOC (Verenigde Oostindische Compagnie), which explains why Phra Narai sought an alliance with Louis XIV which temporarily triumphed over the Dutch. Lastly the irresistible rise of the Greek Phaulkon, introduced into Asia by the English East India Company, cannot be understood if one is unaware of the English presence in Siam and the interloping trade conducted by the British employees of the company.

The historian of the period comes up against a formidable problem: the virtual absence of authentic Siamese documents going back to the seventeenth century, which is in such contrast to the wealth of Dutch and French documents, and to a lesser extent Portuguese and English ones, both published and unpublished. The anti-French revolution of 1688 and the pillaging of the ancient capital, Ayutthaya, by the Burmese in 1767 destroyed the documents which, even without these events, would have indubitably been ravaged by humidity and insects. It will be seen that a European historian in the tradition of Herodotus is confronted with a totally different historiography in Asia. Political disturbances and the ravages of the climate do not explain everything; the Orient, with its cyclical (and metempsychotic) viewpoint of history, is far from attaching the same value to events. Historiography, a science in the West, was until not long ago an art in the East, an art where the reality had to be recreated by adding miracles to facts.

Apart from a few very rare Siamese documents of the seventeenth century, studied and translated in 1921 by Georges Coedès, author of the monumental *Recueil des inscriptions du Siam* and then librarian at the Vajirañâna National Library in Bangkok,[14] the historian is mostly reduced to the *Phra Ratcha Phongsawadan* (royal chronicles) and to the *Khamhaikan chao krung kao* (accounts of the Siamese transported to Burma in 1767). The oral nature of these texts, their recent publication in written form, and the predilection for the marvellous have to be emphasized here. In the opinion of contemporary Thai historians, European documents, notably those of the Portuguese, the Dutch, the English, and the French, are more reliable than the poetic texts which give an idealized chronicle of the kingdom of Ayutthaya.

La Loubère noted that "The Siamese History is full of Fables."[15] The *Phongsawadan* relate that during the stay of the Siamese ambassadors in France in 1686, they demonstrated their magic powers by inviting five hundred elite marksmen to hit them, without a single bullet being able to reach them; this was in the marble courtyard before the astonished eyes of Louis XIV and his court. When prostrating themselves before the king in the Mirror Gallery during their solemn audience, the Siamese mandarins noticed that his throne was studded with huge rubies, emeralds, and diamonds which illuminated the king's person with a supernatural light, alternately red, green, and white.

A fragment of the journal of the first Siamese ambassador, Kosa Pan, is held in the archives of the Missions Etrangères in the Rue du Bac, Paris. Thanks to a facsimile edition it is known in Thailand, but the number of specialists capable of reading it is very small. More than delighted at having a Siamese voice among the cacophony of French, English, Dutch, and Portuguese accounts, it seemed to me essential to have this text translated in Bangkok, though this was not an easy undertaking. The complete English translation of Kosa Pan's journal is forthcoming, published by Silkworm Books. Details and extracts of this document appear in chapter 18.

For the same reason I have included extracts from another Asian text, similarly unique in its way, *The Ship of Sulaiman*, a florid Persian account by the scribe Muhammad Ibrahim Muhammad Rabi of an embassy sent by Shah Sulaiman to Ayutthaya in 1685, at the same time as the Chaumont-Choisy embassy was in the country. This Persian mission proposed to convert Phra Narai to Islam, and was very preoccupied by the French embassy hoping to convert the king to Christianity. The summary of this text[16] provides the "Persian interlude" of chapter 15.

The relationship between France and Siam from 1662 to 1690 was very complex, involving diplomatic, ecclesiastical, commercial, naval, and colonial history. But above all, these are embedded in contrastive attitudes and mentalities. The turbulent history of the evangelization of South-East Asia occupies an important place in some chapters in this book. They were written with both admiration and perplexity, as they reveal generosity worthy of the "century of noble souls" and terrifying intellectual myopia. What can one think of missionaries who go to the ends of the earth to combat a religious culture much more ancient and in some respects more deeply implanted than theirs, and about which they had not the least conception? Their descriptions of the "idolatry," "evil practices," and "ridiculous superstitions" of the Siamese show no effort at all to understand Theravada Buddhism. Herein lies in part the reason for their feeble returns.

When one considers, three centuries later, their strategies, quarrels, and suffering, when one reads their accounts and letters, one cannot avoid asking questions about this attempt at "colonization of souls" conducted with so much intolerance. Our perspectives are no longer the same. The historian of attitudes is obliged to reflect on the documents exhumed from archives. Michelet said, "History judges the world, and has as its first duty to shed its respect . . . Everyone and everything has to be reappraised, men and ideas, kings, laws, peoples, dogmas and philosophies . . ."[17] These questions raised in relation to chapter 8 are precisely those which concern specialists of "missionology" or *Missionswissenschaft*, established as a science in 1902.

A few terms need to be defined before concluding. Everyone knows that present-day Thailand was called Siam until 1939. European texts of the sixteenth and seventeenth century use the term Sião or Siam to designate both the kingdom and the capital. Ayutthaya, also known as Odia, Iuthia, or Iudea, was destroyed in 1767, and has only recently been partially reoccupied. King Narai made the city of Lopburi or Lawo his secondary residence, where he passed two-thirds of the year. Our texts speak of Noccheboury, Louvo, or Louveau. To avoid all confusion, I use the term Siam to designate the kingdom, and Ayutthaya and Lopburi to indicate the capital and the secondary royal residence. When other Siamese cities are mentioned, their ancient name is followed by their modern name, as with Pourcelouc (Phitsanulok), Singor (Songkhla), Joncelang (Phuket), etc.

PART ONE
THE PORTUGUESE, THE DUTCH, AND THE ENGLISH

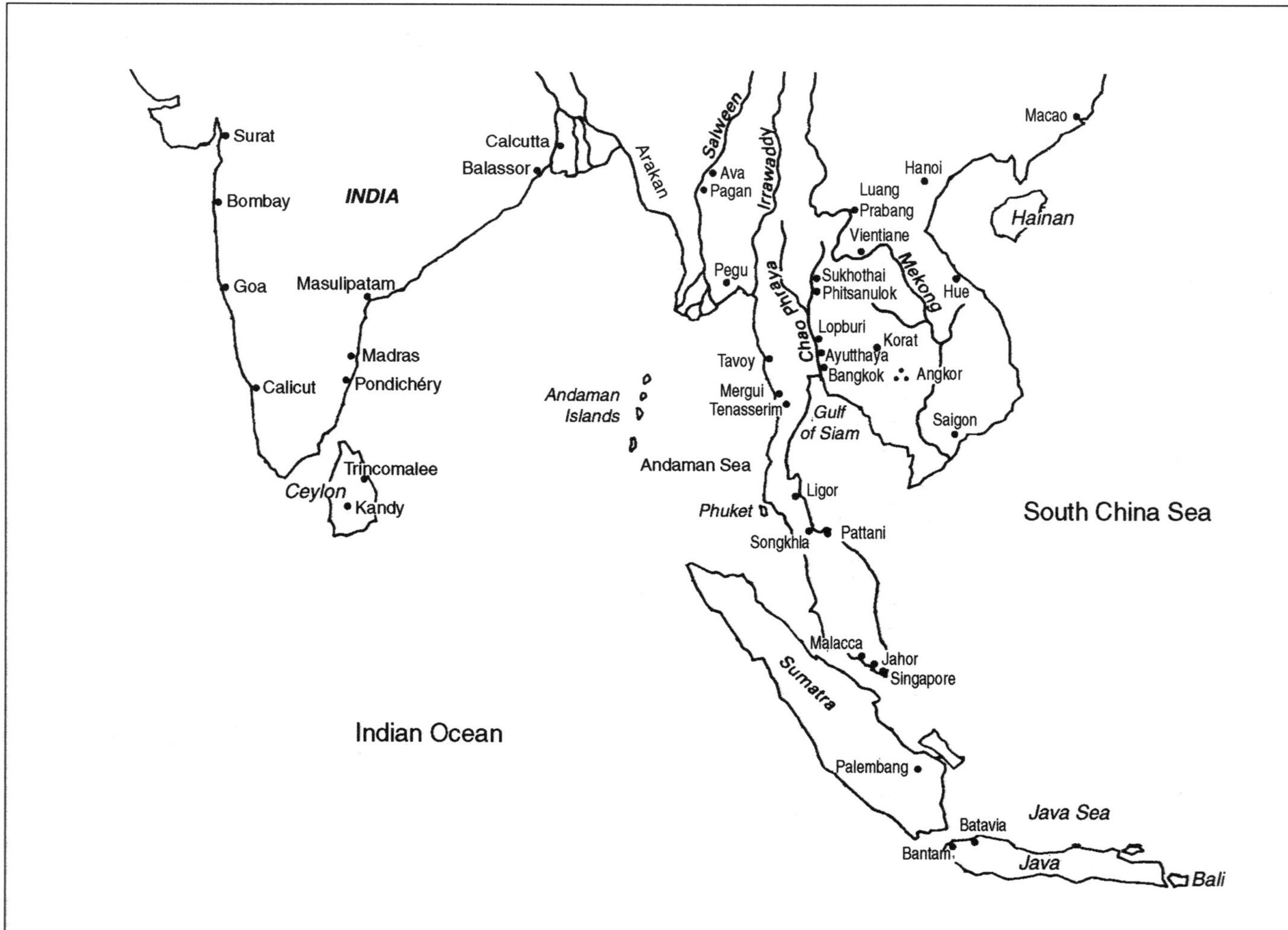

Surat
Bombay
INDIA
Goa
Masulipatam
Madras
Pondichéry
Calicut
Trincomalee
Ceylon
Kandy
Calcutta
Balassor
Arakan
Salween
Ava
Pagan
Irrawaddy
Pegu
Chao Phraya
Andaman Islands
Andaman Sea
Tavoy
Mergui
Tenasserim
Phuket
Songkhla
Pattani
Ligor
Gulf of Siam
Luang Prabang
Vientiane
Sukhothai
Phitsanulok
Mekong
Lopburi
Ayutthaya
Bangkok
Korat
Angkor
Saigon
Hue
Hanoi
Macao
Hainan
South China Sea
Malacca
Jahor
Singapore
Sumatra
Palembang
Indian Ocean
Batavia
Bantam
Java Sea
Java
Bali

CHAPTER ONE

PORTUGAL'S GOLDEN AGE AND SIAM (1510–1580)

SPARE A thought for Nicolo di Conti. This travelling Venetian merchant seems to have been the first European to have visited and described Siam, three-quarters of a century before the discovery of the sea route to the East Indies by Bartolomeu Dias and Vasco da Gama. Clearly enamoured with Asia and speaking several oriental languages, he travelled through Persia, India, and South-East Asia for twenty-five years. He experienced numerous exotic adventures and only saved his skin and the lives of his family by abjuring Christianity.

Thanks to this event which troubled his conscience, we have the account of his travels. When he returned to Venice in 1444, full of remorse, Nicolo went to throw himself at the feet of Pope Eugenius IV. He obtained his pardon on condition that he dictated an account of his Asian peregrinations to the pontifical secretary, the Florentine humanist Poggio Bracciolini.[1] This narration revealed an unknown world, and disclosed the existence of the kingdom of Siam, then governed by Phra Borommaracha II (1424–1448), the eighth king of Ayutthaya.

Between 1425 and 1430 Nicolo di Conti visited Mergui and Tenasserim, the chief towns on the west coast of Siam:

> Leaving the island of Taprobane [Sumatra], I reached in seventeen days with much trouble and travail the town of Tenasserim which is situated at the mouth of a river of the same name. All the land around is full of elephants, and sappanwood grows there in abundance. From there, after a long sea journey, I reached the mouth of the River Ganges . . .

He remarked chiefly on the elephants, numerous on the Kra isthmus—the "elephant's trunk" which separates the Andaman Sea from the Gulf of Siam. Elephants were to continue to fascinate European travellers who devote many enthusiastic and sometimes unbelievable pages of anecdotes to this animal both real and mythical, and so profoundly embedded in the collective conscience of the Siamese people.

PORTUGAL'S OVERSEAS EXPANSION

In spite of the isolated explorations of some enterprising merchants like Nicolo di Conti, and some brave missionaries (like the Flemish Franciscan William of Rubruck, sent by Saint Louis to the court of the Great Khan in 1253),[2] Europe was only aware of one-third of the globe at the end of the Middle Ages. Thanks to the dynamism of the Portuguese people, small in number, and the vision of a junior prince of the House of Avis, the infante Dom Henrique (1394–1460), surnamed *O Navegador* (the Navigator), in scarcely two generations the techniques of naval construction and sea-going exploration were invented or perfected, allowing for a formidable geographic expansion around 1500, the extent of which is even now astonishing.

The scarcity of precious metals in mediaeval Europe and the immense spread of Muslim lands paralysed commerce and made Asian products—silk, precious stones, and spices—virtually inaccessible.[3] The elimination of the intermediaries, who pushed up the prices of exotic merchandise transported by caravans to the Mediterranean commercial hubs of Byzantium and Venice, was the principal objective which fired the imagination of the audacious Portuguese.

Henry the Navigator had read Raymond Lull, who, at the beginning of the fourteenth century, was already suggesting thwarting the Muslim stranglehold on commercial enterprise between Europe and Asia by going round Africa. This rather advanced idea of a consuming country attempting to break up monopolies and seeking its supplies directly from producing countries underlies the great Portuguese exploratory leap in the fifteenth century, by a people who about 1400 scarcely numbered one million.

There were numerous obstacles to be overcome. First of all, vessels capable of sailing the high seas had to be constructed. Then more reliable navigation techniques had to be discovered so that the practice of hugging the coasts could be abandoned. The calculation of the meridian height of the sun, which established the latitudes, provided the key which opened to the Portuguese their great discoveries, though the exact calculation of longitudes would remain a crucial problem until the middle of the eighteenth century. The first navigators who explored the Atlantic only had an approximate idea of its extent.

Progress in naval sciences (navigation, scientific observation of the winds and maritime currents) inspired cartographers who finally woke from their long Ptolemaic slumber. Innovations introduced by the Portuguese (like the graduated meridian, the graduation of longitudes marked on the equator, and before long the theory of loxodromics) led directly to the cylindrical projection of Mercator, and the maps on which the islands and outlines of continents were marked according to the explorations made.[4]

With the impulse of the Navigator (in spite of his acquired name, the prince never travelled on the high seas himself), so-called "round" or "Latin" caraks and caravels were fitted out and crews sent over the Atlantic. The archipelago of Madeira was reached in 1419, the Azores in 1427, the islands of Cape Verde in 1456. In parallel, the systematic exploration of the African coast took place under the supervision of Dom Henrique. The infante moreover established his all-male court at Sagres, at the southernmost point of the Algarve, facing the immensity of the ocean.

The Navigator adopted the French motto "*Talent de bien faire*" (roughly "the ability of doing well"). This ability was very useful to him in combating a curious prejudice firmly entrenched in men's minds that white men who travelled below the equator would immediately be turned into blacks. No doubt the prince had persuasive skills, for Cape Bojador was reached in 1434, and Guinea in 1460, the year of his death. Each discovery was marked on the maps which were used in the following exploration. The boundary stones of the royal arms of Portugal (*padrões*) erected on the beaches symbolized the annexation of new territory in the name of Kings D. João I, D. Duarte, D. Afonso V, and D. João II.

From *padrão* to *padrão*, with a very heavy cost in human lives and ships, Portuguese explorations reached the equator in 1477. Diogo Cão led several expeditions along the coasts of the present-day Congo Republic (the mouth of the Congo was explored in 1483), Angola and Namibia, leading to the historic event of the exploration by Bartolomeu Dias of the bays and capes of South Africa. The discovery of the Cape of Storms (rebaptized Cape of Good Hope) realized an old European dream: finding a sea route to the Indies.

PORTUGUESE MARITIME SUPREMACY AND THE *"ESTADO DA ÍNDIA"*

The expedition led by Vasco da Gama only got under way in 1497, nine years after the return of Bartolomeu Dias. Meantime, Christopher Columbus, who had been unable to convince King D. João II, had found in Spain the means of realizing his dream of crossing the Atlantic and landing in the Indies in 1492. It hardly mattered that he mistook the West Indies for the East Indies, the accomplishment was just as important. The rivalry which the discoveries aroused between Portugal and Spain (finally free of the Moors) inevitably increased.

At the beginning of the fifteenth century, Pope Martin V Colonna had accorded to the Portuguese all the lands they were to discover as far as the Indies "inclusively." This gift was confirmed by Popes Eugenius IV Condulmer, Nicholas V Parentucelli, and Sixtus IV della Rovere. The Treaty of Tordesillas, arbitrated by the Spanish pope Alexander VI Borgia and signed in 1494, accorded to the Spanish a slice of the cake. He fixed a demarcation line which crossed Cape Verde and granted Spain all the lands it discovered 370 leagues to the west of this line. The lack of precision of longitudinal calculations was to lead to serious disputes; it gave rise to the "Molucca question," among others, each of the two crowns situating the spice-producing archipelago on its side of the pontifical longitude.

This division of the planet between the two Iberian nations as though it were an apple becomes comprehensible when one understands that the Holy See, being unable to ensure the evangelization of continents newly discovered or about to be discovered, believed it was acting in the interests of Christianity in dividing them between Portugal and Spain since these countries undertook in exchange to introduce the Gospels (and the Inquisition) in their new possessions. The division of Tordesillas and the exclusivity of missionary work accorded by the popes was doubtless less important in contemporary eyes than in ours. The map of the world, without the Americas,

Oceania, or three-quarters of Africa, seemed almost uninhabited on both sides of the line traced, except for a few oriental kingdoms wreathed in legends.[5]

A year after the Treaty of Tordesillas, D. João II passed away, inconsolable at having lost his heir, the infante D. Afonso, who died as a result of a riding accident at the age of sixteen. It therefore fell to his nephew and successor, D. Manuel, to follow up the discovery of Bartolomeu Dias, in spite of the hesitations of his advisors. One can understand the relief expressed by Vasco da Gama at the beginning of the *Roteiro* (ship's log): "In the name of God, Amen! In the year 1497, King D. Manuel, the first of this name, sent four vessels to make discoveries and go in search of spices . . ." The principle of self-financing was established.

Historically, but without complications, the first voyage of Vasco da Gama took him in five months to Cape Padrone, where Dias had placed his last *padrão*. Going along the coasts of present-day Mozambique, Tanzania, and Kenya, the expedition arrived at Malindi where it found an Arab pilot who in a month made the crossing to Calicut, reached in May 1498. Vasco da Gama returned there in 1502, sporting the grandiose title of *Almirante da Índia* and ready to found, with a brutality which would find competitors, the Portuguese empire of the Indies, the *Estado da Índia*.

One is still astonished at the rapidity of the spread of the Portuguese presence in Asia. Numerous indications point to the fact that this had long been prepared in advance. Avid for geographical information, the infante D. Henrique quizzed Berber, Arab, and Persian merchants. D. João II had sent Pedro de Covilhão to Aden to prepare for the first expedition of Vasco da Gama. Covilhão was able to reach Ormuz, Calicut, and Goa, whence he sent detailed reports to D. João. It was no doubt not accidental that Vasco da Gama found at Malindi an experienced pilot ready to take him to Calicut.

Leaving no doubt as to his intentions, Dom Manuel solemnly assumed the title of "Lord of the navigation, conquest, and commerce with Ethiopia, Arabia, Persia, and India." The *Estado da Índia* was founded and put on a firm footing by the viceroys Francisco de Almeida (1505–1509) and above all Afonso de Albuquerque, the "Portuguese Mars" (1509–1515). The numerous principalities which abounded in the Indian subcontinent facilitated the installation of *feitorias* (factories, or fortified warehouses) on the Malabar coast, at Calicut, Cochin, and Goa, henceforth the capital of Portuguese India.

Albuquerque wrote to D. Manuel in April 1512, "Goa will be my seat forever, and it is here that our chief forces must remain. It is a stronghold, a territory and a port from whence one can conquer the Indies, and can withstand all attacks against it."[6] This declaration was prophetic. It was only in 1962, four centuries and a half later, that India annexed Goa, to which it had long laid claim.

Dom Manuel and his viceroys appreciated the enormous problems posed by the conquest by a small European nation of a vast colonial empire at the other end of the world. If the armaments, the vessels, and nautical prowess of the Portuguese were superior, they had to be careful that military expenditure did not absorb all the profits brought by trade. From this came the decision not to limit themselves to exchanges between the parent state and its colonies, but to corner inter-Asiatic trade routes, all to the profit of the crown which financed the military effort. With the same concern for profitability, Portugal in principal renounced territorial conquests, being content with a network of fortified *feitorias* well placed to take part in commercial dealings as peacefully as possible. This atmosphere of armed détente was to facilitate the evangelization of Asian people; Portuguese soldiers, traders, and missionaries were to travel hand in hand.

The royal monopoly led to the establishment of the *Casa da Índia* in Lisbon. This was charged with the accountability of the commercial activities in the Portuguese outposts and the organization of the *Carreira da Índia*, that is, the fleets of armed caraks which left every year in March or April, reached India in September or October, departed from India around Christmas, and returned to Lisbon in the middle of summer. The profit margins sometimes reached five thousand per cent and were the envy of all Europe.

The heroic conquest of Malacca in 1511, a hub of the spice trade and a strategic place for the control of the straits between Sumatra and the Malay peninsula, was Albuquerque's achievement. Even before taking the city, the viceroy received envoys from Sumatran and Javanese sultans, and sent ambassadors to the court of Phra Ramathibodi II of Siam, the twelfth king of Ayutthaya. Other envoys established contacts the same year with the kingdom of Pegu and the Moluccas. A first delegation, in the form of a Portuguese junk loaded with spices, set off for China in 1513. On the death of Albuquerque in 1515, the prestige of Portugal was such that all Asian sovereigns, from the Persian Gulf to the South China Sea, maintained deferential relations with its viceroy.

THE ESTABLISHMENT OF THE PORTUGUESE IN SIAM

The conquest of Malacca placed Portugal within the Siamese sphere of influence, for the city was governed by a Malay sultan who was a vassal of the King of Siam. The sultan had rebelled against the king in 1489, but Phra Intharacha II had given him a lesson in good behaviour and constrained him to submission.

Albuquerque did not wait for the fall of Malacca to send Duarte Fernandes, who spoke Malay, to the court at Ayutthaya, the Siamese capital. Fernandes embarked on a Chinese junk, bearing a most polite letter justifying the Portuguese conquest. Received in audience by Phra Ramathibodi II, he presented the king on behalf of the viceroy a golden sword in a sheath studded with diamonds. The Siamese king was not opposed to the Portuguese conquest of Malacca.

Fernandes returned to Malacca accompanied by a Siamese envoy bearing presents for Albuquerque, and charged with observing the "Oriental Lisbon" which Malacca was becoming; the King of Siam clearly wished to evaluate the military and technical superiority of the Portuguese. The letter brought by the ambassador showed the king so well disposed that in 1512 Albuquerque sent off a second envoy, António de Miranda de Azevedo. He was accompanied by Manuel Fragoso who spent two years in Ayutthaya, and returned to Goa in 1514, accompanied by a Siamese envoy bearing a letter from Phra Ramathibodi II addressed to the King of Portugal.

Two years later, the Portuguese governor of Malacca sent a third embassy to Ayutthaya. It was led by Duarte de Coelho who had taken part in the embassy of Miranda de Azevedo and had returned to Ayutthaya because the junk on which he should have left for China had been shipwrecked. Coelho signed a treaty of friendship and commerce between Portugal and Siam; it was the first time Siam had allied itself with a European nation.

Portugal undertook to supply muskets, powder, and munitions to Siam; it obtained in exchange the right to establish godowns (warehouses) in Ayutthaya, Ligor (Nakhon Si Thammarat), and Pattani in the south, and Tenasserim and Mergui on the west coast. These last two towns, now in Burmese territory, were located at the end of the route linking the capital with the Andaman Sea, and could control commerce in the Gulf of Bengal as far as the Coromandel Coast. These *feitorias* prospered very quickly. We know that the one at Pattani, founded in the year of the treaty by Manuel Falcão, by

1538 had three hundred Portuguese who were actively engaged in trade.

The treaty of 1516 also granted the Portuguese the right to practise their religion without hindrance, thus opening the door to missionaries. This spirit of tolerance, so foreign to their own culture (think of the anti-Semitism of D. João II and D. Manuel), filled the Portuguese ambassadors with admiration. It doubtless explains why they consented without objections to the establishment of Siamese merchants and artisans in Malacca. Phra Ramathibodi II for his part authorized Duarte de Coelho to erect at Ayutthaya a *padrão* surmounted by a cross;[7] the king was certainly unaware of the symbolism of this action.

The Siamese had observed the Portuguese for five years and finished by understanding that their ambitions were commercial rather than territorial. They desired no more than to trade with these Europeans and buy their firearms. The intermittent wars of the kings of Ayutthaya against the rulers of Chiang Mai, Pegu, Ava, and Cambodia created a pressing need for the latest military equipment. The Portuguese did not limit themselves to selling arms to the Siamese; they assisted in the organization of the Siamese army and even took part in their military campaigns.

João de Barros informs us that Francisco de Castro was sent by D. João III to Siam in 1540 to claim from Phra Chairacha, the fifteenth king of Ayutthaya, the return of Domingo de Seixas who was thought to be held captive in Siam since 1517. But, far from being detained against his will, Seixas commanded a Siamese army which was bringing to heel mountain tribes in the north. Phra Chairacha allowed him to return to Portugal with sixteen of his companions, after having generously compensated them for their services.[8] Fernão Mendes Pinto relates for his part that 120 Portuguese mercenaries distinguished themselves in the army of Phra Chairacha in 1538, when the king marched against the redoubtable Burmese from Pegu. Not content with reinforcing the Siamese army and familiarizing its soldiers with European weapons, the mercenaries apparently also taught them how to make muskets and cast cannons. But the Portuguese, still according to Mendes Pinto, provided the same services to the Burmese.

Phra Chairacha granted a plot of land to the south of the capital between the Chao Phraya and the western canal, to 120 Portuguese mercenaries who had fought against the Burmese at Muang Chiang

Kran in 1540. A fairly numerous Portuguese community subsequently developed there, constituting the *Mu Ban Potuget*, the Portuguese village or "camp."

Everything points to the Portuguese presence in Siam being felicitous and profitable throughout the sixteenth century. From their godown in Pattani, the Portuguese established contact with the Ming Chinese; the first arrived in Canton in 1517. This new expansion was to lead to a durable success. In 1557 the Ming emperor Shih-tsung authorized "the people from the other shore" to establish themselves in Macao (at first named Porto do Nome de Deus), advantageously situated at the mouth of the Pearl River, some hundred kilometres from Canton. Active trade soon linked Macao, Japan, and the Philippines. Macao formally remained Portuguese until 1999.

"SURROUNDED BY SO MANY INFIDELS"

The huge Portuguese colonial enterprise in Asia in the sixteenth century was matched by an equally energetic effort to Christianize the continent. Portugal did not forget the condition attached to its share of half of the world. Camões summed up the situation: "They come to propagate the law of Christ and impose new customs and a new king."[9]

The *Padroado*, or *Ius Patronatus,* an agreement between Spain and Portugal arranged by the pope, granted the Portuguese crown an exclusive authority in religious matters between the Cape of Good Hope and Japan, since it was to supply missionary cadres. Very strict regulations required the presence of at least one missionary on each ship leaving for the East Indies. Documents indicate that in some cases captains, impatient to profit by favourable winds, seized priests in the streets of Lisbon in order to be able to set sail. Taken to Asia willingly or by force, these missionaries sowed the good word with indubitable success. They were reproached, it is true, with being more sensitive to the quantity of infidels they hastily baptized (some champions boasted of having officiated at a thousand baptisms in a single day) than to the quality and solidity of their conversions.

The great Asian proselytizing effort began in tandem with the Portuguese conquests. When he left Lisbon in 1503, Afonso de Albuquerque was accompanied by five missionary Dominicans. Among them was the indefatigable Domingo de Souza who combined the functions of the viceroy's confessor, counsellor, and inseparable companion. The order of Preaching Friars, or Dominicans, was to have an important role. The first bishop to administer the Church in the Indies, Eduardo Nuñez, was a Dominican. One of the two fleets which left in 1503 transported a dozen Minor Friars or Franciscans, and the other, a dozen Preaching Friars.

The progress these two orders made was impressive. By 1549 there were no less than eighteen Dominican churches or convents in the Malaccan peninsula and neighbouring islands. The first Portuguese Dominicans soon entered Siam, Cambodia, and China. In 1557 Pope Paul IV Carafa created three sees in the Portuguese possessions: Goa, the metropolitan and primate of the East, with suffragan bishops in Malacca and Cochin (Malabar). The first archbishop of Goa, Gaspard de León Pereira, was archdeacon of Evora, but his two suffragan bishops were Dominicans.

The Jesuits, founded by Ignatius Loyola in 1534 and recognized by Pope Paul III Farnese in 1540, followed in the steps of the Dominicans and Franciscans. When Francis Xavier disembarked in Goa in 1542, he noted his first impressions in a letter to Ignatius Loyola: "It is an entirely Christian city. We must thank our Lord God, when one realizes how much the name of Christ is venerated in a such a distant land and in the midst of so many infidels."[10] Ten years later, when he wanted to enter China, he died exhausted near Macao, after preaching the Gospel and baptizing with all his might in Malabar, the Moluccas, and Japan.

The young Company of Jesus (the official name of the Jesuit order) played an important part in the missionary effort in Asia, but it was the Dominicans who were to try and introduce Christianity into Siam. The early days of the Dominican mission in Ayutthaya were related in 1865 by a French Dominican, Fr Meynard. His epic account, which is presented like a martyrology destined for the *Guinness Book of Records*, was corrected in 1931 by a less impassioned German colleague, Fr Biermann.[11]

Fathers Jerónimo da Cruz and Sebastião do Couto arrived from Malacca in Ayutthaya in 1555 according to some, 1567 according to others. "They needed little time to study the Siamese language, and . . . converted a great number of infidels. The Muslims, jealous of the progress of Christianity and fearing for their trade, given the power of the Portuguese, resolved to kill the missionaries." Jerónimo da Cruz was assassinated with a thrust from a lance soon after he arrived, and three of his companions were massacred in February 1569 during the siege of Ayutthaya by the Burmese, who eliminated Phra Chakkraphat and installed Phra Maha Thammaracha on the throne. These Fathers were not cut to pieces by the Buddhist Siamese whose reputation for tolerance was well established, but by the powerful colony of Muslims, "Moors," who, fearful for their influence and their trading interests, profited by the confusion in 1569 to eliminate the Dominicans. These misfortunes and the troubles which shook Siam during the following years explain the Portuguese Dominicans' departure from the kingdom about 1575. The Spanish Franciscans, who tried to establish themselves in 1582, were likewise constrained to abandon Siam after two years.[12] But the consequences of Phra Naresuan's wars, and notably his 1593 conquest of the capital of Cambodia, Lovek, brought the Dominicans back to Siam.

Two Fathers, Jorge da Mota and Luis da Fonseca, were among the prisoners of war deported from Lovek to Ayutthaya. They gained the confidence of the king, who authorized them to preach the Gospels. The version of events offered by Fr Meynard is subject to caution:

> A few years later, Fathers Jorge da Mota and Luis da Fonseca, taken prisoner in Cambodia by the King of Siam, profited by their exile to evangelize this kingdom once more. Their success was not to last. Luis da Fonseca was massacred at the altar, and Jorge da Mota died of wounds when returning to Malacca. . . . Belchior da Luz . . . arrived at the port of Martaban, a dependency of Siam, without suspecting the recent martyrdom of his colleagues. The king, still furious at the escape of Fr Jorge da Mota, had sworn an oath that, if he could be taken, he would be roasted in a frying pan . . . The arrival of Fr Belchior and his resemblance in dress and appearance to the fugitive appeared to the governor of Martaban a good occasion to pay court to the king, providing him with the means of assuaging his passion and satisfying his desire for vengeance. But God provides for all things. This prince, until then hostile to the missionaries, received this Dominican very well and granted him full authority to preach the Gospel in his realm and even to build a church, the expenses of which he would defray.[13]

This apparent miracle touching the soul of an Asiatic despot thirsting for Christian blood can be better understood in the light of the Spanish *Vida* of Jacques de Coutre from Bruges, then present in

Ayutthaya; we shall touch on this in the next chapter, but let it be said for now that Fr Jorge da Mota seems to have been, rather than a martyr with a halo of glory, a bold intriguer with sybaritic tastes who would have richly deserved the frying with which Phra Naresuan justly menaced him.

The liberal welcome accorded to Fr Belchior da Luz proves that the king had nothing against Christians. After the Dominican, other Fathers worked among the Portuguese living in Siam rather than among the Siamese, who were not easily converted. "They maintained in Siam [Ayutthaya] in the Portuguese camp a convent and a church whose chief was a commissioner of the Great Inquisitor in Goa."[14] The Dominican effort continued with high and low points in the seventeenth century. About 1640, Father António de São Domingo and Jacinto Piminès animated the mission.

The following anecdote, in the distinctive prose of Fr Meynard, will not fail to edify the reader.

> As a consequence of a revolt in the kingdom, there were many executions. Touched with compassion for the infidels, the Fathers . . . obtained permission to visit the prisoners and accompany them to the scaffold. They then instructed these unfortunates, exhorting patience and resignation, and making fervent Christians of them. All died full of confidence in the merit of the Saviour, murmuring with love the holy name of Jesus. It was really admirable! The jailors themselves became apostles and when they had not enough time to warn the Fathers of an execution they cried to the condemned persons, without understanding what they said, "Jesus! Jesus! Jesus!" This name of love fortified the condemned in their anguish and mitigated their last moments.[15]

In the seventeenth century, other orders and congregations, principally the Jesuits and the Missions Etrangères (Foreign Missions) based in Paris, were to appear in Siam alongside the Dominicans. Their coexistence was not always easy. Meanwhile, the Portuguese were not content to trade and evangelize. They gave considerable service to Siamese historiography by compiling colourful accounts of this exotic kingdom. Let us pause before the most important portrait of Siam compiled by a Portuguese in the sixteenth century.

SIAM SEEN BY FERNÃO MENDES PINTO

We have already mentioned Fernão Mendes Pinto, who spent some ten years in Siam in the middle of the sixteenth century. The credibility of his account of the country has been questioned, especially by people who have only read him in translation. We should rather trust a Portuguese Jesuit, Fr Cardim, who spent three years in Ayutthaya from 1626 to 1629:

> Though the book of *Peregrinação* of Pinto is considered to be apocryphal, he is correct in that which he relates about the kingdom of Siam. I say he does not depart from the truth, because a mandarin who taught me to read and write Siamese told me what the history and records of the country recorded about the coming of the Portuguese to that kingdom and the heroic deeds in which they helped the king to conquer many kingdoms. He told me especially the story of Ok-khun Chinnarat, telling me that it was true and whoever is interested in it can look it up in Pinto's book.[16]

Fernão Mendes Pinto says he saw Francis Xavier in Japan in discussion with Buddhist monks. Captivated by the Jesuit apostle, he accompanied him to Malacca, from which he left alone for Goa. Many years later, when he was waiting for a boat to take him back to Portugal, he saw the body of Francis Xavier, venerated as a saint, arrive in Goa in the middle of lavish ceremonies. This event changed his life; he decided to devote his fortune and the years remaining to him to the Christianization of Japan, and entered the Company of Jesus as a lay novice. But this splendid zeal was short-lived, and our hero returned to Portugal in 1558. He died there in 1583, after having written his prodigious *Peregrinação*.

Throughout the twenty-one years of his Asiatic travels, Mendes Pinto was taken prisoner thirteen times and sold seventeen times "in the regions of India, Ethiopia, Arabia Felix, China, Tartary, Macassar, Sumatra, and other places." He practised almost all the professions imaginable: adventurer, gentleman's squire, mercenary, slave, trader, pirate in the China Seas, doctor, ambassador, and novice. But he is above all in our eyes the author of the *Peregrinação*, published in 1614, in which one can read the earliest Portuguese description of the "Kingdom of Sornau[17] which is commonly called Siam."

Nine chapters of this huge book are devoted to Siam. The first eight (181–188) describe the arrival of Mendes Pinto in the capital Ayutthaya in the middle of the 1540s; the part he played with other Portuguese in the failed attempt of Phra Chairacha (1534–1547) to take the kingdom of Chiang Mai, then allied to the King of Pegu; the death of Phra Chairacha, poisoned by Queen Si Sudachan (Mendes Pinto slips up here, as it was not Phra Chairacha who was poisoned but his successor Phra Yot Fa, in June 1548); the usurpation of the throne by the dreadful Ok-khun Chinnarat, lover and accomplice of the queen (June–July 1548); their assassination at a banquet and the advent to the throne of Phra Thienracha, the half-brother of Phra Chairacha, who left his monastery to reign with the name of Phra Chakkraphat; the siege of Ayutthaya by the Peguan king Taben Shwehti at the beginning of 1559; the heroic but fatal sortie of Queen Suriyothai on a war elephant; the withdrawal of the Burmese who captured the princes Ramesuan and Maha Thammaracha on their return; then their exchange for two war elephants.

This exchange was not at all surprising. The invasion of Siam by Taben Shwehti, one of whose titles was "Lord of the White Elephant," only aimed at possessing a white elephant which the King of Siam considered the apple of his eye, and which died in 1551. The inconsolable Phra Chakkraphat spent a fortune on the royal obsequies for the beast.

The account of Mendes Pinto is as colourful as it is confused. He passes over exact dates and the names of the persons involved in this tumultuous period. But his description of Ayutthaya, which he was the first to call "the Venice of the East," corresponds on the whole to reality. The numerous canals crossing the capital were covered with countless barges and swarmed with crocodiles. The king left his palace twice a year in unimaginable oriental splendour, surrounded by his courtesans and superbly harnessed elephants. The monarch tolerated the practice of every religion in his capital; the Moors or Persians had seven mosques there and their "nation" comprised thirty thousand households. Pinto's chapter 189 outlines the economic resources and military potential of the country under the rubric *On the great fertility of the Kingdom of Siam, and other particularities relating to it.* This gives a better understanding of Portugal's interest in Siam. Its lowlands were fertile and rich, producing more than the country consumed, and the highlands were wooded and provided inexhaustible reserves of huge trees to build "thousands of ships of all kinds." Gold, silver, iron, steel, lead, tin, saltpetre, sulphur, rubies, and sapphires were all mined "in great quantity" there. Ivory, silk, cotton, sealing wax, gum benzoin, alum, indigo, honey, and sugar were so abundant that the country filled "more than a hundred junks" each year with goods sent to China and South-East Asian countries. And, as if that were not enough, this heaven-blessed kingdom was full of ginger, cinnamon, camphor, tamarind, and cardamoms.

To this list are added very relevant military considerations.

> Most of the Siamese communities have no fortifications of any kind, except for some wooden palisades, which means that they could easily be taken by anyone who attacked them with a minimal show of force. The inhabitants of the towns, besides being by nature a very weak breed, do not ordinarily possess defensive weapons.[18]

It is thus evident that "this country would be more profitable to us than anything else we possess in the Indies, and would be easier to seize."

The Portuguese spirit of enterprise conquering Asia by force of drawn sword and holy water sprinkler is cast aside in the conclusion:

> This is one of the finest kingdoms in the world, and one that is easier to conquer and hold than any other province, no matter how small. Moreover, I can say in all truth that of things that I saw in this city of Ayutthaya alone, there is so much more I could say than I have told of the entire kingdom. However, I prefer not to do so, so as to spare my readers the pain I feel when I think about how much we have lost there, for our sins, and how much we could have won.[19]

Mendes Pinto was clearly sufficiently sure-sighted and self-possessed, indispensable qualities for those who travel the world to build empires. Capable of discerning what was hypocritical in the official line of Portuguese imperialism, which wrapped itself in the banner of a crusade concerned only with planting the cross in the most distant corners of Asia, he was not afraid to bring the epic to its real dimensions, which were military and economic.[20]

The tone is different in the letters he wrote under the influence of religious fervour after his meeting with Francis Xavier, thus a long time before writing the *Peregrinação*. A letter, written in Malacca in 1554 and addressed to the Portuguese Jesuits, gives a summary description of Siamese beliefs and superstitions. This text illustrates the fundamental inability of Europeans to understand religions other than their own or to recognize the undeniable nobility of Theravada Buddhism, a religion which had been able to assimilate, like early Christianity, elements of local beliefs wherever it was introduced:

> The inhabitants of this country consider the elements as divinities and, when they die, the person who believed in Water is thrown naked into a river; he who believed in Fire is burnt on a big funeral-pyre; the person who adored the Earth is buried; and the person who believed in the Air is abandoned near a watercourse where he is eaten by vultures and other birds. And yet, most dear Brothers, there are in that city of Siam [Ayutthaya] seven mosques whose worshippers are Turks and Arabs, and thirty thousand Moorish households. This is something which should shame the soldiers of Christ: that the perverse sect of Muhammad should be so widespread in these regions, and that the zeal of its malice knows no limits. These Moors recite the Koran of Muhammad often. The king leaves to each individual whether he wishes to be Muslim or pagan, advancing a very poor reason, to wit that he is only the temporal ruler. At the end of winter, the king goes to wash himself in the river so that this remains sacred and that the people can drink from it without harm. The water in which the king washes his feet is brought ceremoniously by the nobles into their homes. During my stay in Siam, there was an eclipse of the moon an hour after midnight. These people think a cobra is eating the moon. They shoot many muskets into the air, they make a noise banging doors, they cry over land and water, entreating the snake to free the moon and not to swallow it. There was such a din that we Portuguese who were there, thought that treason and revolution possessed the city.[21]

Like many other Europeans after him, Mendes Pinto only observed the most superficial and caricatural aspects of this exotic religious culture, without being able to see in it a particular way of placing man in relation to the sacred and the mundane. This incomprehension will be met with often, and is so characteristic of Westerners, convinced of being the sole trustees of a truth which excludes any other.

CHAPTER TWO

NORTHERN EUROPE DISCOVERS SIAM (1580–1600)

"OUR EXHAUSTED HANDS COULD NO LONGER KEEP ALOFT THE FLAME"

THE CONQUEST and exploitation of Portugal's overseas empire cost much more than just human lives, goods, and sunken ships. Towards the end of the sixteenth century, and notably after its enforced union with Spain in 1580, Portugal seems to have lost some of its soul. The indomitable energy which made the era of Portuguese discoveries one of the most fascinating chapters in the history of the world seemed to have evaporated. As much as it was strong and resolute when it was carving out a colonial empire in Asia at the beginning of the century, the Portuguese became the cross-bred and sybaritic victim of their own conquests, more Asiatic than was justifiable, abandoning what distinguished them from other European nations around 1500. What had begun as a crusade resembled, by the end of the century, moral decline. "Our exhausted hands could no longer keep aloft the flame," as Jaime Cortesão explains it, "with which we illuminated the world . . ."[1]

The observation of Portuguese decline in Asia becomes a kind of leitmotiv in the accounts of numerous travellers who reached the East Indies. Thus in book 4 of the *Voyages* of Jean Mocquet, who spent a long time in Goa about 1610, we are given an almost revolting spectacle of Portuguese depravity.[2] The Manueline dynamism of the beginning of the century was no more than a distant memory when in 1580, two years after the disaster of Alcazar-Kibir where D. Sebastião and the flower of the Portuguese nobility perished, the death of the cardinal-king D. Henrique, the last monarch of the House of Avis, created a dynastic lacuna which was filled by Philip II of Spain, the grandson through his mother of D. Manuel. In spite of some pockets of resistance, the Duke of Alba annexed Portugal in three months, along with its vast Asian, African, and Brazilian empire.

The establishment of a double-headed monarchy and the loss of Portuguese political identity (the country would only regain its independence in 1640 under the new Braganza dynasty) created an ambiguous situation in Asia, from which other seafaring nations were ready to profit. Enterprising and possessing considerable naval experience, the Calvinist United Provinces were at war with Philip II from whose heavy yoke they had shaken themselves free. They therefore had an ideal pretext for seeking out the *Estado da Índia*, that is, the formerly Portuguese godowns and commercial networks. The destruction of the Invincible Armada by the English, the Dutch, and storms in 1588 had shattered Iberian supremacy at sea. Henceforth the colonial empire "on which the sun never set" was exposed to the activities of the northern maritime powers.

VAN LINSCHOTEN AND NAUTICAL ESPIONAGE

The Low Countries, both Calvinist and Spanish, had closely followed the Portuguese conquests and commercial success in Asia. Numerous Flemings and Dutchmen went to Portugal, where they learnt the language and tried to embark on the vessels of the *Carreira da Índia* as merchant, missionary, cannoneer, each according to his capacities or his creed. Francis Xavier's request addressed to Ignatius Loyola, "Da mihi Belgas" (Send me men from the Low Countries), is well known.

Among the men from the Low Countries who transited through Portugal on their way to Asia, the most famous is Jan Huyghen Van Linschoten (1563–1611). He arrived in Lisbon in the fatal year of 1580 at the age of seventeen, and was taken on as secretary by a priest who had been appointed Archbishop of Goa. He lived six years on the Malabar coast, where he collected a mine of information on the country, its inhabitants, flora and fauna, reserves of gold and precious stones, as well as its commercial and industrial establishments, climate, and sanitary conditions. He was particularly interested in what the Portuguese had most jealousy concealed: nautical details of the sea route to the Indies. He was able to complete his spying activities thanks to the observations of his compatriot Dirk Gerritszoon Pomp (also known as Dirk China) who had twice gone to China and Japan as cannoneer on Portuguese ships.

The publication in 1596, at Amsterdam, of the *Itinerario, voyage ofte schipvaert van Jan Huyghen Van Linschoten naer Oost ofte Portugaels Indien* (Itinerary, voyage or navigation of J. H. V. L. to the Orient or the Portuguese Indies) was an important event. This encyclopaedic work supplied invaluable information about the East Indies and the route to get there at the very time the United Provinces were preparing to dismember the Portuguese colonial empire. At the beginning of the twentieth century, the Netherlands decided to honour Van Linschoten by creating the Linschoten Vereniging; like the famous Hakluyt Society, it publishes a prestigious collection of accounts of Dutch voyages which are still in manuscript form.

JACQUES DE COUTRE: A NATIVE OF BRUGES IN SIAM IN 1595

Neither Van Linschoten nor Pomp set foot in Siam. This privilege fell to Jacques de Coutre, a native of Bruges, whose *Vida* (written up in Spanish by his son Estebán and printed in Madrid in 1640) was published a few years back in a Dutch translation, and also recently appeared in a new Spanish edition.[3] Jacques de Coutre was a picaresque merchant who had many adventures; in 1591, aged "fifteen or sixteen years," he departed his native city for Lisbon which he left the following year for the East Indies accompanied by his brother Joseph. For thirty years he wandered over Asia, amassing and losing almost as much wealth as Mendes Pinto. He was also captured and sold almost as many times as Pinto, but had neither his invention nor his satiric verve. What we lose literarily we definitely gain historically. The account of his eight months spent in Siam in 1595 in the reign of Phra Naresuan (1590–1605) is mostly believable, even though our man seems to have magnified the historic events in the kingdom.

Jacques de Coutre had the good fortune to arrive in Siam at a crucial moment and to see the way Phra Naresuan (also known as Phra Naret or Phra Naresvara) ruled. This important Siamese historical personality, a contemporary of Queen Elizabeth of England and Henri IV of France, received the name of *Maharat* (great king) for having restored the independence of the kingdom which, from 1569, was only a vassal state of the powerful Burmese kingdom of Pegu, ruled over with an iron fist by King Bayin Naung.

Phra Naresuan was able to shatter Burmese hegemony and conquer the kingdoms of Cambodia and Chiang Mai. Every Thai schoolchild knows by heart the circumstances of the glorious battle of Nong Sarai which took place on 18 January 1593, in which Phra Naresuan destroyed the powerful Burmese army that had invaded Siam. Mounted on his favourite war elephant, the king noticed in the fray the elephant of the Burmese crown prince, Mapa Ratcha, who commanded the enemy forces, and cried out, "Come, let us fight on our elephants for the honour of our kingdoms!" and then killed him with a powerful blow from his lance. Displeased with five princes who had refused him their assistance in his war against the King of Pegu, Phra Naresuan was going to deal with them when a delegation of Buddhist monks implored him to pardon them and instead charge them with reconquering the provinces of Tavoy and Tenasserim, then still occupied by the Burmese, which was done.[4] According to Jacques de Coutre, the king had burnt on a vast bonfire eight hundred men guilty of not having gone to the front against the Burmese.

This was the redoubtable hero of the Siamese *risorgimento* whom Jacques de Coutre had the opportunity of observing close at hand. His account is all the more valuable because it is the only one we have. It was above all in the reign of Phra Ekathotsarot (1605–1611), brother and successor of Phra Naresuan, that solid relations were established between Siam and the West, more particularly with Holland and England, and printed accounts started to appear offering European readers exotic tales. The adventurer from Bruges introduces us to a kingdom of Siam which knew nothing of the West except the Portuguese, apart from some occasional contacts with the Spanish Philippines, and whose existence was still very little affected by Europe. We can but summarize here the thirty or so pages he devotes to Siam.[5] Jacques de Coutre was in Malacca when he learnt that Phra Naresuan had conquered Cambodia and deported several thousand Cambodians to Siam. Among them were some Portuguese mercenaries and some Dominicans, including Frei Jorge da Mota.

This information is correct. Phra Naresuan had sought to punish King Satha of Lovek, who had profited by the Burmese attack on Ayutthaya to invade Siam and seize Prachin. Satha, fearing reprisals, had attracted Portuguese mercenaries to his land, even "adopting" their leader Diogo Veloso, who had formed a praetorian guard. The King of Cambodia had written to the Portuguese governor of Malacca seeking additional troops, but the governor had neither the men nor the money to spare. Satha then approached the Spanish governor of Manila, Gomez Perea Dasmarinas, sending a letter written on gold leaf seeking Spanish aid against Siam in exchange for giving a completely free hand to the missionaries and commercial privileges. But Dasmarinas temporized and merely sent vague promises.

Meanwhile Phra Naresuan invaded Cambodia with three army regiments, taking Siemreap, Battambang, and the capital Lovek in 1594. King Satha fled with two of his sons to Luang Phrabang in Laos, where he died in 1596. Phra Naresuan deported huge numbers of Cambodians to repeople his kingdom decimated by war, taking at the same time all the Portuguese and Spanish missionaries and mercenaries who were found in the Cambodian capital. The victorious king appeared to wish to deal with the Spanish tactfully, and to this end sent Diogo Veloso back to Manila.[6]

The flexibility of Phra Naresuan concerning the Portuguese, as revealed by Jacques de Coutre, corresponds to what we know of his relations with the Spanish. The king sent Fr Jorge da Mota (a martyr according to the sources cited in chapter 1, a rank liar according to Jacques de Coutre) to discuss the freeing of the Portuguese with the governor of Malacca. He in turn sent a delegation to Ayutthaya comprising a personal envoy named Manuel Pereira de Abreu, ten merchants (Fr da Mota had held out prospects of enticing profits), Jacques de Coutre, and the enterprising Dominican.

On 8 May 1595 these persons embarked on a heavy junk, the *Santo Domingo*, and anchored after encountering the usual difficulties at "the bar of Siam," the mud bank thrown up by the Chao Phraya, the Siamese Nile, also known as the *Maenam* or "mother of the waters." They went upstream in a small craft and arrived after a week in the Siamese capital. They learnt en route that the Portuguese captured in Cambodia were walking the streets of Ayutthaya in complete liberty, but were killing each other without the king lifting his little finger. Worse, the Japanese converts had massacred a Dominican. Other Fathers had taken refuge in a church, but some Portuguese had despatched them at the foot of the altar.

There indeed occurred a massacre of Portuguese missionaries in Ayutthaya in 1595, as in 1569; however their assailants were neither Portuguese nor Japanese converts, but hotheads in the Muslim-

Persian community, who, encouraged by the progress of Islam in Malaya, Java, and the Philippines, hoped to convert Siam and its king. The Portuguese missionaries were, in their eyes, rivals who had to be discouraged by whatever means. It must be said that the means of dissuasion chosen were more expedient than conforming to the Koran which does not stop emphasizing the merciful nature of God.

Phra Naresuan was willing to grant an audience at once to the delegation, but Fr da Mota insisted on being received in private audience with the envoy, "having to discuss extremely secret matters." António and Miguel Ans, sons of a Fleming who had taken a wife in Malacca, served as interpreters and discreetly informed their compatriot. The Dominican presented the envoy of the governor of Malacca as a cousin of the Portuguese king (there had been no "king of Portugal" for fifteen years) who had conquered the island of Ceylon single-handedly, and who was ready to put his redoubtable talents to the service of the King of Siam. The king declared himself to be as delighted as if he had received a white elephant (the comparison was extremely flattering) and offered, as a monarch who knew how to behave, a quantity of rich stuffs so great that eighteen men were needed to take them away.

The solemn audience, which took place a few days later, was closer to a bad farce. The members of the delegation prostrated themselves in front of Phra Naresuan in a great hall in the palace where all the *khunnang*, the mandarins of the kingdom, were assembled. The illustrious envoy did not open his mouth and left everything to the Dominican, who carried the letter from the governor of Malacca, written in Malay and enclosed in a sealed gold cylinder. He knew that it contained only a request for the freeing of the Portuguese detained in Siam, sprinkled with protestations of friendship. Finding this message too stark, Fr da Mota declared that he had a Portuguese version which he would translate at once into Siamese. Then he took out of his pocket a document he had compiled in Portuguese which he paraphrased in Malay to a Spanish renegade, Miguel de Pina, who transposed it for better or worse into vulgar Siamese for the benefit of the mandarins, who then repeated it to the king in court Siamese, *rachasap*. The result was grotesque gibberish full of lies and extravagant promises.

Phra Naresuan was so impressed that he at once decided to send an embassy to the King of Portugal, bearing rich presents and fifteen hundred tons of trade goods of considerable value. These were to be loaded on the delegation's junk and handed over to Fr da Mota. Meanwhile, the priest edified everyone by having himself transported on a royal palanquin surrounded by slaves and wearing the pointed hat used by the mandarins. But some members of the delegation, including Jacques de Coutre, were worried, because they had been assured that the king would fry all the Christians "like sardines" as soon as the Dominican's lies became apparent, which would certainly happen when the original letter of the governor of Malacca was translated from Malay. They decided to confide in a royal concubine whose piety was much admired, for "she made great pilgrimages to their idols and devils which had their shrines outside the city."

The king halted the preparations for the embassy as soon as the concubine revealed the truth to him, and summoned Jacques de Coutre and his friends. They went to the palace carrying on red lacquer trays the accustomed presents: gold and silver coins, twelve flasks of perfume, and six bunches of bird-of-paradise feathers. "These birds only live in dried trees in the Moluccas; they live in the air and have no feet. The peoples of the East Indies greatly appreciate them." They prostrated themselves before Phra Naresuan, their hearts beating. The king was perched on a throne three ells (three and a half metres) high at the foot of which were two chained tigers. The king received them graciously, listened to their explanations, and authorized them to return to Malacca; he offered them a junk filled with sappanwood to take with them, and allowed them to take all the Portuguese who wished to leave.

The good Fr da Mota and the envoy Pereira de Abreu, fearing for their own future, tried to stop them by revealing that the captain of the junk, Luis de Freitas, had stolen some gilded statues of the Buddha. On learning this detail, Phra Naresuan was so furious that he had some fifteen mandarins executed who were deemed guilty of not revealing the intrigues of the Portuguese. He forbade their departure and went on an elephant hunt to take his mind off this affair. The Dominican, "crying like a baby," implored Jacques de Coutre to help him flee the country. But our hero did not want to be embroiled with so compromising a person. He decided to join the royal hunt with his friends and to slip away at the first opportunity.

This stratagem provides us with a detailed account of an elephant hunt involving twenty thousand persons in the region of Lopburi, and a description of the vast elephant stables at Sapampur (present-day Kamphaeng Phet) housing three thousand war elephants. The region was so infested with tigers and enormous mosquitoes that Phra Naresuan had to spend the nights in a temple bedecked with red hangings and surrounded by regiments of his personal guard who stoked huge fires. Too bad for anyone who, bitten by a blood-thirsty insect or attacked by a hungry beast, troubled the royal slumber; he was massacred without pity.

On returning to Ayutthaya in the king's train, Jacques de Coutre and his companions finally received, at the beginning of 1596, permission to leave for Malacca. A few months later, they saw arrive there the envoy Pereira de Abreu and Fr da Mota who both died shortly afterwards as a result of wounds received when fleeing Siam.

"OF THE CRUELTIES AND OTHER THINGS I HAVE SEEN IN SIAM"

The adventurer from Bruges finishes the account of his travails in Siam by declaring, "I have seen in Siam such cruelties that they stunned me by their improbability. This is the reason why I have not mentioned most of them." The two chapters which follow offer a description at once savage and exotic of Siam and its sovereign. They are entitled, "Of the cruelties and other things I have seen in Siam during the eight months I was prisoner of this king," and "Of the justice and tyranny exercised by the King of Siam, and how they burnt and venerated a dead elephant, because the king considered it was his father."

First of all, by way of introduction, a snapshot of Phra Naresuan going through the streets of the capital accompanied by his brother Ekathotsarot:

> His guard marched in two ranks. He followed on an elephant and was quite naked; just a small piece of cloth covered his genital parts. He wore on his head a mitre like our bishops, fluted at the top and entirely made of gold, studded with numerous precious stones and other jewels. He directed the elephant with the aid of two golden crooks which he held in his hands . . . His brother followed him on another elephant, his hands held together above his head and bowed low, like someone being blessed. Around them walked all the trumpeters, horn players and drummers . . . There were four large

parasols, symbols of royal rank. Everything took place in absolute silence and we met no one in the streets . . . The people were warned when he would leave the palace and by which roads he would proceed. At that moment not a soul was to be seen in the streets, not even a dog. You could not even hear them bark, for they would have killed the dog and its master in the cruellest fashion in the world.

The description of Ayutthaya, the capital crossed with canals, recalls Venice or Bruges, give or take a few details:

The king has his court in the city of Odia which is girded with a brick wall and located inside two deep canals. This city is located some forty leagues from the sea on the bank of a tributary of the Ganges [*sic*]. The biggest ships come close to the outworks. Medium-sized vessels can enter the city which is traversed by canals in which swim innumerable and sometimes enormous crocodiles.

The royal palace built of gilded wood and dominated by five *chedi* covered with gold leaf (*Wang Luang*) is barely described, but the stables where the favourite elephants of Phra Naresuan were cossetted fascinated our tourist.

Out of curiosity I went to see them. There were numerous elephants, and two among them were particularly valued and pampered. They all had their silk cushions on which they slept like puppies. You can imagine that these cushions were as long as six ells and even wider. The animals were attached by a chain as thick as those of a heavy door and covered in gold. At first I thought they were in solid gold, but when I came closer I saw that in some worn parts they were plated. Even the tassels were made of silk. Each elephant had six large golden basins, as thick as the front of a Spanish *real*; their size will surprise no one. One contained oil with which they were anointed, a second water with which they were sprinkled. For the four others, they were used for food, drink, urine, and needs of nature. The elephants were so well trained that when they wished to urinate or defecate, they got up from the cushions. The mahouts immediately understood and passed them their basins. Their residence was always perfumed and fumigated with benzoin and other fragrances. Thus they lived magnificently. I would not have believed it if I had not seen it myself.

We can trust Jacques de Coutre. Jeremias Van Vliet, describing Ayutthaya forty years later, confirmed the abundance of man-eating crocodiles in the Chao Phraya and the royal treatment of the palace elephants, emphasizing in his turn that it all seemed "unbelievable to those who had not seen it."[7] Nicolas Gervaise also refers to the gold dishes of the royal elephants in his *Histoire naturelle et politique du Royaume de Siam* (1688), and concluded, "As the written accounts confirm these gold dishes . . . I shall add nothing to this."[8] But none of the important witnesses of the seventeenth century, not even Simon de La Loubère, described the royal funeral for an elephant. The death of the war elephant on which Phra Naresuan had won the battle of Nong Sarai two years earlier was the occasion of bizarre ceremonies.

> The day of its death, the king was wracked by grief; he even said his father had just died. He ordered the people and all the grandees of his kingdom to come and worship the elephant. For this, they carried the corpse outside the city to the opposite bank of the river and placed it in front of a temple . . . They built above the elephant an enormous dais of blue damask, disembowelled it, took out the viscera which they treated with perfumed balsams and covered with a huge quantity of flowers and roses. They placed golden stakes inside the stomach to hold it up. Four talapoins—their priests—took up position there; they were dressed in yellow and told their beads or rosaries. Numerous candles were lit. Some went in, some came out after a few minutes. Then they built all around a vast square wooden gallery which was gilded and painted . . . The elephant already stank for more than half a league around. Then all the grandees and the mandarins came to worship at the gallery, the balustrades of which were lit with a mass of candles. Everyone worshipped the animal on their knees. These barbaric practices lasted eight days and nights in the midst of non-stop dances and an infernal din of bells, kettle drums, saucepans, and other instruments worthy of Pandora. Many men were dressed as tigers, devils, and white horses. The horses were made of paper, and there were wooden birds, painted yellow, exactly like ostriches. All the talapoins mounted one; they were as big as a horse. They placed around numerous painted and sealed containers full of food; these barbarians said that the elephant needed to eat too in the next life. When eight days had passed, the talapoins buried it beneath faggots of wood. The king arrived, went around the elephant

three times, lit the pyre, and ordered that the ashes be collected in golden vases after the cremation. These urns were placed among those of his parents and ancestors. Two mahouts of the elephant then presented themselves before the king and told him that since their master, the elephant, was dead, they wished to go in their turn to the other world to serve him. The king thanked them effusively, unsheathed his sword, cut them in two and had them cremated with many honours . . . Thus ended these barbarous ceremonies for the elephant.

These "human" funeral ceremonies for an elephant were not however astonishing in the Buddhist context, for the elephant is considered the most intelligent and thus the most human of animals. La Loubère affirms that, "They speak of an Elephant as of a Man; they believe him perfectly rational, and they relate such rational things of him, that he only wants Speech."[9] The descriptions of Siamese funerals in Bouvet, La Loubère, Kaempfer, Turpin, Pallegoix, and Bowring show that the elephant was accorded rites reserved for princes, the chief priests, and senior mandarins. The wooden birds resembling ostriches which the monks mounted when presiding over the transmigration of the elephant's soul were clearly *kinnari*, lower deities of a half-female, half-bird shape. The art of Ayutthaya excelled in the representation of these fantastic beings, for which a greater freedom of expression was permitted than the great Buddhist statuary, which was hieratic and bound by canons which evolved only slowly over time.[10]

Our tourist had the good fortune to arrive in Ayutthaya at the time when the king was having the Buddhist *wat* or temples of his capital restored to celebrate his victory over the Burmese and to accumulate merit. The imposing *chedi* or stupa of Wat Chai Mongkhon had just been constructed (1593).[11]

Each pagoda had a very high tower of stone and masonry. They were gilded from the spire to the middle and had four stairways of gilded lead. The king kept his gilded idols, covered in jewels, in these pagodas. He alone mounted inside the towers built in the middle of very large square and tiled courtyards. Each patio had in the four corners a pool bordered by many trees. The tower was surrounded by a small masonry balustrade. The walls were studded with carbuncles, topazes, and many other less precious stones. Inside there were many

> lamps and bronze statues the size of an adult man placed along the wall. They were dressed like ancient Romans; some had sticks in their hands, others held chained lions. These solid bronze statues seemed to be alive. They were found forty years ago in a destroyed city in the kingdom of Cambodia. The inhabitants discovered the city in the mountains and did not know what people had lived there. The city that was discovered received the name of Angkor. To judge from the statues, the inhabitants were probably Romans. When the King of Siam conquered the kingdom of Cambodia, he took these statues away, and many others of the same size carved in stone, to place them in front of his palace.[12]

Jacques de Coutre, who confuses Roman and Khmer art, poses an insoluble archaeological enigma, for the bronze statues he speaks of have disappeared, and were probably melted down. But the persons brandishing sticks make one think of Khmer statues of Vishnu whose club (*gada*) is his usual attribute. The rediscovery of the ruins of Angkor about 1550 is confirmed by Diogo do Couto, the author who continued the *Décadas da Índia* of João de Barros.[13]

Our guide next describes the galleries which surrounded the inner courts of the shrines. The faithful came to worship the numerous Buddha statues there twice a week, though the name of the Buddha is never mentioned. The statues were either of gilded bronze, or painted stone; some were squatting down, some lying on cushions; the alert reader will recognize here the *bhumisparsa mudra* and *parinirvana mudra* positions. "They had ears as big as the Singhalese on the island of Ceylon and the coast of Malabar." The atmosphere in the middle of these hundreds of Buddhas was that which prevails in the important *wat* in Thailand today, like Wat Pho in Bangkok where the faithful burn candles, offer sticks of incense and flowers, and release birds from cages. A great marble statue represented a king on a three-headed elephant. "I also entered a chamber, accompanied by a mandarin, who showed me a very important chapel such as we have in our churches. The chapel was filled with idols decked with gold and silver. Many of them had diadems on their heads, streamers in the hands, and many other objects."

As a conscientious tourist, Jacques de Coutre even visited shrines located in the countryside.

> Outside the city walls, I saw on the ground a statue seated on a

> cushion. It was made entirely of stone and bricks covered with painted and gilded mortar. It had above its head a large parasol of gold thread. From its huge dimensions, and also because it was located in a plain, it could be seen at a distance of four leagues. Out of curiosity I measured one of the thumbnails: it was five palms wide, and that of the right hand likewise. The natives recounted that a king of Pegu had caused it to be made in one night when he seized the kingdom of Siam . . . I think this is a lie . . .

This could be the huge Buddha statue at Wat Phanan Choeng, on the left bank of the Chao Phraya, or a statue which has now disappeared and was placed near Wat Phu Khao Thong, built in 1569 during the Burmese occupation of Ayutthaya.

But Jacques de Coutre seems above all to have retained the memory of the cruelty of Phra Naresuan's justice; he makes him out to be an oriental despot thirsting for blood and tortures. He had condemned persons locked in cages with wild beasts for the pleasure of the spectacle. One day it was discovered that a little girl aged eight who was serving the queen had stolen a small piece of gold. The king condemned her, with twenty-seven of her companions who were guilty of not having denounced her, to an atrocious death in the presence of our nauseated witness.

> They had one of their eyes removed; then the skin from their hands was detached and their nails were torn out. After a certain time, a piece of their flesh was cut from their backs and stuffed in their mouths. So that they should suffer slowly, they were roasted over a low fire, each in her own pan, until they died.

Another day, the Portuguese witnessed with Fr da Mota the execution of an adulterous woman who was ripped to pieces by a mastiff which belonged to them (and which they provoked) and by tigers.

In spite of the oriental splendours seen in Siam, Jacques de Coutre returned with a stock of obsessive memories. The cultural codes of his world and that which he had visited were too different. His memories are not an isolated example of such disorientation. Jean Mocquet, the apothecary of Henri IV, keeper of Louis XIII's collection of unusual objects and above all an impenitent adventurer, visited the Portuguese Indies about 1610. He did not explore Siam, but became friendly during his long stay in Goa with a Chinese who spoke to him about a king of Siam (it is not known if it was Phra Naresuan, who died in 1605, or his brother Phra Ekathotsarot, who died in 1611) who treated his enemies with unbelievable cruelty. "He had some put entirely naked in big copper cauldrons over a fire, and had them slowly roasted in them; others he had placed seated, likewise completely naked, between two great fires, who died in great torment." Relating some stories whose details of butchery are enough to make one's hair stand on end, Mocquet concluded: "These were the cruel torments that these gentile kings applied pitilessly to those on whom they wished to take revenge. The Chinese who told me all these stories was called João Pay, secretary of Dom André Furtado."[14]

The disenchantment is evident; the dream had turned to a nightmare. Images of impossible cruelty overcome those, now well-worn, of an oriental paradise. Seen close to, the garden of Eden lost and rediscovered was only a terrible den of tortures.

CHAPTER THREE
THE DUTCH SET UP SHOP IN SIAM (1601–1608)

"TAKING THE GAME FLUSHED OUT BY OTHERS"

IF THE spirit of enterprise shown by the Portuguese in Asia throughout the sixteenth century stirs the imagination, the rapidity and audacity with which the Dutch dismantled the Portuguese colonial empire to their own profit takes one's breath away. "The Republic of Holland," wrote the Abbé Raynal towards the end of the eighteenth century, "offers in its origins a formidable spectacle to other nations and should remain a powerful object of interest for us, and curiosity for our most distant posterity. Its industry and boldness are seen everywhere, but most particularly on the seas and continents of the Indies."[1] More cynically, the Dutch explorer Willem Bosman, at the end of the seventeenth century, noted in his *Voyage to Guinea* that the role of the Portuguese conquerors consisted in "setting off the dogs to flush out the game which will then be taken by others."[2]

This is precisely what the inhabitants of the young United Provinces did, not content with having seized their independence from Philip II of Spain in the 1580s and wishing to avenge themselves for the persecution they had endured. On 29 May 1585 Philip II had decreed that all Dutch ships should be seized in the ports of the Malay peninsula, but three years later, after the loss of his invincible armada, he had to make use of Dutch caraks to transport corn that was in extremely short supply in his two kingdoms after suffering disastrous harvests.

The Dutch were therefore able to observe close to hand the diminution of power of the Iberian kingdoms deprived of their naval striking force. They understood that an enormous colonial empire was there for the taking and only had to be plucked. Living close to the sea, they felt just as much at ease on their ships as on their polders. For half a century they had been the chief distributors of exotic merchandise arriving at Portuguese ports and sought to take over the trading routes to and from Asia.

The Portuguese, of course, vigorously protested at this encroachment of their Asiatic empire by the stronger upstarts, pleading the Treaty of Tordesillas and their right of being the first there. They had clearly forgotten that there were already Asians in Asia before the arrival of Vasco da Gama and the old story of the burglar burglarized was being replayed. Frei Serafim de Freitas expounded the Portuguese arguments in his treatise, *De Iusto Imperio Lusitanorum Asiatico* (The just Asian empire of the Portuguese), published in Valladolid in 1625 and dedicated to the young Philip IV.[3]

Thus began a premature world war, for the struggle ranged over four continents and seven seas. It also took on the flavour of a religious conflict, since the two belligerent parties considered each other to support the devil. In the eyes of the Dutch Calvinists, the Church of Rome was the Great Prostitute of Babylon, and the pope the personification of the Antichrist. The Portuguese, for their part, as good Catholics kept under control by the Inquisition, could not envisage salvation outside the one, holy, catholic, and apostolic Church. In 1624 a Portuguese author expressed a conviction widespread among his compatriots: "The Dutch are only good cannoneers; for everything else they are only worthy of being burnt as reprobate heretics."[4]

Dutch vessels had begun to distance themselves from the coasts of Europe and North Africa about 1580, to travel as far as Bahia and Pernambuco in Brazil. Ten years later, they explored the coasts between the mouths of the Amazon and the Orinoco. In 1593 Barent Erickszoon of Enkhuizen visited Guinea for the first time where he snatched a cargo of gold and ivory from under Portuguese eyes.

But it was above all the riches of Asia which attracted the United Provinces. In 1592 a few enterprising traders from Amsterdam had sent Cornelis and Frederik de Houtman to Lisbon to obtain details about the maritime route to the East Indies. They returned in 1594, and the success of the nautical espionage mission was so great that the same year a *Compagnie van Verre* (the Company of Distant Commerce) was created. The publication in 1596 of the *Itinerary* of Jan

Huyghen van Linschoten mentioned above was to complete this wealth of information which was to open all the major Asiatic seaports.

The first expedition financed by the new company set sail on 2 April 1595. Four small ships, of two hundred tons burden on average and counting in all 247 crew members, set sail from Texel under the command of Cornelis de Houtman. They needed fifteen months to reach Java, where, notwithstanding the protests of the Portuguese and the arrogance of the Dutch admiral, a trade treaty was concluded with the Sultan of Bantam and the holds filled with spices. Houtman would have liked to continue to the Moluccas, but his men, after seven months spent exploring the Indonesian islands and markets, preferred to return to Europe. That took another seven months. Of the 247 who left twenty-nine months earlier, only 94 landed at Texel at the end of August 1597.

The commercial benefits of this first expedition were rather disappointing. But the information obtained and the perspectives opened justified the equipping of a second fleet of eight vessels manned by 580 men, commanded by Jacob van Neck. They left in May 1598 and returned two years later with precious cargoes which made the shareholders so wealthy that several new private companies were set up to advance trade with the East Indies.

In the year of 1598 alone, five Dutch expeditions, numbering in all twenty-two vessels, set off for Asia. Three went via the Cape of Good Hope, and two (including that commanded by Olivier van Noort) went via South America and the Magellan Strait. Van Noort returned via the Cape of Good Hope after a very agitated voyage and was the first Dutchman to navigate round the earth. He published in 1602 his *Beschryvinghe vande voyagie om den geheelen wereldcloot* (Description of a voyage around the whole world), the reading of which remains enthralling today.[5]

Such intensive maritime activity directly created the need for a new ship capable of crossing the oceans, replacing the heavy barges used in Holland, the too small caravels, and the caraks which rode too high in the water. This new commercial vessel, the store ship, was designed by Pieter Janszoon Liorne from Hoorn and was to give valuable service for two centuries. The store ship was to be used above all in inter-Asian trade, bringing goods to the overseas godowns to be loaded onto the great stern-framed vessels (*spiegelschepen*), also called "returning ships" (*retourschepen*).

PATTANI, THE THRESHOLD OF SIAM

The fifth expedition sent by the *Compagnie van Verre* to Java was to open thrilling perspectives. Six ships sailed in 1600 under the command of Admiral Jacob van Neck. In order to gain time, he went ahead with the three fastest vessels and anchored ten months later after a particularly troubled journey. The cargo of spices waiting at Bantam was loaded onto one of the vessels which returned to Holland; van Neck left for the Moluccas with the two others, the *Amsterdam* and the *Gouda*. Being unable to buy spices in sufficient quantity, he decided to go to Pattani on the Gulf of Siam, but contrary winds and misleading maps led him to Macao. He was thus the first Dutch admiral to visit the Chinese coast. The Portuguese prevented him from trading there and van Neck, his holds still empty, had to set sail for Pattani where he dropped anchor on 7 November 1601. This southern province of Thailand was at the time a small Malay state which was a vassal of Siam, and ruled by a queen.

In spite of the protests of the Portuguese, Chinese, and Japanese merchants, van Neck signed an advantageous treaty with the queen three days after arriving. She allowed the newcomers to set up a godown in Pattani and trade in pepper. The three ships which van Neck had left behind had arrived in Bantam after a thirteen-month voyage. One immediately returned with a cargo of spices. The two others, commanded by Jaspar van Groesbergen, wanted to go on to China but in error went up the mouth of the Mekong; they were the first Dutch ships to reach Cambodia. Not being able to trade in that kingdom, Groesbergen went in his turn to Pattani, where he found van Neck supervising the construction of the Dutch godown.

Van Neck left Pattani in August 1602, his four holds stuffed with spices. Before that, two other Dutch ships had come to anchor in the port, readily found cargoes, and set up eight merchants in Pattani. Three days before their departure, Jacob van Heemskerck arrived with two ships; he was able to fill his holds and left ten men on shore with orders to sell the goods he had left in the godown. At the end of 1602, the Dutch colony at Pattani comprised twenty-six men working for three different trading companies. They were unaware that an historic decision taken in Amsterdam had radically altered the basis of the irresistible rise of the Dutch in South-East Asia.

THE *SANTA CATARINA* AFFAIR

Jacob van Heemskerck had distinguished himself searching in vain for the north-east passage, and was one of the heroes of the famous winter spent in Novaya Zemlya in 1596–1597. He then took part in the second expedition to the East Indies (1598–1600) under the command of Jacob van Neck. After returning to Europe in May 1600, he left again for Asia in April 1601, this time as admiral of a fleet of eight vessels armed by two combined companies. One of the vessels we have already mentioned as being in Pattani in the autumn of 1602.

The expedition of van Heemskerck made history because the Dutch admiral attacked several Portuguese vessels in the Malay and Indonesian straits. If the acts of bravery of André Furtado de Mendonça have above all caught the attention of Portuguese historians,[6] on the Dutch side the interest has been in the political, legal, and moral consequences of the most famous exploit of van Heemskerck in Asiatic waters—the seizure of the carak *Santa Catarina* and its rich cargo.

The Dutch admiral had obtained from the Sultan of Johor, the traditional enemy and neighbour of the Portuguese in Malacca, information about the schedules of and routes taken by Portuguese inter-Asiatic trade. In February 1603, he went with two armed vessels to intercept the caraks coming from Macao to Goa passing through the Singapore Strait, laden with Chinese and Japanese goods, especially silk, gold, and porcelain. On the morning of 25 February, he came across the *Santa Catarina*, an enormous carak of fifteen hundred tons, whose captain was Sebastião Serrão. It was carrying 750 crew and passengers, including a hundred women and children. The Portuguese defended themselves valiantly throughout the day, but the superiority of the Dutch vessels kept their heavy prey under strong pressure. At dusk, after losing seventy men, Serrão hauled up the white flag of surrender. An honourable capitulation was negotiated; van Heemskerck promised to respect the life and liberty of the passengers, and was to honour this agreement.

Contemporaries, even Portuguese, praised the magnanimity of van Heemskerck, which proves that respecting a promise was the exception rather than the rule. The Dutch admiral, who had let his prisoners disembark at Malacca, received letters of thanks from the chamber of commerce and the governor, and even from Captain

Serrão, who congratulated himself on meeting such a generous adversary, and humbly asked for charity.[7]

These reactions illustrate the depths to which the Portuguese in Asia had fallen. Letters were not written in this style at the time of the great Afonso de Albuquerque, the intrepid conqueror of Goa and Malacca. It seemed as though the Mandate of Heaven had passed from the Portuguese to the Dutch. This defeatism and the arrogance of the new arrivals would soon alter the statistics of the *Carreira da Índia*; while there were still six Portuguese merchant ships leaving every year for the East Indies in the middle 1620s, the figure was halved after the mid-1630s.[8]

The object of this act of piracy by van Heemskerck, the *Santa Catarina*, was brought back surrounded by other returning vessels. The value of its cargo was enormous. The Jesuit Fernão Guerreiro noted in his journal:

> The 30th June in the year 1603, between eleven o'clock and midday, there arrived in Macao a junk from Siam with the news that, last March, the ship from China going to Malacca, the richest and the most heavily laden for many years, was captured by the Dutch in the Straits of Singapore.[9]

The news of this prize had preceded the arrival of the *Santa Catarina* in the Netherlands, where people's minds were singularly perturbed. One of the most famous polemics in the history of international law took place around the notion of the freedom of the seas, that is, of international waters. Furthermore the question was asked if Dutch vessels had the right to attack and seize a ship which had not provoked them and which flew the flag of a nation which was not at war with the United Provinces. The Netherlands was at war with Spain, it was true, but the kingdom of Portugal was considered a sovereign nation associated with Spain.

These questions plunged the shareholders of the *Oude Compagnie* and the *Noord-Hollandse Compagnie*, which had jointly financed the expedition, in a curious dilemma of conscience. Some refused to touch immoral dividends and claimed the return of their shares; others foresaw the creation of a new company, to be set up in France under the protection of Henri IV, which would be exclusively given over to peaceful trade.

In order to overcome these scruples, the public prosecutor of the

United Provinces sought the advice of the Admiralty, which alone was competent in this affair, to adjudicate on the legitimacy of the prize. The decision, made public on 9 September 1604, justified the action of van Heemskerck who had been pursued on the outward journey by armed Portuguese vessels near the Canaries. Furthermore, the East Indies had for several years past been the seat of contest with the Portuguese, which had caused the death of several Dutch sailors serving under Jacob van Neck. The Admiralty's council of war and the stadtholder Prince Maurice of Orange-Nassau had for this reason authorized van Heemskerck to attack the enemy and cause as much damage as possible. The admiral had done no more than carry out these secret orders; it was therefore proper that he had taken a Portuguese carak and the goods it transported, and these should be considered as spoils of war, to be sold to the highest bidder and the returns divided among the shareholders according to legal provisions. The document concluded piously, "In truth, the seas should be free so that the Indies trade, so important to the United Provinces, can continue without acts of war."

The auction had begun in August (everyone expected the decision of the Admiralty) and continued for several weeks. It was above all the superb and plentiful Ming porcelain which attracted buyers, to the point where this porcelain was called for a long time in Holland *Kraakporselein*, carak porcelain. While collections of it were being formed, Dutch cabinet makers began to design and make oak or gnarled walnut display cupboards which would be the focal point of wealthy middle class interiors. The revenue from the sale came to the colossal sum of three and a half million guilders, and the shareholders pocketed dividends of two hundred per cent. The finest pieces were put to one side to be offered to important individuals. The French ambassador suggested that Henri IV should not be forgotten; this advice was taken.

However, doubts continued to torment some delicate consciences. The legal expert Hugo Grotius, already the official chronicler of the United Provinces although only twenty-one years old, was invited to study all the documents relating to the affair, and to put his conclusions to paper. The voluminous essay *De Iure Praedae Commentarius* (Commentary on the law of seizure) would only be published in full in 1868; just one chapter was published in 1608 under the title *Mare liberum, sive de Iure quod Batavis competit ad Indiana Commercia* (The open seas, or the right of the Dutch to trade in the Indies). Resolutely anti-Portuguese, Grotius maintained that the seas were free and thus open to all, and no nation had the right to claim them on the pretext of having been the first to explore them.[10]

The *Santa Catarina* affair did much more than fill the pockets and the display cases of a certain number of Calvinist bourgeois. It constituted a decisive moment in the relations between Portugal and Holland in Asia. The spirit of enterprise of the young republic saw no further obstacles; the princely dividends and the strong arguments of Grotius had convinced those who still had doubts. Dutch merchants, sailors, and investors now knew that the East Indies with their spices and treasures belonged to them. Knowing their Bible well, they meditated particularly on the lines of St Matthew: "the Kingdom of Heaven suffereth violence and the violent take it by force."[11] They were certainly violent, but they also had this quality which makes violence compelling: they kept a cool head. Their violence was not to produce pyrotechnics but solid cash. One can go far with such principles.

The Dutch could face the future with all the more assurance now that a formidable commercial enterprise had just been created, the *Verenigde Oost-Indische Compagnie*, the United East India Company.

THE VOC: "WEAKEN THE ENEMY, ASSERT THE FATHERLAND"

At the end of 1602, three Dutch companies were operating out of Pattani. Such a situation ran the strong risk of creating rivalry which would weaken the intrusion of the United Provinces in Asia. The representatives of the three companies were unaware that an historic agreement had been concluded in Amsterdam on 20 March. After difficult negotiations between the States General (represented by Oldenbarneveldt) and the directors of six companies operating in the East, and after the personal intervention of the stadtholder, it had been decided that the "precompanies" would unite into the *Verenigde Oost-Indische Compagnie* or VOC.

The chief reason behind this decision to force the somewhat reluctant companies to join forces was to eliminate internal competition which would reduce profits, but the companies were also aware that the armed struggle against the Portuguese would require means which individually they would have been unable to provide.

Van Oldenbarneveldt summarized the programme of the new company in these words: "to weaken the enemy and assert the fatherland." Another no less cogent reason was the formation in London, at the end of 1600, of the English East India Company, founded to break the monopoly of trade in spices which the Dutch had appropriated to themselves in Asia. The Hollanders were aware of the formidable maritime and commercial skills of the English, and of the need to do everything in their power to sustain their interests.

Contrary to the very centralized structure of the East India Company, the VOC was an amalgam of six regional chambers, submitting to the authority of an administrative council consisting of seventeen representatives, the Heren XVII or "Seventeen Gentlemen." They met twice a year, in spring and autumn, to decide on the annual volume and division of investments, the number of vessels and their armament, as well as the sale of cargoes on their return. The working capital was six million guilders, ten times that of the English company. From 1650 the Heren XVII freed themselves of the obligation of reading and drafting replies to their voluminous Asiatic correspondence by setting up a permanent commission in The Hague.

The first godowns of the VOC remained autonomous until 1609, when the Heren XVII decided to appoint a governor-general, whose mandate ran in principle for three years but was easily renewed. In 1619 Batavia (present-day Jakarta) became the seat of the governor-general and the Council of the Indies. The first holder of this prestigious post was Pieter Both (1610–1614), but the most famous governor-general in the history of the VOC is without any doubt Johan Maetsuyker; his rule of a quarter of a century (1653–1678) coincides with the company's golden age.

The people employed by the VOC comprised merchants, pastors, soldiers, and sailors. The merchants were more important than the army personnel, because military action was always subject to commercial needs. The pastors devoted themselves less to the conversion of the natives than to the salvation of the souls of the sailors and soldiers in the VOC's employ. Everything points to their being fully occupied; their flock, too frequently recruited from among adventurers with something to hide in their past and with somewhat uncouth manners, had much need of spiritual succour. The salaries were so modest that the employees of the VOC were almost constrained to defy formal prohibitions and to trade on their own account to the detriment of the company. The directors dealt with these interloping practices with draconian severity, as they constituted a real menace for the East India Company whose very existence they threatened.

In spite of these problems, the VOC soon became the principal maritime power in Asia. In 1619 Jacatra was taken by assault from the Sultan of Bantam and rebaptized Batavia. Given its advantageous location, the city was predestined to become the capital of the VOC colonial empire. Fortified godowns were established with increasing rapidity: Ayutthaya (1607), Hirado in Japan (1609), Pulicat on the Coromandel Coast (1613), Surat in Gujerat (1616), Moka in Arabia (1616), Palembang in Sumatra (1619), Taiwan (1624), Shiraz and Isfahan (1625), etc. The island of Ambon in the Moluccas, famous for its pepper and cloves, was taken from the Portuguese in 1605 without a shot being fired, to become the centre of the spice trade. The conquest of Malacca, taken after a stiff fight from the Portuguese with the aid of the Sultan of Johor (January 1641), finally broke the power of the Portuguese, who would henceforth no longer be considered a menace, rather an embarrassment to be accommodated. According to a tradition relayed by the Abbé Raynal, Antonio van Diemen, governor-general from 1636 to 1645 and planner of the seizure of Malacca, mockingly asked the vanquished Portuguese commander when he would return. The answer given in all seriousness was, "When your sins are greater than ours."[12]

Anglo-Dutch rivalry in the East broke out in 1619 in undeclared but violent war, followed by a brief defensive alliance against the Spanish and Portuguese. The relations between the two northern maritime powers remained strained; jealousy and fear of the Dutch even led England to sign a peace treaty with the Portuguese in 1635.

Smoke from its gunpowder did not stop the VOC from prospering insolently. It brought to Europe precious spices, like cloves and nutmeg from the Moluccas or cinnamon from Ceylon, pepper in great quantities from Sumatra and Pattani, raw or made-up silk from China and Indochina, cotton from India, indigo and other colouring substances, pharmaceutical products like borax, benzoin, and musk, sugar from China, Siam, and Bengal, silver and copper from Japan, porcelain from China. Like the Portuguese in the sixteenth century, the Dutch company was very active in inter-Asian trade, the volume of which was superior to the exchanges between the homeland and its colonies. Few European products were exported to Asia: modest quantities of mercury, lead, arms, red cloth, African ivory, and Mediterranean coral. The holds of the VOC vessels were so desperately empty on leaving for the East that their ballast was heavy Dutch bricks which were used for the construction of Batavia.

THE FIRST CONTACTS BETWEEN THE NETHERLANDS AND SIAM

The first VOC agents from Pattani to arrive in Ayutthaya no doubt benefited from the prestige of the very efficient commercial and military undertakings they had conducted. In spite of the blunders of some, they succeeded better in Siam than the Portuguese or the English, and this success is due to their national character which allied Calvinist sobriety with a trader's pliancy.

This is how François-Henri Turpin explains, in his *Histoire de Siam* (1771), the unequal situation of the first three European peoples to establish themselves in Siam.

> [The Portuguese] offered the spectacle of dreadful poverty. Their natural laziness, made worse by the vice of the climate, prevented them from profiting by the advantages of a country to which they brought their vices but without absorbing its virtues. . . . England set up the basis of an establishment, but the pride of this race, jealous of its independence, could not get them to bow before the yoke of a despot who had unlimited power. Their lack of docility brought them disgrace and they were constrained to abandon the country.

But this is how their rivals are described:

> The flexible Hollanders, ever prepared to receive the impressions of those who can enrich them, were the only Europeans who had built establishments with solid foundations. Everything suits them when everything is useful to them. The simplicity of their manners inspires the confidence of a nation which believes it has the right to be wary of all those who are surrounded by luxury.[13]

The history of Siamese-Dutch relations began under a favourable star.[14]

One of the first fleets armed by the VOC set sail at the beginning of 1603 under the command of Admiral Wijbrant van Waerwyck.

On arriving in the Indies, he sent off two vessels to Pattani, where they dropped anchor in December 1603; he arrived only a few months later. The Dutch considered Pattani to be the gateway to China, and when van Waerwyck met in Pattani an ambassador of Phra Naresuan, who told him that Siam sent an embassy to China every year, he had the idea of adding a company envoy in order to obtain trading privileges from the Chinese. To this end he wrote a letter to the King of Siam, charging Cornelis Speckx and his nephew to take it to Ayutthaya in June 1604. They were well received by Phra Naresuan, but an expedition against the Burmese, the death of the king in April 1605, and the advent of Phra Ekathotsarot to the throne delayed their mission. Speckx was recalled in 1606. He returned to Pattani where he was joined by some courtiers of the new king bearing presents for Prince Maurice of Orange-Nassau. They travelled together to Bantam, in the west of Java, in December 1607.

A second delegation consisting of Jacques van de Perre and Willem Tonnemann arrived in Ayutthaya at the end of 1606 to explore Siam's economic resources and prepare to open a godown in the capital. Contacts with the court were excellent up to the time when two Dutchmen had the unfortunate idea of requesting from the king some golden *sirih pinang* (betel boxes), a distinction reserved for the greatest Siamese mandarins. This insolence antagonized Phra Ekathotsarot and the impertinent pair had to be recalled, their superior Sprinckel had to write a letter of apology, and presents had to be sent for the incident to be overlooked.

The clumsiness of these Dutchmen, however, could not change for long the favourable disposition the king had for their country. Knowing with what success they had fought the Portuguese and the Spanish, he authorized them in February 1608 to open a godown in Ayutthaya. Its director (opperhoofd) Lambert Jacobszoon Heijn was the first of some fifty VOC employees to occupy this post over more than a century and a half, until the destruction of Ayutthaya by the Burmese in 1767.

THE KING OF SIAM SENDS AN EMBASSY TO THE "KING OF HOLLAND"

The favour shown by Phra Ekathotsarot to the Dutch alarmed the Portuguese who disparaged them on every occasion and in every way, going so far as to say they were a nation of unprincipled pirates. It seems that these allegations gave the King of Siam the idea of sending an embassy to the ruler of these strange people. No one tried to explain to him that Holland was a republic without a king where the legislative power was exercised by the States General and the executive power by a stadtholder, the Prince of Orange-Nassau.[15]

The *Journal* of Cornelis Matelieff, admiral of the returning fleet which left Batavia in January 1608, contains important details about this embassy, the first sent by a king of Siam to a European nation. Matelieff was preparing for the return journey when, on 19 December 1607, one of his vessels, the *Mauritsius*, arrived in Bantam. On board were

> ambassadors from Siam, whom Cornelis Speckx had brought, without the admiral understanding with what purpose he had taken them, since the directors [of the VOC] had recommended that no one took on ambassadors because of the expenses involved. Before they landed, therefore, Speckx was summoned and as this problem was explained to him, he said that he could but do that; that the king desired to send them, and he had asked why the Dutch did not wish to receive them, when they received those from Johor and Achin, whose rulers were only kinglets compared to him.
>
> These ambassadors, having nonetheless disembarked on 21 December, the admiral summoned a council to consider if they should be taken to Holland. It was concluded that too much contempt would be shown to a great king if they were to be sent back, and that the kings of Bantam and all the neighbouring kings would have occasion to think that the Dutch did not wish to trade with the King of Siam, even though he was one of the most powerful kings in the Indies. According to this resolution, the admiral received the ambassadors, who gave him a small sabre as a present, the handle and scabbard of which were gilded, and they were housed in one of the small lodgings until the vessels were ready to leave.[16]

There could be no question of taking all the Siamese embassy of fifteen persons; Matelieff accepted the two chief ambassadors and sent the rest back to Siam with many compliments. During the return journey, from January to September 1608, the admiral had problems with the Siamese. Cornelis Speckx and his nephew Jan Volkertsz both died; the Siamese envoys apparently profited by the occasion to appropriate some precious stones belonging to Speckx. On 23 July Matelieff threatened the first ambassador, called "Conchi" in the texts, with having his ears cut off if he did not hand over the jewels. Conchi returned them through his colleague, thus saving both his face and his ears.

A ten-page brochure in French, discovered and published by Paul Pelliot, tells us about the Siamese ambassadors' stay in Holland. Entitled *Ambassade du Roi de Siam envoyée à l'Excellence du Prince Maurice, arrivée à La Haye le 10 septembre 1608* (The Embassy of the King of Siam sent to His Excellency the Prince Maurice, which arrived in The Hague on 10 September 1608), this curious account is worth quoting.

> On 10 September in the evening the two most directly affected in the great transactions of the East Indies arrived here, presenting themselves to His Excellency the Prince Maurice, taking with them the gentleman Corneille Matelieff, admiral, who having been courteously received by His Excellency . . . was invited to sup with His Excellency, relating in full the success of affairs in the said Indies, and the combats he had fought on several occasions with the Portuguese, having burnt thirteen of their large galleons. . . . Furthermore he related to His Excellency that the affairs of the Dutch were in very good order in the said Indies, going ever from better to better, several kings each day associating with them. In proof of which he had brought two men from the King of Siam, who had purposely come to find out if the Dutch were pirates as the Portuguese gave out to them, or if they had cities and dwellings on land.
>
> These two men of the said King of Siam were introduced to pay their respects to His Excellency the following day, and having arrived at the door of his chamber, both fell to their knees, joining their hands and placing them before their foreheads, lowering their heads several times to the ground. And although it was indicated to them they should rise, they moved three or four paces on their knees, and on rising kept their heads lowered, until His Excellency held out his hand to them, but after they had touched it, they stood up straight . . . They are brown in hue, with squashed noses, thick hair, black and rough like horses' manes, and did not wish to wear hats.
>
> Their dragoman is a young Dutchman who has spent six years there to learn the language, through whom they gave His Excellency

to understand that they were sent by their king to see his country and to offer him their friendship, sending him some presents which they had brought with them, to wit: two pikes having damascened blades, two rattan javelins, two harquebuses like ours using tinder, damascened cannons with gilded wheel-locks, which they use to kill elephants, having a big bullet like our muskets, two swords with beaten gold scabbards, two fans, and two boxes.

In one of these, being of wood, covered with cloth and sealed, was another box of ivory, and in this was the letter from the King of Siam to His Excellency in letters inscribed on beaten gold, in length three-quarters of an ell, rolled up like tinplate, the said letters being quite similar to the Syriac alphabet. The other box was made of gold contrived with much artifice in the shape of a cup, in which were sealed two small wooden boxes covered with pearls; in these were a ring of heavy solid gold, and with eight mounted rubies, with a pointed diamond in the middle, and in another gold box a ring with a ruby as big as a man's thumb-nail.

They gave His Excellency (whom they always called the King of Holland) to understand that their king was sending him these said presents, with the assurance of wishing to be his friend. At this His Excellency thanked them, declaring that for his part he was prepared to render all kinds of services to the said King of Siam.

They are simple people, and say that the said King of Siam wished to send another person, who, having disobeyed him, he had roasted in a heated cauldron in which he languished a month until he expired. He is a very powerful monarch, having under him four or five vassal kings. He can send into the field three hundred thousand men and two thousand elephants, and has active links with the King of China who is the most powerful of all. The Dutch hope to effect entry through him into China, which country is contiguous to the said kingdom of Siam to the north, and Malacca being to the south. The said kingdom is so extensive that in two months one can hardly complete crossing it.

The said two men from Siam were sent by command of His Excellency to Amsterdam, to embark on the first vessel and return to their king with presents that are being got ready. Their language is most barbarous and very difficult to interpret, the letters likewise, the words not being separated from each other. Their tunics of white cotton lack any pomp.[17]

Paul Pelliot pointed out that the list of presents and the letter engraved on gold leaf according to ancient Siamese custom prove that "Conchi" and his colleague were indeed official envoys despatched by Phra Ekathotsarot. The king therefore sincerely wished to establish diplomatic links with the United Provinces, probably to inspire awe among his neighbours. But the account of the audience granted by the stadtholder to the Siamese ambassadors does not beat about the bush; the United Provinces and the VOC, for their part, were only interested in Siam to the degree to which the country could open the enormous Chinese market to them. They had already understood that trade with Siam would not really be profitable except when subordinate to trade with China: European products, which China had no use for, would be bartered in Siam for skins which would be traded in China for products esteemed in Europe, like porcelain and silk. This idea would be taken up again in the nineteenth century by the British who forcibly imported Indian opium into China in order to pay for tea which the swift tea clippers transported to Europe.

However, Matelieff himself did not think that the VOC should enter China through Siam. He declared in a report written shortly after his return to Holland, "It had been suggested that the friendship of China should be obtained through the intermediary of the King of Siam . . . but this means does not seem to me necessary, for I do not doubt [the success] of trade with China . . ."[18] It was only later that the Dutch would discover the specific value of Siam, especially after the break in relations between the courts of Ayutthaya and Peking as a consequence of the deposition of the last Ming emperor by the Manchus in April 1644, and the installation of the Qing dynasty.

The Siamese envoys spent seventeen months in Holland, from 2 September 1608 to 30 January 1610. Only two documents allow us to follow their progress. This is in striking contrast with the avalanche of texts relating the least act and gesture of the Siamese ambassadors to France in 1686.

A resolution of the Amsterdam Chamber of the VOC dated 4 June 1609 indicates that "it was resolved that the Siamese envoys could proceed to Hoorn and Enkhuizen to visit these towns, and that they would be provided with an allowance of one hundred guilders which would cover their travel expenses and stay, and of which Evert Dircksz would give account." It seems that the suspicions of theft which clouded their arrival in Holland had moderated and they were permitted to visit these two small towns on the Zuyderzee which were important centres of the Asian trade. Their cicerone Evert Dircksz was most probably the "young Dutchman" who had served as their interpreter and who would return with them to Siam.

A decision of the Heren XVII, dated 5 September 1609, ruled on the return of the ambassadors.

> It has been resolved to send back by the next fleet the embassy of the King of Siam . . . so that commerce with China can be prepared through the favour of the King of Siam, and the said persons will offer reasonably (*ter redelycker wyze*) some presents in the name of the Company; likewise to submit to His Excellency a request for some presents which His Excellency will send to the said king, and in addition to have the ambassadors accompanied by an agent—a capable and competent person—who will offer the presents to the king in the name of His Excellency and the Company.[19]

It would seem that the "capable and competent person" charged with accompanying the ambassadors on their return and offering to the king reasonable presents (a merchant company does not commit acts of extravagance) was the selfsame Evert Dircksz, now promoted counter-ambassador.

The Siamese envoys and their Dutch colleague embarked on the VOC fleet which sailed from Texel on 30 January 1610. Its admiral Pieter Both had just been appointed governor-general of the Indies by the Heren XVII. Article 24 of his instructions recommended that he seek out the friendship and form an alliance with the King of Siam. The voyage was awful; eight vessels were scattered in a tempest in the southern seas and the new governor only set foot on land at Bantam on 19 December after a crossing lasting nearly eleven months.

Meanwhile, Phra Ekathotsarot did not stop asking what had happened to the ambassadors he had sent to his Dutch counterpart in 1607. The letters of the first director of the Ayutthaya godown, Lambert Jacobszoon Heijn, return to this many times. He informed his colleague in Pattani on 9 November 1609: "The king . . . each time he summons me, asks me when his ambassadors will return. Please bear this in mind, and advise us as soon as you have any news on this subject, so that the king can be satisfied." A year later, on 20 September 1610, Heijn told the same person: "Since the king has returned here, he has summoned me on several occasions and asked if I had not yet received any news of his ambassadors, and also if I had any reply about whether or not the Dutch desired the region of Mergui." The proposition of Mergui would be repeated in 1613, but rejected by the VOC. This refusal proves that the Dutch had no great expectations of trade with Siam and that they were chiefly thinking of China.

There is an unfortunate lacuna in the correspondence between the godowns of Ayutthaya and Pattani. A letter of 26 December 1612, written by the new director at Ayutthaya, Maerten Houtman, indicates that the ambassadors had still not returned and states, "The king here is waiting impatiently for his ambassadors and the persons His Excellency the Prince sent him." Phra Ekathotsarot had meanwhile died and been replaced on the throne by Intharacha (it is not known if the new king was his son or a usurping monk) who adopted the name Phra Song Tham, "the just king." The new sovereign, who would reign until 1628, was still unaware of the fate of his ambassadors who had left Bantam five years previously, but had learnt that the Prince of Orange had sent him a counter-ambassador.

For want of documentation, we do not know what became of these ambassadors. Could "Conchi," his colleague, and the Dutch envoy have died during the dreadful return journey of 1610? It would seem, if that were the case, that Pieter Both would not have omitted to inform the King of Siam (unless the message were lost during the troubles which preceded the advent to the throne of Phra Song Tham). Could they have been shipwrecked at the beginning of 1611 between Bantam and the bar of Siam? Or were Conchi and his accomplice afraid that the story of the stolen jewels would have reached the king's ears and he would fry them like sardines? One can appreciate that they would prefer to disappear into the jungle after their arrival in Bantam rather than try out the cauldrons in which their colleague had "languished" for a whole month. Love of one's country has its limits.

CHAPTER FOUR

THE DUTCH AND ENGLISH GODOWNS IN AYUTTHAYA (1609–1664)

THE EAGERNESS with which the King of Siam invited the Dutch company to establish itself in the port of Mergui can be understood, because he would obtain important advantages from the Dutch presence in his kingdom. The godown at Ayutthaya supplied him, on demand, shipwrights, founders of cannons, and numerous other artisans. The VOC sold him European products: firearms, engravings of ships, textiles, and glassware. Of course the king levied direct and indirect taxes on all the commercial activities which the imaginative enterprise of the Dutch devised, and they supplied him with assistance at critical military junctures. When in 1620 Phra Song Tham waged war on the King of Cambodia, Chey Chettha II, who was trying to free himself of the Siamese yoke, the governor-general Jan Pieterszoon Coen sent him two warships from Batavia equipped with Dutch cannoneers.

The VOC imported technology and European products to Siam, but its vessels left with almost empty holds, as the country produced almost nothing that was worth exporting to Europe. The establishment of a Dutch godown at Hirado in Japan somewhat redressed the situation, for the persons responsible in the VOC discovered that the export to Japan of deerskins and dried rays, which were abundant in Siam, gave rise to worthwhile trade. Joost Schouten, to whom we shall return, indicates that 150,000 deer were killed in Siam every year and their skins prepared for export. The demand for these skins was constant (the Japanese used them for leather bucklers which formed part of the samurai's outfit). But the cost of transport and the duties to pay in Japan ate into the profits to such a degree than the governor-general asked himself if this trade justified the continuation of an outpost at Ayutthaya.

THE "SITUATION IN THE KINGDOM OF SIAM"

Cornelis van Neijenrode, director of the trading station since 1617, was summoned to Batavia in 1621. His superiors considered him an authority in Siamese affairs, for he had worked in Pattani and Ligor before going to Ayutthaya. At their request he wrote a long report entitled *Vertoog van de gelegenheid des koninkrijks Siam* (Account of the situation in the kingdom of Siam),[1] the first of an important series of descriptions of Siam compiled by employees of the VOC.

Van Neijenrode was clearly convinced of the commercial interest of this country which produced more than it consumed. He lacked words to describe the oriental splendour of the court of Phra Song Tham:

> The emperor or king of Siam is surrounded by as much magnificence and such splendid ceremonial as any other king in all the Indies. His foot never touches earth; wherever he wishes to go, he is carried on a golden throne, and he shows himself once a day to the lords and nobles of his court with a display of ostentation which exceeds that of any Christian king . . . This magnificence and grandeur cannot be imagined or believed by those who have not seen it, and though I have often observed these at the court and elsewhere, and have been invited to pay my respects to His Majesty, I am unable to describe adequately the scene.

His comments on the goodness and tolerance of the Siamese "pagans" are surprising from the pen of a seventeenth-century Dutch Protestant. This is how he describes the monks:

> Their food, clothes, and other needs are generously and abundantly supplied by all, great and small, who look after their learned persons or priests very well (and more than is done in our lands for teachers), and it is a cause for sincere admiration for those of our nation to see the considerable charity which the pagans show towards each other.

Likewise, he is surprised by the tolerance these "pagans" show towards the believers of other religions, and by the gentleness of parents who only rarely beat their children, who nonetheless are obedient and submissive. The physical and moral hygiene of the Siamese, who wash three times a day, marry without having seen their spouse beforehand, and despise flirting philanderers, visibly astonished the honest man who was Cornelis van Neijenrode. What was the world coming to if the behaviour of pagans was more edifying than that of Christians?

This enthusiastic plea in favour of maintaining the godown at Ayutthaya seems to have convinced nobody in Batavia. The outpost was temporarily closed in 1622, greatly to the annoyance of Phra Song Tham. But the company changed its mind in 1624, sending Pieter van der Elst to Ayutthaya, ordering him to buy rice for Batavia and skins and sappanwood for Japan. Trade remained very indifferent though; Batavia was contemplating closing the post again when in 1628 a letter and presents arrived for Phra Song Tham from the new stadtholder, Prince Frederick Henry of Orange-Nassau.

The letter, according to custom, was translated from Dutch into Portuguese, from Portuguese into Malay, and from Malay into Siamese. The director of the godown in Ayutthaya, Adriaan de Marees and his assistant, Joost Schouten, were charged with presenting the letter and gifts to the king, as the ambassador sent by the previous stadtholder had died during the outward journey. Joost Schouten was very impressed by the audience granted by Phra Song Tham in the presence of the mandarins. The king enquired about the health of the new "king or prince of Holland," and wished to know if the transfer of power was conducted peacefully. The question was all the more pertinent since these transitions in Siam traditionally led to bloody disorders.

Phra Song Tham departed this world in December 1628 and his death led to the usual carnage. The eldest son of the dead king, Prince Chettha, mounted the throne with the name Phra Chetthathirat, but was assassinated in August 1629 by the minister of war, Ok-ya Kalahom Suriyawong, a distant cousin of Phra Song Tham. Prince Athittayawong, who had the audacity to succeed his brother, suffered the same fate in September. The usurper then placed himself on the throne, and reigned until 1656 with the name Prasat Thong, "the king of the golden palace."[2] During his brief reign, Phra Chetthathirat had shown his sympathy towards the VOC, conferring on de Marees the title of *Ok-luang* accompanied by a silver betel box, and Joost Schouten was granted the title of *Ok-khun* with which went a golden sword. The two returned to Batavia, leaving the godown in the hands of underlings.

COMPETITION FROM THE EAST INDIA COMPANY

Before having completely pushed the Portuguese into the background, the Dutch had to confront the English, who were also trying to establish themselves in Siam.[3] The first Englishman who went to Siam was Ralph Fitch whose voyage to Aleppo on board the *Tiger* is mentioned by one of the witches in *Macbeth*,[4] and whom Jan Huyghen van Linschoten snatched from the clutches of the Portuguese Inquisition in Goa in 1584 by persuading him to abjure Protestantism. Taking the view that his life was well worth a mass, Fitch left Goa without delay for Burma, where the King of Pegu, Nanda Bhureng, was preparing to invade Siam, then governed by Phra Maha Thammaracha, the father of Phra Naresuan. Fitch followed the Burmese army and visited Chiang Mai and the Shan States in 1586–1587. His account seems to have inspired Sir James Lancaster to organize in 1591 the first English expedition to the East Indies; it put into port in Malaya and perhaps Pattani in June 1592.[5]

In 1608 William Keeling, who had turned grey exploring the eastern seas, commanded three vessels of the East India Company, the *Dragon*, the *Hector*, and the *Consent*. He dropped anchor in the roads of Bantam, where he met an ambassador of the King of Siam. He invited him to dine on board the *Dragon* and, seeking openings for English goods, enquired about trade and Siamese markets. The diplomat assured him that "a million lengths of red stuff would sell in his country in two days, and in great quantities each year, because they use it to adorn their elephants and horses."[6] Gold was found there in great abundance and its purity was such that it was worth three times its weight in silver; precious stones were legion and sold cheaply. His king would be happy to enter into commercial dealings with so great a king as that of England to whom "the King of Holland could not be compared."[7] The English heard that Phra Ekathotsarot had burst out laughing when he learnt that the Dutch had no king.

After returning to England in May 1610, Keeling transmitted to those responsible in the East India Company his information about this El Dorado where the elephants wanted nothing more than to be dressed in English stuff. It was decided to explore the Siamese market and send the *Globe* there, commanded by Anthony Hippon. He set sail in February 1611 and cast anchor in Pattani in June 1612. After some difficulties, and in spite of the objections of the Dutch, its queen permitted the English to open a godown. Anthony Hippon died in Pattani and was replaced by Thomas Essington.

Essington left shortly after with some English factors for Ayutthaya, where they arrived at the end of August. On 17 September they were received in solemn audience by Phra Song Tham to whom they presented, placed on a golden container, a letter from James I, "King of Great Britain, Ireland, Scotland, and France." The King of Siam was delighted to see other Europeans set up in his capital. He gave each Englishman a small gold goblet and a jerkin, authorized the East India Company to open a godown in Ayutthaya, and himself bought a large part of the English goods they had brought. The representatives of the VOC did not put out the flags, but they knew they could not oppose the installation of the intruders. Frictions of all kinds soon soured the relations between the Dutch and English godowns.

The profits were perhaps not as great as those the Siamese ambassador had dangled before the eyes of William Keeling, but the English soon discovered that Siam had an unsuspected advantage: the country maintained excellent commercial links with Japan. The shogun Tokugawa Ieyasu, in power since 1603, had just written to Phra Song Tham asking him for muskets and perfumed wood known as eaglewood (*aquilaria agallocha*). The English had met several Japanese at Ayutthaya and Pattani. They had the reputation of being clever sailors and intrepid soldiers. Their unswerving loyalty was so esteemed that the kings of Siam had formed an elite Japanese palace guard. They played an important and sometimes decisive role in the dynastic troubles following the deaths of Kings Ekathotsarot (between 1610–1611) and Song Tham (between 1628–1629). The head of the Japanese community in Ayutthaya, Yamada Yizayemon Nagamasa, seems to have contributed substantially to the seizure of power by the usurper Prasat Thong in September 1629.[8] The artistic quality of Japanese goods imported into Siam impressed the English and inspired in them the strong desire to trade with so cultivated and disciplined a race.

William Adams, perhaps the first Englishman to have lived in Japan, had arrived there in 1600 as a pilot on board a Dutch fleet whose vessels had the names of the three cardinal virtues (*Het*

Gheloove, De Hoop, and *De Liefde*).[9] They visited Ayutthaya in August 1612 at the very time Thomas Essington and his companions were presenting the letter from James I to Phra Song Tham. His enthusiasm for Japan seems to have taken hold of his compatriots who had set up shop in Ayutthaya. Will Adams had been retained in Japan by the shogun Ieyasu, who appreciated his knowledge of naval construction and nautical skills. Adams had been offered a small domain at Miura, near Yokosuka; the Englishman, who had taken a Japanese wife, was known in Japan as Miura Anjin, the pilot of Miura. He had ships built for the shogun; one of them went as far as Mexico in 1610. After his return from Ayutthaya to Osaka, he obtained the authorization for the East India Company to open a godown on the small island of Hirado (1613) where the Dutch had established themselves four years previously. Their frustration could be understood. Miura Anjin died in 1620 in his house in Yokosuka without having seen his native land again.[10]

The installation of the English in Japan deprived Ayutthaya of its principal attraction in their eyes. Worse, the profits of Siamese trade were so meagre that the British company decided to abandon its outpost in Ayutthaya in 1623. The bribes demanded by Siamese officials and the interloping trade conducted by the English employees to the detriment of their company seem to have been the chief reasons of the failure of the English godown in Ayutthaya in the reign of Phra Song Tham.

For their part, the Dutch did all they could to discourage the English. A particularly dramatic moment in this commercial war occurred on 17 July 1619 in the Bay of Pattani. Three Dutch warships commanded by Hendrik Janszoon attacked about midday two English merchant ships, the *Hound* and the *Sampson*; they had arrived from the Coromandel Coast with merchandise and men to give new impetus to the failing godowns of Pattani and Ayutthaya. The bitter fight lasted a good five hours, at the end of which John Jordan, the captain of the *Sampson*, hauled up the white flag and sent his second-in-command on board the lead ship, *De Engel*, to parley. Jordan was killed with a musket shot while leaning against the mainmast to observe the unfolding of the negotiations through his telescope. His death ended the fight. The two English vessels were seized by the Dutch, who tipped the dead overboard and put the survivors, even those severely wounded, in chains.[11]

The two rival companies provisionally left the Siamese capital in

1622 and 1623, perhaps because they had both set up there for the wrong reasons. The English at first saw Siam as the key which would open to them the Japanese market, from which they expected so much; and the Dutch, who only dreamt of Chinese silks and porcelain, persisted in considering Siam as the antechamber to the Middle Kingdom, *Zhong guo.*

The English were not to reopen their godowns in Ayutthaya and Pattani until after 1660, but they did not neglect, on leaving, to ensure themselves of Phra Song Tham's friendship. The list of farewell presents they offered him in the name of their king is preserved:

> some curious pictures of men and women; a picture of the people and habits of all countries; and a picture of all wild beasts, which a fair map may sufficiently express; a curious perspective glass, fair and good; a fair and neat case of pistols; an English watch; six yards of fine scarlet; scarlet baize so much as will cover his oliphant [elephant], which may be some fifteen yards; with any other novelties of no great value.[12]

The Dutch soon returned to Ayutthaya, but the English were not to reopen their godown until 1661, just in time to see the first French arrive. Meanwhile, the Danes also arrived through the opening presented by Siam to the outside world.

THE DANISH EAST INDIES COMPANY DISCOVERS SIAM

During the reign of the shrewd Christian IV (1588–1648), Denmark, inspired by the example of the Dutch and English, became interested in Asian trade. In expectation of added prosperity for his kingdom and an increase of his personal fortune through trade, Christian IV encouraged the foundation in 1616 of the *Dansk Ostindik Kompagni*, the Danish East Indies Company. It was to last, under different names and after surviving difficult moments, until 1843.

The idea of this establishment came from two Dutch merchants, Herman Rosencrantz and Jan de Willum, who in 1616 obtained a monopoly on trade between Denmark and the East Indies, China, and Japan for twelve years. The capital of 190,000 Danish thalers was rather modest. The first fleet sailed from Copenhagen on 14 November 1618, comprising two warships, the *David* and the *Elefanten*, a reconnaissance vessel, the *Øresund*, and two merchant ships, the *Kristian* and the *København*. The Dutch captain of the *Øresund*, Roland Crappé, played a leading role throughout the voyage. The ships either belonged to the Danish crown or to the new company.[13]

A Dutch factor, Boschouwer, had lived some years in Ceylon at the court of King Senerat of Kandy, who had made him a prince and head of his council. These honours had gone to his head; as the United Provinces made fun of his princely airs, he went to offer his services to the King of Denmark. Boschouwer gave him to understand that the King of Kandy wanted nothing more than to open his states to the Danes and shower gold and spices on them. Of course, he took part in the expedition, but his death during the outward voyage ruined the Singhalese expectations of the Danes. They were very badly received in Kandy, and their leader, Gjedde Tommerup, decided to try his luck on the Coromandel Coast.[14]

On 9 September 1620 the Danish expedition dropped anchor in the small port of Tranquebar. The Raja of Tanjore granted them, in return for an annual payment, a small plot of land near this port, where they built the fortified godown of Dansborg. Afterwards, they set up the godown of Frederiksnagor at Serampur, and then a third establishment in the Nicobar Islands. The Danes soon were involved in commercial exchanges with Siam through the port of Tenasserim, which then went by the name of Nakhon Tranauwasri. There they landed their goods (mostly firearms) which they exchanged for elephants to be sold at Tranquebar.

It was the enterprising Dutch captain Roland Crappé who made the first journey to Tenasserim. He arrived there in December 1621 in the reign of Phra Song Tham. Three Siamese letters, preserved in the National Archives (*Rigsarkivet*) at Copenhagen, relate to this journey. The first, dated the thirteenth of the first lunar month in the year of the cock, the third of the decade (or 10 December 1621), was written by the governor of Tenasserim, Ok-ya Chaiyathibodi Srironnarongaliichai Aphaiphiriyabarakromaphabu. It granted all commercial facilities to Captain Crappé, called Karabek de Dilamas, and waived the usual customs duties of eight per cent to be paid in kind, in the name of friendship between the Danes and Siam. It also indicated that victuals and provisions would be graciously provided by His Excellency to the captain and the *farang* soldiers. The two other letters, from a functionary of lesser rank, deal with the same subject. It is clear then that the Siamese were only too anxious to break out of their economic isolation and trade with the Danes. These letters, written in pencil, contain the first known references to the word *farang*. The term probably derives from the Persian *feringhi*, meaning "Franks," and more generally "Westerners," and was to be used in the reign of Phra Narai particularly in reference to the French.

We do not know if the voyage of the *Øresund* to Tenasserim was followed by others. It seems likely that they were, for the Danish company, in spite of its modest funding, conducted quite substantial trade from its godowns of Dansborg and Frederiksnagor. But this success soon incurred the displeasure of the Dutch company which succeeded in excluding the Danes from the markets it controlled.

To add to its woes, the Thirty Years War which ravaged Western Europe so preoccupied Denmark that it was unable to defend its interests at the other end of the earth. The moribund Danish company was finally obliged to cede its privileges and installations to the Danish government, and pay back the sums it had been advanced. A new company was created out of the debris of the old in 1670, but its role was to be extremely modest. Although as unfortunate as the first, it nonetheless prevented the French from setting up at Tranquebar in July 1672.

THE NEW DUTCH GODOWN AT AYUTTHAYA

The Dutch returned to the Siamese capital in 1624, but their affairs did not prosper. The new governor-general Jacques Specx (1629–1632) decided to close the establishment there as soon as he assumed office. In 1632 his successor Hendrik Brouwer sent Anthony Caen to Ayutthaya to seek privileges for the trade in deerskins and sappanwood. He was also to find out if the King of Siam was disposed to guarantee an annual delivery of a fixed quantity of rice to the company.

The unfortunate Caen had to submit to the interminable waiting for and the painful gymnastics of a royal audience, because not everyone can crawl three hundred paces doubled up without intense backache. Prasat Thong, the successor of Phra Song Tham, appeared behind a golden lattice, listened to the reading of the translation of the translation of the translation of the letter from the governor-general, spoke of this and that and the health of the envoy, told him that the *Phra Khlang* (the chief minister in charge of contacts with foreigners) would deal with his affairs, and drew his curtain. The *Phra*

Khlang exhausted himself in vague promises and florid compliments. Caen finally learnt from the mouth of the interpreter that he would obtain nothing without sweeteners for the *Ok-luang* who would draw up the documents, the *Ok-ya* who would check them, and the *Ok-phra* who would seal them.

Caen returned to Batavia, but his bitter report[15] did not stop the godown at Ayutthaya being reopened once more. The new director, Joost Schouten, returned there in May 1633 with Jeremias van Vliet as his deputy. He was well received, for Prasat Thong was seeking the military assistance of the Dutch for an expedition he was planning against the Queen of Pattani who had shaken off Siamese tutelage. He obtained the concession of a plot of land located at the "distance of a musket shot" from the capital, on the left bank of the Chao Phraya, with a quay on the river one hundred metres long. He immediately began the construction of a new godown which was completed in April 1636. Batavia sent the construction materials which could not be found in Siam. The cost of the work (more than ten thousand guilders) was considerable, but the result brought cries of admiration from European travellers, notably Gijsbrecht Heeck, who visited the godown at Ayutthaya in 1655 and left a detailed description of it.[16]

The ensemble, located opposite the Portuguese and next to the Japanese trading establishments, was protected by a canal which was traversed by a bridge. In addition to the main warehouse one hundred feet long, and the principal residence of the director and his assistants, other brick buildings housed a surgeon, a butler, a cook, a trumpeter, a sculptor, carpenters, two blacksmiths, some sailors, a bookbinder, a baker, and a groom. The lack of a pastor confirms that the Dutch were not there to save souls. There was a pavilion with a billiard table for the "young employees." The presence of a prison behind the kitchens suggests that the billiard room was not patronized by all. Bamboo stables housed a dozen horses which were ridden in the dry season. Sheep, goats, geese, ducks, pigeons, and cranes had their appropriate quarters. A garden filled with pomegranate, orange, and lime trees separated the living quarters from a small cemetery. The foundations of the main building (*tuk daeng*) still remain; in 1956 the Netherlands placed a commemorative plaque there indicating: "Here, from 1634 to 1767, was the VOC godown."

In exchange for his square dealing, Joost Schouten was able to convince Batavia in 1634 to send, under his orders, a fleet of six armed vessels to Pattani in support of an army sent there by the King of Siam. This joint punitive expedition was to conquer by sea and by land the *n*th attempt at freedom by the queen, Raja Ungu, who had joined forces this time with the Portuguese, who were very out of favour in Ayutthaya. But the synchronization of the operation was faulty, and the Siamese army had already failed completely and withdrawn when Schouten arrived with his fleet off Pattani. The admiral could only round up a few stray inhabitants who he sent in halters to Ayutthaya as proof of his good will. Prasat Thong raged, convinced the Dutch had betrayed him. The accounts of the prisoners from Pattani and the sight of them tied up like sausages mollified him and made him understand that Schouten and his men were above reproach, but that his military leaders had bungled the operation. He had a few heads cut off, his good humour returned, and he conferred, unprecedentedly, a gold betel box and the corresponding rank on Schouten; he became the first European to take part in private audiences at which only the *khunnang* of high rank were present.

JOOST SCHOUTEN, A WELL-INFORMED OBSERVER

No employee of the VOC played a more important role in Siam than Schouten. King Prasat Thong regularly consulted him and protested when he was recalled by his superiors in 1636. But Schouten returned to Ayutthaya the same year for a last time, bearing a letter and presents from the prince stadtholder Frederick Henry of Orange-Nassau. It was during this stay that he compiled his small book on Siam which was to be published in The Hague in 1638: *Notitie vande Situatie, Regeeringe, Macht, Religie, Costuymen, Traffijquen ende andere Remerquable Saacken des Coninghrijcks Siams* (Notice on the situation, government, power, religion, customs, commerce, and other remarkable things in the kingdom of Siam).

This account of a well-placed individual is precious. A brief geographic exposé precedes a striking description of the absolute power and oriental pomp of the court of the King of Siam. Here he is at the end of the monsoon, taking part in the solemn procession on land (*kathin bok*) or over water (*kathin nam*) at Wat Si Sanphet.

> Once every year, about the moneth of October, the King of Siam shews himself by water and land in state to his people, going to the principal Temple of the Gods, to offer there for the welfare of his

Person and Kingdom, the manner follows:—When he goes by land, the procession is led by two hundred Elephants, each attended with three armed men; these are followed by many Musitians with Gomnies [gongs], Pipes and Drums, and a thousand men richly armed, and provided with Banners: Then march the great Lords of the Kingdom on horse-back, many of them wearing Crowns of Gold upon their heads; and every one waited upon by sixty, eighty, or an hundred men on foot: Two hundred Japan Souldiers follow these with bright Arms and rich Colours, and much noise of Instruments; then comes the Lifeguard with the King's Horses and Elephants, richly adorned with precious Stones and Gold furniture; which is followed by many Servants loaded with fruits and presents for the Sacrifice, accompanied with a sweet consort of Musick: These are again followed by many of the great Ones on foot, with folded hands; as also some Crowned Grandees, whereof one carrieth the gilded Standard, and the other the Sword of Justice; his Majesty follows next in person in his royal Robes, sitting upon an Elephant, or else a gilded Throne, carried upon mens shoulders, and waited upon by many Lords and Courtiers; the Prince, or Heir of the Kingdom, followeth him; and then in order the Kings Wives and Concubins, seated upon Elephants in little enclosed Cabinets; lastly the ordinary Courtiers follow; the whole provision consisting of fifteen or sixteen thousand persons, having its rear brought up by six hundred armed men.

But if the King go by water, then two hundred Lords, each in his Barge, seated in a gilded Cabinet, with eighty or ninety Rowers lead the van; these are followed by ten extraordinary rich figured Praws, or Barges, the which, as also the Oars, are all gilded, each having ninety or an hundred Watermen: The King is in the richest of them, sitting like an Idol upon a golden Throne, with his Lords in the humblest posture at his feet: the royal Banner is born by one of these Grandees, at the head of the Barge, in state. The King's Brother followeth next with his Train; and after him his Majesties Wives and Concubins, in gilded Cabinets and Tents, each in their Barges apart: lastly the Gentry, Courtiers, Guards, and other Attendants follow, the whole amounting to five or six and twenty thousand persons. The River is bordered on both sides with Boats, and an infinite number of People, who reverence and adore their King in his passage, with bended heads and folded hands. [17]

Siamese justice is presented as severe but correct. Schouten must have been aware that Prasat Thong was in the process of overhauling the kingdom's legislation, and had notably introduced a law of appeal (1633), a law of succession (1635), a law determining the status of slaves or *that* (1637), and a law governing debts (1648).[18] The manner of deciding uncertain cases by ordeal remains surprising.

> Where the case is doubtful, no witnesses appearing, nor no strong presumptions against the accused, so that the Judge knows not how nor what to do, he then permits both parties to try it out by common purgation; either by ducking under water, holding their hands in boyling oyl, to go bare-foot upon hot coals, or to eat a mess of charmed rice; this conjured mess being made up into balls, is given them by the Priest with much ceremony; and he that can swallow it without casting it up again, and behave himself in this and the other trials with most courage, is esteemed most innocent and acquitted, whilst the other, whether accusor or accused, is most severely punished, according to the nature of the crime.

The elephant hunt (an inevitable topic in the descriptions of Siam in the seventeenth century) is described with a wealth of details which reveal an attentive witness invited by the king to an impressive spectacle where domesticated elephants were used to attract, capture, and tame wild elephants in special enclosures, the *phaniat.*

The success of the *Notitie des Coninghrijcks Siams* of Joost Schouten was considerable. It was soon translated into several languages and brought fame to its author. His ignominious end is in complete contrast with his career as an important official of the VOC and an early ethnographer. After a brief stay in the Netherlands in 1638, the year in which his work was published, he returned to Batavia, where he served the company as counsellor to the governor Antonio van Diemen, who employed him in various diplomatic missions to Malacca, Aceh, and other places.

He was accused in 1644 of indulging in the "silent sin," that is, sodomy. During his trial, he confessed to having started this practice during his stay in Siam, but the Calvinist traders of the VOC called to judge him showed themselves far from understanding the exotic habits of their colleague. Considering that "this filthy and evil sodomitic sin" was so abominable in the eyes of God that He had "destroyed with the fire of Heaven countries and towns to warn the whole world," they condemned him to death. Schouten was strangled at the stake, his body burnt, his ashes scattered to the winds, and his goods confiscated to the profit of the company. What a splendid windfall for the just was the end of this miscreant, especially as he was not poor! Let us shed a tear for Joost Schouten, guilty of having loved Siam to excess.

JEREMIAS VAN VLIET AND THE "PICNIC AFFAIR"

The new director, or *opperhoofd*, of the godown at Ayutthaya, Jeremias van Vliet, does not seem to have possessed the diplomatic qualities of his predecessor. During his period of office (1636–1641), several incidents came close to seriously compromising relations between the company and the King of Siam. The most important is known as the "picnic affair."

On 10 December 1636, the Dutch under-factor Reynier van Tzum, nine assistants, and some servants profited from the fine weather to organize a trip on the Chao Phraya. They landed near a temple for a bibulous picnic. Two tipsy assistants, Joost Laureysen and Daniel Jacobsen, began to cause trouble with some monks. If only they had stayed quietly at the godown playing billiards! Soldiers at the residence of the *fai na*, the brother of the king, alerted about the trouble, came to the scene. Abuse and stones were hurled and fisticuffs ensued. The Dutch tried to get on board their barge, but all of them were arrested, tied up, and delivered to the *Phra Khlang*.

News of the incident soon came to the ears of Van Vliet at the same time as troubling rumours. The affair had been greatly blown out of proportion to the king who was so enraged that he was ready to have the Dutchmen trampled to death by his elephants. Van Vliet ran to the *Phra Khlang* to inform him that the execution of his men would violate the honour of the VOC governor-general and the consequences would be terrible. He also got to work on a *khunnang* who had the king's ear. The king finally calmed down and had the prisoners released, but Van Vliet had to submit a month later to a dishonourable ceremony.

This is his own account of it:

> After we had crossed the inner gate of the palace, [the interpreter] Trompanit gave me . . . a wooden tray covered with flowers and uncooked rice. He told me to hold it in both my hands and carry it in a humble and supplicating manner to the king. However, as it is an admission of a crime which all offenders are required to carry when they beseech the king's pardon and show their gratitude in spite of their guilt, I politely refused, protesting in truth that I personally had not offended His Majesty.

But there was nothing for it, and Van Vliet was compelled to submit.

> I have never seen the court so crowded . . . When we had come within some sixty metres to the place where the mandarins were assembled, I had to crawl with the above-mentioned tray in one hand to approach the assembly. When I arrived there, the king appeared on his throne . . .

The *Phra Khlang* then proclaimed aloud that Van Vliet had come "to express his guilty gratitude for the generous pardon which Your Majesty has granted his companions." Prasat Thong gave a short speech, which ended with these words: "You will henceforth carry the weight of your men. I shall hold you personally responsible. Since you are their head, it is just that you look after your members and you assume responsibility for them." Van Vliet was constrained to sign an undertaking that the Dutch would henceforth respect the laws and customs of the kingdom and that he would be personally answerable for them.

The VOC godown in Ayutthaya thus did not enjoy extraterritoriality and the immunity this implies. For that we have to wait for the show of force and the treaty of 1664. Van Vliet was summoned to Batavia to justify himself; he took along the two now sober assistants responsible for the picnic affair. They were severely punished, and Van Vliet was upbraided for having submitted to an humiliating ceremony and for having signed a document which was incompatible with the honour and prestige of the company.

THE "DESCRIPTION OF THE KINGDOM OF SIAM"

Van Vliet is well known to Thai historians for his precious historical accounts. His first text, the *Beschryving van het Koningryk Siam* (Description of the kingdom of Siam)[19] is conceived like the short works of van Neijenrode and Schouten, but is much more extensive. His other works are less well known. *The Short History of the past events and the succession of the kings of Siam* taken from ancient histories[20] draws on Siamese chronicles which have since disappeared and oral traditions. *The historical relation of the illness and death of Phra Interra-Tsia, the twenty-second king of Siam, and the present king now reigning, Phra Ongh Sri*[21] relate the last days of Phra Song Tham (or Intharacha) and the way in which Prasat Thong seized the throne. This last text seems to draw on the testimonies of well-placed eyewitnesses of the dynastic drama.

The *Description of the Kingdom of Siam* comprises short well-documented chapters on the country's geography, history, defences, politics, and economy. We are given glimpses of the Portuguese, the Spanish, the Dutch, the "Moors," the Japanese, and Chinese in Siam and very detailed descriptions of the capital and the court. The chapters describing the *kathin* and trials by ordeal confirm the accounts of Schouten. His remarks on education, family and sexual life, and the written and spoken language are comparable to the pages La Loubère would write at the end of the century. The passage concerning the legendary white elephants runs thus:

> Sometimes it happens that a white elephant is caught in Siam. This nation considers it a marvel of nature, and to its neighbours it is a prince of elephants. The kings of Siam often have one in their court; it is sumptuously housed, bedecked and treated, and well provided with attendants and train. His Majesty regularly visits it, his mandarins and vassals worship it, and its table service is of pure gold. At the beginning of the reign of the present king, a young white elephant was captured who suddenly died in the year 1633. His Majesty was so indisposed by this death that all the slaves who had looked after and watched over the animal during its illness were executed. Furthermore the king paid homage to the deceased beast; he had it interred in one of the finest temples and had constructed a small pyramidical structure over its tomb. But after having spent some time in the ground, it was disinterred and cremated with a

> pomp which exceeded that I have seen for the greatest of the mandarins. What the fire did not consume was gathered into a coffin and buried in the above-mentioned temple; a fine pyramid [*stupa*] was built over it.
>
> The Siamese believe, in addition to its princely rank, there is something divine about these animals. They tell many stories about them, saying that they not only respect them for their pale colour, but also because of their supernatural intelligence. It glories in its condition and treatment, but is however sad and melancholy when it has them not and the black elephants do not revere it. All that seems incredible, but the Siamese, having much experience of these animals, believe it to be true.
>
> In the month of May of the year 1635 a strange miracle occurred in Siam. The king was informed that at some twenty leagues upstream from the city of Ayutthaya a white elephant had been born in the middle of the forest. His Majesty despatched in haste Oya Poucelouq [Ok-ya Phitsanulok] with four of the greatest mandarins to the place to confirm the news. On arriving there, the said lords observed that the animal was indeed such as had been indicated and immediately sent him news of this. Transported with joy and considering that a great good fortune had befallen him, His Majesty went to the place with many nobles and a magnificent retinue to admire the venerable animal and bring it back in great pomp to his capital. But as soon as he landed to come close to the elephant, it turned black, filling the mandarins with mortal terror, astonishment and fear that the king would think he had been deceived. But Oya Poucelouq summoned up all his courage, ran to His Majesty and told him what had happened. The king was as much surprised as astounded; he went to see the animal and had it taken to Ayutthaya. After spending a night there, it became as red as copper and has not changed since. It was Oya Poucelouq himself who told me this . . . [22]

The inability of Van Vliet to understand Buddhism and present it other than as frankly ridiculous idolatry is typical of the seventeenth century, even if he is full of admiration for the pure life of its monks. He recognizes clearly that the tolerance shown by the Siamese towards other religions is the chief cause for the lack of success of the Portuguese missionaries:

> They maintain that Heaven can be attained by different religions

> provided one does good, and that the Lord favours all religions . . . so that it is not easy to bring them to change theirs, and still less for the Christian religion, as the Portuguese have observed for many years and after the efforts of many religious orders to introduce the Roman religion . . . [23]

This plain merchant from Schiedam who turned his hand to the history of Siam remarked on the indifference of the Siamese towards their own history and that of others—an indifference which surprises a European in the tradition of Herodotus.

> Although the ancient chronicles and credit-worthy stories are harbingers of the past, the testimonies of the centuries, the arbiters of the present and the portents for the future, the Siamese have little truck with them. The situation, government, power, religion, customs, trade and other remarkable aspects of foreign nations are totally unknown to them and they are incurious about them. So they have few descriptions of the antiquities in their country as causes of war, peace treaties, conquests, or loss of provinces and towns, victories or defeats, battles, intrepid heroes, persons who have excelled in their accomplishments or their knowledge, etc . . . There are few persons among the nobility or the rich bourgeois who know anything more than the chronicles or orally-related stories.[24]

The Western concept of history is linear and irreversible, and comes from the Greeks. Each single event is unique and irreplaceable, and worthy of being recorded. Siamese traditions are shaped by Buddhism and Hinduism and thus by the belief in reincarnation. The concept of history is circular; events of the past are reproduced in the future and thus lose much of their interest.

Van Vliet was obviously not the only Westerner to be struck by this Siamese trait. Anna Leonowens, the English governess who lived six years at the court of King Mongkut in the 1860s, noted that "The libraries of the monasteries are rich in works on the theory and practice of medicine; but very poor in historical books, the few preserved dealing mainly with the lives and actions of Siamese rulers, oddly associated with the genii and heroes of Hindoo mythology."[25]

Thai historians only discovered the considerable contribution of Van Vliet to the history of their country in the twentieth century. The author left Ayutthaya in 1641 to be named director in Malacca, which the Dutch had just seized from the Portuguese. But suspicion of corruption and interloping trade marred the end of his career. The company granted him an honourable discharge but required his departure. In 1647 he returned to Schiedam, his native town, where he was elected burgomaster before dying in 1663.

His successors in Ayutthaya managed, for the most part, to maintain excellent relations with the court of Prasat Thong. The Dutch were without doubt the most favoured nation in Siam, but they had constantly to try and free the VOC from involvement in military expeditions which the king undertook against his neighbours or insurgent vassals. This neutrality though did not help the commercial interests of the company; from 1648, the annual accounts of the Ayutthaya godown too often showed liabilities in spite of the export of deerskins to Japan and rice to Batavia.

PHRA NARAI AND THE DUTCH

During the dynastic tensions which followed the death of Prasat Thong, the VOC seems to have maintained the strictest neutrality so long as a strongman did not emerge from the conflict. Only from the time it was obvious that Phra Narai was clearly in control did the newly arrived director Jan van Rijck (1656–1662) go to "drink the oath of allegiance" before the new king, the Persian *Phra Khlang*, and the ministers. For some years, relations were satisfactory, but Narai's wars against Lanna and Burma disturbed the trade in deerskins which the king exported on his own account to Japan in spite of the privileges granted by his predecessors to the Dutch company. The re-establishment of the English East India Company (EIC) in Ayutthaya in June 1661 did nothing to calm the situation.

A conflict arose in 1662 when a VOC ship, the *Rode Hert*, seized a Portuguese junk near Macao which was trading on behalf of the Siamese crown. Phra Narai, outraged, demanded an indemnity of 84,000 guilders. Johan Maetsuyker, whose very long term of office as VOC governor-general (1653–1678) coincides with the peak of Dutch power and prosperity in Asia, reacted energetically. Considering the negative trade balance in Siam, the substantial indemnity required by Phra Narai, and the fact that Batavia was less in need of Siamese rice, he ordered the closure of the godown at Ayutthaya in May 1663. In September he sent the *Princesse Royale*, the *Hoogcaspel*, and the *Elsenburg* to Siam to bring back to Batavia the fourteen company employees and the goods and chattels remaining there. The captains of the last two named ships were ordered to drop anchor at the bar of Siam and "selectively" blockade river traffic. Obeying their orders, they seized, among others, a cargo of a Chinese junk armed by Phra Narai which was returning from Japan. The blockade from October 1663 to February 1664 effectively created a state of war between the VOC and Siam. Dutch sources dispute the term "war" and speak rather of "preventative measures": colonialism has its reticences.

Meanwhile the *Princesse Royale* had arrived in Ayutthaya with secret instructions for the director of the godown, Enoch Poolvoet. He was ordered to announce to the king that a special envoy of the VOC would soon arrive to discuss the question of the indemnity, and to conceal from him as long as possible his departure and the closure of the Dutch establishment. He had his men and the company's most valuable possessions placed in a barge on the pretext of going on a trip, and then went a little upstream to go on board the *Princesse Royale*, which set sail and began to go down the Chao Phraya. Phra Narai despatched mandarins who asked "with a contrite air" why the company had closed its godown. No longer able to flee the scene as he had hoped, Poolvoet replied that as the envoy promised by Batavia had still not arrived, he had become "most melancholy" and had withdrawn to a company vessel fearing hostile acts.

The mandarins explained to him that Phra Narai had nothing to do with the untoward treatment the Dutch were complaining of. On the contrary, he had imprisoned Abdur-Razzaq or Ok-ya Phichit, a minister of Persian origin who had contributed to inflaming relations between the crown and the VOC. The man had been dragged with a rope round his neck to the foot of the throne and forced to eat pork; for good measure he had been smeared from top to toe with pork fat, and the king had threatened to have him executed "in a most unpleasant way."

These touching proofs of good faith suggest that Phra Narai realized he had gone too far and could not do without the Dutch. It is certain that the king feared reprisals from the company, of whose striking force he was well aware. It was agreed that Poolvoet and his men would return to Batavia and that the king would send ambassadors to decide on the clauses of a new treaty between Siam and the VOC.

The governor-general indeed received the Siamese mandarins and sent off a personal envoy, Pieter de Bitter, armed with complete authority to sign an agreement. He learnt on arriving that Phra Narai, fearing an attack by the company, had precipitately concluded a peace treaty with his enemy, the King of Pegu. Bitter could therefore negotiate from a position of strength, and took advantage of it.

The treaty between the Siamese crown and the Dutch company was signed on 22 August 1664. It guaranteed considerable commercial and diplomatic advantages for the Dutch. Their monopoly in the trade in skins was confirmed, and they agreed on their part to pay an indemnity for the seized junk. Memories of the picnic affair of 1636 and the affront suffered by Jeremias van Vliet and the VOC remained strong in Dutch memories. Pieter de Bitter required and obtained a concession:

> If—may God prevent it!—an employee of the company commits a serious crime in Siam, he will not be judged by the king nor the courts of Siam, but will be brought before the director of the Honorable Company to be punished according to Dutch laws. And if the said director himself should commit a capital crime, His Majesty could have him arrested until the governor-general be informed of the matter.[26]

The company, like a sovereign nation, had thus obtained diplomatic immunity and the prerogatives of extraterritoriality. The behaviour of the VOC employees based in Ayutthaya was to be such that recourse to this clause was never necessary, but the prestige of the Dutch was considerably enhanced thereby. The king complained that they had caused him to lose face.

Phra Narai showed himself more inflexible in relation to Chinese sailors serving on Siamese junks; this practice had always irritated the Dutch, for it allowed the Siamese themselves to export their products to Japan. The king also refused to consent to the departure from Siam of children born of Dutch fathers and Siamese mothers, considering that they were his subjects; he only allowed the departure of children of less than seven years.

The treaty of 1664 normalized relations between Siam and the VOC, but the company from this point only played a discreet role in the country. Phra Narai constantly took back with one hand what he gave with the other, and the return of the English, invited by the king, made the Dutch less indispensable. The appearance of the French was soon to shuffle the cards, for Phra Narai counted on them to counterbalance the different powers.

THE ENGLISH EAST INDIA COMPANY RETURNS TO SIAM

The second attempt of the East India Company to set up shop in the Siamese capital was in response to an initiative of Phra Narai, who felt he was threatened by the Dutch. The EIC had been operating in Lovek in Cambodia, but the invasion of the country by Annam in 1659 had forced the English to withdraw to Ayutthaya, where they were warmly welcomed by the king. He ordered that their head, Rawlins, be given an official invitation addressed to the English company, whose headquarters were still at Surat. The president, Matthew Andrews, consulted his colleagues, the three Lambton brothers, and decided to give the proposal a try. The *Hopewell* was fitted out, and three company employees were put on board, together with goods destined for the Siamese market.[27]

The Ayutthaya godown which had earlier been abandoned was reopened in June 1661. The results of the succeeding years were less than brilliant in spite of the privileges granted by Phra Narai, whose chief desire was to annoy the Dutch who had forced his hand with their blockade of 1663–1664. The EIC then decided to organize direct commercial exchanges between Siam and its base in Madras on the Coromandel Coast. Siamese elephants, greatly esteemed in India, were traded for muslins, taffetas, and cotton loincloths which the English sold in Siam. The Dutch constantly put spokes in their wheels, especially during the brief period when war in Europe broke out between England and the United Provinces (1672–1674), when Louis XIV invaded Holland with the tacit (and paid) agreement of Charles II.

The private trading in which the English (who were supposed to defend the interests of their company) in Ayutthaya indulged put the EIC at such a disadvantage that Phra Narai in the end understood that he would need the assistance of another nation to counterbalance the influence of the Dutch. The French were to arrive at the right moment.

THE SIAMESE INTERLUDE

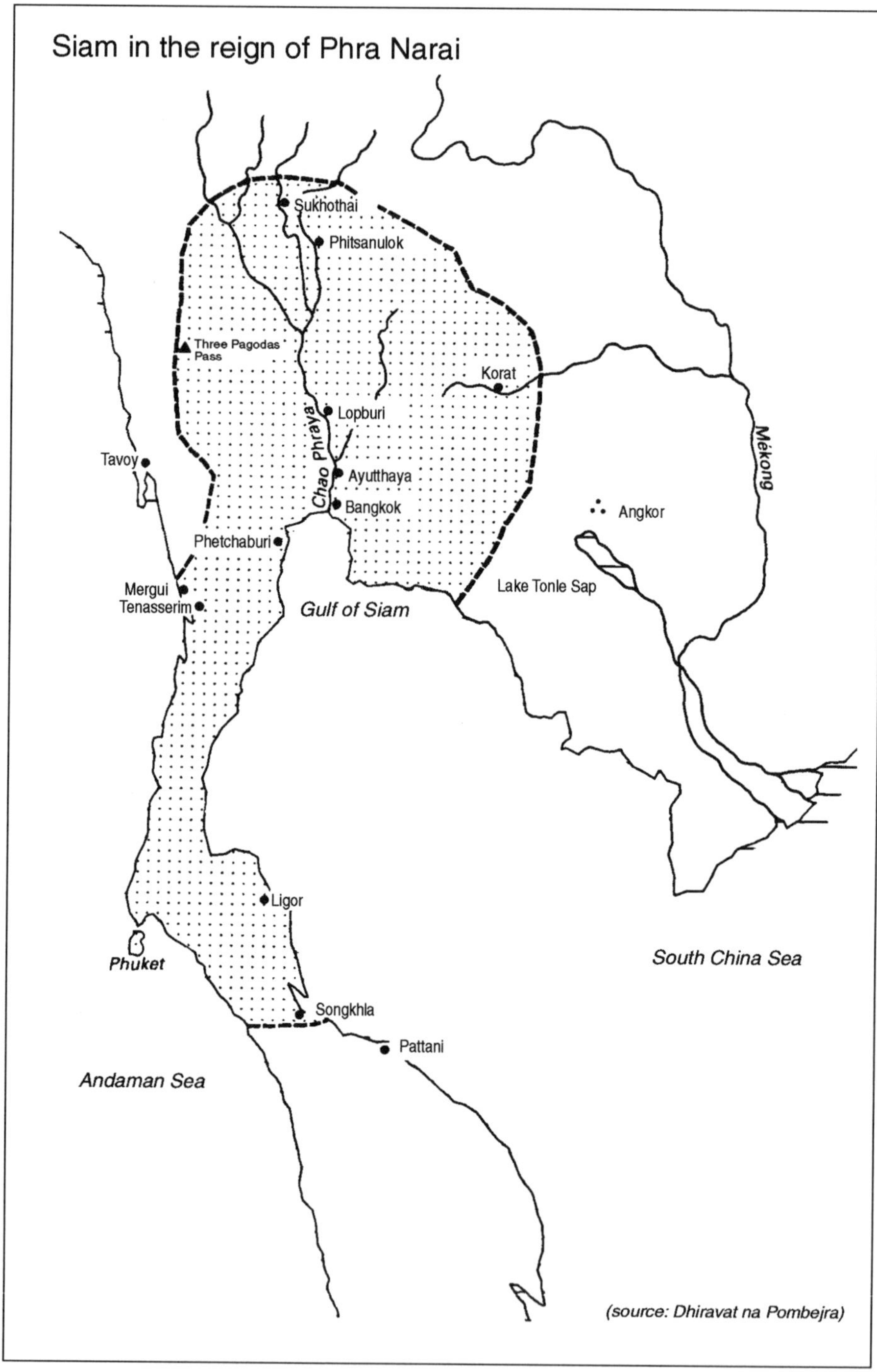
Siam in the reign of Phra Narai
Sukhothai
Phitsanulok
Three Pagodas Pass
Korat
Lopburi
Chao Phraya
Tavoy
Ayutthaya
Bangkok
Mekong
Angkor
Phetchaburi
Mergui
Tenasserim
Lake Tonle Sap
Gulf of Siam
Ligor
Phuket
South China Sea
Songkhla
Pattani
Andaman Sea
(source: Dhiravat na Pombejra)

CHAPTER FIVE

SOMDET PHRA NARAI MAHARAT

PHRA NARAI'S ASSUMPTION OF POWER

PRASAT THONG—king since 1629, founder of the dynasty which bears his name, and father of Phra Narai—kept himself in power by terror. Like every usurper, he felt threatened by murky plots. His adored daughter died in 1649; at her cremation in February 1650, fire did not consume some of her remains. The king thought this was the effect of magic or poisoning and ordered the execution of 2,900 persons among the *chao* (princes) and the *khunnang* (mandarins) of the kingdom.[1] This excuse allowed him to eliminate a good number of potential rivals at one fell swoop.

The king was deeply disturbed with the approach of the end of the Chulasakarat era (April 1639) when the thousandth and last year would coincide with the year of the tiger (*khan*). The Siamese calendar was divided into cycles of twelve years, each placed under the sign of an animal, beginning with the rat, followed by the ox, the tiger, the rabbit, the dragon, the snake, the horse, the goat, the monkey, the cock, the dog, and the pig. Fearing that the year of the tiger at the end of the millennium would bring about an era of calamities (*kali yuga*) for the kingdom and himself, Prasat Thong organized a Brahmin ceremony lasting three days, during which he changed the year of the tiger to the year of the pig (*kun*), making the end of the millennium coincide with that of the cycle.[2] In order to avert the disastrous consequences of the end of the Chulasakarat era, the king had constructed or repaired a good hundred or so temples and ordered a period of abstinence of three months during which hunting, fishing, and the consumption of alcoholic drinks were strictly forbidden.[3] All these preventive measures may have allowed him to retain the throne and die peacefully in his bed on 7 August 1656 after a reign of twenty-seven years.[4]

The history of the Ayutthayan dynasties is cyclic. Successions were always uncertain, bloody disputes regularly wracked the kingdom the moment a king closed his eyes for the last time. Fr Tachard explains in his first *Voyage to Siam* that "in the Kingdom of Siam, the Kings Brothers are preferred before his Children in the Succession to the Crown, but it returns to these after the death of their Uncles."[5] Each time a sovereign started to show signs of weakening, a swarm of brothers, uncles, sons, and nephews, each with their supporters ready for anything, began to try their luck, willing to give the king a helping hand if he delayed his appointment with his ancestors for too long. The *Kot Monthien Ban* ("Law of the Palace"), promulgated in 1456 by King Borommatrailokanat, had tried to regulate the succession by fixing the rank of each person in the royal household, but the text was not a model of clarity. Furthermore, it often happened that an ageing king designated his successor by conferring on him the title of *Upparat*,[6] thus encouraging the most ambitious to seize quickly the other pretenders to the throne. Some were implacably massacred; others suddenly espoused a fervent desire for monastic life and the saffron robe, leaping into the first monastery to hand, never to leave it; yet others remained alive only at the price of abject submission. There were few kings who were not considered usurpers by some of their subjects.

As in 1628–1629 after the death of Phra Song Tham, in 1656 three kings occupied the throne of Ayutthaya in the space of a few months. The first was the eldest son of Prasat Thong, Chaofa Chai, who seized power in a military coup. No good came of this, for his younger brother Narai overthrew him the following day (8 August 1656) and had him executed in the royal manner at Wat Khokphraya; he was secured in a velvet sack and beaten to death with cudgels of sandalwood so that not a drop of royal blood fell to the ground.

It is difficult to decide which of the two sons of the deceased king, Chaofa Chai or Phra Narai, had greater claim to the succession. The royal chronicles, *Phra Ratcha Phongsawadan*, declared that Chaofa Chai was born "outside the reign," meaning he had been born before his father mounted the throne. The date of his *chulakantamangala* or Buddhist tonsure (1632) places his birth about 1622, some seven years before Prasat Thong was crowned.[7] Born in 1632, Narai was indeed born "inside the reign." He was, in addition, the son of a queen of superior rank, a daughter of Phra Song Tham. Royal blood from the earlier dynasty of Maha Thammaracha, which had been on the throne since 1569, flowed in his veins.

However, not yet supported by a sufficiently powerful faction after the elimination of his elder half-brother, Narai then installed his uncle, *fai na* Sri Suthammaracha (the younger brother of Prasat Thong), on the throne, only to topple him two months later (August–October 1656). From 1644 Prasat Thong, who preferred as his successor one of his sons rather than his brother, had relegated Si Suthammaracha with his entourage to Phitsanulok, near Sukhothai, in this way preventing him from staging a surprise attack when the question of the succession arose. Narai no doubt had few scruples in overturning an uncle so little esteemed by his father.

According to the *Phongsawadan*, which cannot be verified, Narai only decided to dispose of his uncle after he had tried to rape (or take as his wife) his younger sister, Princess Si Chulalok, or Phra Ratcha Kanlayani. With the complicity of her nurse, she had escaped from the Grand Palace (*Wang Luang*) hidden in a cupboard under Buddhist manuscripts. She ran to complain to her brother who was residing in the Palace of the Front (*Wang Na*) beside the river. This was his official residence as *Phra Maha Upparat*, first prince of the blood and heir presumptive. He was furious and rounded up his supporters to go and attack his lewd uncle in the Grand Palace. After a fierce fight in the palace inner courtyards, Suthammaracha took refuge in the Palace of the Rear (*Wang Lang*), where he was seized and dragged to Wat Khokphraya to be put to death immediately in the royal manner. The *khunnang* who had supported him were at once mercilessly purged.

Se non è vero, è bene trovato (even if not true, it makes a good story). The reality was probably less romantic, for Volcker Westerwolt, the *opperhoofd* of the VOC in Ayutthaya, informed Batavia that Phra Narai had sought from the Dutch "some men with muskets." We know that the new king brought about his coup d'état with the aid of some of the Siamese *khunnang* and the support of the Japanese, Pattani Malays, and Muslim Persians.[8] The nomination of a Persian "prime minister," called Abdur Razzaq, is mentioned in *The Ship of Sulaiman*, a Persian account by Ibrahim Muhammad Rabi written about 1690.[9] This information is not absolutely correct since the post did not exist in Siam, but it confirms the important part played by foreign colonies in Ayutthaya when Narai assumed power, and notably the "Moorish" and Persian communities. The fact that the new monarch married his sister immediately after his advent to the throne suggests that, like his uncle, he was desirous of consolidating his legitimacy by marrying the daughter of the previous king.

Whatever the case, on 27 October 1656, Prince Narai, who was then twenty-four years old, ascended to the throne of Siam as the thirtieth ruler of Ayutthaya. He was to reign for thirty-two years with the name Somdet Phra Narai. Later the title of *Maharat* or "great king" was added. His reign is marked above all by increasing interference by the West in Siamese affairs, which in the end became intolerable. The entire history of French intervention in Siam took place under this sovereign.

ROYAL ELEPHANT LULLABIES

It is not easy to write the history of Somdet Phra Narai Maharat or of any other king of Ayutthaya. The destruction of the royal archives when the capital was sacked by the Burmese in April 1767 means we lack essential documents, though humidity would probably have destroyed them even if they had been spared the flames. Some of these chronicles were reconstituted, for better or worse, at the beginning of the Rattanakosin era (the Bangkok period), but it is particularly difficult to distinguish between fact and fiction. La Loubère has already been quoted on this point; even Prince Damrong Rachanuphap, the "father of Thai history," was to write in a preface to a new edition of a classic text, "Having compared the manuscript with earlier versions, we have noted the variations, but kept those which seemed more harmonious than the original version."[10] Such principles allow for great freedom of interpretation.

Having never been colonized, Thailand had never felt the need to define its cultural identity and determine its history in relation to former colonizers. This explains the numerous uncertainties which blur the Ayutthaya period chronicles, notably in the reign of Phra Narai. Thai historians frequently disagree over essential questions, be it the reasons which led Narai to select Lopburi as his second capital, or the nature of the internal difficulties which influenced his foreign policy.[11] Dhiravat na Pombejra, a specialist in the history of the Prasat Thong dynasty, does not hesitate to write that "European evidence of the seventeenth century, however flawed, is still more valid as a primary source than, say, the Siamese royal annals (*Phra Ratcha Phongsawadan*), most of which were compiled over a century after the demise of the Prasatthong Dynasty."[12]

Prince Narai, younger son of King Prasat Thong, was born in 1632. His mother Phra Ratcha Thewi was a titled queen and daughter of King Song Tham. The *Phongsawadan* surround his birth with extraordinary events. As he had four arms, his father declared it was a miracle—he could be forgiven—and gave him the name of Narai or Narayan, the Siamese form of Vishnu, the Hindu god who had four arms. Phra Ratcha Thewi died nine days after giving birth, and the young prince was placed in the hands of his wet-nurse Dusit whom he loved as a mother. Her real name was Bua, but as she lived at Wat Dusit near the Khaosan canal, she was known as Chao Mae Wat Dusit.[13] Dusit had two sons: Lek (the future *Phra Khlang* Chao Phraya Kosathibodi), and Pan (Kosa Pan or Phra Wisut Sunthon, later ambassador to Louis XIV). Phetracha, the future head of the royal elephant corps and Narai's successor, was the son of another wet-nurse of the prince. He was to have alternating affectionate and suspicious relations with his foster brothers. Events show that he had every reason to be on his guard.

The young prince (who appears soon to have shed his two surplus arms) early showed much intellectual aptitude. He learned to read and write with the monks, and seems to have acquired a good knowledge of Sanskrit and Pali. La Loubère was to note the lively curiosity and solid literary background of the king, who had translated into Siamese *The History of Alexander* by Quintus Curcius Rufus and had said "that the Art of Ruling is not inspired, and that with great Experience and Reading he perceived that he was not yet perfect in understanding it."[14]

This avid reader seems to have been in addition a gifted poet. Several works are attributed to him. Among them are three didactic texts, including the *Ratcha Sawat* which teaches royal counsellors the rules of protocol to be observed in the presence of the sovereign. Here is a translation of the first stanza:

> The monarch whose power radiates over the whole world
> Has announced a truthful lesson which can be compared
> To the honeyed words which enchant everyone
> And which tell of his glory and power over all.[15]

The passion Phra Narai had for elephant hunts (the beasts were caught but not killed) inspired him to write a treatise on the capture of elephants and—a particularly delightful genre—*klomchang* or lullabies for elephants.[16] Intended for white elephants, the sign of the kingdom's prosperity, these lullabies were composed to calm the wild elephant tied up after its capture. The writing of royal poems devoted to white elephants is not unusual in Thailand. H.R.H. Princess Maha Chakri Sirindhorn, daughter of H.M. King Bhumibol Adulyadej, in 1990 published a volume of youthful texts containing two *Kham Chan Dusadi Sangwoei Klomchang* (Psalms for white elephants), written at the request of her father.[17] The lullabies of Narai are unfortunately not preserved, but anonymous compositions of the mid-eighteenth century survive.

Phra Narai encouraged and protected other poets, making his reign a golden age of Thai poetry. But the relations between the king and the poets are wreathed in legends and the texts so corrupted by successive transcriptions that sorting out the truth is difficult. Gilles Delouche, in his thesis on Siprat, showed that the chief poet at Phra Narai's court was legendary rather than real. Whatever the case, Siprat's stories and poems are known by all Thai schoolchildren, and most poetry of the time, although anonymous, represented an undoubted peak of Thai literature.[18]

"HUMANE BY INCLINATION AND SEVERE BY POLICY"

Several physical descriptions of Phra Narai have come down to us. At the end of 1680, André Deslandes-Boureau observed the king carefully when he was forty-eight years old: "The king is of medium height, neither white nor black, aged about forty years, a broad and pleasant face, and high forehead, beardless, with a broad flat nose which moves a little when he speaks. His lips are quite thick."[19] Nicolas Gervaise gave this sketch of him a few years later:

> As I have had the honour of seeing this prince quite close at hand, I can describe him to you. He is of medium height, has rather high shoulders, a long face, a tanned complexion, bright, lively eyes which indicate a lot of intelligence, and in all his person there is a certain air of grandeur and majesty accompanied by much gentleness and

goodness, that it is impossible to see him without greatly respecting him, and without liking him still more."[20]

Still according to Gervaise, the sovereign married his sister shortly after seizing power: "As soon as he saw that he was in peaceful possession of the kingdom, he solemnly married the daughter of his father. He had her proclaimed queen with all the customary ceremonies."[21] This sister appears to be the same Si Chulalok or Kanlayani mentioned earlier. La Loubère for his part says that, "The late Queen, who was both his Wife and his Sister, was called Nang Achamahisii."[22] This marriage, as noted above, appears to have been a precautionary action on the part of a younger prince who had eliminated several of his elders, and who, because of this, felt the need to strengthen his position and enhance his legitimacy by marrying the daughter of his predecessor. The queen-sister Si Chulalok seems to have been the only *akkhamahesi*, or chief queen, raised to this position. She died about 1680 after having produced only one child, Princess (*Kromluang*) Yothathep, about whom the French living in Siam spoke a great deal without ever having set eyes on her. She was said to be haughty and cruel, having the mouths of her ladies-in-waiting sewn up if they chattered too much or slit to their ears if they did not speak enough. She was to become the wife of Narai's successor.

The chief factors governing the internal and external policies of Phra Narai cannot be understood if one underestimates the feeling of insecurity which haunted the king from the time he mounted the throne. Having ridden roughshod to get there, the young king was condemned to be on his guard against important factions among the Siamese nobility loyal to his uncle or his elder brothers who considered him a usurper.

Phra Narai had only been able to assume the crown with the help of groups of foreigners established in Siam, and they did not wait long before presenting their bill. Confronted in the eighth year of his reign by the gunboat diplomacy of the Dutch blockading the Chao Phraya, the king felt obliged to approach other European nations capable of holding the Dutch company in check. The French missionaries who arrived in Ayutthaya in 1662, preceding the diplomats, traders, and soldiers of Louis XIV, seemed to have been sent by heaven. The passion which Phra Narai showed for the person of Louis XIV, which brought forth tears of emotion in French eyes, was not entirely inspired by love of the Sun King.

The start of the reign was not easy. A half-brother (*chaofa*) of the king, Phra Trai Phuwanathittayawong, supported by his mother and a clique of *chao* and discontented *khunnang*, plotted to kill Narai when he had to pass through a narrow passage to leave the Grand Palace. But the plot was revealed to the king, who immediately had arrested the young prince and his accomplices who had withdrawn to the Palace of the Rear, the residence of the third prince of the realm. Found guilty of high treason, they were executed in January 1657 with the usual cruelty; as for the Palace of the Rear, it was given to the sovereign's foster brother Phetracha for his residence. He commanded the elephant brigade and the tens of thousands of men who trained, rode, and looked after the thousands of elephants belonging to the king.

Phra Narai's lukewarm religious feelings disturbed some of the Buddhist clergy who also fomented a plot which was thwarted. We shall return to this later when dealing with the king's attitude to the Catholic missionaries.

French witnesses have described Phra Narai as an affable, almost easy-tempered person. His lullabies for elephants incline one to this view, but he was a man who had not been afraid of shedding blood to seize power, and was certainly prepared to do anything to retain it. Cosimo de Medici was wont to say that one does not govern by telling one's beads, and Machiavelli wrote in a chapter concerning cruelty and clemency that "a new sovereign can hardly avoid the reproach of cruelty, each new dominion being full of dangers."[23]

The chronicle of the reign of Phra Narai proves that the king shared these beliefs. Turpin, the author of an eighteenth-century *History of the Kingdom of Siam* describes the sovereign as

> ambitious of glory and carried along by the agitation of his spirit . . . His troubled throne . . . required an energetic hand to strengthen its foundations, and his first conquests were over his subjects. The seeds of intestinal wars were swamped by the blood of the rebellious. Humane by inclination and severe by policy, he understood he always needed to be armed with the sword to bring to heel his people, ever ready to break loose from the restraint of obedience were they not held in check by fear.[24]

Both Gervaise and Turpin relate a delightful oriental story

illustrating the subtlety of Phra Narai at the beginning of his reign in his relations with his advisors who dared to try and teach him a lesson. The word *sancrat* or *sangkharat* used in the story comes from *sangharacha* (literally, chief of the *sangha* or Buddhist clergy) and designates the abbots of the four royal monasteries in Ayutthaya.[25] La Loubère explains that "the *Sancrat* of the Convent of the Palace is the most reverend of all."

> There was even one *sancrat* some time ago who took the liberty of declaring with pride to him that his subjects murmured against him and that they did not deserve his punishments. The king received this charitable remonstrance with a good grace, but a few days later he sent to the *sancrat* one of the large and evil monkeys of which the Siamese are in such horror, with the express command that it be well fed and be allowed to do as it pleased in his house until further notice. He had to receive this great monkey. But as soon as it had entered the house it began to do terrible damage. It broke many pieces of the finest porcelain and gnawed the costliest carpets; it bit some people and attacked others, until at length the *sancrat* could endure it no longer, and in great distress went to His Majesty to beg him most humbly to deliver him from so vicious a guest. The king replied with a smile, "What is this? You cannot endure the mere inconvenience of a monkey in your house for three or four days and yet you expect me to put up for the whole of my life with the insolence of my subjects, who are a thousand times more unbearable than the most mischievous monkey." "Now go," he added, "if I know how to punish the wicked, you may be sure I know even better how to reward the good."[26]

The anecdote is charming, and clearly points the moral.

PHRA NARAI ON THE WARPATH

To Phra Narai's ability to snuff out the slightest disturbance and bring to heel importunate monks was added a vigilant and aggressive policy beyond his frontiers when the need arose. He did not wait, like several of his predecessors, to see the Burmese appear under the walls of Ayutthaya, but carried the war into their lands. The Mons of Martaban, oppressed by King Maha Sihasurasu Thammaracha, sought his protection. Only too willing to help them, the king raised two armies in 1661, commanded by his foster brother Lek (Chao Phraya Kosathibodi) and Phraya Siharat Decho, and ordered them to march against the Burmese. His adversaries were defeated on several occasions in the course of a rather confused campaign. The Burmese even invaded Siamese territory through the Three Pagodas Pass in 1663, but the Siamese repulsed them, and the following year took Rangoon and Chittagong before going to lay siege to Ava, then the Burmese capital, close to Mandalay. This siege was a long series of ruses and false retreats, for both armies were severely short of victuals. The Siamese did not succeed at Ava, but they decimated the Burmese troops and withdrew without being pursued. Phra Narai was not to be disturbed again by the Burmese who would think twice before entering Siamese territory.

Closely connected with the Burmese war, the campaigns against Lanna and its capital Chiang Mai likewise had high and low points. Saen Luang, the King of Chiang Mai, overturned his alliances with the Kings of Pegu and Siam in reaction to the reversals of a war between the Ming Chinese expulsed by the Manchu Qing dynasty and the King of Ava. Phra Narai decided to put paid to this fickle ruler, but it took an initial campaign begun in 1660, commanded by the king in person, and another in 1663 to subdue Lanna temporarily, which was only to be definitely annexed in 1727 in the reign of Phumintharacha.[27]

According to the *Phongsawadan*, on the return journey Phra Narai became enamoured with the daughter of his prisoner, Saen Luang. She presented him with a son, Dua, whom the king gave to his foster brother, Phetracha, asking him to raise the child as his own son. It was only later, when he was admitted to the royal page corps (*mahatlek*), that Dua learnt the secret of his birth, and allowed himself liberties which would have cost anyone else their head. But the king forgave his pranks, especially as he had observed the courage of his natural son who succeeded in taming the wildest elephants. Delighted to have so brave a descendant, Phra Narai ennobled him and gave him the title of Luang Sorasak. It seems much more likely, however, given his later career, that Sorasak was indeed the son of Phetracha. We shall meet him again in the fatal year of 1688.

"THE KINGS OF THE INDIES ARE THE CHIEF MERCHANTS IN THEIR STATES"

The wars against the Burmese and Lanna had seriously eroded the human and financial resources of Siam. The Dutch posted to Ayutthaya wrote that a huge area around the capital was virtually depopulated, and that the royal treasure amassed by the extremely rapacious Prasat Thong had gone up in smoke. The *Phra Khlang* introduced new taxes which restricted trade; at the end of 1662 he had proclaimed a royal monopoly on all exports from Siam, notwithstanding the monopoly on deerskins granted to the VOC in 1634, 1645, and 1647. We have already seen that this measure led in May 1663 to the decision of Johan Maetsuyker, governor-general of the VOC, to close the godown in Ayutthaya and a few months later to blockade the estuary of the Chao Phraya.

This crisis did not come from the fact that the King of Siam lay claim to all commercial activity in his kingdom; that was in the order of things. But the Dutch, who knew of the contempt in which European princes and nobles held trade (a gentleman demeaned himself by trading), accepted with difficulty that Phra Narai directly entered the trading arena through intermediary commissioners, and vitiated competition by protecting the most lucrative sectors with royal monopolies. The European merchants who plied in Asia had to adjust to royal trading ventures, for, as André-François Deslandes-Boureau would note in the eighteenth century, "all the kings of the Indies are the chief merchants in their states, and assign several articles of trade to themselves exclusively."[28]

Dhiravat na Pombejra, in an article on crown commerce in the reign of Phra Narai, explains that,

> On a formal level, the Kings of Siam were above active participation in trade. Tradition (and they themselves) portrayed kings as *avatars* of Hindu gods, aspiring *bodhisattvas*, or as *cakravartins* (Buddhist wheel-turning, world-conquering monarchs). Waging war, promulgating laws, and making merit: these were the main responsibilities of kings . . . But, in order to make merit, to live in godlike splendour, and to acquire arms and ammunition for warfare, the Ayutthaya kings had to rely on international trade . . . The Siamese crown thus had to develop an efficient trading mechanism, and during the seventeenth

century this branch of the administration became more extensive than ever before.[29]

The king's trading enterprises and diplomacy were closely linked. Most of the embassies sent and received by Phra Narai chiefly concerned commercial exchanges. This explains why Europeans had some trouble in understanding the functions of the *Phra Khlang*, since this important functionary dealt with foreign affairs, royal trade, and the levying of taxes at the same time. La Loubère summarized his duties thus:

> The Pra-Clang, or by a corruption of the Portugueses, the Barcalon, is the Officer which has the appointment of the Commerce, as well within as without the Kingdom. He is the Superintendent of the King of Siam's Magazines, or if you will, his chief Factor. . . . He is the Minister of the foreign affairs, because they almost all relate to Commerce; and 'tis to him that the fugitive Nations at Siam address themselves in their affairs, because 'tis only the liberty of Trade that formerly invited them thither. In a word, it is the Barcalon that receives the Revenues of the Cities.[30]

Prasat Thong, Phra Narai's father, had amassed a fortune by fitting out vessels and trading as far as China and the Coromandel Coast, without neglecting either internal commerce. His *khunnang*, who drew no salary, lived off illicit commissions and traded on their own account, ready to be deprived of their wealth by the king if they became too rich and thus too dangerous.

Just like his father, Phra Narai was very interested in trading, particularly since the wars at the beginning of his reign had emptied his treasury. Following in the steps of his predecessors, he vitiated the nature of fair competition by the arbitrary use of royal monopolies. He had at first allowed his subjects to buy and sell freely all products except tin, lead, sappanwood, elephants, and ivory. But this liberal approach was modified after 1662, as we have seen, and the traders of the VOC constantly complained when they saw agents of the king cut the grass from under their feet in the trading of copper, cotton, rice, deerskins and cow hides, areca nuts, and so on. The king had allowed them in 1671–1672 to export tin from Ligor (Nakhon Si Thammarat) but they saw on the spot that the *Phra Khlang* Chao Phraya Kosathibodi, the king's foster brother, was their chief competitor.

Kosathibodi, who was to remain *Phra Khlang* until 1683, had amassed a considerable fortune but his position and his wealth did not protect him from royal brutality. He was publicly whipped in 1683 for having accepted a huge bribe. His punishment led to his death soon after. At court, Kosathibodi was implicated in intense rivalry with the Persian Aqa Muhammad or Ok-phra Sinaowarat, the respected chief of the Persian community since the fall from grace of Abdur Razzaq in 1663. He had the ear of the king, who had a penchant for everything Persian, and he spoke court Siamese fluently. The death in 1679 of Aqa Muhammad seems to have diminished the role of the "Moors," Muslims engaged in trade in Siam, and opened the door to other foreign influences.

After having pitted himself against his northern neighbours and acquired more glory than long-lasting advantages, Phra Narai became actively preoccupied by external trade, intensifying the relations (and sometimes the confrontations) between Siam and certain Asiatic and European powers. Less well prepared for this peace which had all the implications of economic war, he ended by calling to his side a European advisor and confidant as clever as one could wish, and destined to play a very important role in the history of Siamese-Western relations.

These concerns did not prevent him from enjoying the pleasures of an almost pastoral residence far from Ayutthaya and its intrigues and foreign godowns.

"LOPBURI IS FOR SIAM WHAT VERSAILLES IS FOR FRANCE"

After reigning for ten years (thus, in 1666), Phra Narai began enlarging and improving the town of Lopburi, located fifty kilometres upstream on the Lopburi River, a tributary of the Chao Phraya. It was an important centre in the Dvaravati period (sixth to eleventh centuries), and became one of the provincial capitals of the Khmer empire at the height of Angkor's power (eleventh to twelfth centuries), until being incorporated into the Sukhothai kingdom shortly before 1200.

The reasons which led the king to abandon the capital in favour of Lopburi for stays which became ever longer each year have often been questioned. Its altitude makes it more agreeable in the summer monsoons and places it above flood waters. There, the sovereign could indulge more freely in his favourite pursuit of elephant hunting, since the beasts were legion in the forests that stretched as far as the eye could see to the east of Lopburi. He could organize there more frequently the spectacle he particularly appreciated: combats between tigers and elephants. According to French witnesses at the end of the reign, the king almost never left the Grand Palace in Ayutthaya, but moved around freely and hunted almost every day in Lopburi, then called Lawo by the Siamese, and Louvo or Louveau by Europeans.

But these reasons alone do not explain the huge architectural and hydraulic works Phra Narai undertook in the town which he was fond of, nor the fact that certain documents of the period refer to him as "the King of Lawo" when it is clear that Ayutthaya remained the ceremonial and cosmic centre of the kingdom. A simple summer residence and hunting lodge did not require forts, enclosing walls complete with towers, and vast reservoirs of drinking water which the king had constructed. There was no need either for the new road fifteen kilometres long which linked it to Phra Phutthabat, where the court went once a year to worship at the Buddha's footprint above which Phra Song Tham had constructed a magnificent temple, which today is flanked by rows of bells which pilgrims ring with bamboo sticks.

A voluminous collection of documents, known under the general title of *Khamhaikan chao krung kao* relates the testimonies of high-ranking Siamese prisoners of war deported to Burma after the fall of Ayutthaya in 1767. Their conquerors, who wished to obtain information about the history, customs, and administration of the kingdom of Ayutthaya which they had just destroyed, questioned them closely and recorded their replies. In that we learn that Phra Narai began the work on the Lopburi palace ten years after his coronation. The reason for the construction of what was to become the second capital of the kingdom was the menacing attitude of the Dutch company after the blockade and unfavourable treaty with Siam which the king had been obliged to sign in 1664. Phra Narai realized that Ayutthaya, located only eighty kilometres from the mouth of the river, was exposed to attacks from Dutch warships. Hence the decision to shift his capital to the north.[31]

This reasoning, compiled a century after the Lopburi's enhanced status, for a long time convinced Thai historians, and notably Prince Damrong. It was only in 1979 during a seminar on the history of

Lopburi, that this interpretation was refuted by a number of Thai specialists. Professor Kobkua Suwannathat expressed the opinion, shared by several others, that Thai historical documents do not explain the reasons why Lopburi was raised to the rank of second capital, except the preference Phra Narai had for this town and the pleasure he took in staying there. Dutch documents of the period show that between 1665 and 1673 relations between the two countries were quite cordial. There was therefore no occasion to fear war and no need to flee Ayutthaya for Lopburi.[32]

Specialists of the history of the VOC confirm that the Dutch acted prudently and discretely after the treaty of 1664.[33] The fact that in 1673, when the Dutch were involved in a costly war with France and England, Phra Narai had granted the company an important quantity of lead which was indispensable for their armaments industry, and that the Dutch assisted him by training in Batavia Siamese artisans sent by the king and by supplying him with Western technology, prove that there was nothing menacing in the relations between Phra Narai and the VOC.

Nicolas Gervaise, who noted that "Louveau, which the Siamese commonly call Nocchebouury, is a town which is, so to say, for the kingdom of Siam what Versailles is for France,"[34] was therefore right. Louis XIV did not like Paris because of its association with the civil war during the first years of his reign; he preferred to place the monarchy in another town which he could arrange in his fashion, where he was his own master and where he could follow his tastes of a hunting Bourbon. Likewise, Phra Narai felt more at ease far from Ayutthaya, where one always felt as though one were living between two palace revolutions and where a highly elaborate ceremonial controlled his least movements; he preferred a town which he could reshape a few steps from the forests where tigers roamed and elephants trumpeted. In addition one can deduce from certain witnesses that Phra Narai was asthmatic and the cleaner air of Lopburi suited him better than that of an overpopulated city surrounded by water like Ayutthaya.

Both kings were thus building at the same time palaces in the middle of gardens featuring fountains. They would have similar hydraulic problems. Louis XIV had to build the Maintenon aqueduct and the Marly "machine." Phra Narai would be forced to dig a canal to bring water from the Thale Chupson lake (the magic lake in which Rama dipped the tip of his arrow) to the Phra Chan canal and then to the Sa Kaeo reservoir. Gervaise explained that, during the dry winter months, the level of the river was at its lowest and "the elephants who washed there made it so dirty it was impossible to drink from it."[35] To each man his own problems.

All of Gervaise's chapter 11 in the first part of his *Natural and Political History of the Kingdom of Siam* deals with Lopburi. The royal palace (*Narai ratchaniwet*) built on the left bank has not the magnificence of the palace in Ayutthaya, but greater charm. Protected by a high crenellated wall, numerous buildings are separated by courtyards and gardens in which fountains play in the middle of tropical thickets and heavily scented tuberoses. Some only give off their scent at night because the heat of the day dissipates their fragrance.[36] The doorways and walls separating the courtyards are decorated with carvings and hollowed with innumerable niches in the shape of leaves which are decorated with Chinese porcelain or fairy lights for great occasions.

Like grandees of Spain, Phra Narai's elephants are divided into classes. Four pachyderms of the second class are correctly lodged in pavilions in the first courtyard while those of the first class wallow in oriental luxury inside pavilions arranged in the second courtyard, closer to the throne hall where the king grants audiences to ambassadors.

More secluded and spacious, the central courtyard encompasses the royal apartments which, decorated in a profusion of gold and covered with varnished yellow tiles, sparkle in a brilliant sun to such a degree that one needs good eyes to withstand their reflection. Niches are arranged in the parapet going around the royal residence and four pools are located in the corners, where His Majesty bathes under rich canopies in the midst of innumerable flowers which scent the air. Flower beds with the rarest specimens of the Indies are tended by the sovereign with his own hands. Behind the residence is a garden planted with orange, lime, and other exotic trees, the dense foliage of which provide relief to the hottest hours of the day. At night, lights of bronze lanterns are placed in the niches and on small altars where perfumed pellets and aromatic timbers create a fairy-like atmosphere. In short, it is not surprising that His Siamese Majesty was so attached to his pleasure dome.

It is to be wondered if the *khunnang* shared love of this Lopburi. Neither the town nor the palace could lodge them all.

> When the court is in residence, the most important mandarins . . . stay there in their boats, which are usually eight brasses [a span or brasse is five feet or 1.60 m] long and one or one and a quarter of a span wide, on which they have small plank bedrooms a span and a half or two long, very neatly covered. They are in truth more convenient than those in town, but more removed from the court, and there are so many boats that when there is water in the river, which runs dry every year, it can be seen covered with two or three rows of them for a good quarter of a league.[37]

After leaving the palace enclosure and passing on the north Wat Sao Thong Thong, the modern visitor can find the remains of numerous buildings. He will come to the imposing residence of Okya Wichayen, the Greek adventurer who would become an all-powerful minister at the end of the reign. Phra Narai not only had his Versailles, but he was to have his Mazarin. We shall discuss him further in chapter 11.

PART TWO
THE MISSIONARIES AND MERCHANTS

CHAPTER SIX

THE FRENCH ROYAL EAST INDIES COMPANY

THE CALL OF THE SEA AND SPICES

THE FIRST French commercial enterprise in Asian seas which is documented to some degree goes back to the time of François I (r. 1515–1547). In 1529 some daring sailors (who cultivated the muses in between serving at the tiller) left the port of Dieppe to evade the Portuguese monopoly and fill their holds with oriental spices. The men of Dieppe had been travelling the high seas from before the birth of Henry the Navigator; they had gone to the western shores of Africa at the beginning of the fourteenth century.[1] The inspiration for the 1529 expedition was Jean, the elder of three Parmentier brothers who had together discovered in 1520 "the island of Pernambuco," Fernando de Noronha Island located four hundred kilometres from the Brazilian coast.

Jean Parmentier had heard talk of "the great islands beyond the Indies"—that is, the Moluccas—which produced spices in abundance. He succeeded in convincing the ship-owner, banker, and entrepreneur Jean Ango of Dieppe to finance a voyage to these distant lands. The journey was a success; the Parmentiers even went, according to some, as far as the Chinese coast.[2] They returned in 1529 with two heavily laden ships, wanting nothing more than to repeat their exploit. Only a few months later, the adventurous brothers were ready to leave again for the East Indies.

Jean Parmentier was one of the pillars of the Academy of Dieppe; his *Very elegant morality with ten characters, in honour of the Assumption of the Virgin Mary*, was, it seems, appreciated. It was therefore not surprising that he incited his friend Pierre Grignon, another poet from Dieppe, to take part in the new expedition. It was an excellent idea, not because Grignon had won some poetry prizes and his verses appeared in printed collections of the Academy of Dieppe, but because he was to write the record of the expedition.[3] Among those taking part were Raoul Parmentier, the younger brother of Jean; there is no mention of the third brother, who had perhaps died or was tired of long voyages.

The *Pensée* and the *Sacre* left the roads of Dieppe on 3 April 1529. The two Parmentier captains had on board an "astrologer" (pilot) who did not take his eyes off "the variation of the magnetic needle." On 25 April they landed on São Tiago Island at Cape Verde. On 11 May, they passed the Line (the equator), marking the event by singing the mass *Salve sancta parens* "with music." This great show of devotion reaped its benefits; after mass they caught a large fish which they called "albatore" and bonitoes. A festival was organized in which those who had crossed the Line for the first time were initiated. On 29 May they discovered at 21 degrees 7 minutes an island they named "the French Island, in honour of the Most Christian King of France, because it was the first unknown island we had met." They were unaware that the southern island of Ascension, much visited by sea turtles, had already been discovered by the Portuguese João de Nova on Ascension Day 1501. On 23 June they passed the Cape of Good Hope.

But a week later a storm broke. The mythological jests of the tempest-tossed sailor-poet Grignon can be appreciated. "This Thursday, 1 July, we had the greatest torment and biggest wind since our departure from Dieppe, and I think that the god Eolus, accompanied by Favorinus and Africus Libo, created or celebrated the marriage between him and Thetis, just to make her dance well. And several large fish, like porpoises and 'cauldrons', assembled in shoals, jumped and paraded under our very noses, and we all, in this, jigged mightily."[4]

They reached Madagascar on 26 July. The longboats were sent ashore to take on water and buy victuals from the natives in exchange for bonnets and rosaries. But the history of Franco-Madagascar relations soured the very next day, perhaps because the natives considered they had been bilked. Two sailors who landed were savagely despatched with javelins, and the *Pensée* and the *Sacre* weighed their anchors in haste. This was not to be the end of the troubles of our men from Dieppe, because scurvy and other illnesses afflicted them. They cast into the sea the bodies of some ten men who had languished a few days before dying, "very worn out and dry."

Lost in the immensity of the Indian Ocean, they searched the heavens and the seas for indications of land. On 16 October, a bird they called the "hochecul" (bobbing arse) sat on the anchor shanks and they caught two snakes joined at their tails which were floating in the sea. They were approaching the Batu Islands (Kepulauan Batu), off the west coast of Taprobane, that is, Sumatra. They generously provided French names for the islands whose outlines they saw on the horizon: Louise, Marguerite, and—why not?—Parmentier. At the end of October, they dropped anchor before Batu, a hundred or so kilometres north of Padang. They were well received by the *shahbandar* or harbour-master, but found no spices. They attributed the hot fevers suffered by many men to the poor quality of the water, and set sail on 27 November. Jean Parmentier died on 3 December after being sick for a week, at the age of forty-nine. He was buried on a desert island. His brother Raoul died a few days later and his body thrown to the sea. Jean left behind a long poem which Grignon was to publish on his return to France describing the marvels of the sea and sky in six hundred alexandrines.

Decimated and leaderless, the remaining crew sailed off Sumatra; they spent Christmas in a place they called "Selagan, in the kingdom of Indrapura." The inhabitants refused to sell spices to them, which greatly surprised Pierre Grignon who noted that "we had always treated them lovingly." The demoralized men from Dieppe saw themselves confronted with the choice either of sailing on to Java in search of spices, or of returning to France after having bartered their merchandise (lengths of waterproof cloth referred to as "bougran," iron dies, mirrors, ivory and tin rosaries, and something called "Rouge de Paris") for edibles as best they could. After voting on the matter, they decided to return. The natives, who had become more accommodating, accepted their goods and supplied them with rice, honey, chickens, and fruit, as well as a little gold and two bahars (some eight hundred pounds) of pepper. The expedition departed on 22 January 1530; the return journey was not related by a discouraged Grignon.

The failure of the last Parmentier expedition explains in part why the French did not play any further role in the exploration and exploitation of the East Indies in the sixteenth century. They were more interested in the Americas, Canada, and Brazil,[5] but the French

Bourbons maintained an interest in Asia through the zeal of the missionaries. The French monarchs could not overlook the substantial advantages which the VOC obtained from its trading ventures in the Indies, nor the fact that they had to obtain their Asiatic products from the Dutch, in so doing increasing the prosperity of this republic of Calvinist traders.

THE FIRST FRENCH COMPANIES IN THE SEVENTEENTH CENTURY

The idea of a French Company of the East Indies, provided with a charter guaranteeing it a trading monopoly and royal prerogatives, was in the minds of French leaders from the beginning of the seventeenth century. In 1604, Henri IV had granted such a charter to the merchants of Dieppe, Rouen, and St Malo, who had embarked on trade in the Indies in the spirit of the Parmentier brothers a century earlier. This first attempt remained without tangible results, although the privilege was renewed in 1611, and the society reorganized in 1615 with the name of the Company of the Moluccas. Shortly before his death in 1642, Richelieu transformed this into a chartered company to establish ports of call in Madagascar, half-way to the Far East, and for trade in the Indies. The Dutch and the English were interested in South Africa and the island of St Helena for the same reason. In 1652 the Dutch founded a colony at the Cape "in the interests of greater security and refreshments" for its fleets, and ceded St Helena to the EIC. But what seemed clear on a terrestrial globe became practically impossible on the spot, since the inhospitable coasts, the hostility of the natives, and the limited resources of Madagascar worked against Richelieu's project. The idea was finally abandoned, but it explains the interest under Louis XIV in Madagascar, aroused by the travels and over-enthusiastic accounts of François Cauche and Etienne de Flacourt.[6]

The Foreign Missions in Paris (Société des Missions Etrangères de Paris, MEP) was quick to recognize the interest of Richelieu's company in their evangelical efforts.[7] It is not known who established the first contacts of the MEP and the Madagascar company, but a written agreement with the company was signed by Bishop Pallu who was to play a leading role in the history of the Foreign Missions in Paris. An expedition was envisaged from Madagascar to the Celebes, and from there to Tonkin. The company and Mgr Pallu would each provide half of the eighty thousand livres necessary to the commercial and evangelical enterprise, to be reimbursed from the eventual profits. But the two parties could not come up with the capital and the project was dropped. Just as well for the missionaries, for the *Maréchale*, on which they were to have embarked had the project gone ahead, was shipwrecked in January 1660 near the Cape of Good Hope.

This first setback led to the formation of an equally ambitious project in the minds of some gentlemen of the Company of the Holy Sacrament, formed in 1627 as a congregation of Catholic lay and clerical figures, and soon to be wound up because of what was seen as its excessive zeal in furthering works of charity. In its assembly held on 7 August 1659, it proposed to form a China company "to aid the missions." A brochure sought the participation of lay persons; a cavalry officer, Philippe de Chamesson, offered his services and was taken on. At first it was proposed to build five ships, then two. The English Catholic Edward Arney, who had five times gone to Batavia, was employed. The sum of 140,000 livres was raised with difficulty from thirty-three shareholders.

A first frigate of three hundred tons was ordered at Amsterdam and its construction started. The idea was excellent, for "a boat cost twice as much in France than the price in Holland."[8] Named the *Saint-Louis*, the vessel was to make its maiden voyage in October 1660, having on board Mr de Chamesson, Captain Arney, and a Dutch pilot named Henk Jans. But the Dutch understood only too well that the frigate would tread on their Asiatic trading toes. They were paid by the ship's commissioners; then, in spite of the fact that Jacques de Thou, the French envoy in The Hague, had taken possession of the boat in the name of Louis XIV, the *Saint-Louis* was detained in the roads until 10 December.

Were they counting on the unfavourable season to thwart the French projects? Whatever the case, the ship was driven against a jetty and suffered damage. The Dutch embargo was only lifted when the French gave assurances that the vessel would not be employed against the United Provinces in times of war. The *Saint-Louis* left Amsterdam six weeks late and was caught in a violent storm near the island of Texel as soon as it entered the North Sea. It sank on 19 December 1660, abandoned by its crew who escaped in a longboat.

The China company sank with the *Saint-Louis* before having got under way. It was not the only victim at the end of 1660. Six days before, a decree of Parliament, granted at the request of Cardinal Mazarin, had dissolved the Company of the Holy Sacrament, too powerful for his taste, too enterprising, and too intolerant.

Thus we return to the point of departure, since the efforts of Mgr Pallu and his friends had aborted and the kingpin of the enterprise was shattered. The first teams sent by the Foreign Missions to Asia would take the overland route.

THE BEGINNINGS OF THE "COMPAGNIE DES INDES ORIENTALES" (CIO)

In spite of privileges granted and renewed and the desire to beat the Dutch and the English at their own game, nothing concrete had emerged by the time Louis XIV took complete charge of affairs of state on the death of Mazarin in March 1661. He knew he could count on the vision and energy of Colbert. This minister, who was aware of the equal importance of a merchant navy as well as a military naval force, dreamed of outwitting the Dutch, whom he detested, and the affair of the *Saint-Louis* mollified nothing in his attitude. With his redoubtable energy, he buckled down to creating a French company capable of equalling the VOC (and perhaps the EIC). "He desired nothing more passionately—he who put so much passion in so many desires—than to ruin it,"[9] wrote Lavisse, who noted that the minister spoke to everyone about the Dutch company which he both hated and admired.

Colbert charged the academician François Charpentier with drawing up a brochure to publicize the project and attract shareholders. The *Discours d'un fidèle sujet du Roi touchant l'établissement d'une Compagnie française pour le commerce des Indes orientales, adressé à tous les Français* (Treatise of a faithful subject of the king concerning the formation of a French company for trading in the East Indies, addressed to all the French) came off the press in April 1664. The document was particularly directed to the merchants of the Atlantic ports, detailing the advantages the French would obtain in trading in the Indies by freeing themselves of the duties which they paid to foreigners, citing the huge dividends distributed by the Dutch company to its shareholders, and singing the praises of Madagascar where commerce with the Indies would be started; there lodes of gold were to be found, laid bare by the rain coming down the mountainsides. The academician boasted:

> Among all the trading ventures conducted in the different parts of the world, there are none richer nor more important than that of the East Indies. In those fecund lands under a warmer sun than ours one can obtain what is most precious to man and what contributes most, either to the amenities of life, or to luxury and magnificence. From there one obtains gold and precious stones; from there come such famous trade goods which sell so readily, such as silk, cinnamon, ginger, nutmeg, cotton fabrics, wadding, porcelain, pepper, exotic woods which provide all kinds of dyes, ivory, incense, bezoar, and a thousand other commodities . . .[10]

In spite of this tempting rhapsody, the first reactions were rather lukewarm. The traders of Rouen, for example, congratulated Colbert on his project but excused themselves from contributing to it, as their province was poor. Those of Antwerp, also sounded out, were politely evasive, fearing not unreasonably that the running of the company would be controlled by the king to the detriment of the shareholders.

A second brochure by the same Charpentier, the *Relation de l'établissement de la Compagnie française pour le commerce des Indes orientales* (Account of the establishment of the French company for trade in the East Indies) was published one year after the first. It was above all aimed at Parisian merchants and informed them that "several persons of considerable quality" had joined with the chief merchants in Paris to set up together a project with articles of association. There is no point in mentioning that the minister drew up the articles and no time was lost in the matter. Louis XIV received the delegates at Fontainebleau in May 1665 to agree to all the articles proposed. The king named nine officials, the signatures of the adherents were collected, and the capital of the new company fixed at fifteen million in shares of one thousand *livres*.

An order under the king's private seal enjoined the mayors and municipal magistrates of the chief towns in the kingdom to assemble the inhabitants and seek out subscriptions. This unsubtle dirigisme was completely the opposite of the spontaneous initiatives of the Dutch or English merchants. "In short, under the guise of shares issued, it was a kind of forced loan, destined to supply funds for a royal enterprise."[11]

The king subscribed one-fifth of the capital, that is, three millions, and his example was followed willingly or under pressure by the queen, the queen mother, the court, financiers, the sovereign courts, and the main towns. The result could not be considered a success: eight million livres out of the fifteen million which had been sought.

Louis XIV had meanwhile made official the existence of the company by a declaration of August 1664, registered on 1 September. This charter of the "Compagnie des Indes orientales" (CIO) detailed the various privileges granted by the king, and set out the organization of the management which drew inspiration from the Dutch company and the Heren XVII; there were to be twelve directors for Paris and nine for the provinces, to be elected by the holders of at least six shares, reporting to an annual general meeting of shareholders. The company was given the monopoly of navigation and trade in "the Indies, the eastern and the southern seas" for fifty years, the concession in perpetuity of lands and places occupied, notably Madagascar and its neighbouring islands, on condition of propagating Christianity.

These privileges were complemented by various fiscal advantages and the right to send ambassadors to the kings of the Indies, to conclude treaties, declare war, fly the royal flag, and establish garrisons. The arms granted carried, on an azure background, a gold fleur-de-lys surrounded by palm and olive branches, surmounting the device *Florebo quocumque ferar* (I shall flourish wherever I am carried), supported on either side by the allegorical figures of Peace and Abundance.

Within the first months of being established, the new company was torn between private shareholders who wanted to trade with the Indies, and Louis XIV and Colbert who wanted to colonize the island of Madagascar, then called Dauphine Island. It is true that a stopover point and trading post were essential, but nothing obliged the company to expend the bulk of its resources in colonizing and peopling a land which was difficult to exploit, and had nothing to offer France. This error was to cost them dearly.

The purchase and construction of the necessary vessels was not accomplished without difficulty. Notices were plastered around Paris seeking settlers. There were so many interested in the proposal that the directors, given a choice, selected primarily tradesmen and not labourers. In their eyes, the peopling of Madagascar was therefore less important than the strictly commercial objectives of the company. In

1667 they sent a memorandum to the king explaining that they desired "to make the land suitable to serve as an entrepot and general emporium for the commerce which the said company desires to establish in Greater India, China and Japan,"[12] knowing however that the "Instruction for the engagement of settlers for Dauphine Island" only spoke of setting up a colony. The enterprise, as can be seen, was ill-defined and started badly.

The engagement of employees already familiar with the Indies trade turned the company's eyes northwards. Commissioners sent to Holland signed up twenty-two Dutch pilots and merchants, almost all of them Protestants; they received their naturalization papers in August 1665. Count Godefroy d'Estrades, the French envoy in The Hague, managed to recruit the most important of them, the famous François Caron. His career is worth summarizing.

Born in Brussels in 1600 of Huguenot parents who soon after left for the United Provinces, François Caron set off in 1619 for Japan in a VOC vessel. He was employed in the godown at Hirado, where he quickly learnt Japanese and served as interpreter for several directors of this important Dutch godown. He was subsequently charged with diplomatic missions to the court of the shogun Iyemitsu at Yedo, and in 1636 wrote his famous *Rechte Beschryvinghe van het machtigh Koninghrijck van Iappan* (A true description of the mighty kingdom of Japan). Caron was named *opperhoofd* (director) of Hirado in 1639, a year before the explosion of xenophobia which resulted in the persecution of Christians, the expulsion of the Portuguese, and the transfer of the Dutch godown from Hirado to Deshima. We next find him in Batavia, where he was entrusted in 1643 with the command of a Dutch expedition against the Portuguese who had settled in Ceylon. He was named governor of Fort Zeelandia, the Dutch stronghold which controlled Taiwan (1644–1647), and finally commercial director-general of the Dutch company, having only the governor-general, Cornelis van der Lijn, over him. But the size of his personal fortune which he flouted indiscreetly in Batavia, where he lived like a prince with Constance Boudaen, whom he had married after dismissing his Japanese concubine, allowed people to think he had enriched himself at the expense of the company. The Heren XVII recalled him in April 1650; back in Holland, he set up home in The Hague, having obtained an honourable discharge.

This was the old hand who, having chafed at the bit for fifteen years, agreed to enter the service of the new French company. He set himself up in Paris, placed his wife and seven children under the protection of the king, and began to submit to Colbert plans which would facilitate the entry of France into Asiatic commercial trading circuits. At the same time, the company sent off three representatives via Aleppo and Baghdad, with the object of obtaining favours from the Shah of Persia and the Great Mogul. Louis XIV sent with them Lalain, gentleman ordinary in the royal household, and La Boullaye Le Gouz, who had travelled in Persia and the Indies in his youth, and published his *Voyages and observations* in 1653.

The first CIO squadron left Brest on 7 March 1665. It comprised four vessels bought in Le Havre, St Malo, and La Rochelle: the flagship *Saint-Paul*, the store ship *Taureau,* and the frigates *Vierge de Bon-Port* and *Aigle Blanc*, carrying altogether 212 crew and 279 merchants, clerks, and settlers. Among the passengers on the *Aigle Blanc* was François Martin, taken on as under-merchant with a salary of six hundred livres a year; he was to play an important role in the history of the company. But the *Taureau* and the *Aigle Blanc* sank off Madagascar and the *Vierge de Bon-Port* was sent to the bottom on its return by two English frigates near Guernsey. Only the *Saint-Paul* returned to Brest.[13] These misfortunes were not calculated to reassure the existing shareholders or likely to attract others, and explains why the merchant vessels of the company were soon to sail in convoy with warships sent by Louis XIV in order, according to Colbert, to "carry to the Indies the first knowledge of the arms and the power of His Majesty."[14]

Thanks to the funds advanced by Louis XIV, a second important fleet was armed at La Rochelle. It set sail on 14 March 1666. The squadron was placed under the command of the Sieur de Montdevergue, "the king's lieutenant-general in Dauphine Island," and consisted of the flagship *Saint-Jean-Baptiste*, three other vessels of between three and six hundred tons (the *Marie,* the *Terron,* and the *Saint-Charles*), two lighter frigates (the *Mazarine* and the *Duchesse*), and four transport ships of between sixty and eighty tons. Faye and Caron, directors-general, watched over the company's interests; they had just obtained their letters patent of nobility and an annual pension of six thousand livres for as long as they stayed in the Indies. According to his instructions, Caron was to go immediately to India to set up godowns; Faye, for his part, was to occupy Fort Dauphin, the principal seat of the company on the south-east coast of

Madagascar, and to explore Bourbon Island (Reunion). The lawyer d'Espinay was charged, as procurer general, with setting up a supreme council in Dauphine Island. The Montdevergue squadron carried a total of 1,688 men, of whom 421 were crew, 212 officers and soldiers forming four infantry companies which the king wished to place on the island, and 1,055 merchants and settlers. The fitting out of the squadron had cost two million livres, half in trade goods. It can be seen that the effort aimed at trading in the Indies and at the same time establishing a French colony on Madagascar, with its administrative and judicial apparatus, and forces of law and order.

The company was now launched. But, in spite of circulars in which the directors, with optimism suited for the occasion, congratulated themselves on "the solid and successful establishment of our affairs," the young company was in a difficult position. The suspicion of the public was such that a number of shareholders neglected to take up their reserved second and third tranches of shares. The king was himself obliged to advance sums over and above the three million subscribed. The company "changed itself purely and simply into a royal enterprise, in which the directors merely provided an official justification."[15] This evolution was made clear in 1667 when Louis XIV forbade the calling of a general meeting of shareholders, wishing "to avoid recriminations of those concerned whose money, destined for the Indies, was uselessly swallowed up in Madagascar"[16] and hoping that good news from Dauphine Island and especially India would reverse the then deplorable situation.

The return to Brest on 7 June 1667 of the *Saint-Paul*, the flagship of the first fleet, was not likely to restore confidence. It was disclosed that the colony of Madagascar had lost many people, the situation was critical, and the squadron of Montdevergue had not arrived eleven months after its departure from La Rochelle (it was tossed up on the coasts of Brazil by a storm, and only reached Fort Dauphin on 10 March 1667, three weeks after the departure of the *Saint-Paul*). Its cargo—sixty logs of ebony—cruelly emphasized the limited resources of Madagascar, while the shareholders were dreaming of spices, silks, and precious stones. One can understand that the public did not jostle in front of the company's offices to snap up new shares.

The discouraged directors bombarded Colbert with memoranda detailing the company's worrying financial position. They told him without beating about the bush "that we have to go directly to the

Indies, open godowns and start trading, without stopping any more half-way there to clear a huge primitive island."[17] They proffered sound common sense.

A little later came letters from Montdevergue complaining of the sterility and unhealthiness of Dauphine Island, adding that it was impossible to colonize and no one else should be sent there. The settlers lacked everything, and to feed them, half the trade goods destined for sale in the Indies had to be sold on the spot. Montdevergue received a withering reply from Louis XIV:

> You seem to imagine that the company will always send, from France or the Indies, the necessary victuals to support the number of my subjects who have settled there, without extracting any advantages. This thought seems so extraordinary that one cannot believe it could come to anyone's mind, howsoever little enlightened he be.[18]

The directors pleaded once more with Colbert to abandon the tiresome idea of settling Madagascar, and set up instead a simple depot on Bourbon Island, and concentrate on trade in the Indies, where Caron had gone with two vessels to establish French godowns from Surat. It was decided that more explicit news would be awaited from Caron before taking a decision, and meanwhile the essential aid demanded by the settlers in Fort Dauphin would be sent. To finance this, the hesitant shareholders were invited to loosen their purse strings. Louis XIV personally pressured courtiers who had imprudently subscribed to the company, dreaming of the treasures of the orient. But the king went further; he promised an additional two million, and authorized the treasury to disburse a first instalment of half a million livres in November 1668.

The company's second general shareholders' meeting was convened by order under the king's private seal. It was held on 15 December 1668 in the Tuileries in the midst of extraordinary pomp, presided over by Louis XIV flanked by the princes and chief officials of the crown. Colbert read out a report, showed a balanced budget thanks to royal generosity, and then admitted that a mistake had been made in sending the fleets to Dauphine Island. He passed over the miserable condition of Montdevergue's expedition, indicating that Caron had reached India to set up godowns there. The *Saint-Jean-Baptiste* was returning with a rich cargo. Complete success, he concluded, could now be expected for this great enterprise.

Louis XIV then took the floor himself to approve the management of the directors, remind people that the enterprise pleased him, and confirm his support. His Majesty added nobly, "that his finances were in a sufficiently good state to be able to tell them that he would not fail them in all their needs." The end must have caused shivers among recalcitrant shareholders. The king showed his satisfaction with those subscribers who had fulfilled their obligations, and his irritation with those who had abandoned the enterprise. He had been shown, he said, the names of various people, and had "too good a memory to forget them." The new directors and the commissioners charged with auditing the accounts were then proposed by Colbert and "selected and named" there and then by the king.

The shareholders had at no point any say in the proceedings. They expected to participate in some degree, but were simply told, in effect, "Pay up and shut up." Those who expected a distribution of dividends were disappointed; the matter did not appear in the agenda.

The arrival of the vessel from Surat announced by Caron did nothing to dissipate the anxieties of the shareholders. The *Saint-Jean-Baptiste* anchored at Port-Louis at the end of January 1669, but its mediocre cargo aroused no enthusiasm. François Caron might well explain in a letter that it contained only samples and there had not been time to send anything better, and Louis XIV might well express his joy to the directors; they, though, expressed their displeasure to Caron at what they called this "miserable merchandise."

The indispensable François Caron had gone to Surat, from where he had begun to set up a network of godowns in Rajpur, Mirza, Tellicherry, and Masulipatam, and was already thinking of extending his area of operations to Bantam in Java. But he took nobody's advice, and his high-and-mighty manners irritated his French colleagues who called him "this f . . . old Flemish idiot." Furthermore, his being a Protestant had put him on bad terms with the Capuchin friars in Surat. Colbert preached the virtues of charity and kindness to everyone, requesting Caron to convert to avoid difficulties, but he too seems to have entertained doubts about his man's ability. Immediately after the arrival of the ship from Surat, he wrote in a despatch addressed to Faye, the other director-general, "Even if you consider the behaviour of the said Sieur Caron blameworthy . . . you should conceal this . . . until you have acquired the necessary experience to support all the establishments which have been created."[19]

Meanwhile, the minister mulled over the views of Caron, who

repeated that trading in the Indies and colonizing Madagascar were incompatible. The idea of abandoning this enterprise began to form in his mind. His instructions of 8 March 1669 suggest establishing the company's port of call at the Cape or elsewhere. Six months later, Dauphine Island was discretely transferred to the royal domain and an order from the Council of State in November 1670 abolished the island's sovereign council. Madagascar was not yet entirely abandoned, but it was only a question of time. France left the island in 1674, just maintaining an establishment on Bourbon Island.

The CIO experienced a crisis of confidence. Louis XIV was the first to admit this, writing in 1669, "The company is compromised in the opinion of the whole of my kingdom."[20] The reasons for this uneasiness? The Madagascan mirage had proved very expensive. The shareholders, lured by a publicity campaign that was more eloquent than true, expected Dutch dividends of twenty-five or thirty per cent immediately, and were cruelly disillusioned. The mountains of gold did not exist. As Lavisse noted, "we do not, in France, like affairs that do not succeed immediately."[21]

"IT WILL BE UP TO THE KING TO BE MASTER OF THE INDIES"

From now on the CIO could concentrate on its commercial undertakings alone. For the first time in its history it sent vessels direct to the Indies. The *Saint-François* set sail on 7 July 1669 with orders to steer a course to Surat without stopping at Madagascar. It carried a letter from Louis XIV to the Great Mogul, Aurangzeb, in which he announced the foundation of the French company, offered his friendship, and asked him to protect the French. Caron was charged with explaining their needs.

Having decided on creating a French presence in the Indies in every way comparable to the Dutch and the English, Colbert carefully studied the reports he received from Asia. The memorandum of François de La Boullaye Le Gouz, who had been sent to Surat in 1664, contained everything to please the minister: "The king's vessels should be sent to be seen on the coasts, and above all do not be niggardly with the powder and shot, as it is extremely important to lay low the pride of the Dutch . . . Once the company is established, it will be up to the king to be master of the Indies, as all these monarchs are without a navy."[22] La Boullaye was probably not proposing the conquest of the Indies, but he demonstrated clearly that Asian trade was inconceivable without territorial establishments protected by cannons of the French navy. Other advice he proffered seems very judicious. "Small children must be sent to the offices to learn . . . the four chief [languages] which are used everywhere, namely Turkish, Persian, Arab, and Malay. And if the king changed the College of Four Nations to become a College of Four Languages, we would have by this means interpreters in France and this would be a great advantage, even for the missionaries."[23] The idea of the School of Oriental Languages arose from this.

The suggestions of François Bernier received Colbert's close attention. Bernier had studied medicine before leaving for Asia in 1656, and became Aurangzeb's private physician for twelve years, and an interested observer of India through which he travelled widely. In 1670–1671 he published his *Mémoires sur l'empire du Grand Moghol* (Memoirs of the empire of the Great Mogul). He suggested prudence rather than sending troops. The Dutch had given the Great Mogul to understand that France was a warlike nation which would try to establish fortresses. The power of Louis XIV therefore had to be underplayed, and Caron sent to head an embassy without any show of strength: "He will have no problems if everything smells of trade." It would be good if Caron, admitted to the presence of Aurangzeb, did his *salaams* in the Indian fashion, placing his hands three times above his head and bowing down to the ground. A similar embassy was to be received by the Raja of Golconda and the Nabab of Bengal. Everywhere presents were necessary to secure the benevolence of the principal governors, for everything depended on them.

In January 1669 Colbert also studied a memorandum from François Caron who insisted on the importance of the spice trade—the preserve of the Dutch—and proposed the establishment of fortified godowns. One could be set up, for example, on the east coast of Ceylon, at Trincomalee or Batticaloa, where cinnamon could be bought from the king of Kandy, under the nose of the Dutch; on the Malabar coast, the centre of the pepper trade, the Dutch dominated all the princes except the Zamorin of Calicut; in the Moluccas, there was Ceram, the large island to the north of Ambon which the Dutch did not yet control, and from where came cloves in particular. France could trade with impunity in all these places providing it had sufficiently powerful ships to protect its interests. Caron was in short proposing the sending of a royal fleet to Asian waters.

This idea seems to have pleased Colbert right away, who had it approved by Louis XIV without difficulty. In May 1669 the minister sent instructions to Rochefort that a squadron be formed which the king had decided to send to the East Indies "with the unique aim of demonstrating a small sample of his power to the princes of Asia." It was important that "all the infantry be carefully selected, and the arms handsome and fine, and finally that everything should be as perfect as possible, in both beauty and quality."[24] While preparing this prestigious gilt-edged operation, Colbert sought, without much success, an anti-Dutch alliance with the Portuguese in the forthcoming struggle for Asian markets.

The command of the royal squadron was given to Sieur Jacob Blanquet de La Haye; he was no genius. His instructions, drawn up in December 1660, ordered him to look for places on the African coast where the company could establish ports of call, and to spend only one month in Madagascar where he was to remove Montdevergue from office (his perpetual complaints wearied the royal ear) and look for the causes of past misfortunes. After this, he was to proceed to Surat from where, in concert with the company directors, he would stimulate and protect the establishment of new godowns in Ceylon and elsewhere. If he met with opposition on the part of the Dutch or the English, His Majesty considered his squadron sufficiently strong to impress them. La Haye was thus to carry out the proposals of Caron and La Boullaye. The Dutch or the English were not to be pointlessly provoked, but neither were they to be avoided. Each was to have his place under the Asian sun!

The squadron comprised five vessels, the *Navarre*, the *Triomphe*, the *Jules*, the *Bayonnais*, and the *Flamand*, as well as the frigate *Diligente* and the storeships *Indienne* and *Sultan*. Altogether they carried 2,100 men and 238 cannons. The company for its part armed three merchant vessels, the *Dauphin Couronné*, the *Phénix*, and the *Vautour*. This fleet, the most powerful ever to appear in the Indies, set sail at the end of March 1670.

Wanting to maintain as sure and speedy communications as possible between France and its future possessions in the Indies, Colbert consulted François Baron, the consul in Aleppo; was not the old overland route better than that via the Cape, prone to storms and pirates? It was decided to set up a rather complicated system of posts and relays, making use of the French Capuchins and Carmelites in Aleppo, Baghdad, Bassora, Isfahan, and Ormuz, since, after all, they had the honour to be the king's subjects. Through this Middle Eastern network went all future correspondence between the directors in Paris and the Asian godowns, which, informed of the departure of vessels, could prepare their cargoes and gain precious time.

François Caron seems to have collaborated loyally with La Haye when he appeared in Surat with his squadron in September 1671, bearing the pompous title of viceroy of the Indies. The entry of the French into Ceylon was made possible by the personal relations going back a long way between Caron and King Rajasingha II of Kandy. The company began to set up a cinnamon godown at Koddiyar in the Bay of Trincomalee in March 1672. If it was dislodged shortly after it was not Caron's fault. French sources gloss over the reasons for this setback, but we have the testimony of Robert Knox, an Englishman detained in Ceylon for twenty years from 1659 by Rajasingha II, who published after his escape an important *Historical Relation of the Island Ceylon in the East Indies*.[25] He was at the Kandy court when the French arrived; his account suggests that their contempt for local customs ruined the venture. They were apparently too preoccupied with demonstrating the king's "power to the princes of Asia" to worry about their susceptibilities.

On 22 March 1672 La Haye arrived with fourteen vessels in sight of Trincomalee. He noticed with chagrin that the Dutch, alerted to his project, had built a fort which controlled access to the bay. Caron, on board the flagship, urged the viceroy to act. "If, on arriving, La Haye had attacked the Dutch, it is certain that he would have dislodged them without difficulty."[26] But the indecisive admiral made shift with avoiding the fort, occupying two small islands in front of Koddiyar at the south of the bay, and beginning their fortification. The bigger was grandiosely named "Sun Island," and the other "Caron Isle." On 15 May the Dutch fleet arrived, commanded by Rijckloff van Goens, governor of the Dutch possessions in Ceylon and future governor-general of the VOC. Badly victualled, La Haye avoided an encounter and set sail on 9 July for Tranquebar on the Coromandel Coast with five vessels and two frigates.

As soon as he had arrived at Trincomalee he sent Sieur de Boisfontaine and two companions to Kandy, charged with preparing a formal embassy. Rajasingha II received them graciously and presented each with a gold chain, a damascened sword, and a breech loader. They at once informed La Haye of the favourable disposition of the king. The admiral prepared an embassy to send to Kandy, where it would wait for his return.

The delegation comprised the ambassador Lanerolle and six gentlemen, among whom Knox cites Mr du Plessis and Mr de La Roche. The ambassador, as cocky as a rooster,

> came riding on Horse-back into the City. Which the noble-men observing, dissuaded him from, and advised him to walk on foot, telling him it was not allowed, nor the Custom. But he regarding them not, rode by the Palace Gate. It offended the King, but he took not much notice of it for the present. [27]

In spite of this blunder he was admitted to the court for his audience, but refused to wait the two hours which etiquette required, saying he was insulted and wanted to return to his lodging.

> Some about the Court observing this, would have stopped him by Elephants that stood in the Court, turning them before the Gate thro which he was to pass. But he would not so be stopped, but laid his hand upon his Sword, as if he meant to make his way by the Elephants. The People seeing his resolution, called away the Elephants and let him pass. As soon as the King heard of it, he was highly displeased, insomuch that he commanded some of his Officers that they should go and beat them [the French], and clap them in Chains, which was immediately done. [28]

Lanerolle was kept in chains for six months; he had plenty of time to meditate on the virtues of diplomatic subtlety. His companions avoided him like the plague. They were lodged and fed at the king's expense, and permitted to walk freely in Kandy until the return of La Haye's squadron.

But the "viceroy of the Indies," detained in São Tomé, did not return to Singhalese waters, and the Dutch, with the blessing of Rajasingha II, forced the fortified isles off Koddiyar to capitulate on 18 July. "We stupidly wasted our time in Trincomalee," concluded Louis Pauliat.[29] This disastrous venture cost the royal squadron the loss of four ships and five hundred men. The French who were stranded in Ceylon made shift as best they could while waiting to be evacuated. Some, veterinarians for the occasion, looked after the king's horses; others distilled arak and opened taverns which Knox praises highly.

This unfortunate episode helps us understand why the subjects of Louis XIV fared so badly in the East Indies. Poorly led and poorly organized, unfamiliar with the local cultures and little inclined to understand them, they considered the flexibility of the Dutch and the English as perhaps suitable for a race of heretics, but incompatible with French grandeur.

The forbearance of Louis XIV is surprising when, learning that La Haye had lost Koddiyar, the king wrote to him that it was impossible to hold this outpost "for lack of men and sufficiently good officers to confront all the difficulties and overcome all the obstacles in so distant a land." Informed a little later that La Haye had taken the former Portuguese godown of São Tomé de Meliapur, a few leagues from Madras, he congratulated him royally: "I have great hopes that you will . . . succeed in holding a post whose importance I appreciate fully, and by the means of which I shall make my power felt in a land where it is scarcely known."[30] But the ink on this letter was not yet dry before São Tomé was besieged by the Dutch, who were in earnest and had friends in the region.

La Haye had first of all dropped anchor at Tranquebar, which was in Danish hands, but they had refused to revictual him. He found there a letter from Louis XIV, already thirteen months old, announcing his intention of attacking the United Provinces. Caron learnt the news with consternation and from that point seems to have cooperated less willingly. He refused to show his precious maps of India which he kept in his cabin, saying he had left them behind in Surat. La Haye treated him with so much arrogance and suspicion that Caron decided to return to Europe.

The admiral left Tranquebar and seized São Tomé without difficulty on 25 July. This godown had been taken back from the Portuguese ten years earlier by the Raja of Golconda; it was therefore necessary to be on good terms with him. François Martin, the future founder of Pondichéry, arrived at the beginning of 1673 in São Tomé and offered his services to La Haye. He went to negotiate with the Raja of Golconda and obtained a draft treaty without difficulty. The raja granted the ownership of São Tomé to the French company, even promising to come to its aid if attacked. All that was necessary were monetary gifts to the raja and his ministers. But La Haye, instead of embracing Martin with tears of joy, was uncompromising. He declared disdainfully that "a Frenchman does not buy peace from his enemies with money, but seizes it from him by force."[31] The Dutch were able to profit by this stupidity and paid the sum sought by the raja, who signed an agreement with them; together they dislodged the French. A long blockade was established by Rijckloff van Goens's fleet and troops supplied by the Raja of Golconda. The decimated French defended themselves valiantly, only capitulating on 6 September 1674, with their squadron now destroyed, and reduced to famine.

This was the cruel end of the grandiose French projects in India. La Haye left São Tomé on 25 September with his 530 remaining men, scarcely a quarter of those who had set out with him four and a half years previously. The Dutch—a particularly humiliating detail—lent him two vessels to bring the remnants of his expedition back to France. He observed, when passing Fort Dauphin in December, that the port was completely deserted, and that all the French settlers, after the massacre of seventy-five of them by their Madagascan servants, had withdrawn to Bourbon Island. He arrived on 6 March 1675 at Port-Louis in France. Louis XIV did not hold a grudge for his blunders, but gave a military command to the former viceroy of the Indies, who was killed in 1677 in Lorraine when his convoy was attacked. He was luckier than Montdevergue who, removed from office and brought back to France like a criminal, had died in prison in Saumur in January 1672 while undergoing trial.

François Caron had left in October 1672. This old Asian hand, who was only too well aware of the power of the Dutch in India and the weakness of the French, did not wish to take part in the final disaster which he considered inevitable. While working for the French, he had not neglected his own affairs. The seventy-year-old Caron left for France carrying a considerable fortune in pearls, amber, and precious stones. But the *Jules*, the company vessel on which he had embarked, broke upon a reef at the entrance to the harbour of Lisbon on 5 April 1673, with loss of vessel and all hands.

It has to be said that the situation of Caron had he returned to France would have been extremely delicate, for Louis XIV had declared war on the United Provinces in April 1672. Two months later, French troops had swum across the Rhine and the republic was close to being overrun. True, Amsterdam was saved by flooding the polders, but dozens of Dutch towns had to open their gates to the king's armies. The seizure of Maastricht, twelve weeks after the death of Caron, was the culminating point of a particularly brilliant military campaign.

Without going as far as Louis Pauliat who maintained that the war in Holland had "no other justification than the desire of the great king to place in the hands of the [French] company founded in 1664 all the possessions the Dutch had in the Indies,"[32] it is difficult not to see a connection between the invasion of the United Provinces and the CIO which the king passionately supported. In June 1672, only a few days after the crossing of the Rhine, Colbert had drawn up his *Proposals concerning the advantages which could be obtained from the Dutch States for increasing commerce in the kingdom.* One of his suggestions was that "His Majesty seek from them one of the Moluccan islands, at his choice, and one or two places on the Malabar Coast."[33] A few days later he did not hesitate to suggest to Louis XIV that he demand half the shares in the Dutch company which would be ceded at double their original selling price (only a fraction of their real value) and bought up by individual Frenchmen designated by the king.

But this fine dream was soon dissipated. The new stadtholder, William of Orange, took charge of matters, an anti-French coalition was formed, and France paid dearly for crossing the Rhine. The VOC, for its part, used its far from inconsiderable resources to prevent the departure of French ships for the Indies. The attack on Holland had only untoward consequences for the CIO.

The La Haye squadron, which had set out in 1670, had been followed every year, more or less regularly, with the despatch of the king's ships or company vessels until 1676. None left in 1677 or 1678. The financial condition of the CIO was not brilliant, even if few ships or cargoes were lost. The directors did not always have in hand the necessary funds to pay the crews who returned from the Indies. They were then obliged to borrow and to repay after the sale of their cargoes, and these costs were sometimes disproportionate in relation to the original expenses of fitting out. The financial problems of the company did not allow it to continue its activities indefinitely. Hence the interruption in 1677–1678.

The attempt to organize a French company along the lines of the successful Dutch company failed for several reasons. There was first of all the strong-armed dirigisme of the new company which frightened off potential investors; state control even decked out in wigs and lace was not universally popular. The idea of colonizing "en route" a country as extensive and as poor in resources as Madagascar was fatal. Lastly, the project of installing the company militarily in the Indies by calling on the resources of the state, at the very time it was invading Holland, could only set the whole of Europe against France and was particularly ill-conceived.

The Compagnie des Indes Orientales seemed to be dying but it was not yet dead. Its activities were to resume after the signing of the peace of Nijmegen. Learning by experience, it would restrict itself to purely commercial ventures. The first vessel to leave for Surat after the truce of 1677–1678, the *Soleil d'Orient*, was to play an important role in the history of Franco-Siamese relations.

CHAPTER SEVEN

THE JESUITS IN SIAM, FOLLOWED BY THE FRENCH MISSIONARIES

THE PORTUGUESE, Dutch, and English who set up in Siam were merchants primarily concerned with the markets and the kingdom's economic potential. The first Frenchmen on the scene were missionaries. Their perspective of Siam was quite different, and probably responsible for the misunderstanding at the start of the French adventure in the kingdom of Somdet Phra Narai. In earlier chapters we discussed the Portuguese Dominicans in Siam from 1567. They worked chiefly among the Portuguese and half-castes, and converts from other Asian countries, especially Japan and the Vietnamese kingdoms of Tonkin and Cochin-China. Their religious contact with the Siamese proper was minimal, not to say nil.

But the work of these forerunners is little known. The great evangelizing effort among the Siamese started at the beginning of the seventeenth century. In parallel with the Portuguese secular priests reporting to the Bishop of Malacca, himself suffragan of the Archbishop of Goa, two missionary orders played a capital role in the effort to convert Siam to Christianity: the Company of Jesus and the young Society of Foreign Missions (MEP). The first Jesuits in Siam were mostly Portuguese, but counted a few Frenchmen among them. They preceded the French bishops and priests of the Foreign Missions, and both were solidly established in Siam by the time the Jesuit mathematicians arrived, escorting the ambassadors of Louis XIV.

THE FIRST JESUITS IN SIAM

The first Jesuit sent from India to Siam was Fr Balthasar Sequeira.[1] Born in Lisbon about 1550 and admitted to the Company of Jesus in 1566, he received orders and left for India in March 1578 on board the *São Luis*. One of his companions on board was the famous Matteo Ricci. They reached Goa in September the same year. Golden Goa, the city of eighty belfries, had been the political and spiritual capital of Portuguese and Catholic Asia since 1534. Fr Ricci studied theology there and was ordained priest. He left Goa in April 1582 on his famous "Christian expedition to the kingdom of China."[2] The era of great missionary enterprise had begun.

After twenty-eight years of religious work in India, Fr Sequeira was chosen by his superiors to go to Siam to check if the conditions were favourable for the propagation of the Gospels. In the previous year, Phra Ekathotsarot had succeeded his brother, Phra Naresuan. He had just sent an envoy to the viceroy to renew the ancient bonds which existed between Portuguese India and Siam. The moment therefore seemed opportune to send a missionary to Ayutthaya. At the end of 1606 Fr Sequeira set sail from São Tomé across the Gulf of Bengal, and then went via Mergui and Tenasserim to Ayutthaya, where he arrived at the end of March 1607. His stayed just over two and a half years, during which time his state of health deteriorated from day to day. He wished to return to India, but died, exhausted after thirty years spent in the tropics, in November 1609 at Pipili, present-day Phetchaburi.

From Siam, Fr Sequeira had corresponded with his colleague André Pereira, then rector of the Jesuit college in Malacca. Pereira seems to have been sent to Ayutthaya in 1619 as ambassador of the viceroy, João Coutinho, but the details of this embassy remain obscure. Whatever the case, Phra Song Tham not only authorized the Portuguese to practise their religion freely, but even personally requested the Bishop of Malacca, Gonçalves da Silva, to send a priest who could look after the Portuguese colony settled in his capital.[3]

The first attempt at establishing a permanent residence of the Company of Jesus in Ayutthaya (1626–1630) failed in spite of the efforts of the two superiors, Fr Pedro Morejón, from Castille, and Fr Giulio Cesare Margico, an Italian. The moment was badly chosen. In August 1624, Don Fernando de Silva, captain of a Spanish galleon, had seized a Dutch yacht, the *Cleen Zeelandt*, on the Chao Phraya, arousing Phra Song Tham's anger; he had the galleon attacked by a mixed Siamese and Japanese force. Don Fernando and 150 of his men were killed, and the 30 surviving Spaniards were cast into prison.[4] In reprisal, Don Juan Niño de Tavora, the governor of the Philippines, ordered the capture in 1628 of a Japanese junk transporting Siamese merchandise, and the burning of a junk belonging to Song Tham which was returning from Canton. The King of Siam was furious; he seriously considered burning alive all the merchants and the Spanish and Portuguese Jesuits, since they were the subjects of the same king. The affair was complicated by the death of Phra Song Tham in December 1628 and the subsequent palace bloodbath, then the death in prison of Fr Margico, poisoned by a half-caste whose irregular life he had criticized. The details of the affair would fill a volume, but the reader will have gathered that the climate in Siam was hardly conducive to missionary activity.

The first Jesuits in Ayutthaya seem to have concentrated their efforts on the Japanese converts established in the capital. One of the Fathers, Romain Nixi, was himself Japanese; he left Siam about 1632 to return to Macao. Throughout the following years, some Jesuits sent from Goa to Laos or Cambodia passed through Ayutthaya, but without staying. It was only in 1655 that the company decided to return to this mission where the Christians, largely Japanese, "demanded a Jesuit, and even two."[5] The expulsion of missionaries from Tokugawa Japan decreed in 1614, and especially the Christian insurrection in Nagasaki in 1637, followed by bloody reprisals, had considerably swollen the number of Japanese Christians who had taken refuge in Siam.

The founder and first superior of the new residence was a Sicilian, Fr Tomaso Valguarnera, who had studied to be an engineer before entering the Company of Jesus. The residence was opened in 1656, the year Phra Narai came to the throne. It benefited a little later by the gift of 14,000 Roman crowns bequeathed by a Portuguese merchant named Sebastião André, who died in Ayutthaya where he had become a lay member. The pious legacy helped the construction of a fine church with a painted and gilded facade, and a few years later the College of São Salvador in Siam.

In 1658, Fr Valguarnera compiled a brief description of Siam which shows great lucidity.[6] He attributes the difficulties of converting the Siamese to the pyramidical political structure of the kingdom: "The king alone is free, and all his vassals are slaves, from the lowest to the next, the bigger to the biggest, and from these to the king." This implies, given the optic of the *Padroado*, that the Siamese who might be baptized would no longer be the slaves of the King of Siam, but of Portugal. Other missionaries explained the impermeability of the Siamese by the Gospels, by their indifference to religion in general, or, to the contrary, by their excessive attachment to their own Buddhist religion. We shall return to this, but it has to be admitted that the political argument was real.

The work and abilities of Fr Valguarnera impressed Phra Narai so much that the Jesuit was named in 1663 "superintendent of the city walls." This function, more martial than sacerdotal, occupied him almost completely; it brought him uncharitable criticism from the missionaries who laboured peacefully in the vineyard of the Lord and who saw little connection between military architecture and the Gospels. Fr Valguarnera let them grumble and had sent from Macao a porcelain fountain with a jet of water which he offered Phra Narai, knowing that his conversion would entail that of the whole kingdom.

Among the other Jesuits then active in Ayutthaya were the Portuguese João Cardoso, who had worked a long time in Tenasserim and died in 1677 in a shipwreck, and the Frenchmen Joseph Tissanier and Pierre Albier who arrived at the end of 1663, expelled from Tonkin. We shall return to Fr Tissanier and his essay on the commercial practices of the missions. Later, after the death of Fr Valguarnera in January 1677, the pillar of the residence and one of its most remarkable members was Fr Jean-Baptiste Maldonado, who arrived from Macao in 1673.

FROM THE *PADROADO* TO THE *PROPAGANDA FIDE*

The "caravels of Christ" had left throughout the sixteenth century to storm pagan Asia, depositing on its shores only Spanish or Portuguese missionaries and foreigners who had given them their allegiance. The Iberian crowns had divided the East and West Indies according to the famous demarcation line of the Treaty of Tordesillas; the *Ius Patronatus* (*Patronato* in Spanish and *Padroado* in Portuguese) permitted them to organize the conversion of their vast possessions without the least interference from the Vatican. But what in the sixteenth century had been an impulse to vitality (the tidal wave of missionary energy released by St Francis Xavier comes to mind) had become in the seventeenth century the cause of paralyzing rigidity. Worse, the division of missionary zones between Spain and Portugal had resulted in antagonisms which deterred the indigenous peoples from embracing a religion which claimed to be pacific.

Before being the spokesmen of Christ, the missionaries were in the first instance subjects and agents of the Kings of Spain or of Portugal, and the joining of the two crowns between 1580 and 1640 had aggravated rather than appeased rivalry in the field. What a calamity if Portuguese clerics dared preach the Gospels to pagans coming under the Catholic king of Spain, or vice versa! Californian gold diggers defended their concessions, picks in hand, with equal ruthlessness. If the Spanish and Portuguese missionaries were seen to unite, it was solely to eject non-Iberian intruders, especially the French, from their respective zones of influence. Unedifying quarrels between the different missionary orders, more absorbed in protecting their petty interests than consumed by holy emulation inspired by apostolic zeal, completed this bleak picture.[7] It is well known that the quarrel over Chinese rites would not have occurred if the brilliant success of silk-dressed Jesuits at the imperial court and among the ruling classes had not aroused jealousy among other missionary orders which laboured more obscurely in China.

The sight of missions linked to temporal administrations enjoying enormous privileges which greatly encroached on the spiritual sphere was of considerable concern to the Holy See. From the end of the sixteenth century, many clear-sighted persons had considered that the papacy should take over the general direction of missions. Inspired by the centralizing influence of the post-Tridentine era, Clement VIII Aldobrandini had created in 1600 the Congregation of the Propagation of the Faith, comprising ten cardinals and charged with all matters which could aid the conversion of infidels. But the representatives of Philip III of Spain had invoked the *Patronato*, and the congregation was dissolved in 1604.

The idea was taken up again during the brief reign of Gregory XV Ludovisi. It ended in January 1622 with the creation of the pontifical congregation, *De Propaganda Fide* (soon to be termed the Propaganda), composed of thirteen cardinals and charged with the expansion of the Catholic faith throughout the world. Under a secretariat, the Propaganda became an efficient organization which replaced the anarchic empiricism of the past with careful management. The first secretary, Mgr Francesco Ingoli, occupied this important position from 1622 to his death in 1649. He devised the policy of the congregation by drawing on the detailed annual reports which each of the superiors of the missionary orders compiled at his request. A polyglot printing house was set up to produce catechisms and liturgical manuals in non-European languages; in 1651, it was to print the Latin-Vietnamese catechism of Fr de Rhodes. In addition, following the request of the Propaganda, Urban VIII Barberini created in 1627 the Urban College which was to train future missionaries and indigenous young men who intended to become priests. It was set up at the southern end of the Piazza di Spagna, a few steps from the residence of the Spanish ambassador. Some cynics might have considered this a provocation.

But this new impulse to missionary enterprise was to encounter serious obstacles, like conflicts between loyalties, and, above all, opposition in the name of antiquated rights of the *Padroado*. The Propaganda soon realized that in Asia the Portuguese Archbishop of Goa and the Spanish Archbishop of Manila overtly sabotaged the missionary reform stimulated by Rome. The directors of the Propaganda would have preferred to make use of priests both zealous and independent of the obsolete *Padroado*, linked with none of the missionary orders already working in the field.

The return to Europe of the French Jesuit Alexandre de Rhodes in 1652 was to prepare the ground for the creation of a new congregation of French priests, devoted more particularly to the Far East. Fr de Rhodes had worked many years in Cochin-China and Tonkin, where he had been very successful, with the help of his remarkable gift for Asian languages. He had formed networks of devoted local catechists and brought about three hundred thousand conversions. But after being expelled five times, he understood that these young churches could not survive the bouts of xenophobia which regularly convulsed them (the Japanese example was in everyone's mind) as long as they did not have native priests recruited from among their catechists. But bishops were needed to ordain them, and bishops could not be nominated in Asia because of the *Padroado*, which was little inclined to support the creation of autochthonous clergy. Mgr Ingoli had noted in a memorandum of 1644: "The bishops in the East Indies do not wish to ordain any indigenous priests."[8] Fr de Rhodes therefore came to entreat the

Propaganda to gather persons from among whom, in its view, bishops might be selected who would consecrate native priests. Rome listened to him and authorized him to recruit volunteers.

The Portuguese Asian empire was in complete decline, and the Propaganda knew this as well as Fr de Rhodes. The accession to the throne of the eighth Duke of Braganza under the name of João IV in 1640 had, it is true, restored Portugal's independence, but its overseas territories were still more exposed to the activities of the Dutch and the English with the end of the enforced link with Spain. The house of Braganza succeeded in expelling the Dutch from Angola and Brazil, but Portuguese Asia was in tatters. Hardly had the Duke of Braganza been acclaimed king in December 1640 than the Dutch seized Malacca in January 1641. They then took possession of Ceylon (1658) and the Moluccas (1666), while the English laid hands on Madras (1640) and Bombay (1661).

Portuguese bishops and priests were immediately expelled by the new Protestant occupiers, while the Lusitanian *Padroado*, to which João IV clung just as much as his predecessors, prevented Rome from replacing them with non-Portuguese. Philip IV of Spain had been unable to prevent Portuguese independence, but tolerated no pontifical concessions to the new king of Portugal. He was opposed in principle to the investiture of Portuguese bishops in the lands of the *Padroado*. Innocent X Pamphili, the former nuncio in Madrid, did not dare ruffle the Catholic monarch whose Neapolitan armies were stationed on the frontiers of the Papal States.

The world had indeed changed since Tordesillas, but not everyone was prepared to admit this.

THE VICARS-APOSTOLIC

After arriving in France, Fr de Rhodes published his *Histoire du royaume du Tonkin et des grands progrès que la prédication de l'Evangile y a faits depuis l'année 1627 jusques à l'année 1646* (The history of the kingdom of Tonkin and the great progress in the preaching of the Gospels there from 1627 to 1646) in Lyons at the end of 1652. His reputation had preceded him to Paris, where he arrived in January 1653. His Jesuit colleagues and the powerful Company of the Holy Sacrament, established in 1630, welcomed him with open arms. His charismatic personality, his oratory, and his writings gave rise to numerous vocations for missionary work in Asia among the young Jesuits in the capital and the members of an association of ecclesiastics devoted to spiritual life among friends, the Bons Amis (Good Friends). Among these were the Norman, Pierre Lambert de La Motte;[9] the archdeacon of Evreux, François de Laval; the Breton, Vincent de Meur; as well as a young canon from Tours, François Pallu.

The idea of converting the Vietnamese kingdoms and China inspired the Bons Amis.

> But as only three bishops were needed, those who were not to be chosen should become Jesuits. For sure, the Superior General of the Jesuits would allow them to complete their novitiate en route. Not so. The Superior General required that at least some of their novitiate be completed before taking any decision. At this point the young priests hesitated.[10]

It was decided that those who were not to be invested with episcopal rank would accompany the bishops as secular priests.

In this way the shape was established for an initiative which was to revolutionize Catholic missionary history—the appointment of vicars-apostolic by the Church.

> In the fourth century, one called a vicar-apostolic, that is, a vicar of the pope, a bishop charged with visiting a nearby diocese in the name of the Roman pontiff. In the twelfth century, the term no longer designated a visitor, but a provisional administrator of a diocese, delegated by the Holy Father.[11]

Since the success of converting Asia depended on indigenous clergy, and since the Iberian bishops, within the jurisdiction of the *Padroado*, refused to ordain such persons, bishops permitted to do this had to be established in missionary lands not yet elevated into dioceses.

The idea had developed over time—Rome has never been accused of rushing things—but it seems that it was above all due to the activities and entreaties of Fr de Rhodes that the Propaganda decided in favour of the following subterfuge: let us allay Iberian susceptibilities and not create resident bishops, but vicars-apostolic, incumbents of dioceses *in partibus infidelium*, that is, ancient episcopal sees situated in the Middle East and long since invaded by Islam.

The death of the indecisive Innocent X at the beginning of 1655 and the election of Alexander VII Chigi seemed to unblock the situation. But the new pope was as fearful of the King of Spain as his predecessor; two more years were needed before the matter of the bishops destined for Asia would progress. It required all the Breton tenacity of Vincent de Meur, whom friends called "the Apostle." He invited François Pallu to accompany him to Rome; they would go as mere pilgrims and see if, with God's help, they could further the matter of the vicars-apostolic.

During their journey, the two received the electrifying but unconfirmed news that five missionaries in Tonkin had baptized seventy thousand pagans in one year, that the Tartar emperor was now master of China which he opened freely to the preaching of the Gospels, that missionaries had entered Korea where in a short time they had converted twenty thousand, etc. The need for bishops for such promising missions was more urgent than ever. They arrived in Rome at the beginning of June 1657, and were received in pontifical audience on 17 July. They told Alexander VII that French priests were ready to leave for Indochina and three vicars-apostolic could be selected from among them; their influential friends in the Compagnie du Saint-Sacrement proposed perpetual annuities to ensure the maintenance of the vicars, and the good functioning of their missions. The pope promised them his help and seemed touched. "He had the goodness to tell them that God, from his earliest years, had given him a particular inclination for the conversion of infidels."[12]

Given the proverbial Roman circumspection, things were proceeding quite well. The new secretary of the Propaganda, Mgr Mario Alberici, had just taken up his post and was following the case. The arrival in Rome of Pierre Lambert de La Motte in November contributed to further progress in the affair. This former magistrate, who had sold his practice to be ordained a priest, understood better than his friends the reason for the reservations of the Propaganda, especially when it came to providing financial guarantees.

At the beginning of 1657, Louis XIV had requested the creation of a bishopric in Canada and proposed François de Laval as the first holder of the new see. This request seems to have facilitated the matter of the three bishops destined for the Far East. The Propaganda indicated its agreement in April 1658, and the pope signed several bulls during the summer. François de Laval was named Bishop *in partibus* of Petra in Arabia, and vicar-apostolic of Canada; François

Pallu became Bishop of Heliopolis (Baalbek) and vicar-apostolic of Tonkin and five northern Chinese provinces; and Pierre Lambert de La Motte was created Bishop of Berythus (Beirut) and vicar-apostolic of Cochin-China and four southern Chinese provinces. Since Vincent de Meur wanted to look after the organization of the logistics base in France for the vicars-apostolic and their priests, his companion Ignace Cotolendi, vicar in Aix-en-Provence, was made Bishop of Metellopolis and vicar-apostolic of Nankin, several provinces of eastern China, Tartary, and Korea. "We can appreciate on reading these listings how incomplete was the knowledge of these regions in Rome," remarks Alain Forest.[13] Whatever the circumstances, they took the long view in those days.

The Propaganda, though, had few illusions about the Portuguese reactions to this initiative. It went as far as advising the vicars-apostolic against reaching their sees by the Portuguese maritime route, advising them to conceal their movements and their titles until they arrived, and to correspond with Rome in code. The margin of manoeuvre of the new bishops *in partibus* was thus very limited. It was clear that they needed all their prudence and diplomatic skills to succeed.

The three young priests invested with unlimited ecclesiastical powers throughout South-East Asia, Korea, and China had an average age of only thirty-two years. The Propaganda sent them detailed instructions which advocated renunciation and disdain for temporal affairs. Rome knew that numerous missionaries were more concerned with their trading than their flock. The Jesuit, Joseph Tissanier, whom we have mentioned in relation to Ayutthaya, was even to draw up a *Religiosus Negotiator* (The Trading Priest), suggesting that the missions could not function without the revenues from their commercial enterprises. In addition to disinterest and simplicity, Rome recommended to the missionaries prayer and patience.

They were to need all these virtues, especially the last-named. The Portuguese did not content themselves with protesting vehemently; they conducted in the field a real war in which every trick in the book was permitted. The attitude of the missionary orders already established on the ground was scarcely more charitable, forcing the vicars to appeal constantly to Rome or go there in person. Even the protection of the Holy See did not prevent the chapter of Goa from threatening excommunication against Mgr Lambert de La Motte for having violated the sacrosanct privileges of the *Padroado*. The lives of the vicars and apostolic missionaries in Asia would not be a bed of roses.

One remains struck by the breadth of the ideas developed in the instructions given by the Propaganda to the vicars-apostolic in November 1659. This document, which proposed a vision founded on the theology and history of the missionary duties of the Church, elaborated the ideas dear to Fr de Rhodes and the secretaries of the Propaganda. Still more important than the promotion of indigenous clergy or the expression of the desire to finish once and for all with the *Padroado* and its links between the missions and colonizing powers, the instructions of 1659 outline a clear strategy of conversion efforts in exotic countries.

The experiences of Fr Matteo Ricci with the Chinese mandarins and the successes obtained by Fr Roberto de Nobili among the Indian Brahmins encouraged great flexibility in relation to traditional cultures as long as they were not explicitly contrary to Christian precepts. The instructions go very far in this sense:

> Beware of any effort and any advice to these people to make them change their rites, their customs, or their habits, providing they are not very clearly contrary to religion and good morality. What would be more absurd than introducing France, Spain, Italy, or any other part of Europe to the Chinese? It is not that which you should introduce; it is the Faith, which does not reject nor endanger either rites or customs, providing they are not evil, but which, on the contrary, desires that they be protected.[14]

Not to compare indigenous customs with those of Europe, to respect exotic cultures, to preach the Gospels without the thick Western veneer which had covered them for centuries, this was the state of mind recommended to the French bishops and priests who were preparing to leave for South-East Asia. Missionary history would have been quite different if the debate over Chinese rites had not obliged Rome to abandon these commonsense precepts, which it refused to apply itself. "On many occasions, the vicars-apostolic would request Rome for permission to use Chinese in the liturgy . . . but each time Rome refused."[15]

THE FOREIGN MISSIONS IN PARIS

The nomination of four apostolic bishops chosen from among the Bons Amis was the origin of the foundation of the oldest specifically missionary society in France, the Société des Missions Etrangères. Created in 1659, at the time when the first vicars-apostolic and missionaries were already preparing to leave for Asia, it was only to receive its definitive statutes in 1700. Its members did not pronounce vows, but undertook to devote themselves to the conversion of infidels (meaning those who did not recognize the faith) and more especially those in China and South-East Asia.

During their stay in Rome, Pallu and Lambert de La Motte had drawn up a project for the establishment of a seminary in Paris to attend to the task of the conversion of infidels, for they realized that the applicants who desired to work under the authority of the vicars-apostolic would need adequate training. This seminary was to be the kernel of the MEP. Mgr Pallu and Vincent de Meur returned to Paris at the beginning of 1659 and were actively involved in this, with the aid of the Compagnie du Saint-Sacrement.

The first problem to resolve was the choice of a large house to lodge the applicants. Mme de Miramion, whose aunt was Mgr Pallu's sister, placed at their disposal the Château de La Couarde, on the road to Brest, fifty kilometres from Paris. The missionaries stayed there eighteen months, before moving back to the capital in 1660 and installing themselves first in the Rue Quincampoix, then in the Rue du Bac.

In truth, others had foreseen before Pallu and La Motte the need for a seminary to train secular priests who would be involved in missionary work. Jean Duval, a Carmelite, had considered the matter and acquired from rich penitents several houses for a seminary destined for missionaries who would go to Persia. Seeing his project would not succeed, he agreed to cede his buildings and land to the young MEP society.

In July 1663, Louis XIV signed letters patent for the society which Parliament recorded on 7 September; the seminary existed legally and juridically. The king specified, "We wish it to be called the 'Seminary for the conversion of infidels in foreign countries,'" but in the end the name "Seminary of Foreign Missions" prevailed. On 27 October the same year, the attorneys acting in the name of the vicars-apostolic were put in possession of their premises. Bossuet preached a sermon which took as its text the line of Psalm 57: "I will praise Thee, O Lord, among the people." The following 7 December, the attorneys and future missionaries moved permanently into the Rue du Bac.

Vincent de Meur, superior of the seminary from 1664, had to face the problem of recruiting applicants. The congregations of the Holy Virgin which flourished in the Jesuit colleges were considered breeding grounds for the individuals who would fill the seminary, but the Company of Jesus, solidly established in Portugal and in missions of Portuguese allegiance, refused to assist a rival missionary congregation which wished to overturn the privileges of the *Padroado*. The seminary of St Sulpice, sounded out about a union which would have made the MEP the missionary branch of St Sulpice, raised a thousand objections.

It was therefore, above all, the propaganda works published by the seminary which were to arouse missionary vocations. Among these were *Relation du voyage de Mgr de Béryte . . . jusqu'au royaume de Siam* (Account of the journey of Mgr de Berythus . . . to the kingdom of Siam) of Jacques de Bourges (1666) and the *Relation abrégée des missions et des voyages des évêques français envoyés aux royaumes de la Chine, Cochinchine, Tonkin et Siam* (Short account of the missions and travels of the French bishops sent to the kingdoms of China, Cochin-China, Tonkin, and Siam) of Mgr Pallu (1668). Jacques de Bourges, apostolic missionary, invited his readers to pray to God "that He arouses the zeal of several good workers who could render great service to our holy religion in distant nations" and asked "what can restrain so many virtuous ecclesiastics?"[16]

Perhaps the account of the privations and dangers to which the missionaries who ventured into the East Indies were exposed provides an answer to his question.

CHAPTER EIGHT

THE DISCOVERY OF BUDDHIST TOLERANCE

"ACCOUNT OF THE JOURNEY OF MGR DE BERYTHUS TO THE KINGDOM OF SIAM"

PIERRE LAMBERT de La Motte was the first French bishop to leave for Asia with the see *in partibus* of Berythus, and had a vast region to cover including Fukian, Kiangsi, Hainan, Cambodia, Cochin-China, and Champa (but not Siam). His consecration took place in Paris on 11 June 1660. A week later, the new prelate was on his way, but had to spend two months in Lyons where he fell seriously ill.

The instructions given by the Propaganda were very explicit as to his itinerary: "The land route, through Syria and Mesopotamia, will be much safer for you than the sea route via the Atlantic and the Cape of Good Hope, and you must at all costs avoid regions and places which depend, in whatever fashion, on the Portuguese."[1] Having been refused Portuguese laissez-passers allowing free passage just in case he needed them, and unwilling to provoke "the jealousy of nations who have become formidable in the seas of the Indies,"[2] Mgr Lambert had every reason to follow his instructions from Rome. He embarked at Marseilles on 27 December 1660 with two priests from the MEP, Jacques de Bourges and François Deydier.

The *Relation du voyage de Mgr l'Evêque de Beryte, vicaire apostolique du royaume de la Cochinchine, par la Turquie, la Perse, les Indes, etc., jusqu'au Royaume de Siam et autres lieux, par M. de Bourges, prêtre, missionnaire apostolique*[3] (Account of the journey of the Bishop of Berythus, vicar-apostolic to the kingdom of Cochin-China, through

Turkey, Persia, the Indies, etc., to the kingdom of Siam and other places, by Mr de Bourges, priest, apostolic missionary) gives the details of this journey and contains a description of Siam. This was the first text about the country printed in France, twenty years before the great Siamese vogue of 1685–1690. The small volume of 250 pages is worth careful reading, and gives one of the earliest descriptions of the overland route.

It should be noted that these missionaries were imbued with the scope of evangelization which they describe in the first chapter:

> We are dealing with the conversion of an empire which surpasses Europe in grandeur, and which we are told contains in its extent more than two hundred million souls, not including the neighbouring kingdoms which are very considerable. Our Lord Jesus Christ seeks the zeal of the French for the conquest of these great countries . . . [4]

THE BAGHDAD CARAVAN AND THE REVELATION OF COFFEE

In Marseilles, the missionaries boarded a small three-master which took them to Alexandretta in Turkey, where they arrived on 5 January 1661. The journey from there to Aleppo via Antioch greatly affected the sensibilities of the priests who saw all the ancient churches converted into mosques. "Among these sad sights, we could hardly restrain our tears and lamentations. Each of us offered himself to God to . . . repair . . . the disgrace of the Christian religion, violated and dishonoured by the sacrilege of a blasphemous sect."[5]

They reached Aleppo on 25 January, and joined the caravan leaving for Babylon (that is, Baghdad). Jacques de Bourges, who wished in writing his account to give useful advice to "missionaries who would be called to follow them, or who wished to undertake the journey," does not spare his reader: "In short, if there is any place in the world where one has to live by adroitness and sobriety, being always on one's guard, sleeping little, always having one's eyes open and being ever courageous, it is on the stages of a caravan, where each person mistrusts his neighbour as if he were a thief."[6] Of course, the desert was crawling with "carnivorous hungry beasts" who, licking their jaws, watched these missionaries dressed like Turks without taking any notice of the muskets fired in the air, nor the furious barking of the dogs.

But the journey by caravan gave rise to interesting discoveries. Jacques de Bourges is one of the first to describe in detail that hot beverage which would delight the court and the town after the visit to Paris in 1669–1670 of the Turkish ambassador, Soliman Agha.

> As the water in these wells is often bad and stagnant, to correct the discomfort it causes the stomach, the Turks serve a beverage they call *caphé* which is beginning to be fashionable in some European towns. This drink contains a little bean which grows in Arabia near Mecca in such abundance that it is carried from there all over Asia and in almost every place where there are Muhammadans, who make use of this drink instead of wine, whose effects are similar, having the properties of fortifying the stomach and facilitating digestion. It also purifies vapours in the head. They roast this bean in a pan, then grind it into a powder with a pestle, and after separating out the bran with a sieve, they boil this black and burnt flour in water for the length of time it takes to say a Miserere, then one drinks it as hot as one can. Although this liquor does not have an agreeable taste, being rather bitter, it is none the less much esteemed by these people. [7]

The time for making the coffee is the time it took to recite Psalm 50, about two minutes.[8] People often said, "I shall return in a Miserere."

FROM BAGHDAD TO ISFAHAN: "ALL THE GRACIOUS OBJECTS OF THE ORIENT"

The caravan arrived in Baghdad on 5 March. The missionaries rested there some ten days with the French Capuchins before taking their places on the "vessel of a janissary" to go down the Tigris. They disembarked at the end of May at Bassora, where they lodged, after the usual hassle of customs formalities, with the Carmelites. The asphyxiating heat did not prevent Jacques de Bourges, a budding botanist, describing at length the rather complicated sexual reproduction of date palms, and piously praising "the Author of the wealth and variety of nature." Bassora (Basra), half-way between the confluence of the Tigris and the Euphrates and the Shatt-el-Arab estuary, was famous for its thousands of date palms; some even placed the Garden of Eden there. According to the *Thousand and One Nights*, it was the base of the legendary sailor, Sinbad.

At Bassora, Western and Eastern religious cultures met, and all were tolerated. Mgr Lambert and his companions conscientiously visited mosques and Hindu temples, feeling pity for what they called "evil cults" and "tumultuous ceremonies," "miserable representations" and "the errors of idolatry." They were clearly unable to appreciate the wealth and exotic exuberance of these religions which coexisted peacefully under a leaden sky. The same incomprehension will be found when they meet Siamese monks, but perhaps it is unreasonable to expect more flexibility on the part of very dogmatic priests who lived in a century which did not count religious tolerance among Christian virtues.

Without knowing what route they were to take, they embarked on 22 April to go in five days to Banderric (Bandar Rig), "which is a port in the state of Persia in the Persian heartland." Jacques de Bourges had a low opinion of this "wretched ship" and its crew of frightened Moors who, at the first gust of wind, went weeping to the bottom of the hold.

They then went to Shiraz, crossing a lunar landscape on mules, the great heat forcing them to proceed only at night. Shiraz, with its gardens where fountains babbled among roses in the bluish shade of huge cypress trees, seemed to them a heavenly spot. They arrived on 14 May at midnight. Even the mosques and the madrassahs, the Koranic schools, decorated with multicoloured tiles, aroused cries of admiration in them. Based on admirable generosity and probably inevitable misunderstandings, missionary history relates the shock of fundamentally different cultures. The search for a common tongue would be the most difficult.

The group resumed their journey after a week. Travelling north through the mountains, they arrived on 11 June at sunrise in that marvellous city of Isfahan, then the capital of the Persian Safavid empire. They had the luck to discover the city some thirty years after the death of Shah Abbas I (1628), who had provided it with sumptuous monuments: mosques, madrassahs, minarets, palaces, bazaars, bridges, and mausoleums, hastily built but decorated with shimmering tiles. The Isfahan they saw was that of Shah Abbas II, who died in 1667; it is well known through the accounts of Sir John Chardin and J-B. Tavernier.

Before describing the marvels he saw, Jacques de Bourges relates his visits to the representatives of the English and Dutch Indies companies, and the perplexity of Mgr Lambert, hesitating over what route to take. The land route to the Indies was full of uncertainties and the missionaries avidly questioned "the oldest and most experienced travellers." They thought of going directly to China by the old Silk Road. The people they consulted indicated the innumerable difficulties that entailed, but Jacques de Bourges declared, his hand on his heart, "We consider ourselves sufficiently happy, being the first to go, to sacrifice ourselves in opening a new route for the conquest of souls."[9]

However, the project was made impossible "by the unforeseen event of the incursion of thirty thousand Tartars who came from Yousbec [Uzbekistan] to swoop down on Persia and who occupied the places through which it was necessary to pass." They were consoled over this contretemps when apprised that they would have had to cross over terrifying mountains so high and with such frightful abysses that travellers had to be carried by sherpas rolled up in carpets, from which they dare not poke their heads. They happily accepted the suggestion of an agent of the EIC who had to go from Bandar Abbas to Surat in India in the autumn, and who offered them passage on an English ship.

The missionaries therefore spent the summer in Isfahan which they visited diligently. Jacques de Bourges lovingly describes its tourist attractions, notably the royal square (Meidan-e-Shah), flanked by the superb mosques of Shah Abbas and Sheik Lotfollah (which Byron was to admire), the palace of Ali Kapu (from where Shah Abbas watched polo matches), and the imperial bazaar (Bazar Kaisaryeh) "filled with all the gracious objects of the Orient and Persia."[10] The famous Middle Eastern hookah, so dear to romantic authors on a traditional voyage to the region, is not overlooked; Persians of rank voluptuously gargle perfumed water with it while indulging in philosophical discussions.

"CROSSING THE INDIES"

At the end of September, Mgr Lambert and his companions left Isfahan with the obliging English agent who would not allow them to eat at a table other than his throughout the journey. His consular position exempted them from tolls. The good man had only one fault: "as much as English gentlemen are civil and helpful, so they are troublesome in insisting on making one drink."[11] On 8 October they reached Shiraz; the twentieth they were at Lar, where Bourges described the lively bazaar and the water full of parasites which enter the human body. He recommended avoiding this water and only drinking wine. The helpful Englishman was proved right.

They left Lar the following day, to arrive on 30 October at Gomeron (Bandar Abbas), where they stayed in the residence of the EIC. They spent the whole of November in this sleepy port, opposite the island and strait of Ormuz. They finally embarked on an English ship at the end of the month; they were very amused during the crossing when a sailor threw a piece of pork at the head of a Muslim passenger, who washed this defilement away with much water, after wanting to throw himself into the sea. This "superstitious simplicity of a gentile" brought tears of laughter into the eyes of these good missionaries, who had come from Europe to put a stop to such ridiculous prejudices.

They disembarked two days before Christmas near Surat, to the north of Bombay, in the states of the Great Mogul Aurangzeb who had just deposed his father, Shah Jahan. The town had been ravaged a year before by the Hindu leader Sivaji who, at the head of rebellious Marathas, threatened Mogul power from the eastern Deccan. The CIO was to open a godown at Surat five years later.

Blithely accustomed to defrauding customs inspections by concealing their money and objects of value under their clothes or at the bottom of their trunks, the missionaries were scandalized when their luggage and persons were minutely inspected. "There were no pleats nor folds, no places about us which they did not search in a most shocking manner."[12] Jacques de Bourges advises his readers to have all that is most precious transported, under the nose of the customs officials, to a reliable friend lined up on the quay, and piously adds: "On this occasion we had to practise to the letter the advice of Our Lord, that if you are stripped, you should not resist."[13] He ought rather to have quoted the famous, "Render unto Caesar the things which are Caesar's,"[14] the more so as the Mogul customs levied reasonable taxes of between two and four per cent.

With these formalities over, they put up at the residence of the French Capuchins, "a charitable hospice for all the missionaries who go to and come from the Indies."[15] Fr de Rhodes, who had died in the meantime, had stayed here before them. The superior, Fr

Ambroise de Preuilly, informed them that the authorities in Goa had received orders "to seize the three French bishops and send them to Lisbon as soon as possible,"[16] but this information and the threats of the Inquisition hardly impressed Mgr Lambert, who carefully continued to avoid Portuguese zones of influence. During the four weeks he spent at Surat, he had the time to study Hinduism, the morality and asceticism of which he admired more than the temples and their statues: "It is terrible when one enters their temples to see the monstrous figures of their idols . . . or to behold people devoutly paying their respects to such hideous images."[17]

The approach of the monsoon hastened their preparations for "crossing the Indies," meaning taking the land route across the subcontinent. Four bullock carts were hired, two valets and three armed men were taken on, and off they set. On 21 January 1662, the missionaries left Surat to travel a thousand kilometres as the crow flies, taking forty days. They covered an average of twenty-five kilometres a day, which is not bad going.

They passed citadels constructed on basalt outcrops which Marathas of the rebel Sivaji occupied, and towns which they called Oletabal (Koeldabad?), Norinhabal (Nuringabad?) and Deder (Bidar?). The last named fortified town was on the frontier separating the Mogul empire from the kingdom of Golconda. On arriving in the capital of this kingdom (present-day Hyderabad), "as big as Rouen, but with much cleaner air," they dismissed their armed guards. On 6 March they got down from the carts in which they spent their nights, for they had arrived as Masulipatam, the chief port on the Coromandel Coast. They were not too exhausted to cheat the customs, giving out that they were Dutch and exempt from taxes.

The town, where they stayed three weeks, was surrounded by insalubrious swamps. The water was undrinkable, and drinks prepared with fermented coconut milk "are not as good for the health as the water of the River Seine."[18] No doubt. The heat was insufferable ("this is how God wishes to make the merchants pay dearly for the profits they seek in foreign lands"); the people were so poor that they sold their children for one or two *écus* to slave merchants.

IN "THE LANDS OF THE KING OF SIAM"

Impatient to reach their Chinese missions, the travellers sought a boat going to Burma from where they hoped to reach China. But they learnt that this route was closed by the King of Ava and Pegu as he feared an invasion of the Manchu Tartars who had overthrown the Ming. Mgr Lambert then cast his eyes in the direction of Siam, without foreseeing the importance of this kingdom in the project of conversion of South-East Asia launched by the MEP. On 22 March, he embarked with his companions on a "Moorish" (Muslim) vessel sailing to Mergui, the port of Tenasserim.

They had the good fortune to arrive safe and sound, for the Portuguese pilot was criminally ignorant. Thanks to his blunders they nearly ran aground on one of the Andaman Islands, whose inhabitants have the troublesome reputation of roasting shipwrecked persons to eat them with a native sauce which they keep a secret. But what "afflicted and pierced their hearts" were these "strange superstitions, charms, pacts, processions, and profanations" of the Muslim sailors who sought favourable winds from the intercession of their "wretched Prophet." They were afraid that the calms which immobilized the vessel under a heavy sky would be imputed to them, and they would be thrown to the sea like the prophet Jonah. But God looks after his own, and they trod the beach of Mergui and "the lands of the King of Siam" on 28 April 1662, seventeen months after leaving Marseilles.

They were agreeably surprised at Tenasserim, where they arrived on 18 May, by the moderation of the Siamese governor who inspected their baggage "rather superficially" without frisking their persons. They had no trouble in bringing ashore the "little curiosities" they brought with them: watches, small religious pictures, mathematical books, amber and coral rosaries. The Portuguese Jesuit João Cardoso (we have already come across him) offered them hospitality, without taking umbrage in the least at the episcopal status of Mgr Lambert.

AN "ABSURD MONK"

Hardly had the vicar-apostolic landed than he launched into a theological debate with a Buddhist monk, called in the passage below a *talapoin,* a term incorrectly used by some Europeans of the time. Derived from the

Burmese *talapo*, corrupted into Portuguese as *talapão*, the word seems to have the same root as the Siamese *talapat*, referring to a palm tree, the leaves of which are used by Buddhist monks—*bikkhu* in Pali—as fans.[19] The section relating this conversation foretells the difficulties facing the conversion of Siam.

> All the region of Tenasserim professes paganism and idolatry, and lives in extreme ignorance of matters concerning God and eternal salvation. We went to pay a visit to some of their chief priests whom they call *talapoins*, with one of whom we entered into a discussion about the tenets of his beliefs, by means of an interpreter. We found this poor man in complete ignorance, full of contradictions and absurdities, and for each proposition he made, we could extract no reason than that it was written thus in their books. But he listened with some satisfaction to all that we proposed concerning the majesty of the Creator, the universal Lord of all things, the holiness of Christianity, the final day of judgment, future life, and the means of attaining this. He gave us to understand that he appreciated the Christians and thought their religion good, without all the same condemning his own, and that the esteem accorded to the holiness of the Christian religion in this country is the only reason for which complete liberty is extended to those who profess it. Indeed, freedom [of worship] could not be greater . . . [20]

Forty pages later, Jacques de Bourges gives the reader more details of the contents of the discussion at Tenasserim.

> The Bishop of Berythus, while in Tenasserim, went to visit one of the leading priests of that place. A Portuguese acted as interpreter for him. After saluting him in the fashion of the country, in order not to surprise the old man, he questioned him as though he wished to learn from him the articles of his faith. This man began his discourse by saying that one had to depart from the principle that there were seven gods, that their dwelling was in heaven, which was a charming land overflowing with delights and which one had to attain after death. Mr de Berythus expounded for his part the articles of his belief, without stopping to refute his absurdities, which he seemed to listen to with satisfaction, and admitted in the end that the Christian religion was very good, and the God of the Christians and his were brothers; that his was the elder and more powerful than the younger.

> This can be seen in a dispute they had which had caused them to take up arms against each other, and the younger had been conquered, captured, and put to death as punishment for his revolt. This was the fantasy that this learned person told us, which shows clearly enough how far these people are from the knowledge of the true God. [21]

After an exposé on the two forms of Christ, of which the monk doubtless understood little (and one wonders about the quality of the translations provided by the Portuguese interpreter), the monk recommended his visitors to read his holy books (the Tripitaka or "Three Baskets").

The Bishop of Berythus left this "absurd" monk shaking his head in disbelief. The idea that one could tolerate through goodness of heart (and by implicitly accepting the notion of plural truths) a religion one did not have the least desire to embrace did not easily penetrate the Cartesian minds of these priests for whom truth was one thing to the exclusion of all others. They should have read Spinoza, who asked of men, "You who think you have found the best of religions, I shall ask you in my turn have you examined all these religions, both old and new, those of our lands, of India, those of the whole universe?"[22]

The message to be sent twenty-five years later to Europe by Phra Narai was the same, that all religions are meritorious, that each person must achieve his salvation from within the religious culture in which he was born, and that proselytism taken as far as apostasy is a deception, an affront to the dignity of man.

The wisdom of this questioning of the very principle of the attempt at conversion could not affect these generous but dogmatic men, who had not feared the privations and perils of an interminable journey to plant the cross at the other end of the earth, galvanized by the universal mission confided by the resurrected Christ to his disciples: "Go ye into the world, and preach the gospel to every creature. He that believeth and is baptized shall be saved; but he that believeth not, shall be damned."[23]

Tolerance and syncretism are proper to most non-Semitic oriental religions. "The various religions," said the Great Khan Mongka, "are like the five fingers of the same hand," and his grandfather, Genghis Khan, ordered his officials to tolerate and respect all religious persuasions of his subjects, be they Christian, Muslim, or Buddhist, and even to take part in their ceremonies, but to profess explicitly no belief.

The historians of Buddhism have emphasized the tolerance that was so characteristic of the historic Buddha and the order of the world or the Law (*dharma*) which he taught. For 2,500 years in the history of Buddhism, little blood has been shed in the Buddha's name, though the great Asoka did not disdain using the sword to impose the *dharma*. Aldous Huxley reminds us that, "Alone of all the great world religions, Buddhism made its way without persecution, censorship or inquisition. In all these respects, its record is enormously superior to that of Christianity."[24] These remarks need to be somewhat nuanced, but the tolerant and pacific nature of the Buddha cannot be contested.

The Buddha did not accomplish miracles to precipitate the adherence of those who followed him; it is a late tradition that credits him with "the great miracle of Sravasti" where he is supposed to have flown in the air and emitted flames and torrents of water to convince sceptics.[25] On the contrary, after one of his monks had whirled around in the air to demonstrate the superiority of Buddhism, the Enlightened One scolded him and severely condemned such a publicity stunt involving magical powers. Neither did he use his spiritual authority to impose his teaching, relying rather on his eloquence, often ironic, and his ability in disputation. Avoiding imperatives of the type, "You must do this, you must not do that," he preferred advice, suggesting to his disciples, "It would be better if you did this . . ." or "Do you not think, Ananda, that it might be better to . . . ?" The precepts of Buddhism are not presented as orders engraved in stone like the Ten Commandments, but as modes of conduct (*sikkhapada*) freely accepted and followed without constraint. Buddhism does not overlook the concept of expansion granted to missionary monks (*dhammaduta*) who carry the message of the Enlightened One to other Asian countries, but this is done with considerable discretion.

The meeting at Tenasserim was thus a dialogue of the deaf, opposing a tolerant Buddhist monk who serenely refers to his holy scriptures without contesting the nobility of Christian morality, and a somewhat impassioned bishop, burning with the desire to convert Siam and to colonize souls. It reveals diametrically opposed cultural codes. The portraits of Mgr Lambert show a tormented face with intensely burning eyes;[26] Jacques de Bourges tells us that he considered this monk "a poor man full of darkness, contradictions and absurdities," whose "excesses" he refused to refute. What can a man convinced of believing in a unique truth say to another who is content with his own version of truth, without questioning that of his interlocutor?

Jacques de Bourges summarized the discussion in Tenasserim and the observations of the monk. Other objections are known to have been raised by Siamese Buddhists to Christianity. The Count of Forbin noted in his *Memoirs*: "The *talapoins* never dispute with anybody about religion. Talk to them of the Christian or any other religion, they approve whatever you say of it. But when a man offers to find fault with their religion, they answer coldly: 'I have been so complaisant to approve of your religion, why do you not then approve of mine?'."[27] Sir John Bowring, ambassador of Queen Victoria to King Mongkut (Rama IV), cited some other Siamese objections: "If God be the father of us all, why did He not reveal His will to Eastern as well as Western nations? . . . If miracles were worked to convert your forefathers, why do you not work miracles to convert us? . . . How are we to know that your books are true? You tell us so, and we tell you our books are true; and why do you not believe us, if you expect us to believe you?"[28]

Mgr Lambert had just observed what exasperated other missionaries before and after him; the Siamese, affable people while fervent Buddhists, were not ripe for conversion. A Jesuit bitterly summarized the reasons for this irritating impermeability:

> Each person gives his own reasons for this extraordinary inflexibility of the Siamese, but all agree that the extreme stupidity of these people and the beliefs they hold from the priests of their idols are the two principal causes. The desire to learn, so natural in man, seems entirely extinguished in the souls of these barbarians. They have no taste for painting; they are without curiosity concerning the mysteries of mathematics; they set little value on watches and those kinds of jewels which are the passion of all other nations in the Indies and which provided the first entry for the missionaries of the Gospel to all the kings of the Orient.[29]

If all truths are equal, I have no reason to exchange mine for yours; but speak about it, as it interests me. Sir John Bowring noted in the 1850s: "I found no indisposition among the Siamese to discuss religious questions; and the general result of the discussions was—'Your religion is excellent for you, and ours is excellent for us. All countries do not produce the same fruits and flowers, and we find various religions suited to various nations.'" The British diplomat quotes a letter from King Mongkut who, before acceding to the throne, had been a monk for twenty-seven years, as a student at Wat Mahathat in Bangkok and as an abbot at Wats Samarai and Boworniwet: "we cannot tell who is right and who is wrong; but I will pray to my God to give you his blessing, and you must pray to your God to bless me; and so, blessings may descend upon both."[30] These noble dispositions had therefore hardly changed between the seventeenth and the nineteenth centuries.

This heralds the fundamental misunderstanding which was to underlie the relations between France, full of propagating zeal in the second half of the seventeenth century, and the serenely Buddhist Siam of Phra Narai.

THE JOURNEY TO AYUTTHAYA AND THE "INCONVENIENCES ATTACHED TO OUR TASKS"

Mgr Lambert hurried to the Siamese capital from where he expected to reach Cochin-China, to which he had been named vicar-apostolic by Rome. He left Tenasserim with his companions on 30 June after a stay of six weeks. They went upstream on the Tenasserim River swollen by the monsoon in three canoes which were only tree trunks hollowed out by fire and covered with palm leaves. "We had to prepare our food and sleep in these boats, it being too dangerous to leave them and to stop on land, because these continual forests were full of lions, wild boars, tigers, and other carnivorous beasts."[31]

Rapids and waterfalls made the journey particularly adventurous. The efforts of the boatmen who got into the water to push and pull the barges did not prevent Mgr Lambert, Mr Deydier, and much of their baggage falling into the torrent. The missionaries, who did not know how to swim, were carried along by the water, but clung to a large tree overturned in the stream. They sat astride the tree trunk and discovered that the branches hidden in the water retained almost all their waterlogged baggage, in particular a chest which contained "important papers," that is, the papal documents attesting the episcopal rank of Mgr Lambert. But the laissez-passers for which they had waited for so long in Tenasserim were lost, and someone had to be sent to obtain new ones.

This setback did not discourage the visitors, who rented while waiting a hut covered with coconut palm leaves in a village they called Ialinga (Jalang). Jacques de Bourges piously noted, "This wreck was a clear manifestation of the protection of God, for without meeting this tree, Mgr Berythus, who could not swim, would have been indubitably lost."[32] They resumed their journey on 27 July, after exchanging their canoes for bullock carts. But these jolting boneshakers, much less comfortable than the Indian carts they had used, seemed to them "better made to torment passengers than to assist them," and they mostly went on foot. The following extract allows one to appreciate the travelling conditions in Siam in the time of Phra Narai.

> Our carts served as hostels for the night, and as we often camped in the middle of the water, the rough war waged against leeches can be imagined . . . We also had to suffer from wild beasts, which frightened us by day, and fought with us at night. To defend ourselves we built every evening a fortress, composed of our carts drawn up in a circle or a triangle; the oxen pulling them and our baggage were placed in the middle. Often we had to fortify our camp with some thorn hedges; we never ceased to hear prowling around us lions, boars, rhinoceros and above all cruel tigers, who conducted a savage war with the oxen, so that these animals were absolutely terrified at the approach of these tigers. We fired our harquebuses and lit fires all night to keep them at bay. Each of us had to act as guard in turn; we slept nonetheless easily in our small portable tombs, without moving much for want of space, and so we became accustomed little by little to the fatigues and inconveniences attached to our calling. In the daytime we were not completely exempt from the war against the animals. Elephants are frequently met with in the kingdom of Siam and caused us continual alarms, for these beast are afraid of nothing.[33]

The mountains of the isthmus covered with primary forests finally gave way to a fertile and well-cultivated plain. The small group began to accustom itself to the torrid climate. They crossed villages which they called Menam (?), Couir (Kuiburi), and Pram (Pranburi) and arrived on 13 August at Pipili (Phetchaburi), close to the Gulf of Siam. It took them six weeks to cover barely 160 kilometres as the crow flies. As soon as they were lodged there, they set up an altar to celebrate mass on the day of the Assumption of the Virgin Mary with great spiritual consolation. "This blessing was so great for us, that it easily allowed us to forget all our fatigues and all our difficulties which are only in name."[34] They walked two more days, and found places on board a junk which took them in five days to Ayutthaya. The mosquitoes "which bit voraciously" and abounded on the Chao Phraya attacked them each night, but they arrived in the capital on 22 August, safe and sound, praising the Lord and animated by intense apostolic zeal.

SIAM AS SEEN BY JACQUES DE BOURGES

"The period of one year which we were obliged to spend in Siam gave us the time to learn the particularities of the country; this is why we are giving a more exact description of it than the other places which we only passed through." Jacques de Bourges interrupts his account of the journey when the missionaries arrive in Ayutthaya. Four chapters (10: Summary account of the kingdom of Siam; 11: The fruits of the kingdom of Siam; 12: The manners and customs of the Siamese; 13: The religion of Siam) give an overview of the Siam of King Narai,[35] preceding subsequent French authors like Claude de l'Isle (1684), Nicolas Gervaise (1688), and Simon de La Loubère (1691).

The privileged location of the kingdom bordered by two seas, its warm but agreeable climate, the abundance of water which floods the rice fields and teems with fish, the variety and wealth of fruits growing there, the riches of the forests which are reservoirs of precious woods and "serve as the lair of elephants, tigers, wild boars and cows, deer, does, rhinoceros, and other animals found there in herds" made Siam a cornucopia. Jacques de Bourges, for whom life was clearly not a pleasure trip, only regrets that "the Siamese, being hostile to work, only like easy things and leave the very attractive countryside uncultivated." Other missionaries were to reproach them for wasting half their lives in amusements.

"The peoples of Siam are very well built, they are olive coloured and not black, although they inhabit the torrid zone. They have shorter noses than Europeans. Their character is gentle, pleasing to strangers whom they respect rather than despise . . ." Since "a gentle poverty [is] more agreeable than an abundance of goods accompanied by worries," they are happy with very simple houses, furniture, and clothes. They wash frequently, eat mostly rice, fish, and fruit, and drink water. But they are but little cultivated. They neither practice martial arts, nor ride horses, nor dance, and are ignorant of philosophy, medicine, and mathematics (La Loubère was to say that "all application of Mind is so laborious in a Climate so hot as theirs"[36]). "All their knowledge lies in writing and knowing the laws concerning government and justice . . ."

The political system was similar to that in France and so was as good as perfect. "The entire state is monarchical and perfectly well governed. The king is absolute . . . The advantage of their government consists principally in the subordination which exists between the king and his subjects." But nothing is perfect, even in the best of all worlds which is this kingdom of Siam, because

> the respect which is shown to the king is considerable, exceeding the bounds that a human should receive, and honouring him like a god. In this they show their blindness. They only speak to the king on their knees, with their hands joined above their heads, a sign of the greatest respect . . . and bent down to the ground without daring to look on him.

The missionary was not aware that the kings of Siam were considered and treated as *devaraja*, or god-kings. After listing all the royal titles which relate rather to God than to a man, Jacques de Bourges allows himself a lesson in modesty for Christian monarchs (his book after all was dedicated to Louis XIV):

> The Christian religion teaches more modest sentiments, and commands on the part of God that subjects obey their rulers, but it also teaches the same rulers to fear God and to recognize that they are human, and have only received from Him the power which raises them, for the benefit of their subjects who are placed beneath them.

One aspect of Siamese government which Jacques de Bourges particularly admired is the very considerable liberty granted to foreigners who live in their various quarters. To avoid disorders, the king designates for each "nation" a person who answers for the conduct of his compatriots. A senior official (the *Phra Khlang*) serves as intermediary between the king and the heads of the different nations. These take part in an annual ceremony in which the dignitaries of the kingdom renew their oath of loyalty to the king.

And religion? After noting that there is no country in the world where one can find greater religious diversity and liberty ("Gentiles, Christians and Muhammadans . . . have complete freedom to follow whichever cult seems best to them"), and that there are some two thousand Catholics, almost all Portuguese, in the country, Jacques de Bourges questions the reasons for this tolerance. The coexistence of so many different religions seems to him all the more surprising since "it is a received maxim of the most esteemed politics that only one should be permitted, for fear that, should they multiply, the diversity of beliefs would cause spiritual friction, and so lead to conflict." The Edict of Nantes, which had permitted the freedom of worship of Protestants in France, was to be revoked in 1685, and its revocation is heralded here. It was appreciated that the King of Siam obtained too many economic advantages from the presence of foreign artisans and traders in his kingdom to forbid them practising and even proselytizing their religions. But there was a more basic reason: "this is the view which is held by the Siamese that all religions are good, which is why they show themselves hostile to none . . ."

He quotes this comparison:

> they say that heaven is like a great palace to which several paths lead. Some are shorter, some more frequented, some more difficult, but all in the end arrive at the palace of bliss which men seek . . . The gentleness of their character, the presence and frequentation of so many foreigners . . . has committed them to this pernicious opinion, which means that, despairing of finding the truth, they do not concern themselves with seeking it. This indifference is one of the greatest obstacles to their conversion.

Perhaps, but that does not stop the image of a celestial palace accessible to all men of good will, whatever path they wish to take to reach it, from being magnificent. It is a pity that the missionaries, entrenched in their dogmatic pedantry, did not appreciate this. After all, Christ himself said, "In my Father's house are many mansions."[37]

There follows a totally confused account of the "idolatry" of the Siamese, meaning Theravada Buddhism. The missionary did not understand that the tens and even hundreds of "idols of different heights, all gilded and shining brightly" lined up in the *wat* were representations of the one Buddha, and their great number is explained by the conviction that "to have a religious image cast is, in short, an act of devotion and a means of acquiring merit."[38] The Chinese monk I-Ching had written about this in the seventh century: "Even if someone can only produce an image the size of a grain of barley, he would have created thereby a reason as vast as the seven seas to obtain an excellent reincarnation, and the merits will last as long as the first four reincarnations to come . . ."[39]

One has to say in Jacques de Bourges's defence that Brahminical practices, which from the point of view of Buddhism are of secondary importance, complicate the statuary and the religious viewpoint. He is less excusable when he speaks of the "crime of idolatry," adding that "it is a matter worthy of compassion to see these deluded people render so much honour to masses of stone." The iconoclastic Protestants made the same reproaches to Roman Catholics worshipping the statues of saints.

The Buddha is nowhere mentioned. The catechism of Fr de Rhodes designates him by the name *Thicca.* French sources at the end of the seventeenth century (Tachard, Choisy, Gervaise, La Loubère) call him *Sommonokhodom* or *Sommona Codom. Sommana* is a Siamese term designating a monk; *Codom* seems to be a corrupted form of *Gautama* (the princely name of the Sakyamuni Buddha was Siddartha Gautama). Little progress was to be made between 1660 and 1680 in the comprehension of the person of the Buddha, erroneously taken to be a god having a brother called Thevatat.

Jacques de Bourges seems to have understood nothing of the belief in reincarnation and the interminable succession of *samsara* which is finally broken with the obliteration of *nirvana.* Yet this was the very foundation of Buddhism. He is more positive in respect of Buddhist morality. "The precepts which the religion of the Siamese prescribes for moral conduct are in conformity with the natural law which God has implanted in men's being for the conduct of their actions." In spite of the conditional admiration he seems to have felt for the monks and the austerity of their life, he was unable to resist calling them "impostors" who drink a concoction of areca and renounce their monastic vows and their yellow robes whenever they wish. "In this country the robe forms the monk."

The conclusion of the chapter on religion in Siam indicates that the missionaries would have their work cut out:

> Although the Siamese, both the *talapoins* and the people, are not particularly zealous in respect of their religion, which is only an inveterate superstition to which they are accustomed from birth, one cannot all the same deny, in a sense, that they are very attached to it, making it difficult to get them to abandon it to follow a better one.

These pages reveal an almost complete incomprehension of the religious belief system of the Siamese whom the missionaries were proposing to convert. A more perspicacious observer would have predicted that they were labouring to no purpose.

CHAPTER NINE

THE FRENCH MISSION IN AYUTTHAYA (1662–1670)

THE INSTALLATION OF THE MISSION

THE PRIESTS of the Foreign Missions (MEP) were delighted with the Siamese capital. Located at less than one hundred kilometres from the Gulf of Siam, Ayutthaya was readily accessible to junks which were used throughout the Far East and South-East Asia, to Indonesian and Malay prahu, to the dhows which plied between the Middle East and India, and to European caraks, caravels, galleons, frigates, storeships and the like, of three to four hundred tons, which unloaded merchandise in the city from the four corners of Asia and Europe. Jacques de Bourges noted that vessels "came there from everywhere, from Japan, China, the Philippine islands, Champa, Cambodia, the Javanese islands, Sumatra, Golconda, Bengal, and the whole of the Coromandel Coast."[1]

Mgr Lambert would soon realize that this hub where all the nations of the East met, and where all oriental languages were spoken, was the perfect place for him to set up a native seminary.

Mostly situated on an island in the Chao Phraya River, Ayutthaya glittered with its five hundred gilded temples and royal palace, built in the north of the island in the midst of well-watered gardens and surrounded by a double brick wall. The rest of the island comprised canals, shady streets, artisans' quarters, shops, and markets animated by multicoloured crowds. To the south lay the foreign quarters lining the river on both sides. In addition to the Portuguese, Dutch, and English godowns, there were also the substantial "nations" of the Japanese, Malays, Chinese, and Cochin-Chinese.

The arrival of the vicar-apostolic and his two French priests caused some unrest among the Portuguese colony where the Jesuits, Dominicans, and Franciscans had their churches and monasteries. According to Fr Deydier, two thousand Christians (mostly Portuguese) were then living in the capital; there were three secular priests, four Jesuits, two Dominicans, and two Franciscans to look after them.[2]

Thanks to the Calouste Gulbenkian Foundation, excavations were conducted in 1984 in *Mu Ban Portuget*, the Portuguese "camp" in Ayutthaya, particularly at the site of São Pedro where the São Domingo church[3] of the Dominicans was located on the western bank of the Chao Phraya, a short distance from the churches of the Franciscans and the Jesuits. This was the physical layout when the bishops and priests of the Foreign Missions arrived from Paris. Archaeologists have discovered some 250 European and Asian skeletons at the site. To date these are the only human remains found in Ayutthaya from the historic period; those buried were Christians and were thus not cremated in the Buddhist tradition. It is thought that the dead who were buried inside the church at the foot of the altar were priests. One of them had his skull smashed; he could have been one of the Dominicans who came from Malacca to Ayutthaya and who was assassinated by Muslims ("Moors") in 1567–1569. The various objects found on the skeletons (crucifixes, medallions, and rosaries) movingly evoke the funeral rites of the small Catholic community of the sixteenth and seventeenth centuries living at the furthest ends of Asia.

The "captain" of the Portuguese community allocated lodgings to the French missionaries, and the ecclesiastics then in Ayutthaya came to greet them. They proffered numerous guarded compliments, and everything went off very well. Mgr Lambert did his best not to alarm anyone. He informed Johan Maetsuyker, the governor-general of the VOC, of his arrival, indicating that the French missionaries had not come to the Indies to indulge in "temporal commerce." He wrote other letters announcing his holy enterprise to the Spanish archbishop and the governor in Manila, as well as the head of the Jesuits in Macao. These letters set out the intentions of the French priests; they had no other aim, said Mgr Lambert, "than the glory of God and the salvation of souls," and to "live with you like brothers and die for Jesus Christ." One letter addressed to the French Jesuits in Cochin-

China elicited after a few months a polite reply advising against going into his see, which was then convulsed with religious persecutions. The Fathers also sent some presents with their letter, since these cement friendship: "a cutlass which had been used to cut the head of one of four martyrs, a braid of hair covered with the blood of another, and linen soaked in their blood."[4]

But this brotherly atmosphere was troubled four months after they landed when the order arrived from the viceroy in Goa "to prevent the French from proceeding to their missions by all the means at their disposal." The Portuguese showed themselves immediately so hostile that there was resort to fisticuffs, and Mgr Lambert had reason to fear for his life. Enoch Poolvoet, the new director of the Dutch godown, offered him shelter in his residence, but the prelate declined this offer, not wishing to exasperate the Portuguese by taking refuge with a Dutch heretic.

It was the Cochin-Chinese converts who flew to the aid of "their" bishop. Their community was a league away from that of the Portuguese, and they came to take away Mgr Lambert and his companions, servants, arms, and baggage in broad daylight, to settle them in their community. This act warmed the heart of the vicar-apostolic, the more so as the Cochin-Chinese, for good measure, were to build a modest residence and a chapel dedicated to St Joseph on the river bank.

These events doubtless gave Mgr Lambert to understand that prudence and temporizing would not serve much purpose. His exasperation only increased when he noticed abuses which had crept into the methods of evangelization of other religious orders, which he considered henceforth as harmful rivals. He was particularly angered with the Society of Jesus for he observed that the Christian Cochin-Chinese, previously baptized by the Jesuits, had not the least notion of the Christian religion which they had embraced for God knows what reason. They told him that they were baptized the day they requested it, without the least preparation.

Mgr Lambert, who knew that the Jesuits sent to Europe exaggerated accounts full of the numbers of "rice Christians" they baptized by the armful, was disgusted by these practices which he considered "disorders" (the word comes frequently from his pen). He reproached the Jesuits with authorizing "dissolute morality" and of indulging in trade. The loss of a merchant vessel belonging to them was, of course, divine retribution. Later, in October 1667, he was to publish a pastoral instruction against clerical trade in which he did not mince his words.

On 11 July 1663, Mgr Lambert wrote a despondent letter to the pope, suggesting a radical solution: removing all the priests from the missions, and replacing them with other clerics who would depend directly on the Holy See and the Propaganda. "I admit," he added, "that this advice is extreme, but the evil from which Christianity suffers is likewise."[5] Aware that the proposal he was suggesting would not be implemented, he requested the pope to relieve him of his episcopal responsibilities.

JACQUES DE BOURGES RETURNS TO EUROPE

Mgr Lambert added to this letter numerous others, giving them to Jacques de Bourges to carry to Europe, with the secret hope that de Bourges would be named bishop to succeed him. According to his biographer, Fr de Bourges was "one of those balanced persons whom nothing troubles and causes no trouble to anyone,"[6] and had been persuaded to go under duress. "Although I have made an effort to submit to the orders I have been given," he wrote, "I feel that I should stay where I am."[7]

After reserving a place on board an English vessel which was going to Madras, he left Ayutthaya on 14 October 1663. The excellent relations between Louis XIV of France and Charles II of Great Britain allowed the missionary to avoid the Portuguese zones of influence and the exhausting journey across the Indian subcontinent and the Middle East. His ship was stopped once by three warships of the VOC which had just started their blockade of the Chao Phraya to force the hand of Phra Narai. One of the Dutch captains explained "that they were there to oblige the King of Siam to make amends for some insult they declared they had received."[8] Jacques de Bourges, manifestly ever a practical soul, profited by this encounter to obtain from a Dutchman a letter of introduction to the governor of Malacca, where he arrived on 27 November.

En route, the missionary observed the heroic efforts of the VOC to maintain commercial relations with Japan at all costs:

> A little before our arrival in Malacca, we met the Dutch fleet

> returning from Japan. Of eight vessels sent there, five arrived, and three others had been shipwrecked; and of those five two sank during the return. The three which remained had their mainmasts shattered, and yet we were assured that there remained sufficient riches in these three vessels to compensate the losses the fleet had suffered, and not to regret the voyage to Japan.[9]

Jacques de Bourges reached Masulipatam on 6 January; five days later he was in Madras, where the English governor Edwards found him a private cabin on one of six vessels of the returning EIC fleet. They agreed, after some discussion, on the price of 140 écus (around some seven or eight hundred US dollars today). Bourges only had half a day in which to buy his victuals; the sails were already hoisted. They rounded the Cape of Good Hope on 7 April and stopped three weeks later at St Helena; "a more delightful port of call could not be imagined."

Ascension Island, where they dropped anchor on 5 May, lacked fresh water and fruit, but the waters around the island were full of huge sea turtles weighing between three and five hundred pounds. "The meat is quite agreeable and good for one's health; it is as though one were eating veal. They live thirty or forty days on board ship without dying."[10] The English sailors caught seventy in one night; all that had to be done was to turn them on their backs so they could not move, immobilized by the weight of their shells.

Jacques de Bourges finally landed in London at the end of July. The overland journey from Marseilles to Ayutthaya had taken twenty-one months; the return sea route from Ayutthaya to London scarcely ten. He congratulated himself on his successful journey; during the voyage, the English fleet had not lost a single man; the captain, though a heretic, had treated him with every consideration; fresh fish was never lacking; and there even remained on board some decidedly peripatetic fowls which had travelled from London to Madras and back from Madras to London.

This priestly globetrotter spent some ten days in the capital. He was received by the queen mother and by her younger son, the Duke of York (the future James II). He bombarded Bourges with questions about the state of the Indies, and presented him to his brother Charles II, who graciously granted audience to the missionary. He left London on 6 August, narrowly escaped shipwreck between Gravesend and Dieppe, stopped in his native Paris, and there paid visits to "pious persons in that great city" who financed the first journey of the MEP to Asia. He learnt with delight that a seminary had been established in the Rue du Bac, the MEP's headquarters.

But nothing holds back a man of zeal. He immediately set off for Rome, where he arrived on 9 October. After delivering the various petitions of Mgr Lambert to the congregation of the Propaganda, he was received in audience by Alexander VII on 1 February 1665. The pope gave him a brief authorizing the bishops of Berythus and Heliopolis to consecrate one of their priests in Ayutthaya to succeed the Bishop of Metellopolis, who had died in the meantime. The pope extended for a further period of seven years the authorization to ordain indigenous priests who did not know Latin.

Jacques de Bourges considered himself satisfied, even if the Holy See had refused to extend the jurisdiction of the vicars-apostolic to the kingdom of Siam. Bourges was disturbed by the presence in Rome of the Jesuit Philip Marini, a missionary in Cochin-China and Siam, for Fr Marini had come to defend the privileges of his company in South-East Asia. He maintained that, "for the good of the missions, it was necessary that there be only one kind of worker, and this maxim was based on experience, and that it should be the base of good management of these Eastern missions."[11] The end of the tension between the different groups of missionaries was not yet in sight.

On returning to Paris, Jacques de Bourges found the time to complete the definitive text of his *Relation du voyage de Mgr de Beryte* . . . When this fascinating book appeared (the date of the completion of the print run was 7 January 1666), the author prepared for his return, with five companions from the MEP, on one of the vessels of the Montdevergue squadron which was going to set sail on 14 March. It was only in 1669 that they landed in Ayutthaya, after a particularly turbulent voyage which had taken them to the coasts of Brazil.

THE SECOND TEAM FROM MEP ARRIVES IN SIAM

Without waiting for Jacques de Bourges's departure for Europe, Mgr Lambert had embarked with Fr Deydier for Canton, which came within his jurisdiction. But a violent storm had cast their junk on the coasts of Cambodia, and the two missionaries had been obliged to return to Ayutthaya.

They were joined there on 27 January 1664, four months after their return, by the Bishop of Heliopolis, François Pallu, four priests

(Louis Chevreuil, Pierre Brindeau, Antoine Hainques, and Louis Maneau), and a lay person, Philippe de Chamesson. They were not expected so soon, for the Portuguese had intercepted all their letters. They had taken the land route which Mgr Lambert knew so well. Their companion, Ignance Cotolendi, consecrated Bishop of Metellopolis, had succumbed to the fatigues of the journey in the hamlet of Palacol, two days' walk from Masulipatam, in spite of the attentions of the French doctor Montval attached to the Dutch godown there. Only thirty-one years old, he had died murmuring, "All is well . . . eternity is nigh."

The joy of their reunion and their sadness at the death of Mgr Cotolendi unsettled the two teams from the Foreign Missions. "They agreed after their meeting that no news would be discussed for five days, and they would be solely concerned with giving thanks to divine goodness."[12] After this retreat of five days, and a few more to exchange news and impressions, the two bishops now reunited in Ayutthaya were anxious to reach their missions in Cochin-China and Tonkin. But the persecutions which were raging there retained them in Siam.

Meeting in synod with their companions, they discussed the future of their programme of conversion, its priorities and modalities. They resolved to open a permanent residence in Ayutthaya and there to build a native seminary, whose establishment had been decided in Rome. All oriental languages could be learnt there, and the religious tolerance which prevailed in Siam made it an ideal place for the preparation for the priesthood of young Asians destined to swarm over South-East Asia and supply native cadres for the Church.

The synod of Ayutthaya triggered an important reflection on missionary strategy and rhetoric. The MEP set itself apart from the methods of the Society of Jesus, which had been defined in 1588 by the Spanish Jesuit José de Acosta. In his treatise *De procuranda Indorum conversione*, he distinguished three categories of people: savages deprived of any civilization, people partially civilized whose education was wanting, and lastly highly civilized people, such as the Chinese, who were to be respected and whose usages and customs were to be assimilated in so far as they did not contravene the Gospels.

The vicars-apostolic and their priests set themselves clearly apart from this hierarchy and the appropriate steps they invoked. Since the equality of individuals before salvation was a notion acquired since St Paul, it followed that degrees of civilization were denied. The French missionaries started with the principle "that all peoples are susceptible to demonstrations of reason and that it was necessary, in the first instance, to make use of this to demonstrate the falsity of their beliefs."[13] These considerations were to govern the MEP in its attempts to convert South-East Asia.

Mgr Pallu had two brothers in the Society of Jesus. More conciliatory than Mgr Lambert, he made an effort to improve relations with the Jesuits in Ayutthaya and suggested communal pastoral work. There was some hesitation, but nonetheless a general procession was organized in the first Sunday in Lent in 1664, and the Jesuits came with all their musicians to celebrate the feast of St Joseph in the chapel of the MEP.

A few baptisms and occasional confirmations did not fill the days of the two bishops and their clergy. Since the establishment of a seminary could not be lasting, so long as the prelates had not received jurisdiction over Siam, it was decided that Mgr Pallu would return to Rome to seek this. The bishop remembered the pressing request of Mgr Alberici, the secretary of the Propaganda, who had indicated to him that his journey would already be successful if he could bring back precise information about the itineraries which allowed travellers to avoid regions coming under the *Padroado*. "The greatest obstacle to progress," he had written, "is our ignorance of the routes, paths and means of making the journey."[14]

The Bishop of Heliopolis therefore packed his bags and set off on 20 January 1665, after a stay of exactly one year. Mr de Chamesson accompanied him. They took the difficult land and river route to Mergui, "where there are usually several ships returning in March to the Coromandel Coast, from where every year English vessels leave for Europe."[15] As the missionaries were unable to embark for the east coast of India for want of ships, they crossed the Indian subcontinent in order to find a vessel in the Mogul port of Surat in the north-west. The traveller Jean Thévenot met them at the beginning of March 1666 between Aurangabad and Surat "under some mango trees a short distance from a small stream."[16] Pallu and Chamesson were unaware that during their stay in Siam, the decision to create a Compagnie des Indes Orientales (CIO) had been taken in France, and that French missionaries could soon travel to Asia in French bottoms. It will be recalled that both Mgr Pallu and Chamesson, before their departure from Europe, had played a part in the preparation of this project.

Jacques de Bourges had learnt of this "great and noble plan" during his stay in London. He noted:

> I considered from that moment that it was pointless to look for advantages from foreigners which I could henceforth expect from the new company which had been created in Paris on the king's orders for trading with and navigation to the East Indies, and I gave thanks to God that He had inspired this great monarch with such a fine venture, the success of which would not only be a source of profit for the kingdom, but still more so would be an advantageous means of extending the Faith to all parts of the world, since there was no country from which such zealous workers for the propagation of Christianity could be obtained as France.[17]

Henceforth the French missionaries would travel together with merchants, often protected by the warships of His Most Christian Majesty, also known as Louis XIV.

FRANÇOIS PALLU IN ROME AND PARIS

The Bishop of Heliopolis only arrived in Rome in April 1667, after a voyage of twenty-seven months across India, Persia, Mesopotamia, and Syria. His lucid judgment, conciliatory character, and good personal relations with the Society of Jesus made him a better negotiator than the rigid Lambert. But he did not arrive at a good time: Alexander VII Chigi was dying (he expired on 27 May) and it was necessary to wait for the election of Clement IX Rospigliosi on 20 June before being able to deal with matters Siamese. Pallu only presented the different memoranda he had prepared to Girolamo Casanata, the secretary of the Propaganda, in October. He was granted audience the same month by the new pope who decided that a commission of four cardinals would examine the petitions of the vicars-apostolic.

Seeing his affairs well in hand, Mgr Pallu left for Paris where he arrived in January 1668. Louis XIV received him on the twenty-eighth at St Germain and promised him his help for "the great undertaking" of the Foreign Missions, "which His Majesty considered to be very advantageous to the progress of the Gospels and to the reputation of the French."[18] Mgr Pallu discussed with Colbert possible cooperation between the CIO and the MEP. After crossing Asia twice on foot, the bishop was in a position to give the minister first-hand information.

He returned to Rome on 10 November 1668. He had learnt during his absence that the pope and the Propaganda had been exposed to Portuguese intrigues and Spanish pressure, and the Roman distrust of the French, maintained by the Jesuits, was hardly favourable to the mission of the French bishops. But he was confident, knowing that the Propaganda would not abandon an undertaking it had created. Indeed, the brief *Cum sicut accepimus* of Clement IX, dated 4 July 1669, extended the jurisdiction of the vicars-apostolic throughout the kingdom of Siam. On 7 June, the brief *Sollicitudo* had renewed the condemnations of trading missionaries proclaimed by Urban VIII. This decision of Rome was a personal victory for Pierre Lambert de La Motte who eight months earlier had published a pastoral letter vehemently denouncing the trading activities of clerics.

But the most important success of Mgr Pallu was the brief *Speculatores* which Clement IX signed on 13 September 1669, and which fixed once and for all the relationship between the vicars-apostolic and the ordained missionaries established in their territories. On reading this document it can be seen that the pope was not niggardly; men of the cloth sent by their superiors to missions under the authority of the vicars-apostolic could not exercise their ministry before presenting their letters patent to the vicars; the priests could not build churches where these prelates or other religious orders were already established. As delegates of the Holy See, the vicars were made judges of conflicts between the religious orders operating in their jurisdiction. Finally, catechists were entirely answerable to the vicars to whom they had to swear an oath of obedience. It was a victory all along the line, and one can understand that Pallu, after receiving a certified copy of the brief, should have returned very satisfied to France. He expected to leave as soon as possible for Siam.

The occasion arose soon after. Accompanied by six priests of the MEP, the Bishop of Heliopolis embarked on 11 April 1670 at Port-Louis on the *Phénix*, a vessel of the CIO leaving with the *Dauphin Couronné* and the *Vautour* to join the La Haye squadron. François Pallu carried in his luggage, in addition to three briefs of Clement IX, who had meanwhile died, two other precious documents: a letter in

Latin from the pope and a letter in French from Louis XIV, both addressed to Phra Narai.

A SCARCELY EDIFYING SPECTACLE

We left Mgr Lambert immobilized in Siam when he wanted to proceed to Indochina. The difficulties he faced do not seem to have mollified his intractable humour. Lambert was incapable of making the least concession to human weakness. His blind obedience to the Holy See and his rigid mysticism prevented him from understanding in the field the cases of conscience of missionaries who had been obliged to bend to circumstances. He ordered perpetual fasting to his priests, as if the change of climate and food were not already sufficiently demanding. He admitted to Mgr Pallu in a letter of October 1666, "I have had my coffin prepared, and it is in my bedroom, covered with a black cloth. I find this sight a useful reminder for me."[19]

Such an attitude worried Bishop Pallu and people at the MEP. Even before returning to Europe, Pallu had written to his friends in the Rue du Bac: "I consider in particular the long prayers and the perpetual fasting which [Mgr Lambert] practises as exceedingly pernicious temptations in a missionary, and I was rather unhappy at having to brace myself, in opposition, when I saw my brothers were inclined to follow his example."[20]

In the meantime the intransigent prelate managed to fall out with the Dominicans and the Jesuits; this former magistrate from Rouen, a town which has the reputation of loving chicanery, retained a delight in wrangling. The quarrel over competence which pitted him against the Dominicans of Ayutthaya (and thus the Goanese chapter) was purely technical. It hinged above all on the fact that Mgr Lambert had no jurisdiction in Siam, through which he was passing, and that he refused to produce apostolic documents confirming his episcopal rank.

The conflict which caused him to grapple with the Jesuits was more serious. From July 1663 he had written and given to Jacques de Bourges a long letter accusing the Jesuits and destined to be read before the assembly of the clergy in France. But this philippic was so violent that the gentlemen of the MEP wisely decided to bury it at the bottom of their archives. The Jesuits, the vicar-apostolic asserted, only went to the missions to lead a licentious life and amass wealth. The rapturous accounts they sent to Europe gave an absolutely false picture of their activities, which were in reality nothing more than "disorder" and "irregularity." Filled with the same indignation as Pascal showed in his *Provinciales* six years earlier, he declared that "they are lax in their morality, which is the greatest shortcoming to be encountered in an order, since to be lax in one's doctrine is to stray from that of the Son of God."[21] He added, "It would be desirable that the Jesuits were no longer in the Indies, for they have corrupted the Gospels; I know that God wishes this society to be humiliated and that Europe should be disabused of its opinion of these Fathers."[22] The words "I know that God wishes . . ." clearly show that the fiery Bishop of Berythus believed himself to be party to the secret designs of the Almighty.

Among the complaints he brought against the Jesuits, Mgr Lambert particularly emphasized their commercial practices. We have already indicated that the problem of clerical trading was not new. The Jesuits maintained that the alms sent from Europe were insufficient to sustain their missions, and it was necessary for commerce to supplement the little money they received. In 1580, the Jesuits in Macao had requested their general superior, Fr Claudio Aquaviva, to seek the opinion of Gregory XIII Buoncompagni. He had approved the participation of the Jesuits in the profitable Sino-Japanese trade in silk, saying "that in his opinion that should not be called commerce, since it was done not for a desire for lucre, but out of pure necessity."[23]

It is true that the stern brief of Urban VIII Barberini (*Ex debito pastoralis*, 1633) had subsequently condemned clerical trading, but the Jesuits, considering they were covered by Gregory XIII's approbation and that Urban VIII was misinformed, continued their commercial practices. The Macao Fathers, reduced to the sad extremity of selling their sacred vessels and leaving unrepaired their church which had lost its roof in a typhoon, were shocked to see themselves blamed for their "passion for riches."

A few Jesuits, though, entertained some doubts. This explains the theological dissertation of some thirty pages drawn up in Ayutthaya during 1665 by Fr Joseph Tissanier with the title *Religiosus negotiator* (The commercial priest) on the question of whether members of the Society of Jesus were permitted to trade in the East Indies. The dissertation, written in 1664 as a consequence of a series of friendly conversations between Fr Tissanier and the accommodating Mgr Pallu, attempted to take all things into consideration in a delicate and complex question. It opted rather against clerical trading, but admitted exceptions and cases of necessity.

Fr Tissanier noted bitterly in his report to Rome dated 25 October 1666:

> The French bishops have loudly inveighed against traders. To satisfy their desires, I drew up . . . a little treatise to show to those who were blamed on that account. These gentlemen wished to see it, and I think they made a copy. This lack of sincerity which I observed in them from the beginning gave me to understand that they wished to have us under their feet. They have completely broken with us . . . Mgr de Berythus says out loud to those who visit him that the Fathers of the Society [of Jesus] are not missionaries but merchants; that they do not in the least obey the pope, and they will be punished. Those who speak evil of us are well received by him . . . I do not think we can live with them in the same mission[ary field].[24]

Nothing could satisfy the tormented conscience of Mgr Lambert, who probably had visions of Christ chasing the merchants from the temple. Considering all circumspection as weakness, and saying with St Paul that "the word of God is not bound,"[25] on 15 October 1667 he had posted up a pastoral letter in Latin and Portuguese vehemently attacking clerical trade.[26] "Carried along by his fiery nature, he went so far as to propose that it would be better for the good of the East Indies missions if the Society of Jesus had never gone there."[27]

This put the cat among the pigeons. The Dominicans and the Jesuits were angry, memoranda flew from both sides to Rome full of complaints and counts of indictment, everyone censured the "very pernicious maxims" of everyone else, and Mgr Lambert declared, in the purest evangelical spirit, that Luigi Fragoso, the commissioner of the Holy Office, deserved to be sentenced to the hulks.

Such propositions do not win over people's hearts, the more so as it was affirmed that the prelate did not regulate his conduct according to his rigorous propositions. It was given out that he bought up partisans for hard cash, that he sold gold, that he lent money on interest, in short that he engaged in trade.[28] The Bishop of Berythus did not set foot inside the Portuguese quarter, and the Dominicans and Jesuits refused to go and visit the troublemaker withdrawn into the midst of the Indochinese.

The Indochinese were in particular to be pitied. Mgr Lambert decided in 1668 that confessions heard by the Jesuits were no longer valid. The Cochin-Chinese therefore had to confess to their bishop or his priests. As none of them spoke nor understood Vietnamese, their penitents were obliged to give the details of their sins to a Portuguese interpreter installed next to the confessional. These three-sided confessions were all the more embarrassing as the Indochinese seemed to have a propensity for sodomy, and the confessors of the MEP were not content with vague avowals. They went straight to the point, asked pitilessly precise questions, and showed themselves less indulgent than the Jesuits.[29] The poor Cochin-Chinese would certainly have preferred a little more discretion in the administration of the sacrament of penance, but Mgr Lambert was unshakable. He even refused absolution to dying Christians if they did not promise under oath never to confess themselves again to the Jesuits.[30]

On 16 December 1668, Fr Tissanier drew up an annual report full of indignation.

> This year Mgr de Berythus . . . ordained a Cochin-Chinese priest who cannot read, who learnt by heart two or three masses, substituting instead of the breviary a part of the rosary. This prelate . . . has principles which make several fear he may be a Jansenist. He forbids the Cochin-Chinese who are here to eat eggs on Fridays and Saturdays throughout the year. He has virtually required these poor Christians to confess through an interpreter . . . without any necessity, since these Cochin-Chinese could confess to Fr Felipe Marini and me. He wants to change in the missions what our Fathers have already introduced . . . He proclaimed in his chapel that our confessions are void . . . He thinks that by virtue of his fastings he has the right to defame the religious orders.[31]

The tone was even more bitter a year later in the report of 10 September 1669. "It seems that our French bishop has a plan to exterminate us. The passion he displays against us, his extravagant principles and his mode of living make many think he is a Jansenist. I have been told that he avers he reads no book coming from our Society."[32] The term "Jansenist" was the worst insult which a Jesuit could throw at the head of an adversary in the seventeenth century.

The report of 7 November 1669 was probably intercepted, since it is found not in the archives of the Society of Jesus in Rome, but in those of the Foreign Missions in Paris. The tone is more or less the same as that of the previous year:

> I have seen things over four or five years which one has difficulty in believing: Mgr de Berythus, without showing his apostolic letters nor the authority he says he has obtained from Rome, wished to declare himself bishop of these countries and had given orders without the consent of the diocesan bishop; he has usurped the authority of the Inquisition in Goa . . . and had caused to be proclaimed in his church that the confessions made in ours and in that of the Dominicans are void, and has tried to stain our reputation and has boasted that he came to these missions to reform the abuses introduced by our Fathers. If he is not a Jansenist, he is not far off it.[33]

The least one can say is that the evangelization of Siam by the French bishops did not begin under a favourable star. Tension continued to mount; the anti-Berythus Portuguese and the pro-Berythus Cochin-Chinese confronted each other in armed barges playing trumpets and drums. It was only in November 1670 that Mgr Lambert, summoned by the Goan chapter and threatened with excommunication and heavy fines, finally consented to show his patents and bulls of nomination which clearly revealed that he had no jurisdiction in Siam. (No one in Ayutthaya at that point knew that Clement IX had granted this sixteen months previously.) The Bishop of Berythus wrote, "I thought that the interests of God and the Church required that I avoided a scandal."[34] It was rather late in the day to realize this.

CHAPTER TEN

PHRA NARAI AND THE FRENCH (1665–1679)

MGR LAMBERT and his priests were probably unaware that they had landed in Siam at a propitious moment. Shortly before their arrival, the indifference to Buddhism which Phra Narai was said to have shown had incited a group of diehard monks to hatch a plot against the king's life. But the conspiracy was exposed, and monks hiding daggers under their saffron robes were seized and mercilessly executed.[1] There is little information available about the incident; it is clear, though, that relations between the king and the Buddhist *sangha*—between the throne and the altar if one wishes—were undergoing a period of crisis.

It would seem that Phra Narai was not particularly attached to his role of *bodhisattva* and *chakravartin*, the monarch who causes the Wheel of Buddhist Law to turn. He presided without great enthusiasm, when he did not send a substitute, over the great processions on water (*kathin nam*) and on land (*kathin bok*) which were supposed to guarantee harmonious relations between the heavens, water, and land. He was clearly not as tormented as his father, Prasat Thong, by the need to acquire merit by constructing or restoring *wats* and Buddha statues. If the king and his clergy had been more united, the French missionaries would doubtless not have so readily gained royal favour.

PHRA NARAI AND THE CHRISTIAN RELIGION

Given the unedifying disputes which rent the Catholic community in Siam, it is surprising that the king did not withdraw his sympathy for the European priests who were established in his capital. He was regularly informed about the activities of the missionaries whose arrival had created such a stir. The mission journal of 1665 records that when he learnt that the MEP priests only wished to train young people, "the king ordered that ten of his subjects be sent to the house of the missionaries to be instructed there, adding that they were free to preach and go anywhere they wished, except inside the royal palace."[2]

Mgr Lambert thanked Phra Narai in a solemn letter of 29 May 1665 which was a succinct summary of the Christian faith, and in which he presented himself as "one of the great priests of the All-Powerful God and one of the princes of his Church." He promised the king that two of his priests would teach in a college the "sciences of Europe . . . which are necessary to a state to make it estimable before all nations on earth." He concluded: "These, Sire, are the motives which brought us to these lands. If Your Majesty accepts the offer of our services, we hope, from your royal bounty—and this is the only boon we seek—that you will grant us a temple in which to practise our religion."[3]

The king gave the missionaries a piece of land located on the right bank of the Chao Phraya to the south of the capital, near the Cochin-Chinese quarter, at a place called Ban Plahet, and conveyed to them the news that he would give them the necessary building materials for the construction of a church. The Siamese unfortunate enough to live there were ordered to disassemble their houses within eight days and build them elsewhere. The missionaries constructed a fairly large building in brick and wood, covered with tiles. It contained a chapel and six bedrooms. Mgr Lambert, who looked far into the future, foresaw this grant of land as the kernel of a French colony which would also include the godown of the CIO. At the end of 1666 he wrote to Mgr Pallu, then in France: "If other Frenchmen come to set themselves up in this country, where they are greatly desired, they could stay on a plot which belongs to our nation. You can assure the directors of the CIO and offer [the services of] our ecclesiastics wherever they are."[4]

The relations between Phra Narai and the French missionaries go back a long way. They had prepared "a book of images in copper-plate engravings of all the mysteries of the life and passion of Our Lord, the twelve apostles, the four evangelists . . . which we have had bound in France with blank pages between the images, to write down what they mean." With a finesse which could be envied by the Jesuits, they foresaw that these blank pages would arouse the curiosity of the king, to whom the volume was offered in 1667. "Indeed, two or three days after he had received it, he sent to say that he greatly desired to know what these portraits signified, and they would oblige him by writing on the blank pages the explanations in the language of Siam."[5]

Louis Laneau, who from his arrival had applied himself to the study of Siamese and had even lived some time among Buddhist monks to understand their religious discourse and modes of thought, was charged with this task, which took him two months to complete. Phra Narai flipped through the texts with interest and gave them to the monks in the royal monasteries of Ayutthaya. They told him, after carefully examining them, "that the Christian religion was good, that it taught very noble things, but that which the king professed was equally good." A characteristic reply.

A half-brother of Phra Narai, Chaofa Aphaithot, who was considered by the missionaries to be the king's successor or *Upparat*, soon after showed a great interest in Christianity. With the king's approval, this "second brother" invited a missionary (probably the polyglot Laneau) to the palace at the end of 1667, and informed him of two reasons which attracted him to the Christian religion: "The first was because it seemed noble; the second because he hoped that the God which we adored, being all-powerful, as we told him, would cure him of paralysis which for twelve years had taken from him the use of his feet and hands."[6]

It was a delicate situation, for the poor crippled prince visibly expected a miracle. But the missionary knew that faith moves mountains, and began the prince's religious instruction without delay; Aphaithot declared to him after a few sessions that "there was only one God, to whom he would render his prayers henceforth." He went further; he invited Mgr Lambert to Lopburi where Phra Narai was hunting tigers, and affirmed to him on 1 December 1667 that "he only recognized a single God, the creator of heaven and earth, whom he worshipped several times a day." He repeated this modified profession of faith a month later in the palace in Ayutthaya.

On learning about all this, the king summoned his "chief astrologer," a Brahmin who had taken part in the religious conversations between the prince and the priest, and told him to go and ask on his behalf for the missionaries to perform a miracle to prove the truth of their religion. This person transmitted the message, and added that, if the miracle occurred, the king would believe in their God, and he, too. He also indicated that, as Phra Narai had no male offspring, he passionately desired the cure of his paralyzed brother. This great show of brotherly love has however been questioned. Nicolas Gervaise, writing twenty or so years later, mentions "the other brother is paralyzed," adding that he

> leads an obscure and monotonous existence in a little palace in the capital, where he lives as a recluse. He is not allowed to go to court, and whenever he has appeared there he has always pretended to stammer and behaved in a deranged manner, perhaps because he is frightened that the king, who has always distrusted him and disliked him, will put him in such a position that he will never be able to undertake anything against his interests.[7]

At all events, the challenge was laid down, and the stakes high. Everything was dropped while Mgr Lambert and his priests lent a hand. The Holy Sacrament was exposed and the whole community, fasting even more than usual, sent ardent prayers day and night towards heaven.

The mission journal relates:

> It nevertheless pleased God to defer the miracle to test the faith of many, which was the occasion of several importunate reminders to the missionaries [from the king] informing them that the prince was still in the same state of paralysis, and the effect of their promises was awaited, and this was all that was needed for several to embrace the Christian religion.

This blackmail sorely pressed the priests. They replied to the Brahmin who shuttled between the palace and their residence that they did not doubt the miracle they had promised, "but they only doubted the faith of those who demanded miracles more for their personal interest and to satisfy their curiosity than for the desire they had to convert."

They continued their prayers all the same, and behold, "when one least expected it . . . blood began to enter the veins of the legs of the paralytic prince, and the flesh to grow a little for the whole court to see." The missionaries, who were doubtless very relieved, gave to understand that "they had kept their word, and that was sufficient to show the supreme power of God, [and] they thought things would remain thus until the prince had completed for his part what he promised God, which was to make himself a Christian at the first extraordinary sign which might appear." Considering themselves now masters of the situation after the half-miracle they had obtained by the sweat of their brow, they promised the other half "if the king and the prince wished for their part to fulfil their promises."

But there the matter remained, for Phra Narai had understood that he was being asked for nothing more nor less "than a general change in religion throughout the country, and this matter was of the greatest consequence." It is obvious that the king, as a *bodhisattva* or future Buddha, could not consider changing religion without overturning the political, religious, and even cosmic order of his kingdom. Being brought back to earth, the missionaries had to acknowledge the evidence; the condition they laid down for the miracle to be achieved was unacceptable. "This was the cause," the mission journal explains, "why the whole subject was dropped, and communication between the court and the missionaries on the subject of religion was completely ended."[8]

The king's brother therefore remained Buddhist and paralyzed. Phra Narai noted with surprise that the French did not seek, like the Dutch or the English, commercial concessions, but were preoccupied with his soul and that of his subjects, and he could obtain much from them by holding out prospects of an eventual conversion. This was his first experience, in 1668, of religious blackmail.

THE LONG RETURN JOURNEY TO SIAM OF FRANÇOIS PALLU

The exalting enterprise of converting Phra Narai and the tussle with the Portuguese and the clergy of the *Padroado* had not deflected Mgr Lambert's attention from the kingdom of Tonkin where he had sent François Deydier with the title of vicar-general. He had met with the hostility of a group of Jesuits sent from Macao who were also trying, in spite of the persecutions of the *chua* Trinh Tac, to obtain a foothold in northern Vietnam. Dressed as merchants, Mgr Lambert and Fr de Bourges went there in 1669 on a French vessel. In Tonkin the bishop found the same competition, the same refusal to profess allegiance, and showed his usual harshness towards the Jesuits.

He secretly confirmed a number of Christians on board his ship anchored at Hanoi. After asking them, as ritual required, if they renounced the devil and all his works, he added: "Do you renounce the Fathers of the Society of Jesus?" He ordained seven catechists and held a synod which was supposed to organize the young and sorely tried church of Tonkin. A series of articles was approved. One of them specified that it was necessary to ask of God "a spirit of submission in the Jesuit Fathers in these regions so that, with this great obstacle removed, one could advantageously work for the conversion of souls." The bishop left Bourges in Tonkin and set sail on 14 March 1670; a month later he was back in Ayutthaya.[9]

He was unaware that a few days earlier François Pallu had embarked in Port-Louis on the *Phénix* for a very long return journey to Siam. Mgr Pallu and his six companions arrived at the Cape of Good Hope on 8 November. They disembarked in February 1671 at Fort Dauphin in Madagascar for what turned out to be a stay of six months, because the *Phénix* had suffered in storms and needed extensive repairs. They arrived in Surat at the beginning of October.

At the Capuchins in Surat, the bishop found a voluminous correspondence which detailed the vexations the Portuguese and the Jesuits heaped upon the Propaganda missionaries in the name of the *Padroado*. What he learnt seemed to him so serious that he sent one of his companions, Charles Sevin, to Europe, charged with seeking in Rome sanctions against the Inquisition in Goa, which had dared to imprison Louis Chevreuil, an MEP priest, who had been seized in Cambodia on the instigation of the Jesuits and sent first to Macao, then to Goa, suspected of heresy. Fr Sevin was also given a letter for Colbert; the prelate implored him to obtain from Louis XIV energetic protestations addressed to the prince-regent Dom Pedro about Portuguese injustice towards the French.

Other letters were addressed to the directors of the CIO. Mgr Pallu had followed enthusiastically the creation and first efforts of the company to set up in Asia. In 1667 he had written a long memorandum to the directors, entreating them to resist colonialist abuses. Pallu wrote:

> It seems that everything is permitted beyond the Line, that the people found there are not men like us, and their houses, persons and goods can be seized with impunity. I could produce evidence of a multitude of injustices committed throughout the Indies, not only by heretics

who have no more faith than legal constraint, but also by those who proclaim themselves . . . faithful Catholics."

In 1671, in the interests of harmonious cooperation between the French missionaries and merchants, the bishop invited the CIO to undertake "the glorious design of the conversion of barbarians, and in that way to sanctify its trade and enlarge the Church at the same time as enriching France."[10] In his eyes, there was no contradiction between saving souls and providing dividends for delighted shareholders.

Charles Sevin went to Rome to obtain fresh and powerful support from Clement X Altieri for the vicars-apostolic. The eighty-year-old pope signed a whole series of very stern briefs addressed to the inquisitors, the archbishop, and the chapter of Goa, reprimanding them for having dared question the bulls of the Holy See. The important brief *Decet romanum,* signed 23 December 1673, solemnly reconfirmed the subordination of missionaries of the religious orders to the vicars, striking a decisive blow at Portuguese pretensions to spiritual hegemony. The pope ordered all the bishops in the East Indies and the superiors of religious orders to publish the brief to those under their jurisdiction, to see that it was observed by their subordinates, and to send to Rome a signed act of acceptance. A month later, the general superior of the Jesuits, Fr Gianpaolo Oliva, swore on oath that the pontifical briefs concerning the vicars-apostolic would be observed by all Jesuits.

Pallu meanwhile had left Surat on the *Vautour*, one of the ships of the CIO. He landed in Bantam in west Java at the end of April 1672, and could have gone on board a small Portuguese ship sailing for Siam, but chose to take an English vessel which dropped anchor at the sleepy outpost of Balassor on the Bengal coast in August. He left this port on 8 March 1673 on a Siamese junk, and on 17 May returned to Ayutthaya, after a voyage lasting more than three years. He had been away eight years and four months.

A BISHOP IS CONSECRATED IN AYUTTHAYA

His reunion with the missionaries was both pious and moving. A witness wrote that "joy was great on both sides."[11] The two bishops, together again after so many years, had so much to relate about their struggles and sufferings that several days of conversation and outpouring were needed.

The first problem which claimed the urgent attention of the vicars-apostolic was the succession of Ignace Cotolendi, Bishop of Metellopolis, who had died in India in August 1662. It will be recalled that a brief of Alexander VII of 1665 authorized the Bishops of Berythus and Heliopolis jointly to choose and consecrate one of their priests to succeed their departed colleague. Mgr Pallu preferred Louis Chevreuil, the martyr of the Goa inquisition who had returned with him to Siam. Mgr Lambert, for his part, thought Louis Laneau the better choice; he appreciated his humility and apostolic zeal, and everyone considered him a saint. Each remaining firm in his convictions, the two prelates decided to act like the apostles in the first chapter of Acts where Matthias was designated the successor of the traitor Judas. They wrote down the two names on slips of paper which they placed in a hat, prayed to the Holy Ghost, and twice drew out the hat the name of Louis Laneau, who was thus elected Bishop of Metellopolis at the end of September. The Siamese court was immediately informed of this selection.

Laneau was an exceptional person. A gifted linguist, he spoke Portuguese, Spanish, Siamese, and Vietnamese. He had studied Pali, the sacred language of Theravada Buddhism, with Buddhist monks, and published a catechism in Siamese and Pali. Later he compiled a remarkable Siamese-Latin dictionary. His willingness to share the life of Siamese monks and his open-mindedness in regard to the country's religious practices had earned him the sympathy of Phra Narai and his *khunnang*. His colleagues only reproached him with a certain lack of firmness and rash liberality which risked compromising the mission's finances.

But the work of Louis Laneau, who did not spare himself for the salvation of infidels, compelled the admiration of all. This noble cause, he wrote, "fires the hearts of true missionaries and . . . gives them wings to abandon everything, to cross the high seas, go to the ends of the earth, to take no notice of danger, to dare to do anything, take on anything, and work day and night . . ."[12] This extraordinary man, who had started the mission of Pourcelouc (Phitsanulok), also tended the sick, and had the reputation of being a good doctor. The *Relation des missions et des voyages des évêques vicaires apostoliques* (Account of the mission and the travels of the episcopal vicars-apostolic) frankly explains his medical-cum-apostolic strategy:

> God visibly condones Mr Laneau's cures and remedies for healing the sick, and he is held by the Court and the Town a very able doctor. It was considered therefore that the opportunity should be taken to use this reputation to save souls under pretext of healing bodies, and with this in mind a small hospice was built next to the seminary for the poor who suffered from certain illnesses.[13]

Born in May 1637, Laneau was only thirty-six at the time of his election.

The episcopal consecration of Mgr Laneau, originally scheduled for 27 December 1673, finally took place on Easter Day, 25 March 1674. Mgr Pallu deferred the honours of the ceremony to Mgr Lambert, the consecrating bishop. The new bishop, after having sworn the canonical oath of fidelity to the Holy See, was consecrated Bishop *in partibus* of Metellopolis, and installed as vicar-apostolic of Siam at the same time, by virtue of the brief *Cum sicut accepimus* of Clement IX. All the Roman ceremonies were observed as far as possible "at the extremity of the world." The mitre, crozier, pectoral cross, ring, and other episcopal ornaments "were not very valuable, but were correct. And one could say that the poverty which appeared in all this in the midst of an idolatrous kingdom had . . . the rich simplicity of the first centuries of the Church."[14]

Another more political project occupied Pallu's mind since his return to Siam. The bearer of letters for Phra Narai from the pope and the King of France, he considered himself their ambassador and desired to surround his diplomatic mission with as much lustre as possible. He had travelled, negotiated, and frequented the antechambers of power too much not to understand that the French missions in Siam would benefit from closer links between Phra Narai and Louis XIV.

Mgr Lambert must have been delighted on learning of the existence of these letters in Mgr Pallu's strongbox. He had written to Pallu in 1667 suggesting that one could imply to Louis XIV that an ambassador sent to the court of Siam would urge Phra Narai "to wish to embrace our religion, as being most holy, and the most appropriate for reigning monarchs who profess it in supreme authority, because it obliges Christians by its laws to be faithful and very obedient to their sovereigns *for fear of being damned*"[15] (emphasis added). Rarely has the connivance of the throne and the altar been expressed with so much cynicism. The letters which Pallu brought appeared in the eyes of his colleague a first step towards this desired aim.

The bishops were sufficiently familiar with Siamese customs to know that a letter from a foreign ruler was treated with as much respect as his person, and that delivery of royal (or pontifical) letters was no slight matter. From the time of Pallu's return, Lambert had indicated to the *Phra Khlang* Chao Phraya Kosathibodi, foster brother of the king, that the prelate brought letters and presents from the King of France and the Sovereign Pontiff, "common father of all the Catholics." A delighted Phra Narai consented to receive the ambassador-bishop in public audience "with extraordinary pomp."

Charged with organizing this great event, the *Phra Khlang* informed the vicars-apostolic about Siamese ceremonial, notably of the fact that they would have to present themselves before the sovereign barefooted and with their faces bowed down to the ground. The requirements of the *kow-tow* have often troubled European-Asian diplomatic relations. The bishops protested that this custom was incompatible with their episcopal rank, with the diplomatic status which the circumstances endowed them, and with "the glory of France, whose great monarch at that moment was reaping such brilliant victories, the echoes of which were heard to the extremities of the earth."[16] A diplomatic incident was in the offing. Negotiations dragged on for months, but the *Phra Khlang*, not in the least impressed, was inflexible.

Phra Narai was informed of the objections of the vicars-apostolic. He decided after a moment of perplexity that etiquette would be bent for them. The ambassadors "would retain their shoes and would be separately seated on a richly embroidered carpet, [and] would present their compliments in the European fashion." The obstacle was thus removed without face being lost, and the day for the audience was fixed for 18 October 1673. The history of ambassadorial exchanges between France, the Vatican, and Siam was beginning. It would last exactly fifteen years.

"WHAT OCCURRED DURING THE PRESENTATION OF THE LETTERS"[17]

The day before the audience, Mgr Laneau, surrounded by missionaries and other Frenchmen, carried the letters of Louis XIV and Clement IX into a room in the palace set aside for the receipt of letters from kings and foreign princes. They remained there a few hours, before being placed in two great golden basins and transported into the council chamber. The *Phra Khlang* and a great number of *khunnang* listened with every sign of respect to the Siamese translation read by the Bishop of Metellopolis. The two missives were then placed on a sort of throne and carried to the royal palace, "to the sound of hautboys, drums, and trumpets," by armed soldiers who held ceremonial umbrellas above the basins.

The following day at five in the morning, two sumptuous ceremonial barges (*balões*, "balons") with fifty oarsmen brought Mgrs of Berythus, Heliopolis, and Metellopolis to the palace. Their missionaries and nine Frenchmen followed them in four other barges. Among them were the Sieur du Hautmesnil "who had come to Siam on the orders of the directors-general of the Royal Indies Company."[18] The bishops wanted to involve him in the event, since the trader and the missionary could, each in his own sphere, unite the greater glory of God and the Most Christian King. They arrived towards half-past seven in the outer courtyard of the palace where the last remaining details concerning etiquette were decided.

After an hour, trumpets and drums sounded the expected signal. The bishops in surplices and copes, followed by their people, slowly crossed the second and third courtyards filled with ceremonial elephants and "seven or eight thousand soldiers in very good order, all prostrate with their hands above their heads and their faces to the ground."[19] The number seems somewhat exaggerated, but the sight must have been impressive. The famous white elephant for which Phra Narai had written lullabies, and the elephant he normally rode, were waiting with their rich harnesses in the fourth courtyard.

At the end of this was the main building, "gilded withall on the outside," which contained a huge audience chamber, "entry to which is forbidden to any foreigner, and to most persons in the kingdom, and in which no ambassador had previously been received." Yet it was in this sacrosanct place that the king, to the great surprise of his court, had decided to grant an audience to the bishops. They found there the *khunnang* prostrate on Persian carpets, and Somdet Phra Narai royally seated "on a very high and most magnificent throne, bearing a crown on his head, dressed in an extraordinarily rich jacket which shone with all kinds of precious jewels."

The bishops sat on silk carpets embroidered with gold and silver, and then bowed three times to the king. The *Phra Khlang* and the *khunnang*, who wore conical tapering headdresses, got up on their knees to make three profound inclinations, their hands joined and raised above their heads, and prostrated themselves once more afterwards. A *khunnang* charged with introducing the ambassadors said a few words to the king; another came to place himself in front of the bishops to read out the Siamese translation of the letters of the pope and the French king.

The Latin letter of Clement IX Rospigliosi was dated 24 August 1669,[20] and began "*Serenissime Rex, salutem et lumen gratiae* . . ." The pope expressed satisfaction at the prosperity of the kingdom of Siam under the enlightened reign of Phra Narai, and the protection he had granted to those who preached the Gospels. After a few well-turned phrases concerning the grandeur, wisdom, and "thousand other brilliant qualities of your august person," the letter described the zeal with which Mgr Pallu had broadcast praises of Phra Narai in Europe. The gift to the mission of a plot of land and construction materials had warmed the heart of the Sovereign Pontiff who announced the return to Siam of Mgr Pallu with some modest presents. The pope did not cease to pray to God, night and day, to extend the light of divine truth to the King of Siam, so that he might, after having reigned long on earth, reign eternally in heaven.

Louis XIV's letter said more or less the same thing in French. The complete text, the first diplomatic exchange between France and Siam, reads:

> Most high, most excellent, most powerful prince, our very dear and good friend:
>
> Having learnt the favourable reception you have granted to those of our subjects who, through burning zeal for our holy religion, were resolved to carry the light of the Faith and the Gospels to the extent of your realms, we have taken pleasure in profiting by the occasion of the return of the Bishop of Heliopolis to show our gratitude to you and to indicate at the same time that we feel ourselves obliged for the gift you accorded him and the Bishop of Berythus, not only a field for their dwelling, but even materials to construct their church and house. And as they might have frequent occasions to seek your protection and your justice in the execution of a design so pious and so salutary, we thought it would be agreeable to you that we ask you on their behalf and that of all our subjects every kind of good treatment, assuring you that the grace and favour which you accord them will be most dear to us, and we shall embrace with joy the

> occasions of expressing our gratitude to you, praying to God, most high, most powerful, and most excellent prince, and very dear and good friend, that he will increase your grandeur with a happy ending.
>
> Your very dear and good friend, LOUIS.
>
> Written in the royal city of Paris, 31 January 1670.[21]

After this double reading was over, Mgr Pallu, to whom Mgr Laneau acted as interpreter, apologized for not being able to bring the king the presents sent by Clement IX and Louis XIV; difficulties in communications had obliged him to leave them at Bantam where the CIO had a small godown, and from where they would be sent on the first safe occasion. (The Dutch seized them in the end, to the great anger of the Siamese court.)[22] To thank the bishops, Phra Narai addressed the person introducing the ambassadors, who repeated the sacred words to Mgr Laneau, who translated them into French; the episcopal replies reached the royal ear by the same route. The introducer must have had a terrible backache by the end of the audience. "Each time His Majesty finished speaking, this mandarin profoundly prostrated himself three times in the manner of the country, and he did the same before giving him the bishops' reply."

After saying he would receive the presents with pleasure when they arrived, Phra Narai expressed his sympathy for the pope and the French king, and promised his protection to the missionaries and other Frenchmen. He then enquired after the health of Clement IX (he had to be informed that he had died four years before) and Louis XIV (excellent). The king then asked a series of questions about the invasion of Holland and the French military successes, the royal house, and the magnificence of the French court. "He then praised the magnanimity of this great monarch who carried in this way to every corner his name and his glory."

Officials presented in golden cups areca nuts and betel leaves, which the bishops politely masticated during the rest of the audience, praising, with their mouths full, Louis XIV who had triumphed over the insolent Dutch. Soon after, other officials brought in a trunk containing two violet Chinese silk robes for Mgrs Berythus and Heliopolis, and a set of black clothes for Mgr Metellopolis who had not yet been consecrated bishop. The prelates received these presents with effusions of thanks and bows in the direction of the king, who told them they could apply to the *Phra Khlang* if they needed anything. He then turned to Mgr Lambert, telling him that "as it was he who had the advantage of beginning the liaison between the two kings, it was also his charge to seek the means to sustain it." The message was important; the King of Siam desired to strengthen links with the King of France.

Phra Narai remained immobile on his throne and the *khunnang* prostrated themselves before him, while a small concert lasting some ten minutes allowed everyone to regurgitate discreetly the reddish ball of areca and betel in their mouths, at the same time savouring the importance of the inauguration of Franco-Siamese diplomatic relations. A curtain was drawn to conceal the king; two other larger curtains then concealed the throne and ended the audience. The *khunnang* raised themselves and sat chatting on their Persian carpets, whilst the bishops and their companions, bowing left and right, were led out the same way they had come.

"IT WAS ON THIS SOLEMN DAY"

Some ten days later, Phra Narai demonstrated his esteem for the Catholic missionaries during the great annual procession on the Chao Phraya (*kathin nam*), though this was a Buddhist ceremony. Jeremy Kemp notes that "the *kathin* is of purely Buddhist origins, and consists in offering alms and robes to the monks. These offerings are usually made in the month following the Buddhist lent (*phansa*) in the middle of the eleventh lunar month."[23] The great royal barge, so covered with gold that it seemed to be entirely built of the precious metal, solemnly glided over the waters of the river, surrounded by more than two hundred lesser barges carrying the *khunnang*, each more colourful than his neighbour. An enormous crowd jostled on the two river banks, hoping to catch a glimpse of the king "shining with an infinity of jewels like the sun."

An MEP witness relates the unexpected event which occurred on that occasion:

> It was on this solemn day that His Majesty gave orders to the oarsmen to depart from the route they customarily took and to go upstream of the river instead of down it. He came close to the place where the French house is located, and there, stopping awhile to look carefully at their building and their grounds with an attention that indicated his benevolence, he decided that they did not have enough land, and gave them on the spot another plot close by, where he

> declared he wished to build a magnificent church which would one day be the first cathedral in his realm.[24]

Since Ayutthaya now had its bishop in the person of Mgr Laneau, one had to think of building a cathedral for him. It can be imagined that the monks, performing over the *kathina* robes which the king had just presented them the rite of *pravarana* prescribed by the *Vinaya* texts,[25] did not rejoice on learning that the monarch who caused the Buddhist Wheel of Law to turn (*dharmachakravartin*) had just offered the competitors a fine plot of land and a cathedral.

The "other plot close by" was that of the Cochin-Chinese, who were requested to vacate the area without delay. The building materials sent by the king soon piled up in the grounds. He had decided that nothing would be spared, "neither in beauty nor grandeur of design, nor in solidity and ornament of the structure, whose plan he demanded to see." It was drawn up by the bishops and their priests, and submitted mid-January 1674 to Phra Narai, who ordered it to be built. The construction lasted a good ten years. Aumont describes in 1683

> the church, which is very big . . . has a rather fine entrance supported by four brick pilasters facing the river bank. On each side of the entrance is a square tower finishing in a spire topped by a fairly high ball. The church is entirely built of bricks and plaster, well constructed . . . very well lit by great crossings whose frames are embellished with linen cloth, glass being unknown in this country. The roof is shaped in the manner of the temples of the country's idols.[26]

The building was so vast that Constantine Phaulkon wrote in 1682 to Innocent XI Odescalchi, "But when it is finished, I know not where the Christians will be found to use it."[27] The project was indeed on a grand scale.

THREE BISHOPS IN LOPBURI

Soon after the audience, the rumour was spread that the king had the intention to send an ambassador to Europe bearing replies to the pope and the King of France. This news was confirmed in a letter from the three bishops to Louis XIV dated 8 November 1673.[28] The prelates were invited soon afterwards to Lopburi, and a barge with twenty-six oarsmen was provided to take them. They arrived on 20 November and were put up at a house prepared for them in the town. Early in the morning of the twenty-second they went to the palace.

> Hardly had they arrived than an officer brought them two elephants which the king sent, to take them to the place where His Majesty customarily indulges in the pleasure of the hunt. The Bishops of Heliopolis and Berythus mounted one of these elephants, where there was a seat with a balustrade half a foot high all around. They were seated in front in surplice and cape, and the Bishop of Metellopolis mounted the other, in his cassock and long coat.[29]

They were thus transported to Phra Tinang Yen where Phra Narai had a hunting lodge near the enclosure (*phaniat*) in which wild elephants were tamed.

They found the king on a hillock close to the palisade, from where he was observing the taming of an elephant caught the day before.

> This monarch, wearing that day on his bonnet a golden crown studded all over with diamonds, was mounted on a magnificently adorned black elephant. Several court officials accompanied him, all on foot and showing the greatest respect . . . As soon as the bishops were seen, the minister came before them and accomplished his task of introducing them to the presence of the king. On arriving they made three low bows. The monarch received them very courteously, had them come close to him so the trunks of their elephants could touch him, which greatly surprised the court.

The meeting lasted about three hours, "which was all the time filled with taming the furious elephant." So their conversation took place with the background noise of panic-stricken trumpeting, mahouts' shouts, and perhaps soothing lullabies. Clearly fascinated by the person of Louis XIV, whose portrait in enamel Pallu had presented to the king, Phra Narai asked a thousand questions about his French counterpart, particularly about the composition of his family and his feats of arms, "opening up in this way a fruitful area for agreeable replies." The detailed description with Mgr Laneau gave of the innumerable qualities of this "incomparable monarch" brought forth from the King of Siam the remark that "nothing seemed to him more majestic." He then asked why His Most Christian Majesty sent his subjects to the other end of the world. The prelates were quick to explain to him that "zeal for the salvation of souls was the only cause," and that Louis XIV "had much desire to extend the kingdom of God."

Phra Narai replied that

> he would be very happy to contribute to his glorious designs and that, to give him an indication of the particular esteem in which he held his qualities, he had resolved to make him an offer of a port, in the extent of his realm, where a town could be built in the name of Louis the Great, which would even become—if the king judged it appropriate—the residence of one of his viceroys.

This surprising proposition—rebounding from the back of one elephant to another—was going to place Franco-Siamese relations on a new phase, exceeding everything that Louis XIV and Colbert had hoped for from their diplomatic initiative. The bishops, through Mgr Laneau, wore themselves out with thanks and promised to transmit this generous offer.

They next talked about the pope, and the bishops took advantage of the occasion to relate the story of the conversion of Constantine and "the great benefits this emperor and his successors provided to the Holy See and the Church." If the cap fits . . . The king listened politely and dismissed the bishops on their elephants, declaring they would meet again before their departure.

The following day, the prelates had a long conversation with the *Phra Khlang* who said he was concerned about the presence of the La Haye squadron in the seas of the Indies; the admiral had seized São Tomé sixteen months earlier in July 1672. A Siamese vessel flying the Dutch flag had had its mainmast and rigging torn to shreds by the French near Ormuz. The bishops vaguely invoked the "laws of war." While declaring "they were not wrong," the *Phra Khlang* requested them to write to La Haye, which they willingly did. The minister then asked numerous questions about the Christian religion. The bishops replied as best they could, whilst wondering if the minister would profit by their replies, for his devotion to Buddhism ("the cult of his idols") was well known.

A few days later, the king sent the prelates a generous selection of fruit, preserves, and game in forty large silver basins. The bishops received the same day a letter from Tenasserim with the news La Haye had seized a "Moorish" vessel at Masulipatam, only to free it the moment he learnt that it belonged to the King of Siam. A compliment from the "viceroy of the Indies," saying he was more than anyone the devoted servant of His Siamese Majesty, accompanied the letter. The prelates immediately transmitted the news and the compliments to Phra Narai who expressed his satisfaction.

The following day, the king invited the bishops to watch a fight between a tiger and an elephant, but they declined this invitation to a cruel spectacle which they judged incompatible with their calling. Phra Narai received this excuse very well, and the following morning sent them three elephants to bring them to the palace where he wished to grant them a final audience. It was spent entirely in satisfying the king's curiosity. "This monarch desired to know how many Christian kings and kingdoms there are, what they are called, if there were no difference between them on the subject of religion, and several other similar things." The king ended the audience after an hour and a half, saying they could remain in Lopburi if they desired to. They thanked him as they should, but said they were impatient to return to Ayutthaya.

Hardly had they reached the capital than Mgr Lambert fell seriously ill with kidney stones. His condition, which delayed the consecration of Mgr Laneau, alarmed the king who hastened to send him two of his best doctors. The cleverer, a Chinese, had him on his feet in a few weeks, and showed a sincere interest in Christianity, thus warming the heart of the bedridden prelate.

The remarkable favour the French bishops enjoyed did not make all the other nations established in Ayutthaya dance for joy. The Moors (Muslims) in particular, who secretly hoped to win over Phra Narai and his kingdom to Islam, gritted their teeth. The Dutch, implicated in a war with France which was almost fatal for them, saw in the vicars and their people the advance guard of an invasion of French traders, diplomats, and soldiers. "To the other foreigners in Siam, the priests must have seemed to be promoting the glory of Louis XIV as much as the glory of God," as Dhiravat na Pombejra neatly has it.[30] Their contacts with the court and the tendentious information about the whole of Europe with which they filled the ears of the king and the *Phra Khlang* preoccupied everyone. In his report of 20 November 1672, De Rooij, *opperhoofd* at the VOC godown in Ayutthaya, sought regular news of Europe because "the bishop [Lambert] and his Frenchmen have spread a mass of information, but perhaps it is not in accordance with the facts."[31]

"PROFIT BY THE GOOD GRACES OF THE KING"

The year 1674 saw the bishops very concerned with exploiting the royal favour they enjoyed for the greater glory of God. They conferred in February on "how to procure advantages for religion and profit by the good graces of the king. The means which seemed the easiest was to ask His Majesty for some fifty families to serve the missionaries, and in that way make known the esteem he showed them in giving them vassals."[32] At the beginning of this year, Mgr Laneau completed a book "in which he dealt indirectly with many errors found in the Siamese religion."

Mgr Lambert for his part occupied himself with what comes close to being a bit of blackmail. He noted that Phra Narai was still considering sending an embassy to France, and was wondering about the kind of presents to offer Louis XIV. The king considered the bishop to be the head of the French in Siam, and so an indispensable person in the preparation of the embassy. After his journey to Tonkin in 1669–1670, he had visited Cochin-China in 1671–1672, where the situation was less troubling and where he was vicar-apostolic.[33] Letters from Cochin-China informed him that King Hien-vong, the ruler of the south who had his court in Hué, wished the bishop to come and settle in his realm. Mgr Lambert considered that Siam now had its own vicar-apostolic and the moment had come for him to take up residence in the missions Rome had accorded him. But he needed to obtain the authorization of Phra Narai.

To this end he travelled to Lopburi in style in May 1674, accompanied by Mgr Pallu who was seeking permission to leave for his mission in Tonkin. No less than eight elephants were needed to transport the two bishops, their domestics, and baggage from the landing stage to the palace. Phra Narai granted leave to Pallu to depart Siam in August, but was vexed at the request of Lambert whom he wished to accompany his ambassadors to France. After several months he agreed to his departure, but only after receiving the bishop's promise that his absence would last not more than one year.

Noting the king's fondness for him, Mgr Lambert described in somewhat exaggerated terms the benefits and privileges which Hien-vong promised the Christian mission in Cochin-China. He gave the king to understand that he hoped for the same treatment for the young church in Siam, and that perhaps he would not leave if he were completely satisfied on this score.

But it would seem that Mgr Lambert's demands were unreasonable, for in July 1675, positioned between two crates of goods on a junk, he left for a voyage which was to last ten months. During his stay in Cochin-China he observed that the church was not as free in its movements as he had thought, but that the Cochin-Chinese embraced the Christian faith with an ardour which would have made the Siamese blush for shame.[34]

The accounts of the MEP for the years 1676 and 1677 paint a rosy picture of the continual kindnesses of the king. Not content with building a cathedral at his own expense, he also took in charge the construction of the large two-storey principal building, big enough to house the priests and the seminary which Pierre Langlois directed. Even before the cathedral was finished, Phra Narai ordered some of his officers to carry a magnificent gilded pulpit there. They took part in prayers in the mission's chapel and then related to the king all that they had seen and heard. After listening carefully to their report, "this monarch declared in the presence of some mandarins that he did not oppose any of his subjects embracing the Christian religion."[35] This declaration was not likely to improve relations between the king and the Buddhist monks who must have muttered that he truly went too far in Buddhist tolerance. Dutch and French sources relate that the sovereign lost the little credit he still had in the eyes of the Buddhist *sangha*.

At the end of 1676, Phra Narai decided to suppress the ceremony which was supposed to favour the withdrawal of the waters, for a prolonged flood could affect the rice harvest. The ceremony required that he strike the surface of the water symbolically with a long-handled fan, thus reversing the flow of water (one of the king's titles was "He who controls the world's rainfall")[36] and guaranteeing the harmonious continuity of the seasons and the prosperity of his subjects. In spite of the predictions of his astrologers, it rained on the day of the ceremony, and the king considered he had lost face. The Abbé de Choisy noted in 1685: "about twelve years ago the king fixed the day for dividing the waters, and it rained, and all the fine barges were spoilt. The astrologers were dismissed, and since then the ceremony has not been observed."[37] La Loubère for his part wrote that the kings of Siam performed a ceremony

> to conjure the River to return to its Channel, when the Agriculture requir'd it, and when the wind inclining to the North assured the return of fair weather. The present King was the first that dispenc'd with this troublesom work . . . because, say they, that the last time he perform'd it, he had the disgrace of being surpriz'd with rain, altho his Astrologers had promised him a fair day.[38]

Was it because of this humiliating incident that Phra Narai had the temples closed as a form of reprisal? A report of the MEP indicates that in 1676

> during the overflowing of the river which floods the country, just at the time when the people are in the habit of frequenting the temples for their god, [the king] ordered that their doors be closed, and forbade with great penalties anyone to enter them. Everyone was extremely surprised. And as from that time he was not seen to go to a temple in the manner of his predecessors, it was generally said that he was of the religion of the foreigners.[39]

Was this an exercise in wishful thinking on the part of the missionaries or an expression of royal anger for having suffered a cosmic affront? The incident suggests that Phra Narai was reconsidering the Buddhist and Brahmin culture of his kingdom, and the role he was supposed to play in it. Given this, one can understand the ambiguity in the king's religious sympathies. This was to justify the great conversion projects at the base of the French effort. "A king who becomes a Christian, a million souls following his example," Choisy foresaw when travelling towards Siam with his head full of impossible dreams.[40] Phra Narai had done nothing to dissipate the misunderstanding.

"HERE WE ARE ENTIRELY CAUGHT BETWEEN THE HAMMER AND THE ANVIL"

The quarrel between the vicars-apostolic supported by Rome and the clergy coming under the *Padroado* now entered its final phase. In October 1672 Louis Laneau had taken the text of the brief *Speculatores* to the residences of the Jesuits and the Dominicans in Ayutthaya, but the Fathers had replied that they could not receive a document from the Holy See which had not first passed through the chancellery in Lisbon. Summoned by Mgr Laneau, the priests explained that to receive a brief from the pope would be an act of rebellion against the King of Portugal. They were going round in circles. Mgr Laneau would have avoided a lot of futile exasperation on both sides if he had waited for the moment when the Jesuits and the Dominicans had received from their own superiors the text of the pontifical documents and the order to submit.

The arrival in Ayutthaya in June 1676 of Charles Sevin, bearer of the briefs of Clement X, clarified the situation. His return journey had been adventurous. Attacked by pirates in the Mediterranean, he had spent the winter on the Anatolian plateau and taken passage on a Portuguese warship disguised as a representative of the CIO. The priests depending on the Portuguese king could no longer doubt the authenticity of the pontifical briefs, nor their acceptance by their superiors, for very specific orders had come from them. But, as the Jesuit Sotomayor wrote at the beginning of 1676 to his general superior Oliva, the Portuguese viceroy had threatened with prison the Fathers who carried out the orders of the Holy See. Fr Oliva knew for certain that Dom Pedro, the Portuguese regent, was ready to expel from the Indies the Jesuits who recognized the authority of the vicars apostolic. The situation was difficult for everyone.

Portugal meanwhile sought to consolidate its position in the Siamese court. On 19 September 1676 there arrived at the bar of the Chao Phraya a Portuguese ship bringing a formal letter from the prince regent to Phra Narai. Barreto de Pina, the leader of the Portuguese colony, went to announce the great news to the *Phra Khlang* and then decided on the ceremonial of an audience which was very similar to that accorded to the French three years previously. Full of satisfaction, Barreto could write: "I have lived in Siam for twenty-one years, and I have never seen a letter delivered by any ambassador from any monarch with so much honour and acclaim."[41] One imagines that Mgr Laneau did his utmost to explain to the king, in his best Siamese, the reasons for the Portuguese alacrity, and why the Lusitanian monopoly for the organization of missions henceforth belonged to the past.

The Jesuits in Ayutthaya, and notably Fathers Tomaso Valguarnera, Manuel Soares, Joseph Tissanier, and Jean-Baptiste Maldonado, wished to gain time, torn as they were between the instructions of Fr Oliva and their oath of fidelity to the Portuguese king. This loyalty placed them painfully at the heart of the conflict of jurisdiction raging between the French bishops sent by the Roman Propaganda and the Archbishop of Goa acting in the name of the King of Portugal.

The arrival in Goa, in September 1675, of the new archbishop António Brandão, who succeeded the unbending Cristóvão de Silveira, was to unblock the impasse. On 8 May 1677, in a conciliatory letter to the vicars-apostolic, he informed them he had ordered his suffragan bishops of Malacca and Macao to adhere to the decisions of Clement X. As for the question of knowing if the Portuguese colony in Siam fell within the jurisdiction of the Bishop of Malacca or the vicar-apostolic of Ayutthaya, it was up to the pope alone to decide after having listened to Portugal's point of view. It is clear that "a breach had been made in the fortress" of the *Padroado*,[42] and that the archbishop was holding out a lifebuoy to the Jesuits who could henceforth put themselves in line with Goa without breaking their vow of obedience to the pope.

As a consequence of this opening the Jesuit and Dominican superiors in provinces located in South-East Asia required their subjects to submit to the vicars-apostolic, threatening to recall them if they did not obey. Carrying out this order gave rise to several cases of mental torment, for there were many who were most unwilling to submit to the French prelates whom they considered hot-headed Jansenists.

In Ayutthaya, which Fr Tissanier had left in June 1675 to return to Macao, and where Fr Valguarnera had died at the beginning of 1677, Fr Maldonado had considerable difficulty in taking this step. At one time he wrote to his general saying he would make every effort to obey the pope; at another time he considered with his colleague Manuel Soares the possibility of continuing their ministry under the jurisdiction of Goa alone. Not being French (he was born in Mons in

Flanders) he was opposed to the vicars-apostolic and attached to the Portuguese *Padroado*. He had been active in Siam since 1673 and observed at close hand the untoward consequences of the conflict, and finished by accepting, not without personal anguish, the authority of the French bishops imposed by Rome. In 1682 he wrote to Charles de Noyelle, who had succeeded Oliva: "*Aspera sunt tempora* . . . the times are harsh. Here we are entirely caught between the hammer and the anvil, assailed on one side by the decrees of the Sacred Congregation [of the Propaganda], and on the other by the edicts of Portugal."[43] Maldonado's loyalty to the vicars from 1681 was to earn him the hostility of Goa under Brandão's successor.[44]

The Dominicans settled in Siam made their act of submission to Mgr Laneau on 27 November 1678. The Jesuits followed only on 10 October 1681.[45] It would seem that this turn of events, which the French vicars in no ways expected, left them perplexed. They had assumed the Jesuits in Ayutthaya would prefer to leave rather than submit, and did not conceal their desire to have the missionary field in Siam to themselves. But this satisfaction was denied them, and an uneasy collaboration followed. The Jesuits had lost the battle but certainly not the war. Circumstances and their ability would soon bring them a splendid revenge.

THE DEATH OF MGR LAMBERT

The embassy which Phra Narai wished to send to France escorted by the Bishop of Berythus preoccupied Lambert from his return from Cochin-China in May 1676. He wrote the same year to the Archbishop of Paris, Harlay de Champvallon:

> I do not despair of having the honour of seeing you, since it has been decided in this court to send ambassadors to France, and I shall not be able to resist the pressure being applied for me to accompany them. This project would have been carried out this year, but for the Dutch refusing the necessary laissez-passers. The purpose of this embassy is that the King of Siam, replying to a letter which His Most Christian Majesty had written to him . . . expresses his desire for an alliance, and makes very considerable offers, the chief one of which is, if he considers it desirable, to be given a port in his realm, where the

> French could build a town for the safety of their commerce. We believe that our notification of this sent to the king and Mr Colbert has arrived in France."[46]

In October 1677, Mgr Laneau on his part informed his friend the parish priest of St Jacques de La Boucherie: "The King of Siam still continues to think of sending an embassy to the courts of France and Rome; his presents are already prepared. He would have sent them, had it not been for the war with the Dutch."[47] The war with Holland does indeed seem to have been the chief reason for the delay in sending the embassy, but Phra Narai did not stop thinking about it, knowing that this conflict would not last for ever.

Mgr Lambert wrote to Mgr Pallu at the beginning of September 1678:

> The King of Siam summoned, two or three days ago, his mandarins in the council chamber and ordered them to select the ambassadors for France. They named two, and reported their choice to the king. He became angry on account of their not being important enough, and ordered them to choose others. We do not know if he has in mind to send them this year; carrying out the project seems difficult because of the Dutch. It was Ok-phra Krai who gave us this news.[48]

Phra Narai of course could not have known that the United Provinces and France had just begun negotiations and that the peace of Nijmegen would be signed on 17 September, hardly a fortnight after his order for the selection of ambassadors.

The king could finally bring off his diplomatic project, but Mgr Lambert was not to see its realization. He had not laid down his arms, in spite of the conciliatory attitude of the Archbishop of Goa, and even seems to have intended bringing the *Padroado* priests who had not submitted before a Siamese tribunal to force them to obey him.[49] The advice of moderation which the priests at the Rue du Bac regularly sent him only served to irritate the intransigent bishop who would rather have broken with his Parisian friends than ceded. Indeed, he desired the absorption of the MEP seminary into that of St Sulpice. This rigour deterred some priests around him. Charles Sevin, who had permitted himself to suggest to the bishop rather more pliability, was pushed to one side and not given any duties. To console himself, he said that the state of health of the bishop, seriously afflicted with kidney stones, excused his hypochondria. It is certain that this extremely painful illness had not softened the character of the unbending Pierre Lambert. A humiliating urinary incontinence confined him more and more to his bedroom where he endured serious bouts of depression. Claude Gayme, who looked after him to the end of his life, wrote to Sevin that "lassitude and melancholy were his greatest torment, and until two months before his death he could not be contradicted in anything whatsoever, and he was of a very difficult humour . . . For forty or fifty days, I took him on a barge on the river, seeing that distracted him somewhat from his lassitude."[50]

This tormented man finally died of lassitude—and the stone. These two afflictions caused him to suffer terribly in the last months of his life. Mgr Laneau wrote:

> It was pitiful to hear the cries which he uttered when the pains began, and they did every quarter or half hour. He often said that was nothing in comparison to lassitude and bitterness which filled his soul, for Our Lord deprived him of any inner consolation . . . Finally he gave up his soul to God as a true man in torment, as he had always lived, in the midst of crosses and suffering, less external than internal.[51]

Death, benevolent here, relieved Lambert of his sufferings and torments on 15 June 1679 at the age of fifty-five. When an autopsy was conducted, "three big stones, coagulated together" were found, and "these stones had destroyed and ulcerated his bladder, and one of his kidneys was as large as one's fist with an ulcer."[52]

The death of this undoubtedly admirable man, who yet inspires pity rather than sympathy, seems to have brought the Portuguese and French communities in Ayutthaya together; the entire Portuguese colony came to attend the funeral of the Bishop of Berythus. The occasion was grand. The *khunnang* and the chief monks attended on the king's orders.[53]

This death coincided with the end of the first period of relations between France and Siam. The French mission in Ayutthaya and those established in the provinces (Phitsanulok, Tenasserim, Bangkok) were well entrenched and enjoyed royal favour, while the clouds generated by the dispute between the Propaganda and the *Padroado* were dispersed. The news of the peace of Nijmegen at last allowed Phra Narai to send an embassy to France, and this was at the time when the CIO was preparing to establish a godown in Siam. French missionaries would be followed by traders, diplomats, and officials sent by the royal company and the court at Versailles. Franco-Siamese relations were entering a decisive phase which seemed to justify the highest hopes.

THE GREEK INTERLUDE

CHAPTER ELEVEN

PHAULKON, THE GREEK FAVOURITE

CONSTANTINE PHAULKON, CHARLATAN OR MARTYR?

THE HISTORY of the person the French were to call "Monsieur Constance" or "His Excellency Mr Constance" is not easy to compile. He inspired hagiographies written in rose water and diatribes inked in vitriol, and his character does not seem to constitute a whole. Several biographical novels, starting with *The Falcon of Siam* by Axel Aylwen; a Japanese hoax, the fictitious memoirs of Phaulkon's Japanese wife by Reiko Hada entitled *The Moonlit Palace*; and more recently *Le Ministre des Moussons* (The monsoon minister) by Claire Keefe-Fox (1998); not to pass over *A la plus grande gloire de Dieu* (To the greater glory of God) by Morgan Sportès, complicate the historian's task. It is enough to read the unpublished and very precise reactions to the naive and edifying *Histoire de M. Constance, premier ministre du roi de Siam* (The history of M. Constance, chief minister to the King of Siam) of the Jesuit Pierre-Joseph d'Orléans,[1] to realize that things did not all pass as the good Father would have us believe. Moreover this author never went to Asia, but was happy to repeat the inventions of his colleague Guy Tachard, who made himself Phaulkon's grey eminence during two stays in Siam.

The anonymous author of the *Letter of an English Catholic to the Rev. Fr Pierre d'Orléans* (written in French) traded in Asia and was well aware of Phaulkon's reputation. He does not beat about the bush:

> To make a man whom everyone who has been in the Indies knew to

> be the biggest charlatan ever to emerge, not to speak of his other vices, to be a saint and a martyr, a man whose principal concern had always been the implantation of the Christian religion; to call his death holy and precious and the crowning of a most Christian life; to make out his wife's relations, people of infamy and scandal, to be confessors of Jesus Christ and virtuous women, is something never before seen . . . Your book, Reverend Father, is in short nothing but a novel . . . Your credulity must have been cruelly abused.[2]

Such indignation rings true.

In 1756, André François Deslandes-Boureau also published a *Histoire de M. Constance, premier ministre du roi de Siam* (History of Mr Constance, chief minister of the King of Siam). It is based on the letters and memoirs of his father, André Deslandes, who arrived in Siam in 1680 as the first representative of the CIO and knew Phaulkon well. His opinion of the little book of Fr d'Orléans is the same:

> I do not think I am mistaken in saying that his *History* is a complete fabrication . . . What is extraordinary in this *History* is that Fr d'Orléans wants to pass off the chief minister of Siam as a martyr and even a saint. But he was neither the one nor the other . . .[3]

The *Letter of an English Catholic* is followed by a *Short Life and Habits of Mr Constance*, a good forty pages in length, the pages large and closely written.[4] It reveals a fascinating character, it is true, but bearing no resemblance to the confessor and haloed martyr of Fathers Tachard and d'Orléans. The true personality of the Greek adventurer, one of the protagonists of this book, is better found in the pens of the Englishmen who were his first employers than those of the French Jesuits who wanted to make use of him, without realizing he intended to make use of them.

Phaulkon was without doubt the king-pin of French involvement in Siam, and it is necessary to remove the accretions of hagiographic varnish that make him unrecognizable, but finding the real person underneath remains difficult. There seems to have been deliberate mystification, and the person mostly responsible for this was the Jesuit who had the complete confidence of Louis XIV and who penned two *Voyages de Siam* (Journeys to Siam), Fr Guy Tachard.

The "English Catholic" gives invaluable evidence of the close relations which cemented the European trading community scattered across the Indies and which allowed its members to be well informed about events and reputations:

> Although the places where Europeans trade in the Orient cover more than a thousand leagues of coastline, they are not so numerous; and they know more at one end what is happening at the other than in a couple of towns in Europe three or four leagues distant from each other . . . These merchants are not like those in European towns, always in their stores and always busy. They are only employed when their vessels arrive or depart. The rest of the time, while seeking some occasion to obtain profit or pass the time, is for discussing what is valued here or there, visiting each other, drinking together, and relating stories in Portuguese, the lingua franca of all the Europeans in the Indies and the Orient . . . Although Mr Constance only lasted a few years, there is hardly a merchant who did not complain about him and believes he had caused him some injury.[5]

It is therefore in the name of public notoriety that this Englishman offers a very different account from the myth which the French Jesuits peddled around Europe.

THE OBSCURE BEGINNINGS OF THE "LITTLE GREEK"

Since we are told that Phaulkon was forty or forty-one in 1688,[6] it must be presumed he was born in 1647 or 1648, though some have him born in 1650.[7] He was not yet ten years old when Phra Narai came to the throne. He was born in a small settlement of Argostoli on the island of Cephalonia (Kephallenia), the largest of the Ionian Isles which were then in Venetian hands. The Count of Forbin, who knew him well, had little affection for him, and visited his family in Cephalonia in 1695, said he was the son of a tavern-keeper.[8] Fr Tachard, and in his wake Fr d'Orléans, assure us that Phaulkon was born of "a Venetian noble, son of the governor of that island, and daughter of the oldest families in the land,"[9] but Turpin justly observes that the name Phaulkon nowhere appears in the "golden books" listing the Venetian nobility. The Jesuit Claude de Bèze, who stayed in Siam in 1687–1688, notes that "his father was Greek, of an honest family, and he had, on his mother's side, ancestors who had governed the country for the Republic of Venice."[10] He further notes that this person was not called Constance Phaulkon, but Constantin Hierachy. Since *hierax* means "falcon" in ancient Greek (*geraki* in modern Greek), he had the idea of changing his name to Phaulkon, close to the English *falcon* and Portuguese *falcão*.

This hero himself, who repeated that he knew nothing about his origins and did not attach the least importance to the subject, made fun of Fr Tachard who ennobled him with the sweat of his brow. The English Catholic specified:

> As for his extraction, he said he did not know from whence he came. On the occasion of differences with Mr de Forbin, this gentleman complained of the indignity with which he treated a man of his rank. He [Phaulkon] said: "Knighthood and rank count for nothing in this country; as for me, I have no rank and no birthright, I am nothing!" Furthermore he always had certain ways of acting which revealed his true character. Fr Tachard had often heard him repeat these words at table.[11]

Whatever the case, life was not exciting and the future seemed hopeless on a barren island like Cephalonia, which only produced goat cheese, olives, and some paltry vines. Tired of the uncouth peasants and goatherds who went to get drunk in his father's tavern, the youth seems to have felt at a very young age an irresistible desire to travel the world. "His pride," wrote Turpin, "could not tolerate remaining where everything reminded him of his humble origins, and at the age of twelve, he set sail for England."[12]

The English Catholic is more specific:

> He was of Greek nationality, and most often was called "the Greek" or "the little Greek," and this is still the name the Siamese give him. When you ask of them satisfaction for a transaction, "Go," they say, "seek out the Greek." He was probably born on the island of Cephalonia. The captain of an English vessel passing there, a poor woman presented him with this boy to serve him. They say she gave him away, and it was his mother who did so.

One can imagine the scene on the quay reeking of fish in the sleepy port of Argostoli: a woman dressed in black seeking to dispose of a restless youngster she can no longer feed, who is ready to leave without a backward glance. An anonymous English publication which appeared at the end of the century placed this departure "about the year 1660."[13]

The English Catholic continues:

> He went to England in this vessel, and it appears he then, and in the first few years afterwards, became a cabin boy . . . These are poor small boys found in the ports who simply seek a living. They are taken on, and, although nothing is settled for them, they are given food. They are given to three or four sailors to serve them, and live off their leftovers. They are charged with scrubbing down the decks of the ship and other similar tasks. However, they go to sea, and often become sailors.[14]

The little Greek was extremely resourceful and a fine talker. Fr de Bèze calls him "a man of the world who had the most engaging manners."[15] An anonymous Dutch text, published in 1692, says he was "a crafty, cunning character, a liar and deceiver, artful and always capable of landing on his feet, with a slick, enchanting and ever-ready tongue."[16] Until he left for the Indies in 1670, he seems to have lived principally in England. According to Fr de Bèze, he had made "some voyages to the Mediterranean" before going with his captain to England. In a letter of 1686 he would speak of this country as "a kingdom where I breathed from my childhood to the time I was brought here."[17] With very Levantine flexibility, he had adhered from the beginning to the Church of England.

From 1670, Phaulkon made three journeys on vessels of the EIC to the East Indies. The first trip on the *Hopewell* he was a sailor, the second quartermaster, and the third scrivener in charge of buying provisions. If it is true, as Fr de Bèze affirms,[18] that he took part in the war of 1672 serving in the fleet of the Palatine prince Rupert, it must be supposed that he signed on for a time in the British navy after his first journey to Asia.

He is next found on the Asian commercial circuit, spending several years in Bantam, west Java. There he learnt Malay without difficulty "which is of great use in the Indies."[19] His linguistic abilities, which everyone acknowledged, enabled him to learn other Asian languages, notably Siamese, which he mastered in two years. Of course, he spoke

Portuguese as well as he did English, but a reading of his letters in Portuguese suggests that his knowledge of that language was not perfect.

In Bantam, according to Fr de Bèze, he held the "job of minor clerk in the [English] godown," and distinguished himself by an heroic action which was at the origins of his fortune.

> It happened on the king's birthday which the English were celebrating with great gusto. The gunner, while loading the cannon, by an accident set fire to the gunpowder and the blaze rapidly spread to the well-stocked powder magazine nearby. To make matters worse, the cask from which the powder had been drawn stood open, and at no distance from the place where the fire had started. The danger was apparent to all, and with the exception of Constans, all present took to their heels . . . He plunged into the magazine through the opening in the wall by which the fire had entered. Flames were literally licking the open cask as he moved it away from them . . . he saved the magazine and the whole factory from destruction.[20]

The head of the godown rewarded him with the considerable sum of one thousand crowns and he decided to set himself up independently as soon as possible.

PHAULKON DISCOVERS SIAM

According to the English Catholic (whose account is not in complete conformity with that of Fr de Bèze), Phaulkon used his knowledge of Siamese in 1680 when one of the English merchants in Bantam, Richard Burnaby, was sent to Ayutthaya to take charge of the moribund godown of the EIC. Phaulkon was on the same ship as sailor-cannoneer ("it was the custom on those kinds of ships to choose a sailor with some wit and give him to the cannoneer to provide assistance if the need arises").[21] This suggests that Phaulkon's career, in spite of his gift of the gab, his cleverness and ambition, was stuck in the mesh of the EIC. Is it for this reason that he succeeded in impressing Richard Burnaby during the voyage from Bantam to Ayutthaya? The Englishman, who only spoke a few words of Siamese and who knew he could expect stiff competition from the Dutch, perhaps desired to acquire the services of such a useful person. He succeeded, not without difficulty, in persuading the captain to hand over to him this polyglot sailor who was too gifted to prime cannons.

In spite of the reliability of this witness, it is evident that he makes a mistake in placing this event in 1680. This anecdote raises the most difficult question in Phaulkon's chequered career: the date of his arrival in Siam. No other details about his life have given rise to such divergent opinions. According to Pallegoix, he became *Phra Khlang* in 1658;[22] according to the English Catholic, he arrived in Siam only in 1680. The difference is considerable.

Engelbert Kaempfer, who visited Ayutthaya in 1690, indicates that Phaulkon was raised to the rank of *Phra Khlang* nine years after his arrival in the kingdom,[23] which therefore occurred about 1675. A summary history of Siam drawn up in the nineteenth century by King Mongkut, and published as an appendix by Sir John Bowring, places the ministry of the Greek in the 1660s, since he explains that Phaulkon persuaded Phra Narai, "the most famous of all the Siamese kings," to restore Lopburi and build a palace there. Likewise, Phaulkon would have built "about 1675" a fort in Bangkok to control the Chao Phraya estuary.[24] But quotations of this nature, which could be multiplied, only confuse the issue.

What we know for certain about the relations between Phaulkon and a few Englishmen who only served the English company to swindle it provides a better point of departure. Among these specialists of interloping commerce are the White brothers, George and Samuel, and Richard Burnaby.[25] George White had been captain of the *Hopewell,* the vessel on which Phaulkon made his first journey to Asia.[26] A Dutch source, *Het leven en daden van d'Heer Constantyn Phaulkon* (The life and actions of Mr Constantine Phaulkon), reveals that a Mr White lent him when he started out a sum of money advanced from the coffers of the EIC, with which to begin to trade privately,[27] but this could be in fact the thousand crowns which he had been given to reward his courage the day he risked his life and saved the godown at Bantam.

It was probably in 1678 that Richard Burnaby, accompanied by Phaulkon, arrived in Ayutthaya. There he found George White, who had swapped the service of the EIC with that of the King of Siam. As noted earlier, Phra Narai had appropriated important monopolies and was the leading trader in his kingdom on this account. He exported articles under his monopolies from the port of Mergui on junks crewed by Indians or Chinese, since the Siamese did not make good sailors. In the context of the Anglo-Siamese reconciliation which followed the reopening of the English godown in Ayutthaya in 1661, Phra Narai had recruited several English captains for his merchant fleet, like John Coates, Howell, and one Williams who was for a time admiral of the Siamese fleet. George White was one of these, which did not prevent him from tending to some of his own personal business. Now a servant of the King of Siam, he felt protected from the agents of the EIC who chased after him asking embarrassing questions about his conduct of affairs when he still worked for the company, for he was inclined to make little distinction between his own funds and those of his former employers. In short, George White felt on top of the world in Siam.

Then his old accomplice Phaulkon arrived in the wake of Burnaby, whose reputation for deriving his income from two sources only made the situation more intriguing. The cronies were joined soon after by Samuel White, the younger brother of George. A complicated ballet with many entrées soon started between Mergui, Masulipatam, and Ayutthaya, between the bureaux of the EIC in Madras and those of the *Phra Khlang* Chao Phraya Kosathibodi.

What we know about the Siamese operations of the White brothers also applies to those of Phaulkon, who established the basis of his fortune at the end of the 1670s. The export of elephants from Mergui to Masulipatam on the Coromandel Coast was particularly profitable. The King of Golconda was implicated in several wars with his neighbours, and Siamese elephants trained for battle—the tanks of the period—were in great demand. But this trade was not without its dangers. Tough vessels with a specially arranged flat bottom, like the *Derea Dowlat* which Samuel White commanded, took on between fourteen and twenty-six more or less drugged pachyderms, plus seventy banana trees per animal for a voyage of between sixteen and twenty days. The captains needed to be particularly vigilant, as it was essential that the elephants were not panicky, for they could destroy the ship. Once an angry beast had pierced the hull with its tusk, a ship sank in five minutes in the midst of the most unholy din, while the crew jumped into a longboat.

The unfortunate John Struys relates in his *Perillous and most Unhappy Voyages* that in 1650 he was a sailor on an English elephant ship, the *Posthorse*, in the Gulf of Bengal. One day he was going to serve hot soup to his comrades when a mischievous elephant entwined its trunk round his legs and made him stumble. The soup tureen landed on the back of the elephant whose panic-stricken trampling dangerously shook the ship which was only just spared disaster.[28] Perhaps the sailors sang appropriate lullabies in chorus.

The White brothers, Burnaby, and Phaulkon do not seem to have encountered such picturesque difficulties. Their affairs prospered, in spite of two shipwrecks which Phaulkon suffered, according to his Jesuit protagonists. At all events, they did less and less business for their company, and more and more for the king and themselves. Phra Narai and his Siamese *Phra Khlang* were very satisfied, so much so that Richard Burnaby was promoted to be a second class *khunnang* and appointed governor of Mergui at the beginning of the 1680s, and Samuel White became a third class *khunnang* and *shahbandar* (harbour-master) of Mergui and Tenasserim. Everyone was therefore satisfied, except the influential "Moorish" community, comprising Arabs and Persians as well as Muslim Indians. They had controlled important sectors of the Siamese economy for many years, and viewed with a jaundiced eye the joint ventures of the interloping Englishmen and Phra Narai. The death of Aqa Muhammad in 1679 further reduced the role played by the Muslims in the commercial and political life of the realm.

Phaulkon was in his element. And was grasping. His first mishaps and profits made him bold, to such an extent that he had the idea of mounting a most dangerous if very profitable operation: to arm a coastal vessel and sell rice, gunpowder, arms, and other contraband goods to the inhabitants of Singor (Songkhla), then in revolt against the King of Siam. It was during one of these extremely risky journeys that he was shipwrecked on the Malay coast and lost his ship and its cargo. Richard Burnaby, no doubt in order to refloat him, then presented him to the *Phra Khlang* as a very useful interpreter in relations between the minister and the English, and a most gifted man for supervising the complex accounts of the commerce in which the king was involved.

This is the version of the English Catholic, and seems probable.[29] Fr de Bèze for his part relates that "Mestre Ouits" (George White) lent Phaulkon a thousand crowns after this shipwreck "to console him in his misfortune," and that the Greek used the money to buy the good will of the *Phra Khlang* Kosathibodi, seeking but one favour, that he be employed in the service of the King of Siam. The good father justifies this corrupt act of a high official by explaining that providence destined Phaulkon "to be one of the most influential supporters of religion in the Indies."[30] But let us move from the illicit arms trade and bribes to the hagiography embellished by visions. This is the version of the facts according to Fathers Tachard and d'Orléans; it is rather long but most instructive.

> He arrived in the kingdom of Siam with these noble sentiments, and it was clear he remained true to himself by the little wealth he had gained over a rather long period of time. He acquired some all the same after many long years of service, as much as he needed to negotiate on his own account. Tired of being in a subaltern position, he bought a ship and, ever full of courage which never left him, he set off to sea to trade in the neighbouring kingdoms. Two shipwrecks which he suffered at the mouth of the river of Siam would have disheartened anyone else, and a third he subsequently suffered on the Malabar [in fact: Malay] Coast would have brought to despair anyone less resolved than he. He thought he would die, and only retained two thousand crowns of his capital.
>
> Having been thrown on the shore with the remains of his fortune, he was so exhausted that he fell asleep to recover his strength. He himself related several times that at that moment he saw, either in a dream, or else otherwise—for he was never able to unravel if he were awake or asleep—a person with an extraordinary form and an air full of majesty, who, looking on him with a smile, ordered him to return whence he had come. These words, which he heard or imagined he heard, echoed in his head for a long time, and as he lay stretched out at the approach of night, he spent it entirely reflecting on what had happened to him.
>
> He continued his reverie in the morning while walking at the water's edge, when he saw in the distance a man coming towards him with big strides. He had no difficulty in recognizing that it was a traveller who had escaped from a shipwreck like himself. His pale face and clothes still dripping water were the too visible signs for him to have any doubt. The similarity of their fate made both of them impatient to meet and know each other . . . The stranger was an ambassador whom the King of Siam had sent to Persia and who, returning to his country, had been shipwrecked at the same spot where Mr Constance had been beached . . . Of all that he had on board his vessel, the ambassador had only saved himself. Among his feelings of pity that such a sad condition gave rise to in Mr Constance, he had some joy to be able to assist, even in his own

> distress, an unfortunate man . . . He at once offered to bring him back to Siam; the ambassador accepted his offer, and with the two thousand crowns that remained to him, he [Phaulkon] bought a boat, victuals, and clothes for himself and his companion.
>
> Their voyage was successful as they had nothing further to lose; they arrived in Siam without any untoward encounters . . . The Siamese was not ungrateful for the assistance he had received from the Greek. He had no sooner given an account of his mission to the barcalon [*Phra Khlang*] than he spoke of his benefactor, and related to him in detail the obligations he had. He said so many good things about him that this minister, who himself was a well-meaning man and liked honest persons, had the curiosity to meet him. He had no sooner seen him than he was charmed by him, and decided to take him into his service. Then the experience he acquired of his ability in several matters and the probity he found in him made him consider that he was a man who should serve the king.[31]

It is as though one were reading the episode of St Paul on the road to Damascus combined with the parable of the good Samaritan. The English Catholic is particularly caustic:

> The ambassador from Persia he brought back to Siam and the vision he had are visions of Fr Tachard himself. What was this Siamese ambassador returning from Persia doing on the Malay coast? If a Siamese ambassador had gone to Persia, he would have embarked at Mergui, and would have returned that way, without ever approaching, either close to or from afar, the place where Mr Constance lost his ship. But it was necessary to link matters, to have Mr Constance knowing the barcalon and the king . . . This artifice is rather gross for people who know a little about such matters.[32]

The anonymous *Remarques sur l'histoire de M. Constance composée par le P. d'Orléans Jesuite* (Remarks on the history of Mr Constance written by Fr d'Orléans, Jesuit) relates that

> Mr Constance, on reading that in the *Relation* of Fr Tachard, said he had never been on the Malay coast. "It's all the same," Fr Tachard told him. The same Mr Constance, asking Fr Tachard for his *Relation*, said to him: "Where are your lies?" It was Mr Vincent who was present who related this to me.[33]

Fr de Bèze, though a Jesuit, had the good taste not to mention any vision. He differs markedly from the account of his two colleagues by explaining that it was Phaulkon himself who was sent by the *Phra Khlang* on an essentially commercial mission to Persia, which the Greek accomplished to the satisfaction of everyone, especially of the minister, "who was heavily involved in the merchandise."[34] It was after this first successful mission that the Greek was presented to Phra Narai and began to take the management of crown affairs into his hands.

But in the end, what does it matter? We shall examine later the reasons for Fr Tachard wishing to create a devotee and martyr out of Phaulkon. This person never existed, and in no ways resembles the devilishly clever adventurer we have seen worming his way into the Siamese court. "It's all the same," the good Father would have said, muttering in his beard; the only thing that mattered was the usefulness of Phaulkon in the dangerous game of poker which the Society of Jesus was playing in Siam.

The little Greek had arrived where he was to fulfil his destiny. Phra Narai had just discovered an indispensable man who would cross the most famous reign in Siamese history like a comet. The falcon had landed.

PART THREE
THE FIRST EMBASSIES

CHAPTER TWELVE

THE DRAMA OF THE FIRST SIAMESE EMBASSY (1680–1681)

ANDRÉ DESLANDES VISITS THE SIAMESE COURT

THE EXCELLENT relations between the MEP and the CIO are easy to explain. The conquest of souls and markets in South-East Asia depended on the same infrastructure: the financial means provided by the home country, French vessels transporting missionaries and merchandise, and the support of Louis XIV which facilitated everything. The return of peace enabled the CIO, based in Surat, to renew its activities in the seas of the Indies, and above all to extend trade from one part of Asia to another, that is, finding new trading posts for inter-Asian commerce.

François Baron, the CIO's director-general in Asia, allowed himself to be easily convinced by Mgr Laneau and decided to send to Ayutthaya the young trader André Deslandes-Boureau (the future son-in-law of François Martin, who directed the CIO's activities in Pondichéry). He was charged with evaluating the situation on the spot, then with organizing the journey of the ambassadors whom the king wished to send to France. Deslandes himself noted in a detailed report of his mission that "one thing could check the King of Siam from sending the embassy: that was not having appropriate persons to take a ship to France, since they have the habit of following the coasts, where little knowledge of the science of piloting was needed."[1]

Deslandes left Surat on 2 May 1680 on the *Vautour*, a supply ship of six hundred tons. The thirty-first it was at Pondichéry, in possession of a modest sum of money with which François Martin bought goods destined for Siam. His delight in seeing commercial activities resume was so great that he ordered the hymn of thanks to God, the *Te Deum*, be sung in the small chapel of his colony.

Martin had left the besieged São Tomé with a hundred inessential persons in January 1674. After having done everything he could to provide food and assist the stronghold, he learnt with a heavy heart that La Haye had capitulated in September the same year. "This," he wrote bitterly, "was the success of the squadron which His Majesty sent to the Indies, and from which one could assuredly expect something more if we had managed our advantages better."[2]

During the almost complete interruption of the CIO's activities because of the Franco-Dutch war, Martin had laid the foundations of Pondichéry's prosperity with the help of some sixty Frenchmen who had escaped from São Tomé. He understood that this favourably located port with a roadstead that sheltered it from the monsoon had a future. With admirable perseverance, he had persuaded the natives to trade, had established cloth factories, allocated land to his colonizers, built houses and shops "a musket-shot from the sea" in an enclosure defended by two bastions sporting cannons, constructed vessels, and formed a small army to defend the new colony. After two years, he could write to the directors in Surat that he was able to send them every year cloth worth more than a million livres.[3]

Martin had merchandise destined for Siam loaded on the *Vautour*, which set sail for Ayutthaya on 16 June 1680. The same day the *Vierge* left for Tenasserim, carrying other goods (mostly fabrics). The *Vautour* arrived at the bar of Siam on 3 September; it was the first time a ship of the CIO showed the French flag at the mouth of the Chao Phraya. Deslandes wrote that the court at Ayutthaya "was moved" on receiving the news. According to another unpublished account, "the whole court showed much joy, and the king thought that this event would facilitate an embassy to France."[4] André Deslandes was charged with letters and presents sent by Baron in the name of the CIO to Phra Narai and the *Phra Khlang*, which gave his prospecting mission the appearance of an embassy.

The *Vautour* dropped anchor in the estuary. Its captain Cornuel then sent word to the king asking if he thought it proper that his vessel should salute the fort at Bangkok when passing it, in the European manner. The governor of the fort, a Turk, received the order to return the salute, and the French ship sailed up the Chao Phraya, proudly flying the fleur-de-lis flag. Siam having no special flag (later the white elephant on a crimson background would be used), the governor raised the Dutch flag. Cornuel, who did not fool around when the honour of his country was at stake, informed the governor through an intermediary that the Dutch flag had to be lowered and any other substituted. The governor raised a red flag and repaired his gaffe by ordering a round of fifty cannon shots "and more, without being stingy." Another witness even speaks of "more than one hundred and fifty shots."[5] These resounding honours made a few Portuguese grit their teeth. For good measure, "this governor then requested the captain to come and eat at the fort; he was well entertained there. On leaving fifteen rounds of cannon were fired."[6] In short, everything went off very well.

Mgr Laneau, who prepared the ceremonial with the *Phra Khlang* Kosathibodi, would have liked Deslandes to present to Phra Narai himself the letter and presents from Baron, but Siamese protocol absolutely forbade it. For three weeks the matter was discussed, and Deslandes, who did not have time to waste, finally resigned himself to being received by the *Phra Khlang*.

On the appointed day at the beginning of October, three *khunnang* came for Deslandes and his travelling companions at Mgr Laneau's residence, where they were being put up. The French were taken in ceremonial barges to the residence of the Chao Phraya Kosathibodi. The letter and presents were carried before them with great signs of respect. In addition to Deslandes and Cornuel, the delegation was composed of Claude Gayme of the MEP, who was to serve as interpreter, and some twenty French soldiers whose polished arms shone in the sun. The *Phra Khlang* was surrounded by a number of *khunnang* and senior monks. After the reading and translation of the letter to the king and the presentation of the gifts (two chandeliers and two crystal girandoles), the conversation mainly turned on the French court. Deslandes replied to the minister's questions with so much assurance and wit that he drew praise from the assembled company; it could be heard said that "this young man has been well brought up."

The audience over, the *Phra Khlang* took the gifts to the king, who "appreciated them more than any other presents he customarily received," since well-wrought crystal was almost unknown in Siam. Phra Narai decided "to show favour to Deslandes above all other nations," and to show himself to the French delegation; it seems it was Mgr Laneau who obtained this favour. "He went out one day with a guard of more than six hundred soldiers and came into a great courtyard where Deslandes and Cornuel were waiting for him seated on a carpet. He had a conversation with them, and on withdrawing gave each of them a present of a Persian brocaded jacket."[7]

Deslandes observed the king closely. We have already given the physical portrait he described on this occasion. The clothes, arms, and jewels of Phra Narai are detailed with remarkable precision.

> His dress comprised a jacket of red Persian satin, sprinkled with small gold flowers, sleeves like a cassock without buttonholes, and above a jacket made of material similar to very fine and clear Bengal cloth, with lace-like decoration at the seams. A kris with a golden handle covered with precious stones was on his left side; a richly decorated Japanese sabre was on his knees, and his fingers were half-covered with rings and jewels of all sorts of colours, and very big.[8]

Here can be seen the sharp eye of a trader curious about the luxury with which an oriental potentate surrounds himself.

"MAY OUR AMBASSADORS COME AND GO WITHOUT FAIL"

Preparations for the Siamese embassy were going ahead well. Baron had ordered the captain of the *Vautour* to sail without delay to Bantam where it would meet the *Soleil d'Orient* which was to take the ambassadors to France. Meanwhile as the king had gone to Lopburi, Mgr Laneau went there to join him, with Claude Gayme who was to accompany the Siamese ambassadors. They had a long private conversation with the king, without interpreters, since the two missionaries both spoke court Siamese fluently. "The Bishop of Metellopolis was placed facing the monarch on a small carpet brocaded in gold. The prime minister was on his right, prostrate in the manner of the country on a silk carpet, and Fr Gayme was at his left."[9] The conversation first dealt with questions of astronomy, geography, and mathematics "about which the king sought elucidation." Mgr Laneau had compiled treatises in Siamese on these subjects; Phra Narai had carefully read them and was now asking numerous questions which his reading had prompted. "Three mandarins wrote down all these discourses; they came close to being chastised for not being able to follow the whole conversation."[10] The king did not cease to impress his visitors with his mental agility and curiosity.

They then spoke of kingdoms and European monarchs, "the king showing his surprise that, with so many kings and princes who ruled in Europe, he only heard speak of that of the French. That, he added, increased his desire to send him ambassadors, "in spite of all the difficulties which the Moors, who are powerful at court, and some other envious persons of different nationalities, raised to divert him from this plan."[11] The Moors and the Brahmin astrologers who resided at court had indeed made considerable efforts at dissuasion, predicting the worst possible misfortune to every Siamese who would board a *farang* vessel.[12] But Phra Narai did not allow himself to be deflected and took all necessary measures with the French ecclesiastics. It seems though that the embassy he was to send to Persia in 1681 was intended to win round those who had been ill-disposed to the embassy to France.

Fr Gayme was charged with the selection of presents to be sent to the French court. Several gold and silver objects were shown to him, "but he replied it would be difficult to send finer ones than were already to be found in the king's cabinets . . . which infinitely surpass in number and perfection all the works of the Orient," and selected Chinese and Japanese lacquer furniture. The king's officials urged him to take more, but he declined, saying "none of these works was lacking in France, and more beautiful ones too."[13] Claude Gayme was perhaps an excellent ecclesiastic who spoke Siamese well, but he was for sure a wretched diplomat.

Phra Narai, who one might expect to be somewhat offended, then decided to add to these lacquer pieces things which they certainly did not have in France, and "sent everywhere for a small rhinoceros to send, but did not find any." He then had the charming idea of surprising the French king by sending two young elephants, male and female, without thinking of the enormous quantities of food which would have to be taken for such a long journey, and that the beasts, which would have been fully grown by the time they reached France, ran the risk of demolishing the vessel transporting them. But it is intentions that count.

The choice of ambassadors posed fewer problems. The king nominated as first ambassador an old hand of sixty-two years, Phraya Phiphat Kosa, who had already led three embassies to China, and who was thus well placed to compare the court of the Most Christian King with that of the Son of Heaven. The other ambassadors were Luang Si Wisan and Khun Nakhon Wichai.[14] "It is to be presumed," Deslandes wrote, "that these ambassadors would be obliged to repeat what the Queen of Sheba said: 'I have seen something grander than I have heard said of Solomon.'"[15]

Lastly, it was necessary to think of the composition of the letters from Phra Narai to the pope and the French king. The letter to Louis XIV looked fine:

> Letter of the royal and remarkable embassy from the Great King of the Kingdom of Ayutthaya, which he sends to you, O Very Great King and Most Powerful Lord of the Kingdoms of France and Navarre, of supereminent rank, whose brilliance and splendour shine like the sun . . . The report and renown of your victories has spread throughout all nations in the universe . . . We send presents to you, O Very Great King, so that between us there might be a true understanding, a perfect union and friendship, and that this friendship might be solid and inviolable in times to come . . . Moreover, we beseech you, O Very Great and Powerful King, to send us your ambassadors, and that our ambassadors may come and go without fail, requesting you that our friendship be firm and inviolable for ever. And I entreat the all-powerful God to keep you in every kind of prosperity. . .

The title of Very Great King given to Louis XIV was that which the King of Siam used when he addressed the Emperor of China. The letter to "the holy pope, who is the first and father of all the Christians"[16] was written in the same style.

These letters were translated into French by Mgr Laneau. An unpublished account says, "One can still see the style of the old kings of the East. They are very elegantly written, and although the Bishop of Metellopolis took trouble to make a faithful translation, it was not possible for him to retain all their elegance."[17] One could have observed that the letters were not signed; the names of the kings of Ayutthaya, held to be sacred and secret, were only revealed after their deaths.

The missionaries took advantage of the departure, at the end of November, of an English vessel to send letters to Europe, in which they insisted on as sumptuous a reception as possible for the Siamese ambassadors. Mgr Laneau requested the Archbishop of Paris to advise the court of the imminent departure of the embassy, mentioning that "the good reception which this king expects, given the magnificence of our great monarch, will be made better known in all these countries since here is the only place where all the Orientals gather in great number, and remain in liberty."[18] Fr Gayme for his part reassured the directors of the MEP seminary: "As they are people from another world, you will have no trouble in ensuring that the king will settle their expenses. These will not be great; they are not people to regale themselves. . . . The news of this embassy will be spread throughout the world . . . it will not fail to appear in the gazettes."[19] He explains in another letter that, "as the ambassadors which this monarch sends to China and to the Great Mogul are paid as soon as they enter the realms of these monarchs, it would be appropriate for the grandeur of the king that he order they be treated no less favourably on arriving in France."[20]

The two royal missives, engraved on very thin sheets of gold forty-five by twenty centimetres, were rolled up and placed in golden (for Louis XIV) or sandalwood (for the pope) cases. Translations, written on paper, were included with the originals. The two cases were then placed in caskets covered with gold brocade—violet for the pope, and red for Louis XIV "to mark his victories." The royal astrologers set about making complicated calculations and designated 1 December 1680 as the most auspicious day to carry the two letters on board the *Vautour* in the presence of the ambassadors, the *Phra Khlang*, and the *khunnang*, who redoubled their prostrations to the sound of trumpets. The two caskets were ceremonially received on board ship, laid on a rich Persian carpet placed under a canopy on the highest point of the stern, and illuminated each night by numerous torches. During the three weeks the *Vautour* remained at anchor in the Chao Phraya, "all the vessels which passed in front of the royal missives had orders to salute them, their sails furled; the oarsmen of the galleys had to row standing with their heads bowed."[21]

The fifty cases of presents destined for Louis XIV, Queen Maria-Theresa, the Dauphin, the king's brother the Duke of Orléans, Colbert and his right-hand man Louis Berryer, were put on board during December, the most cumbersome—the baby elephants—last. The ambassadors had learnt "with surprise and as though it were something entirely new" that they would have to pay their respects to the queen. This was a profoundly shocking perspective for an oriental courtier who did not have the right to raise his eyes to the wives or concubines of his sovereign, of whatever rank they might be.

A LONG STOPOVER AT BANTAM

The *Vautour* set sail on 24 December and arrived in seventeen days, "the fastest which could be done," in Bantam on the western tip of Java. François Caron had established the French godown on this strategic location near the Sunda Strait in 1671. This rapid and successful journey put the lie to the disturbing prophecies of the Siamese court astrologers. The ambassadors and their suite only landed four days later, 14 January 1681, when the house being prepared for them was ready. Mr de Guilhem, the head of the French godown "having prepared as best as he was able a house belonging to the godown, and placed coloured hangings on the walls and covered the floor with big carpets, went himself, with as many Frenchmen as he could muster, to take the ambassadors from their ship. They left with their letters to the sound of French and English cannon, with several ceremonial umbrellas. He entertained them that day to his best."[22] The ambassadors thanked him for his civilities, telling him they would remember this in "the right time and place."

A letter which Guilhem sent to the directors of the CIO on 29 January gives an idea of the importance of the ambassadors' retinue and baggage:

> The three ambassadors of the King of Siam are bringing many presents . . . All these presents consist of Japanese desks, sideboards and cabinets, chests, tables and curious boxes, Japanese dressing gowns, silk items, and gold and silver vases, Chinese screens of different sizes and many other pieces . . . All this takes up a great deal of space on the ship, in addition to two young elephants, one male, one female. The son of the first ambassador is in the suite of this embassy with twenty attendants. A missionary [Claude Gayme] and a young priest [Emmanuel Picaredo] accompany the ambassadors. So much food for all this crowd who bring their stews with them, likewise the provisions needed for the two elephants and the quantity of water they need, demand a ship well supplied and well equipped with men and victuals. All this is lacking on the *Vautour*.[23]

It was clear that with its six hundred tons, the *Vautour* was not very suitable to transport to France the ambassadors and their retinue, their presents, and their elephants. The *Soleil d'Orient*, the pride of the company, was of one thousand tons burden and because of this better suited for the journey. Built at the beginning of the 1670s, it had made its maiden voyage to Asia from March 1672 to July 1674. It was the first of the company's vessels to return to Surat after the interruption in 1677–1678 caused by the Franco-Dutch war. It had set sail on 1 February 1679 from Port-Louis and remained in the seas of the Indies, mostly plying between Surat and Bantam. A little before the arrival of the *Vautour*, the *Soleil d'Orient* had been careened. On 17 March Baron sent it to take on board the ambassadors and transport them to France. It dropped anchor in the Bantam roadstead on 24 June.

One month later, Gayme wrote from Bantam to the directors of the seminary of the MEP:

> The *Soleil d'Orient* having arrived here from Surat on St John's Day to go to France, we shall depart at the end of August . . . and we shall be able to arrive in France at the end of March. The third ambassador is seriously ill; he is beginning to suffer from paralysis. I am taking special care to have him treated.[24]

Were the sinister predictions of the astrologers about to be realized after all?

THE LAST VOYAGE OF THE *SOLEIL D'ORIENT*

The ship only weighed anchor, as Gayme had foreseen, at the end of August 1681; it was taking goods worth more than a million crowns for the CIO. After waiting for nearly eight months, the ambassadors, burdened by the royal presents, and the priestly interpreters, were happy to be able to begin the journey to France. One wonders why two months had to pass between the arrival of the ship at Bantam and its departure. Did the troublesome state of health of the third ambassador, Khun Nakhon Wichai, cause the delay? Or were they simply waiting for the end of the summer monsoon? The delay is all the more inexplicable as the safest period for rounding the Cape of Good Hope began in September, at the beginning of spring in the southern hemisphere, and the ship, if it had left at the beginning of July, could still have hoped to reach the Cape at the right moment.

It would be interesting to know if, in spite of the non-disclosure of Guilhem, the two elephants were put on board. Indeed, one would like to know everything about this voyage, but we know almost nothing. The *Soleil d'Orient* made a stopover at Mauritius in November to unload some goods and take on victuals and fresh water. It then set sail for Fort Dauphin and the Cape but was never seen again by anyone. It vanished into the sea with all hands, goods, and elephants in December 1681 or January 1682, according to some overtaken by a furious storm off the coasts of Madagascar or near the Cape, or according to others the victim of an attack by Dutch pirates in southern waters.[25]

The *Mercure Galant* was to publish in July 1686 two mutually concordant accounts extracted from a letter from Surat dated 14 November 1685:

> A man named Croizier, son of a merchant from Morlaix, who had gone to the Indies on Mr du Hautmesnil's ship called the *Coche*, left this vessel to embark on an English bottom called the *Bristol*, which left Surat at the end of last January to go to Europe. The young man said that this vessel, having met with bad weather, had been obliged to put into port on the island of Madagascar, in the bay of Fort Dauphin . . . They learnt from some blacks, among others one called Jean, who had formerly been the servant of Mr de Saint-Martin and who speaks French very well, that a few years back the ship the *Soleil d'Orient* had come into the bay of Fort Dauphin in a very bad condition and shipping a lot of water. This person gave them the names of the ship's chief officers, and told them that there were on board ambassadors from the King of Siam; that these officers had made peace with the blacks, and after having repaired their vessel and taken on victuals, had left Fort Dauphin, and four or five leagues from there had been overtaken by a storm which had sent the vessel to the bottom of the ocean, without anyone being saved . . . If I were to advance my opinion on this, I think that the vessel, on leaving Mascarene [Mauritius], had wanted to pass the Cape of Good Hope, was overcome by the storm, and a broken mast or some leak had made it necessary to seek the nearest land it could, where it was lost in the strait on the side of Madagascar [the Mozambique Channel], which would have allowed most of the men in the crew to reach land.

> It is true that one has to fear that if they landed on the coast of Fort Dauphin, the inhabitants, who are our mortal enemies, might have murdered them . . .
>
> This information relates quite closely to what I have heard said to Mr de Hautmesnil, that when he came into the Indies in 1683 on the *Heureuse*, he had met in the Mozambique Channel an English vessel which was coming from Mazelages, a place to the north of Madagascar where one goes to trade with the blacks, and the captain of this vessel, who was French, had shouted to them in passing that he had been told that a French ship carrying sixty cannons had been sunk on the coasts of that island. The weather did not allow them to obtain further details.[26]

Whatever the case, the astrologers had the last word: *farang* ships did not bring good fortune to the Siamese.

It was only two years later, in 1683, that the news of this shipwreck reached the Siamese court. On 13 September, Mgr Laneau received letters from Paris via a vessel which had come direct from London informing him that at the beginning of 1683 the *Soleil d'Orient* had still not arrived in France, that not the least news of it had been received, and one had to fear for the worst. Extremely put out, the Bishop of Metellopolis "greatly feared to pass this news to the sovereign." One can understand why. But after considering the matter and informing Phra Narai of "this untoward news, instead of causing any ill effects in the mind of this monarch, [it] only served to obtain more certain token of the desire he had to entertain a close friendship with His Most Christian Majesty." The king went so far as to say that, "even if the ambassadors had been shipwrecked, as was feared, he still desired, notwithstanding that, to maintain an inviolable friendship with the King of France."[27] Martin notes in his memoirs that Phra Narai "knew that sea voyages were full of risks and are not always successful . . . [and] that even if an accident had befallen his people, he would send a second embassy and would not cease to do so."[28] The drama of the *Soleil d'Orient* was not therefore to hinder Franco-Siamese relations, in spite of the king's comment on learning of the loss of the presents sent to Europe, "that the royal treasury could never supply similar ones."[29]

Mgr Laneau wrote at the beginning of 1684 to the directors of the seminary of the MEP:

> All the displeasure the king has shown at the loss of his ambassadors and his presents has been to observe that the great desire he has to learn that his ambassadors had arrived in France has not been accomplished. He resolved at the same time to send others, protesting that he would do so until some of them arrived safely.[30]

The chagrin of the Bishop of Metellopolis was clearly greater than the king's. When in 1698 Laneau on his deathbed drew up a list of his accomplishments for the Foreign Missions in Siam and dictated a moving letter in Latin to the cardinals of the Propaganda, he was to write:

> Most Eminent Fathers, fortified by the last sacraments of our Holy Mother the Church, feeling death close at hand and ready to give my soul to God and the account of my stewardship, having already written so many letters to Your Eminences, I write to add this final missive to express my last feelings and the profound sadness which is in my heart . . . Some will go so far as to say that the Siamese embassies in Europe have provided the occasion to spread sinister suspicions about me. If only it had pleased God that the first one—that which was shipwrecked—had arrived, or that Your Eminences could have learned the truth from those who might have survived . . . But extreme weakness prevents me from writing further.[31]

In the meantime, Mgr Laneau had occasion to observe the disastrous consequences of the loss of the first embassy. The initiative for the important embassies which were to come was to be highjacked by the Jesuits, and the bishops of the Foreign Missions were henceforth condemned to watch impotently a game of diplomatic and colonial poker where others held the cards which were to decide the outcome. If the *Soleil d'Orient* had arrived safely, the rest of this book would have been different, and its issue undoubtedly less dramatic.

CHAPTER THIRTEEN

BETWEEN TWO EMBASSIES (1682–1684)

"PERFECT LOVE AND INVIOLABLE FRIENDSHIP"

ANDRÉ DESLANDES was not content with organizing the voyage to Bantam of the ambassadors, their numerous retinue, fifty crates of presents, and two baby elephants. In conformity with his instructions, he had obtained from the king complete freedom for French trade. He next noted on the spot opportunities for European and Asian goods in which the CIO traded, and Siamese products to export to other Asian countries or to France.

A close study of the kingdom's resources brought him to the conclusion that Siam had almost no goods to export, but one could readily obtain there at advantageous prices products from China and Japan, then closed to European trade. "It was therefore above all as an entrepot of Far Eastern trade that the godown could be very useful."[1] The only Siamese product likely to interest France was pepper. Deslandes was able to persuade the *Phra Khlang* to develop the planting of the pepper vine, and to assign the harvest to the company for a very moderate price. François Martin was to note in his *Mémoires* of March 1685 that thirteen thousand men were employed in growing pepper, and each man was in charge of two hundred plants.[2]

The *Phra Khlang* at the end of 1680 sent a letter and presents to François Baron in Surat, confirming the benevolence of the king in regard to the CIO. He invited the company furthermore to "foresee the means which are necessary so that between him [Baron] and me there could be perfect love and inviolable friendship in the future."[3] It is evident that Deslandes had worked hard. The company could confidently count on the future of its Siamese godown so long as ships plied regularly between Surat, Pondichéry, and Siamese ports. These were the "necessary means" mentioned in the letter of the *Phra Khlang*. But it can be seen, from reading Deslandes's letters to his superiors, he had nothing left to do, since the *Vautour* was not followed by other CIO merchant ships.

He even let it be understood that Phra Narai, displeased with the limited transactions of the CIO, was drawing closer to the Dutch and the English, who were better established and more actively trading, either for the company which employed them or on their own account. The Dutch, closely supervised from Batavia, belonged either willingly or by force to the first category. The English, specialists in interloping trade in spite of the control of Madras, gaily fleeced their company which once again seriously considered withdrawing from Siam after the fire (probably criminal) at the EIC godown in Ayutthaya in December 1682. Deslandes was therefore witness to the tensions and intrigues which perturbed the trading nations in Ayutthaya, and the relations they had with the *Phra Khlang* Kosathibodi. While being the official link between the king and the groups of merchants trading in Siam, he controlled the commercial activities of the Siamese crown without overlooking his own, which were considerable. Deslandes—his letters prove it—did not understand much of the complicated dance which was going on between the department of the *Khlang* and the Dutch and English godowns. But he was able to observe the beginnings of the meteoric career of Constantine Phaulkon, the "little Greek" whose background we have given earlier.

THE IRRESISTIBLE RISE OF CONSTANTINE PHAULKON

Phaulkon had arrived in Siam in September 1678 in the company of his superior and future associate, Richard Burnaby. Although an employee of the EIC, he immediately launched into high risk and high profit interloping activities, like supplying arms to the Songkhla rebels. Soon after the shipwreck which inspired the hagiographic flights of imagination of Fathers Tachard and d'Orléans, he entered the service of the *Phra Khlang* "probably in late 1679."[4] His experience of commerce within the Indies and the internal workings of the EIC, from which he had separated, made him a man both well informed and independent. His knowledge of Portuguese, Malay, and Siamese, to which he would soon add court Siamese with its hieratic Khmer formulae and florid circumlocutions, considerably increased his usefulness.

The *Letter of an English Catholic,* already quoted in chapter 11, explains that Phaulkon was "loaned" by his associates or accomplices, Richard Burnaby and George White, to the *Phra Khlang* since they hoped "to have a man of their own who was in the service of the king, and who would act as an intermediary on their behalf if the need arose." It was with the money they advanced that he "succeeded through the Barcalon [*Phra Khlang*] in becoming *caluan* [*kha luang*], a servant of the king, and the position the Barcalon gave him was in his *gudans* [godowns], the king's stores, and concerned commerce, since the king was the biggest merchant in his realm."[5]

The presence of this enterprising, ambitious, and extremely clever European in the control post of external commerce troubled the powerful faction of "Moors," Muslim Persians or Indians, because they traditionally controlled the king's affairs which they arranged with a generous cut. Phaulkon was soon in a position to reveal their malversations and then prove that the crown, far from owing them reimbursements which they claimed when presenting their confused accounts, was in a position to claim from them the considerable sum of sixty thousand crowns.[6]

The *Phra Khlang* was involved over many years in merciless rivalry with the Moors, who were unassailable as long as their leader, Aqa Muhammad, retained the king's complete confidence. His death in 1679 exposed them to the grudge of Kosathibodi, who used the Greek as a heaven-sent instrument of vengeance. He gave Phaulkon in 1680 the conduct of a commercial rather than diplomatic mission to Shah Sulaiman's court in Isfahan.

Fr de Bèze explains:

> The custom prevails in this East Indies whereby missions are exchanged between rulers of diverse states from time to time with the object of fostering trade rather than to maintain political relations. The King of Siam often received such missions from Persia and reciprocated them.[7]

These missions were traditionally given to the Moors who advanced to the king and the *Phra Khlang* the money necessary to send to Persia a merchant vessel loaded with Siamese products, to be reimbursed only on its return from the profits from the merchandise. One needed commercial flair, nautical experience, and financial reserves to accomplish such a mission successfully.

Bèze went on to add:

> Constans accepted the undertaking and, with the help of his friends, carried it through by the exercise of his own dexterity in the teeth of strong opposition by influential Moors. Assuming charge of the envoys, Constans conducted the business entrusted to him with such success that the profit realized on the goods exported was equal to twice that obtained when the Moors where in charge. The reason for this was that the successful conduct of the king's business was Constans' aim rather than his personal share in the profits. The Barcalon had a considerable stake in the business and was unspeakably delighted with the result; he so lauded Constans' services in the hearing of the king that His Majesty expressed a wish to see the Greek.[8]

Phra Narai was literally charmed from the first conversation he had with Phaulkon, by his insinuating wit, his worldly wisdom, his encyclopedic knowledge. The portrait which the Jesuit Claude de Bèze draws of his personality explains the royal infatuation:

> He possessed every quality required for such as conquest, being of a lively temperament with the most diverse talents. With but little schooling he was yet acquainted with all that a man of parts should know; he had learned no end of things from the men of breeding he had encountered and he had the wit to make the most of it. The ease with which he discoursed upon almost any learned subject was a marvel to those most intimate with him. Few better instances can exist of the height to which compelling genius can aspire unaided by any technical knowledge. Joined to all this was the winning manner by means of which Constans would worm his way towards any whom he sought to convince. Moreover his hot and inflammable temper was so well under control that, when it suited him, he might be taken for a model of cool self-possession. The king sent for him frequently . . .[9]

A less flattering portrait, probably drawn by the Abbé Artus de Lionne, survives in the archives of the MEP:

> A mind which wants to dominate everything, bold, enterprising, generous in making a show of spending, proud, irascible, changeable, on whom one could rely for nothing; inventing a thousand things and making them out to be true, with a thousand magnificent incidents; promising everything and holding to nothing; only concerned with himself . . . of a haughty and insupportable humour to everyone . . . who was supple when he counted for little, but who now takes on grand airs which turn everyone against him.[10]

The Phaulkon of the Jesuits is painted in more luminous colours than the person described by the gentlemen of the Foreign Missions after the first infatuating moment had passed. His name begins to appear in their letters and accounts from 1682; a reference going back to February 1674 is a mistake on the part of Adrien Launay, editor of two volumes of extracts from the archives of the MEP.[11]

The subsequent favour of the Greek was not just due to his lively and instructive conversation, but also to his practical talents. According to the *Phra Ratcha Phongsawadan* (royal chronicles), he first caught the attention of the king by devising an ingenious way of taking a newly constructed crown junk out of the graving-dock. The English Catholic attributes to him the invention of a mechanism capable of raising a heavy beam to buttress the high pyramidical pyre erected for the cremation of the body of Si Chulalok, the half-sister and queen of Phra Narai, who died in 1680 or 1681.[12] The favour "Monsieur Constance" enjoyed was almost instantaneous. Given a title from 1680, Luang Ritthi Kamhaeng, he would soon be raised to the rank of *Phra*, and then to *Phraya (Ok-ya)* and known as Okya Wichayen.[13]

André Deslandes mentions Phaulkon in a letter to François Baron dated December 1682.

> This gentleman has a lively, active, and penetrating mind, which has caused him to rise so high in favour in the two years since he has been in the king's service that he is now called in jest the second Barcalon. He undertakes more trading than all the individual merchants put together, goes twice a day to the king's audience, and the monarch is pleased with his conversation and is curious, and often retains this mandarin for two

> or three hours together. You can judge the usefulness friendship with such a person could be for us . . . I have struck a very close relationship with him, and I have also helped to include him in the service of Messeigneurs [Laneau and Pallu], in such a way that they do nothing and ask for nothing except on his advice and through his means.[14]

This testimony, confirmed by the English Catholic,[15] goes directly to the crucial problem of the relations between Phaulkon and Catholic France.

"SCUM, LISTEN TO THAT!"

The coming together of Phaulkon, the French, and Roman Catholicism occurred in 1682. One of the major topics of the Greek's interminable conversations with Phra Narai was France, where he had never set foot. The *Phongsawadan* simplifies things by saying that Phaulkon, by his rapturous descriptions of Louis XIV, his victories, and his preeminence in relation to other European rulers, inspired the king to exchange ambassadors with him, for the French bishops had sung his praises for many years.

Fr de Bèze's testimony goes in the same direction, but with a few nuances:

> These discourses gave rise to the marked friendliness and admiration which King Narai conceived and maintained to the end for His Most Christian Majesty . . . It was the time when the Indies were resounding with tidings of French victory over a league of mighty monarchs in Europe and Constans entertained the king with details of it: Constans had no particular affection for France at that period; he felt confident however that naught would accord better with the king's martial taste than to hear tell of actions which had won world-wide admiration for the victorious hero whose example the king minded to follow. . . [16]

This indicates that Phaulkon's Francophilia was simply pure opportunism. Having broken his links with the EIC, which he had cynically robbed and which did not cease to claim compensation from him, and for long very hostile to the Dutch, he sought European allies against the increasing jealousy of the Siamese *khunnang*, irritated by the rise of this *farang* with unscrupulous ambition. The Portuguese presence in Asia was only a shadow of its former self in the sixteenth century. Phaulkon therefore had hardly any choice in courting France, represented in Siam by missionaries for twenty years, and by the recently established godown of the CIO.

He had very quickly understood that he had to share the religion of His Most Christian Majesty. His shift from Anglicanism to the bosom of the Roman Catholic Church, into which he had been born, was therefore necessary. This decision was taken at the beginning of 1682 and is perfectly comprehensible, but it is difficult to explain why Phaulkon, instead of turning to the French bishops with whom he had excellent relations, chose to abjure his heresy at the hands of the Jesuits. The role they played in Siam was somewhat effaced, especially since they had to submit to the authority of the vicars-apostolic in October 1681. But Phaulkon was certainly aware of Jesuit influence at the French court, and the powerful credit of Fr de La Chaize, the king's confessor from 1675.

The honour for the "conversion" of Phaulkon was to go to two Jesuits born in French Flanders, Fathers Jean-Baptiste Maldonado and Antoine Thomas. Fr Tachard relates that Phaulkon had embraced Protestantism in his youth under English influence, but "since he had had some discussions with Fathers Thomas and Maldonado of our Society, for which he has always had much sympathy, and recognizing himself the false faith which he had been made to follow, he abandoned it when he was fully convinced."[17]

In reality, things did not occur so simply. Seeing his fortune well established through the favour he enjoyed with the king, and being close to thirty-five years old, Phaulkon wanted to find a wife. His eyes fell on a pretty part-Portuguese and part-Japanese woman named Maria Guyomar de Pinha, or "Marie Guimard" to the French. She was then sixteen years old. Her parents were called Master Phanick and Ursula Yamada; her grandmother claimed to be the granddaughter of the first Japanese baptized by St Francis Xavier near Kagoshima in 1549.[18] Fr d'Orléans speaks of Phaulkon's fiancée as a "young Japanese, of note because of the nobility of her family and still more because of the blood of martyrs from which she had the honour to descend."[19]

But one does not marry a young lady of such irreproachable pedigree without embracing her religion, especially if your future father-in-law invites you to do so in pressing terms. Master Phanick, who "had an inconceivable attachment to his religion which he preferred above all worldly goods," declared to Phaulkon without beating about the bush: "The maiden is a pauper compared with you, but nevertheless I cannot persuade myself to give her hand to you in marriage until the day when I behold you practising the Catholic faith openly and with no reservation."[20] God was to use Phaulkon's passion for Maria Guyomar to save him from heretical darkness.

The detailed and precise testimony of the English Catholic, who was living in Siam, presents quite a different picture. His unpublished account plunges us into a complicated intrigue of Siamese and Burmese concubines, bastard children, promises of marriage given at the same time to two different women (the natural daughter of a Spaniard from Manila called Catona and Maria Guyomar), and the tortuous proceedings of Fathers Thomas and Maldonado who, for five catties (three kilograms of silver), bought the discretion of the dishonoured Catona, who then married a black named Hilary, "who is even now the choirmaster of the Dominican Fathers in the Portuguese camp." These are details which are not invented.

As for the parents of Maria Guyomar, the anonymous English Catholic traces their portrait for Fr d'Orléans:

> The father of this girl is called Fanick. He is black, half-Bengali and half-Japanese, very poor at the beginning, but a man of probity, a good Christian and very intelligent. With these qualities, which are rare in that kind of person, he acquired sufficient worldly goods by the means of the English who always employed him usefully both for themselves and for him. He was only unfortunate in his wife (this is the "virtuous wife" whom you praise . . .), but he bore this affliction generously and in a Christian manner. He withdrew some time to Ligor in order not to be witness to his dishonour, and nearly died there of sickness.

The rest, blurred in implications, suggests that the mother of Maria Guyomar, "the virtuous wife," had children of very different colours, and that one of them, "fairly white," had for father a Jesuit priest recalled by his superiors after this exploit. "Your Society," the Englishman charitably says to Fr d'Orléans, "is too involved—although this was only the error of one person who was in the end recalled—to provide you with the details."[21] The least that could be said is that Phaulkon's mother-in-law, in spite of her great affection for the Society of Jesus, was not a model of virtue, and the family was not as brilliant as Fathers Tachard, d'Orléans, and de Bèze would have us believe. The Englishman protested vigorously against their lies:

> To make of the parents of his wife, people of infamous and scandalous lives, confessors of Jesus Christ and virtuous women, is something never seen before, and it brought our Protestants to exclaim: "Here are the truths of the Roman Church!" and the most moderate among them to say: "Here are the saints and martyrs of the Society of Jesus!"[22]

The efforts of Fr Maldonado had already prepared the return of Phaulkon to the faith of his childhood, but it was Fr Thomas, recently arrived in Ayutthaya, who completed the task. This Jesuit astronomer, who had been in Siam eight months, was to continue his journey in May 1682 to China, where he distinguished himself as successor to Fr Verbiest at the Mathematics Tribunal of Peking. Thomas's biographer indicates that,

> it was only after having had serious discussions with Antoine Thomas, and after a journey they made together to Louvo on the same ship, that Phaulkon took his decision. Their discussions covered the real presence, the authority of the pope, indulgences, purgatory, and the intercession of the saints.[23]

According to de Bèze, a letter from Phaulkon's mother decided his conversion:

> Great was the good lady's delight, so she wrote, to hear of her son's first steps upon the path leading to preferment in Siam, but her gladness had been eclipsed by reports which wrung her heart when she learned that his manner of living was unworthy of any good Catholic.[24]

A few days' retreat and general confession preceded the return of the lost sheep to the Roman fold; on 2 May 1682, Phaulkon pronounced his abjuration and profession of faith to Fr Thomas in the Jesuit church located in the Portuguese camp, in the presence of the Portuguese governor of Macao and some friends. It can be supposed that Master Phanick, on the front row, did not miss a word of the ceremony. "God alone knows," concludes the English Catholic, "the true motive he [Phaulkon] had in taking this righteous step."[25]

A few days later, Phaulkon took, to have and to hold, for better and for worse, Maria Guyomar, henceforth "Madame Phaulkon" or "Madame Constance," before God and mankind. The couple do not seem to have been very happy; the husband had a brusque and imperious nature, and the wife's dominant characteristic does not seem to have been tenderness.

Was Phaulkon vexed with his father-in-law for having made him pay through the nose? The two men certainly got on very badly. According to the English Catholic, Master Phanick followed the career of his son-in-law with concern: "On what he was told in the subsequent years of the fortune of Mr Constance which visibly increased, he replied: 'He will be the cause of the ruin of my family. He is,' he said, 'like these papyrus which grow suddenly, and a breath of wind fells them.'" The father-in-law died in 1686. "Before dying, he many times requested Mr Constance to come and see him in order to be reconciled, but he let him die without ever wishing to give him this satisfaction."

According to the English Catholic, Phaulkon treated Master Phanick as a madman and picked quarrels with those who went to buy things from him. "Among others, one named Mr de La Brosse . . . brother of Mr Deslandes, received a reprimand from him for having bought from his father-in-law some Chinese and Japanese curiosities." This animosity suggests that Phaulkon was not very satisfied with his marriage, nor with the counsels of moderation which Master Phanick proffered. Phanick amassed enough wealth to leave his five children, whatever the colour of their skin, an inheritance of twenty catties (twelve kilos of silver).

No one, however, doubted the Catholic zeal of Phaulkon, not even the priests of the MEP in Ayutthaya, though they had taken no part in his abjuration. Pierre-Joseph Duchesne, in Siam from 1679, left a picturesque account, written six months after the conversion of "Master Constance." He obtained from him the following anecdote:

> The king having condemned to death twenty-eight thieves, Mr Constance summoned his courage to seek their pardon. This was granted, but the king asked if there was as great a number of thieves in Europe. To which the mandarin replied that in truth they were not lacking, but that Jesus Christ had established in the [Catholic] religion a

> means which greatly reduced their number. “What is that?” asked the king. “Confession of one’s sins,” answered the mandarin, “and the obligation of the thieves to hand back . . .” Then the king, turning to his mandarins, said, “Scum, scum, listen to that! I shall send you to the bishop to confess.” Then he asked Master Constance if all could be relied on to confess their sins and make restitution. “In truth,” replied this mandarin, “the devil so takes possession of the hearts of some of them, that they do not; but the greater number do so.” “Oh!” said the king, “if that is so, I fear that my scum will be among the first lot!”[26]

Phra Narai was clearly amusing himself, but one wonders if the *khunnang* present laughed as much, hearing themselves treated as scum and thieves. They carried out administrative duties without receiving any salary or pension. Their only revenues were bribes from the persons they administered, and what they skimmed off from the crown’s commercial transactions. The *farang* favourite was going about things the wrong way if he wished to gain their sympathy, but that seems to have been the least of his concerns.

“A POOR UNFORTUNATE PRELATE”: THE RETURN OF MGR PALLU

Two months after Phaulkon’s abjuration of faith and marriage, François Pallu, Bishop of Heliopolis, returned to Siam after an absence of eight years. One would need a fat tome to relate his adventures and misfortunes. The *Coche* of Mr du Hautmesnil, on which he had left Ayutthaya in August 1674 for Tonkin, had been obliged to seek shelter in the port of Cavite near Manila because of a violent typhoon. The Spanish authorities of the Philippines, upholders of the *Patronato* and very hostile to France, accused him of spying and placed him under arrest. In spite of his energetic protestations, it was decided to bring him before the Sovereign Council of the Indies in Madrid. Fr Luis Pimantel, the chief Jesuit in the Philippines in whose care the bishop had been placed, suggested that his liberty not be restored in order to discredit and ruin the missions of the vicars-apostolic, but the Sovereign Council of Manila did not listen to him.

Mgr Pallu left Manila on 1 June 1675 on a Spanish galleon, to reach Madrid through New Spain. He arrived on 17 January 1676 in

Acapulco, crossed Mexico, and at the end of June embarked at Vera Cruz on the flagship of a fleet of sixteen galleons which dropped anchor five months later at Cadiz. He immediately sent letters written during the crossing to Louis XIV, Colbert, the papal nuncio in Madrid, and the widow of Philip IV, the regent of Spain during the minority of Charles II. He presented himself in his letter to the queen mother as

> a poor unfortunate prelate, already advanced in years [he was fifty], crossing the high seas for sixteen years, after visiting the whole of the Orient with its infinite perils, after passing through the same troubles throughout Turkey, Persia, the States of the Great Mogul, the King of Golconda, [and arriving in] the kingdom of Siam . . . [27]

The Spanish government, to which the Holy See had sent a strong protest over the arbitrary arrest of Mgr Pallu, treated the captive bishop with consideration and actively concerned itself with his case. He was able to write on 11 March 1677 to his friends in Paris that he had been exonerated. He went via Bayonne to Rome where he arrived on 5 June. The new pope, Innocent XI Odescalchi, received him in audience and showed himself very touched by his misfortunes. The Holy See appeared more determined than ever to impose the authority of the vicars-apostolic over those who still clung to ancient privileges.[28] But the activities and protestations of the Portuguese and Spanish champions of the *Padroado* were to immobilize François Pallu in Rome for three more years until May 1680.

On his arrival in Paris in June, the Bishop of Heliopolis observed that Fr de La Chaize had done him a disservice in relation to Louis XIV by maintaining the right of the French Church to be independent in certain respects of papal control. Relations between the Holy See and the king were already poisoned by the quarrel of the royal prerogative to enjoy the revenues of vacant sees and abbacies. In a general climate of Gallicanism, the Jesuit had convinced his royal penitent that the submission of the French missionaries to the "ultramontane" vicars-apostolic, even if they were French, was incompatible with the freedom of the church in France. Speaking about the Jesuits in a letter to a friend, Pallu wrote in September 1680, "One has everything to fear of people who have no moderation, and of a king as absolute as ours who is not and does not wish to be informed of our affairs except through their mouths."[29]

Yet the situation became clearer in October, when a letter from Fr

Oliva to Fr de La Chaize and the conciliatory moves of the latter with Louis XIV resulted in the king authorizing his missionary subjects to take the oath required by Rome, adding simply that they did so "with the permission of His Majesty."[30] Having had read to him the memorandum Mgr Pallu had addressed to the Council, Louis XIV agreed that a letter be sent from him to the King of Siam recommending the French missions and the royal company, the CIO; the Bishop of Heliopolis would take the letter and presents.

The prelate was received in audience by the king, who promised him money for his missions. Mme de Montespan, the Marquis de Seignelay (the elder son of Colbert), and the Dukes of Beauvillier and Chevreuse (sons-in-law of Colbert) generously untied their purse strings. His problems resolved and his money bags full, François Pallu thought only of leaving. He put to sea at the end of March 1681 at Port-Louis for his third and last voyage to Asia, taking with him on the *Blancpignon* and the *Président* ten new missionaries to work in Siam and Tonkin.

The two vessels of the CIO entered the Surat roadstead on 15 October the same year. The party from the Foreign Missions had to wait until the end of spring 1682 before continuing their journey to Siam on the ketch *Saint-Joseph*.[31] An MEP account notes:

> It was on 4 July 1682 that Mgr of Heliopolis arrived at the seminary [in Ayutthaya] after evening prayers . . . As he came at night, it was not possible to receive him as we desired and should. We contented ourselves with a *Te Deum* and an *Ave maris stella* in the church, and took him to his room to rest. He embraced us all so affectionately that we could not contain our joy.[32]

Mgr Pallu brought from the pope for Phra Narai four religious pictures with rich frames and appropriate subjects: the adoration of the Magi, the ascension, the apparition of the cross to Emperor Constantine, and the retreat of Attila from Rome. The presents from Louis XIV were more profane: several mirrors with gilded bronze frames, pieces of brocade, a large chiming clock, an enamelled watch decorated with miniatures, two small gold enamelled trees in gilded bronze boxes, two big Savonnerie carpets "which were only to be considered as samples and not presents, since they were both spoilt on board." For good measure, the Bishop of Heliopolis had added a sumptuously bound book containing prints of the life and death of

Christ. The *Phra Khlang* Kosathibodi was given a large mirror and several bolts of French and English cloth.

The King of Siam, then in Lopburi, received these presents with much delight. The English Catholic notes that

> the king did what he could to please this bishop. He overrode all customary practices to receive the letters he brought. He told him to look in the town [of Lopburi] or nearby for any place where he desired to build a church, and he wished to have built for him the most magnificent which was possible . . . He offered to get him into China, which these bishops had not been able to do for twenty years, being prevented by the intrigues of the Jesuits in Macao.[33]

These royal promises were kept. Mgr Pallu laid the foundation stone of the Lopburi church on 15 April 1683; a month later he obtained a passage on a junk belonging to the King of Siam going to Macao.

Phra Narai was also ready to grant the CIO the outpost of Johor, close to Singapore. This was announced to Mgr Laneau by the *Phra Khlang* three weeks after Pallu's return. André Deslandes, who knew the Dutch desired this exceptional strategic position, conveyed the news to François Baron at the end of December 1682.[34] After discussing the matter with Mgr Pallu, he decided without waiting for orders from Surat, to send an unofficial agent to Johor to look over the place.

Deslandes also emphasized in his letter to Baron the necessity of sending new presents to Phra Narai, and in particular an imposing lion which was kept at the Surat godown, "formerly given to Baron by a Portuguese gentlemen."[35] The king had heard about this animal and greatly desired to add it to his menagerie in Lopburi. The lion was sent by Baron to Siam on the *Saint-Louis* in May 1684. According to the Jesuit Joachim Bouvet, who arrived in October 1685, this much-travelled lion was a magnificent specimen with the appearance of a hero:

> We saw outside the palace a lion which the French Company had presented to the king. It seemed to me to be bigger, more handsome and stronger than those at Vincennes, but not so yellow. I found, as did several others to whom I made the observation, that this lion resembled the late Marshall of Turenne, and if it is true what is

commonly held, that each man has his beast, then I would think this brave lion would be that of our great hero if he were still alive.[36]

The Francophilia of Phra Narai was also seen in other forms. François Pallu had brought in his luggage a large portrait of the Dauphin. The king heard about this and asked to see it. "After seeing it, he immediately ordered clothes to be made for him like those of Monseigneur, to see if they would suit him well."[37] This fantasy of dressing like Louis XIV's son indicates in the King of Siam a strong attachment for everything French, even for powdered wigs, jabots, and lace ruffles.

After leaving Siam for China at the end of June 1683, Pallu, accompanied by an MEP priest, nearly failed to arrive. Their junk was attacked by Chinese pirates, and the two missionaries were taken to the island of Formosa (Taiwan) where they were detained five months. Freed after the payment of a ransom, they finally arrived at Fukien in January 1684. Worn out by years of struggle and lengthy voyages, Mgr Pallu had to confront the Dominicans, Franciscans, and Augustins who were already working there and refused to submit to his authority.

He died, exhausted, nine months after his arrival in China, on 29 October 1684 in the village of Mo-yang. The apostolic authority which the Holy See had given him had poisoned the whole career of this itinerant missionary bishop, preventing him from devoting himself to what was his vocation and his justification—the conversion of infidels.

THE FALL OF *PHRA KHLANG* KOSATHIBODI

During the eleven months he spent in Siam before leaving for China, the Bishop of Heliopolis had noticed the great favour which Phaulkon enjoyed. He had served him as interpreter in the audiences the king granted him, and had observed the degree to which the Greek favourite had captivated the mind of his xenophilous master who only saw through his eyes and spoke through his mouth. A witness at the Foreign Missions noted that "Mr Constance makes one of the chief points of his policy to prevent any European speaking directly to the king . . . Mr Constance is known to wish to control everything and impose his will."[38] Phaulkon placed himself in the tradition of favourites who shut up their sovereign to govern in his stead, like the Duke of Olivares, the favourite of Philip IV of Spain, and Cardinal Alberoni, favourite of Philip V.

The *Phra Khlang*, whilst treating his former protégé with the consideration due to a man who clearly would go far, secretly opposed his projects without understanding he was digging his own tomb. The English Catholic is full of praise for this person: "This Barcalon was pure Siamese, very devout in his religion and very attached to his temples. For the rest, he was the most accomplished person to be seen in Siam for many years, having a good brain and being very assiduous, just, and equitable as much as a pagan can be."[39]

The *Phongsawadan* are silent on the fall of *Chao Phraya Phra Khlang* Kosathibodi. The one source is Fr de Bèze, who arrived in Siam only in 1687 and was probably informed by Phaulkon himself. His account is as detailed as one could wish:

> Constans was no engineer, but he had a fine bent that way which, with his strong desire to satisfy the king, made up for his lack of expert knowledge. By calling to mind all that he remembered of the strongholds he had seen in Europe, Constans was able to devise plans for such fortifications as he judged appropriate to the nature of the place and the terrain.

Phra Narai liked this project and ordered it to be carried out by the *phrai luang*, the free men who had to render corvée service. These were not liable to tallage, but they received no remuneration for their work, not even food for the six months of corvée service they had to provide each year to the crown. It can be imagined that this ambitious architectural project did not make them dance for joy.

> The forced labour entailed in this new corvée terrified them and protests against it were presented to the Barcalon in the usual way—that is to say, fifty catties (worth 1,500 of our francs) were offered to him as a present, to the end that he advise the king to desist from the undertaking.

The *Phra Khlang* pocketed this considerable sum and went to explain to Phra Narai that fortifications were not so useful in Siam as in Europe, since the Siamese did not know how to withstand sieges. He added that "Constans, who had drafted the plans, had not been long in the country and was too young to be a judge in a matter which might involve His Majesty in a whole chain of expenses." But the king, who had his ear close to the ground, knew that "it was not the unbiased advice of a loyal servant, but an opinion for which the Barcalon had received payment." The *Phra Khlang* denied having accepted a bribe; he ought to have known better.

The king reproached him for his venality and his attacks on Phaulkon whom he had nevertheless recommended, and dismissed him in great anger. He had him followed soon after by a *khunnang* who had orders to beat him with a rattan.

> Flogging is a common form of punishment in Siam, but is only administered to persons of high degree for the most serious offences. The offender, stripped to the waist, is suspended by both hands above his head while his bare back is thrashed—the implement being a rattan, tightly bound around with string. The number of strokes administered depends upon the gravity of the offence, but sufficient cuts are usually given to strip the skin from the offender's back completely.[40]

Kosathibodi, foster brother of the king, victorious general of his armies at the beginning of the reign, and as *Phra Khlang* one of the most important *khunnang*, was profoundly affected by this public affront which caused him to lose face forever. He fell ill and died soon afterwards in July 1683, after making the king his unique heir in the hope that he would leave something to his family, whom he entrusted to Phaulkon. His widow ("the Barcalonne") and brother (Kosa Pan) tried to rescue something from his immense fortune and eight thousand slaves, but Phra Narai left them not a crumb. According to Fr de Bèze, Kosa Pan was also in disgrace for a time, but regained royal favour thanks to Phaulkon. It was also through the Greek that Kosa Pan would be designated two years later *ratchathut*, or first ambassador, to France.

An accomplished courtier, speaking as many languages as one could wish, experienced in diplomacy, international trade, and accountancy, Phaulkon had all the qualities needed to make an excellent *Phra Khlang*. According to de Bèze, Phra Narai offered him the position, but the favourite "had no desire to attract the jealousy of the chief courtiers . . . The influence he possessed already without the office was all he wanted."[41] The office was given, at his suggestion, to Okya

Wang, a *khunnang* of Malay descent who had spent three years as Siamese admiral in Pattani, but Phaulkon directed the *Khlang* department himself.[42]

To have accepted the post in his own name would have pointlessly provoked the Moors and the numerous *khunnang* who were vexed at his enormous prestige. Phaulkon had no support or faction at court apart from the king's favour, and realized he had to humour the adversaries he could not eliminate. His ambition did not consist in amassing in Siam a huge fortune to return to Europe to buy a nice plot of land and hunt with the hounds to the end of his days. The wealth he was amassing—which was considerable—was only to finance his political ambitions, which knew no bounds.

Claude de Bèze also relates that Okya Wang, displeased with being only a front man, sought to cause Phaulkon to lose the king's favour. With the help of an assistant still more obtuse than himself, he accused the Greek of misappropriation and other crimes, but Phra Narai was swift to see through the manoeuvre. Okya Wang was removed from office, his lieutenant had his head cut off, Phaulkon refused once again the honour of being *Phra Khlang*, and a Siamese *khunnang* in the pocket of the Greek was raised to the prestigious post.[43]

The English Catholic, ever well informed, gives the details:

> Another Siamese mandarin was put in his place, called Oya Phra Sadet, meaning the chief mandarin of the talapoins; he had been given to them previously because he had an extremely gentle and quiet nature. Mr Constance, who was then at the peak of his favour, encroached a lot on his authority. That grieved him somewhat, but he endured it to avoid trouble. Whilst waiting, like many others, for his rice to cool before eating it, he was patient. This proverb, very common among the Siamese, signifies that when one has a powerful enemy, one has to dissimulate until the right moment.[44]

One should note that Phaulkon was never *Phra Khlang* in name; he occupied the position without having the title. But no one was deceived; numerous French sources call him the "Barcalon," without heeding his inoffensive man of straw, making the situation perfectly clear.

Phra Phetracha, another of the king's foster brothers, and head of the elephant corps, was without doubt the one among all the important *khunnang* who acquiesced least in the rise in fortune of the Greek favourite. His xenophobia was well known. With the help of his son Sua (sometimes Dua, and also known as Luang Sorasak), he also tried to overthrow Phaulkon by instigating several behind-the-scenes affairs, but he learnt in time the futility of his efforts. His son received a dose of the rattan for his efforts, and Phetracha, who appeared to disapprove this attempt at character assassination, decided to wait for a more propitious moment.

After this setback, no one dared declare his opposition to a man so well entrenched. "The king entrusted all affairs of state to his care and he governed the whole country as deputy for His Majesty with full powers."[45] When he wanted Phra Narai to espouse his viewpoint, it was sufficient, according to a Persian witness, to say that monarchs in Europe in such a situation would act in such a way.[46] For his part Fr Bouvet noted in 1685:

> The king . . . made him, about three years ago, his chief minister of state, and united in his person all the important crown offices, because he occupies at the same time the posts of high constable, chancellor, trade supervisor, etc. It is he who makes the fortune of all those who share His Majesty's favour, and who can ruin them with just one word, which makes the greatest mandarins inferior and humble before him.[47]

His Excellency Mr Constantine Phaulkon was particularly interested in foreign affairs. The love of glory and foreign monarchs which he observed and encouraged in his master suited him down to the ground. The procession of embassies and the signing of alliances strengthening the influence of foreign powers, notably of Louis XIV, at the Siamese court could only be profitable for him. He hoped in this way to neutralize the nationalist resentment of the Siamese *khunnang* who, whilst prostrating themselves before him with their hands raised above their heads, hated him like poison. They were "waiting for the rice to cool before eating it."

CHAPTER FOURTEEN

THE SECOND SIAMESE EMBASSY (1684–1685)

A MINI-EMBASSY

PHAULKON TOOK no part in the decision to send the first Siamese embassy to France and the Holy See on the fatal *Soleil d'Orient* in 1681, but he was in complete control of the situation when, in September 1683, Phra Narai learnt that his ambassadors had most likely suffered shipwreck. He had no trouble in maintaining the favourable disposition of the king towards France. So he succeeded in convincing the king to send a fresh and much reduced delegation to transmit his offers of alliance to Louis XIV, if it materialized that the first embassy had indeed perished en route. At the end of 1683, the king asked him to write on his behalf to Colbert (it was not known in Siam that the minister had died in September) and to his brother, Colbert de Croissy, in charge of foreign affairs since 1679.

Not wishing that, in the event the first embassy had arrived, two Siamese delegations should meet in the galleries of Versailles, Phra Narai decided on sending only two *khunnang* for a mission at ministerial level. They would take a few presents to the two Colberts and would request them to transmit to the King of France their king's congratulations on the birth of the Duke of Burgundy. This first of Louis XIV's grandsons was born on 6 August 1682, but the news only reached Siam a year later. Phra Narai nominated Khun Phichai Walit and Khun Phichit Maitri for this task; the first was much more corpulent and advanced in years than the second.

In January 1684 Mgr Laneau informed the director of the MEP that the king,

> after considering that he was not entirely certain that the said ambassadors had perished, decided to send two officials with letters from the chief minister addressed to Messers de Colbert and de Croissy, to inform them of what he had done three or four years previously, and at the same time to request them to inform him what they considered most appropriate to do to establish this friendship [between the two monarchs].[1]

Phra Narai asked the Bishop of Metellopolis for two priests to accompany his envoys and serve as their ciceroni and interpreters. Mgr Laneau, who could not decline this service, selected Bénigne Vachet and Antoine Pascot. Vachet, in Siam since July 1671, is the author of precious *Memoirs*, still only partially published,[2] which relate the details of this mini-embassy in which he played a major role. He suffered from kidney stones and hoped to find in France remedies which would relieve the terrible pains this malady caused. Fr Pascot, in Siam since 1679, enjoyed robust health and taught philosophy at the Mahapram college, two leagues from Ayutthaya. But he had adjusted with difficulty and had so often requested to return to France that it was decided to profit by the first opportunity to despatch him. Phra Narai accorded Vachet the honour of being the chief envoy, which he could not refuse.

Remembering the repeated offer of Mgr Pallu that he could order anything he wanted in France, the king gave his envoys a list of things to acquire, notably a large order for huge mirrors to be placed in the audience chamber in Lopburi, the dimensions of which he gave them. He also wanted a "machine for seeing eclipses clearly," but omitted to give them anything to pay for these purchases. It is true that crowned heads are little concerned with such trivial details. This explains the anxious note of Mgr Laneau writing to the directors of the MEP: "I am afraid that this will give you a lot of trouble and difficulty in paying for all these expenses."[3]

The king also sent four Siamese boys to France to learn to become constructors of fountains, architects, goldsmiths, etc., and be brought up in the French manner. Bénigne Vachet regretted that those selected were "very uncomely in shape and appearance, and [had] an equally unpleasant disposition" and was surprised: "There is no place in the world where one could have a better choice than in Siam; the temples are crammed with very pretty boys."[4] The Bishop of Metellopolis was also anxious: "What I recommend . . . is to have the goodness that these young people . . . be raised in piety, and only placed in houses where they can acquire virtue." He hastened to add though: "As for the King of Siam, he has the best intentions in the world, and thought he would do us a favour to act in this way."[5] The conquest of souls, it can be seen, can lead the toilers for the Gospels into situations which they would happily have avoided.

Mgr Laneau wrote to Colbert at the same time, explaining that the envoys of the King of Siam would travel on an English ship, "because to send to France one of his own ships is not possible, seeing he did not have one capable of undertaking such a long journey, and still less people who could take it there."[6] This is why the two *khunnang*, the two priests, and the four ill-shaped and ill-disposed youths embarked on the small vessel of an interloping English trader they called "Mr Obones"—probably Holmes or Jones.[7] They set sail on 25 January 1684.

FROM AYUTTHAYA VIA LONDON TO PARIS

The voyage went off very well. The winds were favourable, allowing the travellers to cover the seven thousand leagues separating them from Europe in six months. They were unable to stop at the Cape of Good Hope or St Helena, for the VOC and the EIC had agreed to arrest interloping vessels and confiscate their cargoes. At the entrance to the English Channel, they encountered two Algerian pirate ships, but were saved by English warships which appeared in the nick of time. They stopped one night at the Isle of Wight, where Fr Pascot went ashore at last to go as quickly as possible to London to announce the arrival of the vessel. Thanks to his moves and those of Paul de Barrillon, the French ambassador in London, the envoys of the King of Siam were able to disembark at Margate and travel to the capital.

They arrived in September. On the 26th, Barrillon presented Bénigne Vachet to Charles II at Windsor Castle in the chambers of his current mistress, the Frenchwoman Louise de Kéroüalle. The king was curious about China and listened closely to his replies.

> Only the lady interrupted me five or six times, and often I pretended not to hear her. She approached me and, taking my hand, said: "Let me tell you that if you do not satisfy my curiosity, I shall give you no rest." The king made a sign indicating I should satisfy her. "Well,

> Madam," I said, "let us know what you would like to know." "It is, sir, to know the real reason which makes Chinese men abandon their country, their families, and their possessions in order not to have their hair cut . . ." "Madam," I replied, "I know of no other reasons, except that the Chinese men are as enamoured of their hair as ladies in our countries are of their healthy complexion." I had hardly stopped when the king, tapping her on the shoulder, said: "Madam, madam, you want to sell coals to Newcastle!" And turning to me, said: "Continue, for what you have to say interests me."[8]

It would seem that Charles II thought Vachet had come from China, and that Vachet did nothing to dispel this impression. John Evelyn, the author of a *Diary* as famous as that of Samuel Pepys, seems hardly better informed: "26th September [1684]. There was now an ambassador from the King of Siam, in the East Indies, to His Majesty."[9]

When taking leave of the king, Fr Vachet requested an order to the customs supervisor to return to his party, without inspection, their bales which were still held in Margate. Charles II signed a note to this effect on the spot, ordering in addition that the envoys and their effects be transported to Calais on the royal yacht, the *Charlotte*. The order to prepare the yacht was sent to Samuel Pepys, superintendent of the Royal Navy.[10] There were some dilatory procedures for the sake of form, England having a parliamentary government, but in the end everything was settled, and the Siamese delegation was finally able to cross the Channel at the beginning of October.

On his arrival in Calais, Vachet learnt that the directors of the MEP and the court did not consider it appropriate that he retain his position of chief envoy, and the post should be accorded to the elder of the Siamese. So he handed over to the *khunnang*, not without foreseeing embarrassing consequences "because of the brusque and choleric disposition of my companions who think they are free to do what they want when they have no one over them." In the subsequent activities of the embassy, Vachet was to occupy the position of advisor and interpreter, but he pulled strings energetically without disguising the fact. As for Fr Pascot, he seems not to have joined the Siamese delegation after his return to France.

On landing in Calais, the travellers from Siam were magnificently received by the Duke of Charost, governor of Calais, and a great supporter of the Foreign Missions. The Duke of Elbeuf, governor of

Picardy, had taken all the necessary measures to ensure that the journey to Paris would be a long succession of receptions, speeches, compliments, and presents. Vachet was not insensible to all this: "It seems very pleasant to live among so much glamour, to hear nothing but applause, to see the most important personalities of the towns jostle to meet us."

But this pleasure was somewhat spoilt by the Siamese, who, exposed to a heavy dose of culture shock, did not in the least appreciate the pushing and shoving going on around them. Vachet noted with a sigh:

> It is a hard thing to digest when one is with people who become vexed at the most praiseworthy actions, whom one has to prod like cattle to get them to be in the least gracious, and who are as readily shocked as others simply try to please them. Perhaps I shall repeat this lament on several occasions.

He must have been very relieved to see at Beaumont, Mr Brisacier, the head of the seminary of the Foreign Missions, and other gentlemen from the MEP.

Two magnificent carriages with six horses, bearing the arms of Colbert, were waiting for them near St Denis, flanked by the captain of the guards and smart cavalrymen who proudly cut capers in their blue helmets, with their blunderbusses slung crosswise over their shoulders. In this manner they arrived at the gates of Paris in the second week of October, followed by a dozen other carriages and carts transporting their baggage.

"THESE ARE THE AMBASSADORS OF THE KING OF SIAM!"

The guards took care to explain to the curious assembled at the St Denis gate who the exotic persons were in the first carriage, with the result that the cry was heard in all the streets: "These are the ambassadors of the King of Siam!" The shops magically emptied and the crowds in the streets were so great that the most curious ran the risk of being crushed under the horses or the wheels of the cavalcade. The crowds grew and carriages, sedan chairs, and horsemen turned back to satisfy their curiosity.

After crossing the finest streets of Paris in the midst of the hubbub, the procession stopped in the Faubourg St Germain in front of the Hotel de Taranne, near the Charity Hospital (the present Faculty of Medicine). The Marquis of Seignelay, who had succeeded his father Colbert, had prepared for them this elegant private residence which was spacious and sumptuously furnished. Vachet, who describes its luxury with some naivety, also appreciated its proximity to the Rue du Bac and the Foreign Missions. Two officers, four valets, an equerry, two cooks, and a porter, all loaned by Seignelay, looked after the well-being of the delegation. A dining table set for twelve places, always abundantly served at the king's expense, and a carriage with its horses, coachman, and postilion, complemented the comfort of Phichai Walit, Phichit Maitri, and their attendants. Vachet would have been happy if the two mandarins had shown less indifference to the efforts of their French hosts. But the Siamese scarcely concealed their antipathy to Western customs which they did not try to understand.

A STUDENT FARCE

It was the first time that Siamese had come to France and their arrival seems to have provoked good-humoured agitation. Some sharp wits even had the idea of putting on a farce, clearly inspired by the fourth act of the *Bourgeois Gentilhomme* in which Mr Jourdain becomes *Mamamouchi* in the middle of a deafening "Turkishness." The details of this rag are found in the *Mandarinade* of the Abbé Charles-Gabriel Porée.[11]

The victim was an old Normandy abbé, Michel de Saint-Martin, professor emeritus of the University of Caen, who lived comfortably in that town. His furs and his bed built above a stove in the Chinese fashion had given him a reputation for eccentricity. His nephews profited by the advent of the embassy to concoct a "Siamese" letter addressed to their famous uncle, called "The King of Stoves," and in which the first ambassador announced to him that the King of Siam, who had heard a great deal about him, had named him "inspector-general of stoves and furs in Siam," and had ordered a statue to be raised to him in the great royal temple of Ayutthaya.

If the abbé had doubts about the authenticity of this surprising document, the arrival of a second "Siamese" missive dispelled them completely. This letter announced that some Siamese were travelling to Caen, from where they would take him directly to Siam, where he would be made a first class talapoin and Marquis of Miskou. Both flattered and troubled—he had no desire to leave Caen and his comfortable bed—the abbé consulted his friends who advised him to seek the protection of Louis XIV. He was unaware that they were involved in the plot, and the letter under the king's private seal signed LOUIS which came immediately after his petition was false. It ordered him to remain in Caen and dissuade his Siamese visitors from their project by offering them a banquet at the Croix de Fer, the best inn in town.

The supposed Siamese arrived in the evening of the same day, bearing on a velvet cushion a triple ceremonial tiara. The terrified abbé waved his royal letter. The "Siamese" confiscated it to show it to their king, placed the tiara on his head, saluted him with profound salaams, muttering compliments in Siamese with a Normandy accent, dubbed him on the nape of his neck with the flat of a sword, and magnanimously consented to follow the new first class talapoin to the Croix de Fer. The abbé gave there a grand speech and quaffed several glasses to the health of Their Majesties the Kings of France and Siam. His example was copied without him having to press the "Siamese," and the evening ended in general drunkenness. The abbé-talapoin was taken back unconscious to his home and placed in his heated bed by his guests who tipsily disappeared. The following day, the incident seemed forgotten.

This Molièresque pleasantry, helped by the irresistible attraction of novelty, shows an infatuation for things Siamese. We shall see that the following embassy was to cause enthusiasm bordering on delirium, but this time round the embassy was to arouse signs of racial hostility in the Parisian populace.

THE ABBÉ DE CHOISY COMES ON STAGE

Vachet was more familiar with the conversion of infidels than the Byzantine complexities of a private diplomatic mission with official standing. Very perplexed and not knowing what to do about presenting his sullen Siamese to Louis XIV, he consulted the gentlemen at the MEP who advised him to speak with the Abbé François-Timoléon de Choisy, who was then taking a retreat at the seminary of the Foreign Missions.

Choisy was the younger son of a whimsical mother in good standing in the court, who, to console herself for not having a daughter, had dressed her son in his youth as a girl without thinking of the indelible effects which this transvestism would have on the delicate rather than strong character of her son. François-Timoléon, who was intimate with the king's brother, Monsieur, could say that the court had been his "schoolmistress." It was difficult to find in Paris an abbé better acquainted with the inner corridors of power or knowing better the ins and outs of the court. Bénigne Vachet, knowing that "only one false step, or one taken with indiscreet zeal, would delay or even ruin matters which are easily undertaken when embarked on with the advice of a wise and prudent man,"[12] had found the man he needed.

"The Frills and Furbelows Abbé" was then forty. Having only taken minor orders and acquired comfortable livings, he had given himself over without hesitation to the ambiguous game and joys of transvestism. He wallowed in a flood of head combs, patches, earrings, diamonds, ribbons, lace, skirts, and extravagant dresses, called himself "Madame de Sancy" and went so dressed to seek alms for the poor in the quarter of Saint-Médard. In the same outfit and with various excuses, he drew into his bed very young girls who were not too put out when they discovered that "Madame de Sancy" had a trick or two up her sleeve. He candidly relates these naughty adventures in his *Memoirs of the Abbé de Choisy dressed as a woman.*[13]

But a sudden illness gave him a glimpse of the tomb in 1683. After collapsing in the Place Royale (now the Place des Vosges), the enforced leisure of a long convalescence had made him consider his past and his future. The abbé had then renounced cards and feminine trinkets to throw himself into religious devotion. In the Rue du Bac, at the Foreign Missions, he tried austerity, penance, and compiling edifying works. With his friend the Abbé Dangeau who encouraged him in his path to conversion, he had just published *Four Dialogues on the Immortality of the Soul, the Existence of God, Providence, and Religion*;[14] after his return from Siam he was to write *Stories of Piety and Morality, An Interpretation of the Psalms, Christian Thoughts,* and *A Life of St Louis.*[15]

In short, Bénigne Vachet had met an unusual man and a good counsellor, and congratulated himself: "It is impossible to say how much enlightenment one receives from people like the Abbé de Choisy, who have spent all their lives at court. I obtained from him opinions which were the basis of most things which were successful." He explained in detail the matters he had come to negotiate, and then related all the particulars of the history, then unknown in France, of the first Siamese embassy which must have been totally wrecked.

Very garrulous—the volubility of his *Memoirs* is striking—and mistaking his own desires for reality, Vachet dangled in front of Choisy's eyes the possibility of the conversion of Phra Narai which would bring about that of the whole kingdom. All that had to be done was to send a prudent ambassador who would invite him formally to convert on the part of the Most Christian Majesty, the monarch he so much admired. Choisy noted:

> He related in conversation that mandarins from the Indies had come and there was talk of sending an ambassador to the King of Siam to invite him to become a Christian: that he had much predilection for this, and that it was an occupation worthy of a clever and zealous priest.[16]

The misunderstanding was there for ever. It promised a fine future—and a sad ending.

The idea of converting an oriental despot and his subjects quickened the abbé's pulse. The project appeared just as exciting as transdressing in order to seduce little girls. Sainte-Beuve considered Choisy "as a seventeenth century curiosity and a pleasant oddity in nature."[17] Rather, the century was remarkable in being able to produce people like Choisy who could be so zealous in such disparate occupations. He wrote: "I need no more to fire my heart with apostolic ambition to go to the end of the earth to convert a great kingdom."[18]

FR VACHET AT VERSAILLES

Choisy himself introduced the missionary behind closed doors to the Marquis of Seignelay, who fired a dozen questions at him without giving him the time to reply. They spoke for a good three hours. Vachet had much difficulty in convincing the minister of the fact that the King of Siam had sent a first embassy to France but this had been lost in a shipwreck; the Dutch had given out that this story was untrue. He finally said to him: "Are you not, sir, at the head of the

Royal Indies Company? Nothing is easier for you than to have presented to you the expense accounts which were run up at Bantam for the three or four months the Siamese ambassadors were fed and lodged in the French godown. The person who was then the head is now in Paris. You can summon him; his name is Guilhem and he lodges at the Lion Inn. He will tell you how they embarked on the *Soleil d'Orient* for France . . . If they were shipwrecked in a furious tempest and nothing more has been heard of them, should the fault be laid at the door of the King of Siam who, for his part, omitted nothing which might contribute to the success of the embassy, and should one not consider things as if, in reality, it had arrived?" Seignelay reflected a few moments and then said: "I think you will persuade the king that he should send an ambassador. That is enough for today. Return with as little ado as you came. I shall let you know the king's decision; I am going now to inform him of all that you have just told me."[19]

These first contacts took place during the annual stay of court at Fontainebleau from 14 October to 15 November 1684. The Marquis de Dangeau noted in his *Journal* in October, without indicating the day: "The envoys of Siam arrived in Paris to negotiate something concerning trade with the king's ministers, to whom they were sent. Their ambassadors perished the previous year and these will have no audience with His Majesty."[20] Dangeau and the court had thus clearly understood the unofficial rather than official nature of the Siamese mission.

Soon after the court's return to Versailles, Seignelay presented Fr Vachet to Louis XIV. The missionary paid his homage and explained that, "although I wished to appear as an individual, nevertheless in the envoys' commission my name appears at the head; but since I am French, I gave way to others in my country. The king, laughing, told me I was a very honest person, and had me sit on his left side, as it was during his dinner." Monsieur, the Duke of Orléans and the brother of the king, bombarded him with questions during the meal, notably asking "why the King of Siam appears to be so anxious to seek the king's friendship." Vachet replied as best he could, and then followed Louis XIV after his meal into his cabinet. There he spoke about Siam, its sovereign, the first shipwrecked embassy, and the opportunity for France and the Church to send an ambassador to Siam. He left after an hour with the feeling that his words had made an impression on his monarch.

The following day, Fr de La Chaize invited Vachet to dine at Versailles in the presence of his friend Fr Antoine Verjus, the bursar of the missions. After the meal they had a long conversation "in front of a good fire," during which the confessor requested his guest to give him details of the quarrel between the vicars-apostolic and the Jesuits. Vachet spoke at length, Fr de La Chaize listened attentively, and then dismissed him after embracing him "very tenderly," inviting him to write to him henceforth as a friend, concealing nothing. The Society of Jesus was beginning to be interested in Siam and Fr Vachet, charming in his naivety, was not aware of the English proverb, "Who sups with the devil needs a very long spoon."

All this time, Phichai Walit and Phichit Maitri, while considering the French with scorn, were living in clover in the Hotel de Taranne, served on silver platters belonging to the crown, warming themselves beside eight fires burning day and night, transported like princes in their carriage or taken like duchesses in sedan chairs. All the court and the town came to pay them visits, but they feigned sometimes a headache, sometimes a stomach-ache, to hide from the distinguished company wanting to know what a Siamese looked like. Poor Bénigne Vachet died a thousand times over and implored them to show themselves more amiable. "I well know that on that subject I was more than ten times extremely angry, and their excuses were nothing more than coarseness, alleging as a pretext that the King of Siam had not ordered them to go out in company."

The Siamese, to whom it had been hoped to show the fortified places in Flanders, flatly refused to leave their fireside in spite of the pressure of Seignelay who had organized the journey. Vachet exploded:

> Oh! These people are good at being professional layabouts! I think it is easier to enter the Capuchins than to get them to leave their rooms. So I have not spent much time without receiving the reproaches of our minister, for I was the moving spirit of the household; he had brought to me all the . . . impertinences of the Siamese. But what is worse, was that I had continually to find pretexts to conceal their faults and excuse them.

"ASSURE THESE GENTLEMEN THAT I AM DELIGHTED TO HAVE SEEN THEM"

It can be seen that Bénigne Vachet's mission was no walkover. He had his worst moment on Monday, 27 November, the day set aside for the audience with Seignelay and Croissy at Versailles. The Siamese would afterwards have the honour of seeing from afar His Most Christian Majesty going to mass. Vachet set them up as best he could for the great day and made them put on their best clothes and each his "white, very high, pointed bonnet, with a circle of gold three fingers wide at the base." He then had them mount a carriage after stuffing them with instructions, prayers, and threats in very precise Siamese.

Everything went off very well. The two mandarins went to Seignelay and then to Croissy where they pronounced before a numerous and distinguished gathering a short discourse which was translated by their cicerone. We shall never know what they actually said, but Vachet summarized their mission under three heads: "The first, to enquire about the Siamese who set out in 1680; the second, to request Their Excellencies the ministers to congratulate His Majesty on behalf of the King of Siam on the birth of the Duke of Burgundy; the third, to convince the same ministers to engage themselves to discover the shortest and most solid means of linking the two crowns in solid amity and correspondence." Each in his way, the two ministers replied particularly on the last point, saying "that the most assured of all the means consisted in the unity of religion which would provide an indissoluble link, and to which neither the distance separating the two kingdoms nor the jealousy of other nations could bring any alteration at all."

It is thus clear that Vachet had spoken to the ministers of a possible, or even probable, conversion of the King of Siam, a conversion which an embassy from Louis XIV would hasten. Fr Maldonado would reproach him about this later in very precise terms.[21] Let it be said in Vachet's favour though, that Phra Narai had spoken to him in scarcely veiled terms about a conversion. In a memorandum destined for Seignelay and Croissy in which he refers to himself in the third person, Fr Vachet declared that "in the last audience which [the King of Siam] gave Mr Vachet in the presence of the whole court, he said in very clear terms that *on his return he wished to carry out a plan which he had discussed with no one, and which would give joy to many*"[22] (emphasis added). These words had only one meaning for the good Vachet: Phra Narai intended to make himself a Christian.

An affirmation, difficult to corroborate, of the English Catholic complicates the matter. According to him, Phra Narai had made this declaration, not in person, *but through the intermediary of Phaulkon*, which changes everything. "It was said to this missionary, Mr Vachet, who accompanied these two mandarins who went to France via England in 1684, that Mr Constance, speaking to him on behalf of the king before he left, had told him that this monarch assured them that, if they succeeded, *he would on their return do something which would greatly surprise all his neighbours, and give great joy to the whole of Europe*. In a word, he gave them to understand that he would convert. He only relayed, he said, the very words of the king"[23] (emphasis added).

The royal message is virtually identical in the two accounts. The good faith of Fr Vachet appears to be above suspicion, but it can be supposed that Phaulkon, whose extraordinary favour brought him daily more hostility, was seeking European protectors. As the English and Dutch had seen through his game, he could only turn to the King of France, who the sibylline words attributed to the King of Siam were meant to entice.

To return to Vachet and his two *khunnang* received by Seignelay and Croissy, the Siamese offered the presents sent by Phra Narai. Croissy showed the gifts the following Friday to some courtiers, among whom was Dangeau, who mentions the fact without registering any appreciation of them.[24]

The audiences with the two ministers were over by ten in the morning. In spite of the early hour, a splendid meal was served because it had been decided that the same day the *khunnang* would be presented to the king after the council meeting, and would watch His Majesty dine later. The first meeting would take place in the great mirror gallery. Its whole length was filled with courtiers and ladies who were waiting amid much hubbub for the moment when the king would leave the council chamber to go to the chapel. The Siamese envoys had their breath taken away.

> Our Siamese, who were used to the profound respect and incredible silence maintained in the presence of their king, were completely astonished to hear a confused murmur and to see the frantic jostling

going on to come close to the monarch's person. Some went ahead of him, some followed, but most were at his sides, so that it was only when he was five or six feet away from us, that we were told "Here is the king."

Vachet had the reflex of a dog trainer:

> I immediately had the Siamese prostrate themselves with their faces down to the ground and their hands joined, in the manner I had seen them when before the King of Siam. As I wished to give the little discourse which I had composed . . . the king, unwilling to let the Siamese remain in that posture, told me to have them stand up. This being done, I pronounced these few words: "Sire, the Siamese whom Your Majesty sees before you are envoys sent by the King of Siam from his kingdom to come to France and request your ministers of state to help them in their task, in order to obtain from Your Majesty what that monarch so greatly desires. They [are] only too happy to have found so favourable an occasion to present Your Majesty with their most humble and most profound respects."

Louis XIV replied royally: "Assure these gentlemen that I am delighted to have seen them and I shall undertake for the King of Siam, my brother, indeed with much pleasure, that which he would desire of me." He bowed slightly and continued on his way.

Vachet and his Siamese visited the apartments of Versailles during the king's mass, and then went to watch His Majesty dine. They were placed—a signal honour, this—on a crimson velvet bench. "During the whole meal, there was a concert punctuated from time to time by the single voice of a girl." Amid the music, the king charged Vachet to show his gardens to the Siamese, and to bring them back to Versailles to see the opera *Roland* "which he wished to bring forward for them." This was the new opera of Lully and Quinault and was going to be performed in November 1685 in the riding school in the Great Stables.

Fr Vachet and the mandarins therefore went to see the gardens and fountains of Versailles in bath chairs drawn by Swiss guards. The fountains were turned on in their honour, but the two *khunnang*, observing these European gardens with their trees devoid of leaves (it being winter), suppressed bored yawns. "These marvels, which are the admiration of the whole earth, were observed by my Siamese with an indolence which froze my heart; and as if they were wearied, they said to me at each new sight, 'That's enough, let's go.' Fortunately only I was there to notice their depraved taste."

THE SIAMESE AT THE OPERA: A CULTURAL INCIDENT

But the poor man was not yet at the end of his tribulations. When the day came, he returned to Versailles with the envoys. Louis XIV had ordered Seignelay to have them seated opposite him on the front row, without realizing that he was thus creating what one can call a "cultural incident." The Siamese, "who did not know that the lowest row was the most esteemed and the most convenient, went to place themselves at the highest point in order to have no one above their heads," profiting from a moment of inattention among the guards charged with placing them at the front of the fourteen raised tiers. As soon as they saw this error, the guards tried to get them to be seated in conformity with the king's orders, but they resisted, in spite of the repeated efforts of Vachet, who ran around like a madman from top to bottom of the theatre. "The Siamese thought that an affront was being shown to them, and without wishing to listen to me, they went off on foot like brutes to the hostelry where our carriages awaited us, and returned to Paris, in spite of all the remonstrances and advice and threats I made."

Louis XIV arrived shortly after and was surprised not to see the mandarins. Vachet, who was running after his Siamese, did not have the time to explain to Seignelay what had happened. The king, thinking the guards had offended the mandarins, told his brother that those responsible had to be severely chastised. Monsieur did all he could to calm him down, and the following day sent one of his gentlemen to the Hotel de Taranne, requesting Vachet to go to St Cloud to consider together how they could save the supposed guilty from the galleys.

Bénigne Vachet was fuming with anger.

> God knows what I said or did not say to these Siamese who thought they had done something wonderful. I threatened I would complain to the King of Siam, but they shook their heads and said: "What could he do? The worst thing would be to be condemned to death. Our lives are less valuable to us than our honour."

Vachet dropped his arms and went to see the Duke of Orléans, who promised to use his good offices. "Effectively, Monsieur explained the situation to the king, who considered it inappropriate to become embroiled with such unreasonable persons, and His Majesty had the goodness to tell his brother that I had to abandon this particular matter, and he hoped I would succeed."

The incident, insignificant in itself, illustrates the difficulty in the relations between two worlds conditioned by fundamentally different cultural codes. Pitched into a civilization which they could not understand, the Siamese envoys appeared bewildered or, as Louis XIV said, "rather unreasonable." Their tense attitude when they went a little later to see a performance of *Roland* on the express command of the king, who could not conceive that one might not like an opera by Lully, shows to what degree the incident had traumatized them.

Vachet this time had reserved seats for them on the dress circle "which was almost in front of the king's seat, and consequently a point from where everything in the theatre could be observed, and all the spectators could easily see us." Being both spectators and spectacle, the mandarins wriggled about, very uneasy on their red velvet chairs with gold fringes.

> I had to tell them two times to stand up when the king entered, and he had the goodness to turn towards them and greet them. Monseigneur [the Dauphin] and the whole court did likewise, and it was only after many remonstrances that they returned the salutation. It is hard to believe that during the whole performance, they did not look at the king or the actors, but kept the eyes lowered, except when they turned them from time to time towards the door.

They detested being taken around on a lead like strange animals. Can they really be blamed?

ST CLOUD IN FLOWER AND CHANTILLY IN THE SNOW

Fr Vachet had occasion to be more pleased when his Siamese, invited by the king's brother, went to visit the Palais Royal and St Cloud. They were first of all received at the Palais Royal by Monsieur and his Palatine spouse, surrounded by a brilliant assembly. Vachet played his usual role: "I had our envoys prostrate themselves in the Siamese manner, and only had them stand up after Monsieur had ordered it three or four times." The amiability of Monsieur, passing "a thousand compliments in favour of the King of Siam," overwhelmed the priest. They then got into their carriages to visit the château of St Cloud which had been completed in 1678. The country retreat of Monsieur was marvellous and the object of sincere Siamese admiration, and seems to have inspired Vachet's chatterbox style. "The palace seemed to us captivating. Everything there is grand and magnificent; the azure, gold, paintings, statues, silver, fountains, house, gardens, and orangery exceed all the images of those who have only read descriptions of them." The envoys were first led into the apartment of the Duke of Chartres, the son of Monsieur, and the future regent. The young prince was then ten years old and his very lively mind must have been overwhelmed by this exotic visit.

A sumptuous meal served with plenty of wine preceded a visit of the gardens in their carriage. Vachet, not very blasé in such matters, could not believe his eyes.

> I must confess, for myself, that I was so surprised that I hardly believe what I could touch with my fingers. It seemed as though we were there in June, but November was coming to its end. I touched fruits and flowers as though in the middle of spring. Fresh objects constantly presented themselves for our admiration. The boscages, grottoes, labyrinths, cascades, perspective views, and a thousand other curiosities made five hours pass more quickly than five minutes.

But the biggest surprise was the enthusiasm of the Siamese, who did not stop expressing their admiration, to such an extent that Vachet suspected them of having drunk too much at table and having "light heads." It was in any case a compliment for the refined taste which Monsieur showed in all things.

The envoys were present on All Saints' Day at a pontifical mass in Notre Dame at which the Archbishop of Paris, Harlay de Champvallon, officiated. As they had said they would refuse to prostrate themselves or even to kneel at the moment of the elevation of the host, they were placed in the gallery. They also saw from a gallery a solemn session of Parliament in the presence of the king "dressed all over in purple, ermine, and scarlet." Monsieur le Prince, the head of the Condé branch of the royal family, invited them to

Chantilly where an unusual sight awaited them. "Although it had snowed a lot, all the fountains and cascades were working as though in summer. Our Siamese did not let me down, and I was content with their conduct."

But it was time to think of returning and, above all, of the embassy Louis XIV had decided to send to Phra Narai. The directors of the MEP seminary were naturally thinking about it—after all, it was thanks to the Foreign Missions that the court and the town had been able to see the Siamese—but they discovered a bit late in the day that the Jesuits were still more actively thinking about it. The moment had come when the Society of Jesus was to snatch the Siamese monopoly from the Foreign Missions.

THEOLOGY AND MATHEMATICS

Who was the first to have the idea of applying a Chinese-style missionary strategy in Siam? It is known that the Jesuits, who believed they should practise evangelization at the top, had gained entry to the imperial court in Peking as silk-dressed astronomical and mathematical mandarins. The successes obtained by Fathers Matteo Ricci, Adam Schall, and Ferdinand Verbiest were in everyone's mind. Verbiest, president of the mathematics tribunal in Peking, had neatly written that "our holy religion, under the star-spattered cloak of astronomy, is easily introduced to the princes and provincial governors, and shelters churches and missionaries under their protection."[25] Seeing the ranks of the Society of Jesus thinning out in China, Fr Verbiest had issued an appeal through the Flemish Jesuit Philippe Couplet, bursar of the Chinese missions and co-author of the famous *Confucius Sinarum philosophus* which was later published in 1687. On 15 September 1684, a month before the arrival of the Siamese envoys, Louis XIV had received Couplet flanked by a Chinese curiously named Arcade Wang.

Moreover, since his first contacts with the French missionaries, Phra Narai had shown a genuine interest in astronomy, physics, mathematics, and geography. It was therefore natural that one should think of exploiting this thirst for knowledge in the interests of the evangelization of Siam and China.

A similar idea could have been sown in Phaulkon's mind from 1682 by his converter, Fr Thomas. He indeed was preparing to continue his journey to Peking where his talents in mathematics and astronomy were to shine. We have indicated earlier the amicable relations between the Greek and the Jesuits after his abjuration in May 1682. In November the same year, Fr Maldonado had sent a letter in Latin to Fr Charles de Noyelle, the new Society of Jesus general, explaining Phaulkon's great affection for their order (*"Societatis nostrae amantissimus"*), and requesting him to write an official letter to encourage this agreeable disposition.[26]

It was probably in reply to this letter that Phaulkon wrote to Fr de Noyelle in January 1684, at the time when the mini-embassy escorted by Vachet was preparing to leave for Europe. After congratulating his correspondent on his election, he continued: "I have no less satisfaction in indicating to Your Most Reverend Paternity the great esteem in which the Reverend Fathers are held in the broad spread of the Chinese empire, particularly in the court at Peking." His greatest desire was to support a similar situation in Siam.

> I would point out to Your Most Reverend Paternity that manner in which, in the great empire of Siam, the holy Society of Jesus could be esteemed: by sending into this empire ten or twelve persons of approved conduct and saintly morals: be they Italians, Venetians, or Flemings, men versed in mathematics and other liberal arts.

They would be better placed than others (by which he meant the Foreign Missions) to introduce Christianity into Siam. "For my part, I shall here take care of the Church and shall give my support to the Reverend missionary Fathers in the vineyard of the Lord . . . Your Most Reverend Paternity's unknown humble servant, Phaulkon."[27]

It is not known if Fr de Noyelle wept tears of joy on reading this letter, but it is known that, taken short, he did not have the time to assemble the Italians, Venetians, and Flemings Phaulkon requested. The decision to send French Jesuits who were versed in mathematics to Siam was taken in Versailles before the middle of December 1684. Louis XIV, Louvois (who controlled, in addition to war and buildings, everything concerning the sciences and the arts), Fr de La Chaize, and Fr Jacques Pallu, the Jesuit director in Paris and brother of the late Bishop of Heliopolis, seem to have settled matters between themselves. Louvois supported the project and organized it with his usual energy. The young Duke of Maine, natural son of Louis XIV, was also enthusiastic about this scientific expedition. He spoke to his father about it on several occasions and offered the astronomical missionaries a very luxurious geometrical instrument.

On 22 December, an uneasy Fr Pallu explained in a letter to the Jesuit general in Rome that things had been taken in hand by Louvois and were out of his control, and he had to bow before the will of the king and his minister.[28] On 29 December, the confessor La Chaize wrote in his turn to Rome, plunging Fr de Noyelle into a state of perplexity. The most important parts follow:

> Most Reverend Father:
>
> I think the time has come when God wishes to use our Society for his glory. . . provided one can supply a sufficient number of good workers for the more than Christian zeal of the king who . . . has decided to carry the Gospels by means of our Fathers to all the places where his vessels touch land to favour his subjects' trading. As Fr Couplet, whom I presented to His Majesty, gave him to understand the rich harvest one can gather in China, if people of intelligence and virtue can be introduced there, and His Majesty moreover being greatly in favour of the sciences and all that one can acquire in knowledge of foreign lands, he ordered me to seek among his subjects a number of good missionaries with sufficient mathematical knowledge to travel there and conduct on the spot all the necessary observations to rectify maritime and geographical maps, and above all to become familiar with the sciences and arts, chiefly of the Chinese, to form a collection of their books to enrich his library, to form some interpreters who can make translations of them, and under pretext of being the observers and mathematicians of the king, instruct the people in the truths of the faith—which is [a task] so glorious and so advantageous to our Society that I thought there was no need to hesitate about this, nor any occasion to doubt that Your Paternity would give your joyous consent.
>
> The favour I have to seek is that you permit everything to be done in the king's name, so without fearing that the French vicars-apostolic cause us concern, nor that we should do anything which might reasonably shock the gentlemen of the Congregation of the Propaganda.
>
> The king is sending an ambassador to the King of Siam at the end of February, and desires that four of our Fathers go to that country with him. And at the same time measures are being taken, on his

> orders, for them to pass through Macao and then to China. The intention of His Majesty is that a similar number of our Fathers should travel through Surat on our vessels, and he even wishes others to undertake to assist these missions, either through Persia and the land route, or through the Great Tartary . . . [29]

This letter is essential to understand the scientific, commercial, and evangelizing strategy of the French of the period. First of all, efforts apparently concentrating on Siam were in fact aimed at China. We have already indicated that the EIC, the VOC, and the CIO were principally interested in Siam because they saw the kingdom as a gateway to China and Japan.

The expedition of 1685 was to inaugurate the capital role of the French Jesuits in the China of K'ang-si and Yong-cheng, but also the untoward outcome over Chinese rites. Everything that the eighteenth century knew about the Middle Kingdom derives from information supplied by the Jesuits in their *Lettres édifiantes et curieuses* (Edifying and curious letters), which began to appear in 1702, or the encyclopaedic information about China found in the four large in-folio volumes of the *Description de l'empire de la Chine et de la Tartarie chinoise* (Description of the empire of China and Chinese Tartary), compiled under the auspices of Fr Jean-Baptiste du Halde (1735).

Setting out to conquer souls, knowledge, and markets at the same time, the expedition sent to Siam and China appears a very complex operation. One wonders whether the scientific and commercial aspects were a pretext for missionary activity, or vice versa. In any case, the programme, as defined, was ambitious. It foretold the vogue in the following century for expeditions of discovery over the face of the globe. The enlargement of the royal collections reminds one of the efforts of Lucas in Egypt and Galland in Asia Minor at the beginning of the reign to bring the king medals and other antique curiosities.

Finally one should note that the evangelization programme envisaged by Louis XIV fits into the general pattern of conversion which spurred him on in 1684–1685, and which was to end in October 1685 with the revocation of the Edict of Nantes, whereby Protestants lost their right to practise their faith. The letter of La Chaize also invokes, in the part not quoted above, the "pre-revocation" action of French Jesuits who would have converted fifty thousand heretics in two years.

Charles de Noyelle must have reflected carefully while turning the three pages of this letter. It undoubtedly opened interesting perspectives, but it risked above all bringing back the ghosts from the past, notably the rivalry which, under his predecessor Oliva, had humiliated the Society of Jesus when it dared contest the authority of the vicars-apostolic who brandished their pontifical briefs. The Father General first of all dictated a reply in Latin to La Chaize, which was not sent. Ten days later, after consulting his advisors, he compiled another version. The archives in Rome of the Society of Jesus have the two texts.[30]

The first version, dated 10 February 1685, begins with the usual compliments and some pious reflections on extending the glory of God to the ends of the earth. But the Father General does not conceal his disquiet. Without being specific, he recalls the dangers the projected expedition holds for the Society of Jesus. "This is why, except for the departure of the four Fathers which has already been decided upon, Your Reverence should reflect on other ways and means. We are entirely convinced that we must make haste slowly." But the matter was delicate. By refusing to act, the Society risked losing Louis XIV's support and perhaps his confessional. On the other hand, carrying out the orders of His Most Christian Majesty would provoke the anger of the autocratic Innocent XI and the cardinals of the Propaganda.

After carefully weighing the pros and the cons, Noyelle decided to give primacy to good relations with the Holy See above all other considerations. On 20 February, he dictated a fresh letter in which he observed that the decision to send Fathers to Siam had been taken without his knowledge and without his being consulted (*"me inscio ac inconsulto"*). After speaking again of the dire consequences for the Society, he insisted: "It is absolutely essential that Your Reverence and the Provincial Father carefully explain to the king, notable for his wisdom and his love of the Society, the reasons which constrain us to abandon an expedition to the Indies, while waiting to see what we can do later. The project is still being studied, but one can justly fear that it will be used to denigrate the Society."

The reply of Fr de La Chaize, written eleven days after the departure of the embassy, confronted Fr de Noyelle with a fait accompli.

> As soon as I received the most recent letter with which Your Paternity honoured me, I thought I should inform Mgr the Papal Nuncio, who is here, of all that occurred in the despatch of *six* Fathers of our

> Society, who have set off for China on the same vessel transporting the ambassador to Siam. I gave him to understand that the little time the king had given us. . . had obliged us to take from the Paris college the professor of mathematics and five other virtuous and knowledgeable priests in the same college, without having the leisure . . . to wait for the orders of Your Paternity.

The royal confessor went on to indicate that he had explained all the details concerning the embassy in a letter to Cardinal d'Estrées, charged with overseeing French interests in Rome "so that, as our intentions in this enterprise are entirely beneficent and holy, as well as those of His Majesty who ordered us to do this and who originated the project, Your Paternity will find in it no displeasure."[31]

Clever, and almost convincing, this letter allayed the concerns of the Father General who seems to have closed the dossier with a sigh of resignation. It is clear that the decision had not been taken in Rome, but Versailles. The astronomers of the Society of Jesus were destined to play a major role in the unravelling of the Siamese drama.

The Foreign Missions, who were sending some priests to Siam under the tutelage of Bénigne Vachet, were of course neither consulted nor informed. Vachet wrote in his *Memoirs*, "As everything was being prepared, I learnt that the Jesuits would be part of the company, and that six had already been named for the journey."[32] Clearly he was not overjoyed.

A GREAT EMBASSY IS ASSEMBLED

The preparations for the "brilliant embassy"[33] which Louis XIV was sending to Phra Narai were well in hand. It was the first one that His Majesty, then at the peak of his power, had sent to an oriental monarch; he considered himself, a king by divine right, more and more as God's lieutenant on earth. The great movement of religious intolerance and proselytism which was to characterize the second half of his reign favoured, a few months before the revocation of the Edict of Nantes, a large-scale diplomatic, missionary, scientific, and commercial expedition. As soon as he learnt that the decision had been taken, the Abbé de Choisy, dreaming of being appointed ambassador extraordinary, ran to his childhood friend the Cardinal de Bouillon, chief almoner of France. The abbé writes:

> Without losing time, he [Bouillon] went to the Marquis de Seignelay, his friend, to propose me. This minister told him he came too late; that the Chevalier de Chaumont, a man of quality and virtue, was named ambassador; that it had been rather difficult to find a man worthy of this mission . . . and that two days earlier my affair could have been concluded.

But this upset did not cool the abbé's apostolic zeal:

> The idea of a mission was too advanced. I told him that the Chevalier de Chaumont could die during the journey, and that the embassy could fall into the hands of some sailor with little acquaintance with such matters . . . that moreover the King of Siam wishing to convert, the Chevalier de Chaumont, an indifferent theologian, would give him rather superficial instruction.

So he requested the cardinal to obtain for him "the coadjutancy of the Chevalier, and ambassador ordinary in the case that the king undertook instruction in the Christian religion." Louis XIV granted this request, saying "I have never heard before of a coadjutant ambassador, but it is justified, given the length and dangers of the journey."[34]

While collecting the money and contracting loans at usurious rates (he needed more than twenty thousand livres), the abbé carefully prepared for his mission, as is shown in a signed memorandum overflowing with enthusiastic projects and kept in the Archives Nationales in Paris.[35] He foresaw satisfying the curiosity of the French and set out to know Siam "at least as well as France." He even intended, in spite of his limited finances, bringing to Ayutthaya a painter who would make portraits of the king and "the whole court, sketch the finest views in the country, its handsome houses, the temples of the gods, and the dress of the men and the women." A man of taste, the abbé selected an artist with talent but with only a very vague idea of what was involved in such a long journey. On arriving at Brest, where he saw the sea for the first time in his life, the artist was seized with panic. The abbé had to embark without him, mocking "my little painter, who, at the sight of the sea, fell sick, and was cured as soon as I told him he could return to see the towers of Notre Dame and his god-mother."[36] This was a great pity, for the "little painter" (we would like to know his name) would probably have left us drawings or paintings less mediocre than the plates illustrating the volumes of Tachard and La Loubère.

The Chevalier de Chaumont, the ambassador, was one of those persons whom everyone respects but who has few friends. Michel Jacq-Hergoualc'h considers him "a narrow-minded fool [who] all the same had great singleness of mind."[37] Born into a Huguenot family and bearing a very ancient name, Alexandre de Chaumont had distinguished himself in the army and the navy and came to the king's notice in abandoning Calvin for Rome. Pious, rigid, and austere, this ship's commander and major-general in the army in the Levant seemed predestined for this embassy. "It was because of that," Fr Tachard explains,

> that his Majesty, who proposed to himself chiefly the good of Religion, and the Conversion of the King of Siam by the Embassie which he resolved to send him, pitched upon the Chevalier de Chaumont for so glorious an employment; being persuaded that the good example, which he would give in that Country, would be so many proofs of the sanctity of Christianity, that might fully convince that King of the truth of our Religion.[38]

Much was expected of Chaumont, but this person was very conscious of his dignity and lacked pliancy, a troublesome fault in an ambassador. The official *Gazette* of 16 December published his nomination.

Mr Desclouzeaux, the intendant at Brest, had received orders from the Marquis de Seignelay to advance the preparation of the *Oiseau*, one of the king's ships of six hundred tons burden, on which the ambassador and his "coadjutant" were to embark together with the two Siamese envoys and a group of missionaries. The *Oiseau*, partly armed for war, partly geared for trading, carried thirty-six cannons. It had the reputation of sailing well and carried a crew of 132 men; Seignelay had ordered that they be "good and shapely persons." The captain, Mr de Vaudricourt, was an old hand who had served under Abraham Duquesne. Among his lieutenants was the impetuous Claude de Forbin. He was to stay one year in Siam and gives in his *Memoirs* a less flattering image of the kingdom than those of Tachard or Choisy. We shall read his protests against what he called "the blunders of our compilers of accounts."

The Chevalier de Chaumont took the Abbé de Jully as his personal almoner, the Sieur de La Brosse-Bonneau (a brother of André Deslandes-Boureau) as secretary, and Mr Billy as butler. A dozen young gentlemen, all naval officers, accompanied him. They were bubbling with impatience to make a trip to the East Indies and regale their mistresses on their return with exotic tales enlivened with saucy details that they would not read in the *Mercure Galant.* Seignelay had ordered a capable engineer, La Mare, "to demonstrate hydrology to the marine guards and the young officers, and to make plans of the towns to which he travelled." La Mare would stay on in Siam at the request of Phra Narai, very impressed with his competence.

Apart from the amusing Abbé de Choisy whose conversion had—thank goodness—not made him ponderous, the dozen priests who completed the expedition formed a more serious contingent. Their interests ranged from converting infidels to the precise calculation of longitudes and latitudes under which the latter practised idolatry. Fr Vachet brought two colleagues, Jean Basset and Etienne Manuel. The Abbé François de Langlade du Chayla travelled as an independent tourist and was going to return with the ambassador; he would be massacred by Protestants in the Cevennes in 1702 (Robert Louis Stevenson, in his donkey-borne travels through the Cevennes, supplies ample details about his death).

The six Jesuits sent to Siam and China constituted a genuine "brains trust." It had been decided that, in addition to the four mathematician-astronomers who had been discussed from the beginning, two fairly young Fathers would be selected to learn Chinese more easily. Their superior, Jean de Fontancy, was a remarkable man. An avid mathematician and astronomer, he had taught mathematics for eight years in the famous College Louis-le-Grand, the Society of Jesus' Parisian college. While comparing his calculations to those of Jean-Dominique Cassini of the Paris Observatory, he repeatedly asked his superiors to be sent to China or Japan. He had never forgotten his meeting with Cassini and Colbert a little before the minister's death. Colbert had told him: "The sciences, Father, do not deserve that you take the trouble to cross the oceans . . . but as the desire to convert infidels and gain souls for Jesus Christ often makes you Fathers undertake such voyages, I would hope that they would use the occasion and that, during the time when they are not preoccupied in preaching the Gospels, they make on the spot a lot of observations which we need for the perfection of science and the arts."[39]

This is exactly what Fr de Fontaney was proposing to do when he learnt on 13 December 1684 that he would leave for China, passing through Siam. In addition to a list of observations which the gentlemen of the Academy of Science had given him, he took a huge selection of memoranda of the academy on physics, astronomy, anatomy, and botany, copies of the best maps in the royal library, as well as tables of the satellites of Jupiter established with infinite care by Cassini and considered indispensable for the calculation of longitudes.

Among his mathematical colleagues teaching in the same college, Fr de Fontaney and his superiors had designated Jean-François Gerbillon, Louis Le Comte, Guy Tachard, Claude de Visdelou, and Joachim Bouvet. The last two were appointed because of their youth. They had finished their studies in theology and were rapidly ordained. They said their first mass on 14 January.

Fr Bouvet was later to write important works on China; he would work there forty years and would be profoundly affected by the quarrel over Chinese rites. His generous synthesis of Chinese and Christian thought—he is the author of an *Essai du mystère de la Trinité tiré des plus anciens livres chinois* (Essay on the mystery of the Trinity taken from the oldest Chinese texts)—did not convince everyone. Since the publication in 1963 by Janette Gatty of the *Voyage de Siam du P. Bouvet* (Journey to Siam by Fr Bouvet), he is no longer unknown. But it is above all Fr Tachard who monopolized people's attention, relegating his five colleagues to obscurity. His two *Voyages de Siam* published with considerable success (1686, 1689), explain this fame. It is not generally realized that the first *Voyage* owes a lot to the account of Fr Bouvet, which was moreover written for this purpose; numerous long passages reappear without change in the first volume of Tachard which fails to indicate their source. Born in Marthon near Angoulême in 1651, Guy Tachard had entered the Company of Jesus when young and taught mathematics in several colleges. This did not stop him from travelling to distant lands, particularly as almoner from 1680 to 1684 in the expedition to the West Indies commanded by Marshall Count d'Estrées. Full of his experience of distant travel, he "was very pressing to be among the number of those who were to be chosen."[40]

The six learned Jesuits were given the signal honour of being received into the Academy of Sciences and took their seats a few days before their departure. In addition they obtained letters patent "sealed with the great seal in yellow wax," which conferred on them the title of "the king's mathematicians in the Indies and China."[41] Louis XIV furthermore granted his mathematicians a travelling allowance of twenty thousand livres and pensions.

The two ambassadors and their attendants, the *khunnang*, the missionaries, the King of Siam's six workmen, the valets, and guards came to a total of seventy-seven persons. The *Oiseau* thus had in all 209 crew, soldiers, and passengers.

The volume of baggage, presents, and purchases for Phra Narai piling up in the hold of the *Oiseau* was considerable. There were first of all the scientific instruments supplied by the Academy of Sciences and paid for by the king: repeater clocks measuring the seconds, various types of sundials, geometric slide-rules, barometers, compasses, tubes, etc. Among these scientific curiosities were two globes, celestial and terrestrial, of gilded copper, two and a half feet in diameter and mounted on silver bases, remarkable for their sumptuousness and the refinement of their complex movements regulated by hidden mechanisms concealed in the hollow of the globes. "They had to be seen to be believed," remarked Fr Vachet, adding with a note of resentment for the celestial globe, "This little marvel was enough to gain the entrance into the palaces of the greatest monarchs, and in consequence, the person who was in charge of it was always needed."[42]

The presents from Louis XIV to Phra Narai were numerous and magnificent, as to be expected: mirrors embellished with gold and silver, silver candlesticks and girandoles, crystal chandeliers, twelve rich lengths of gold brocade, one hundred ells of linen, two clocks "showing the movements of the moon, very curious," three more clocks, eight pairs of pistols, twelve "very fine" muskets, a purse of medals and French gold coins, a large portrait of the king mounted on horseback and two small ones in enamel and embellished with diamonds, three marquetry writing desks and three tables, six pedestal tables, four large Savonnerie carpets, a great bowl of rock crystal embellished with gold, two sets of embroidered clothes with several pairs of silk stockings, ribbons, beaver hats, cravats, and lace ruffles, "everything very French."[43] Monarchs who know their role are not stingy.

There were lastly the mirrors ordered by Phra Narai. Dangeau explains that the mandarins "were taking away a great number of very fine mirrors for a gallery which their king had recently built."[44]

"THE WHOLE OF EUROPE HAS ITS EYES TURNED ON US"

An order drawn up by Seignelay on 21 January 1685 unequivocally underlines the religious objective of the expedition which eclipsed its commercial and scientific considerations.

> The principal object of His Majesty, in his resolution taken to send an ambassador to Siam, is the hope that the missionaries have given of the advantage religion would draw and the hopes they have conceived on reasonably likely foundations that the King of Siam, touched by the marks of esteem from His Majesty, will complete, with the help of the grace of God, his determination to embrace the Christian religion for which he had already shown much inclination . . . His Majesty desires also with this voyage to procure all possible advantages in commerce for his subjects in the Indies, and to take certain information of what can be done in Siam. The Sieur de Chaumont should be informed that the King [of Siam] has offered the French Indies Company to trade with him, that is to say that the vessels of Siam will continue every year to travel to China and Japan, and that on their return, the said king, who alone conducts all trade in his country, will supply merchandise through barter or for money. . . . As it is likely that the King of Siam will send ambassadors on the vessel which will have taken the said Sieur de Chaumont, His Majesty desires that he conduct them to France, and entertain them during the journey with the best treatment he is able to provide.[45]

Seignelay therefore speaks, in connection with the conversion of the King of Siam, of *the hopes they have conceived on reasonably likely foundations*. It would seem that the person who had chiefly nourished these "hopes," Bénigne Vachet, had moments of doubt before re-embarking for Siam. He writes in his *Memoirs*:

> It would be boldness to wish to reach the bottom of the king's heart; one can only judge by externals. Never has any negotiation been more delicate nor more weighty. The whole of Europe has its eyes turned on us. From the result of this commission will result either enormous good, or very heavy crosses to bear.

What follows, which turns on the equivocal role played by

Phaulkon in this project of conversion, and the jealousy which caused him to make Phra Narai inaccessible to every European except himself, is of prime importance. "If it had been possible for Mgr de Metellopolis, after being well acquainted with all these facts, to have a private audience with the king, I do not doubt that we would have succeeded incomparably better, than if we had only acted through the intermediary of Mr Constance."[46] These remarks seem to confirm the testimony of the English Catholic quoted above. Vachet was perhaps loquacious and sometimes naive, but he did not lack common sense.

"YOU WISH TO LEAVE, MR VACHET"

A few days before the departure of the members of the embassy from Brest, the chief luminaries of the French navy, like Tourville and Châteaurenault, were explaining to Louis XIV the time needed to travel to Siam and return. They envisaged the ships laying up for winter at the Cape, and told the king that he would not see his ambassadors for another four years. As Seignelay, informed by Vachet, had maintained that two years would be more than enough, Louis XIV summoned the priest to Versailles. "Have you assured Seignelay that my vessels will only be twenty months at sea, both for the journey out and return?" he asked. The missionary, who had recognized Tourville and Châteaurenault, replied that it was still too much, and that "without unforeseen accidents," sixteen or seventeen months were plenty.

Tourville, extremely ruffled, retorted, "You speak of the sea as if you were only concerned about your breviary." But Vachet, sure of his ground, gave the king a long speech, citing the monsoon cycles and the nautical experience of the Dutch, without knowing that the ambassador of the United Provinces was present. Hardly had he finished than the diplomat, who had twice travelled to Batavia, said he was right. Let it be said now that the Chaumont-Choisy embassy was to return after an absence of exactly fifteen months and fifteen days. Louis XIV, remembering this discussion then was to confide in Vachet who had gone to pay his respects, "You have paid your debts sooner than you promised!"

But they had to set out first of all. At the end of February, Vachet went to take leave of the king in Versailles where he saw him sup. He went down on his knees and kissed his hand. The monarch, laying down his knife and fork, put his hands on his shoulders. "You wish to leave then, Mr Vachet," he said. "Go, I pray to the Lord to grant a happy outcome to all our plans. I know they are good, and I hope we shall meet again." Vachet got up and replied with a profound bow: "Sire, I hope so. But, if it pleases God, it will be in paradise, and not in your kingdom."

On 17 February, Louis XIV had decided that the *Maligne*, a frigate of one hundred and fifty tons, would be added as support vessel to the *Oiseau*. It was commanded by Charles de Joyeux, lieutenant of the port of Brest, who had travelled several times to the Indies. This news, which delayed the departure, was received with joy in Brest by all those making the voyage.

On 1 March 1685, the Chevalier de Chaumont, accompanied by Châteaurenault and many of the nobility then in Brest, entered one of the king's longboats and went on board the *Oiseau* to the sound of trumpets and cannons. The crews of the two vessels cried "God save the king!" at the top of their voices. The following day was set aside for taking on board the last victuals and a few latecomers who were unable to release themselves from the embraces of their loved ones.

Fr Tachard piously concludes:

> Thus we left in France the gentle repose of a religious life which we had enjoyed up to then, to go and seek at the end of the earth the occasion to procure the greater glory of God and to devote ourselves to the conversion of infidels, while carrying out the orders of our Great Monarch.[47]

Few episodes in French diplomatic and maritime history are as well documented as the first embassy sent by Louis XIV to Siam. One has only to cite the accounts of Chaumont, the *Mercure Galant,* Choisy, Vachet, Forbin, Bouvet, and Tachard. While these people were travelling towards the Siamese Indies, their hearts puffed up with grand projects, a Persian embassy was raising its anchor at Bandar Abbas for Siam, hoping to convert Phra Narai to Islam. It was to inspire a flowery account which is unique in its genre.

Phra Narai surrounded by eight prostrate *khunnang* (Tachard, *Voyage de Siam*, 1686).

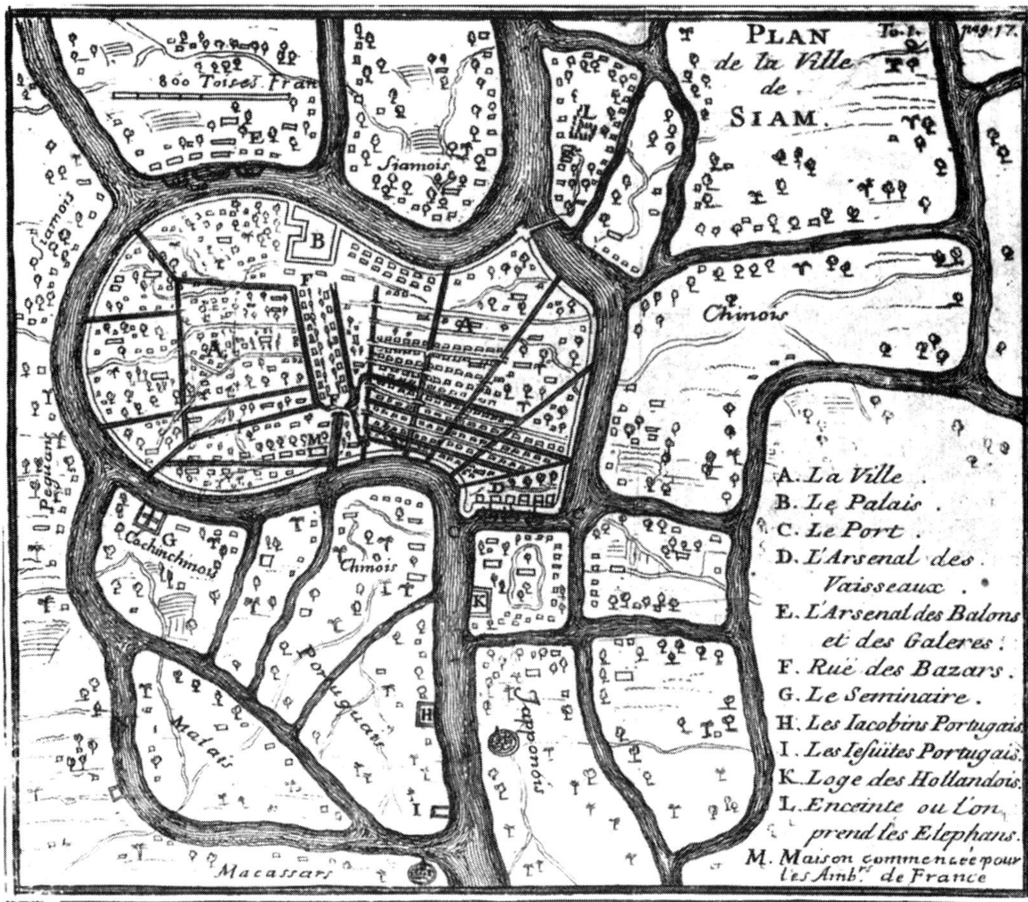

Plan of Ayutthaya (La Loubère, *Du Royaume de Siam*, 1691).

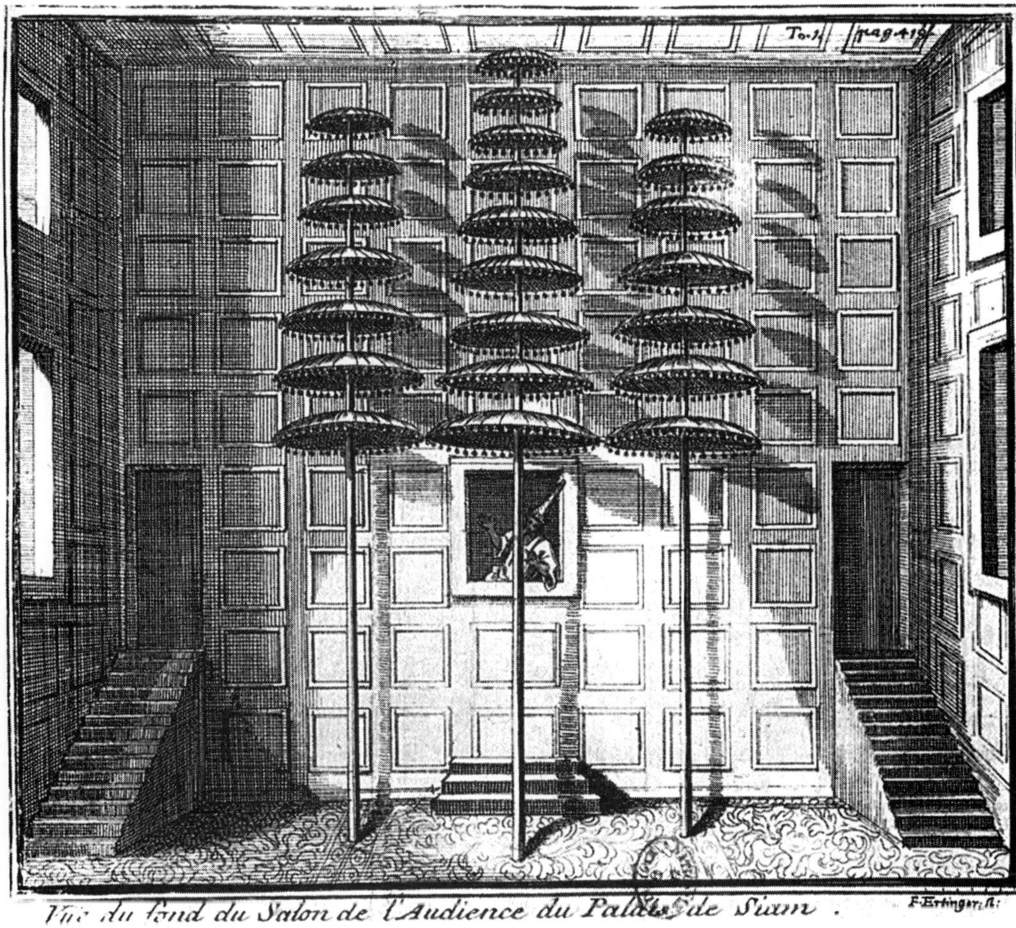

Audience hall in the Palace of Ayutthaya (La Loubère, op. cit.).

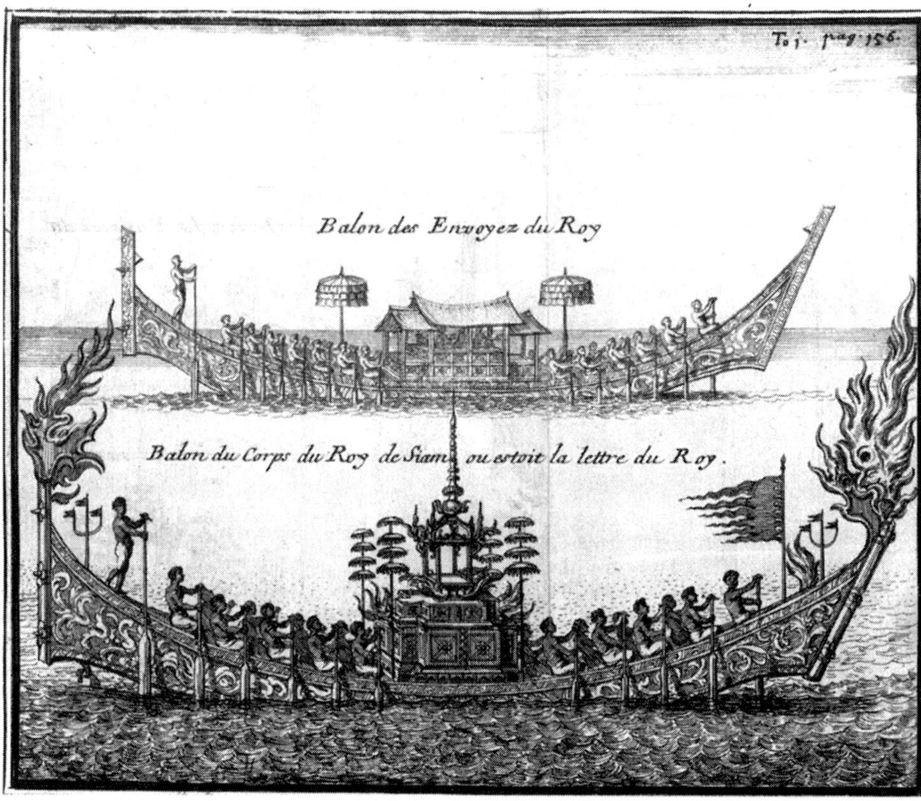

Siamese *naga* and dragon barges.

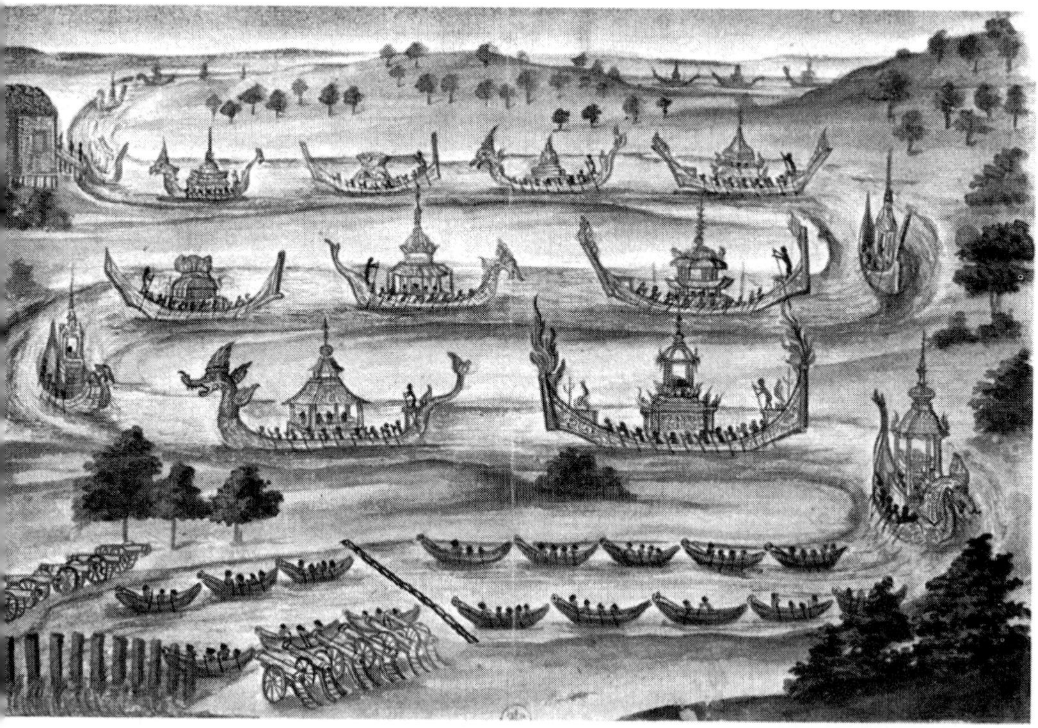

The French ambassadors' entry to Ayutthaya on 18 October 1685 (BN, Cabinet des estampes).

The moment of presenting Louis XIV's letter to Phra Narai on 18 October 1685 (BN, Estampes).

The "machine" containing the King of Siam's letter on 1 September 1686, at Versailles (BN, Estampes, Hennin collection, t. 63, 5548).

The three Siamese ambassadors during their stay in France (June 1686–February 1687) (ibid., t. 62, 5495).

The *ratchathut* Ok-phra Wisut Sunthon (Kosa Pan) (ibid., t. 62, 5500).

The *trithut* Ok-khun Siwisan Wacha (ibid., t. 62, 5504).

The *uppathut* Ok-luang Kanlaya Ratchamaitri (ibid., t. 62, 5502).

The Siamese ambassadors befo[illegible] the throne of Lou[illegible] XIV on 1 Septem ber 1686 (ibid., t. 63, 5550 and 5551).

Phra Narai observes a solar eclipse at Lopburi (BN, Estampes).

A *talapoin* and mandarin (La Loubère and Tachard, op. cit.).

THE PERSIAN INTERLUDE

CHAPTER FIFTEEN

THE SHIP OF SULAIMAN (1685–1688)

THE YEAR 1685 marks a high point in the annals of Siamese diplomacy. While the Chaumont embassy was passing by the southern coasts of Africa, a Portuguese embassy, sent by the viceroy of Goa, was arriving in Lopburi. It was led by Pero Vaz de Siqueira, a trader in Macao, and sought to obtain concessions from the King of Siam, namely, complete liberty of Portuguese trade in respect of royal monopolies, the right of the Portuguese to be judged by the head of their nation and not by Siamese judges, and lastly the support of the king in the quarrel pitting Portuguese priests against the French vicars-apostolic.

Vaz de Siqueira and his men were received in solemn audience in Lopburi in May. Phra Narai granted them the freedom to trade but refused juridical extraterritoriality, as well as intervention in the dispute between Roman Catholics. On 23 June, the Portuguese left Ayutthaya, where they had gone with the court at the beginning of the monsoon. One suspects they were disappointed in spite of the declarations of satisfaction given to their Dutch rivals, who relayed the news of this embassy to Batavia. As was his wont, the King of Siam made a point of returning the compliment. He sent an embassy to Portugal the following year. We know that three Siamese ambassadors were on board the ship *Nossa Senhora dos Milagros* which, after leaving Goa, was shipwrecked near Cape Agulhas in April 1686.[1] One of them, Ok-khun Chamnan, survived and will reappear in these pages.

"MAY ALLAH GUIDE HIM INTO THE FOLD OF ISLAM!"

On 27 June in the same year, 1685—the *Oiseau* and the *Maligne* had passed the Cape three weeks earlier—a Persian embassy sent to Siam by the Safavid ruler, Shah Sulaiman (1666–1694), set sail from Bandar Abbas on the Persian Gulf. The intermittent relations between the two countries since the beginning of the Prasat Thong dynasty had given rise to the exchange of letters, presents, and commercial missions. The influential Mauro-Persian community, established in Siam from the beginning of the century, encouraged these exchanges which it organized at the request of the *Phra Khlang* and from which it obtained as much profit as the crown. Phaulkon, at the beginning of his Siamese career, had exposed the malversation of one of its leaders, Haji Salim, who had led a commercial mission to Isfahan.

According to the chronicle of the Persian embassy which was setting out, the King of Siam had on several occasions sent courtiers bearing magnificent presents and affectionate letters to the King of Persia to seek his friendship.

> Alas, some drowned in nameless seas and left no sign behind, others caught by pirates on the main failed to reach their Destination. But in [1682], Haji Salim Mazandarani was delegated to attempt the great voyage and present to our king a letter of friendship which professed all forms of good will and sincerity, and was accompanied by the finest gifts the Siamese king could procure. The letter prayed that the limitless sea of true affection be stirred up with happy waves as delegates and embassies passed between the monarchs, that love and lasting attachment rejoice in the freshing breezes thus created.[2]

Touched by these poetic propositions, Shah Sulaiman designated Muhammad Husain Beg, an administrator in the *Khassa* which oversaw the crown revenues, to lead a delegation to Shahr Nav, that is, Siam. Husain Beg formed a delegation of civil and military officers, and charged the scribe Ibrahim Muhammad Rabi to make an account of the chronicle of the embassy, destined for the shah. Brought up on elegant Persian metaphors which predisposed him to wrap up the bald facts of events in florid if somewhat mechanical poetry, the author divided his account into "jewels" rather than chapters.

> . . . No captain sets sail for his destination without some goods of value. So I have loaded the ship of my account with all kinds of priceless wares, tales which sparkle like bright gems and thus we call each anecdote which comes before the elixir of our king's gaze, a threaded jewel.[3]

He called his chronicle *Safina'i Sulaimani* or the Ship of Sulaiman, playing on the double meaning of the Persian word *safina* which means "ship" as well as "account" or "anthology." The manuscript of this unique text, acquired long ago by the British Museum, was translated into English by John O'Kane and published in 1972.[4] The 240-odd pages are divided into four "jewels." The first relates the voyage from Bandar Abbas to Chinapatan (Masulipatam); the second describes the rest of the journey to Tenasserim and Lopburi, followed by the account of the embassy at the Siamese court until its departure; the third gives a well-documented picture of the kingdom of Siam; and the fourth, less coherent than the rest, locates Siam in Asia, the geography of which is summarily outlined, and relates the return to Persia. Almost three years passed between leaving Bandar Abbas and returning to the same port (27 June 1685 to 14 May 1688).

The Ship of Sulaiman is no literary masterpiece, but provides a Persian description of Siam at the very moment the French were trying to establish themselves there. This non-European viewpoint of Phra Narai, his court, his kingdom, Phaulkon, and the trading nations in Siam, is an irreplaceable document in the context of this present work. The avowed intention of converting the King of Siam to Islam at the very moment when the French ambassadors thought he was ready to embrace Christianity adds to the interest of the text. The author of *The Ship of Sulaiman* remarks in his introduction that the Siamese sovereign, "possessor of the white elephant and the throne of solid gold," likes all Muslims, and piously adds: "May Allah bless him and guide him into the fold of Islam."[5]

"ENTRUSTING OUR SOULS TO THE LIMITLESS SEA": FROM BANDAR ABBAS TO LOPBURI

After a six-month wait at the port of Bandar Abbas, the Persian delegation went aboard an English ship sailing for India, "entrusting our souls to the limitless sea." The captain raised the anchor on the twenty-fifth day of the month of Rajab 1096, 27 June 1685 in the Christian era. Removing the stylistic embellishments so dear to Ibrahim Muhammad Rabi, one realizes that the journey was no pleasure trip. They had their share of storms, alarms over reefs about to pierce the hull, calms, heat waves, and shortages of water, before arriving after two weeks sailing at Muscat on the Gulf of Oman. The Portuguese had been chased out of this port by the Karijit troops in 1649, and our scribe does not refrain from recalling this exploit with pleasure, without concealing his scorn for this sect.

They needed a month to reach Masulipatam on the Coromandel Coast. An Indian Muslim, who had got on board at Muscat after performing the pilgrimage to Mecca, fell into the water during a violent storm. "That night of the storm he fell into a sleep of neglect and with all the sea and wind, the ship of his being plunged into the waves like a bubble and the fox of his life swam off into the dim waters of non-existence."[6] Abandoning describing all the misfortunes which overcame the passengers, the author of *The Ship of Sulaiman* says merely, "Let it be sufficient if my pen writes out this final phrase: 'I was sore afflicted, struck with every kind of misery, misery enough to turn bright light of day into the darkest of nights.'"[7]

His account becomes brighter when the vessel reaches Masulipatam, the port the King of Golconda rented to the English. The ambassador and his suite were received magnificently by the *gundar*, the English governor. They were carried in ebony litters, offered banquets, installed in a splendid house in the middle of a perfumed garden, lent servants, and sent food and fruits in abundance.

It was during the stay of the Persian embassy at Masulipatam that the news was received of the death of Charles II on 6 February, and the advent to the throne of his brother James II. Or, as our scribe has it: "The king's soul threw the body's transitory cloak to the ground. On the chessboard of time his soul was checkmated by the raging elephant of death." In clear, the king was dead. According to our chronicler, the Duke of York had proclaimed to his subjects: "The puppeteer, Fortune, has smiled his bounty on me from behind the double coloured veil of the chess game, and the backgammon player, Chance, has shaken the dice of hope and thrown the number of my wish. So I am king."[8]

The date fixed for the coronation, 22 August 1685, being known in Masulipatam, the British colony joyfully celebrated the accession of its new sovereign. As it was during Ramadan, the English waited for sunset so as to allow the Persians to join them without breaking their fast. Musicians placed behind a screen played harmonious music, and wine flowed generously. The assembly drank to the health of Their Gracious Majesties the Kings of England, Persia, and Siam. The Persians were shocked to see these ill-bred Westerners walk on carpets without removing their shoes, but the appearance of the Frank ladies made them thrill with pleasure.

The English *gundar* apologized to his guests:

> Although it is a Muslim practice to keep women from associating with men outside their kin, we feel that to keep the dazzling Frank women, whose faces beam like the sun and are round like the moon, hidden with veils of modesty would be the height of blasphemy and exceed the bounds of all propriety. Such a sin would be inexcusable, pure abomination.

Our scribe fully supported this distortion of Islamic customs:

> Suddenly these moon-faced idols entered and an indescribable charm was radiated throughout the room. They were all joy from head to toe. The magic of their eyes bewitched our sight and this gathering became the very envy of eternal paradise. Their flashing appearance was the key which opened up the doors of paradise. The garden of joy and spiritual union stood before us. [9]

It would seem that the good fellow had done credit to the *farang* wines.

The celebrations of the Franks amazed their Persian guests: affectionate embraces, dances in which men and women held hands, the huge wine goblets they raised to their lips when giving a toast. The perilous leaps of rope dancers brought in for the occasion brought forth cries of fright from the ladies while the tables were being prepared for the banquet. Our chronicler, who seems to have greatly appreciated the dishes and the drinks, could not find words for a white cockerel, "a skilfully executed masterpiece of sugar confectionery. Every single feather was in place." He had a moment of fear when a Brahmin soothsayer whispered in his ear that the ambassador Husain Beg would die soon after arriving in Siam.

The Persians re-embarked on 16 September for Mergui, where they arrived after the usual travails. Indeed, exhausted by the journey, Husain Beg "set out for the regions of the Ruler of all men" on 19 September 1685. The delegation, which still comprised seven persons, observed with astonishment the ceremonies and marks of great respect which the Siamese showed the shah's letter, placed on a throne "like a message from heaven." The governor of the province of Tenasserim, a Persian who had made his fortune in Siam, put them up in his palace of overwhelming luxury, while waiting for Phra Narai's instructions.

These arrived at the end of December: the king desired that the Persians go from Tenasserim to Ayutthaya in barges and on elephant back. So they traversed the isthmus of Kra following the dangerous route taken by Mgr Lambert and Jacques de Bourges in 1662. After three weeks spent on the Tenasserim River in the middle of virgin jungle, they reached the village of Jalang where they found elephants ready to transport them to the capital. "Our royal letter was placed on top of the best-looking elephant."[10]

This journey on the backs of elephants took a fortnight. The Persians passed through Paj Puri (Phetchaburi) and Suhan (Suan Sampran or "rose garden"), the gardens and orchards of which they describe and which today are tourist attractions. They learnt en route that Phra Narai was not at Shahr Nav (Siam, that is Ayutthaya), but at Lubu (Louvo or Lopburi); so they went to that city on river transport provided by their compatriots. After explaining that this place was a former capital which had fallen into ruin, the Persian scribe indicates: "Recently the present king rebuilt the city, being very pleased with its climate, and now he resides in this comfortable spot and had made it the base of his power. He regularly spends nine months of the year in Lubu."[11] A little before reaching Lopburi, they were greeted by the chief of the Persian community, Hassan Ali. He had succeeded Aqa Muhammad, who had died in this office in 1679.

"TO FORTIFY THE FOUNDATIONS OF UNDERSTANDING AND AFFECTION"

The disembarkation at Lopburi brought the Persians a series of surprises. The magnificence of the gold throne on which the royal letter was placed, the procession accompanying it, elephants dressed in their finest raiment, contrasted greatly with the near-naked Siamese.

> Except for the king himself, all the natives of Siam of whatever station in life, men or women, consider their bare flesh to be sufficient clothing and they expose their bodies without concern. The sole blessing of clothing they avail themselves of is the lungi, a small cloth which veils their private parts. Their apparel is the same through spring and autumn and, despite the fact that they stumble though the rocky wadi of idolatry, they wear no shoes on their unsure feet.[12]

The soldiers placed on both sides of the route from the landing stage to the palace gates seemed to them hardly formidable with their bamboo helmets and small red muslin tunics.

Going into the first courtyard, the Persians saw a marvellous, recently constructed pavilion destined to house the letter and presents sent by Shah Sulaiman. The interior was decorated with carpets, silk cushions, and Chinese screens. They were taken into two pavilions which were to be their lodges. A messenger from Phra Narai came to ask the seven Persians to select one among themselves to be first ambassador. To the great disappointment of our scribe, who, "with the help of God," thought he was best fitted for the post, his companions chose Ibrahim Beg.

The account of the parleys with Siamese officials over the preparations for the royal audience causes the author of *The Ship of Sulaiman* to return to the death of Aqa Muhammad, the stupidity of his sons who caused the collapse of the Mauro-Persian community's influence, and to speak of the rise of Phaulkon.

> When Aqa Muhammad passed away, the king was in need of foreign support. Taking advantage of the situation, an ill-begotten Christian rose to power and filled the empty position. Formerly this Frank had been employed as a humble worker on ships. Thus he illustrated the true saying, "Once the lion leaves the jungle, the jackals venture forth." In a very short time this Christian learned the language, customs and laws of Siam and day by day, in the eyes of the king, he cultivated a reputation for managing affairs. The Siamese king has made this man his chief minister and confidant, without bothering to test the coin of his character or establish to what degree his opinions or abilities are an advantage to the state . . . The Frank has endeavoured to weaken the king's character and encourage the royal

> fickleness. He causes the king's sight to stray from the straight path of practising justice.[13]

Phaulkon seems to have fanned Phra Narai's suspicions of the Persians. Having exiled Aqa Muhammad's two sons to an island, and relegated the Moors in Siam to almost total insignificance, the king feared assassination to such a degree that he refused to accept the shah's letter from the hand of Ibrahim Beg. Isolated from their compatriots and unfamiliar with Siamese susceptibilities and protocol, the envoys did not know what to do. Weeks passed. Finally Phaulkon summoned our scribe and questioned him on the reasons for their journey to Siam. "Our king, the benefactor of mankind, has sent us to this country for the purpose of increasing goodwill and strengthening the foundations of accord and love and there are absolutely no other motives attached to our mission." The minister replied, "If what you say is true you should put aside the idea of Ibrahim Beg handing your document directly to the king and, as is the practice in Iran, you should stand at a respectful distance from the king and let the honourable chief minister make the actual presentation." The Persian ambassador, on being informed, accepted the proposal, sighing, "If you make friends with elephant drivers build your house big enough to admit the elephants."[14]

There was no further obstacle to the solemn audience. Dressed in their finest clothes and followed by their servants, the Persians went on horseback to the palace between rows of richly caparisoned elephants and soldiers wearing small loincloths, a spectacle the visitors had difficulty in adjusting to. Bearing the letter of their king placed on a golden casket decorated with pearls and preceded by Siamese officials, they moved towards the audience chamber. As soon as they saw the throne through the half-open door, they threw themselves to the ground and continued their progress on their elbows and knees in the midst of a great immobile crowd, prostrate, faces to the floor, which reminded our Persians of a large congregation of Muslims saying their prayers.

The throne hall had a teak floor covered with carpets. The pink and vermilion interior was reflected to infinity by six huge mirrors ordered from France. The throne at the end of the hall comprised a projecting balcony closed off by folding panels, reached by two staircases, one to the left, one to the right. Everything was gilded and "decorated with pictures of devils." The interior of the royal niche was panelled with gold brocade. Phra Narai was already seated on his throne when the ambassadors and their attendants entered the chamber. They saw it was filled with rows of prostrate *khunnang*. A sofa, opposite the throne, was waiting for the Persians. It was whispered in their ears that they could pay their respects in the manner of their country, which they did by bowing respectfully before the king.

Two officials rose to their knees to take the shah's letter from the hands of the ambassador. It was placed on a golden platter fixed at the end of a gold handle and offered to the king, who leaned forward slightly to take it in both hands. He took it to his lips, raised it to the height of his crown, pressed it against his eyes and his chest, and then placed it beside him.

A conversation took place between intermediary *khunnang* and interpreters, and the florid formulae flew between the Siamese throne and the Persian sofa. Addressing his god-king, or *devaraja*, the *khunnang* said: "Divine protector of Heaven and earth, your command hangs over my head. Be merciful to me." The Persians considering these words as sacrilege, said for their part: "Oh my lord and my refuge, your indulgence is the essence, the very height of mercy."[15] Phra Narai asked about the health of Shah Sulaiman, then if he were involved in any wars. Ibrahim Beg replied that "all the enemies of our blessed state perish in the desert of their error" and that his king had sent a huge army into Azerbaijan. To end the audience, Phra Narai said that the appropriate season for their return journey had not yet arrived, and the Persian envoys would be his guests until their departure. "Then the king closed the door of his throne and the audience was over."

The Persians were invited the following day to an elephant hunt. Their elaborate description is similar in all respects to the Portuguese, Dutch, English, and French accounts which we have already met with. Our scribe observed with malicious pleasure that Phaulkon was prostrate on the ground at the foot of the royal elephant, ready to receive "on his head" the orders of his monarch. A banquet was given for the visitors a few days later but only aroused disgust:

> The food of the Siamese . . . in no ways resembles normal, proper foods and the natives are not familiar with intelligent methods of preparing meals. In fact, no one in Siam really knows how to cook and eat or even how to sit correctly at table. The Siamese have only

> recently arrived "from the world of bestiality to the realm of humanity."[16]

It does not seem that our Persians, very full of their own culture, made great efforts to understand the exotic civilization they beheld. No European visitor passed such Philistine remarks. La Loubère simply notes that "the table of the Siamese is not sumptuous" and observes that, in relations with distant countries, words like "good," "fine," "magnificent," "grand," "bad," "ugly," do not mean much. "It would not be just," he writes, "to contemn every thing that resembles not what we do now see in the Court of France."[17] The remark is true for the court of Isfahan.

Invited in the following weeks to tiger hunts and fights between elephants and tigers, the author of *The Ship of Sulaiman* describes these amusements with a luxury of details which is absent from the accounts of European travellers, who did not appreciate these cruel spectacles. The Persian embassy remained in Lopburi until the beginning of the monsoon in June 1686. It then followed the court to Ayutthaya.

Four months later at the end of the monsoon, the time had come to think of the return journey. In spite of their horror of the sea, the Persians opted for the maritime route from Ayutthaya to Bandar Abbas. Phra Narai sent them presents of cloth and silver catties on silver platters. The scribe received ten catties and twenty-eight rolls of cloth estimated to be worth four catties; he showed himself only marginally satisfied. The Persians were invited to a final elephant hunt. At that occasion Phra Narai announced his intention of sending several young captured elephants to the shah and offered a very small one to the scribe. He declined the offer with profuse thanks, explaining that "it is impossible to take care of such a beast and the transportation would be very difficult."[18]

The farewell audience took place like the first. The king asked the Persians if they had accomplished their mission and if they desired to return to their country. They replied in the affirmative, and the ambassador received a letter for his king. Before closing the shutters of his throne, Phra Narai said to them by way of farewell:

> May God look over your lord's life and increase his prosperity. May he live a thousand years, for that would give me the greatest joy. Make every effort to communicate my good will and sincerity and

> convey my wish that, God willing, his friends may prosper and his enemies be destroyed. May the King of Iran not forget us in time to come.[19]

The ambassador and his suite finally went on board the English vessel *Satisfaction* which left for Moka under the command of William Rand. It set sail on 18 January 1687; the Persians had stayed more than a year in Siam. They returned to Bandar Abbas in May 1688, after a journey as eventful as the outgoing voyage.

"HIS PAGAN BELIEFS ARE NOT AS STRONG AS BEFORE"

"Now that our pen has sailed through the straits of a condensed report and the official events of our embassy have been described, it is permissible if we turn our attentions to recording some facts about the local conditions."[20] The third "jewel" of *The Ship of Sulaiman* offers a precious overview of the politics, society, religion, and economy of Siam. We shall highlight the pages describing the role played by the Mauro-Persian colony at the time of the advent to power of Phra Narai, and the attitude of the king to Islam.

According to this account, Narai, after installing his uncle Si Suthammaracha on the throne, behaved as though he were already king, deciding on affairs of state without consulting his uncle, and knocking down a minister one day in the presence of the king without any apparent reason. Feeling himself threatened, Suthammaracha decided to dispose of his nephew, but one of the king's servants, who had grown up with Phra Narai (probably one of his foster brothers) came to him and said, "Take care not to go before the king or if you do, be on your guard lest he kill you." Narai then decided to eliminate his uncle and "drew the Franks and the Iranians into his plot."

As it was in the month of Muharram (October), the Persians had completed the Shiite religious ceremony of *ta'ziyat* in honour of the martyr Hussain, son of the caliph Ali. They profited by this pretext to enter the palace and divert attention at the moment when the partisans of the young prince in revolt set fire to the surrounding houses. The palace guards, sent to put out the fire, met Narai and his supporters, and were won over to his side. They joined forces to attack the palace, while the Moors and Persians, already inside, rushed into the royal apartments crying: "Oh Ali!" Overwhelmed by events

Suthammaracha succeeded in escaping by the river, but was caught soon after and killed by his nephew, the new king. The Persian scribe makes a mistake though in placing the advent to the throne of Phra Narai at 17 October 1657; we know he assumed power in October 1656.[21]

The new king did not forget those who had helped him. He immediately named the Persian Abdur Razzaq as chief minister and principal counsellor (with the name Ok-ya Phichit), but he so abused his position that the king, who heard of nothing but his despotism and extortion, had him imprisoned. We have seen earlier that he forced him to eat pork. The fallen and humiliated minister died shortly after; he was replaced by Aqa Muhammad, whose noble character, political wisdom, and unwavering loyalty our scribe praises. Very familiar with international affairs, Aqa Muhammad apparently broadened the king's outlook by speaking to him about the outside world. Phra Narai showed himself a good student, going so far as to prefer Persian dress, arms, and dishes. All this, our witness relates, contributed to "refine his character."

The king however turned a deaf ear when his Persian counsellor tried to win him over to Islam.

> He delved into the precepts on the natural disposition and lusts of man but when it came to beholding the beauty of the true Beloved [the Prophet] and mastering the Perfect Subject [Islam], which consists in knowing the one God, his inner eye of understanding remained limited to the bare exterior of this world. Despite the breadth of his studies, the king held firmly to the path of ingratitude before his Maker and to this day he continues on the road of ignorance. However, a certain degree of change did take place. Contrary to the fixed attitude which his father displayed, the present king has made certain concessions and the most basic beliefs he held have been shaken to their foundation. His pagan faith is no longer so firm and the hatred which usually exists between the non-believers and the faithful has disappeared.[22]

This important passage could well explain the failure of Catholic and Muslim attempts to convert Phra Narai. French and Persian texts say the same thing. Carried forward by unsatiated intellectual curiosity and possibly suffering from a cultural inferiority complex, the king continued to explore foreign metaphysics. This curiosity could not bring him to change his religion. In renouncing Buddhism, the monarch who caused the Wheel of the Law to turn would have undermined his own throne. It was just as unthinkable for Phra Narai to become a Christian as for the pope to convert to Islam.

The incursions of the King of Siam into other religious cultures had no other consequence than a vaguely deistic indifference. The Persian scribe prudently noted: "What faith the king really holds in his heart, God knows best the secrets of his servants."[23] According to Fr Tachard, Phra Narai had declared: "It is certain that if I had no religion, I would not chose Muhammadanism."[24]

Tossed between his own culture, of whose limits he was aware, but which he incarnated, and foreign cultures which were on this account forbidden him, Somdet Phra Narai appears an uprooted person. One can understand from this that some of his frustrated and impulsive remarks were interpreted as intentions to convert, and that embassies were despatched to obtain a notable proselyte. Bénigne Vachet and Ibrahim Muhammad Rabi were victims of the same delusion.

As soon as they were able to speak to their compatriots living in Siam, the Persian ambassadors clearly saw that the hope of enrolling the king among the true believers was vain, and that, influenced by Phaulkon, he had clearly more sympathy for Christianity than Islam. *The Ship of Sulaiman* constantly regrets the darkness of idolatry which surrounded the sovereign, but also notes that the position of Aqa Muhammad was not unassailable. Following a scandal over the unequal and excessive salaries paid to the two hundred Persian bodyguards recruited in India, Phra Narai had the lips of Aqa Muhammad sewn up with threads of bamboo. He died shortly after this treatment. The stupid behaviour of his two sons and the split in the Persian colony helped Phaulkon's rise. With this, the hopes of the Persians and the Moors living in Siam were definitely ruined.

Although our scribe does not say so anywhere, one gathers the impression that the embassy of Shah Sulaiman was not a success, in spite of the florid compliments uttered on both sides. Moreover the elephants which the King of Siam had promised to send to the Shah of Persia never arrived in Isfahan.

The Persian embassy only arrived in Siam after the return to France of Chaumont's embassy which we shall discuss now, and it had already left the kingdom by the time La Loubère's embassy set sail from Brest. It seemed better to incorporate the chronicle of the brief Persian interlude here before beginning the account of the two French embassies and the important Siamese embassy which separates them. This triptych constitutes the high point of this book; the scenes described in *The Ship of Sulaiman* are but a modest foretaste of what was to come.

PART FOUR
THE GREAT EMBASSIES

CHAPTER SIXTEEN

"THESE POOR PEOPLE WHO ARE GOING SO FAR" (MARCH–SEPTEMBER 1685)

CRUISE OR CRUSADE?

DOUBTLESS THE travellers had difficult moments, but a reading of the accounts of the "brilliant embassy" sent by Louis XIV to Siam gives a generally pleasurable impression, at least as far as the first part of the journey was concerned. Grateful for the trade winds which took the two vessels to the Cape without over-agitating the sea, Fr Tachard exclaimed: "If sea journeys are never more uncomfortable nor more dangerous, travel to the Indies would be but long and pleasant promenades."[1]

They attributed their luck to the numerous pious activities which punctuated the days on board. Fr Bouvet, a newly ordained priest, does not doubt this for a moment: "It was a great blessing for the ship that up to eight or nine masses were said each day, and it is to that above all that I attribute the successful sea journey we completed."[2] Even the Abbé de Choisy agrees: "Still a following wind: what a blessing! I was right to tell you God had a hand in it, and I think the trade winds went to find us in Brest, and will take us to Siam."[3] Choisy's "little painter" was wrong to stay close to his godmother.

The Chevalier de Chaumont did not content himself with hearing several masses each day with exemplary piety; he required everyone to be present at mass each day. Vespers were sung on Sundays and holy days before the whole crew. For good measure, His Excellency had expressed his desire that before vespers a short sermon be given "for the edification and instruction of those poor people who, ordinarily bereft of such succour, have great need of it."[4] As the *Oiseau* carried a dozen ecclesiastics who were itching with impatience to go and convert infidels, they asked for nothing better than to try their hand on the sailors, to such an extent that a roster had to be devised.

In addition, a Jesuit had the idea to have the litanies of the Virgin recited by two groups of sailors and soldiers, placed on top of the bridge and the prow, so true is it that one should not do things by halves when saving souls. Lastly Fr Tachard took on the charge of teaching the catechism three times a week to the officers' valets, the soldiers, and the sailors, and "they finished by an uplifting canticle which two sailors with quite good voices sung, and everyone else replied to them on their knees before the main mast."[5] The *Mercure Galant* did not exaggerate when it explained to its readers that "the whole day was filled with pious devotions, and they lived with the same regularity as in a monastery."[6]

As no sailor has left an account of the journey, we do not know what the crew thought of this floating monastery. Reading the Abbé de Choisy, one has the impression that the sailors were less than enthusiastic, at least during the first weeks. "There is much zeal among the preachers, and considerable docility among the listeners. There is not a cabin-boy on board who does not want to go to paradise."[7] Having listened to an exhortation to the sailors delivered by Fr Basset, he explained: "How easily everything brings us to God, when one is in the middle of the seas on five or six planks, ever between life and death!"[8] But there can be too much of a good thing:

> The service is conducted here as in Notre Dame. There is singing and preaching, and if we were to believe all our ecclesiastics, they would be preaching four times a day. They would like to practise, but our poor crew can take no more. When a sailor has sung for all his worth the litany and the prayer for the King, he is happy and asks for his mess bowl.[9]

The accounts we have show an impressive evangelical fervour among the missionaries going to Siam and China. Because of this their journey took on the nature of a crusade. The Abbé de Choisy already saw himself converting the King of Siam; on Easter Day he wrote in his journal: "A king who becomes a Christian, a million souls following his example; this is perhaps what we are going to see; this at least is what we are going to attempt. Could a nobler idea, a more magnificent thought, enter man's mind?"[10] And having observed the progress in the eloquence of Fr Basset, a mediocre orator in the seminary but "a torrent of eloquence" on board the *Oiseau*, he concluded: "If that goes on as started, I shall cease to be surprised at the progress of the Missionaries in the Indies."[11]

It can be guessed though that there were frictions between the six Jesuit Fathers and the three gentlemen of the Foreign Missions. Bénigne Vachet noted in his *Mémoires* that the intendant at Brest had decided to spread the twelve priests among the two vessels, and had ordered three Jesuits who should have been on the *Oiseau* to go on board the *Maligne*. But "these Fathers made such an issue to the ambassador of not being separated that the council decided to put Frs Basset and Manuel on the *Maligne*."[12] It seems, though, that these two soon joined the *Oiseau*, for they appear regularly in Choisy's journal. The priests of the MEP then suggested to the Jesuits that they conduct their pious devotions in common and draw up "a timetable to organize daily life on board throughout the journey," but Fr de Fontaney politely declined this ecumenical proposal.

FROM BREST TO THE CAPE

The *Oiseau* and the *Maligne* set sail on 3 March 1685, leaving the Brest roadstead with a good north-north-east wind. Thus began a memorable journey because it is so well documented. The travellers rarely contradict each other, complement each other on many points, and confirm each other often. The events related are not without interest, but the aridity of these numerous documents is often overwhelming. For Sainte-Beuve, the *Voyage* of Tachard is a "solid work, but heavy and dense . . . It can be consulted, but it is very difficult to read."[13] The geniality and wit of the engaging Choisy seem almost miraculous when set beside the ponderousness of his travelling companions. Here is someone who can instruct and edify his reader without boring him. If timelessness in writing and a dislike of taking oneself seriously are literary criteria—and I am convinced they are—then Choisy is a great writer. He will be our star witness.

It took several days for those unaccustomed to sea travel to get over seasickness. Only Fr Tachard, who had been to the West Indies, and Fr Vachet, who had already crossed the Line four times, were good sailors. The others miserably threw up "half their souls" while waiting for better days.

The 209 men on board the *Oiseau* jostled each other in the very limited space available, reminiscent of Noah's ark. There was an immense gulf between, on the one hand, the officers, gentlemen accompanying the ambassador, and ecclesiastics, who had their cabins and ate reasonably adequate food, and, on the other hand, the sailors and troops who had to make do with a hammock slung up in the between-decks and meals where ship's biscuits were doused with various sauces. The ship carried live sheep and pigs which ate bread and shared the between-decks with the sailors. Chickens were piled up in cages on the poop along with salted provisions, ship's biscuits, water, wine, brandy, wood, and cannon balls. Gunpowder was kept under lock and key, as well as all the gear needed for the ship's maintenance and repairs. Choisy, the only one to mention these details, notes in his journal:

> I went this morning to visit the hold of the ship. It is a vast region. Sheep here, pigs there; water on one side, wine the other. Mr de Forbin was my guide. We found at the bottom of the hold some salted beef tongues and some good wine. I ate the crew's biscuit and found it very good, and was very pleased to see the powder so firmly locked away.[14]

A few days were needed to get used to the ship's rolling and pitching. Then life began to get organized. The travellers were surprised not to be bored a single moment. Apart from the frequent religious activities, learning what life was like on board, meteorology, and the sea overwhelmed those in search of exotic impressions. Marine terminology delighted Choisy; he amused himself explaining to his friend Dangeau (for whom his journal was written) terms like squalls, sailing close-hauled, parrot's perch, topsail, taking in sail, etc. "How easy it is for one to talk nautical! You have to get used to it. I tell my valet to moor my collar."[15]

The atmosphere on the *Oiseau* was studious. Fathers Basset and Manuel began to learn Siamese with Fr Vachet, Choisy studied Portuguese and algebra before tackling Siamese and geometry, and the Jesuits "spend their time drawing lines and making calculations; that is their mission. They know it is through mathematics that they prosper in China."[16] The abbé particularly appreciated the learned exposés of Fr de Fontaney: "We shall learn . . . astronomy; we ought to profit by the presence of the six Fathers who will in China be many Verbiests." And a month later:

> This morning Fr de Fontaney began a public lecture on the sphere. It will not be said that we let him go without getting all that we could from him, and when he is a great mandarin and favourite of the Emperor of China, I shall say: "It is he who taught me the daily movement of the heavens."[17]

The evenings were filled with astronomy. "We do not need the sun to consider the moon and the stars; we are already beginning to recognize the Milky Way and the Great Bear; and we shall see, beyond the Line, other stars which you are most unlikely ever to see."[18]

This love of the stars did not prevent the abbé from learning about Siam from Fr Vachet, whom he appreciated with some reserve.

> I often talk to Mr Vachet. He little by little tells me everything I should be aware of, and I hope on arriving in Siam to know more or less the people we shall have to deal with . . . You do not know Mr V, and to know him, you should hear him speak about public affairs. No one speaks better than he . . . It is true that everything is lost when he wants to be amusing; it is his weakness, not his talent. I listen to him when he speaks seriously, and when he wants to be funny, I absent myself.[19]

Opportunities to relax after such studious application were not lacking. First of all there were the surprising phenomena to observe at sea, like St Elmo's fire (corposants) or the "water dragons" (whirlpools). Then there was fishing and the discovery of exotic fish which were conscientiously dissected and then tasted. The travellers could only talk of porpoises, flying fish, bonitos, sharks, dolphins, turtles, rays, and pilot fish, which the sailors caught or harpooned under their eyes. "The sea is alive with fish; some swim, others fly. Those which swim leap to catch those flying; they all do battle with each other, and eat each other when they can. We too eat them when we can."[20]

When he was not passing his time watching the fish and those who caught them, the abbé played chess with Forbin, whose southern enthusiasm he appreciated. He resumes his days on board thus:

> I discuss Portuguese with Fr Visdelou; Mr Basset explains the sacred orders to me; I look at the moon with Fr de Fontaney; I talk about steering with our ensign Chamoreau, who knows a lot about it; and all that incidentally, without any haste, while walking about. And when I want to relax, I call Mr Manuel . . . who has a mighty fine voice, and knows music as well as Lully. You know how much I like music . . . We sing hymns which are as fine as *Roland*. After that, are you still sorry for these poor people who are going so far away?[21]

Few external events disturbed the peace of this floating city of God, the *Oiseau*. The equinoctial line (the equator) was crossed on 7 April, after five weeks' sailing. The pilots organized a baptism for those crossing the Line for the first time. Given the choice of forking out into a pan or being doused in sea water, the travellers loosened their purse strings. The amount collected, sixty crowns, would be used at the Cape to augment the crews' commons. Those who had already crossed the equator had to swear to the fact on the Gospels, but the pious ambassador saw profanity in that and had people swear on a globe, which was perhaps not such a bad idea. Those who refused to pay were generously daubed and then drenched in quantities of water. By mistake a bucket drenched a Jesuit who had already paid; the error caused general hilarity.

On 10 May, Choisy wrote: "A ship! We can see a ship! We were beginning to think that there was only us on the sea."[22] It was a small English vessel which passed close to the *Maligne* to inform the crew of the death of Charles II and the accession of James, Duke of York. Fr Bouvet and his copier Fr Tachard indicate that "this ship was coming from the West Indies, and was going to take on slaves in Madagascar,"[23] without taking exception in the least, as though the slave ship were a banana boat.

It was realized that the *Oiseau* and the *Maligne* had to reach the Cape by the end of May if they wished to arrive in Siam the same year; after this date, it would be impossible to profit by the summer monsoon in the Indian Ocean blowing towards land. A calm at the beginning of May worried the travellers, but everything turned out well in the end. The abbé noted on 30 May: "Land! Land! All is well; we can see land, see the Cape! We are about twelve leagues away. What a pleasure after being so long away! We shall eat vegetables!"[24] On 31 May at daybreak, the two vessels carefully entered the bay of the Cape of Good Hope. The west wind suddenly dropped and a dangerous current took them towards a rock but an accident was just avoided. They anchored close to the Dutch fort after a successful crossing of three months, during which they had only lost a single sailor who was already sick when they set out. Four big Dutch vessels were anchored in the roads. The admiral, the Baron van Reede tot Drakestein, was travelling to Batavia where the VOC was sending him with the title of commissioner general armed with considerable authority.

THE CAPE: "WE ARE WELL OFF HERE, BUT MUST GO TO SIAM"

The Chevalier de Forbin went ashore the following day to pay his respects to the governor Simon van der Stel and decide on the manner in which the king's vessels, the Dutch ships and the fort would salute each other. He was also charged with negotiating the purchase of the victuals the French needed. "It was decided," Forbin wrote, "that the salute would be gun for gun, and that we should be furnished with all manner of refreshments for our money."[25] After a lengthy concert of carefully counted cannon shots, the longboats were put to sea and the travellers could only think of feeling solid ground beneath their feet and "eating salads." The Abbé de Choisy was in less of a hurry, for Baron van Reede sent the ambassador a present of fruits, vegetables, and sheep. "Our invalids, our Jesuits, and our Missionaries went on land. I shall go tomorrow in good company, for they say there are some bad-tempered lions and extremely impertinent elephants on the mountainside . . . We shall eat some salad; I do not care about the rest."[26]

He disembarked the next morning to visit the fortress with five bastions topped by cannons. He also saw the nascent town at the Cape. The whitewashed thatched houses were so clean one would have thought one were in Holland. But what Choisy and the other French admired most was the botanical garden, the pride of the colony, where had been planted "all the good fruits of Europe and the Indies. These on one side, those on the other, and all survive very well."[27] Fr Tachard, who describes the garden very precisely, explains that "The gentlemen of the [Dutch] East Indies Company . . . have created it so as to have always in this place a store, as it were, of all kinds of refreshments for their vessels going to the Indies or returning thence."[28] The Chevalier de Chaumont recognized as the chief person responsible for this marvel a Frenchman who had formerly been gardener to the Duke of Orléans at St Cloud.

But this one-time servant of the king's brother, in spite of the consideration he enjoyed in the land and the numerous slaves he commanded, was not without cares; baboons in great numbers lived on the mountains and adored his melons. Their strategy is revealed by Choisy:

> Sometimes two hundred of them commandeer them from the gardens. First of all they place four or five guards on some rocks or in the trees; these send up a special cry when they see people. The bravest macaques come into the garden one behind the other, and pass the melons down the line. They return on three legs, each holding a melon, and when they are chased, they put the melon down very carefully, and defend themselves by throwing stones. This happens here several times every year.[29]

The stopover of a week at the Cape allowed the members of the crew suffering from scurvy to revive; they had "become vigorous again" in four days after a cure of vegetables and fruit. The young officers organized hunting parties and returned dog-tired, loaded with game. "They walked all day up to the neck in grasses and reeds; they will sleep soundly," the paternalistic Choisy noted.[30] The abbé gave himself over to less exhausting distractions. He walked in the botanic garden, went to fish in the bay, visited the Baron van Reede (they spoke Portuguese and French), or assisted the Jesuits absorbed in their astronomical observations.

Profiting from the benevolent attitude of the Calvinist Dutch, Fr de Fontaney declared to the governor that, to thank the Dutch gentlemen for their hospitality, he proposed to determine with his companions the exact longitude of the Cape, based on the table of the satellites of Jupiter established by Cassini. Very impressed, van der Stel put at their disposal a magnificent pavilion in the botanical garden, where the Fathers installed their scientific paraphernalia. Choisy wrote:

> Their quarters are between two terraces, where there is plenty of room for the biggest telescopes; bread, wine, fruit, they lack nothing. They keep a good table. Are they foolish? They show the Dutch

> Jupiter's satellites, Saturn's belts, and the Milky Way . . . The intellect is a fine thing in all countries.[31]

Fr Bouvet explains the methods and the results of the observations, indicating that "The Abbé de Choisy found us so well placed that he turned observer as well, and always remained with us."[32] With charming modesty, the abbé explains that he counted the seconds out loud whilst the Fathers busied themselves with their instruments before the eyes of the Dutch. The combined efforts allowed them to conclude that the longitude of the Cape was three degrees less than was thought. "Three degrees in longitude in these lands means forty-eight leagues, and that is most important when sailing . . . This single observation justifies all the instruments which the king has caused to have made. Do you not consider me a great astronomer?"[33]

During this time the other members of the expedition gave themselves over to observations of the hinterland. Their descriptions of the native "Hottentots" (Khoikhoi) are very summary. Forbin writes:

> The natives are Kaffirs . . . there is not a more unpolite and brutish people under the sun. They speak inarticulately, so that nobody could ever learn their language . . . They live without religion, feed up on all sorts of insects that they find in the fields, and go naked, both the men and the women, with only a sheep's skin over their shoulders, that breeds vermin, which they eat without loathing. All the ornament worn by the women is the guts of sheep fresh killed, which they roll about their arms and legs . . . They lie all together, higgledy-piggledy, without distinction of sexes, in sorry cottages, and couple with one another indifferently like beasts, without any regard to consanguinity. [34]

The description given to the readers of the *Mercure Galant*, provided by people in Chaumont's entourage, is still more repulsive:

> The inhabitants . . . are ugly, ill-formed, small, and live more like beasts than men. Their faces are all wrinkled, their hair is covered with grease; as they cover themselves with whale fat and only eat raw meat, they smell so much that they can be discerned from afar. They only eat their cattle when an animal has died diseased, and it is a great relish when a dead whale is thrown up by the sea on their shores, or they have the fresh intestines of some animal. They shake them

> gently, and eat them with the filth, after removing the excrement, which some of them use to rub on their faces. They bear the name of Kaffirs, and the men and women have only a triangular-shaped skin to cover what nature teaches them to conceal.[35]

There was a long way to go before serious ethnography got under way! The absence of any anthropological interest is striking. These gratuitous appetizers, inserted in travel accounts which reveal no serious bent of mind, reduce men to the level of beasts because their language was impenetrable. There is total incomprehension. Chaumont writes: "These people have no religion; yet during the full moon they perform certain ceremonies, *but which signify nothing*"[36] (emphasis added). The era of the "noble savage," whose purity and natural virtues would made the corrupted European blush for shame, had not yet arrived.

The stopover at the Cape was most agreeable and instructive, but time pressed; the monsoon would not wait. "We are mighty fine here, but must go to Siam," wrote Choisy.[37] The crew had not been idle while the travellers observed the natives, the thieving baboons, and the satellites of Jupiter. Water, wood, sheep, pigs, chickens, fruit, and vegetables had been taken on, everything needed for crossing the Indian Ocean. The refreshed invalids and the royal telescopes were put on board again. The hospitable Dutch were thanked in bad Portuguese. The departure was set for 6 June, but there was not enough wind. They had to wait for the next day to set sail. "We were the better for it by small suckling pigs and wine from the Canary Islands, which the Commissioner-General sent us."[38] Good can come of misfortune.

FROM THE CAPE TO BATAVIA: "LET US PRAY TO GOD AND DRINK OUR SPANISH WINE"

As soon as they were at sea, the travellers realized that the second ocean crossing would not be as easy as the first. The swell was considerable, the winds strong, and the *Oiseau* rolled dangerously. The Abbé de Choisy had trouble in keeping his journal: "We carry on, but roll badly . . . Yet again, my inkstand has turned over. This entry will be short; where to get ink? The rolling serves as an excuse."[39]

But they took consolation, for the ship skimmed over the water and travelled sixty leagues a day with just its foresail.

A few whales spouted, but there were no fish on the surface of the ocean, which troubled the cooks for they had counted on replenishing their stocks at sea. But the professional or amateur astronomers had the good fortune to observe a lunar eclipse. This phenomenon even flushed out the two *khunnang* who remained obstinately invisible. "Our poor mandarins, who make much ado about the moon, came out of their lair, from which, in parenthesis, they never emerge, and came to see the piteous state it was in; they could not bear the sight of it and went back to bed."[40] One is reassured to see them mentioned for the first time since setting out, for one began to wonder if, by oversight, in the flurry of the departure, the two uncouth Siamese had not been left on the Brest quayside.

After a week, the wind abated, and then reversed. They hardly moved for a fortnight, and the Jesuits organized a novena to obtain from the Virgin Mary a favourable wind. As one novena was not enough, they began another. In order to speed things up, two sailors from St Malo made a solemn vow to go on a pilgrimage dressed in shifts to the church of St Saviour in St Malo. But nothing came of it, and the Fathers consoled themselves by saying that if their prayers had been answered, the vessel would surely have run up against an uncharted island and been shipwrecked.

But the anxiety of the travellers can be understood. The summer monsoon was already blowing further north, and they were afraid of not arriving at their rendezvous. The discovery, at dawn on 25 June, that the *Maligne* had disappeared from the horizon, added to the general unease. They could only hope to meet the lost frigate at Batavia. At the beginning of July Choisy summarizes the anxiety which racked the passengers on the *Oiseau*:

> Now the lamentations start again. We shall not reach Siam this year. For a fortnight we have advanced not a jot; we are going backwards . . . There are still more than one thousand leagues from here to Batavia. When we arrive, the monsoon in Siam will be over. What a pity! To spend winter in the hands of the Dutch, who do not like us as much as they say. Oh, poor France, when shall we see you again? In this way a year will be lost.[41]

The abbé was more optimistic: "Pray to God and let us drink our Spanish wine . . . The good winds will come." To maintain his cheerful disposition, he reread the description of the joys of paradise in the *Essais de morale* (Essays on morality) of Pierre Nicole. "In truth, one must be mad not to wish to go there."[42]

The oratorical eagerness of the Jesuits seems to have cooled since the journey began. Fr Tachard did what he could, but Choisy considered that "his appearance is not imposing. His zeal makes him speak with too much effort." The prize went to Fr Le Comte, who preached with the sweat of his brow, acclaimed and coddled by an enthusiastic audience. After his sermons, "everyone embraces him, mops his brow, no one wants him to catch cold, because they want to hear him again."[43]

The situation on board became worrying. The bad weather and above all rotten victuals brought down sixty of the sailors attacked by the plague of long sea journeys, scurvy, "an illness which paralyzed the legs and the mouth, and caused their teeth to fall out," Bouvet notes. The surgeons cut gangrened gums "up to the palate" and disinfected them with vinegar. The Jesuits consoled the poor devils by having them understand "the obligation they had to God who afflicted them in this world instead of reserving a punishment for them in the next."[44] In short, they did everything they could to cheer them up.

The rough seas and variable winds obliged the pilots of the *Oiseau* (there were six) to shift to forty degrees south to find west winds. They caught them at last on 8 July and went north, covering more than four hundred leagues in a week. On the tenth day they passed the Tropic of Capricorn again.

A sad accident then troubled the pleasant journey. The facts as related by Choisy are:

> Robin is dead, and we shall eat him. He was a sheep famous among all others for his long voyages. He had gone through several campaigns very successfully, and seen the American islands, always between two bridges, at the head of the others to whom he taught how to withstand the pitching and rolling; and after passing the Line, the Cape of Good Hope, and five hundred leagues from Batavia, the stupid beast fell, and damaged one of his rear legs. Robin was very fat; it was feared he would get thin, and so he was handed over to the butcher.[45]

He was the talk of the table, and someone considered "that Robin was only a machine." This indelicate proposition—one does not speak ill of someone whose haunches one is consuming—provoked a heated debate about the souls of animals between those who held to the machine theory and those who opted for souls. The question, which had already pitted Descartes against Gassendi, was very delicate because to consider that an animal had an immortal soul was a terrible heresy incurring the direst anathemas. Fr Vachet, a convinced believer in souls, cited anecdotes about the intelligence and memory of Siamese elephants which cut into the machinist side. They were agreed on one point though: the well-travelled Robin was the most famous sheep of his kind.[46]

But life went on. Batavia and Siam approached, and the Abbé de Choisy prepared himself for them. His study of Siamese made progress. "The Siamese is coming along beautifully, and I begin to gabble with the mandarins," he wrote on 6 July. And on the nineteenth,

> The mandarins wrote me this morning a letter to congratulate me on my progress in the finest language on earth. I read the letter very carefully, and understood almost all of it; and immediately replied in pure Siamese. It is true, I was aided in my task . . . I am beginning to take pleasure in it, and am sure, morally speaking, to speak Siamese in Siam.[47]

While studying Siamese with Vachet and geometry with Tachard, Choisy did not forget that he was making the journey as coadjutor to the ambassador. But Chaumont did not treat him as such and never spoke of any details concerning the embassy. The abbé relates in his *Memoirs* how he finally brought round the touchy ambassador:

> But we were already five months at sea, without the Chevalier de Chaumont making any overtures to me. This began to tire me. I foresaw that if this continued, I would count for nothing in Siam, when, through the partition which separated my cabin from his, I heard him pondering over his discourse [for the day of audience]. I said to him a week later (for he continued with the same song) that I had heard the most splendid things in the world. Upon that he took me into his cabin and repeated it to me; I found it faultless. From that day he began to speak to me about what had to be done in that

> country; I gave him my humble opinions. He is a goodly man, and truly a person of standing and quality, but he does not understand geometry. I did not have much trouble in letting him understand that, as it happened, I could be useful to him in some degree. From that day on he did not even spit without warning me first.[48]

He then had "an interesting thought": if Chaumont should die at sea, he would have to address the King of Siam. Seduced by the idea, he wrote down his discourse. One wonders if it would have convinced Phra Narai to worship the same God as Louis XIV, but Choisy was sufficiently pleased with it to insert it in his *Memoirs*.[49]

At dawn on 3 August, the passengers on the *Oiseau* observed a few leagues away to starboard the "Isle of Mony," a low-lying island which Captain Cook would rename Christmas Island. It is located forty leagues south of the western tip of Java. Choisy noted the event and the confusion of the pilots who were forced by cartographic uncertainties to navigate by guesswork, and who did not expect to find it there.

The ship went north, helped "by a fairly fresh breeze," towards the Sunda Strait between Sumatra and Java. Land was close by; everyone had visions of salads and exotic fruits. Large birds soared in the sky, and came to perch unafraid on the rigging. "They are taken, stroked, and then eaten."[50] They then entered the strait, "plumb line in hand," but contrary currents halted their progress or caused the *Oiseau* to move back. Passing through Sunda took a week which seemed like an eternity. Provisions were virtually exhausted and the sick, ever more numerous, suffered the tortures of Tantalus seeing coconut and fruit trees on the shores. Finally on 15 August they dropped anchor in the Bay of Bantam, hoping to find the Dutch there as hospitable as those at the Cape.

Chaumont sent Forbin on shore to compliment the sultan and request him to provide them with "refreshments" which they badly needed. Bantam had no godown of the CIO since 1682. The Dutch had profited by a dispute between the old sultan Abdulfatah and his heir Abdulkahar (known as Sultan Haji) to depose the father, install his son on the throne, and govern the country in his name. They had expelled the English and French traders, and jealously held on to the small sultanate because of its strategic location. As for Sultan Haji, he dared not even sneeze without their consent.

Forbin learnt from the mouth of a low-ranking Dutch officer that the "king" could not receive him, having withdrawn into the apartments of his wives, that the resident representing the VOC was sick, that there were no provisions for sale, and that the king had absolutely forbidden the disembarkation of the French. But a pleasant discovery softened this refusal; on returning in his longboat, Forbin discovered, anchored in the roadstead behind a small island, the *Maligne* which had arrived four days before them. He went on board the frigate, embraced the captain Joyeux, and returned with him to the *Oiseau*, "where the pleasure we had of seeing one another made amends for the repulse we had met with from the Dutch."[51]

Fortunately they could buy some provisions from the Javanese who loaded their dugouts with chickens, ducks, bananas, figs, and coconuts. In Choisy's eyes, these good "Javans," who were disinterested in money and were content with pins, needles, and knives, were "not in the least disgusting like the Hottentots." Suddenly the two resuscitated Siamese *khunnang* were unrecognizable. "Now they are always on the bridge, they smile at the angels in the sky, and play little games. They also ate betel and areca; these are their foibles. I think that in Siam we shall find them lively enough; may God grant that we shall not be the ones who are stupid."[52]

The two vessels set sail the following day for Batavia, only twelve leagues away. They dropped anchor in the roadstead on Saturday, 18 August at sunset. The crossing of the Indian Ocean had not always been a pleasure trip, but the certainty that the monsoon was still blowing and that they would be in Siam in a month comforted them.

BATAVIA, CAPITAL OF THE DUTCH INDIES

Forbin, sent ashore at once, returned on board "overcome with joy." The new VOC governor-general, Johan Camphuys, granted all they desired and even more.

> As soon as we had cast anchor, I went ashore to make my compliment to him, and was received at my landing by an officer of the port, who conducted me to the palace. At my arrival, the common guard, which was very numerous, stood under their arms in two lines, through which I was introduced into a gallery adorned with the finest porcelain of Japan. There I found His Excellency . . . standing with his hat down to the ground, a reception which made ample reparation for the repulse I had suffered at Bantam. The only

> language he spoke to me was in French . . . I had nothing to do but to ask a favour, and it was granted, the general having assured me, at the very first, in express terms, that there was nothing he was not ready to undertake to show the ambassador the veneration he had for his character, and for his person in particular.[53]

Hardly had he completed his report than the officers of the governor-general came to offer on his behalf twelve large baskets of vegetables and fruit, as well as cattle and sheep. Camphuys maintained this politeness for the week the French were to stay in Batavia. The sick were disembarked and the reprovisioning of the ship started.

Our sources contradict themselves on one particular point. Whilst Bouvet, Tachard, and Choisy declare that the French vessels and the Dutch fort saluted each other shot for shot (Choisy even declared that this had "never happened before in the Indies"),[54] Forbin is categoric:

> We could not agree upon the salute to be gun for gun, as I would have had it; therefore I cannot imagine how Fr Tachard came by that account in his narrative, where he is so particular as to tell how many guns were discharged; for 'tis very certain that we agreed that there should be no salute on either side.[55]

He should know; after all, it was he who negotiated with the Dutch.

The French travellers saw Batavia at the beginning of Camphuys's mandate; he had been installed as governor-general only some ten days previously. They were visibly impressed:

> Batavia is the capital city of the Dutch nation in the Indies, whose power here is formidable, for they commonly keep in pay five or six thousand men of regular troops, composed of different nations. The citadel, which lies near the middle of the road, is built upon piles of wood . . . The town is well built, all the houses are white, after the manner of Holland; and among the numberless inhabitants there are a great many French Huguenots and Catholics who live there for the sake of trade. The general of the India Company who resides here has the command over all the Dutch Indies, and no king has a court more numerous and splendid . . . The embassies of all the Indian princes are to apply to him, and he sends ambassadors to them in the name of his nation. He makes peace and war at his own pleasure, without control from any power whatsoever.[56]

One finds the same admiration in Tachard: "It is the most agreeable city in the Indies, and it would seem very handsome in Europe . . . The streets are long and broad, all perfectly straight, between two rows of local trees which are always green."[57] The town crawled with people all preoccupied with making money. The Chinese, comprising three-quarters of the population, were most successful at this. The Malays and Javanese, less pushing, passively observed the Chinese, who traded from dawn to dusk, and the Dutch, who controlled everything and skimmed their share from the transactions, imposing prices at their pleasure and causing gold to pour into the coffers of their company.

The Jesuits went to pay their respects to the governor-general who treated them with every possible consideration. They spoke about Louis XIV (whom Camphuys seemed to have sincerely admired), China, and astronomy. The Fathers mentioned their longitudinal calculations at the Cape; they offered their services, were given a pavilion in the middle of a garden, and went off to get their instruments on board the *Oiseau*.

They returned to their temporary residence where they met with an aged colleague, Fr Domenico Fuciti, who had worked for thirty years in Tonkin and Cochin-China, where he became embroiled with the vicars-apostolic whose authority he challenged. The Jesuit general had recalled him to Rome to explain his refusal to obey the instructions of the Holy See.[58] Desirous to return through Siam where letters from his provincial superior in Macao were awaiting him, he joyfully accepted the offer of travelling with his colleagues on the *Oiseau*. Tachard and Bouvet relate Fuciti's virtues, travails, and tribulations at length; they consider him a saint, the victim of false rumours spread by the Foreign Missions, and gloss over his insubordination "with Jesuitical skates."[59] The Fathers installed themselves in their garden, but the overcast sky prevented them from making astronomic calculations. They were often seen in town where they discreetly administered the sacraments to the Catholics they found there, for the practice of Roman Catholicism was forbidden in the Dutch Indies.

The Abbé de Choisy went about Batavia as a tourist. He visited the citadel, the streets, the canals, the tropical garden of the Jesuits, where, made blasé by the fountains at Versailles, he mocked a little jet of water: "They make much fuss of a gee-gaw which pisses when the pump has functioned." He was served at table by black lackeys who "brought us a dry wine for the right hand and a well-lit pipe for the left," in the presence of ladies. "But what ladies, always chewing betel and areca! You know that this betel produces a red liquid like blood; and these ladies have mouths as though they have just had four large teeth removed." He even went book hunting: "I went to the only bookseller in Batavia to look for local books. He did not stock them, but he was very pressing in his desire to sell me the *Mercure Galant.*"

On 24 August, the ambassador sent Fathers Tachard and Bouvet to the governor-general to advise him that the French were going to celebrate the feast of St Louis at nightfall with cannon shots. Camphuys thought they were celebrating Louis XIV's birthday, and said he was ready to have the artillery in the fort and on the Dutch ships participate. But on learning that it was a question of a saint's day with the same name as the king, he expressed his regret. "I am very sorry, Fathers," he said to them, "but I cannot honour St Louis," and he dismissed the Jesuits after drinking to the king's health.[60] The Dutch soldiers also indicated their regret at not being able to take part in the celebrations in honour of a Catholic saint: "We should have drunk plenty of wine and smoked many pipes on the ramparts of the citadel, to the sound of all the cannons."[61] It is true that the life of guards in the tropics lacks distractions.

Two days later, the *Oiseau* and the *Maligne* set sail. The sick, all by then recovered, were on board, as were the provisions. The governor-general lent them a pilot who knew the route like the back of his hand. The travellers were aware that the last stretch would be the most pleasant and the shortest.

FROM BATAVIA TO THE BAR OF SIAM: "WHERE ARE THE SABRES?"

On Monday, 26 August, the two vessels left the Batavia roadstead early in the morning with a favourable wind, in the direction of the strait between the north-east tip of Sumatra and Bangka Island. At ten in the evening, the watch on the *Oiseau* suddenly noticed, at a distance of a couple of musket shots to port, a large ship which came from nowhere in the dark with a rear wind and was coming straight at them with the clear intention of boarding them. The alarm was sounded. They cried out; no one replied. A cannon was fired at the ship, which did not change its course. A strong turn of the tiller just avoided a collision, but the mast of the assailant's bowsprit knocked off some of the taffrail of the *Oiseau*'s forecastle, and broke the porthole window of the cabin where the venerable Fr Fuciti was sleeping. Forbin, posted on the poop, fired several rifle shots, but no one was to be seen on the bridge of this ghost ship.

Thinking they were going to fight, the watch soldiers and sailors quickly took up their arms. A Jesuit Father came up on deck with a sabre in his hands, "resolved to defend his life and ours, to lose them on a better occasion in the midst of infidels,"[62] but the attacker was already far off. Choisy, woken by the cries "To arms, to arms, prepare the cannons, prime the muskets, where are the sabres?" went up on deck. "I myself have not fought in many battles, but to look at the faces of our soldiers and sailors, we would not have been taken without striking a blow. The Jesuits and Missionaries had already declared themselves. Some were on their knees at the bottom of the hold, and others proudly on deck, sabre in hand."[63] Bouvet concludes, "I leave you to consider what impression this adventure made on our minds, particularly on those who had never seen a battle except in paintings or books."[64]

Much of the night was spent in discussing the event. The vessel, clearly European, could only be English or Dutch. The absence of anyone on deck made the ambassador think that the unknown intruder had no hostile intentions, but they were only an inch away from colliding due to the inattention of a possibly drunken pilot. Chaumont was right. The ship was Dutch, the *Berckmeer*, which was returning to Batavia from Palembang in Sumatra loaded with pepper.

The keels moved with difficulty over the muddy floor of the Bangka Strait which was crossed with plumb line in hand. The two vessels crossed the Line on 3 September in intense heat. Two days later, seeing in the distance the tip of the Malacca peninsula, the travellers had their first sight of continental Asia; up to then they had seen only islands. But they were concerned; the young Herbouville, a gentlemen in the ambassador's suite, received the last sacraments on the *Maligne*, and his death was seen to be imminent. Handsome, well-turned, only son of a Normandy gentleman and heir to a considerable fortune, he had wanted to undertake the voyage to the end of the earth before entrenching himself in a pampered life. On 6 September, at nine in the morning, the frigate sent up the flag announcing his death; five cannon shots were fired in the evening, when the weighted body slipped into the water.

The *Oiseau* and the *Maligne* then passed between the Malay peninsula, which those on board could constantly see to port, and islands with exotic names. Fr Vachet explained to the passengers that the small kingdom of Johor, as well as those of Pattani and Ligor further north, were tributary to the King of Siam, to whom each year they sent a gold and silver flower as a symbol of their allegiance. The two *khunnang* became more lively as they approached Siam. According to the *Mercure Galant*, "the two mandarins who were returning from France to Siam had only left the lubber's hole into which they had placed themselves throughout the voyage on two occasions, but when black men began to be seen near the Bangka Strait, they got up on the deck and showed great signs of joy."[65]

A succession of sudden winds and calms had the captains constantly raising and dropping their anchors, fearing contrary currents might make them go back over the distance they had already covered. On 12 September, level with Pattani, they lost a soldier who was both a carpenter and a fountain-maker, and should have built waterfalls at Lopburi. "That poor soldier died this morning; so the King of Siam will do without fountains."[66]

Bénigne Vachet is the only person to mention that he suggested to Chaumont that he take possession, in the name of the King of France, of the outpost of Singor (Songkhla), which the King of Siam had ceded to the CIO, and leave there a dozen or so men because it was the ideal spot for a godown. He added that he had spoken about this to Seignelay who had approved the idea. Chaumont at first appeared convinced, then hesitated (his instructions said nothing about this), and finally decided not to stop at Singor, wishing to do nothing before consulting Phaulkon. Vachet did not forgive him in light of the dramatic events of 1688: "This is what the Chevalier de Chaumont's conduct cost us, with the terrible consequences of the revolution in Siam, which would never have occurred if the French had first of all taken possession of Singor."[67] He was probably wrong, but it is certain that a fortified assembly point in the south would have allowed a less disordered withdrawal.

Finally, with much furling and unfurling of sails, lowering and raising of anchors, the two vessels arrived on 24 September at the estuary of the Chao Phraya. They dropped anchor a few leagues from the "bar of Siam," a vast mudbank formed by the outflow of the river two leagues from its mouth. This bar acts as a barrier; when the tides were high the water never rose above twelve or thirteen feet, and the *Oiseau* drew seventeen feet. Our travellers were not worried about this, being only too happy to have arrived. "The view of the kingdom of Siam," says Tachard, "made everyone extremely happy after so many perils and the exhaustion of such a long journey."[68] The passage from Brest had only lasted six months and three weeks.

FORBIN DISCOVERS SIAM: "FRANKLY, I WAS SURPRISED"

The Chevalier de Chaumont immediately sent Vachet and Forbin on shore. After dropping off Forbin, Vachet was to go to Ayutthaya, bearing a letter for Mgr Laneau, requesting him to inform Phra Narai of the arrival of Louis XIV's embassy and to come on board "to discuss all matters." According to Choisy, "for the moment it only concerns our entrance into the capital, but this must correspond to the dignity of the greatest monarch on earth."[69] The mission given to Forbin was more concrete: to go and find the "governor of the bar" and that of Bangkok, and to obtain from them provisions which would permit the French to remain on board their ships until everything was ready for their entrance into the capital. Forbin's account is worth quoting *in extenso*:

> As we were going up, we saw three or four little houses of canes covered with the leaves of palm; Mr Vachet told me that there lived the governor of the bar. We went ashore in our canoe, and found three or four fellows sitting on the bare ground in one of those houses, chewing the cud like oxen, without shoes, stockings or hat, or anything at all to cover their body but a piece of cloth to hide their nakedness. Their house too looked as poor as the inhabitants, for I saw no chairs in it, nor any manner of furniture; upon which I enquired where the governor was, and one of the company said, "I am he."
>
> This first scene very much sunk the ideas I had formed of Siam; nevertheless I had a keen appetite, and asking for food, the honest governor made me a present of some rice, and when I desired to know if he had nothing else to give me, he answered "Amay," which signifies "No."
>
> Having been thus regaled at our arrival, I frankly own that I have wondered more than once how the Abbé de Choisy and Father Tachard, who made the same voyage and saw the same things as I did, should both agree to give such pompous ideas of the kingdom of Siam, with so little foundation. 'Tis true that as they stayed there but

> a few months, and as it was the interest of M. Constance, the chief minister, to cast a mist before their eyes, for reasons which I shall mention in their place, there was nothing in this kingdom capable of imposing on them but what was showed to them; though when all is said and done, they must have been strangely infatuated not to see the misery of the whole country, which is so visible, go where you will, that it is impossible not to perceive it. Having said this *en passant,* we return now to our voyage.
>
> When the tide served, we went aboard again . . . and by ten o'clock at night arrived at Bangkok. The governor of the place, who was a Turk, but cut a better figure than he at the bar, gave us a very indifferent supper . . . Next morning . . . I returned in the canoe on board our ship; but before I went, I asked the governor if, for my money, I might not have some herbs, fruit, and other refreshments to carry on board, to which he answered "No." As our company were impatient for my return, as soon as ever they saw me coming at a great distance, they called out to me to know if I brought any refreshments with me, but I said I had brought nothing except the bites of gnats which had persecuted us all the way.[70]

The dreams of grandeur of Chaumont and Choisy hardly corresponded to the reality of the "real Siam" which Forbin had just discovered. To each man his truths. The comment of Forbin on the over-brilliant image of Siam propagated by the accounts which Tachard and Choisy were to publish after a stay of only three months denounce the creation of a myth responsible for misunderstandings and unfortunate decisions. After living more than a year in Siam, Forbin knew what he was talking about.

Phichai Walit and Phichit Maitri, at last back in their country, considered their mission over. A barge came to fetch them; the men rowing it informed Phichai Walit (whom the French called "the old mandarin" because his hair was completely grey) of the death of his grandmother, who must have been at least a hundred. "The ambassador, seeing him cry like a baby, thought that the old man was mourning the death of one of his wives (he had three). This caused him to say in jest that he could take consolation, since if he had lost one of his women, he still had two in excess."[71]

After many thanks and much bowing and scraping, the two Siamese got into their barge, without leaving behind all the numerous presents they had received in France. Chaumont, a gallant person to the end, fired five shots of cannon on their departure. The French were visibly relieved to see them go.

Fr Bouvet does not mince his words. "This was the last honour shown to these supposed mandarins. I say *supposed mandarins* because they were only such in name. And they only acquired it in France, for they were ordinary Siamese who had been sent to enquire about the first mandarins. So on their return they were quickly de-mandarinized."[72] The Jesuit also relates that the King of Siam, displeased with their conduct in France, had them beaten, and that the younger in particular was "irremediably ruined."

At the end of October Fr Tachard related for his part:

> They began to examine the conduct of the two mandarins . . . who had been sent to France with Mr Vachet. The complaints made about them had reached the king's ears, who was shocked by their conduct. The ambassador spoke in their favour. The older was let off with a month in prison and some other chastisement. We do not know what is the punishment of the other, but it is certain that without such a powerful plea on his behalf he would have lost his head.[73]

Choisy also confirms the poor impression left by the two Siamese. He noted the day before their departure, "The Siamese we have seen up to now are very well turned. I do not understand why they selected the dregs of their country to parade to the end of the earth."[74] Such harsh judgments are rare from the pen of the abbé, who did not forgive the two mandarins for failing to live up to the Siam of his dreams.

The first contacts were perhaps not very encouraging, but the French, having arrived out of the blue, knew that the Siamese would need a few days to organize their reception. The essential was done, though. Here they were at the bar of Siam, at the beginning of their task, ordering their valets to polish the gilded copper of their arms, to air their best clothes and finest uniforms, to iron their lace ruffles, and powder their wigs. Their speeches were written and learnt by heart, the presents and scientific instruments were ready to be offloaded. The "brilliant embassy" which Forbin talked about could finally begin.

CHAPTER SEVENTEEN

"A BRILLIANT EMBASSY" (OCTOBER–DECEMBER 1685)

"WHO IS THE PERSON WHO DECEIVED THE KING OF FRANCE?"

THE REPROVISIONING requested by the French was arranged without delay. Fruit, vegetables, chickens, ducks, and pigs were delivered in ever greater quantities, sent by the Turkish governor of Bangkok, representatives of the CIO, Phaulkon, and lastly the king. "There is not a cabin-boy who did not have for his dinner a chicken or a duck," wrote Choisy.[1] Phra Narai let it be known that he would defray the expenses of the two vessels for the whole time they remained in his kingdom.

The Dutch pilot and one of the French pilots went to take soundings at the bar and concluded that the *Oiseau* could not go up the Chao Phraya, even though it was swollen with the abundant rains of the monsoon, now coming to its end. The *Oiseau* would therefore remain at the bar, and the *Maligne*, which had a shallower draught, would pass over the mudbank at high tide and drop anchor at Bangkok. Siamese craft were needed to take the ambassador and his retinue to the capital.

Not knowing what had occurred in Siam since the departure of Fr Vachet and the two *khunnang* at the beginning of 1684, the French received encouraging news. The King of Siam was in good health and continued to treat the French and the missionaries well; the favour in which Mr Constance stood was greater than ever; the king had not yet decided to change his religion.

Bénigne Vachet left for Ayutthaya on 23 September in the

company of Mr Véret, a Parisian jeweller designated head of the godown of the CIO there. This shady successor to Deslandes will have his day later. The Siamese customs made available to them a barge with fifteen oarsmen which took them to the capital in a single day "with unbelievable rapidity." As soon as he learnt of the safe arrival of the embassy, Mgr Laneau informed the king. In spite of the late hour (it was ten in the evening), the king summoned the Bishop of Metellopolis and Fr Vachet. In a long speech, the missionary related the success of his mission to France; an ambassador from Louis XIV was waiting with his retinue at the bar of Siam for His Majesty's orders to advance to greet his royal person.

Phra Narai listened "with such transports of joy as I can scarce describe," congratulated him on the successful result of his representations at the French court, and immediately decided to send an embassy to Louis XIV which would return with the French ambassadors. "'Father Vachet,' he said, 'do not attribute to yourself the glory of these things I have just heard, and do not be proud of them. It is to God who rules over heaven and earth to whom all thanks should be given . . . It is true that he used your services . . . Since you have brought me an ambassador from the king my brother and very dear friend, you must reconcile yourself to taking one from me.'"[2] Phaulkon of course attended this nocturnal audience.

Mgr Laneau did not conceal his admiration and surprise at the diplomatic exploits of Vachet. "I did not think that Mr Vachet would have succeeded as well as he has done. I think that, if he did not have this soldier-like appearance, he would have done even better . . . He has something about him, you who know him, which makes him persuade people easily. It is true that in some matters he has moved too far ahead . . . As he sets to work rather quickly and has incurred considerable expenses, he was treated rather coldly after his return."[3]

Whilst Phaulkon took in hand the organization of the reception of the French embassy and the preparation of the Siamese embassy to go to France, two delegations sent by Phra Narai went to pay their respects to Chaumont at the bar of Siam. One consisted of two mandarins (one of whom was Kosa Pan, whom we shall meet again) and the other Mgr Laneau, accompanied by the Abbé Artus de Lionne, son of a former minister. They went on board the *Oiseau* on 29 September. The bishop graciously greeted the ambassador and his retinue. The six Jesuits kissed his hand and said they were "happy to meet a prelate who had such great qualities." They began by attending a mass said by Mgr Laneau before the crew, at the end of which he granted each of them forty days' indulgence. The vicar-apostolic then spoke in private with the ambassador.

Chaumont summarized their conversation in a manuscript account of his embassy:

> I informed him that the subject of my embassy was what had been told the king: that the King of Siam had much inclination to become a Christian and that if the king sent him an ambassador . . . there was no doubt but that he would firmly resolve to embrace this religion, which was the principal subject of my embassy, and that the king was greatly concerned to see this important matter succeed. He was surprised that the conversion of the King of Siam had been made out to be such a simple matter, and told me that things were not so advanced as had been implied.[4]

The opinion of the Abbé de Choisy, who was to remain in Siam if the king agreed to take instruction in the Christian religion, was quickly formed.

> The Bishop of Metellopolis . . . has just come on board; he is a tall man with a pleasant demeanour who is only forty-five years old but looks sixty. Twenty-four years of missionary work does not freshen one's complexion. The Abbé de Lionne was with him . . . From what I could judge from the first discussions with them, I think I shall return to France with the Chevalier de Chaumont. The conversion of the King of Siam is not going to occur immediately. He supports our religion, he likes the missionaries, he has churches built, but he is still very far from being baptized. It is none the less true that the Christian religion would obtain a great advantage from the embassy.[5]

The two mandarins crouched on a carpet before Chaumont and accepted tea and preserves. Kosa Pan congratulated him on his successful voyage, enquired about the health of Louis XIV and "added, in conformity with the notions of metempsychosis with which most Orientals are perversely imbued, that he well knew His Excellency had been formerly employed in great matters of substance, and that more than a thousand years earlier he had been in Siam to renew the friendship which existed between the two kingdoms of

France and Siam."[6] Surprised at this compliment, the ambassador stupidly replied that he did not remember it. The mandarins had a retinue of forty men dressed in loincloths; Choisy nicely put it that "their livery is their skin."

The following day, Mgr Laneau went to see Phaulkon who asked him point-blank what was the object of Chaumont's embassy. The bishop replied that he came, in the name of Louis XIV, to offer the Christian religion to the King of Siam.

> Then my lord Constance, extremely surprised at this news, said 'Who then is the person who has deceived the King of France?' The bishop replied, shrugging his shoulders, that he knew nothing about it and was very put out. My lord Constance retorted that this affair was of the utmost importance, and that he would answer to God for any untoward outcome. He went on: 'Since your lordship has been here, have you observed the least indication on the part of the king my master, if you except his charitable works, from which one might infer the slightest possibility of his conversion?' 'I know of none,' replied the bishop, 'and am very surprised that people were found to dare to give such an assurance to His Most Christian Majesty.'[7]

Before going ashore, Chaumont and his retinue knew that the principal objective which Louis XIV had given them would not be attained. The protection of the French missionaries and traders which they were to "obtain" from Phra Narai would only serve to disguise this failure, for it had already been granted long before.

"WHEN SHALL WE SEE ALL THESE PAGODAS CONVERTED INTO TEMPLES OF THE TRUE GOD?"

Fr de Fontaney had decided that Fathers Tachard, Bouvet, and Visdelou would accompany Mgr Laneau to Ayutthaya. They left the *Oiseau* on 30 September in one of the bishop's barges. Bouvet describes the voyage upstream with a wealth of detail. The lush vegetation, the monkeys, the variegated birds, the fireflies, everything appeared to him "both charming and extraordinary." The swarms of implacable mosquitoes attacked them all through the night, and spoilt the pleasure of the travellers who scratched themselves so vigorously that they looked like lepers. Only Fr Tachard escaped the cruelty of these insects. "I do not know what kind of constitution he has," Bouvet exclaimed.

The sight of numerous Buddhist *wats* and yellow-robed monks caused the Jesuits to suffer even more.

> What grief . . . did we not feel on seeing all those places dedicated to the cult of the devil, and such a great number of his ministers who were only occupied with prayers devoted to idols of clay or metal! How we lamented the ignorance and blindness of these poor people! When will it be, we asked ourselves, that we shall see all these pagodas converted into as many temples of the True God, and all these ministers of Satan adopt the function of the priests of Jesus Christ?[8]

The Jesuits, it can be seen, did not display any greater open-mindedness in respect of the religion of the country which they had come to convert than the priests of the MEP who had landed twenty-three years earlier. But the sight was even more distressing in the light of a total absence of results after so many years of missionary work. "God has his programme for this, but it appears that the moment has not yet come, seeing the little progress the ministers of the Gospels have made up to now, for one hardly sees any converted Siamese."[9]

They passed before Bangkok. The town was then little more than a hamlet protected by an earthwork, but they recognized its strategic importance. "Although it is nothing much, it is all the same one of the most important strongholds in the kingdom of which it is like the key."[10]

They arrived on 3 October in Ayutthaya, where Vachet took them to the Jesuit residence in the Portuguese quarter. They found there only old Fr Soares, alone since the departure of Fr Maldonado seven months before for Macao. As the house was too small to accommodate the six French Fathers, men sent by Phaulkon were busy building them new quarters. Tachard wrote:

> We are being built in the river, on piles, six little rooms to accommodate us, and a gallery in which to keep our instruments. Nearly a hundred workmen are employed at this day and night, overseen by two mandarins. Without this addition, Fr Soares would not have been able to receive us. He had only one room and a study, both so wretched and so poorly enclosed that the *tukkaes*, which are very poisonous lizards, were everywhere behind his chests and under his furniture.[11]

Bouvet might well describe him as "a good old man of some seventy years,"[12] but Fr Soares received his colleagues, who upset his ways, with mixed feelings. His displeasure could only increase when they were all installed and spread their instruments out in the new gallery. He saw no connection between this indiscreet scientific invasion and the patient conquest of souls.

A letter from Fr Soares to the Jesuit general, written two months after the arrival of his learned colleagues, leaves no doubt at all about the real feelings of this missionary of the old school:

> Six Fathers of our Society have arrived here with the French ambassador . . . I received them all in this house . . . They say they are sent by the King of France to make various observations with numerous mathematical instruments . . . Several lay persons have already remarked that it is not appropriate for priests of the Society of Jesus to come here, not to be missionaries of souls, but only . . . to observe the stars, the sun, and the moon. I have heard it rumoured that the King of Siam . . . is going to ask for six more mathematical Fathers—something quite pointless, since one would suffice, and the arrival of so great a number will not convince the king to become a Christian. These French Fathers are rarely at home. They often go about, not to convert souls, but to pay visits and busy themselves with secular matters, in particular seeking out and buying objects in silver and Chinese porcelain, to send to France as presents.[13]

The intrusion of six Jesuits into Mgr Laneau's diocese could have opened old wounds, but Louis XIV had done things properly. Chaumont had given the vicar-apostolic, a subject of the French king, a sealed letter which forbade him to require the oath of allegiance of the six astronomers His Majesty was sending to China.[14] No doubt relieved at being able to avoid a confrontation with this redoubtable cohort which humbly kissed his episcopal ring without recognizing his authority, Mgr Laneau permitted the six Fathers to administer the sacraments until their departure for China. "There is a lot of difference between making observations of Jupiter or Saturn, and catechizing and preaching the Gospels," said the bishop, and Fr de Fontaney replied with a little bow, "We shall do nothing concerning spiritual matters in this kingdom except on your lordship's authority."[15]

Whilst waiting for the formal entrance of the ambassador in

Ayutthaya, Fr Bouvet went to look at the capital. His description has the merit of avoiding the manifest exaggerations of Tachard and Choisy against which Forbin had energetically protested:

> I cannot help correcting a mistake of our writers of travels. They tell us every now and then of a pretended city, they call it the capital of Siam, which they make to be very near as big as Paris, and embellish after what manner they please . . . [Ayutthaya] is hardly so big as our towns in France of the fourth and fifth rate.[16]

Bouvet indeed describes a less brilliant city than that seen by Tachard and Choisy:

> We had the curiosity to take a tour by boat . . . The island on which the town is built is cut across by several canals, which make its situation so pleasant that one could easily make it one of the finest cities in the world. Only the Moorish quarter and the Chinese street give Siam the appearance of a town. Even so, the houses of the Moors are few in number, and those of the Chinese so low that they are only fifteen or twenty feet high. All the rest of the town, with the exception of the palace which occupies a good part of it, is filled with orchards and swamps, in which can be seen a large number of huts made of reeds and bamboo, placed about on all sides, in no order, so that the town, properly speaking, is only a pile of villages and cottages enclosed by walls. I shall say nothing about the palace, because I have not yet seen it . . . ; it is not like a palace in Europe. The town is fairly populous . . .[17]

Bouvet also describes the almost total nudity and lack of adornment of the Siamese; only the mandarins wear muslin shirts. "They are good people," he notes, "without serious vices, enemies of labour." Subject to the corvée half the year, they were not in a position to become wealthy and offer themselves treats. "They also need little with which to feed themselves; with twenty or thirty *sous* you can feed a Siamese well for a month."[18]

The wealth of the gilded temples and the innumerable and sometimes enormous statues of the Buddha in them contrasted strangely with the poverty of the town and its inhabitants. "I confess that I was never more surprised than when I saw on all sides, in the middle of the huts of the Siamese—I call them thus, for they do not merit the name of houses—such a great number of pagodas, among which there are some that one would admire in Europe."[19] From his detailed descriptions of Wat Phra Chao Phanan Choeng and the royal temple, Wat Phra Si Sanphet, and the Buddhas in solid gold inside it, the mathematical Jesuit, with his measuring rod in hand, rendered considerable service to later specialists in Ayutthayan period architecture and sculpture.

The three Jesuits sent ahead as scouts met Phaulkon when they went to see the residence being prepared for the ambassador. Tachard was literally charmed:

> We met the Lord Constance, the chief—or rather the only—minister of this kingdom. We already knew him to be a person of merit, and that he held us in esteem, but we found him on both counts to be way above what we had imagined. In that first meeting, he gave a thousand indications of his goodness. We thanked him . . . for the rooms he had kindly undertaken to construct for us . . . He said that he . . . was doing his duty in constructing apartments for his brothers (for this is what we had the honour to be called), our not being able to stay with him.[20]

The first meeting between these two clever men would be followed by others. Their mutual understanding was to shape the future of Franco-Siamese relations, and of Siam's relations with the West in general.

"ONE COULD ONLY SEE BARGES ON THE RIVER"

The rest of the French, who were biting their nails on the ships, waiting for everything to be finished in preparation for their solemn entry into Ayutthaya, received regular news of the progress of the preparations being made under the close supervision of His Excellency Lord Constance. Mr Véret, returning on board, informed them that

> the whole river is covered with gilded barges and mandarins, that Mr Constance is already in Bangkok, that the whole of Siam is astir over the reception of the ambassador, that more than five hundred pieces of gold, silver, and silk cloth had been cut to decorate his palace, that

> all the gentlemen and his suite will have rooms in the French fashion, that our courtyard will be well-stocked, that the king wishes to provide for both the ships without the French having to spend a farthing.

Choisy adds, without really believing it: "All this bodes well, and if at the end of everything he becomes a Christian, would you not love him as much as I do? That says a lot, for I already feel great sympathy for His Siamese Majesty."[21]

Finally, on 8 October, the Chevalier de Chaumont saw Mgr Laneau and the Abbé de Lionne returned, accompanied by two mandarins who, on behalf of the king, requested him to go ashore. After midday he got into the *Oiseau*'s longboat, to witness at the mouth of the Chao Phraya a magical sight: a flotilla of gilded barges decorated with chips of multicoloured glass, sparkling under the tropical sun. Narrow and high in the water, they cut across the surface, propelled by dozens of tireless oarsmen. The prows and poops were bent upwards and carved to imitate the shape of *naga*, the sacred dragon-snake.

His Excellency's barge was magnificent,

> all gilded, seventy-two feet long, rowed by seventy well-turned men, with their oars covered with silver plaques. The chirole, which is a kind of small dome placed in the middle, was covered in scarlet cloth and lined with Chinese golden brocade, with curtains of the same material. The balusters were made of ivory, the cushions of velvet, and under one's feet were Persian carpets.[22]

The ambassador took his seat in this floating marvel with Mgr Laneau and the Abbé de Choisy. Five other stately barges transported the priests and the gentlemen. Dozens of barges belonging to the *khunnang*, without counting those of the governors of Bangkok, Phetchaburi, and their retinues, covered the surface of the Chao Phraya. "One could only see barges on the river," noted Choisy, clearly impressed.[23] Only two leagues were covered on the first day. A house built specially for the occasion was waiting for the ambassador and his retinue at Bangkok, but it was invaded by mosquitoes, and Chaumont went to sleep on the *Maligne* anchored nearby.

The aquatic journey to the capital lasted five days. Throughout, houses of bamboo and red-painted rush matting (Choisy speaks of "resthouses,"

Bouvet of "fragile palaces") had been constructed on piles by twenty thousand corvée workers. According to Forbin, there were only two which were continually put up and taken down: "The houses which served for dinner one day, served for the same purpose the next day; and those in which they lodged one night, served for the same use the next night."[24] They were in any case identical, comprising three wings and filled with gilded Chinese beds, Japanese screens, and Persian carpets. The bedrooms had painted linen hangings; the ambassador's had a gold cloth canopy.

Everywhere were tables with thirty places where a flock of servants served numerous meals prepared in the French manner, accompanied by exotic fruits, the tastes of which the travellers compared: pineapples, mangoes, mangosteens, jackfruit, figs, green oranges with pink flesh, sweet pomeloes with thick skins, durians with their strange odour and taste of roasted chestnuts. At each stage, numerous *khunnang* with ever more important ranks attended the travellers. They prostrated themselves before the ambassador, accompanied him under his canopy, took their leave by prostrating themselves once more, passed the night in the barges and the next day joined the procession which became ever bigger.

The journey upstream had been prepared with particular care. In order to hide unpleasant objects capable of offending the eyes of the ambassador and his retinue, measures had been taken which remind one of Prince Potemkin taking Catherine II through Russia with theatrical scenery shifted all along the imperial route. "We noticed," writes Choisy, "that in front of all the villages along the river, bamboo walls covered with greenery had been built, an honour reserved for the king alone."[25] Nothing spoilt the exotic delectation of the guests.

Choisy describes the splendid banks of the Chao Phraya with a pleasure which will, though, be spoilt.

> Both banks of the river are edged with betel-nut palms and coconut trees, which are green and laden with fruit, monkeys, and birds. Some birds are all blue, others all red, still others entirely yellow. The prettiest are the egrets, which are completely snow-white and have on their heads a true aigrette spray . . . From time to time there are wide canals edged with trees covered with monkeys and parrots. Everywhere the river is about a quarter of a league wide, often more, and there are broad landscapes of rice. But no boats are to be seen on this wide river, not a single little fisherman, and almost no one in the

> villages. I was astonished at this desolation, but the Bishop of Metellopolis informed me that ordinarily the river is covered with boats and the villages are well populated, and if we see no one, it is out of respect for His Excellency. They do this when the king passes, and one sees only those who have not had the time to hide.[26]

Chaumont himself notes: "I had the same honours showed me as to the King of Siam when he is wont to pass on the river. All people were in barges, or on the side of the river, lying flat on their bellies, and their hands joined against their foreheads."[27]

During this time, Phaulkon was also practicing the art of invisibility, chiefly for reasons of etiquette. Omnipresent, observing the French incognito, overseeing the smallest detail in the preparations, he left the spot a few moments before they arrived.

On 12 October, the travellers, overwhelmed with exotic images, saw between the coconut trees, the *chedi* and tiered roofs of the temples of Ayutthaya. They were shown in the distance the outline of the Lopburi hills. They disembarked at a spacious property beside the river, three-quarters of a league from the capital, at a place they called *Ouat Prassat* (Wat Prasat). Work was going on day and night on a magnificent establishment, worthy of the ambassador, but it was not yet finished. Phaulkon had in the meantime requisitioned and filled with furniture the luxurious residence of a *khunnang* of Persian origins. A private chapel had been erected; the gold crucifix on the altar was a present from the king. The bedroom of the ambassador was entirely decorated with a Japanese screen with innumerable panels "of singular beauty." But the finest room was the chamber in which His Excellency received the heads of the English and Dutch godowns who came to congratulate him on his successful journey. "There was a fountain in the entrance hall, inside a platform with a canopy and a very rich armchair . . . On whichever side one cast one's eyes, one saw only fine porcelain of all sizes, placed in niches. In short, everything was fresh and pleasant."[28]

"THE CUSTOMS OF THE ORIENT ARE VERY DIFFERENT"

The week which followed was entirely given over to preparations for the ceremonies of the ambassador's solemn entry and audience. As usual, questions of protocol complicated everything. Phaulkon paved the way for his first visit to Chaumont by sending presents: porcelain, Chinese preserves, and tea, "this famous tea, so expensive, so precious, that only the Emperor of China uses it." The ambassador for his part requested the *khunnang*, who did not stop paying courtesy calls, to describe in detail the manner in which the King of Siam received ambassadors. He explained to them first of all how things were done in France. They politely listened and then replied "that the customs of the Orient are very different, but they did not dare speak of them without the king's express order."[29]

Lord Constance arrived the following day after midday in a flamboyant barge which Phra Narai had just given him. The French gentlemen went to receive him at the landing stage, and the minister and the ambassador shut themselves up for a discussion lasting a good three hours. As Phaulkon spoke in Portuguese, the Bishop of Metellopolis served as interpreter. Tachard wrote:

> After the first compliments, the Chevalier de Chaumont spoke of the conversion of the king as the principal purpose of his embassy. Mr Constance expressed surprise and said to the ambassador that it was the thing he most desired in the world, but he saw no likelihood of bringing this about; that the king was extremely attached to the religion of his ancestors, and he would be very surprised at a proposition for which he had not been prepared. He conjured the ambassador not to speak of this subject which would doubtless cause disorder at the present juncture, and which could lead to no good. The ambassador replied that he would think about it, but he would have much difficulty in suppressing the most important and almost unique reason for his journey.[30]

They then spoke of the ceremonial of the audience. Beginning to understand that he had made a long journey in vain, Chaumont wanted at least to give lustre to his embassy by obtaining unheard-of concessions in protocol. "We had a tedious dispute, and I would abate nothing of the mode of receiving ambassadors in France, which he granted me."[31] Phaulkon, to whom these concessions cost nothing, foresaw a thousand difficulties but promised to do the impossible.

The two principal questions to resolve were the seat with arms which Chaumont demanded, and the manner in which Louis XIV's letter would be carried and presented to Phra Narai. The seat was the less difficult, even though Phaulkon claimed at first he could not even guarantee a cushion. Choisy learnt the day following the Greek's visit that "no one had yet dared to propose to the king that he should offer a cushion to the ambassador; that not one mandarin had dared to make such a novel proposition to His Majesty."[32] There was no further question, in the following days, of cushions or chairs, but they finally learnt that the king, who had decided that "extraordinary and unprecedented things were [to be] done to honour the ambassador of France,"[33] granted the seat. The concession was significant; it will be recalled that in 1673, when Mgr Pallu and Mgr Lambert had presented the letters of Louis XIV and Clement IX in solemn audience, the two bishops crouched on a carpet, and considered themselves lucky to be able to keep on their shoes.

Phaulkon and Chaumont had diametrically opposed ideas about the transfer of Louis's letter from the residence to the royal palace. The former wanted, in conformity with Siamese custom, the letter and its gold casket to be placed under the throne of a state barge to be transported "in triumph" to the palace; there a high-ranking *khun-nang* would solemnly carry the letter through the interior courtyards to the audience chamber. The ambassador did not want to let go of his letter which he intended to hand over from his own hand, as was done in European courts.

The Abbé de Choisy showed in this matter diplomatic flexibility which was not entirely disinterested. He explained to his stubborn superior that one had to adapt to Eastern customs and one could not render excessive honour to the king's letter:

> I proposed to the ambassador that instead of placing it in the hands of Siamese mandarins, it be given to me to show to the people and to carry it into the audience chamber. He agreed, and in that was happy to give me pleasure, and Mr Constance too, who only wanted that the letter be displayed to everybody. In this way I gave myself a most honourable position; whereas before I was rather embarrassed, only being a mere coadjutant, a nominal character. Due honour would have to be shown to the person who had touched the letter from the greatest king on earth. I shall be given a royal barge to myself, shall go to the audience next to the ambassador, and shall have an appropriate and honourable place.[34]

The problem of handing over the letter to Phra Narai was more thorny. Forbin is the person who explains most clearly why

Chaumont's claim to give the letter from his hand to the king's so shocked Siamese protocol:

> As according to them the principal mark of their grandeur and sovereign power consists in being always raised higher than those who appear before them; and as 'tis for this reason that they never grant an audience to ambassadors but through a very high window which looks into the hall where they admit them, the ambassador could not have reached the king's hand without raising a stage for the purpose with several steps, to which they made so many objections as took us up several days.[35]

Impasse. Finally, after much to-ing and fro-ing, someone had the splendid idea of placing the letter in a golden cup, under which a golden handle an ell (roughly a yard) long would be fixed, which would allow the ambassador to raise the precious document to the king's window. One only had to think of it. We have already indicated that a few months later the Persian ambassador was also permitted a sofa and a golden handle.

In the meantime, the French king's presents had been unpacked and cleaned; they had survived the long journey well, stowed in the bottom of the hold. The Dutch, who had occasion to see them, estimated their value at 639 catties or 30,672 rix-dollars.

Chaumont continued to devote much of his time to receiving visitors. On 14 October, the young ecclesiastics of the Foreign Missions' seminary at Mahapram to the north of Ayutthaya, came to salute His Excellency. Choisy, clearly moved, related that they numbered about forty,

> aged between twelve and twenty, from all nations, Chinese, Japanese, Tonkinese, Cochin-Chinese, Peguans, Siamese, all wearing cassocks. I thought I was at the seminary of St Lazare. A Cochin-Chinese made the address in very good Latin . . . They submit theses in philosophy and theology as in Paris.[36]

Indeed, fourteen seminarists had been selected to address the ambassador, each in his own tongue, but Chaumont, after hearing compliments in French, Latin, Siamese, and Cochin-Chinese, asked to be excused the remaining ten which were deferred to "a more favourable occasion."[37]

Phra Narai for his part was also preparing for the audience. He wanted to know of Phaulkon "if the French were clean, if they looked after their teeth, if they washed their mouths and their bodies." Choisy, who relates this curiosity, had already had occasion to be surprised at the physical cleanliness of the Siamese. "This is a rather amusing thing: one sees these swarthy people, almost entirely naked, and they are the cleanest people on earth in their eating, in their dress, in everything, including their discourse." The East and the West, ready to meet, had to cut a path through a forest of prejudices. "The customs of this country are so different from ours that at every moment we have to stop."[38]

The question of hygiene revealed cultural differences of another kind. We owe the details to the English Catholic. As a zealous Christian, Phaulkon did everything possible for the visitors who had come from far away.

> The King of Siam, after learning of the arrival of the Chevalier de Chaumont, asked [Phaulkon] what he should do to make the ambassador happy. He replied that he should give to each of his twelve gentlemen a Siamese girl. The king agreed, and ordered that they be sought. Some of the chief mandarins . . . indicated to the king that it was injurious to the nation (which the Siamese considered incomparably superior to all others), and suggested they be given Christian girls. He allowed them to take those whom they wished.[39]

But the pious ambassador categorically declined this hospitable gesture. One would like to know if the said gentlemen were consulted.

After extremely complicated calculations, the astrologers decided on the day of the audience. The date fixed was Thursday, 18 October, the twelfth anniversary of the first audience granted by Phra Narai to an envoy of Louis XIV, Mgr Pallu. Fate arranges things well.

But with irony. On the same day of this audience, when the King of Siam was asked to open his mind in the name of religious tolerance, the King of France signed the enactment in Fontainebleau revoking the Edict of Nantes which had accorded liberty of worship to French Protestants.

"HEAD RAISED IN THE FRENCH MANNER"

At dawn on the day of the audience, two important grandees sent by the king came to fetch the ambassador. Tachard calls them Oya Prassadet, "the head and protector of all the talapoins of the kingdom," and Piya Thep Decha, "full cousin of the King of Cambodia."[40] They brought some twenty state barges and were followed by forty mandarins, each in his own ceremonial barge. All the *khunnang* prostrated themselves three times, their faces down to the ground, before the letter of Louis XIV. It was enclosed in a golden box placed in a gold receptacle laid on a gold plate on a table covered with gold brocade under a canopy of the same material. They all then returned to their barges; the aquatic procession to the palace could start. It was seven in the morning.

The ambassador, dressed in a rich red brocade edged with gold, took the receptacle, carried it a few paces, and then gave it to the Abbé de Choisy, dressed in a black satin cassock with a surplice and a great mantle. They walked solemnly to the water's edge, where Chaumont took back the letter to place it on the pyramidical throne erected under a canopy on the entirely gilded great royal barge.

The mandarins' barges began the procession, two by two. They were followed by four huge barges bearing the royal presents and the barge carrying the letter. Next came, at a respectful distance, the ambassador and Choisy, each in a barge glittering with gold. "There were sixty men on each side with small gilded oars, which all struck and rose from the water in unison; in the sunlight it made a most impressive sight," wrote Choisy.[41] They were escorted by six barges with the bodyguards together with trumpets, drums, kettle drums, and other Siamese instruments which made "quite a noise." Next came four barges with the ambassador's gentlemen. His domestic staff—secretary, maître d'hotel, wine butler, valets—followed in other barges with twenty men in livery and the trumpeters. "Finally, the procession ended with the barges of all the different nations," Choisy concluded.

The spectacle, unforgettable in the brilliant sunlight that comes after the monsoon, attracted "an infinity of people to see this august ceremony."[42] The cannons of the vessels anchored in front of the Dutch, English, and French godowns saluted the procession, each going better than the other, whilst Fr Soares had the bells of his church rung with all their might. The rhythmic cries of thousands of oarsmen and "the harmony both bizarre and extraordinary"[43] of the oriental instruments completed this sonorous orgy honouring the French letter, ambassadors, and presents.

Lord Constance, mounted on his finest elephant, was waiting for the procession at the landing stage. He got down, saluted the barge carrying the letter with a profound bow, and went before Chaumont. The royal letter was placed with great signs of respect on a gleaming carriage. The ambassador sat in a gilded armchair raised on a platform carried by ten men. Choisy had a red chair decorated with ivory, and eight porters. "I had never been to such a show before, and thought I had become the pope."[44] A third simpler chair was for the Bishop of Metellopolis. Twenty war elephants went ahead of the ambassadors' chairs and the gentlemen on horseback. The trumpeters and liveried servants completed the procession. In profound silence it crossed "a street as long as but narrower than the Rue Saint-Honoré" between two lines of soldiers, to the outer gate of the palace.

Everyone got down. Chaumont took up the letter again, and crossed into the first courtyard. There they saw a thousand soldiers in short muslin vests, seated on their heels, armed with helmets, gilded shields, and muskets. "That is very fine to look at," Choisy observed, "but frankly I think fifty musketeers would easily beat them." The abbé, who noted elsewhere that "two eyes do not see everything,"[45] did not notice that some of these guards who seemed so inoffensive had their arms tattooed with blue bands; these were the *khaen lai*, the King of Siam's executioners. The red painted arms of others indicated his rowers. The Portuguese called them "*os braços pintados*," the painted arms. La Loubère mentions them on several occasions.[46]

The second courtyard contained a squadron of three hundred horse, "rather fine but badly trained," and eighty huge war elephants harnessed in gold. On the first row, surrounded by four mandarins carrying fans, was "the famous white elephant, which in the wars with Pegu cost the lives of five or six hundred thousand men. It is fairly big, very old, wrinkled, and has screwed-up eyes."[47] The third courtyard was covered with rush mats and *khunnang* or mandarins of lower rank, faces down to the ground, resting on their elbows and turned towards the seven steps which led into the audience chamber. Two enormous elephants, dressed in crimson velvet and with gold chains, were on either side of the stairway. The total silence reigning in this huge courtyard filled with so many people was impressive. "No one could be heard to spit or cough," remarked a surprised Bouvet.[48]

Phaulkon and the principal notables stopped at the entrance to give the ambassador's gentlemen time to precede them into the chamber and sit on the carpets. It had been agreed that they would enter with their "heads raised in the French manner, wearing their shoes,"[49] and that, when the king appeared, they would bow without getting up from their places. Forbin—one of them—explained: "All the ambassador's retinue sat . . . on the ground cross-legged. We were charged above all things to be cautious of putting out our feet, that being reckoned at Siam the greatest piece of ill manners that can be."[50]

At the bottom of the stairway, Mr Constance presented Chaumont and Choisy to the old *Phra Khlang* "whom no one had mentioned until then." This is a sign of his insignificance. He politely said that he would have gone to greet His Excellency at the bar if affairs of state had not detained him. Sounds of trumpet and a rolling of drums announcing that the king had taken his position on the throne, put an end to these compliments. Phaulkon and the *Phra Khlang* went up the seven steps crawling and unshod. Inside,

> the mandarins, who had nothing on but a piece of linen, which reached from the waist to half of the thigh, a sort of muslin waistcoat, and a basket cap on their heads in the form of a pyramid, covered with muslin, squatted down upon the ground, leaning upon their knees and elbows. The posture of these mandarins, with their caps seeming as if stuck in one another's arses, made every Frenchman laugh.[51]

Another roll of drums put paid to this inappropriate hilarity. Somdet Phra Narai himself opened the shutters of his raised tribune framed by two huge gilded linen royal umbrellas with seven tiers one above the other, whose gilded staffs almost touched the ceiling. A third, with nine tiers, was placed in front of the throne. The sacred moment of the royal epiphany had arrived. The audience could begin.

"THIS GOOD KING BENT HIMSELF SO LOW"

The Chevalier de Chaumont, with the Abbé de Choisy bearing Louis XIV's letter on his left, solemnly mounted the steps leading into the audience chamber. He had obtained the exceptional privilege of retaining his sword. The envoys saw a spacious square chamber with very low windows on each side. The walls and ceiling were decorated with gilded rosettes. Two staircases in the far corners led to two closed doors, on either side of the tribune for the throne. On entering the chamber and seeing the king, His Excellency removed his hat, crossed the threshold, bowed once in the French manner, walked to the middle of the hall between the prostrate *khunnang*, bowed a second time, went to place himself before the armchair facing the throne, and bowed a third time. The abbé stayed at his side, but without bowing, since he carried The Letter. The ambassador began his discourse to the king standing and uncovered, then, after having said "Sire," he sat down, put on his hat, and continued the speech he had compiled and memorized during the voyage.

> The king my master, who is now so famous in the world by his great victories and the peace he has often granted his enemies [when] at the head of his armies, has commanded me to come to Your Majesty, to assure you of the particular esteem he has of you. He knows, Sire, your princely qualities, the wisdom of your government, the magnificence of your court, the grandeur of your states . . .

As these noble phrases rolled off Chaumont's tongue, Mgr Laneau translated them into Portuguese for the benefit of Phaulkon, who, after prostrating himself three times before the throne, translated them into Siamese. One interpreter would have sufficed, but Lord Phaulkon, who left nothing to chance, pretended that though the Bishop of Metellopolis might speak ordinary Siamese fluently, his knowledge of court Siamese was limited. The Greek above all intended to censor the passages in the discourse too openly inviting Phra Narai to convert to Christianity. He confided afterwards to Choisy that "at the first audience he had not dared convey to the king all that the ambassador had said about religion, because of the mandarins present."[52] Chaumont was exhausting himself quite pointlessly.

Louis XIV, he said, was ready

> to keep a continual correspondence with you, to send you his subjects to undertake and increase commerce with you, to provide you with all the signs of a sincere friendship, but specially to begin an union between these two crowns, which will be the more famous to posterity, by your country's lying so distantly from his and the vast seas which separate them. But nothing will so much keep him in this

> resolution, and more unite him to you, than to live together in the opinions of the same belief. And this is, Sire, what the king my master, who is so wise and enlightened a prince, and who had never failed in his advice to the kings his allies, has especially enjoined me to recommend to you . . .

Forbin, during this time, was carefully watching the king:

> He had on a high-crowned hat, such as they wore formerly in France, but the brim of it was scarce above an inch broad; which hat was tied under his chin with a silk ribbon. His habit was after the Persian fashion, being a stuff of the colour of flame and gold. He had a rich scarf about his middle with a poniard; his fingers were adorned with a great number of costly rings.

The ambassador now entered the heart of the matter:

> He conjures you, as the sincerest of your friends, and by the interest which he already has in your true glory, to consider that this supreme majesty with which you are endued on earth can come only from the true God, that is to say, from a Being almighty, eternal, and infinite, such as the Christians acknowledge Him to be, by whom along kings reign, and who regulates the fate of all peoples. Submit your greatness to this God, who governs heaven and earth: this is what's far more reasonable than to submit to other divinities which are adored in the Orient and of whose insignificancy Your Majesty's great judgment and penetration cannot choose but be sensible . . .

Forbin did not cease to observe Phra Narai. "He was about fifty years of age; a very thin man, of low stature, and no beard, but on the left side of his chin he had a wart from which sprouted two long hairs like horsehair."[53] Chaumont, who could only think of the important evangelizing mission with which he was entrusted, began his peroration:

> The best news, Sire, I can carry to the king my master is that Your Majesty, being convinced of the truth, has taken instruction in the Christian religion . . . since by this means it assures your person eternal happiness in heaven, after having reigned with so much prosperity on earth.[54]

Choisy had remained standing, holding Louis XIV's letter placed in the golden bowl with a gold handle. During his discourse, Chaumont had stood and removed his hat each time he said "Sire" or mentioned "the king my master." No one, except Mgr Laneau, realized that Phra Narai had heard from Phaulkon's tongue only a very attenuated appeal for conversion which the ambassador had just made. The Greek contented himself with saying that, to maintain the good relations between the two kings, "there was no better means than to unite in such a way that they could both have the same heart, and that their liaison could last as long in the future life as in the present one."[55] That did not commit one to very much.

But the most difficult matter, handing over the letter to Phra Narai, remained. The ambassador presented Choisy and the gentlemen in his retinue. Then, observing that the tribune of the throne was higher than he had thought, he "considered that this distance was not suitable to his dignity,"[56] having all the same been exempted from the most humiliating postures which Siamese etiquette required. He muttered to Choisy on taking the golden bowl, "I cannot give him the letter at the end of a stick, and I shall never do it." Choisy was very embarrassed. "I thought of carrying the ambassador's chair near to the throne, so that he could climb up on it."[57] Chaumont then made his decision; he moved towards the throne, holding the bowl by the top, and presented the letter to the king, slightly raising his arm. Phaulkon was crawling behind him on his knees and elbows crying: "Lift it up, lift it up!" but the ambassador did not shift his arm one inch. Phra Narai, who observed this stratagem with amusement, tactfully raised himself from his throne to go half-way, leaned half-way out of his tribune, and, smiling, took the letter, raising it above his head, thus showing his great respect for the person of Louis XIV.

The ambassador made a deep bow and sat down again, very pleased with himself. True, he could not show the king's baptismal certificate to Versailles, but he could at least point to this "victory" of French diplomacy. The seventeenth century, we know, often attached more importance to the form than the substance of diplomatic exchanges. The Abbé de Choisy has carefully emphasized the symbolic meanings of these two vertical movements of Phra Narai.

> This action of the King of Siam rejuvenated me, and I would have willingly embraced the ambassador for the action he had just taken.

> But not only did this good king bend down so low to receive the king's letter; he lifted it up to be as high as his head, which is the greatest honour he could ever show it.[58]

So low . . . so high. It cannot be said that Chaumont had gone so far for nothing.

The audience ended in a less rigid atmosphere. The eighty *khunnang* present, each with his *krob* or betel box—the sign of his rank—in front of him, remained, of course, flat on the ground, but the conversation between the king and the ambassador was almost relaxed. Mgr Laneau, seated on the carpet to the left of Chaumont, translated the questions and the replies. Phaulkon was prostrate between the ambassador and the throne. The king expressed his joy at the arrival of the ambassador and his retinue, but they chiefly spoke about Louis XIV, his victories, his health, and the royal family. Phra Narai mentioned the shipwreck of his ambassadors on the *Soleil d'Orient.* Chaumont replied that "there was a rumour in France that the Dutch had caused its loss; that the king had ordered his ambassador in Holland to made careful investigations to see if anything could be discovered about this, but that nothing had been learnt."[59] There was a short silence. An imperceptible gesture from the king let loose a din of trumpets and drums, then a royal hand, weighed down with rings, slowly drew the curtain before the tribune. The audience was over; it had lasted an hour.

The *khunnang* then assumed more human positions, murmurs filled the room, betel boxes were opened. When they were outside, Phaulkon suggested to the French a visit to the white elephant which lived in a pavilion with golden panelling, served by slaves, surrounded by silk cushions and solid gold plate "of extraordinary splendour and thickness."[60] This oriental marvel did not fail to impress the visitors, especially when it was explained to them that the Siamese were convinced "that a soul of some great king is always lodged in the body of a white elephant."[61] They also learnt that a small white elephant, raised with its mother and aunt, was ready to succeed the old one. This venerable beast was already dead and buried when the La Loubère/Céberet embassy arrived in Siam at the end of 1687.

This visit was the worthy conclusion of a great audience which marked Siamese diplomatic history. When Sir John Bowring, Queen Victoria's ambassador, went to sign a treaty between Siam and Great Britain in 1855, he insisted on having the same reception as the

Chevalier de Chaumont 170 years earlier, and claimed the right to wear his sword like him, when the audience was granted by King Mongkut, Rama IV.[62]

"OUR VERY DEAR AND GOOD FRIEND": LOUIS XIV'S LETTER

The French returned in pomp as they had come, but were taken to a new palace specially constructed for the ambassador and his retinue. To reach it, they had to take the Chinese street and that of the Moors, in the middle of a huge crowd. "The courtyard of our palace is big and very cheerful. To the right is a large columned construction, which is magnificent and noble; full of niches in which there are pieces of porcelain; the yellow, white, and blue mix very well together."[63] This large chamber, the "divan," served as a reception and council room; the Chinese porcelain there, estimated to be worth two thousand crowns, would be given to Chaumont at the conclusion of his embassy. The ambassador had his antechamber, his bedroom, his gallery, and his terrace. A large chapel completed the whole. Numerous domestics, commanded by mandarins, served the king's guests.

In the days that followed, the French delegation had regular conversations with Phaulkon. He had come to live in a residence close to that of the ambassadors, and held open table with the magnificence worthy of an oriental despot. They drank Cephalonian wine, exchanged presents, sounded each other out, and prudently outlined the future of Franco-Siamese relations which Lord Constance had every reason in the world to favour. The health of the king was deteriorating, and the favourite could see the clouds gathering on the horizon.

The day after the audience, a large commission gathered in one of the rooms of the palace to translate the royal letter. There were forty *khunnang* from the council, the *Phra Khlang*, Phaulkon, Mgr Laneau, the Abbé de Lionne, and Fr Vachet. "The letter was translated out loud, word for word, in the most expressive Siamese phrases. After that the chief mandarins took it to the king."[64] This letter, it seemed, made a considerable impression. Here is the gist:

> Most great, most powerful, most excellent and most magnanimous prince, our very good and dear friend. May God increase your grandeur with a happy end. We have learnt with regret of the loss of

> the ambassadors whom you sent in 1681. We have been informed . . . of the urgency with which you desire our royal friendship. It is in answer to this that we have selected the Chevalier de Chaumont to be our ambassador to you . . . We shall be very pleased to demonstrate the gratitude with which we have learnt that you continue your protection of the bishops and other apostolic missionaries who work for the instruction of your subjects in the Christian religion; and our particular esteem for you makes us ardently desire that you would wish yourself to listen to them, and learn from them the true maxims and sacred mysteries of such a holy religion in which one has knowledge of the True God . . . We have given our ambassador the most curious things of our kingdom which he will present to you as a mark of our esteem; and he will explain also what we might desire from you for the increase in trade by our subjects. With this, we pray to God that he desires to increase your grandeur with success in all things. Written in our royal château of Versailles, the twenty-first day of January 1685. Your very dear and good friend, LOUIS.[65]

Louis XIV, it can be seen, had chosen more discreet terms than his ambassador to invite Phra Narai to become a Christian. After reading the letter, the king said to Phaulkon: "I can see clearly that the King of France wants me to be a Christian," and added words of studied ambiguity "to keep me in suspense," as Choisy says, who was unaware if he would remain in Siam or return to France with the ambassador.[66]

To show his satisfaction, the king sent Phaulkon very fine presents for the French envoys. For Chaumont, Japanese kimonos, a hundred gold Manila buttons, and ten pieces of Chinese and Persian gold and silver cloth. There were four pieces of black Chinese satin for Choisy, and forty pieces of gold and silk for the twelve gentlemen. They immediately had clothes made with it, in which they would appear before the king on the first occasion.

"YOU ARE RIGHT: SO HE WILL NOT BECOME A CHRISTIAN"

This occasion came not long after, for the ambassador, accompanied only by Mgr Laneau and the Abbés de Choisy and de Lionne, had a private audience on 25 October. It took place in the innermost gardens of the royal palace, on a shady terrace. The king was seated in an armchair placed on a small platform, the ambassador had his seat, and the three ecclesiastics were seated cross-legged on a carpet. Phaulkon, prostrate as he should be, translated. But the rain came to interrupt the conversation, and they left with the promise of a longer audience in Lopburi. A magnificent meal was served; they ate stews in the Japanese, Siamese, and Portuguese fashion, and drank to the health of His Most Christian Majesty and His Siamese Majesty, perhaps one day to be a Christian.

On the same evening, Choisy had an impromptu conversation with Phaulkon lasting four hours. He only mentions it in the journal of his voyage, but gives a detailed account of it in a secret memorandum written on board the *Oiseau* during the return.[67] The two men, who called each other *Vossa Senhoria*, spoke Portuguese (Phaulkon) and Italian (Choisy), and understood each other perfectly. After having spoken at length of the possible conversion of Phra Narai, Choisy said, laughing, "Frankly I find it hard to believe the King of Siam wants to become a Christian. There is nothing but talapoins here. There is not a single Christian mandarin and if he asked my personal opinion, I do not know what I would advise him." The Greek replied:

> You are right; so he will not become a Christian, and even for the good of the [Catholic] religion, it would not be politic for him to convert too quickly. One has to start by converting a part of the kingdom. Has one ever seen a king change his religion without having [it established] in a large part of his realm? Moreover, the king is old and in ill-health. Everything will change after his death, and perhaps the Christian religion will be persecuted as being the cause of disorders.

The favourite added that, during the first audience, he had not dared translate everything the ambassador had said about religion, and that after the reading of Louis XIV's letter, "His Majesty had opened his heart to him on this subject; that he was persuaded that all religions were good; that he had even said, 'You are a Christian; if you adopted my religion, I would think you a knave.'" They concluded that it was in the interest of everyone that the ambassador took to Louis XIV "letters giving great hope of the conversion of the King of Siam; and that finally God was the master of all things."

The abbé asked himself the reasons why Phaulkon, who was a "Christian and a good Christian," did not permit that the King of Siam be pressed on the question of religion. His analysis seems pertinent. "He is a minister from overseas, hated by all the mandarins. If the king had converted, and the people were against it, would they not have accused the Christian minister? Would they not have attacked him? And does one know if his zeal went as far as martyrdom?"

He repeated this instructive conversation next day to Chaumont and Mgr Laneau, who hardly believed it until Phaulkon confirmed it. The four men decided that Choisy would not stay in Siam, that they would try to obtain an edict of tolerance in favour of the Catholic religion, privileges for the missionaries and their converts, and advantages for the CIO. But the ambassador, a proselyte before he was a diplomat, did not despair of seeing the conversion of Phra Narai succeed one day. Through the Abbé de Lionne, he promised Phaulkon the blue sash of the very prestigious Order of the Holy Spirit if the king became a Christian. The favourite replied that the honour would be too great, and "that he would do everything possible to make this matter succeed with the king his master, and he only had the interests of religion in mind in acting thus."[68] He even declared, according to another source: "I am ready to give my life to contribute to this, if someone convinces me there is the least chance of succeeding."[69] He was bilking them, but they had to make do with that.

Meanwhile, Fr du Carpon, a French priest newly disembarked after a stopover at Surat, informed the French envoys that a great Persian embassy was going to Siam. His considerably exaggerated description of the ambassador Husain Beg and his retinue, on board the "ship of Sulaiman," caused some concern to the French missionaries in Ayutthaya. Fr Bouvet seemed worried:

> This priest, who had seen the ambassador and his retinue, told me that the embassy was magnificent; there were between twenty-eight and thirty persons as gentleman attendants, all very handsome and well dressed, not counting more than a hundred domestics and minor officials; they were bringing the king several fine horses . . . and above all a very rich Koran which they are coming to present him and invite him to become a Muslim. Thus you see the Koran is placed alongside the Gospels. We do not know who will win. What is certain is the

> King of Siam formerly had much esteem for the Muhammadan religion.[70]

Only Choisy was not worried: "This is rather amusing. He says that this ambassador is coming to propose to the king that he convert to Islam. If this is so, I am of the opinion we should have a trial by battle."[71] More and more convinced that the King of Siam would not change religion, the abbé was not afraid of the advent of the Persians. He had had occasion to observe the *devaraja* Phra Narai surrounded with almost divine pomp, and thought that such a person was incapable of submitting to the humility and simplicity of the children of God which the Gospels preach.

> Oh, my God, how he made me feel sorry, this poor king, when I saw him with this pomp, passing in front of two hundred thousand people at the river's edge, who, with their hands joined and their faces bowed to the earth, gave him divine honours! How could a poor man accustomed to such adoration not conceive of himself as being above humanity? And how difficult it will be to persuade him to submit to all the humiliations of the Christian religion![72]

The "Memorandum of Mr Constance, first minister of the King of Siam, on the embassy which the king has sent to invite him to become a Christian," already cited several times, provides in detail a conversation between the king, who had finally understood the purpose of the French embassy, and his favourite, who summarized his efforts to deflect the stubborn ambassador. The dialogue is worth quoting.

> He began, smiling, by saying to me: "Well, well, I do not wish to charge your conscience, but who persuaded the King of France, my good friend, that I could have such sentiments?"
>
> "I know no one, Sire, who could have done this, but this great king did not doubt that Your Majesty had such favourable inclinations seeing the protection which Your Majesty gives to the missionaries."
>
> "That is so, but when you told the ambassador all the reasons you have spoken of to me, what did he say to you?"
>
> "The French ambassador . . . did not consider that any of these

reasons . . . should prevent the execution of the orders of the king his master, especially when he learnt that the Persian ambassador had arrived in the kingdom, and that he brought Your Majesty a Koran for you to follow its injunctions. And as the French ambassador does not doubt that the Persian will present the Koran to Your Majesty, he thought himself obliged to offer Your Majesty the Christian religion."

"Indeed, is it true that the Persian ambassador is bringing me the Koran?"

"It is said so, Sire."

"I would like, with all my heart, that the French ambassador were here to see in what manner I shall treat the Persian ambassador. It is certain that if I had no religion, I would not chose to become a Muslim . . . I am extremely concerned that the King of France, my good friend, is proposing something so difficult, and of which I had not the least knowledge. I would like the Most Christian King to consider the importance of the difficulty in such a delicate matter as changing a religion observed without a break over 2,229 years.[73] I am surprised that the King of France, my good friend, preoccupies himself in a matter which concerns God, in which God himself seems to take no interest. Because does it not depend on divine providence, giving us a body and a soul of the same nature, to give us also the same feelings and the same inclinations for the religion which pleases him most, and so to cause us to be born in the same religion? Since God has not wished this, and on the contrary has permitted to be established in the world over all time an infinity of different religions, should we not believe that his infinite wisdom takes pleasure in having himself honoured by so many ceremonies in different ways, as we see he wished to be glorified by all the creatures in the world, each one of which praises him in his own manner? This variety and diversity of creatures which we admire in the natural order of things, would they be less admirable in the supernatural order and less worthy of the wisdom of God?"[74]

One can only regret that this splendid lesson in wisdom and tolerance was unable to touch the "King of France, my good friend," the monarch who signed away the right of his people to worship as they pleased, and was currently very preoccupied in ordering one of God's affairs, "in which God himself seemed to take no interest."

"IN TRUTH, SIR, YOU PROMISE MUCH"

Reading the accounts of the travellers, one has the feeling that they spent most of their time on tourist trips. They visited the royal temples and the seminary of the Foreign Missions. They took part in elephant fights and festivals organized to celebrate the accession of James II of England and Dom Pedro II of Portugal. They observed and described in detail the great procession on the river (*kathin nam*) to the monks. This brilliant ceremony, related by every visitor from Schouten to Kaempfer, made a profound impression on Choisy. He found it impossible to describe in words the oriental luxury of "the pomp worthy of the King of the White Elephant" which took place before his astonished eyes. "I do not know where to begin. There are no words sufficiently magnificent to express what I have just seen."[75] We regret all the more the absence of the cowardly "little painter" whom the abbé was unable to bring to Siam.

The members of the embassy had the leisure to soak up exotic impressions, for the centre of gravity of diplomatic action had shifted to Phaulkon's offices. The preparation of the treaties on religion and commerce had taken a decisive turn when Phaulkon had given Chaumont to understand, in Choisy's presence, that, naturally, Phra Narai's friendship for Louis XIV was completely disinterested, but that, if the ambassador wished to please him, he would put out the rumour that an offensive and defensive pact had been signed between France and Siam. "That," he indicated, "would be capable of keeping the Dutch in check, if it were true that they had designs on the kingdom of Siam."[76]

The phobia of the Dutch, twenty-two years after the blockade of the Chao Phraya, and twelve years after the Dutch confiscation of the presents sent by Louis XIV to Phra Narai through the intermediary of Mgr Pallu, continued to torment the Siamese. It is true that the VOC tried to avoid irritating the King of Siam,[77] but in ejecting the English and French traders from Bantam in 1682, it had shown that it was capable of anything. When Chaumont's private audience took place at the end of October, Phra Narai had told him "that he knew the Dutch wanted to wage war with him, and he had noticed that the great friendship and understanding which he wished to have with the King of France caused them to be jealous." In November at Lopburi, the ambassador received a memorandum drawn up by Phaulkon on the king's behalf affirming that "here and throughout the Indies there was a rumour that the Dutch were intent on attacking the domains of His Majesty . . . The considerations of His Majesty and his council were founded on secret intelligence which was worthy of credence."[78] One wonders if this fear of a Dutch attack was justified, or if Phaulkon wittingly planted it in the king's mind by presenting "secret intelligence" fabricated by himself. Dhiravat na Pombejra, who has studied the VOC archives, concludes "that there is no VOC document which indicates that Batavia wanted to take Bangkok or Ayutthaya: such a measure would have involved too much expense, especially unjustifiable when the Siam trade was far from crucial to the VOC."[79]

Whatever the case, Chaumont promised Phaulkon, immediately and without hesitation, to speak everywhere of an offensive and defensive pact between the two kings, instead of profiting by this request to obtain as advantageous clauses as possible for his country, for the treaties on religion and trade were not yet signed. "I was surprised," notes Choisy, "he moved so quickly, and could not restrain myself from saying to him in French in a low voice, 'In truth, sir, you are promising much, and this is sufficiently important for us to think about it a little.'"[80]

But it was too late. The following day, the ambassador repeated this undertaking to the king, who, delighted, ordered Phaulkon to include in the treaties everything the French wanted. The favourite prostrated himself before his king, but followed his own inclinations. Chaumont might well ask him for the drafts of the treaties, but the Greek replied in very vague terms that they were working on them in his offices, and deferred the subject to another day. The ambassador only received the text of the treaties the day of his departure; it was by then too late to modify anything at all.

Phaulkon rubbed his hands in delight. He had obtained all he wanted without having to make concessions which would have fanned the hatred that the xenophobic mandarins and monks had of him. Furthermore, rumours of military assistance should prepare the ground for what he most desired: a French military presence in Siam which would protect him the day when Phra Narai's soul would transmigrate into a white elephant, for he knew better than anyone the worrying state of the king's health. But it was not through the naive and stubborn intermediary of Chaumont, but by plotting with the very accommodating Fr Tachard, that Phaulkon unleashed a military adventure which would have disastrous consequences.

THE FRENCH IN LOPBURI

Phra Narai and some of his court left for Lopburi on 8 November. The French, very preoccupied in selecting presents for Louis XIV and the royal family from the state stores, stayed a few more days in Ayutthaya. A detailed list of the presents had to be drawn up ("It will be a book," Choisy declared), their packing supervised, and their transport organized on the two vessels anchored in the estuary. By 13 November 150 bales had already been despatched.

At Lopburi, Phaulkon prepared to involve the six Jesuit astronomers in his plans. After all, it was he who had first requested mathematical missionaries from Fr de Noyelle. He told them to prepare their instruments and sent them three barges. They left Ayutthaya on 15 November, the same day as Chaumont and his retinue. On their way, they saw the funeral ceremonies and cremation of "a famous talapoin."

Fr Bouvet describes with clear reprobation the exotic ceremonies he had occasion to witness. "We saw nothing but burlesque dances and ridiculous farces performed in bamboo and reed huts open on all sides, with horrible masks and contortions of veritable fanatics a thousand times more impertinent that anything done by our charlatans on the Pont Neuf."[81] Bouvet's inability to assimilate the least little particle of Siamese religious culture is surprising. In China, he would be a model of flexibility, to such an extent that K'ang-si would say of him, "Of all the Europeans in China, Po Chin [Bouvet] is the only one to understand a little."[82]

The French arrived in Lopburi on 17 November, at eight in the evening. They were lodged in a "very pleasant" house. This brick structure had been run up in great haste next to Phaulkon's residence. The complex, located inside a surrounding wall, is today known as Wichayen's house. These ruins and the descriptions of the French visitors allow one to form a good idea of the complex. In the western part, near the river, Phaulkon's spacious residence was surrounded by outhouses and a cistern which supplied the bath house. In the centre, an elegant chapel facing east had two side entrances and a main entrance on the western facade under a fine rose window. One entered the eastern side after crossing an internal garden ornamented with two fountains, and went up five semi-circular steps to enter a huge chamber dominated by a full-length portrait of Louis XIV. A building between this hall and the chapel housed the Jesuits. The ambassadors and their staff lodged in two other buildings to the east and north of the reception area.[83] In this surprising city of Lopburi, heavily charged with history, where the monkeys of Sa Kaeo wait for the green light to cross the road, Phaulkon's residence remains a magical place. One needs but little imagination to see our characters moving around inside it, with their telescopes and royal presents, formulating complex projects and chasing after an impossible chimera: Christian unity of the world.

On the next day, Chaumont, accompanied by Mgr Laneau and the Abbé de Choisy, had a long audience described by Choisy.[84] Apart from the inevitable Phaulkon, only eight mandarins were present. After the customary compliments, Phra Narai praised the disinterested friendship of the King of France. They next spoke of the late Bishop of Heliopolis, François Pallu, whom the king said he liked a lot. "All the French missionaries," he said, "had two things in mind, the progress of their religion and the glory of their king." The ambassador then transmitted the compliments of the Duke of Orléans, the king's brother. Phra Narai replied,

> he was delighted to see such solid union in the house of France; that this was its strength, and that when the princes had only the will of the king in view, the state was invincible . . . Raising his eyes to the heavens, he added with a serious and sad look, that he was unaware of what God ordained for his own.

There was suddenly an atmosphere of end of reign, which could not have pleased the favourite.

Choisy observed Phra Narai very closely:

> I had not seen him so clearly before; he was very close to us, and stood from time to time. He is rather thin, with great lively black eyes full of intelligence. He speaks quickly, and mumbles; he has the physiognomy of an honest person. He will not be damned, and half understands the truth: God will give him the strength to continue in this.

The abbé did not despair of the salvation of the king, knowing he had a crucifix in his bedroom and he read the Gospels in the Siamese translation provided by the Bishop of Metellopolis.

Phra Narai also said that most of the ambassadors were only the bearers of letters and compliments. "For example," he said, "the ambassador of Persia who has arrived at Tenasserim will bring me some fine cloth; that is good to wear, but the ambassador of France comes for serious affairs." At the end of the audience, the king promised to do everything the ambassador desired, and indicated Phaulkon would handle the details.

The afternoon of the same day was given over to a new divertissement for the French: a trip on the back of an elephant. Each had his palanquin with its gilded balustrade and his elephant ridden by two mahouts, "one man on the elephant's neck, and another on its tail," using iron-pointed silver sticks. Choisy noted: "The gait is rather rough but steady. These are only females, who go down on their knees when one wants and are only required to walk solemnly."[85] Chaumont was less appreciative of these pachyderms with their solemn gait: "I had rather ride ten leagues on horseback than one on these animals."[86]

Other distractions filled the following days: an elephant fight, the fight of three elephants protected by leather masks with a tiger, the capture of wild elephants. The king, surrounded with oriental splendour, took pleasure in being present at these elephantine divertissements offered to his guests. "I think the Pharaoh on the banks of the Nile must have paraded in similar pomp," Choisy wrote.[87] And, of course, they told each other stories about elephants.

The captains of the *Oiseau* and the *Maligne*, Vaudricourt and Joyeux, came to Lopburi to announce that both ships were ready for the return journey. They left for Bangkok loaded with lavish presents; they had the honour to salute the king mounted on his elephant.

The Abbé de Choisy for his part "examined his conscience" and decided, after a long conversation with Mgr Laneau, to be ordained a priest before returning to France.

> For a long time I have been ready for this; when one is weak one should not expose oneself to danger, and I think these holy chains will tie me to the righteous path. I shall no longer want to go to the opera; as a priest, I hope God will let me live as such. I have livings, and do not wish to leave them; am I not obliged to lead an ordered life? What further decides me is that I can see in front of me seven or eight months of innocent life.[88]

On 7 December he began a retreat at the Ayutthaya seminary; Mgr Laneau ordained him on 10 December. The abbé noted that day: "So now I am a priest. What a terrible burden I have placed on my own back!"[89]

FR TACHARD CREEPS BEHIND THE DIPLOMATIC FRONT

This retreat had important consequences for Chaumont's embassy. Phaulkon had had a conversation with Choisy on a subject which was dear to him.

> Constance suggested giving our king the town of Bangkok which is truly the key of the kingdom, on condition troops, engineers and money were sent. The Chevalier de Chaumont and I did not think such a thing feasible, and we told him frankly that the king would not wish to pledge himself on his word to the extent of spending four or five million which would perhaps be lost. Things would have stayed there. . . [90]

The project, to build a fortress at Bangkok, equipped and controlled by the French, was huge. It consisted of placing the key of the kingdom of Siam in the hands of the French king, for the person who controlled access to the Chao Phraya held the whole of Siam in the palm of his hand. The Dutch threat would be neutralized, and Phaulkon would have his French protection in case of need. True, the ambassador had written to Phra Narai that Louis XIV "had commanded me to offer to Your Majesty on his behalf all his land and sea forces, troops, vessels, and generally everything that would add to Your Majesty's glory,"[91] but one understands why Chaumont and Choisy hesitated to embark on a military adventure on this scale. They must have asked themselves if the offer really came from the king, or if it was a new invention of Phaulkon.

It was the abbé who in the end saw the Greek in his true light. For proof, one has this portrait in his *Mémoires*:

> He was one of the people with the greatest wit, liberality, magnificence, and intrepidity in the world, full of great concepts, but

> perhaps he only wished to have French troops to declare himself king on the death of his master, which he foresaw as coming very soon. He was proud, cruel, pitiless, and with outrageous ambition. He supported the Christian religion because it could support him, and I would never have trusted him in matters in which his own betterment was not involved.[92]

But the Greek, who did not take no for an answer, returned to the charge during Choisy's retreat. He needed an interpreter, and used Fr Tachard. Phaulkon

> found in him a gentle, supple, compliant and yet bold if not to say reckless character. He spoke to him of the idea he had, the idea which we had dismissed as a chimera. Fr Tachard undertook to bring about a successful conclusion to the proposal. He told Mr Constance that we had no credit at court, in which he was not far wrong, and if he wished to write to Fr de La Chaize about it, His Reverence would bring it to fruition.

Fr Paumard of the Foreign Missions got wind of this development, and ran to warn Choisy, who did not want to interrupt his retreat.

> [I] let Fr Tachard get on with it, who, in doing so, pinched a fine golden crucifix which the King of Siam was going to give me at the farewell audience, and to which the good Father was treated in justice since the Chevalier de Chaumont and I were only actors on the stage after that, and he was the real ambassador charged with secret negotiations.[93]

Rarely can a religious retreat of just one person have cost so much.

In this way Fr Tachard was pushed to the front of the diplomatic scene. Hitherto his role had been rather modest; he chiefly confined himself to studying elephants' feet. "The gentlemen of the Royal Academy of Science had asked us to examine if all elephants had nails on their feet. We only saw one which did not have five on each foot, at the end of five big fingers; but their fingers are so short that they hardly emerge from the mass of the foot."[94] This scientific problem resolved once and for all, the good Father could devote himself to matters more worthy of his talents. Phaulkon had found an interlocutor equal to himself.

Of course, the return to France of the enterprising Fr Tachard was presented quite differently to the public at large. This is the official version, as presented by Fr Le Comte:

> The King of Siam, who was interested in astrology, wanted to see us, to know us, and observe the stars with us. He above all admired the accuracy with which we predicted a lunar eclipse; and from that moment, he had in mind to retain us at his court. But being informed of our orders, he allowed four of us to travel to China, on condition that Fr Tachard returned to France to ask the king for fresh mathematicians, and that I remain in his kingdom.[95]

Fr Bouvet mentions the project of a Siamese observatory which would be a copy of those in Paris and Peking, and placed in the hands of the Jesuits. He explains that the King of Siam wanted to charge his ambassadors with requesting Louis XIV to provide twelve Jesuit mathematicians. "As Lord Constance considered, to ensure the success of the project, it would be appropriate for us to return to France to urge this matter *and others of importance*, the decision was made to send Fr Tachard who would suitably undertake this commission" (emphasis added).[96] Tachard himself expressed his heart-breaking regrets: "I then felt extreme grief at seeing myself distanced for a long time from China where I greatly desired to go for so many years. But I had to obey."[97] Obey who?

The version of facts according to Choisy is confirmed by two unpublished letters written in Lopburi on 8 December 1685 (thus during the abbé's retreat), and addressed to the Jesuit General in Rome. The first, written in Portuguese, was from Phaulkon. It reminded Fr de Noyelle of all Phaulkon's efforts in favour of the Christian religion. His Siamese Majesty, encouraged by Phaulkon, protected the missionaries in his states and built churches, but his conversion depended on God, and "God our Lord is not obliged to perform miracles, having so many other means [at his disposition]." Among God's instruments, Phaulkon modestly included himself, saying he was ready to work for this great project, "not only for the conversion of the king, but the whole kingdom." The letter ended by referring to a memorandum addressed to Fr de La Chaize and the indispensable Fr Tachard, who would orally present Phaulkon's proposals.[98]

The other letter addressed the same day to the Father General was from Fr Jean de Fontaney. In Latin it sings the praises of Phaulkon, presented as "a friend of the Society, its very energetic benefactor, and so to say its other father." The Siamese ambassadors were charged with asking His Most Christian Majesty for twelve Jesuit mathematicians who would direct the new observatory, which would be twinned with that in Paris.[99] A year later, Fr de Fontaney would have seen through Phaulkon's game. He then wrote to Fr de Verjus, a confidant of Fr de La Chaize:

> Mr Constance is writing a letter to Fr de La Chaize entirely on his own initiative. The conclusion is that, to convert, it is necessary to send troops here which he will pay for out of his own pocket, and which he would command. He speaks of building French forts . . . He does not speak of having good missionaries, perhaps because they neither bring him authority nor profit. I implore you to believe, and to inform Fr de La Chaize, that I have no part in these expedients.[100]

THE TREATIES CONCERNING RELIGION AND TRADE

Given the great projects of Phaulkon and Tachard, the details of the treaty on religion which had to be concluded before the departure of Chaumont had little importance, the more so as Phaulkon had decided to grant the privileges the ambassador sought but hedge them in with a series of restrictions and not to publish them. These restrictions and this concealment, which Tachard had to get the French court to swallow, rendered null and void the supposed advantages which would remain a dead letter.

The first two privileges accorded in the name of His Siamese Majesty authorized the missionaries to preach freely the "law of God" and to teach European sciences to young Siamese who could be received in their establishments. The last three privileges concerned Siamese converts: they were absolved from performing royal corvée on Sundays and holy days; in case of old age or infirmity they would be completely exempted; finally, they would have their own system of justice. To avoid new Christians being victims of persecution or injustice, a "righteous and just" mandarin would oversee their trials and pass sentence without charge after consulting a professional judge.[101] Dated in one instance 2 December and another the tenth, the text of the treaty was only signed by Phaulkon and given to Chaumont at the moment of his departure on 20 December.

The bitterness of the Abbé de Lionne, a powerless witness to the machinations of Phaulkon and Tachard, can be understood.

> I am the eye witness to the fact that [the privileges concerning religion] were only signed by Mr Constance and placed in the hands of Mr de Chaumont when he was in the roads of Siam and on the point of setting sail. It is said that Fr Tachard, still in the roads of Siam, went down on his knees before the ambassador to try to get him to agree that these privileges not be published. But whether that is true or not, what at least is quite certain is that it was secretly agreed with Mr Constance that they would not be published, and that he was charged with getting the matter agreed in France. Because it could only be from him that it was known in France that they would not be [published], Mr de Chaumont being very far from persuading himself that Mr Constance, after having promised him to do so, would be so bold as to break his word.[102]

In spite of the outrageous favour he enjoyed, Phaulkon had his hands tied. He had told Chaumont that a change of religion would unleash a revolution, and was probably right. He did not wish, by inopportunely publicizing the privileges granted to Christian converts, needlessly to provoke the *khunnang* and the powerful Buddhist *sangha* who were patiently waiting for "the rice to cool." No doubt he thought that the arrival of French troops at his disposal would protect him from their hatred. One would like to know by what unreasonable arguments he was able to impose on Tachard a view so clearly contrary to the real interests of the young Siamese church.

The CIO, through Véret, had formulated a list of privileges it desired to obtain. "A special treaty granted [the company] complete freedom of commerce without paying duties on entering or leaving, though forbidding trade in contraband, and obliging it to buy all its goods only from the royal stores."[103] The captain of the French company was given the privilege of judging disputes between the French, except in cases when they were in the service of the King of Siam. The treaty granted the monopoly of the tin trade in Joncelang Island (Phuket) to the CIO, which had the right to build godowns throughout the kingdom with the approval of the king's ministers. Finally, the company took possession of Singor (Songkhla) which it could fortify as it saw fit.

THE END OF THE EMBASSY

In the night of 10 to 11 December, Phra Narai observed a lunar eclipse in the company of the six Jesuits, who had calculated and predicted with impressive precision the moment of immersion and emersion. The observation posed a delicate question of etiquette, because, to direct and adjust the king's telescope, Fr de Fontaney had to place himself at one moment at the same level as the king, which caused more than one set of eyebrows to be raised in the Siamese court. The Jesuits received on this occasion black satin soutanes damascened with flowers. The king gave the predestined Fr Tachard two large gold crucifixes with silver bases, one for himself and one for Fr de La Chaize.

The Chevalier de Chaumont's embassy was reaching its end. Phra Narai had asked him to leave Forbin and de La Mare in Siam; the former was to command his armies, the latter to reconstruct the fortress at Bangkok which was to receive the troops expected from Louis XIV. Forbin, who did not have a high opinion of Siam and still less of Phaulkon, did not want to stay. He was convinced the Greek feared his perspicacity and direct manner of speaking in France.

> He discovered in me that openness, that character of frankness which rendered it impossible for me to dissemble, or to call things by their wrong names. Therefore he was apprehensive that . . . when I came to France, I should make the same declaration as I had done at Siam, and that, by divulging my entire opinion of this country, I should, with a word's speaking, dash that project to pieces, on the success of which he founded all his hopes.[104]

An order from Chaumont was needed to make Forbin remain in Siam. He was to be given the title of Ok-phra Sakdisongkhram.

Gorged with elephant hunts, tiger fights, Chinese operas, Siamese shows, illuminations, fireworks, visits to royal residences and temples full of gilded idols, weighed down by presents from the king and Phaulkon, the French asked for nothing more than to return home. Chaumont had his farewell audience on 12 December in Lopburi. He went to the audience chamber, the walls of which are still standing, after crossing the palace courtyards filled with two hundred war elephants, each surmounted by two mandarins wearing their ceremonial bonnets.

Serious matters were foremost in the king's mind. "He charged me," writes Chaumont, "to request the king to consider Mr Constance as a person who served him well and who was very dear to him; that as he [Phaulkon] had many who envied him, and that he [the king] was old, on dying things would change in his kingdom, and he [Phaulkon] could be obliged to leave the kingdom and withdraw to France." The syntax is a little tormented, but the message clear: the favourite was having his master recommend him to Louis XIV in case his situation in Siam became untenable. But would he have the time to make his exit? "I told him that I did not doubt, should such a thing come to pass, that the king would receive him very well, and that he should be persuaded that France would always be a refuge for him, where he would be considered according to his merit."[105] Finally, thinking of the poor impression Phichai Walit and Phichit Maitri had made on the French court, the king requested the ambassador to take charge of the three ambassadors he was sending to Louis XIV on the French vessels, and to explain to them "how one conducts oneself when in France." Chaumont and Choisy promised to look after them during the return to Europe.

As a special honour, the king gave the ambassador a large gold betel box called *tiap* or, by the French, *bossette*,[106] which is the outward sign of the high rank of *Oya*. The other members of the embassy also received appropriate presents. On leaving the audience, they were taken into a banqueting hall surrounded by canals, banks of flowers, and fountains. The ruins of this building with ogival windows still remain in the outer palace courtyard. A final magnificent meal, with some dishes coming from the king's table, was served in these enchanting surroundings.

His Excellency had to perform one last duty before leaving Lopburi. "After dinner, the ambassador selected two small pocket-sized elephants, which each weighs as much as a good half-dozen bulls; they will complicate things a lot . . . They are very pretty; may they arrive in Versailles, which I doubt."[107] The king absolutely insisted on offering these baby elephants to the Dukes of Burgundy and Anjou, the Dauphin's sons. The embassy left the palace with the usual pomp, to take gilded barges which travelled throughout the night to arrive the next day in Ayutthaya. The Abbé de Choisy, who thought he had left some pages from his journal under his mattress, sent someone to Lopburi to look for them. He finally found them at the bottom of his trunk; their loss would have been unforgivable.

Phaulkon accompanied the embassy. He offered still more presents to Chaumont and Choisy: Chinese porcelain and two small slaves, "to make them Christians." Chaumont gave him a sedan chair he had brought from France. Choisy wrote with a sigh: "Certainly this man likes to give presents, but it is getting irksome. If we had something to give in return it would be a pleasure; but always to receive and to give nothing is hard to endure. We shall have to send some from France."[108] Forbin was more severe:

> The minister judging that the magnificence of the presents intended for the king and court of France might contribute much to his design, he drained the kingdom for the best of everything that it produced . . . he carried things to excess; since he not only exhausted Siam, but sent also to China and Japan for what was most rare and curious, and was continually loading the king's ships till they could contain no more.[109]

The French only stayed two days in the capital. On 16 December, at nightfall, they embarked on the *Oiseau* and the *Maligne*. The next day, the three Siamese ambassadors, eight mandarins, four secretaries, and twenty valets who accompanied them were divided between the main ship and the frigate. At the king's request, Chaumont visited the fort at Bangkok on which Mr de La Mare was to work, and gave suggestions for his implementation. The taking on board the *Oiseau* of Phra Narai's letter for Louis XIV, written on a thin sheet of gold, was done with the prescribed honours.

The two vessels were loaded to the gunnels, full to bursting with personal baggage, three hundred bales of presents, furniture, and provisions. They were wrong to do this, because the *Oiseau* had the reputation of being unreliable, especially when it was overloaded. Choisy wrote: "You could not imagine the muddle we are in; the bales are everywhere and the *Maligne* has as many as it can take. Yet now there are another twenty-two belonging to the ambassadors, and on top of everything else, two elephants. What to do?"[110] Phaulkon, who came to wish them a safe journey, had to admit it was impossible to embark the two elephants and the last twenty-two bales; they were sent ashore. The Greek on leaving was saluted with eleven cannon shots; that was the least they could do. On the *Oiseau* he had a final secret meeting with Fr Tachard, far from the ears of Chaumont and his deputy.

The ambassador would have wished to leave earlier, but a boat bringing, among others, Vachet and La Brosse on board had been carried off by the tide in the Gulf of Siam, and only reached the *Oiseau* on Friday, 21 December. They were joyfully greeted and His Excellency set sail one hour after midnight. This delay was a concession to sailors from Brittany, who, superstitious without acknowledging it, always arranged not to set sail on a Friday.

Was Chaumont satisfied with his embassy? Frustrated in his hope of convincing Phra Narai to change religion, bearer of a treaty on religion which was a dead letter, and a commercial treaty which raised many questions, the ambassador saw himself dispossessed of true substance in his embassy, which was to examine the future possibilities and concrete forms of Franco-Siamese cooperation. Like a delayed action bomb, a devilishly intriguing Jesuit was returning with him to France. The bearer of secret instructions and letters addressed to Louis XIV's confessor, he was getting ready to short-circuit the normal diplomatic channels.

In spite of the sumptuous presents and flowery compliments with which he had been saturated, Chaumont was now only superficially an ambassador. He had represented his king honourably at the court of an oriental despot, but the future of French involvement in Siam would be decided without him. The era in which the missionaries, diplomats, and traders were the only Frenchmen on Siamese soil was close to its end. Soon to come, with the assistance of the Society of Jesus, was a military phase. Phaulkon had worked well.

CHAPTER EIGHTEEN

THE SIAMESE EMBASSY TO FRANCE (JANUARY 1686–FEBRUARY 1687)

AN UNEVENTFUL RETURN

THE *OISEAU* and the *Maligne* set sail to turn south, travelling along the Cambodian coast. Two days were enough to recover from seasickness, in spite of the strong wind and the swell of the sea. Choisy wanted to say his first mass on 1 January 1686, but a storm and rain moved the event to 6 January, the feast of the Epiphany. The ship was then in the middle of the Bangka Strait, between Bangka and Sumatra. "It is rather extraordinary," the *Mercure Galant* commented, "to become a priest six thousand leagues from one's country and to say one's first mass at sea!"[1] The abbé noted in his *Journal*: "God gave me leave to say today my first mass. How a boat is a good seminary, how good a retreat! You are at peace in your little room; no one comes to interrupt you."[2]

The stopover at Bantam, where they dropped anchor on 11 January, brought them once again in contact with the inexorable Dutch governor who had refused to provide them with victuals on the outward journey. This time he grudgingly sold them six oxen. But it was impossible to take on fresh water. The barrels of Siamese water were crawling with worms; four years later Robert Challe was to describe with considerable precision, the "three illnesses" of water the vessels transported in the bottom of their holds.[3] The Sunda Strait, which took a whole week to pass through on the outward journey, was "slipped through" in one day.

In the immensity of the Indian Ocean, the *Oiseau* was slowed down by its hull covered with half a foot of barnacles, whilst the

Maligne, which had spent three months in the fresh water of the Chao Phraya, sailed along beautifully. The two vessels lost sight of each other one stormy night, at more or less the same position they lost each other on the outward journey. They were to meet at the Cape. The Abbé de Choisy gave his first sermons to the crew and outlined as the days passed a picture of Siam, inserted in his journal between 18 and 30 January.

The long crossing allowed the French to get to know the three Siamese ambassadors and the *khunmun* (mandarins of inferior rank) in their retinue. As Chaumont explains, "We had then with us three ambassadors, the most considerable persons in Siam." Careful not to repeat the error of the preceding Siamese mission, courtiers had been selected who were as distinguished as Phichai Walit and Phichit Maitri were mediocre. Chaumont continues:

> The first, named Ocppra Visut Jurithora, is brother to the late deceased Barcalon, a man of sense, having ever been close to his brother, playing an important role in all matters during his period in office. This person came to receive me at the mouth of the River of Siam when I arrived, and has been ever with me, attending me wherever I went. The first time I saw him he seemed to me an upright person, free from all affectation and reservedness.[4]

Ok-phra Wisut Sunthon, better known as Kosa Pan, was indeed the brother of the *Phra Khlang* Chao Phraya Kosathibodi, who died in 1683, and so like him foster-brother of Phra Narai. The choice of a person as important as he as *ratchathut*, first ambassador, illustrated the importance of this embassy in the Siamese king's eyes.

"The second of the ambassadors is called Ocluang Calaya Rayomaytry Ockkhun Arucha Rarsa, and is very aged, and wants not wit, having been ambassador to China, and acquitted himself to the king his master's satisfaction." The *uppathut*, or second ambassador, Okluang Kanlaya Ratchamaitri, an old hand in Siamese diplomacy, would impress everyone with his wit and very oriental wisdom. He had been selected as he knew China and Phra Narai wanted to know if the court at Versailles could bear comparison with that at Peking. The *Mercure Galant* would cite several of his Sino-French comparisons, invariably favourable to France.

"The third, named Ockhun Jurin Ocman Viset Ppubaan [*sic*], is aged about twenty-five or thirty years, and his father is at present ambassador in Portugal." The *trithut* or third ambassador, Ok-khun Siwisan Wacha, was the son of the unfortunate ambassador[5] sent to Portugal at the beginning of 1686 on the *Nossa Senhora dos Milagros* which was shipwrecked.[6] This son had already been sent as ambassador to the Great Mogul, Aurangzeb.

"These three gentlemen are very gentle, obliging, and good-natured, and have a very equable disposition. They write down the smallest matters they see; I imagine they will be much occupied in France, where they will encounter so many things worth of their admiration," Chaumont concludes.[7] The curiosity of the ambassadors, and their zeal in taking notes, were emphasized by everyone. Choisy observed: "These are quite different from those awful mandarins who did not drink, did not eat, and did not speak. These always have their writing-tablets in their hands, and if you ask them four questions, they ask you six."[8] Donneau de Visé wrote in the *Mercure Galant*: "They keep, day by day, an exact record of what they have seen . . . they even counted the trees of the places they visited," and, "Not only do they write each evening an account of what they have seen during the day, but there is even a mandarin with them who describes their journey in Siamese verse."[9] Nothing has come down to us from this mass of detailed reports intended for Phra Narai, apart from the beginning of Kosa Pan's journal which miraculously survived, and a black folded manuscript in *nirat* verse recently discovered at the French National Library.

The conversations between the Siamese and the French were facilitated by the Abbé de Lionne in the first instance, but also by a Portuguese-Siamese interpreter, António Pinto, called "Mr Antoine." Brilliant but with indifferent health, he had studied at the Mahapram seminary and spoke fluently Siamese, Portuguese, French, and Latin. At the end of the year he was to defend a thesis in theology at the Sorbonne, and would be received in audience by the pope.

The *Oiseau* dropped anchor on 13 May in the roadstead of the Cape of Good Hope, where it found the *Maligne*. Fr Tachard went to see the obliging governor van der Stel, who gave him four tiger skins and a tame mongoose. "He gave me to understand that it was an implacable enemy of snakes and fought a savage war with them."[10] Was the governor aware of the dangerous associations of the Jesuit? Imbued with cleanliness and used to washing in plenty of water, the first ambassador went ashore to wash in the stream which went through the famous garden. The Dutch saluted this hygienic exploit with seven cannon shots. The two vessels got ready for the last lap of their journey.

> Life on board ship is very active. When you are sailing, it is all hauling up, trimming, anchoring, port, starboard, straight ahead, like this, slacken the tiller; there is always work. Hardly have you arrived in the right port, than you hear the hammer at work; the ship has been strained, it has to be repaired, strengthened, caulked, water taken on for three months, and the bottom of the hold had to be put in order. You do not have the time to be bored.[11]

The *Oiseau* and the *Maligne* set sail on 26 March. They crossed the Line again on 28 April, without occasion to complain of calms or heavy seas. Neither Chaumont, Choisy, Tachard, nor Vachet mention any outstanding events; one has the impression they were already thinking of their return to France. The death of a crew member only inspired a distracted passing mention from the abbé: "A sailor has just been thrown overboard. From time to time someone has to leave the company."[12] The death at the end of May of one of the *khunmun* on the *Maligne* seems to have troubled no one.

On 1 June, the outline of Corvo Island, the westernmost of the Azores, could be seen on the horizon. A stormy wind, a rough sea, and fogs obliged the pilots to proceed with plumb line in hand as they approached the coasts of Brittany. According to an extraordinary chapter in the *Phongsawadan* (the late rendition and miraculous nature of which we have already commented on), a terrible whirlwind would have overturned the two vessels if the incantations of the *ratchathut* Kosa Pan, appealing for the magical assistance of the king his master, had not overcome the evil power of the elements.[13]

Choisy mentions nothing of the kind, but wrote on Friday, 14 June,

> Yesterday . . . we carried on with the foresail. At three in the morning the main topsail was raised; we have just added the lower fore topsail, the spritsail and the mizzen topsail. With that, we are advancing. A sounding will be taken this evening, and if it pleases God, we shall touch bottom. Tomorrow we shall see Ushant, and early on Sunday we shall eat salad. I have used rather a lot of nautical terms; we have to celebrate before coming to an end.[14]

They finally saw Ushant to port on Monday, 17 June. The tide carried them the following morning into the Brest roadstead, after a particularly successful voyage lasting fifteen months and fifteen days.

"THE CHEVALIER DE CHAUMONT HAS ARRIVED IN THE ROADS TODAY"

On 18 June, towards midday, Fr Michel Bellanger, a Jesuit in Brest, heard more than fifty cannon shots being fired; he was quite sure they announced the return of the king's ships.

> I went to the port where I met three midshipmen who came up to me, told me the King of Siam kissed my hands, and that they had brought Fr Tachard. I immediately took a longboat to go into the roadstead. After passing the chain, I saw the Father, I took him on board, and brought him to our house, where I was alone. After doing my best to entertain him, we returned to take his chest from a vessel called the *Oiseau*. I gave the compliments of our Society to Mr de Vaudricourt, the captain of the vessel, and to the three ambassadors of the King of Siam. The Abbé de Lionne acted as interpreter for me.[15]

Bénigne Vachet was one of the first ashore to announce their arrival and the presence of the Siamese ambassadors to Desclouzeaux, the intendant at Brest. As the intendant's house was a royal residence and was spacious and richly furnished, it was decided the ambassadors would stay there for as long as they were at Brest. Desclouzeaux immediately went to greet Their Siamese Excellencies, requesting them "not to set foot on land that day, because, as their arrival was unexpected, he had not been able to put things into a suitable state to receive them in France. He spent the whole night issuing orders."[16]

Desclouzeaux sent the same day a report to the Marquis de Seignelay, minister of the navy.

> The Chevalier de Chaumont has arrived in the roads today at midday, on the vessel the *Oiseau*, with the frigate the *Maligne*. I have been on board the vessels and found them in very good condition. The officers and crew are in very good health, and one can in truth say that a journey of this nature has never been done in like fashion,

> nor so favourably, and it seems as though the vessels only come from [nearby] Belle Isle, being clean, taking in no water, having nothing broken nor having lost anything . . . I have seen the ambassadors of Siam to whom I paid my respects and offered everything that was within my power. I agreed with the Chevalier de Chaumont that they would be shown the greatest possible honours when they go ashore.[17]

The *ratchathut* Kosa Pan gave Desclouzeaux to understand that they would only leave the *Oiseau* with the letter from the king his master for Louis XIV, but that the pyramidical pavilion which contained it had suffered during the journey and required some repairs. Fr Tachard described it in detail: "The letter was in a golden box in the shape of a cone; the first box was enclosed in a bigger silver one. This second one was inside a third of varnished Japanese wood, wrapped in a rich gold brocade. All this was inside a gilded pyramid."[18] This pyramid (which the French, for want of an appropriate term, were to call a "machine") was a huge transportable altar surrounded by four fluted columns upholding a square temple roof, the whole gilded all over.[19] Eight Swiss guards were needed to transport it for the ambassadors' solemn audience.

Desclouzeaux wrote to Seignelay: "The machine which was made in Siam for placing the king's letter having been damaged, I sent on board the *Oiseau* workmen to put it aright, the ambassadors not having wished to come ashore without this machine and the letter."[20] The intendant seems to have had some difficulty in understanding that the royal message, written on a sheet of gold, was sacred, and its delivery to Louis XIV was the principal object of the Siamese diplomatic mission. It had to receive attention to the exclusion of all other business.

There is some confusion in the documentation about the precise moment of the official disembarkation of the ambassadors. If one believes the *Mercure Galant* and the *Mémoires* of Vachet, one has the impression that the Siamese envoys left the *Oiseau* as early as 19 June. But the personal journal of Kosa Pan indicates that the ambassadors, while receiving visits on board their ship and paying visits on land, did not disembark with the royal letter before Sunday, 23 June 1685, which Desclouzeaux's letter, cited above, confirms.

THE "BREST JOURNAL" OF KOSA PAN

Having noticed in the National Library in Bangkok the almost complete absence of authentic Siamese documents dating from the seventeenth century, I was delighted when I learnt of the existence of a Siamese manuscript dating from 1686 in the archives of the Foreign Missions (MEP) in Paris. At first sight, the manuscript 1081 seems to be unexceptional. It concerns a seventeenth-century translation in French of a Jataka (an earlier life of the Buddha) in Pali, entitled *History of Naauan*. The careful and regular writing only fills half the volume. Only on turning the volume does one realize that at the other end there are sixty-seven pages covered with Siamese seventeenth-century writing. It turned out to be from the hand of the *ratchathut* Ok-phra Wisut Sunthon (Kosa Pan) and concerns a fragment of his stay in Brest from 20 June (the day after his arrival) to 4 July.

It is fortunate that this document remained in France, even if we do not know the reasons for this omission. It would certainly not have survived the revolution of 1688 or the destruction of Ayutthaya in 1767 if it had returned to Siam with the mass of reports and journals compiled by the Siamese mandarins, none of which has come down to us.

A reproduction of this journal was published in Bangkok, first of all in facsimile, thanks to Mom Luang Manich Jumsai (Chalermnit, 1984), then in facsimile with a double transliteration, old and new, in a special issue of *Silpakorn Journal* (January 1985). The introduction of this last edition, signed by Kongkaew Viraprachaksa of the National Library, suggested that it was not possible to find a competent translator. It seemed to me nevertheless indispensable to have a translation of the *Brest Journal* of Kosa Pan for this book. My first attempts in Bangkok came to nothing; given the extreme rarity of Siamese texts before 1767, specialists capable of translating them can be counted on the fingers of one hand. Finally I had the good fortune, thanks to Dr Dhiravat na Pombejra, to be put in touch with the Translations Centre of Chulalongkorn University, and was able to convince professor emeritus Visudh Busyakul to undertake an English translation of the document.

A comparison of the *Brest Journal* and the *Personal Memoirs of Kosa Pan*, published in Bangkok in 1990,[21] in which it is said, to give a false scent, that they were an approximately contemporary "English translation . . . most likely based on a published French work which has been lost . . . itself a translation . . . from the original Siamese, lost in its turn," clearly shows the latter document to be a gifted pastiche, which is, as the author himself admitted in personal communication, all that was intended. There is no incident in it which is not found in printed sources of the period, but the text does conjecture what Kosa Pan might have felt and thought himself during his travels through France.

The first pages of the *Brest Journal* relate the social visits and curiosity calls the ambassadors had to endure on board the *Oiseau*. Finally, on "Sunday the fourth day of the waxing moon of the eighth lunar month in the year of the tiger, the eighth year of the Chulasakkarat decade" (23 June 1686), the day set aside for the official reception of the sealed message from the King of Siam,

> the intendant, the commissioner, the captain of the vessel, and the chief doctor came on board ship to dine with me . . . At two in the afternoon the priests, sailors, officers, men and women of the town came in thirty longboats to receive the King of Siam's royal letter. Among them was the galley designated to carry the King of Siam's royal letter which was nine *wah* long and two *wah* wide [some eighteen by four metres]. There was a cabin on the poop. Its ceiling was decked with silk woven with threads of gold, knotted at intervals. Other designs were woven in threads of gold. It was also decorated with ribbons, fringes, and pendant tufts of gold thread. The outer wall of the cabin is carved and gilded. The two sides of the galley and the prow were also gilded. The internal wall of the cabin is painted with *bencharong* [five-coloured] motifs. The windows are glassed in. Four cannons of two *niu* [inches] are placed on the prow. A platform covered with a carpet was prepared in the outer part of the cabin for the pavilion containing the royal letter. The boats designated for the *khunmun* [mandarins of lower rank] are covered with a roof lined with white cloth. The back of the seats of these boats are carved and gilded; the cushions are covered with red embroidered brocaded silk . . .
>
> At the moment of departure, the galley carrying the king's letter fired two cannon shots. The governor, the commander and officers came to see me on board the vessel. I said to the commander: "I am very impressed by the magnificent preparations for the reception of the official letter from the king of a great kingdom and by the

> honours accorded me as his ambassador." One of the aforementioned gentlemen replied: "It seems to us that our arrangements for the reception of the royal letter, and of you as ambassador, leave much to be desired . . ." I replied: "What has been done has been well done, and appropriate for a friendly country. As for your efforts to promote the reciprocal friendship between the two sovereigns of our two countries, I beseech you to rest assured of my appreciation. I am extremely satisfied with everything . . ." At two in the afternoon the royal letter was ceremonially carried on board the galley and placed on the carpeted platform described above. We, the three ambassadors, took seats at the end of the cabin. Khun Raksa Phubendra and Khun Narendra Sena remained standing in front of the raised platform on which was placed the pavilion containing the royal letter.

The text continues by counting the cannon shots fired from the vessels anchored in the roadstead and the two forts, to honour The Letter being carried ashore and installed in a room specially prepared in the intendant's house. "In the reception hall, the pavilion was placed on a prepared platform. Four *sappathon* [ceremonial royal umbrellas] were placed in the corners, and a canopy covered the pavilion. After that, the intendant conducted me into my room which had been attractively decorated."

A crowd of some eighty dignitaries, officers, and ships' captains accompanied Kosa Pan, who gave them this short speech:

> Most excellent governor, most excellent commander, and all of you, I sincerely appreciate all that you have done in giving the excellent service appropriate to the king your master. Your efforts are sincerely in proportion to the renown and honour of the two sovereigns of our respective countries. Please allow me to express my sincere thanks to you all.
>
> "We appreciate sincerely all that you have said," said one of the gentlemen to whom I had spoken. "In truth, we had planned a more sumptuous reception for Your Honour, but this is a small town with a limited number of inhabitants. It is all we were able to do . . ."

The *Brest Journal* of Kosa Pan and the *Mémoires* of Bénigne Vachet complement each other (as Choisy had remarked, "two eyes do not see everything"), only contradicting each other in a few details. Vachet wrote:

> About two in the afternoon, the intendant, the governor, and all the officers and captains of vessels in their longboats, accompanying a galley covered all over in gold cloth with a thousand streamers of white embroidered satin, having on the poop a kind of triumphal arch of impressive cleanliness, where ten persons could stand, with fifty very smartly dressed sailors to row, and three small silvered cannons, innumerable trumpets, cymbals, hautbois, and violins—these gentlemen, I say, in this grand party gently approached in marvellous order our vessel . . . Our ambassadors . . . took the seats of honour . . . the letter of the King of Siam was in a golden box on the first ambassador's knees . . . On going ashore, we found all the garrison and burghers bearing arms, forming two rows between which we passed . . . Hardly had we entered the house than the mayor and the magistrates of the town appeared to address the ambassadors and offer them presents, consisting of wine, preserves, sugared almonds, candles, and all the ladies of Brest, dressed in their finest, who saluted the ambassadors on entering the great hall. This was the first time in their lives that Siamese ambassadors had the honour to kiss foreign ladies on the cheek, about which, for fear of surprising them, they had been warned. The first ambassador took the hand of the intendant's lady, who led him into a splendid room, where a magnificent collation was awaiting him . . . Our first ambassador . . . played his part perfectly, which augurs well for the future. It is true that during our journey we had often discussed French ceremonies and customs.[22]

Kosa Pan relates in his journal that in the middle of the afternoon he received the visit of an officer sent by the commander of the barracks, who explained to him that two guards would keep watch day and night for his security, and that he should give the password each day.

> In the town of Brest, the governor is the person who chooses the password each day. Now that Your Excellency is present in this town, and your rank is higher than that of the governor, I am here to ask you to select the passwords. I gave "One kingdom" as the password for the first day, "Long live the King of France" for the second, and "Long live the King of Siam" for the third day.

Fifteen pages were not enough for the *ratchathut* Kosa Pan to relate the rest of the events of his first day on French soil. He details his room and those of the *uppathut* and the *trithut* with an abundance of details which reveal his astonishment at French luxury. A whole page is given over to the description of the bed with its three-metre-high canopy, its curtains, and bedcover of crimson silk edged with gold and silver braid, its four mattresses, its pillows, sheets, and coverlets with lantern-shaped patterns. The curtains at the windows, the furniture, the mantelpiece, the wall hangings, the pictures, the portraits of Louis XIV and "Mu-su Sing-lae" (Monsieur Seignelay), the woodcarvings, everything is listed with an auctioneer's precision. We even learn that the mirror in Kosa Pan's room (that set aside for the king), measures two cubits and one span three cubits (125 by 150 cm), and that of the *uppathut*'s room one *khup* and five *niu* by one *sok* (37 by 50 cm). This last room was decorated with hangings showing battle scenes, four painted portraits, and "banana-leaf green" curtains.

The same concern for precision fills the pages describing the banquet set for seventy-two places offered by the intendant Desclouzeaux. The numerous dishes, often new to him, presented problems. Being unable to use words in his own language to designate vegetables and fruit unknown in Siam, Kosa Pan turns into Siamese the French words passed to him by the intendant, his neighbour at table. We therefore learn that he was served *a-ra-ti-cho* (artichokes), fried vegetable roots called *ka-pe-ra-ya* (possibly "champignons," mushrooms), peas called *pra-chau* ("pois jaunes," yellow peas), and *faeu* ("fèves," broad beans). Among the fruits listed are *fre-se* ("fraises," strawberries), *se-ri-sa* ("cerises," cherries), and *pa-ron* ("prunes," plums).

The following days were given over to visits to the roadstead, the finest ships, the admiralty stores, the naval depots, the arsenal, a cannon foundry, the two forts which dominate the roadstead, the ramparts, the hospital, the monastery of the "Fathers of Saint-Paul," meaning the Jesuits. The ambassadors were furthermore regaled with demonstrations of cannoneering, the making of ropes, dredging rivers, and installing masts on a vessel under construction. The journal of Kosa Pan laboriously describes all these curiosities with the appropriate measurements and numbers.

The *ratchathut* seems proud of having assimilated French manners. "In the evening [of 24 June], the governor and his lady came and supped with me. I took his lady's hand and we washed our hands together. I conducted her to her seat beside me, and sat on her right. The *uppathut* and the *trithut* were seated on her left. I respected French etiquette which Fr Vachet had explained to me."

In the numerous towns which they passed through, the ambassadors would find the same welcome: triumphal arches, addresses from the magistrates, presents of wine and preserves, banquets with elegantly dresses ladies bedecked with all their jewels, and intensive visits of local curiosities.

The sample provided by the fragment of Kosa Pan's journal allows one to conclude that the complete journal must have filled a thousand pages, not counting what the other Siamese noted or dictated with a dedication which astonished the French. The *Mercure Galant* explains that the ambassadors "shut themselves up every evening after supper with several secretaries. They read to each other what they have written about what they have seen, some being able to recall some things which the others had forgotten, and thus day by day they compile an exact journal of what they have seen."[23]

The numerous visits received and mentioned by Kosa Pan indicate the enormous curiosity which the Siamese aroused. They would get used to it during their eight-month stay in France. This curiosity plunged Donneau de Visé, the director of the *Mercure Galant,* into a veritable Siamese frenzy; during this period, he published no less than two thousand pages given over to things Siamese, in five special volumes detailing Chaumont's embassy to Siam (July 1686), the details and gestures of the Siamese ambassadors in France (September, November, and December 1686, and January 1687).[24] At the beginning of the special volume of September, Donneau de Visé downplayed the differences between the Siamese and the French. "If physical distance made us consider those people separated from us by the vast oceans as barbarians, we are no less so in their eyes, since we are as far from them as they are from us . . . The black, brown, or white colour of a person's skin has nothing to do with a man's heart and feelings."[25] Detailed and precise, the Siamese chronicle of the *Mercure Galant* omits nothing about the ambassadors' movements and remarks.

FROM BREST TO PARIS

As soon as Louis XIV and Seignelay learnt of the arrival of the Siamese ambassadors at Brest, their voyage to Paris was arranged. Chaumont, who had taken posthorses with Choisy to go to the court as soon as he could, had sent in haste a memorandum to Seignelay which suggested:

> The king's carriages could be sent to Brest for the ambassadors, and in all the towns through which they would pass, grant them the same honours as I received, greeting them each day at the places where they would dine and sup . . . and lodge them in the neatest houses, since I was not lodged in a single house which was not specially constructed and magnificently furnished . . . One should also fire the cannons in the towns which have them, and when they arrive in Paris, give them a very fine formal entrance, for it would have been impossible to have a better one than that I was granted.[26]

The Marquis de Dangeau wrote on 24 June in his journal about the news of the arrival of the Siamese. Spanheim, the envoy of the elector of Brandenburg in Paris, wrote in a despatch of 28 June to Berlin:

> The Chevalier de Chaumont, who was sent from here to the King of Siam with envoys who came from there nearly two years ago, has recently returned after a voyage of almost eighteen months, with new ambassadors from the said King of Siam, who are charged with presents for the king, the dauphin, and the dauphin's lady. A gentleman ordinary of the king's household has already been sent to receive them.[27]

A gentleman ordinary of the king's household, Mr Storf or Torf (both spellings are given; Kosa Pan called him Mu-su Tro), and Mr de Silly (Mu-su Si-li), in charge of protocol, arrived at the beginning of July in Brest to present the king's compliments to the ambassadors, accompany them while they were in the kingdom, and give them all the honours due to them.

The considerable volume of luggage and bales of presents led to the decision to send them on a frigate from Brest via Le Havre to Rouen, where they would be loaded onto barges and go up the Seine to Paris. Chaumont's secretary, Mr de la Brosse, would look after them. The "machine" for Phra Narai's letter was too big to go by carriage; it would go with the baggage. The letter itself, the ambassadors, and their retinue would travel in carriages. As there was plenty of time and it was desired to show the Siamese the country, it was decided that the shortest route through Rennes, Le Mans, and Chartres would not be taken, but they would go down to Nantes, and up the Loire to Orléans, from where they would reach Paris via Fontainebleau.

The ambassadors left Brest on 9 July for Quimper where they stayed the following day. They arrived on the thirteenth at Vannes, where they were received with much honour by the Parliament of Brittany. In the good hands of the Marquis de Lavardin, they continued to Pontchâteau, staying with the Duke of Coislin. The transport of Phra Narai's letter was done with deference to Siamese etiquette: "As the letter of the king their master had always to be higher than them, they arranged a plank above their heads to place it on. They removed and replaced this plank each time they changed carriage."[28]

They slept on 15 July in Nantes on the right bank of the Loire. All the nobility mounted on horseback lined up to receive them while the cannon shots rang out. The seventeenth, at Ancenis, "they bathed in the river, which was a great pleasure for them, because they bathe often in their country, and even here they wash every day after meals. The eighteenth they dined at Ingrandes, where they bathed once more. They even crossed the river to bathe in peace on the other side."[29]

They arrived therefore very clean at Angers in the evening of the eighteenth. They slept the next day at Saumur, and the day after at Langeais, where the burghers armed themselves and guarded their residence. They dined on the twenty-first at Tours, and slept the same day at Amboise. The following evening they were in Blois, where they spent the twenty-third. A visit to Chambord was obligatory; the ambassadors admired the château and requested its plan. They were at Orléans on the twenty-fifth where, according to Dangeau, their reception was very poor,[30] and where they left their hired carriages to get into the king's coaches.

They were at Fontainebleau on the twenty-eighth. They could not find words enough to praise the forest, the gardens, and the château with its famous galleries. Mr Brisacier, the superior of the Foreign Missions, had travelled to Fontainebleau to greet the envoys. They dined the next day at Melun and arrived in the evening at Vincennes, at the gates of Paris. As work was going on in the château, they stayed in a private house, which gave rise to a characteristic incident. Mr Storf led the third ambassador into his room on the second floor, the window of which provided a view of Paris and the triumphal arch erected in front of St Anthony's gate. The *trithut* admired the view, then asked who was to sleep in the room below his. He was told it was the first ambassador. "Immediately his face altered and, unable to hide the anxiety which agitated him, he suddenly left the room, as if some sudden misfortune had occurred. He was asked the reason, and he said that the King of Siam's letter would be in the room which was below that he was to occupy, and being always required to be lower than the letter, he was unable to sleep above a place in which he knew it would be lodged."[31] It was only with great difficulty that he could be found another room.

The next day the Siamese visited the menagerie and the château at Vincennes. There they met Fr de La Chaize, who came to compliment them on their safe arrival. Well aware of the unlimited influence of the king's confessor, the ambassadors showed him all possible deference. The Foreign Missions and the Society of Jesus wasted no time in reminding the public of the privileged relationship they had with the King of Siam. All this time the bales containing Phra Narai's presents were proceeding upstream on the Seine with a royal lack of haste. As the solemn audience at Versailles was impossible as long as the presents and the "machine" had not arrived, it was decided to install the ambassadors and their men at Berny while waiting to make their solemn entry into Paris. Berny, to the south of Paris, was one of the first constructions of Mansart. The château had belonged to the family of the Abbé de Lionne; furnished from the crown's stores and protected by His Majesty's Swiss guards, it was to house the Siamese for some twelve days.

Berny was only two leagues from Paris. Numerous courtiers and townsfolk went to see the exotic visitors whose ease, gallantry, and witty remarks were the talk of the town. The person designated to introduce the ambassadors at court, Mr Bonneuil, complimented them on behalf of Louis XIV. The Marquis de Seignelay informed them that his duties kept him in attendance on His Majesty, but he went to see them incognito, as a neighbour, from his château in Sceaux. Informed by Vachet of the identity of his visitor, Kosa Pan was still more considerate and witty than usual. He offered preserves and compliments to Madame de Seignelay, presented as "a lady from Brittany," telling her that he had crossed the whole of Brittany but had not seen a lady whose beauty matched hers. He gallantly added, squeezing her hand, that she would be still more beautiful if she were dressed like the women in his country, who were half-naked. "She blushed, the good lady," says Vachet, "and the noble lords made jokes about it."[32]

The solemn entry into Paris took place on 12 August in the midst of considerable crowds and monstrous traffic jams. In the morning, the ambassadors had gone from Berny to a house in the Faubourg St Antoine. The Duke-Marshal de La Feuillade, colonel of the French guards, went to fetch them towards midday, at the head of sixty carriages bearing heraldic arms, each with six or eight horses, sent by the royal house, the princes and princesses of the blood, and other groups of persons who had obligations to the King of Siam, like Chaumont, the Abbés de Lionne and de Choisy, the Jesuits, and the gentlemen of the Foreign Missions.

Trumpets and cymbals preceded a carriage from the king carrying the *ratchathut* Kosa Pan, accompanied by La Feuillade and Storf, and a second carriage in which were the other two ambassadors. "In the third," Vachet explains, "I was alone in the rear part, carrying on my knees the King of Siam's letter in a golden coffer, having before me two of the mandarins in a posture of humility, a gatekeeper, and four royal guards on horseback with drawn swords."[33] The long procession, surrounded by a regiment from the guards, entered Paris by the St Anthony's gate and the Rue St Antoine, and cleared a way for itself slowly to the residence for ambassadors extraordinary in the Rue de Tournon. They arrived there exhausted at seven in the evening. But so what, the Parisian bystanders had been able to see these oriental ambassadors who became the talk of the taverns.

Louis XIV's indisposition (1686 was the year of his fistula operation) caused the solemn audience to be delayed. The ambassadors decided to limit their visits so long as they had not saluted His Majesty. They went to see, though, the Assumption procession at Notre Dame, causing huge crowds to assemble. They were very impressed by the Gothic architecture and the sound of the organ. To thank him for his trouble, Kosa Pan offered betel to the archdeacon de La Mothe who had shown them the interior of the cathedral and explained the ceremonial.

The king's health problems did not prevent him from enquiring each day about the ambassadors and the crowds, not always good tempered, which their outings provoked. On 18 August Seignelay wrote this message to La Reynie, the police chief:

> His Majesty the King, having been informed that the populace gathers to see the Siamese ambassador, that he is proffered insults,

> and that some insolent people dared stop one of the carriages he was using and beat his coachman, orders me to write to you that his intention is that you take measures to prevent this disorder, and if you think it necessary to publish some ordinance to this effect and to punish some of those who could be accused of such offences, His Majesty relies on you to do what you consider best.[34]

The presence of Fr Vachet in proximity to the ambassadors did not please Fr Tachard, very preoccupied in monopolizing negotiations while Kosa Pan charmed his admirers. He arranged it so that Seignelay told the missionary "not to meddle in what concerns the ambassadors of Siam."[35] Vachet swallowed his pride and went on a trip to Burgundy where he had relatives. He received there a friendly letter from the Abbé de Lionne: "Our ambassadors delight everyone far beyond what I could tell you. They are good people, courteous and polite; they are diametrically opposed in their conduct, in their manners, to the first two mandarins who gave you so much trouble. We think their audience will take place next Thursday."[36]

But the king's fever abated only on 24 August, and the date of the audience was finally fixed for Sunday, 1 September.

"THIS HAPPY DAY FOR WHICH WE HAVE TRAVELLED OVER SO MANY SEAS"

On the day of the audience, the Duke de La Feuillade and the official presenter at court Bonneuil went to the Rue de Tournon to take the ambassadors and their retinue in the king's carriages. Kosa Pan told them of his joy "that this happy day, for which they had crossed so many seas, had at last arrived."[37] They learnt with great pleasure that Madame la Dauphine, the heir-apparent's lady, had given birth the day before to a third son, the Duke of Berry. The Siamese arrived at Versailles by the main approach and saw in the outer courtyard two regiments of guards under arms. They were taken first of all into the Ambassadors' Room where they washed their hands and faces, and donned their pointed ceremonial hats covered with white muslin and encircled at the base with a crown of very thin gold leaves. The *khunmun* and secretaries who followed them wore the same hats, but without crowns. They were informed that the king was ready to be seated on his throne.

They went up the marble steps between two rows of Swiss guards. A Siamese touch was added to the ceremony: "They climbed to the sound of trumpets and drums, to imitate the manner of the King of Siam who never enters the audience chamber without this music," the Marquis de Sourches noted in his *Mémoires*.[38] The services of twenty-four trumpeters and thirty-six drummers from the Great Stables had been enlisted. Chaumont had explained to the master of ceremonies, Blainville, that in his audience "there were many instruments, like trumpets, drums, kettle drums, musettes, kinds of little bells, and little horns like shepherds in France use."[39] "Siamese" music would for a time be the rage at court; Delalande, soon to be superintendent of the king's chamber music, was to include two "Siamese tunes" in the ninth suite of his "Symphonies for the King's Suppers."

Followed by trumpeters, the ambassadors next crossed the principal rooms flanked by two rows of bodyguards and a crowd of onlookers. Twelve Swiss guards had carried the "machine" with the King of Siam's letter and the four *sappathon* (umbrellas) which were to surround it to the top of the main staircase. There, Kosa Pan took the golden box which contained Phra Narai's letter to give it to the third ambassador to carry. Surrounded by thirty officers of the guards in blue jerkins, the Duke-Marshal of Luxembourg addressed the ambassadors and took them to the Peace Chamber opening onto the Mirror Gallery.

They entered the gallery at last. At the end, Louis XIV was seated on his silver throne placed on a dais with eight steps covered by a carpet with a gold fleur-de-lis design and flanked by solid silver candelabra three metres high and huge silver vases. As soon as they saw the king, the ambassadors gave three low bows, *thawai bangkhom*, with their hands joined and raised before them. They repeated these oriental salutations many times while traversing the gallery in which were gathered fifteen hundred persons. Three *khunmun* preceded them, carrying their betel boxes, the signs of their rank.

On arriving at the foot of the throne, they prostrated themselves and remained on their knees throughout the audience, "looking very intently at the king," says Sourches.[40] The *Mercure Galant*, outdoing him, wrote: "One could not represent anything in which respect could be more marked than was shown on the faces of the ambassadors and all those in their retinue."[41] The king replied to their prostrations by standing for a moment and doffing his hat. He wore a costume with a gold background studded with huge diamonds worth several million livres. According to Sourches's editor, this dress "was worth more than the entire kingdom of Siam,"[42] which shows that infatuation for things Siamese had not overcome everyone.

Louis XIV, then at the summit of his power, had reason to be pleased in spite of his fistula; for the first time the envoys of a great oriental monarch came to grovel at the steps of his throne. The *Mercure Galant* recalled that "we had not yet seen in France ambassadors extraordinary from the Indies."[43] The sovereign was surrounded by the dauphin, and princes of the royal house. The king's brother, the Duke of Orléans, wore mourning for his mother-in-law; his black dress gave particular brilliance to the diamonds with which he was adorned. The Duke of Maine, the king's son by Madame de Montespan, shone in a dress studded with rubies. The high officers of the king's bedchamber and the royal wardrobe were placed behind the throne.

Kosa Pan, on his knees, pronounced his address: "Very Great King, who by your might have conquered all your enemies: We seek of Your Majesty the favour to be willing to listen to us; and we appear today before your throne with so much more joy, because the throne itself had been gratified by the birth of a new prince which heaven has just given France . . ." The rest detailed the innumerable qualities of the French monarch, well known throughout the Orient and by the King of Siam who had wished to send him ambassadors and presents.

> We confess to Your Majesty that first of all we felt some sadness at leaving our country to undertake such a long journey, because we were not used to this kind of navigation. But today, now that we have the joy to appear in the presence of Your Majesty, to see with our own eyes the brilliance which surrounds your throne, and to recognize for ourselves that everything which reputation broadcasts about your grandeur and heroic qualities is still less than the truth, all our sadness is gone; and we taste a peace so perfect, as if we were still beside the king our master to receive the most touching marks of his kindness . . .[44]

The Abbé de Lionne waited for the end of the discourse to read a French translation which had been prepared beforehand. Kosa Pan then took his king's letter from the hands of the third ambassador, and, bent double, went up the steps of the throne to give it to Louis XIV, who took it standing and with his hat doffed. The letter was written on a rolled sheet of gold, and began with the words: "Letter from the royal and distinguished embassy of the great king of the kingdom of Ayutthaya which he sends you, oh very great king, oh most powerful lord of the kingdoms of France and Navarre . . ."[45] The letter repeated the compliments of the ambassador and proposed an alliance and eternal friendship. Louis XIV asked a few questions about the King of Siam's health, translated by the Abbé de Lionne, and concluded by saying that, if the ambassador had anything to propose to him, he would listen to him.

It was the end of a memorable audience, and recorded with remarkable precision by Antoine Coysevox in one of two bronze bas-reliefs that decorated the sides of the pedestal of an equestrian statue of Louis XIV put up by the States of Britanny in the centre of the Place du Palais in Rennes; it can be seen today in the Museum of Fine Arts in that city.[46]

The ambassadors and their retinue withdrew to the other end of the gallery, moving backwards with their hands joined and with repeated *thawai bangkhom*. They were taken back to the Ambassadors' Room where a magnificent lunch was served them by Swiss guards. Lionne, La Feuillade, Bonneuil, Storf, and Chaumont ate with them. They put on their hats for the audience after the meal with the dauphin. Kosa Pan told him the king his master considered him the worthy son of the greatest monarch in Europe, whose great qualities and victories were known to the ends of the earth. He concluded by declaring that, "The king our master will participate to a considerable degree in the joy at the birth of the new prince that heaven has given you at the same time as we arrived from so far to present you with our profound respects; this we regard as a happy portent . . ."[47]

They then paid their respects to the three sons of the dauphin, the Dukes of Burgundy, Anjou (the future king of Spain), and the newborn Berry. Kosa Pan nicely put it that, "We do not doubt that you will be a most illustrious and most important prince, since you seem to have been born to give audience to ambassadors coming from the other end of the world."[48] The old Maréchale de La Mothe, governess of the French royal princes, replied wittily to these compliments.

The last visits of the day were to the Duke and Duchess of Orléans. The ambassadors found the king's brother in the midst of a considerable court. Kosa Pan congratulated him in the name of his king on the victories he had formerly won, rejoicing in the perfect union existing between the king and his brother. Monsieur replied to these compliments fittingly, and the ambassadors proceeded, between a double row of guards, to his lady, Madame Palatine, surrounded by her ladies-in-waiting. Kosa Pan assured her that it was a very great honour for him and the other ambassadors "to be able to salute a heroine, wife of a hero," and he presented his respects "to one of the greatest, most excellent and most accomplished princesses in the world."[49] It was of course just a compliment, but contained a good deal of truth.

The visits to the royal house now over, the ambassadors took off their hats and returned to Paris in the king's carriages, speaking only about Louis XIV throughout the journey. Mr Storf asked Kosa Pan if he had noticed the diamonds on the royal costume; the ambassador replied that he only had eyes for the king's person.

THE SIAMESE PRESENTS

The selection, itemizing, wrapping, and transport of Phra Narai's presents had, it will be recalled, given considerable trouble to the French sent to Siam. The most precious pieces were wrapped in Persian brocades and placed in Holland linen bags. Everything was placed in boxes of Japanese lacquer, which themselves were put inside trunks made of ordinary wood. These trunks were covered with waxed cloth reinforced by strips of bamboo. The bale was then sewn up in cowskin coated with lime to protect it from worms and insects, and stowed in the bottom of the hold. It will also be recalled that Forbin accused Phaulkon of depleting the kingdom to send to France presents which "were indeed most magnificent."

But these do not seem to have overly impressed the blasé courtiers at Versailles, even if the inventory now seems very impressive.[50] The king received no less than fifteen hundred pieces of porcelain, mostly Chinese, without counting the furniture, screens, and lacquered chests, the numerous gold and silver vases, Persian and Chinese carpets, and Japanese dressing gowns. The list of presents for the dauphin is scarcely less rich. The "princess queen of Siam," that is *kromluang* Yothathep, Phra Narai's daughter, sent for her part sumptuous presents to the dauphine and her sons, the Dukes of Burgundy and Anjou. The latter, who was only three, was overwhelmed with baubles, figurines, and other eye-catching toys.

The pieces of porcelain, objets d'art, and lacquered furniture from China or Japan contributed to launching the fashion for things in the Chinese taste and "pagodas" which were to be the joy of collectors in the following century. The preparation of the exhibition "Phra Narai, King of Siam, and Louis XIV," organized in 1986 at the Orangerie in Paris by the Musée Guimet to mark the three hundred years of the Siamese embassy in France, led to the identification of a great number of these presents in the collections of the Louvre, the Musée Guimet, and the Museum of Natural History. The very small number of truly Siamese items is striking.

The tempered enthusiasm of the French can partly be explained by the fact that most of the gold objects were in reality "tambac," a mixture of gold and copper which, according to Choisy, shone more than gold, and which he compares to the electrum of Solomon's temple.[51] The abbé relates in his *Mémoires* that the presents brought by the ambassadors were put on display in the War Room.

> Mr de Louvois, who did not think much of things in which he had no part, was extremely disdainful of them. "My dear Abbé," he said in passing, "all that you have brought, is it really worth fifteen hundred *pistoles*?" "I have no idea, sir," I replied, very loudly, so everyone would hear me, "but I know for a fact that there is more than twenty thousand crowns of solid gold there, not counting the workmanship. And that is leaving out the japanned cabinets, the screens, and the porcelain." He gave me a disdainful smile.[52]

The same disdain is also found in Sourches: "The presents which the king, their master, sent to the king and to the Dauphin . . . consisted of a great number of rather ugly porcelain pieces, a few Chinese cabinets and screens, rather fine, and a few gold and tambac vases, rather indifferent."[53] A passing reference by Dangeau, the day after the audience, also illustrates the inability of the French to appreciate exotic objets d'art: "Monseigneur [the Dauphin] gave in the evening a supper in his apartments for the Princess of Conti and a few ladies, and then he organized a lottery of some of the presents he received from Siam."[54]

History reserved for two of the Siamese presents a singular destiny. *The Memorandum of the King of Siam's presents to the King of France*, in the 1687 English translation, lists at the beginning, "Two pieces of cast iron cannon six foot long, hammered cold, set out with silver, mounted on their carriages, garnished also with silver, made at Siam." Too luxurious to be used, the Siamese cannons were sent to the king's repository. When the Parisian crowds ransacked the arms kept in the royal stores on 13 July 1789, the two cannons fell into the hands of the revolutionaries. They served the next day in the attack on the Bastille. In sending these dangerous presents, Phra Narai could not have foreseen that they would one day be used to overthrow the Bourbons.[55]

THE TIME FOR VISITS

The following weeks were given over to visits in Paris and nearby. A book would be needed to relate them all, but its interest would be very limited, for the reality of Franco-Siamese relations was being played out elsewhere. Let us mention, as a sample, the visit of 4 September to St Cloud. The summer residence of the king's brother was a marvel, showing the impeccable taste of the prince, with millions being invested in the château, the orangery, the Italian gardens, and the famous water theatre. Aubert, who was to introduce the ambassadors to Monsieur, Duke of Orléans, came to fetch the Siamese envoys in His Highness's carriages, in rainy weather.

At St Cloud they presented well-turned compliments to the Duke of Chartres (the future regent), and Mademoiselle (the future Duchess of Lorraine). Their Royal Highnesses received the ambassadors in the Diana Room under ceilings painted by Mignard.

> They were charmed by the gracious welcome of Monsieur and Madame . . . They were informed that they were annoyed that the heavy rain that day prevented a visit to the gardens, and that a collation was prepared for them at the end of the mall. The first ambassador replied that, even if it were fine, they would have been happy enough with the reception they had just received from so great a prince and princess; that they would come another time to see the gardens.[56]

Madame Palatine, the Duchess of Orléans, related this visit in a letter to her aunt Sophie of Hanover, adding that "the ambassadors know very well how to behave and have much wit; only their faces are rather strange."[57] The same letter explains that the dauphine received fine presents from the princess of Siam: "A collection of small caskets from the Indies and different cabinets, a lot of gold and silver tableware, numerous pieces of porcelain of different types and dimensions, and also a pretty screen to place in front of the mantelpiece." The court of Siam had omitted to send presents to Monsieur and Madame, an oversight which provoked some jealousy.

It was only some twenty years later that Madame spoke to her correspondent of the reply sent by Phra Narai to Louis XIV concerning changing his religion. "When our king gave the late King of Siam to understand that he requested him to embrace the Catholic Christian religion, he replied that he thought one could reach one's salvation in all religions, and that God liked nothing so much as diversity. For this reason, nothing is the same in the world, all the green leaves are different. Thus our king should continue to serve his all-powerful God in the manner he had learnt. As for himself, he wished to praise and serve God in his own way . . . I think he was not wrong in that."[58]

The well-known reaction of La Bruyère is found in his *Characters*:

> If we were told that the secret reason for the Siamese embassy was to provoke the Most Christian King to renounce Christianity, to permit the entry of talapoins into his kingdom, who would have entered our homes to propose their religion to our women, children, and ourselves through their books and their discussions, who would have erected temples in the middle of the towns, where they would have placed metal statues to be worshipped, with what derision and what marked scorn would not we have heard such outrageous proposals! Yet we cover six thousand leagues over the seas to convert the Indies, the kingdoms of Siam, China, and Japan, that is to say to make in all seriousness to all these peoples propositions which must seem very deranged and very ridiculous. They tolerate though our priests and religious orders; they sometimes listen to them, letting them build their churches and conduct their missions. Who causes that to be done in them and in us? Would it not be the force of truth?[59]

Whilst the court and the town spoke in favour or against the attempts to change Phra Narai's religion, his ambassadors did not stop paying visits, admiring and praising everything that was shown to them. They asked innumerable questions, and the white pencils of their secretaries worked hard on their black paper. They saw plays by

Molière, Corneille, and Racine. They heard operas by Lully. They visited the Luxembourg Palace, the Jesuit College of Louis-le-Grand (where they were addressed in twenty-four languages including Canadian Algonquin, Flemish, and Low Breton), the Carthusians and the Foreign Missions, the Bastille and the Arsenal, the royal repository, the Louvre, the academies of painting and sculpture at the Palais-Royal, Cassini's observatory, the Gobelins tapestry factory, Montmartre, Meudon, St Cyr, St Germain, the work on the aqueduct at Maintenon which was to bring the waters of the Eure to Versailles, Versailles itself (including the stables, the kennels, the Trianon, Clagny, and Marly), etc. They went into raptures over all they saw, they tortured the Siamese language with their praises, and their interpreters ran out of French superlatives. In the end they gave up, saying that they were no longer surprised at anything, and that in France everything was possible.

Their residence in the Rue de Tournon was watched over by a company of guards whose chief officer went each evening to ask for the password. For the first three days Kosa Pan had selected "Prosperity," "Royal Alliance," and "Two against all." The idea of a military alliance between the two countries began to take hold.

During a visit to the Condé palace, the prince, known as Monsieur le Duc, asked the ambassadors what they thought of the king's troops.

> The first ambassador replied that he did not think he could see better, but this had not surprised him, because one could not think highly enough of the troops whom the king had taught to conquer. The prince replied that, since he found these troops so fine, it would be desirable if Siam were not so far off, so that they could easily be transported there in case of need. The ambassador replied that God had already created a miracle in bringing together the two kings in close amity in spite of the great distance between their states, and he could perform another for the transport of the troops.[60]

Was he aware that in all seriousness this miracle was being worked on in Versailles?

TACHARD AND SEIGNELAY PREPARE FOR THE FUTURE

We are not well informed about the way the industrious Fr Tachard accomplished in the corridors of Versailles the secret mission Phaulkon had given him, but clearly he was not idle. It is strange that the secret instructions given to the Jesuit only indirectly make reference to the troops the Greek expected from the French king. The document is very instructive, for it reveals Phaulkon actively working towards the French colonization of Siam.

> Sixty or seventy persons very skilled in handling affairs should be brought in the king's ships . . . and if the Father General wishes to send some Fathers of the Society among this number, they have to be dressed like lay persons and even those who they are with should not know them. I undertake . . . to obtain for them the most notable advantages in the kingdom of Siam, like making them governors of provinces, towns, and fortresses; give them the command of the land and sea forces; introduce them into the palace and the government of public affairs; even to give them the principal charges of the king's household, and to use them as counsellors in my negotiations and affairs . . . And so that success is prompt and infallible, the king must be made to understand that Singor [Songkhla] must first be taken possession of, whither it is important to bring two good settlements and men under arms, because once the stronghold is established, there will be nothing to fear . . . It can be objected that, if the King of Siam were to die and these persons arrived at the bar, all these plans will collapse. But I promise and pledge that the successor of the king will be even more disposed to grant everything than his predecessor . . . I ask you, therefore, good Father, by the entrails and wounds of Jesus Christ, to pursue this matter closely with the king and his confessor . . .[61]

This seems unbelievable. It shows clearly that Phaulkon, determined to obtain French protection, followed up his ideas, but it is extremely surprising that a Jesuit should let himself be manipulated by such a megalomaniac adventurer, to the point of linking to the explosive project "the entrails and wounds of Jesus Christ."

It is understandable that the Foreign Missions did not want to touch, even with tongs, Fr Tachard and his dangerous schemes. After the dismissal of Vachet, the Abbé de Lionne confided to a friend:

> I took so little part in all the decisions taken in France that I can swear that my opinion was sought on nothing, except that one day the Marquis de Seignelay asked me if Fr Tachard was such a good friend of Mr Constance, nothing more. It was even my good fortune that neither the king, nor any person on his behalf, asked what I thought of Siamese affairs, and in particular what I thought of Mr Constance; for as I had a very different idea about both than that offered by Fr Tachard, it might have placed me in an embarrassing position.[62]

The increasing frequency of the correspondence exchanged between Seignelay and the intendant at Brest allows one to follow the progress of the idea of a military expedition which has to be considered a colonizing enterprise. Already on 11 September, the minister informed Desclouzeaux: "His Majesty having resolved to send some vessels to Siam at the beginning of next January, it is necessary that you prepare immediately the *Oiseau*, another with thirty cannons, and a storeship . . . Take care that the departure of these vessels be not delayed in any way."[63] On 15 October: "Concerning their apparel, as H.M. desires that they should all be dressed alike, I shall at once send breeches, stockings and hats for five hundred men." Desclouzeaux had remarked that five hundred men would be too confined on three ships. Seignelay replied on 29 November that a fourth vessel had been granted: "The king having considered that it is appropriate that the men H.M. wishes to send to Siam have plenty of room on the vessels transporting them, to preserve their health during such a long crossing, he has resolved to arm another storeship of some three hundred tons."

On 28 December, a letter from the minister concerned the arming of the troops destined to go to Siam, the number of which had been increased to six hundred. "I am also sending you an order for one hundred and sixty cannons which the King of Siam requests. H.M. desires that you put in the ballast of these vessels those which you have among the iron cannons at Brest." A letter of 4 January 1687 announced to the intendant:

> I have sent to Nantes the necessary orders for making without delay eighteen hundred pairs of shoes for the soldiers who are to go to Siam . . . you must have made promptly one thousand tools of all kinds, appropriate for digging earth for making fortifications and sieges. And as some of these arms which you will give to the said soldiers

> could over time be spoilt, the king desires that you have placed on board the vessels which are to make this journey three hundred muskets, two hundred iron pikes, and fifty halberds. I wrote to you today to have placed in the ballast of these vessels two thousand cannon balls. You must add to this number two thousand grenades, and you must prepare twenty thousands of gunpowder for cannons and five thousands for muskets.

Michel Jacq-Hergoualc'h correctly emphasizes the impression of ill-considered haste arising from this correspondence which is "instructive about the extraordinary manner in which this expedition was prepared."[64] Recent history has shown that the transport of troops and their equipment from one end of the earth to the other is no simple matter; military logistics are not improvised. The offensive character of the Siamese campaign suggested by the missives just cited will become even more evident when we examine the instructions given to the military commander and the envoys extraordinary designated to flank this expedition.

THE SIAMESE VISIT THE NORTHERN FORTS

Let us return to the Siamese envoys who were travelling around the Paris basin with open mouths, replete with the grandeur of the French monarch and naively hoping a miracle would transport French troops to their country. Their prayers would be fulfilled.

In 1686, the court went to stay at Fontainebleau for the hunting season from 8 October to 15 November, and it was decided that during this period the Siamese ambassadors would visit the towns and strongholds in the north. It will be recalled that Phichai Walit and Phichit Maitri had refused to undertake the same journey two years earlier. Kosa Pan and his colleagues had seen the king again in Versailles in his study on 2 October. According to Sourches, this private audience "was very long and very tiresome for His Majesty, because it is not pleasant to discuss business through an interpreter."[65] Dangeau said that the ambassadors were "charmed by the goodness of His Majesty," and announced their programme: "They are going to Flanders to see the king's conquests, but they will not go to Alsace or the Rhine, because the journey would be too long and they would suffer too much from the cold. They already suffer from it a lot here and ask if winter will last long."[66]

This explains Seignelay's note to Mr Dumeix at the royal repository:

> The king wishes to have made for the ambassadors of Siam three lined jackets for the voyage they are about to undertake. This is why I request you, before leaving for Fontainebleau, to leave orders at the repository, as His Majesty desires, to supply marten fur suitable for these jackets.[67]

This shows a charming attention to detail on the part of the king, who was at the same time planning an armed expedition whose objectives were not as pleasing.

They left then well protected from the rigours of the winter. The special volumes published by the *Mercure Galant* in December 1686 and January 1687, as well as the letters of Mr Storf to Seignelay, allow us to follow them, listen to the addresses they had to sit through, and appreciate their courtesy and their witty remarks. They left Paris on 14 October for a journey of six weeks, the main stops of which were Beauvais, Amiens, Arras, Béthune, St Omer, Calais, Dunkirk, Ypres, Menin, Lille, Tournai, Valenciennes, Douai, Cambrai, Péronne, St Quentin, Soissons, and Villers-Cotterêts. They returned to Paris on 22 November.

Better than the logorrhoea of the *Mercure Galant*, a witty letter from Mr Storf summarizes the atmosphere of the journey.

> My Lord . . . More than a quire of paper would be needed to relate to you all the honours they received since my last letter. We have had nothing but comedies, music, fireworks, magnificent meals, and above all balls where the Flemish beauties, adorned in jewels both genuine and false, attract their admiration and cause them to confess in good faith the impossibility of being able to describe all this magnificence, and all these things seem to them a dream rather than a reality. But even if they could do so, their supply of black paper would be insufficient. Indeed, My Lord, everyone is everywhere pleased with them. They respond very well, agreeably and with much wit, and the password they give each evening gives pleasure to those who receive them. This is more or less what happens concerning them. I show them in each town the fortifications, the troops and the smallest details.[68]

The conversion of the King of Siam was the leitmotif of most of these addresses. In his replies, Kosa Pan always found a way of avoiding the subject without vexing his hosts. He said at Péronne that "the alliance which has just been concluded between the two kings would last as long as the sun and the moon, that they commended themselves to their prayers, that they thought there would one day be many Christians in the kingdom of Siam, and that the French would become Siamese, and the Siamese French."[69]

On returning to Paris, the ambassadors resumed their merry-go-round of visits, shows, and receptions. They were more fashionable than ever. Their least remarks were repeated, a medal was struck in their honour, their portraits were painted for a room at Versailles, their pictures engraved many times. Their outings created such crowds as became proverbial. Even in 1712, the Marquis de Monteleón, the new Spanish ambassador in England, spoke of the crowds at his formal entrance into London: "The people followed me as though I were an ambassador from Siam, crying out loud 'Long live the King and Queen of Spain!'"[70]

Kosa Pan and his colleagues learnt that Louis XIV, two days after his return from Fontainebleau, had been operated for his fistula. They rejoiced at his convalescence and were concerned when the royal fistula required two further operations. But they would have the pleasure of noting at their farewell audience that the sovereign was definitively cured. Their presence at the great *Te Deum* which Lully had sung at the beginning of January at the Chapel of the Feuillants to celebrate the king's recovery was duly noted. This *Te Deum* was fatal for the musician. He beat the time with so much vigour that he hurt his foot with a violent blow of his staff. The wound became infected and caused his death soon after.

"WHO IS NOT A GOOD SIAMESE, IS NOT A GOOD FRENCHMAN": THE END OF THE EMBASSY

The king desired that the presents for Phra Narai, Phaulkon, and the ambassadors be worthy of his grandeur. The gifts sent in his name, that of the dauphin, and the dauphine, were valued at 175,431 livres; the sum was considerable.[71] The presents sent by Seignelay, Croissy, and Louvois were not included in this amount. The gifts of H.M., taken from the royal repository and bought from merchants, were particularly ostentatious: a gold crown with fleurons ornamented with diamonds, rubies, emeralds, and pearls; crystal mirrors decorated with precious stones; gold watches; a celestial globe on which gold stars marked the constellations, enclosing a clock which sounded the hours and a mechanism which caused the firmament to turn; crystal candelabra and chandeliers; wall-brackets in white, red, and jasper marble, with gold feet; Savonnerie carpets; Gobelins tapestries. There was also a magnificent harpsichord sent to Madame Phaulkon; one wonders in what condition it arrived in Siam, after seven months rolling about in a humid hold.

But that was not all. The King of Siam had given his ambassadors a long list of orders translated into French by Vachet. It is most impressive. Not to mention the 160 cannons which have already been mentioned, two hundred blunderbusses, and twenty quivers with gilded flowers—the provision of arms has always smoothed relations between Europe and the rest of the world. More interesting are the elephant masks lined with velvet and gold, elephant harnesses in red cloth lined with leather and stars of gilded copper, or two thousand crystal objects to decorate a male and female elephant. Two globes, a celestial one to be hung and a terrestrial one on a pedestal, with indications in Siamese, must have given a lot of trouble to the makers. Optical instruments, telescopes, magnifying glasses, suggest that the astronomic panoply of the Jesuits had impressed Phra Narai. Seven huge Savonnerie carpets, greatly appreciated in a country where one moved about much of the time on one's elbows and knees, figured in the list, as well as huge quantities of linen and velvet, lace jackets, and beaver hats of different colours. But the most important orders on the shopping list went to the very new royal mirror factory at St Gobain: 4,264 mirrors of different dimensions to be placed in the palaces of Ayutthaya and Lopburi, and 4,300 pieces of crystal fruits and flowers for Siamese-style chandeliers and candelabra.[72]

The enormous volume of bales of presents and orders made Desclouzeaux blanch when they arrived at Brest, the more so as many objects were in a very poor condition because of negligence on the part of the packers and carelessness by the coachmen. "This was an untoward portent for these projects of an oriental alliance, based in part on such fragile securities!"[73]

On 6 January 1687, the prelate Fénelon gave his *Sermon for the Feast of the Epiphany on the vocation of gentiles* in the crypt of the church of the Foreign Missions, in the presence of Tachard and the Siamese ambassadors. In it, he addressed the King of Siam and his ambassadors:

> Great King . . . why do you delay in creating for the True God, with your own heart, the most agreeable and august of all the temples? . . . Faithful ministers whom he has sent, from the place where the sun rises to that where it sets, to see Louis, take back to him what you have seen with your eyes: . . . this gentle and peaceful majesty . . . but above all this piety which seeks that God reigns rather than man. Be it known in our most distant future that the Indian came to place at the feet of Louis the riches of the dawning day and recognition of the Gospels received through his attentions! . . . May the heavens one day allow among these peoples compassionate fathers to say to their children to instruct them: "Formerly, in a century favoured by God, a king called Louis, desirous of extending the conquests of Jesus Christ beyond his people, sent new apostles to the Indies; it is because of that that we are Christians."[74]

One of the last visits paid by the ambassadors was to the royal printing house established in the Louvre, directed by Sébastien Mabre-Cramoisy. He had the presses run and showed them the different Latin, Greek, Hebrew, and Arabic characters. The first ambassador asked if Siamese characters could also be made for a printing house in Siam. "Yes, you just have to desire it," replied Mr Mabre. At which Kosa Pan raised his eyes to heaven and exclaimed: "Oh France, France!," in Siamese of course.

The ambassadors, who had seen the king at his supper on 12 January, had their farewell audience on the fourteenth. Louis XIV was seated on his throne in the same pomp, but "he was dressed ordinarily."[75] The speech of the first ambassador was greatly admired; the king asked for the text and the court was flooded with copies the same evening. According to Choisy:

> the ambassadors had put in their tongue a part of the thoughts it contained. The Abbé de Lionne had translated this into French, Mr Tiberge [of the MEP] gave it that simple, natural, and noble turn of phrase which he knows how to give everything he touches, and I put in a few full stops and commas.[76]

Kosa Pan finished his compliment in a way which went right to the heart of Louis XIV:

> For us, great king, overwhelmed by your blessings, charmed by your virtues, touched to the bottom of the heart by your goodness, caught by surprise at the sight of your profound wisdom and of all the miracles of your reign, our life seems too short, and the whole world too small, to publish what we think about it. Our memory will be taxed to retain so many things; that is why we have gathered with avidity in faithful registers all that we could observe, and we shall finish them with this protestation, that though we say much, still much has escaped us. These memoirs will be preserved for posterity and placed in safety among the most rare and most precious monuments of state. The king our master will send them as presents to the princes his allies, and in that way the whole Orient will soon know, and all the centuries will come to learn, of the incomparable virtues of Louis the Great.[77]

The "faithful registers" were to be harassed by future troubles. Kosa Pan left behind in France his *Brest Journal*, the small sample of a huge mass which has disappeared for ever. We can only imagine what we would have learnt from the complete report of France and the court of Louis XIV, seen through Siamese eyes. Comparative social history would have had a unique document.

The ambassadors had sixteen other audiences the same day, with members of the royal family, princes of the blood, Colbert de Croissy, and Seignelay. They stayed three more days in Paris, where they received a final visit from Fr de La Chaize, who presented them an equestrian portrait of Louis XIV in miniature by Mignard. Kosa Pan returned the visit the next day, but, says the *Mercure Galant*, "what took place is secret." The eve of their departure for Brest, the ambassadors received the farewell visit of the Duke de La Feuillade who said to them "that who was not a good Siamese, was not a good Frenchman."[78]

Before getting into their coaches the next day, the three ambassadors and the six *khunmun* turned in the direction of Versailles, lined up in single file, joined their hands, raised them to their foreheads, and bowed low three times. Kosa Pan was particularly moved. It had been hoped to send them through Normandy, but winter made the roads impassable. They returned the same way they had come, through Orléans and down the Loire, and arrived on 4 February at Brest. They reoccupied their quarters in Desclouzeaux's residence, waiting for the squadron to leave.

"HIS MAJESTY HAS RESOLVED TO ATTACK BANGKOK"

Dangeau notes in his *Journal* on 9 November:

> I learnt that the king had named La Loubère to go to Siam to take the presents he is sending there and to complete a trade treaty. He will not have the rank of ambassador. Sebret [Céberet], one of the directors of the Compagnie des Indes Orientales [CIO], is going there with him; both of them will have the title of envoys extraordinary.[79]

It is surprising that the two men only received their instructions in January 1687, at the time when the military preparations were already well advanced.

The principal position went to Simon de La Loubère, who, in spite of an honourable diplomatic career, was little known among courtiers. Born in 1674 in Toulouse, this clever but choleric southerner had gone to live in the capital about 1665 where he frequented literary and social circles. A writer and a mathematician, he shone in such society. This was the time when diplomats were chosen in the salons. La Loubère was made secretary of the embassy at Solothurn near Berne (1672–1676), minister-resident in Strasburg (1678), and envoy charged with presenting the court at Hanover with Louis XIV's compliments on the accession of Duke Ernst Augustus, husband of Sophie of Hanover (1680). La Loubère's occupations after his return from Hanover to his nomination for Siam in November 1686 are not known. His irritable and stubborn character, his inability to give way before the opinions of others, and his passion for questions of etiquette promised a rocky diplomatic mission.[80]

The reasons for the choice of Claude Céberet du Boullay are more easily understood. The son of one of the king's secretaries, he had liked the sea from his youth. Robert Challe explains that, during one of his voyages, he had married in Martinique a relative of Madame de Maintenon, the king's morganatic wife.

> It is a good means for lacking neither support nor protection. It is though very true that his merit does not lie in that: it is certainly in his probity, and inexpressible zeal in the service and interests of the king . . . An intelligent, lively, fiery yet ever tranquil mind; so judicious that even now no one has ever complained of his decisions. In a word, a man such as I would like to have as my superior for the rest of my days.[81]

This compliment from a person as independent as Challe is not to be dismissed. From 1685 Céberet was one of the twelve directors of the CIO. He complemented La Loubère, charged with political affairs and unfamiliar with colonial commerce. But the instructions of the two envoys prescribed them to work hand in hand.

La Loubère received his first instructions on 18 January 1687.[82] Among the matters which Louis XIV held most important,

> the first . . . is the establishment of the Catholic religion in the kingdom of Siam; and as it pleased God to bless the efforts which [H.M.] has taken up to the present to unite all his subjects in such a holy creed and even to extend it among his neighbours, he wishes with the same ardour to be able to establish it throughout the Orient.

There was, then, in the mind of the Most Christian revoker of the Edict of Nantes, a direct link between the eradication of heresy in his own kingdom and the propagation of Christianity in Siam, indeed in the whole Orient. As for the conversion of Phra Narai himself, "it is not appropriate to press him on this change, except in concert with Mr Constance." The instructions underline the importance of relations between the two kingdoms and express the hope that, out of a desire for economy, the King of Siam will not send fresh ambassadors to France.

La Loubère, supposed to remain in Siam, was in addition charged with

> applying himself to learn without delay the language of the country, to learn of the differences the King of Siam might have with his neighbours, the forces he has at his disposal, by land or by sea, the manner in which he customarily wages war, the number of fortified strongholds he has, the nature of their fortifications, what are the revenues of the monarch, how far his power over his subjects extends,

if they are free or slaves, and generally everything concerning the government, both spiritual and political—His Majesty desiring that, when some vessels return from the said country, he sends him very exact accounts of all the information he had been able to gather.

La Loubère was not to spend an eternity in Siam, but he brought back enough material to compile the two volumes of his remarkable *Kingdom of Siam* which appeared in 1691 and would be the only lasting result of the expedition which was being prepared.

On 22 January Seignelay signed a letter addressed to Phaulkon, informing him that His Majesty was persuaded that

> you would do everything possible for his service and satisfaction. Fr Tachard will explain to you what H.M. desires of you, and in what way the execution of what will be proposed to you on his behalf depends on the maintenance of royal friendship which H.M. has consented to contract with the King of Siam; he has no cause to doubt . . . that you will do everything which will help him retain this friendship which will be useful to him later. I return to what the Rev. Fr Tachard will explain to you, to which you can give complete credence.[83]

Phaulkon, ready to sell Siam to France, would surely have appreciated a less lofty tone. But La Loubère was taking for him the Order of St Michael, letters of naturalization, the right of bearing three fleurs-de-lys in his arms and, for his son, the title of count and the gift of land bringing in three thousand livres in rent. This letter shows to what degree Tachard, the bearer of secret instructions which he refused to show La Loubère and Céberet, complicated their task. Full of his own importance, the Jesuit treated the envoys with an arrogance which compromised their joint mission.

Fresh instructions for La Loubère and Céberet, dated 25 January,[84] returned to the central role of Tachard and the promises of Phaulkon to "give all the posts requested in the name of the king, to establish Frenchmen to govern in the strongholds belonging to the King of Siam, and to permit complete freedom of trade for His Majesty's subjects." In case these undertakings were not respected, "His Majesty has resolved . . . to attack Bangkok, and to become its master by force of arms." If Bangkok were given to the French, the envoys were not to consent to hostilities, even if the King of Siam refused to cede Mergui to them.

A reading of this flabbergasting document suggests that Louis XIV had acquired a "war mentality." The king and Seignelay did not want Singor (Songkhla) which was being offered them. They wanted Mergui, and above all Bangkok, "the two gateways of the kingdom, one on the Gulf of Bengal, the other on the Gulf of Siam," as Turpin was to write a century later.[85] The minister had sounded out Kosa Pan about the cession of Bangkok, but he had replied that his instructions only mentioned Songkhla, and that this stronghold was excellent. Seignelay insisted, saying that if Bangkok was in the hands of the French, they could defend the country against external attack from the Dutch, for example. But the *ratchathut* repeated that there was only question of Songkhla.[86]

Who had inspired in Louis XIV this passion for Bangkok and Mergui? Phaulkon, it will be recalled, had orally suggested "giving the king the town of Bangkok," but Chaumont and Choisy had not taken seriously this offer which is not found in the written instructions given by Phaulkon to Tachard. Had the idea germinated in the mind of the Jesuit? Bèze was to reproach the gentlemen of the Foreign Missions with having first suggested the idea: "They put . . . the Chevalier de Chaumont off about Singor and persuaded him to ask for Bangkok which, by its situation, put the French in a better position to rule over the whole kingdom and become masters of its trade."[87]

Fr de Bèze, then in France, could only have obtained this information from the very suspect Fr Tachard. Had he not removed from the court Fr Vachet who, indeed, had advised Chaumont to occupy Songkhla? If the MEP had recommended the taking of Bangkok, this could only have been done through the Abbé de Lionne who had already declared: "I can swear my opinion was not sought on anything." The Jesuits and the Foreign Missions accuse each other. The documents make one incline for Tachard. On arriving at the bar of Siam, the Abbé de Lionne wrote: "All the people in the squadron, and the envoys of the king themselves, considered Fr Tachard as the moving spirit of this embassy."[88] Whatever the case, the decision to attack Bangkok was going to have disastrous consequences.

The command of the troops to be landed was given to Mr Desfarges, a former queen's regimental lieutenant-colonel, promoted for the occasion to be brigadier of the king's armies, and usually given the title general. He was doubtless brave, but lacked perspicacity. Lanier considers him "vain and narrow-minded, indecisive, touchy and susceptible, without real friends and without clear ideas, shifting from extreme credulity to extreme suspicion, very self-interested, and seeming to like money more than was proper."[89] The other leaders of the expedition were the regimental chiefs of staff, du Bruant, Vertesalle, de Beauchamp, and d'Alvimare. Du Laric, an artillery captain, had ten bombardiers under his orders.

Desfarges's instructions specified that, with the means placed at his disposal, he was capable "of undertaking everything and bringing terror to all part of the Indies," as if six hundred men could create fear throughout a continent like Asia. No troops were to be disembarked so long as Bangkok and Mergui were not handed over, but Bangkok was to be occupied by force if the King of Siam refused to cede this stronghold. The occupation of Bangkok was to be followed by that of Mergui. These two strongholds were to be victualled for eighteen months and fortified "with all necessary diligence to protect them from any surprise attack, and prevent attempts by the Dutch who might seize them." The King of Siam was to be asked to provide the men necessary for "shifting soil and other fortification works." Desfarges was authorized to detach men to guard the person of the king and to teach Siamese sailors and soldiers, on condition of not exposing the two strongholds to danger. The instructions finished with a familiar refrain: "Although the establishment of trade is the basis of this undertaking . . . he should however be informed that the chief reason which has led His Majesty to obtain a solid French establishment in that country is the project to advance religious affairs."[90]

Of course it was not forgotten that the King of Siam requested a large number of French Jesuits; the military expedition was also a religious crusade. According to the *Mercure Galant*, there were one hundred and fifty volunteers. The fifteen selected received, like their colleagues on the preceding expedition, an official scientific mission from the king, and instruments from the Academy of Sciences. The list of their names and a summary of the destiny awaiting them in Asia is found in the archives of the Society of Jesus in Rome. At the head of the list, as to be expected, is the inevitable Guy Tachard, denominated the superior of the French Jesuits in the Indies. His companions were Jean Richaud, Vénance Bouchet, Jean Collusson, Patrice Comilh, Abraham Le Royer, Claude de Bèze, François Thionville, Henri Dollu, Jacques Duchatz, Marcel Le Blanc, Charles de La Breuille, Pierre d'Espagnac, Pierre de Saint-Martin, and Louis Rochette. The last-named was to die during the outward crossing.[91]

Fathers de Bèze and Le Blanc were to leave detailed accounts of the events which the expedition gave rise to. We shall read of the troubles of the others.

THE DEPARTURE OF THE SQUADRON

Poor Desclouzeaux, constantly taken to task, struggled all the while in Brest to find supplies, to arm the vessels, to take on crews, and above all to keep Seignelay happy. The minister, pressured himself by the king, bombarded him with missives insisting on the use of every possible means, the prompt implementation of orders, and at the same time, of course, the strictest economy. The intendant had finally succeeded in putting together two vessels of 600 tons, the *Gaillard* and the *Oiseau*, as well as three storeships, the *Loire*, the *Normande*, and the *Dromadaire*. The *Gaillard* had been built in 1684 and was held to sail well. Its captain, Mr de Vaudricourt, commanded the squadron. The *Oiseau*, built in 1670, still had a good reputation, but Robert Challe three years later complained of its slowness; it was commanded by Duquesne-Guiton, nephew of the great Abraham Duquesne. The *Loire* and the *Normande*, which were of 500 and 300 tons, had recently come from the naval shipyards at Brest. The *Dromadaire*, built in 1676, had 500 tons burden and was considered "good but heavy." On their arrival at Brest, in February, the envoys decided to add the recently careened *Maligne* to the squadron. The bales of presents and the orders from the court of Siam had arrived in Brest from Le Havre on a frigate of the CIO, and it was clear that not everything could be loaded onto the five vessels already overloaded with men, arms, and tools. The frigate, like the *Oiseau* built in 1670, only had 150 tons burden. It was said to be "an indifferent sailing ship."[92]

The squadron transported in all 1,361 persons: 307 on the Gaillard, 310 on the *Oiseau*, 707 on the three storeships, and 37 on the *Maligne*. A listing drawn up by Desclouzeaux provides full details.[93] Among the 307 persons crammed into the flagship, the *Gaillard*, the list distinguishes between the crew, soldiers, and passengers. With its 158 men, the crew formed the largest group. In addition to Mr de Vaudricourt, 9 chiefs of staff and 37 naval officers, there were 87 sailors, 12 officers' valets, and 12 cabin boys. Among the army people, 3 sergeants and 9 corporals commanded 72 soldiers and a drummer. The 600 troops were spread unequally between the two vessels and the three storeships: 75 on the *Gaillard* and the Normande, 100 on the *Oiseau*, 150 on the *Loire*, and 200 on the *Dromadaire*.

The 74 passengers travelling on the *Gaillard* comprised the most varied group. Among them were the 3 Siamese ambassadors, their interpreter the Abbé de Lionne, 3 *khunmun*, and 2 secretaries. Four Jesuits, including Tachard, watched over the spiritual well-being of everyone. General Desfarges, his officers, and his 10 bombardiers are listed among the passengers. Two sons of Desfarges, the Marquis and the Chevalier, accompanied their father; between the three of them they had 13 domestics. Also listed, in addition to several surgeons and lay brothers destined for the "hospital at Siam," was a group of artisans: a gardener, a tailor, a shoemaker, a carpenter, a "workman for mathematics," 2 painters, and 2 master carpenters.

What were "three musicians for Mr Constance" doing in that crowd? Were they going to teach Mme Phaulkon to play the harpsichord? André Cardinal-Destouches, who was born in 1672 and who is known to have travelled to Siam with Fr Tachard at the age of fifteen, was one of them.[94] It is also known that "The Jesuit Fathers of the Siamese and Chinese mission transported in their baggage, on the royal frigates, the scores of the divine Florentine,"[95] meaning Lully, who died three weeks after the departure of the squadron. This is reassuring; France was not only sending bombardiers and blunderbusses to Siam, but musicians and music as well.

La Loubère, Céberet, and his son travelled with 4 other Jesuits on the *Oiseau*. The 2 envoys took a retinue of 13 servants: a secretary, an aid, a surgeon, a painter, a valet de chambre, an equerry, a cook, a butler, and 5 lackeys.

The Siamese ambassadors, after expressing to the intendant for the last time their satisfaction at the reception they had received in France, bowed low before the portrait of Louis XIV and embarked on the *Gaillard*. The following day, 1 March, the squadron set sail. It was the end of an important embassy in the annals of Louis XIV's diplomacy. It was also the end of the "innocent" period of Franco-Siamese relations.

CHAPTER NINETEEN

THE LA LOUBÈRE/CÉBERET EMBASSY (MARCH–DECEMBER 1687)

"TO CHARM THE BOREDOM OF A LONG SEA JOURNEY"

TO READ the accounts of this crossing, it appears more arduous than that of the preceding embassy. The main source is *The Second Voyage of Fr Tachard and the Jesuits sent by the King to the Kingdom of Siam* in French,[1] which is complemented by the unpublished manuscript *Voyage or Relation of Fr Tachard to Siam.*[2] Since the first edition of the present work was published, Michel Jacq-Hergoualc'h published the *Journal of the Voyage to Siam of Claude Céberet, Envoy extraordinary of the King in 1687 and 1688.*[3]

Hardly had Vaudricourt's squadron rounded Cape Finisterre than a violent storm struck the six ships. The *Loire* had its mainsail torn off and its mainmast damaged. It became separated from the squadron, but commanded by Joyeux, the captain of the *Maligne* in 1685–1686, it arrived at the cape two days before the rest of the fleet. Thinking of other things, Fr Tachard only devotes a few paragraphs to the pious and studious activities of those on board, explaining: "In this way in all our vessels we tried to charm the boredom of the long sea journey, and more important, to banish idleness which is the source of every disorder."[4] We shall do like the Jesuit who excuses himself, after a few hasty lines about the flying fish, and catching bonitos, dolphins, and sharks: "As we have already spoken about these innocent pleasures during our first sea journey, we shall not speak of them here."[5]

Cassini had alerted the astronomical Fathers that a solar eclipse would be partly visible on 11 May. The Siamese ambassadors, fascinated by eclipses, asked the Jesuits if they could observe it through their instruments. "We gave them to understand that we did not think it would be possible to see it at the spot where we would be. But to keep them happy we had to explain the reasons, which did not entirely satisfy them since they did not sufficiently understand them. And as we told them that we had not made the calculations to know its exact size, they requested us to calculate it for love of them." Six days of calculations were needed for Fr Comilh, on the *Gaillard*, to determine the hour, length, and degree the sun would be covered by some five fingers' width. The observation began at eight in the morning, and everything passed exactly as Comilh had predicted. Overcome with excitement, the Siamese "waited a long time on the bridge, telling each other all the time about the hour and minute marked in the calculations." Kosa Pan was delighted; he repeated "that the sun must have had a discussion with the Father, and told him what it would do, so exact had he been in predicting the least circumstances."[6] On the same day, 11 May, the ships passed the Tropic of Capricorn.

The unbelievable overcrowding (the *Oiseau,* which on the previous journey had carried 209 men, now carried 310), the heat, the bad water, and the poor quality of the victuals caused terrible devastation among the crews, and still more among the foot soldiers, less hardened to the privations of a long voyage. Fevers, scurvy, and dysentery put half the sailors out of action. The *Dromadaire*, with its 200 soldiers, suffered the most; in less than a fortnight, on the stretch between the Tropic of Capricorn and arriving at the Cape, 26 soldiers or sailors died on board, and that in spite of the charity, which attracted considerable attention, of its captain, Mr d'Ardennes, who gave his personal provisions to the sick.

The 15 Jesuits, 3 priests of the Foreign Missions, and the almoners formed relays among the sick and the dying. The dramatic circumstances revealed the unexpected consequences of the revocation of the Edict of Nantes. Among the seriously ill were two newly converted sailors and a soldier who confessed they were only nominal Catholics, and that "they had embarked to go to Siam with the intention of moving on to Batavia and the Dutch, that their abjuration had been forced, and that they intended to keep for the rest of their lives the religion in which they had been raised."[7] Naturally the Fathers worked hard on these crypto-Huguenots whose "stubbornness only resulted from ignorance," and they abjured a second time their "false and detestable maxims."

The king's vessels anchored on 11 June at the Cape, where the obliging governor, Simon van der Stel, allowed them to take on water and wood, buy "refreshments," as well as send on shore 300 sick persons. Fr Tachard went to present his 14 colleagues to the governor. He received this learned cohort with much consideration and authorized them to set themselves up in the pavilion where the six Jesuits in the preceding expedition had lodged. Fr de Bèze profited by this putting into port to visit the places nearby. He summarized his impressions in a letter to a friend: "I found the country more beautiful than we had been given to believe, and the Hottentots much more hideous . . . They live more like beasts than men, and I think it would be very difficult to convert them; but with the grace of God one can accomplish everything."[8]

The leaders of the expedition decided to unload the *Maligne* and send it back to France, since the deaths and the consumption of some of the provisions had reduced the cargo of the five remaining ships. The frigate set off for Brest with letters talking of the "good disposition with which we are embarking to continue our voyage."[9] On 28 June the squadron left the roadstead and went to sea.

The second part of the journey was even more distressing than the first. The five ships were dispersed by storms at night, and the mortality increased alarmingly. The death on 17 August of Fr Rochette, who distinguished himself by looking after the sick on the *Dromadaire*, greatly affected the travellers; some considered him a saint amid the misfortune which afflicted the fleet. "He lived," wrote Tachard, "like a true Jesuit, and died like an apostle."[10] The *Gaillard* dropped anchor before Bantam on 24 August, thinking it was the first to arrive, but fishermen brought a letter from Mr Duquesne-Guiton, captain of the *Oiseau* who had arrived a week earlier, announcing that the Dutch had refused to supply anything at all, and he was waiting for them in Batavia.

The welcome at Batavia was not at all the same as that given to the Chaumont/Choisy embassy. The four ships (there was no news of the *Normande*) were barely allowed to buy provisions and send ashore the men most afflicted by scurvy. The rest of the French were requested to remain on board. Unable to believe his ears, Tachard ran to the governor-general Johan Camphuys, whom he calls Campiche. He was only received the following day to hear that, since news had reached Batavia of the revocation of the Edict of Nantes, and of the persecution of French Huguenots, the king's vessels could no longer count on the same hospitality. The good Father was thunderstruck. "I told him I was surprised about what he said concerning religion, that the king had not treated them harshly as he had been given to understand, but on the contrary with every kind of consideration and testimonies of goodness."[11] One can doubt on other occasions the good faith of the Jesuit, but here the evidence is clear: Guy Tachard lied through his teeth.

The disastrous consequences of the revocation were felt even in the Indies. During a third voyage to Asia in 1690, the French squadron, with Tachard on board again, could not even make a stopover at the Cape; the Dutch seized the *Coche* and the *Normande*, both heavily laden, whose captains were unaware that the War of the Augsburg League had started. Louis XIV could not force the consciences of his Huguenot subjects, set the whole of Europe against him, go and destroy the Palatinate, and at the same time count on the benevolence of the powerful VOC which had all the means at its disposal to destroy his grand Asiatic projects. One has to choose.

It can be understood that the squadron did not stay long in Batavia; it set sail on 7 September after only a week in port. After crossing the dangerous Bangka Strait, the leaders assembled on the *Gaillard* at the request of Fr Tachard. He was determined to go ashore and see Phaulkon before the others. "The gentlemen," he innocently wrote, "considered it appropriate that . . . I should go on board the *Oiseau* to go ahead of the rest of the squadron to Siam to seek all the things we needed."[12] The Abbé de Lionne saw the departure of the intriguing Jesuit in a completely different light:

> Fr Tachard, who had until then been on board the vessel transporting the ambassadors, went onto another vessel which immediately set off, to arrive in Siam before the others. Being the first to come ashore, he went to find Mr Constance . . . Fr Tachard always had the chief role in everything; he was the favourite and servant of Mr Constance.[13]

We shall see in the following chapter that the Abbé de Lionne, named as coadjutor of Mgr Laneau and future Bishop of Rosalie, was to behave in a questionable manner, to say the least. The Jesuits for their part were convinced the abbé was chiefly responsible for the

French decision to demand the cession of Bangkok and Mergui, the chief object of this embassy. Fr Maldonado underlined this in an account in Portuguese of the events triggered by this embassy:

> It also has to be stated as certain that [Phaulkon] had not called for troops, but the Abbé de Lionne was the chief author of their arrival, by the repeated requests he made in Paris, promising that the two principal strongholds of the kingdom would be handed over, thus imagining that the trade of the Royal Company would be assured."[14]

The *Oiseau* arrived on 27 September at the bar of Siam, from where Tachard was able to get in touch with Phaulkon. They had a lot to discuss, the more so as Siam had gone through a turbulent period since the departure of Chaumont's embassy at the end of 1685.

FORBIN AND THE MAKASSAR REVOLT

The Chevalier de Forbin had remained in Siam because Chaumont had ordered him to. What he saw and experienced in the kingdom after the departure of the rest of the French had further increased his regret at remaining in the country, the extreme poverty of which he emphasizes in his *Mémoires*. Installed in a tiny house with thirty-six slaves and two elephants at his command, he took his meals at Phaulkon's establishment. In a short time with his straight talking he worked his way into the good graces of Phra Narai, of whom he drew a less flattering portrait than Tachard or Choisy. "I diverted him by telling a thousand stories, after my manner, which he seemed to be pleased with. 'Tis true that a little matter would do it, he being a stupid and very ignorant prince . . . He was so fond of nothing in the world as to be compared to Louis le Grand."[15]

But the favour Forbin enjoyed worried Phaulkon, who had him appointed governor of Bangkok charged with overseeing the construction of the new fort, "which was to be delivered to the French soldiers that the King of Siam had sent for."[16] Forbin was convinced that the Greek had tried to dispose of him by sending some poisoned "curdled milk" which despatched four of his slaves to the other world. It was in Bangkok that Forbin was confronted with an event which shook the foundations of the Siamese throne in 1686: the revolt of the Makassars. Numerous Dutch, English, and French documents speak of this in considerable detail,[17] but the event remains somewhat mysterious. The conquest by the VOC of the sultanate of Makassar in the Celebes (Sulawesi) at the end of the 1660s had caused a large number of its inhabitants to emigrate, being too proud to accept the Dutch yoke. The Makassar prince Dai, sometimes Daen, had found refuge with several hundred of his men in Ayutthaya, where Phra Narai had assigned them a plot of land next to the Malay quarter. Their brutality, fanaticism, and their indifference to death made them formidable.

Ten Makassars armed with wavy-bladed krises would watch unmoved as a hundred soldiers toting muskets advanced on them, and cause terrible carnage. Forbin relates that he plunged his lance into the stomach of a furious Makassar, but

> as if he had no sense of feeling, advanced upon the weapon, which I held fast to his body, and made incredible efforts to come at me in order to run me through . . . I found that my best way was to retreat a little, still keeping the lance in his stomach, without venturing to repeat my thrust, till at length I was relieved by others of the lancemen who laid him dead upon the spot.[18]

The chevalier questioned the Portuguese "born in the Indies" about this strange people. They told him

> that they were schismatical Muhammadans, and very superstitious; that their priests gave them letters written in magic characters, which they tied to their arms, and assured them that as long as they wore them they would be invulnerable; that one thing contributed not a little to render them cruel and intrepid, which was a firm belief that all persons whom they killed in this world, excepting Muhammadans, should be as so many slaves to serve them in the other.[19]

A priest with the Foreign Missions noted:

> I do not know any people in the world as bold as these Makassars. When they have taken opium and they run *amok* . . . there are no dangers they do not face . . . They die happy provided they have killed. Their gaze is frightful; sometimes, after having been felled with a mortal blow, they pick themselves up and return to use the thread of life remaining them to kill an enemy.[20]

As can be seen, Phra Narai should have thought twice before installing these fanatics within a lance's throw of his palace.

According to the same witness at the Foreign Missions, a Makassar deputy chief preached rebellion against the King of Siam in the name of Islam under threat, explaining that this was written in the stars. The Makassars, with their prince at their head, plotted to burn down the capital, seize the palaces in Ayutthaya and Lopburi, and kill the king, Phaulkon, and all the Europeans. They planned to place a half-brother of the king on the throne, after having duly converted him to Islam. It also seems—and this is the most obscure point in the affair—that an important faction of the *khunnang* and the monks were involved in the plot, invisible behind the Makassars, who sharpened their krises and fortified themselves with opium.

The plot was discovered mid-July 1686. Two hundred Makassars were obliged to give themselves up; 53 others boarded a junk which tried to reach the Gulf of Siam. Forbin in Bangkok received Phaulkon's order to close the Chao Phraya River with a chain and "arrest" the Makassars. This was sending him to certain death. The chevalier had under his orders a few dozen Portuguese half-castes and 2,000 Siamese whom he trained as best he could. He tried various ruses when the Makassar junk was stopped by the chain, but they drew their krises and a terrible slaughter took place. At the end of the day, Forbin had lost 366 men; the Makassars, 17. It took another difficult fortnight and further considerable loss of life to track down and despatch the remaining 36 who were hidden in the region near Bangkok and caused terror all around.

A detailed account dated 20 September 1686, sent by Samuel White to his brother George, then in London, related the end of the revolt.[21] At the beginning of September a good hundred Makassars remained in Ayutthaya, having retreated into their camp. As they refused to lay down their arms, Phaulkon encircled them on 14 September with some 60 Europeans, mostly English, French, and Portuguese, and 6,000 Siamese. A first attack was repulsed; Phaulkon himself was only just saved by one of his slaves. A second assault, better organized, evicted the Makassars from their entrenched positions. They hid among the reeds and bamboo bordering the Chao Phraya swollen by the monsoon, but were massacred or martyrized, not before decimating their assailants. The captain of Phaulkon's bodyguard killed their prince.

Several Europeans lost their lives in the mêlée, among whom was a certain Mr de Rohan and the English captains Coates and Henry Udall. The surviving Makassars were put to death with particularly refined tortures, the description of which turns one's stomach. The two young sons of the prince alone were spared, and Phaulkon did not delay sending them to France on a CIO vessel. They would be baptized in Versailles on 3 February 1688.[22]

Véret, director of the French godown in Ayutthaya, sent this warning to the directors of the company:

> Mr Constance is sending to France the two sons of the Makassar prince . . . As it is a nation which lives and breathes sedition and cruel and barbarous acts . . . there is no safety in allowing them to approach His Majesty, because this people is afflicted by such despair as to kill their women, children, and leave their houses to run and kill everyone they meet.[23]

André-François Deslandes-Boureau, the son of André Deslandes, was not soft-hearted about the two Makassar princes.

> Louis XIV saw them, and as he liked grandiose things, he ordered that they be employed in the navy. The fate of the elder was very sad: he killed himself with stabs wounds from a knife. The second I met at Brest: he had the colour, manners and appearance of an uncouth black. Never have the Jesuits made such a bad bargain as to have brought to France these Makassar princes. They were a dishonour to humanity. I should add in passing that Paris and the court have often been deceived by these so-called princes from Asia and Africa. One should have blushed for shame just in presenting them, unless it were as unusual animals.[24]

The Makassar revolt was thus crushed, but worrying questions remained. The motives for the revolt, and above all the identity of those who wished to use the Makassars to overthrow the throne and Phaulkon, remained concealed. The name of the prince who would have profited by the revolt, had it succeeded, is also not known.

Fr de Bèze gives precious details on the two half-brothers of the king. The elder, Chaofa Aphaitot, "was deformed; he had crooked legs and could hardly use them, and was moreover very choleric and much given to wine." This is the paralyzed prince we saw demanding a miracle in 1667. He was accused of being involved in the plot, "which led him to be totally imprisoned in the palace."

The younger half-brother was Chaofa Noi. It seems the people were pleased he be considered the successor, for he possessed all the qualities needed to make a prince liked: "He was handsome and rather pale, which the Siamese appreciate a lot."[25] But in 1683 he had been the victim of a murky intrigue, the strings of which were pulled by the head of the elephant corps, Ok-phra Phetracha. His disgrace was even greater than that of his brother. He was beaten on Phra Narai's orders by Phetracha and the royal favourite Phra Pi.

> Between them they carried out [the sentence] with such a ruthless rain of blows that the unfortunate prince was left for dead at the stake. He came to however, but his whole body was strangely bloated, joined with great weakness in the legs and a form of paralysis in the tongue which hindered him from speaking. Some however have maintained that his dumbness was a mask he wore lest the king's suspicion be aroused.[26]

The succession to the throne was not yet discussed, but the elimination of possible candidates was going ahead nicely, over several years.

The Makassar revolt and the intrigues in the shadow of the throne revealed a greater malaise, provoked by the king's Western sympathies. In a long letter of 20 November 1686 to Fr de La Chaize, Phaulkon mentions a significant incident which can be placed around March or April of that year:

> Three or four months after the departure of the French ambassador, a piece of paper was found hanging from a tree in front of the Lopburi palace gate . . . This paper set out the perilous position of the Siamese religion. Everyone was asked to open their eyes on a matter of public concern. All this was conceived in very insolent terms.[27]

The cry of alarm, uttered in a very oriental way, in favour of Buddhism which was seen to be threatened, was a very serious factor.

One can understand that Forbin, who saw the corpses of the victims of the revolt floating down the river past Bangkok, wanted more than ever to leave Siam. Still convinced that Phaulkon was seeking his death, he sought permission from the king to leave the kingdom. He embarked at the beginning of 1687 on a CIO ship leaving for the Coromandel Coast. His relief was considerable: "I had nothing more to fear from the malice of the minister. In short, we set sail the very next day. I was so glad that I was leaving this cursed country, that I already forgot whatever I had suffered in it."[28]

Forbin was therefore no longer in Siam when the *Oiseau* arrived there on 27 September, followed on 6 October by the *Gaillard*, the *Loire*, and the *Dromadaire*. The *Normande*, separated from the squadron by a storm soon after leaving the Cape, only reached the bar of Siam at the end of November. Of 636 soldiers and officers who had left Brest, only 492 reached Siam. The physical condition of the survivors was so poor that, with the help of the climate, many more died in the weeks which followed the disembarkation. The expedition had not got off to a good start.

FR TACHARD TAKES THINGS IN HAND

The equivocal division of responsibilities between the official envoys, La Loubère and Céberet, and Tachard, the unofficial emissary armed with secret instructions, explains why the embassy started off in an atmosphere of suspicion and ambiguity. Hardly had the *Oiseau* dropped anchor than the Jesuit displayed prodigious activity. The smooth-tongued tone of his published account scarcely conceals the irritation of the envoys, especially of La Loubère.

The *ratchathut* Kosa Pan and his two colleagues had sent charming letters of thanks from the Cape to Seignelay, Lagny, the director of commerce, and Fr de La Chaize,[29] but the French proposals concerning Bangkok and Mergui profoundly worried them. The manuscript *Relation* of Tachard reproaches them for not espousing his views. "When I went to tell them that I did not see any other outpost except Bangkok which could be given to the king's troops, they always protested about this, pointing out that it was the key to the kingdom."[30] The good Father overlooked that it was, after all, their country.

Fr de Bèze explains that the precaution of not letting anyone go ashore before the formal cession of Bangkok and Mergui, was necessary.

> The facts were that the ambassador [Kosa Pan] had never liked to make this promise during his visit to France, and being aware of the

> importance of Bangkok, also of the uneasiness which sight of that stronghold in French hands would occasion among the Siamese, he held out against all pressure brought to bear upon him to promise it.[31]

Bèze did not understand the Siamese; they were being brought eternal salvation, but made difficulties over a miserable place located on the swamps of the estuary of the Chao Phraya.

Tachard's unpublished *Relation* does not bother to disguise the arrogance he displayed when La Loubère expressed his discontent at seeing the ground cut beneath his feet:

> I demonstrated to him that in truth I had no intention in going quickly to Siam [Ayutthaya] other than in predisposing the king and Mr Constance, and inspiring in them the good sentiments for their negotiation to succeed, and that I hoped more than ever to do this without need of the presence of the [Siamese] ambassadors, because it was impossible that this monarch and his minister would not believe what I would tell them, since they themselves sent me . . . Were they waiting for the ambassadors to know from them their views on a matter with which I alone was charged, about which no one had wished to inform them, neither in Siam, nor in France?[32]

This means, in plain words, that the two envoys should not hope to succeed without the preliminary representations of the Father, and that the Siamese ambassadors were of no consequence.

Céberet tried to intervene to support La Loubère, but

> he told us many times that he knew what he had to say and do, and that the king and his lordship the Marquis de Seignelay had explained to him what he should do, that Mr Constance was a man with whom one had to negotiate with an open heart . . . We did all we could, Mr de La Loubère and I, to commit him to some considerations of confidence, but it was not possible to persuade him.[33]

The conclusion of Michel Jacq-Hergoualc'h, the historian of this embassy, is compelling: "One wonders, with that, why Versailles had gone to the expense of sending two envoys . . . who duplicated the work of the Reverend Father."[34]

In conformity with Seignelay's orders, the two envoys drew up secret instructions indicating, in their conclusion: "The Reverend

Father will listen to no moderation on the subject of Mergui, any more than of Bangkok, since the king has categorically forbidden us to listen to any."[35] That, at least, was clear.

The redoubtable Jesuit set foot on shore on 27 September, accompanied by Fr d'Espagnac who spoke Portuguese and who was to act as interpreter with Phaulkon. They learnt in Ayutthaya that the court was at Lopburi, and lodged in the Jesuit house in the Portuguese quarter. Fr Maldonado, who had returned from Macao, gave Tachard a very long letter from Fr de Fontaney, relating in detail the misfortunes that he, Bouvet, Visdelou, and Gerbillon had suffered since they tried to reach China on a leaky junk in July 1686. Off Cambodia, a storm had so badly battered them that they had been forced to return to Siam, doing much of the journey on foot and suffering countless privations. They had arrived on 12 September at the bar of Siam "in a dreadful state," Forbin noted, when receiving them in Bangkok.[36] But, Fr de Fontaney bravely concluded, "one does not come to the Indies for an easy life."

Fr Tachard, whose *Second Voyage to the Kingdom of Siam* is largely a compilation of texts taken from other sources, quotes the long letter of Fr de Fontaney, as well as another to Fr Verjus relating the activities of the French Jesuits in Siam while waiting for a new vessel to take them to the Celestial Empire.[37] The second attempt of the four Fathers, this time accompanied by Fr Le Comte, had more success. They left Siam in June 1687 and arrived in Peking in February 1688, twelve days after the death of Fr Verbiest. The account of their adventurous voyage is found in Le Comte's recently reprinted *Nouveaux mémoires sur l'état présent de la Chine* (A new account of the present condition of China).[38]

The Jesuit emissary met his idol Phaulkon between Ayutthaya and Lopburi. After the customary compliments and an exchange of generalities, Tachard declared that he had particular matters to communicate to him. "He had me go with him on board a large covered barge, where we remained alone for the rest of the day and the following night. In the conversation I had throughout that time with him, he seemed to me equally attached to the interests of his king and zealous for those of ours."[39] Phaulkon immediately drew up a "very long and very rational" memorandum, which he sent to the king, who had it read before his council, which approved the cession of Bangkok and Mergui to the French.

But this agreement was not unanimous. According to Bèze, Okphra Phetracha, a fierce nationalist, dared to disagree.

> In the king's council he set himself passionately against granting the French the two strongholds they were demanding . . . He enlarged upon the fate of each Eastern prince in turn who had admitted European troops into his land—first the Portuguese and later the Dutch—only to be despoiled by them and reduced to the level of slaves . . . "Never will I give my consent to a policy so fatal to the interests of Your Majesty." The king took this outburst as a spontaneous expression of loyalty and excused it.[40]

This courageous and isolated opposition is worth recording.

A messenger the following day brought full powers to the favourite, permitting him to sign a Franco-Siamese treaty in the name of Phra Narai. Fr Tachard was in raptures at this news and immediately returned to the bar of Siam, bearing a letter from Phaulkon in Portuguese which promised everything Louis XIV demanded. The meddlesome priest re-embarked on the *Oiseau* on 5 October, the day before the arrival of the *Gaillard* with the three Siamese ambassadors, as well as the two storeships.

The passengers on the *Oiseau* had champed at the bit during the Father's ten days' absence. The hostility he inspired had intensified after the revelations of Mr Véret who had gone on board. His reports to the CIO directors reveal a person lacking in perspicacity, but who sought to describe, "with the sincerest truth,"[41] Siam seen "as the most wretched affair in the world." His remarks about Phaulkon, "the biggest swindler in the world, capable of the foulest treason," perfectly summarized the delicate situation of the Greek: "He has more to get out of you than you out of him, and every day he is about to lose his life, his wealth, his wife and his children, and this must sooner or later happen to him, if he finds no protection."[42]

This same witness sketched a rare portrait of Phaulkon:

> He is a man of medium height, rather good-looking for this country, aged about thirty-five or thirty-six, who has much liveliness, and a very pleasant exterior, but I rather doubt if the underneath is the same in that, every day, he undertakes a thousand things he does not succeed in. He is ambitious, he loves money, vengeance, flatterers,

> and people who crawl before him. With all that, he is the best person in the world.[43]

These comments on Tachard's hero, like the revelations of Véret about the Makassars and the misfortunes of Forbin, were not likely to cheer up La Loubère and Céberet, who were wondering each day what on earth they were doing there.

Tachard does not disguise "the worst suspicions" which greeted him on board the *Oiseau*, but if one is to believe him, the distrust was changed into delight after reading Phaulkon's letter, and "everyone sought to show their friendliness, and even congratulate me on this success."[44] The envoys were undeceived after the first access of joy. Céberet notes in his *Journal*:

> This letter, and the report Fr Tachard made, gave us to understand first of all that Mr Constance wished to remove from us any hope of negotiating with him over anything, holding to the letter of credence which the said Father carried from the Marquis de Seignelay on the king's orders, and he considered us as persons who had assumed the outward appearance which the Reverend Father could not assume in public because of his religious vocation, but for the negotiation of affairs he would only deal with Fr Tachard.[45]

Faced with a fait accompli, the three Siamese ambassadors asked to be placed on shore as soon as the *Gaillard* anchored, and left to the sound of cannon shots. They first of all gave an account to Phaulkon of their mission to the French court, saying that "they had seen angels, not men, and that France was not a kingdom, but a world . . . They could not retain their tears when they spoke of the person of the king." That is indeed Tachard's style. They then went to Phra Narai, who received them very well and kept the *ratchathut* about him "to read his account every day at a certain hour."[46] It would be interesting to know if Kosa Pan took advantage of these intimate moments in the inner chambers of the palace to reveal to his sovereign what he really thought of the cession of Bangkok.

During this time, La Loubère and Cebéret pressed the Jesuit to carry out Phaulkon's fine promises. But he assumed a mysterious air and told them that the French troops had to swear to obey Phaulkon before their disembarkation and installation in Bangkok. Naturally the envoys protested, recalling that their instructions only permitted an oath to the King of Siam. Tachard went off to find the Greek again.

The situation of La Loubère and Céberet was impossible; their orders forbade them to disembark before the troops, and the troops could not go ashore without swearing obedience to Phaulkon. They were faced with three possible courses of action: to return to France with the squadron and the troops without doing anything; to seize Bangkok by force; or to cede by hedging the articles of the Franco-Siamese treaty with so many restrictions and fine details that they were worthless. Several trips back and forth on the part of Tachard between the bar and the court of Siam were needed before the Portuguese text of the treaty was drawn up, amended, and agreed by all parties.

The fifteen articles of the treaty regulated the French military presence in Siam. The king would not ask for more than half of the expeditionary corps for his personal use (bodyguards, punitive expeditions, training and instruction of Siamese troops), plans of fortifications would be submitted to him, the officers and soldiers would obey him, etc. But the first article stipulated: "The French troops in Bangkok and Mergui may not be commanded by any Siamese nor any foreigners, and will follow the orders sent by the chief minister (i.e. Phaulkon) when they are not contrary to those of His Most Christian Majesty." A secret article amplified the first article:

> This is to be understood in conformity with the stipulation agreed between the most excellent lords Constance Phaulkon and the Father Tachard, *which has been communicated* to the most excellent lords La Loubère and Céberet, by the oath they have sworn on the Holy Gospels to observe, promising not to include it in their journals nor to communicate it to anyone . . . except to His Most Christian Majesty and to the most excellent lord the Marquis de Seignelay, and only verbally, not in writing . . . [47]

One can understand Céberet noting in his *Journal*, "I cannot express the vexation we felt, reduced to signing such disagreeable articles."[48] The envoys understood only too well that these clauses put the troops in Phaulkon's hands. The delight which spread over the face of the perfidious Jesuit when they were signing the document did not leave any cause for doubt.

FROM DISEMBARKATION TO AUDIENCE

But the signed treaty at least allowed the decimated and exhausted troops finally to disembark and enter Bangkok with the pompous Desfarges at their head. The two envoys set foot on land the following day amidst a multitude of barges and gilded umbrellas, "with all the signs of honour due to their position."[49] Among these signs were a fanfare of drums and Siamese hautbois; they "beat together a kind of war march which, heard from a little way off, is tolerable to people who are not over-delicate in musical matters; furthermore, we were assured that this symphony was reserved for the king alone."[50] What they saw in Bangkok pleased them still less; far from being only in the hands of the French, the stronghold also contained a garrison consisting of Asian-born Portuguese and Siamese, all placed under the orders of Desfarges, general and governor of Bangkok.

The envoys indicated their displeasure to Tachard, who "brusquely replied that the king's commission was over, that His Majesty had only given him orders to go ashore the first and see that His Majesty's troops entered Bangkok," and bowed himself out. Céberet adds: "Our astonishment to hear the Father speak in this manner prevented our replying."[51] After this, Guy Tachard conducted himself like an agent and éminence grise of Phaulkon, who had bewitched him, goodness knows how. He even countersigned, as secretary, provisions in which the Greek reserved, notwithstanding the treaties, the right of administering justice to the French troops.

Céberet's *Journal* cites several examples of the abject submission of the Jesuit to his new master. During a dinner Phaulkon gave the two envoys at Ayutthaya,

> he told Fr Tachard out loud to go to the kitchen and give orders for the supper; when the Father returned from his commission, Mr Constance resumed a private conversation and began to complain of several things which the Chevalier de Chaumont had printed in his *Relation* . . . The Father trod on Mr Constance's foot at that point, and he immediately changed the subject.[52]

As the favourite of a Greek, himself the favourite of an oriental despot, Guy Tachard betrayed his king's confidence, which did not stop him dedicating to him both his *Voyages to Siam*, which begin with sickening dedications to the king.

La Loubère and Céberet went up the Chao Phraya in the midst of a great water-borne procession, determined to take things in hand. Like Chaumont, they stopped in "fragile palaces" constructed every four leagues. From the time they arrived at Ayutthaya at the residence in which they waited for their entrance and solemn audience, they observed that they had to swallow further indignities. The *ratchathut* Kosa Pan came to ask them on behalf of the *Phra Khlang* what honours they expected at their audience. It is true that Louis XIV had decided that they would be envoys extraordinary and not ambassadors, but they expected to be received with all the honours accorded to Chaumont. They only obtained satisfaction after days of argument, seeing in that, not the ill-will of the king or the *Phra Khlang*, but rather the intrigues of Phaulkon and Tachard, "this truly infernal duo."[53]

The audience, for which Phra Narai had returned from Lopburi, took place on Sunday, 2 November. The reception given to Chaumont governed the ceremonial. Everything went off very well, except that Céberet, crossing the palace courtyard on foot under a blazing sun, suffered from sunstroke. His son carried Louis XIV's letter in a golden cup placed on a gold basin, La Loubère gave it personally into the king's hand, and pronounced his discourse standing, his hat under his arm. Phaulkon was prostrate (this posture must have warmed the envoys' hearts) and served as interpreter. The letter and the discourse resembled those delivered two years earlier by Chaumont. Phra Narai asked a few questions about the health of the king and closed his window, leaving the *Phra Khlang* and Phaulkon to take care of the details. The king immediately went to another room in his palace where he granted audience to General Desfarges; with his usual verbosity, he introduced a certain number of his officers, "selected persons, well-turned, and very clean."[54] A magnificent banquet awaited the envoys and the officers in a coppice of huge trees at the edge of a moat in the innermost palace enclosure.

Mgr Laneau had taken part in the envoys' audience but remained silent. According to the Abbé de Lionne, "The Bishop of Metellopolis . . . took no part in what occurred, and seemed only to be there to suffer, with patience and gentleness which one could call angelic, the strongest invectives which could come from such a choleric person as Mr Constance, whose pride seemed at this time to have reached its peak."[55] Phaulkon for his part complained, in a letter to the superior of the MEP seminary in Paris, of "wrongs" which he had to endure from the gentlemen of the Foreign Missions, he who "only sought their well-being and the glory of God."[56] Everything points to Tachard considering that the moment had come to make the Foreign Missions pay for the humiliation they had formerly caused the Jesuits. Like Siamese elephants, the Father had an excellent memory.

Two days after the audience, Phaulkon read to the two envoys a few pages of a journal in which he noted in Portuguese his conversations with Phra Narai. "If the king has not already embraced the Christian faith, it is because he had not yet been instructed in it, the fault being that of the Bishop of Metellopolis who spoke the Siamese language so badly, in spite of living twenty-five years in the country, that the monarch could not understand him." Fr Tachard added as modestly as possible: "We have to wait for the Jesuits to learn Siamese in order to instruct him."[57] Of Christ's advice to his apostles: "Be wise as serpents, and harmless as doves,"[58] the Father had at least noted the beginning.

Informed of these words by the envoys, Mgr Laneau protested that he spoke Siamese very well, that the king always replied to him very exactly, and that he had perfectly understood how Phaulkon had altered in his translation the discourse pronounced by Chaumont during his solemn audience. And he added: "Several persons had come to tell me of an aberrant folly, which is that Mr Constance fears I should take his place beside the king if I were to convert him."[59] This open rivalry between the Foreign Missions and the Jesuits did not facilitate the task of the envoys. Neither did it serve the interests of France nor the Church. A long *Memorandum of Mr Constance to the king on the subject of religion*, taken by Fr Tachard to France, is a violent indictment of the Foreign Missions and everything they had done in Siam since the arrival of Mgr Lambert in 1662.[60]

"PRODIGIES OF PERFIDY AND CLEVERNESS"

Phra Narai returned to Lopburi on 5 November, followed by his court. La Loubère and Céberet went there in their turn on 10 November. But the sumptuous welcome given them, the elephant hunts, tiger fights, spectacles of tumblers, and other exotic entertainments could not dissipate the unease surrounding the embassy. Phaulkon, who had also invited Desfarges and his general staff, dazzled them with his Levantine charm and magnificent feasts, increasing the isolation of the envoys. The foolish Desfarges let himself be manipulated like a child, admiring and slobbering to order. He was present when Phra Narai received Vaudricourt and Duquesne, the captains of the *Gaillard* and the *Oiseau*. Putting on airs for his audience, he told the king "that he felt the same joy in seeing His Majesty as when formerly in France, the king his master honoured him with his presence." Phra Narai replied with moist eyes: "The king is not as far as you might imagine. If you saw into my heart, you would discover his portrait engraved there, in prime position."[61]

But these touching remarks could not prevent certain questions remaining unresolved: a new commercial treaty, the promulgation of the treaty on religion drawn up in December 1685, and the installation of French troops in Mergui. Phaulkon, caught in a spider's web of conflicting interests, was not in an easy situation. Lucien Lanier summarizes it well:

> Constrained to please a despot whose favour he had obtained, and holding in check a faction of mandarins secretly jealous of his influence, surrounded by foreigners who he had at the same time to satisfy and restrain, he steered cleverly between opposed religions, rival interests, and implacable hatreds, and only succeeded through prodigious skill and perfidy in maintaining a precarious authority and an already uncertain privileged position.[62]

His position was all the more delicate as the health of the king, who "treated his myriad illnesses . . . [and was] probably already prematurely senile,"[63] caused the greatest concern.

While continuing his Byzantine scheming, the favourite did not forget to satisfy his stooge, Fr Tachard. He obtained letters patent granting the Society of Jesus a house and an observatory (yet to be built) at Lopburi, as well as a hundred slaves, "either to row us in our barges . . . or render us other services." The text, sealed with the great royal seal, notably said:

> We wish that the one hundred persons we grant them, with their children and their future posterity, serve them for ever . . . If anyone, with whatsoever authority, rank or condition he may have, dares to contravene our orders, we declare them damned by God and us, and condemned to eternal punishment in hell.[64]

The good Father accepted this present without hesitation, announcing that "it would be through these persons that we would begin to establish Christianity." Indeed, a life of slavery is little before eternal beatitude.

The promise of a house and an observatory can only surprise those who remember this passage in the *[First] Voyage* in which Fr Tachard mentioned the twelve mathematical Fathers he was to request from Fr de La Chaize and the king: "His [Siamese] Majesty informed me . . . that I could assure them that before their arrival they would find in Louvo an observatory, a house, and a church, as well as at Siam [Ayutthaya]. He gave orders at the same time to Lord Constance to build them without delay."[65] Nothing had therefore been done in two years.

The English Catholic, already quoted several times in this book, notes:

> Fr Tachard returned with his twelve supposed mathematicians, certain of finding these churches, houses, and observatories not only completed, but even furnished with everything necessary. These Fathers were counting on this, and had named superiors for these houses. Yet on their arrival, they found neither a church, nor a house, nor an observatory in Siam, and even the site where they were to be built was not yet known.

Embarrassed, Phaulkon had promised Tachard "churches of unbelievable magnificence; that in Siam would be as fine and as big as St Peter's in Rome. I do not know [why] Fr Tachard did not open his eyes before such exorbitant promises."[66] Meanwhile, the Fathers occupied the house in which the Persian embassy had stayed. Three of them, Le Blanc, La Breuille, and Bouchet, studied court Siamese in a Buddhist monastery.

Instead of concerning himself with the garrison in Bangkok, where his men were dying of dysentery and where the Siamese were muttering against the presence of the French, Desfarges was the braggart at Phaulkon's table in Lopburi. Now only obeying the King of Siam to whom he had sworn his oath of allegiance, the pompous general considered himself the mainstay of the throne, forgetting both his own dignity and that of his king. He was too carried away to understand he was only a pawn on Phaulkon's chessboard, and the

Greek, impressed by Desfarges's bluster, thought himself protected by this redoubtable warrior's sword.

The son of Deslandes does not spare Desfarges:

> A man with a limited and narrow mind, incapable of taking a decision, having no friends and deserving none, only trusting people of the lowest condition, and in addition extremely self-interested and liking money excessively. His excuse was . . . that he had not left France merely for a change of air.[67]

Desirous of informing Seignelay of the condition of the stronghold at Bangkok, Céberet requested Desfarges to tell him if the troops there were safe and if the fortress was capable of repulsing an assault. The general puffed himself up and said "that he would retain this stronghold, though very indifferent; that he would defend himself behind a gauze curtain."[68] It was not possible to extract from him more precise information.

The matter of sending French troops to Mergui was constantly deferred by Phaulkon, who hoped to keep them close to hand in case of need. He cited either the bad weather (the monsoon, though, was over), or the lack of drinking water. It was agreed after long discussions that Mr du Bruant would accompany or follow Céberet there with three companies when the CIO director, obeying his orders, crossed the Kra Isthmus.

THE MERGUI MASSACRE

Long before leaving Lopburi for Mergui, Céberet was aware of the details of a particularly serious incident which had occurred some months previously involving the English living in the port of Mergui. To understand this affair better, one has to go back in time. We have already encountered in this book the brothers George and Samuel White and their accomplice Richard Burnaby. George White was captain of the *Hopewell*, the ship on which Phaulkon had made his first journey to Asia in 1670. It was Richard Burnaby who in 1678 had taken the Greek to Ayutthaya, where he met up with George White again, who had meanwhile left the service of the EIC for that of the King of Siam. Having insinuated himself into the good graces of Phra Narai, Phaulkon appointed his old pals to lucrative positions in Mergui, the hub of Indo-Siamese trade. Burnaby was made governor, and Samuel White *shahbandar* (harbour-master and collector of customs duties).

White, aware that he enjoyed the protection of Phaulkon, who had a hand in the fiddles of the *shahbandar*, enriched himself inordinately. He went so far as to seize cargoes belonging to the EIC in the name of the King of Siam. The directors of the British company in London, informed of White's piracy, ordered their representative in Madras, Elihu Yale, to come to grips with Siam and to recall all the Englishmen employed by oriental sovereigns. In June 1687, Yale sent an armed frigate, the *Curtana*, captained by Anthony Weltden, and the corvette *James*. Weltden was to summon White to give an account of himself in Madras, and demand the payment of compensation from the King of Siam within sixty days.

White succeeded in manipulating Weltden, and promised to follow him to Madras on his own frigate, the *Resolution*. During the following weeks of waiting, Weltden divided his time between his frigate and White's residence, where he enjoyed sumptuous hospitality. The Siamese mandarins in Mergui, who had endured the arrogance and extortions of White, Burnaby, and associates with clenched teeth, were convinced the Englishmen living in Mergui wanted to seize the port with the help of Weltden's men. They therefore decided to act without waiting for Phra Narai's reply to the EIC's ultimatum.

Readers interested in the details of the "Mergui massacre" can consult several excellent standard or recent works.[69] We shall here briefly summarize the events.

The concentration of Siamese boats in the port ought at least to have worried the English, but it seems they suspected nothing. On the evening of 14 July (or the twenty-fourth according to the Gregorian calendar), Captain Weltden left his ship to go and dine at White's house. After the meal, White accompanied his guest and some of his companions back to the landing stage where the boat was waiting to transport them on board the *Curtana*. Suddenly shouts rent the night. Drugged Siamese and Burmese rushed out of the warehouses lining the quay and hurled themselves on the English. One of the attackers struck a sharp blow on Weltden's skull, who collapsed. In the fray which ensued, White managed to escape with a few men in the waiting boat, convinced the captain was dead. But Weltden came to and succeeded in getting into the water, out of which he was hauled, half-dead, into the boat. At this moment, the land batteries opened fire on the corvette *James*. White then understood that it was a matter of an uprising directed against all the English. The boat managed to join the *Resolution* at anchor downstream.

The following morning, while the *Curtana*'s surgeon was attending to Weltden, the survivors wondered if they should go to the aid of those English remaining on land. But the ebbing tide carried with it horribly mutilated corpses of Englishmen. It was soon learnt that at least sixty Englishmen had been killed (the numbers involved vary according to one's sources), including Richard Burnaby who was murdered in his house. The *Resolution* and the *Curtana* repulsed an attempted attack by several dozen Siamese boats without much difficulty, and set sail for the open seas. Samuel White, of course, did not stop in Madras. He shipped his fortune to England where he was largely untroubled. He did not live long to enjoy the fruits of his schemes, for he died on his estate near Bath in January 1689. The subsequent adventures of Captain Anthony Weltden, who recovered from his wound, would take us too far from the subject.

This was the end of the English presence at Mergui, which had been more profitable for the interloping traders than the EIC. When he learnt the details of the Mergui massacre, Phra Narai had some mandarins who had a hand in the affair transferred to Ayutthaya. They were soon released, and that was that. With their summons, the English had committed the unpardonable error of making the king lose face. For his part, Phaulkon thought he could now count on the French who wanted to fill at any price the vacuum created in Mergui by the massacre and flight of the English. Richard Burnaby, Phaulkon's former patron, was replaced by Beauregard, who had succeeded Forbin as governor of Bangkok.

"TIRED OF THESE PERPETUAL SIAMESERIES"

The commercial treaty between Siam and the CIO had to conform to the personal interests of Lord Constance. After having put off the preparation of the treaty for a long time, at the beginning of December he gave the envoys to understand that he was working at it, but that first of all an "association" had to be agreed between himself and the CIO for the sum of 300,000 livres. Tachard used torrents of eloquence to persuade Céberet that this participation was above all advantageous for the French company.

The new commercial treaty was signed on 11 December in Lopburi,[70] and the act of association of Phaulkon to the company two days later. The commercial privileges granted were those which had already been obtained in 1682 and 1685, but without the ambiguities and restrictions which hampered them. Céberet, entrusted to produce a draft, had started from a text amended by Chaumont and Seignelay's ministry.[71] In addition, the company obtained freedom of trading throughout the kingdom, with exemption from import and export duties. The tin monopoly was broadened and the jurisdictional competence of the company heads extended. These privileges were also to apply to foreign vessels which took on goods from French godowns. Lastly, article 9 gave "freely to the French Company the unrestricted property of some suitable island not more than ten leagues distant from the port of Mergui, to fortify it, build on it, and use it as it wished." The French government, the CIO, and Céberet had every reason to be satisfied.

The intransigent Phaulkon showed himself to be a decent fellow because this treaty should increase the volume of his estate. He became one of the biggest shareholders of the CIO by virtue of the act of association of 13 December, which stipulated that Mr Constance, by investing 300,000 livres in the company, "would have his annual dividend of ten per cent" of profits realized, payable to his agent in Paris.[72] The Greek would soon ask, at the beginning of January 1688, to be made one of the ten directors of the company.

The treaty and the convention being signed, Céberet left Lopburi after a farewell audience which the king, even though unwell, granted him. The audience, according to Céberet himself, was accompanied by the usual ceremonial, but was fortuitous and secret according to Tachard.[73] Phra Narai looked at Céberet's son for a long time, asked about his age and the college of Louis-le-Grand where he had studied, and gave him a fine gold chain.

The other directors of the CIO had asked Céberet to examine the location and potential of the port of Mergui on the spot. He went down to Bangkok, where he began the journey to Mergui on a barge taking the canals and rivers, and on elephant back. Céberet describes with evident pride "my elephant, on which there was a gilded seat covered with a kind of dome acting as a sunshade, upheld by four columns, everything very finely gilded and embellished with carpets and gold brocade cushions. The elephant's harness was of scarlet cloth four fingers' wide, decorated with silver studs."[74] Every evening, he found a house specially built and furnished for him and his retinue, which was very numerous, requiring twenty-eight elephants and five palanquins. A guard of fifty soldiers, three hundred porters, and one hundred carts followed, all "travelling in single file."

They arrived on 30 December at Tenasserim, where Forbin was waiting for them, having come from Pondichéry. Kosa Pan, who escorted Céberet, ran up to the chevalier and told him he was right to want to return to his country. He added in bad French: "*La France grand bon, Siam petit bon*" (France big good, Siam little good).[75] On 1 January 1688, Céberet was at Mergui, at the mouth of the Tenasserim River. He found the port very suitable. Fresh water was lacking though, but there were plenty of springs nearby, and the forests supplied excellent wood for shipbuilding on the island of Pulao Tavoy, ceded to the company. Céberet embarked on 3 January with Forbin on the *Président*, a CIO vessel, for Pondichéry, where the *Oiseau* was to call to pick them up. He informed the governor of Mergui, Beauregard, of the imminent arrival of du Bruant, who was coming to take possession of the port at the head of a detachment of 120 soldiers.

"Tired of these perpetual Siameseries" (the phrase is Lanier's, who should perhaps have spoken of Phaulkoneries),[76] La Loubère only thought of leaving as well. The departure of his colleague, with whom he got on well, in spite of the perfidious insinuations of Fr Tachard,[77] did not help matters. Céberet had left satisfied, having obtained a commercial treaty in conformity with the wishes of his government and his company. La Loubère, though, had been obliged to sign a suspect military agreement, and had not obtained the proclamation of the treaty concerning religion of 1685. Phaulkon and Tachard told him there would be time to think about that when there were Siamese Christians.

But his troubles were not over. The moderating influence of Céberet was absent to calm the disputes between the two headstrong personalities of La Loubère and Phaulkon, disputes which were deliberately inflamed by Tachard. The affair of the bombardiers was to afflict the first envoy's nerves considerably. It will be recalled that ten bombardiers, under the orders of Mr du Laric, were part of the expedition. He had formal instructions to return with his men to

France in the squadron, "His Majesty not considering their presence necessary in that country after the departure of the vessels."[78] Desfarges had received the same orders.

In order to court Phaulkon's favour, Desfarges had brought a mortar and three bombs to Lopburi to give the king a demonstration of French fighting power. Three houses had to be torn down, but Phra Narai, who observed "from far off, from one of his palace windows,"[79] was extremely impressed. He told Phaulkon that he wished to retain these redoubtable firearms in Siam, counting on using them against the rebels of Pattani. Unable to dissuade him, the favourite, supported by the good Fr Tachard who was more inclined to pulverize infidels than to convert them, gave no thought to the consequences. They were both able to convince Desfarges to keep Laric, his bombardiers, and his weapons in Siam. The two envoys were formally opposed to this. There were several particularly acerbic disputes, and the insolence of Phaulkon, who shouted "that he only desired Frenchmen in Siam who obeyed him," knew no bounds.

On the eve of Céberet's departure, the envoys sent a declaration to Desfarges:

> The intentions of the king our master and lord are that the bombardiers, bombs, and mortars which His Majesty had sent on his vessels were to return to France with Mr du Laric, commander of the said bombardiers. [We] summon the said Mr Desfarges to send back the said bombardiers in accordance with His Majesty's orders . . . He will be accountable to H.M. for acting in his own name."[80]

Laric and his men would remain in Siam, and Fr Tachard preceded his return to the court in France with a letter to Seignelay, trying to justify this disobedience of the king's orders.[81]

Phaulkon and La Loubère hardly spoke to each other after the departure of Céberet. The announcement by the Greek that Fr Tachard would be sent to France and Rome as ambassador extraordinary of the King of Siam was not calculated to improve the climate. La Loubère wanted to leave at all costs, in spite of Phaulkon's attempts to retain him. Tachard wrote: "Mr de La Loubère thought that the season [for sailing] was passing, and he was sick. The air of Siam did not suit him . . . This obliged him to seek most pressingly his farewell audience."[82] He was granted it on 23 December, and according to Tachard it was "rather short."

La Loubère went to say goodbye to Phaulkon after the audience. Barely polite, he could not prevent himself speaking once more about the bombardiers whom he hoped to bring back to France. Phaulkon declared loftily that the king did not oppose the departure of Mr du Laric, but that the bombardiers and their weapons would remain in Siam. La Loubère, got up from his chair and left the room, throwing over his shoulder an extremely curt "*Adeus Senhor.*" Fr Tachard said he was "aghast" at the incident, noting in his unpublished account:

> Two of our Fathers, who had always accompanied Mr de La Loubère, could not refrain from expressing their astonishment to him at such a brusque and impolite farewell. Then he complained that Mr Constance had insulted him and had uttered harsh words, and that little more was needed to retain his position as the king's envoy, than for him to request the Frenchmen who were with him to attack Mr Constance.[83]

Phaulkon and La Loubère did not see each other again.

Tachard, now the King of Siam's ambassador, had his farewell audience on Christmas Day. Phra Narai gave him his instructions, in which His Siamese Majesty declared himself "persuaded that you would properly appreciate the marks of royal confidence which had convinced him to confide in you, although a foreigner, his powers, interests, and even his honour in the court of his true sovereign, a procedure which should be all the more agreeable to you as it is extraordinary and almost without precedent."[84] But the reader cannot place in him as much confidence as the King of Siam, for the good Father contradicts himself in the published version of his *Voyage* and his unpublished *Relation*. According to the *Voyage*, he then improvised on the spot an explanation of the nativity;[85] in the *Relation*, Phaulkon gave the homily watched by a moved Tachard.

Phaulkon's theological capacities should surprise no one. Tachard noted in his *[First] Voyage* that the Greek one day gave a long speech on the Christian religion which he improvised before the King of Siam. The Jesuit was full of admiration: "I confessed to him, without fear of flattering him, that a consummate theologian could not have spoken better."[86]

"GO, LEAVE JOYFULLY"

Ruffled at the lack of success of his mission, La Loubère had embarked with bag and baggage on the *Gaillard*, where he had to put up with the presence of the ambassador Jesuit, very full of his new rank. The loading of the bales of presents for the royal house, as well as the merchandise the Siamese crown wished to dispose of in France, posed the usual problems. Vaudricourt had been informed there would be three hundred. Remembering the excessive quantity on Chaumont's departure two years previously, he had prepared for four hundred, but there were in all seven hundred and fifty. The squadron commander succeeded in stowing away six hundred, and sent the rest back on land in spite of Phaulkon's protests. Vaudricourt explained his action in a letter written from the Cape to Seignelay: "The officers of the company will inform you, My Lord, of our surprise . . . at the embarkation; it was very awkward for me not to be able to follow the king's orders as all the said bales were sent as presents for the king or for the company."[87]

But this was not all. The King of Siam sent three young elephants to the Dukes of Burgundy, Anjou, and Berry, and a "fairly big" rhinoceros for good measure. Each animal had its mahout; the elephants travelled on the *Dromadaire*, the rhinoceros on the *Loire*. La Loubère had the delightful idea of noting the way the baby elephants were got on board.

> The Siamese who had brought them to our vessels to embark them took their leave of them as though they were leaving one of their friends, and said to each of them in their ear: "Go, leave joyfully. You will be slaves, it is true, but you will be slaves of the three greatest princes in the world, for whom service is as agreeable as it is glorious." They then took them into the ships, and because they lowered themselves to pass under the bridge, everyone cried out in admiration.[88]

But all four animals died during the crossing between Batavia and the Cape, and their guardians were sent back to Siam on a Dutch ship.

In spite of the discreet warning from Céberet to Phaulkon that the constant exchange of presents was wearying Louis XIV, the court of Siam insisted on sending him costly trifles, no doubt to thank him for his bombardiers. Two further silver damascened cannons were sent, two Chinese ladies mounted on peacocks moved by internal mechanisms, a silver crab bearing a goblet on its back, a chest full of birds' nests, and several hundred pieces of porcelain.

Both ambassador and comprador, Fr Tachard was given a long list of French items to buy for the court of Siam. For a start, there were four thousand mirrors for the palace in Lopburi, and 36,660 glass and crystal items; more surprising were the fifty-four hats of different colours (white, blue, green, black, red, violet, "wine, vinegar, dead leaves"), different sizes (from seven to thirteen inches), and different kinds of material (flexible, soft, long-piled, short-piled). Drawings and models accompanied the order.[89] No doubt, as talented a person as Fr Tachard would be as gifted in the hat trade as in diplomacy, but one would like to know what Phra Narai intended to do with all those hats.

The Jesuit ambassador embarked on the *Oiseau* at the very last moment, 3 January, with a retinue of three mandarins (Ok-khun Phiphit, Ok-khun Chamnan, and Ok-khun Wiset)[90] and five sons of mandarins whom Phra Narai wished to study at the college of Louis-le-Grand. Tachard explained that "the king hopes in this way to unite the hearts of the two nations, and to inculcate French manners in his subjects."[91] The young Cardinal-Destouches, who had studied at the same college, returned to France, placed by his parents in the care of Tachard. The *uppathut* Ok-luang Kanlaya Ratchamaitri brought the same day a letter on gold from the King of Siam for his good friend the King of France. It was placed with much ceremony in Fr Tachard's cabin.

Mr de Vaudricourt gave the signal for the departure, and the travellers began their long return journey. Phaulkon, at the bar of Siam to organize the departure and give last-minute instructions to Tachard, returned in time to Lopburi to see his young son João die on 11 January. Fr de Bèze, in his service, tried to console him. He replied that

> this death signified more to him than the loss of a dearly loved child; he looked upon it as a direct intimation that Heaven was giving him some even greater misfortune as his lot; he now espied brewings of the nation-wide reaction against the French which he had dreaded; rumours were now being circulated, warning the people that the kingdom would pass through a radical transformation in March or April.[92]

The future was indeed worrying.

A VERY TENSE RETURN

The *Gaillard*, the *Loire*, and the *Dromadaire* set sail on 3 January 1688. The *Oiseau* had left on the preceding 25 November for Pondichéry where Céberet and Forbin were to embark. The *Normande* had been sent to Bengal where it was to take on trade goods for the CIO.

The three naval vessels followed the well-known route through the Bangka Strait, Bantam (which they reached on 29 January), the Sunda Strait, and the Indian Ocean. The *Dromadaire*, separated from the other ships by a storm, reached the Cape of Good Hope three days earlier than the others. As they were approaching the Cape, Ok-khun Chamnan related the details of the shipwreck he had suffered on the Portuguese vessel *Nossa Senhora dos Milagros* near Agulhas Point in April 1686, and his painful journey on foot across the "Great Caffraria" (the lands of the Kaffirs and the Hottentots) to the Dutch outpost. This detailed account fills Book VII of Tachard's *Second Voyage to Siam*.[93] The *Gaillard* and the *Loire* dropped anchor on 21 April in the bay of the Cape; they found the *Dromadaire* there, having in the meantime jettisoned its elephants. Mr d'Ardennes, its captain, informed them that the *Oiseau* had already stopped over, and had left two days earlier for Brest. The three ships left the roadstead of the Cape on 1 May for the last part of their journey.

The atmosphere on the *Gaillard* was detestable throughout the seven months of the journey. The open hostility between La Loubère and Tachard poisoned the atmosphere, rows and disputes at table came in quick succession, and a man like the Abbé de Choisy was needed to calm the passengers with his easy good humour.

Unable to endure the mealy-mouthed airs of his adversary, Simon de La Loubère spent his time in his cabin located next door to the Jesuit's, working on his masterly book, *The Kingdom of Siam*. As he questioned the mandarins non-stop about the customs and practices of their country, and spent his time writing, Tachard, convinced he was writing memoranda to blacken his character, put all his bile into his manuscript *Relation*. In reality, La Loubère was trying to forget Guy Tachard by closing his cabin door, but the Jesuit accused him of the worst misdeeds: La Loubère had said that Phaulkon and the Jesuits should be hung, he tried to get hold of Tachard's documents, he had cut a hole "through which to insert his finger" in the wall separating their cabins to spy on him. He even (but it is hard to give faith to such a criminal act) tried to cut the Jesuit's beard.[94] In short, Tachard relapsed into complete paranoia. He was more tolerable when, as a mere missionary, he counted the nails on elephants' feet.

The good Father, in addition, was not kind to his own entourage. He had locked up two of his mandarins who had quarrelled. He confiscated André Cardinal-Destouches's pocket money, kept him locked in his cabin, and deprived him of food and even water, when the young musician did not study hard enough or when he read books which the Father considered futile or dangerous. Of course, "La Loubère offered him as much water as he wanted to drink, and gave him books which Tachard had forbidden him to read . . . and slipped him three golden *louis* in his hand so that he could amuse himself at his leisure at the Cape."[95]

To read Céberet and Forbin, the atmosphere was much more friendly on board the *Oiseau*. They had set sail from Pondichéry on 2 February. Forbin wrote in his *Memoirs*:

> Mr Céberet and I were never asunder during the whole voyage; but our ordinary discourse was about the kingdom of Siam, and the manners and customs of the people. He was so astonished to find them so poor, and to see the misery of the kingdom, that it was unaccountable to him how persons could have the assurance to give such a pompous narrative of their wealth and grandeur. "Yet," said I to him one day, "what you saw was the most they have to boast of. The whole kingdom, which is very large, is little more than a vast desert; for as you advance within land, you will find nothing but forest and wild beasts, the inhabitants choosing to live on the banks of the river . . . so that as you went up from the bar to Louvo, you saw everything that was worth seeing in the whole kingdom."

And, of course, the two men compared their impressions of the unspeakable Phaulkon. "I told him all I knew of that minister; and though he had a pretty good guess at his views and politics, I gave him an insight into many things which had escaped him, and which he did not doubt the truth of, when he was enabled to compare what I told him with what he knew before."[96]

It is with these feelings of relief and apprehension that the chief protagonists of the expedition saw the coast of Brittany approach, having plenty to justify and explain. On 25 July 1688, a week after the *Oiseau*, the *Gaillard* and the two storeships dropped anchor in the

Brest roadstead. Desclouzeaux, the intendant, still hard at work, informed Seignelay the following day,

> On the information I was given that the vessels the *Gaillard*, the *Loire*, and the *Dromadaire*, coming from Siam, had dropped anchor . . . I left this morning to go on board . . . We found on board the *Gaillard* Mr de La Loubère in good health, the Rev. Fr Tachard and some mandarins . . . All these gentlemen will relate to Your Lordship their journey.[97]

And four days later, he wrote again to Seignelay,

> Mr Céberet left from here last Saturday [the 24th] to go to Lorient and continue his journey. Mr de La Loubère left Tuesday evening [the 27th] to go to court. Fr Tachard left the following day, Wednesday. But in all the conversations I had with these gentlemen, it seemed to me that they were not at all pleased with each other.[98]

That was the euphemism of the year.

One could devote many pages to the memoranda and letters full of explanations, justifications, insinuations, and accusations which the poor Seignelay had to read in the days which followed.[99] But this chapter would be without interest in light of the events which had shaken the kingdom of Siam while these voyagers were returning to France, sulking with each other.

PART FIVE
THE END OF THE MIRAGE

CHAPTER TWENTY

THE REVOLUTION IN SIAM (1688)

THE FRENCH court did not wait for the return of Vaudricourt's squadron to continue its Siamese policy. The need to reinforce the expeditionary corps in Siam did not allow it to let pass the sailing season at the beginning of 1688. The navy ship, the *Oriflamme,* of 750 tons burden, set sail at the beginning of February, taking two hundred troopers to Siam. Its commander, Mr de l'Estrille, had received very precise orders. He would stop only at the Cape where he would present the helpful governor van der Stel with a ceremonial chain and a gold medal in the name of Louis XIV. He was to remain only a short time in Bangkok, and return through Mergui and Pondichéry, where he would take on merchandise for the CIO.

Mr de l'Estrille carried letters and orders for Desfarges, who could henceforth "count on receiving every year His Majesty's vessels." The king did not lose sight of the missionary dimension of the French presence in Siam. The *Oriflamme* was carrying not only five bales of prayer books and vestments, but also a royal order to the officers and soldiers, in order to edify the idolatrous infidels who lived mostly on rice, to abstain from meat on Fridays, Saturdays, and other fasting days, "except in cases of absolute necessity." Louis XIV prescribed in addition modest behaviour in churches, respect for priests, and forbade the frequentation of bawdy houses "and other places of debauchery."[1]

In the eyes of His Most Christian Majesty, the commercial and military enterprise which he had allowed himself to be persuaded to undertake would only be crowned with success if it were accompanied by a sustained effort at conversion. For him, as for the Portuguese in the sixteenth century, the missionary, the diplomat, the merchant, and the soldier had to work alongside each other. Fr Tachard expressed this ideal in his own way: "Today in France God and Caesar have but the same interests."[2]

"SIRE, THAT PRINCE NEVER ENTERTAINED A THOUGHT OF IT"

Vaudricourt, quoted in the last words of Céberet's *Journal*, had said, "one would have to wait in Paris to be enlightened about everything." Some perplexity in Versailles can be guessed at, given the denunciations, recriminations, and contradictory proposals formulated by the different persons in the expedition which returned to the kingdom in July 1688.

Dangeau noted on 24 July that "Mr Sebret [*sic*], whom the king had sent to the King of Siam, has arrived at Brest. He has indicated that the journey was very successful, that the King of Siam had given to the French the two best strongholds in his kingdom, called Bangkok and Mergui."[3] Céberet had no trouble in obtaining approval for the articles of the commercial treaty he had negotiated, and even the principle of an association of Phaulkon with the royal company. (It is true that no one could then foresee that the agents of Phaulkon's widow would later institute proceedings against the CIO which would drag on until 1717.)[4] Céberet therefore returned satisfied to Brittany, to concern himself with the company's business and entertain his friends with exotic tales about Siam. The following summer, the famous French letter-writer Mme de Sévigné was to relate to her daughter a visit she paid in Lorient: "A Mr Céberet, who has come from Siam and looks after trade there, and his wife who has come from Paris, and who is more magnificent than when at Versailles, gave us a dinner. We had the husband relate his voyage, which is very amusing. We saw lots of trade goods, porcelain, and materials. They are rather nice."[5]

We know very little about the mission of Fr Tachard, ambassador extraordinary of His Siamese Majesty, to the court of France. According to a note in Sourches's *Mémoires*, "it was amusing to see a Jesuit sent from an idolatrous king."[6] We shall never know what was said in Fr de La Chaize's study, but Louis XIV, his minister, and his confessor seem to have had doubts, especially after hearing Forbin, who, in favour in the court and having nothing to justify, could speak with his characteristic forthrightness.

Louis XIV questioned him one day at dinner about Siam, asking if the country were rich.

> "Sire," said I, "the kingdom of Siam neither produces nor consumes anything."
>
> "That's a great deal said in a few words," replied the king . . .
>
> "Now," said the king, "let us talk of their religion. Are there many Christians in the kingdom of Siam? And does the king really think of embracing Christianity?"
>
> "Sire," I said to him, "that prince never entertained a thought of it, nor durst any mortal be so bold as to propose it to him."

Forbin related how Phaulkon had cleverly suppressed all Chaumont's proposals over religion on the day of his audience. "The king, surprised at what I said, heard me very attentively . . . [he] asked me if the missionaries did much good at Siam; and in particular, whether they had converted many of the Siamese. 'Not a soul, sir,' said I."[7]

In a letter to Seignelay, Céberet had confirmed for his part the complete failure of the expedition in matters of religion: "We have advanced nothing concerning religion, although we devoted all our efforts to this."[8] But Fr Tachard charitably hastened to attribute this failure, very serious in the king's eyes, to the gentlemen of the Foreign Missions, who created difficulties with the Jesuits, and sowed dissension among the workers of the Gospels.

Forbin was also questioned by Seignelay. He told him squarely that,

> the establishment begun [in Siam] by sending troops thither, was absolutely unnecessary . . . that as to the fortress of Bangkok, it would remain in French hands as long as the King of Siam and Mr Constance lived; but that when either of them happened to die, the Siamese . . . would not fail to dislodge our troops.

Questioned two days later by Fr de La Chaize about the Jesuits in Siam, he replied that "Mr Constance, who was resolved, whatever it cost him, to obtain our king's protection, had promised more than he could perform," and the advantages enjoyed by the Fathers would cease with Phra Narai. "Your account . . . does not agree with Fr Tachard's,"[9] he was told. Forbin shrugged his shoulders; he did not know what the Father had told him, but he had "told him nothing but the naked truth."

Forbin's chastening revelations perhaps explain why the court at Versailles decided to wait and see. It was resolved to do nothing before returning from Fontainebleau in November. But the presents sent by Phra Narai to the royal house were being unpacked. Dangeau noted: "The king and Mme la Dauphine have had the bales of presents from the King of Siam opened; there is nothing very grand there. The presents are more numerous, but less beautiful than those which came with the ambassadors." The king's brother and his lady, overlooked in 1686, were more satisfied. "Today they opened thirty or forty cases from Siam, in which they found presents both beautiful and agreeable. The King of Siam had not sent them any by his first ambassadors, and they had indicated that they were not pleased."[10]

Louis XIV, whose confidence seemed shaken, let Fr Tachard leave for Rome where he was also going on behalf of the King of Siam. He left Paris at the beginning of November, accompanied by his three mandarins, to present letters and some presents from Phra Narai and Phaulkon to Innocent XI and the superior general of the Society of Jesus. The relations between Versailles and the Vatican were then going through a crisis (the pope had just excommunicated the French ambassador, and Louis XIV had seized Avignon), which made the mission of Tachard, a subject of the King of France and ambassador of an oriental monarch, extremely delicate.

This voyage to Italy fills the last book of his *Second Voyage to Siam*[11] and was a complete success according to Tachard, even if the mandarins, being idolaters, did not wish to kiss the pope's feet, "which is properly a religious act." In spite of this shocking refusal, His Holiness indicated to the Father-ambassador "how much he appreciated the marks of respect from so distant an infidel king," and sent the King of Siam a painting by Carlo Marati and a casket of rock crystal. The mandarins received gold medals, boxes of perfumes, and pots of preserves. They were taken at this Christmas period to see the sights of Rome, and were very impressed by the dazzling nature of the pontifical liturgy and the wealth of the churches. One of them came to the conclusion that the God of the Christians was "the true God, since he was served with so much pomp and majesty," and declared to Fr Tachard that he wished to remain in France and be instructed in the Christian faith. In sum, everything went off very well.[12]

At the beginning of 1689, Tachard returned to Versailles, where he gave Phra Narai's letter to Louis XIV in solemn audience. Projects for a new treaty were elaborated in February–March 1689, showing that French policy towards Siam was becoming clear.[13] The nine articles of the Franco-Siamese treaty, signed on 15 March for Siam by Fr Tachard, "envoy extraordinary of the most high, most excellent, most powerful, and most invincible monarch, the King of Siam," concerned above all the thorny question of the command of the French troops in Siam. They would only be commanded and judged by Frenchmen obeying the orders of the King of Siam transmitted through his chief minister, "in which they would not be contrary to those of His Most Christian Majesty, and that the French alone, except with the consent of the commander, would occupy the fortresses and entrenchments controlled by them." The oath given by the French to the King of Siam was only valid in the measure that it concerned military actions directed against the common enemies of the two crowns. Lastly, a citadel with four bastions would be built at Bangkok; the plan was annexed to the treaty, and the King of Siam undertook to supply the necessary materials.

Phra Narai requested a company of bodyguards, fifty gentlemen cavaliers placed under the orders of a captain who would be Mr Storf (aka Torf), whose virtues the *ratchathut* Kosa Pan had extolled so much. Since the French king did not wish to part with the services of Storf,[14] the command of a new expeditionary corps was given to the Marquis de Ragny, who would reside at the court of Siam and would be at the same time captain of the King of Siam's guard, inspector-general of French troops, and charged with the supervision of religious and commercial affairs in which France was involved. His commission of resident in Siam was issued on 6 March 1689. Shortly after, he signed a convention with Fr Tachard; this document designates him as "commander and inspector-general of the troops, strongholds, and affairs of the [French] king in the kingdom of Siam."[15]

Seen from Versailles, the Marquis de Ragny was called on to play a very important part in Siam.

> Installed in the court, master of the palace and the person of the king, whose bodyguard was under his command, acting at the same time as captain, counsellor, diplomat, and chief judge, combining civil and

> military powers, [he] was, under the appearance of being a respectful and obedient servant, to exercise in this divided kingdom a real protectorate disguised in the name of friendship, and impose if needs be by force the suzerainty of the great Western ruler over this Asian vassal who was at last undeceived.[16]

The terms Lanier uses are rather strong, but they convey well enough the colonization process under way. Ragny, who had to sell his commission to the regiment of guards because his finances were in a mess, would leave for Siam at the head of a company of horse guards and four infantry companies.

At the end of December 1688, James II had fled England, which, after rising up against its Catholic king, had passed to the Protestant rule of William III of Orange and Mary Stuart. Louis XIV had installed the overthrown king in the château of St Germain, and several scenarios were examined in Versailles for putting James on the throne again with the support of French soldiers and sailors. Ragny and his men destined for Siam, and Forbin after returning from Siam, were to play a part in this ill-conceived and poorly executed undertaking. The defeat at the Battle of the Boyne on 1 July 1690 would finally draw a line under French attempts to restore James II to his throne.

According to a note in Sourches's *Mémoires*, the war against England "happily" prevented Ragny and his men embarking for Siam.[17] The term can be understood in light of disturbing and unconfirmed news which had begun to circulate that particularly dramatic events had shaken Siam in 1688. Dangeau mentions them for the first time on 5 November 1689; Sourches spoke of them the next day, noting that it concerned "the confirmation of news which had been circulated four months earlier in a Dutch gazette, but in which credence had not wished to be placed."[18] It should be noted that the intelligence services of Louis XIV worked with appalling inefficiency and tardiness.

What had occurred in the distant kingdom of Siam? We are very well informed about what contemporaries called the "revolution in Siam." Numerous French officers involved in the events wrote up more or less detailed accounts after their return;[19] the most important of these, the *History of the revolution in Siam in the year 1688* by Jean Vollant des Verquains, was published in 1691.[20] Two other witnesses, the Jesuits Claude de Bèze and Marcel Le Blanc, were in

Lopburi when the "revolution" occurred. Their accounts are essential and agree with each other. The manuscript of Fr de Bèze, kept in Tokyo, was published there in 1947; Hutchinson's translation appeared in English in 1968.[21] The more detailed manuscript of Le Blanc (according to Robert Challe, "the only sincere Jesuit") is kept in the Society of Jesus' archives in Rome as *Mémoires secrets sur ce qui s'est passé à Siam dans les années 1687 et 1688* (The secret memoirs of what occurred in Siam in the years 1687 and 1688).[22] It was published in 1692 in an edited version with the title *Histoire de la révolution du royaume de Siam arrivée en l'année 1688* (History of the revolution in the Kingdom of Siam which occurred in 1688),[23] but I have preferred to quote from the original manuscript, which is more confidential and more colourful than the published text. It will be understood, after what has been said in chapter 11 concerning Fr d'Orléans and his *History of Mr Constance, chief minister of the King of Siam and the recent revolution in that state,*[24] that this "novel" has to be treated with considerable caution. More interesting in my view are the English and Dutch accounts,[25] or the two unpublished accounts of Fr Maldonado, then in Siam.[26] The account of La Touche, mentioned by Robert Challe and thought to be lost, was discovered in Munich in an early version of Challe's *Journal*, and published in 1998.[27]

THE SIAMESE COURT AT THE BEGINNING OF 1688

Reading the different accounts of the La Loubère/Céberet embassy one wonders if the French on the spot were sufficiently aware of the end of the reign atmosphere hanging over the court of Somdet Phra Narai and the eruption which was about to occur. The continued illnesses of the king explain why the question of his succession could not be avoided even though he was only fifty-six years old. Bèze noted that "during the past four or five years the king's health had deteriorated owing to an asthmatic cough."[28]

Phra Narai had no sons, and the harshness with which he treated his two half-brothers, Chaofa Aphaitot and Chaofa Noi, had relegated them to obscurity. One was a paralyzed alcoholic and the other a stuttering imbecile, and neither could be considered as presentable successors, the more so as the king's distrust had prevented them from finding supporters among the *chao* (princes) and *khunnang* (mandarins) capable of placing them on the throne.

The king showed himself more indulgent to his daughter, Kromluang Yothathep, who had the reputation of being extremely cruel, having some political influence, disapproving of the xenophilous policy of her father and, naturally, hating Phaulkon. Céberet relates a revealing conversation on this subject which he and La Loubère had with Bèze who demonstrated to them why Bangkok could not be given "purely and simply" to the French. He told them "that Mr Constance would lose his head: if he did what we asked, the whole kingdom would rise up, and a thousand cabals would be formed; it would be the moment for his enemies, who were very numerous, and among whom were counted the princess queen, who was very haughty and had unbelievable pride."[29] The king's daughter could not play a political role directly, but she could give a veneer of legitimacy to a candidate to the throne who was born outside the Prasat Thong dynasty.

Two younger men figured among Phra Narai's entourage. According to the *Phongsawadan*, the first, Dua (sometimes Sua), with the title Ok-luang Sorasak, was a son whom the king had by a Lanna princess. The king was supposed to have given him to Ok-phra Phetracha, asking him to raise him as his own son. But the *Phongsawadan* complicate things by presenting Ok-luang Sorasak sometimes as a secretly recognized descendant of the sovereign, sometimes as the son of Ok-phra Phetracha.[30] The Europeans living in Siam remarked on the very evident favour of Sorasak, but believed him to be the son of Phetracha. Everything leads one to believe they were right.

The *Phongsawadan* describe Ok-luang Sorasak as a champion of the Buddhist cause and resolute adversary of Ok-phra Wichayen, that is, Phaulkon. When the Greek favourite had forcibly defrocked a certain number of monks who had taken refuge in the temples to escape the six-month corvée and the obligation to perform as *phrai luang*, Sorasak had become very angry, considering this an insult to Buddhism and the *sangha*. He went to find Phaulkon and broke two of his teeth with a well-aimed punch.[31]

After the disgrace in 1683 of Chaofa Noi, Narai's younger half-brother, the king found a substitute son in Phra Pi, also known as Mom Pi, son of a courtier Ok-khun Kraisitthisak. Phra Pi, called by the French "Prapy" or "Pra Pit," had been a *mahatlek* or royal page like Sorasak. Bèze, who had his entries into the palace, gives details about the young favourite. "[He] came of low estate from a village upstream above Louvo," and had been taken into the court when very young and raised by a sister of the king together with Princess Yothathep, who had the same age. "He was not conspicuous for sharpness of wit or brilliance, but made up for them by his good-natured air, his winning and easy manners—in particular by his readiness to flatter the king—and by his diligence in learning the way to all he hoped to attain." Phra Pi did this so well that Phra Narai could no longer do without him.

> Phra Pi was ever at the king's side, his eyes fixed upon His Majesty and ready to anticipate His Majesty's orders. The king was wont to say: "Phra Pi spares me speech, he takes the words out of my mouth." His affection for Phra Pi led him to adopt his young favourite. After the fall of the two princes . . . the king actually conceived a project of giving Phra Pi the succession by uniting him in marriage with the princess.[32]

But the haughty *kromluang* refused to marry the favourite and was exiled to the palace in Ayutthaya. In the sulks with her father, she did not wish to return to Lopburi to receive the presents which were sent her by Mme la Dauphine. This open dispute drew her close to Phetracha and his son Sorasak. Phra Pi, lured on by Phetracha, accumulated blunder after blunder which gave Phra Narai to understand that the young man, then aged twenty-two, could never succeed as king. Not wishing to abandon him after his death to the resentment of the *chao* who were jealous of his influence, he was

> resolved therefore to set him up as "Chief," giving him rule over the province of Porcelouk [Phitsanulok] and furthermore, to the end that he might there maintain himself in style, to make over to him all the elephants captured in warfare during that reign. This was kept a profound secret.[33]

Fr de Bèze had this confidential information from Phaulkon.

OK-PHRA PHETRACHA, SUPERINTENDENT OF THE ELEPHANTS, AND "ZEALOUS SUPPORTER OF THE PAGODAS"

As can be guessed, the central character in the drama which was being prepared was the very clever and influential Ok-phra Phetracha, superintendent of the elephant corps and foster brother of the king. That was clear, even to the eyes of a person as recently arrived in Siam as La Loubère. ". . . 'tis Oc-Pra Pipitcharatcha, corruptly called Petratcha, who commands all the Elephants, and all the Horses: and it is one of the greatest Employments in the Kingdom, because that the Elephants are esteemed the King of Siam's Principal Forces." This person, still according to La Loubère,

> is yet a very great Lord. The people love him because he appears moderate . . . his Courage has likewise procur'd him the Favour of the King his Master. His Family has continued a long time in the highest Offices: is frequently allied to the Crown; and it is publickly reported that he or his Son Oc-Louang Souracac may pretend to it, if either of them survive the King that now Reigns.[34]

The French witnesses, who observed that Ok-phra Phetracha served as a rallying point for those who were irritated by the favour enjoyed by Phaulkon and the pro-French, pro-Christian policies of the king, did not like the commander of the elephants. While Vollant des Verquains makes him descend from "a very illustrious family which was said to be the only one which was sustained since time immemorial in the honours and the most important offices of state,"[35] Fr Le Blanc says he "had a birthright to serve on a barge rather than wear a crown." He gave this portrait of him:

> This man is of little above middling height, an open countenance, lively, considered brave, and who, at the age of fifty-five or fifty-six, keeps all his youthful vigour. He was poor, but had much credit among the people for his popular ways, and in the court through his favour with the king. He was bold, always on the go, frank, speaking freely, but with a frankness and a freedom which were a very subtle disguise to conceal his designs, because he showed himself to be the biggest rogue in Siam.[36]

Whatever the case, Ok-phra Phetracha showed consummate ability. Without showing his hand, he had succeeded in compromising the king's two half-brothers and his adopted son Phra Pi, to whom he had secretly promised the crown. He maintained very discreet links with Kromluang Yothathep, who was the guarantor of a more or less legitimate transfer of power, while keeping in the good graces of Phra Narai. The fact that his sister as well as his daughter were *phra sanom*, royal concubines, surely simplified matters.

Affecting great disdain for this temporal world, Phetracha had his head shaved, donned the saffron robe, and withdrew into a monastery. But, Le Blanc assures us,

> the least of his concerns, during his retreat, was to acquire merit . . . he rather thought of forming supporters there and gaining the esteem of the talapoins whose good standing with the people he understood. He established close links with the most important among them, and especially with the *sankharat* or superior of all the talapoins in Louvo.[37]

These connections were essential, for the powerful *sangha*, guardian of Buddhist traditions, was one of the pillars of the throne of the *dharmachakravartin* or monarch who causes the wheel of the Law to turn. This is why he, according to Le Blanc, "assumed the guise of a zealous supporter of the pagodas."[38]

And Phetracha knew how to make himself wanted. One of his courtier friends cleverly insinuated to Phra Narai that the royal council had been deprived for too long of the insights of a man as capable and disinterested as he. "This speech renewed the friendship the king had for this mandarin; he immediately sent for him." But the superintendent of the elephants needed much persuading, declaring "that they were forcing him under duress, and that, if he were left to follow his desires, he would have preferred calm and solitude to all the pomp and circumstance of the court."[39] He returned, of course, in better standing than ever, well supported on all sides, affecting great outward simplicity. The ochre cotton garments he wore were meant to remind one of his supposed monastic inclinations.

His objections to the cession of Bangkok and Mergui at the council of state have already been noted. French control of these two strategic strongholds, the uncertain health of the king, and Phaulkon's intolerable stranglehold on Siamese affairs, decided the superintendent of the elephants to go into action. A swindler and an idolater in the eyes of the French, he appears to us as the champion of traditional Siamese values, of Buddhism under threat, and of national independence. Can one reproach him for that?

"THERE IS ONE OF THE GREAT FALLEN": PORTENTS AND PREDICTIONS

A perfectly orchestrated concert of evil portents and prophesies of sedition preoccupied minds in the first weeks of 1688. Phaulkon himself, in mourning for the death of his son, was affected by it. It was enough, for example, for a *khunnang* to hear "There is one of the great fallen" spoken by a man pulling hairs from his chin, for this phrase to be interpreted as a bad augury for the king's life.[40] Ok-phra Phetracha had this information circulated among the people, having at his command an inestimable means of communication: the monks leaving their monasteries each morning to beg for alms. Instructed by the *sangkharat*, they passed on with a distant look unverifiable information to the faithful who filled their offering bowls with rice and vegetables. Another rumour announcing a revolution at the beginning of April was circulating at the same time, and reached the king's ears, like the first.

Equally disquieting external incidents increased the sovereign's distress. Hardly had the French vessels set sail than the Sultan of Johor, a vassal of the King of Siam but advised by a Dutch minister, sent a letter to his suzerain saying "that he was surprised that a prince as wise as he had called into his kingdom foreigners whom he would no longer be free to remove when he desired; that he had more reason to fear the ambitious nature of the French than he had to hope from an alliance with them; and that if he wished to entertain the idea of chasing out these dangerous guests before they were better entrenched, he offered his services for the enterprise."[41] Phra Narai was so furious that he would have cut off the heads of the two bearers of this insolent missive, had not Phaulkon restrained him by saying that it "would be bruited abroad throughout the Indies." The king calmed down and had a letter sent to the sultan saying he was still very young to give him advice.

Soon after, at the end of January, a Malay passed word to Phra

Narai "that Mr Constance and the French were plotting against [him], public liberty and religion, and he was ready to give him convincing proofs even if it cost him his life." The king refused to listen to him and had him thrown to the tigers. For good measure, "His Majesty seized the occasion to burn the Makassars remaining from the last plot. The execution took place in Siam, in the very camp of the Malays, to create terror among those who might have similar designs."[42]

These incidents seem to have further reinforced the bonds between the king and the French. "He only spoke of *his Frenchmen*, he always wished to see them at his court, he neither went hunting, nor travelled abroad nor witnessed entertainments, except that he was surrounded by officers from Bangkok on horseback beside his elephant, talking with them." The king learnt with chagrin that the French foot soldiers "were dying as much from moroseness as sickness in Bangkok," and charitably exclaimed "that the death of a single Frenchman afflicted him more than the loss of a hundred Siamese."[43] It is unlikely that the king knew the real condition of the French troops quartered in Bangkok. Badly paid and undisciplined, the soldiers begged in the streets, robbing passers-by and molesting the women.[44] Deslandes's son deplores this "conduct of the French who threw themselves at the women in a thoughtless manner without considering the seemliness appropriate for the country. It is known that this was the reef on which the French, letting pleasure get the better of them and doing nothing to restrain its satisfaction, came to grief."[45]

In February, Phra Narai fell seriously ill "of asthma which, alongside his inveterate consumption, gave little hope that he could yet live much longer." This news caused Phetracha to accelerate his preparations; he remained "a supporter of the monkhood among the talapoins and popular among the people, but was even more so a clever courtier among the great." He spoke with utter scorn of the French, "calling them *kijnrha*, which politeness does not allow one to translate." One day, in the presence of one of Phaulkon's informers, he pronounced this little speech: "Here we are captives, and for the crowning misfortune there is no one to liberate us. The king is sick and lets himself be governed, the princes are unfitted to succeed him. For me, I do not have the honour to have royal blood in my veins, but I had royal milk, and I have the heart of a Siamese."[46] As for the people in the street, they only spoke about the prophecies broadcast by the monks.

Phaulkon was, of course, aware of all these movements, but could not act without proof. The king, whose health worsened daily, was of no assistance. The Greek had learned that Phetracha and Phra Pi terrified the sovereign, making him believe that his two disgraced half-brothers had decided to drag his body through the mire after his death, and refuse him the sumptuous funeral ceremonies and cremation which would release his soul. Brandishing this threat, insupportable for a king who also had pretensions of being a *bodhisattva*, they had extracted from him the authorization to assemble Siamese troops who were to prevent this abomination. Phetracha tried to put Phaulkon on a false scent and gave him a series of sham confidences and promises. "If you will but join us . . . I will assemble here at Louvo all the men I should need in order to place the crown upon whose head I list. . . . And why not upon yours? All you need do is make believe that you are adopting the Buddhist Faith. As for me, I swear I will seek rest and retirement in a *wat,* the moment I see all in order in the land and the last rites duly paid to the King's mortal remains."[47] He underestimated someone like Phaulkon to relate such rubbish.

DESFARGES'S TREASON

Considering the joke had gone far enough, Phaulkon summoned Desfarges, busy with fortifying Bangkok. He informed him that the interests of the two crowns urgently required his presence in Lopburi. French troops had come from the other end of the globe to support Phaulkon in case of need. It was time to put them to work, arrest Phetracha and accomplices, give them a trial, and throw them to the tigers.

Desfarges arrived at the end of March with a small escort. He was received in audience by the sick king and had a conversation with Phaulkon who informed him of all the details of the elephant intendant's plot. It was agreed between them that Desfarges would go to Bangkok and fetch a detachment of selected men, returning with them without wasting time. The Greek swore him to secrecy and put him on his guard against false rumours of the death of the king as long as he, Phaulkon, had not informed him of it, for such a rumour could be a trick by which Phetracha would halt his advance and provoke a general uprising.

Desfarges promised everything asked of him, and returned to Bangkok where he chose eighty soldiers and ten officers, "intrepid persons and ready to undertake anything." Ninety courageous men (105 according to La Touche) had in their hands the dynastic succession of Siam and the destiny of Phaulkon. Vollant des Verquains remarks: "It is perhaps surprising that one put so much reliance on a handful of persons in a kingdom as large as Siam. Nevertheless, nothing is more certain than that the small number of Frenchmen introduced there were enough to hold in check the whole Siamese nation."[48] This engineer did not doubt for a moment that this modest detachment could have seized Ok-phra Phetracha without difficulty, and that his arrest would have put an end to the trouble. One is not obliged to share his optimism.

The detachment arrived in Ayutthaya on 15 April, Maundy Thursday. The general stopped at the French godown to have a long conversation with Mr Véret who had just come back from Lopburi where he had been assured about the king's health. Bèze writes:

> Véret did his best to retain the general and deter him from proceeding farther in the direction of Louvo. His most cogent argument was the report, current at the time in the capital, that the king had died; he adduced the danger to which the general was exposing himself on behalf of a person and a policy alike which France was preparing to drop.

Desfarges did not let himself be convinced, even when Véret assured him that Phaulkon was "to be left to his fate," and Phetracha had seized power. They decided to go together to consult Mgr Laneau and the Abbé de Lionne in the Foreign Missions.

> The picture of Constans which he found at the seminary was that of a desperado, clinging to office in despite of the king—a man who, by bringing out the French upon his own initiative, proved that his mind was set upon involving them in his own downfall, or at least upon sustaining himself by French support lest he fall—and this in defiance of the solid weight of opinion united against him throughout the kingdom.

These were the accusations of Fr de Bèze, which Fr Le Blanc echoed.[49]

Lionne, Véret, and Desfarges have each given their version of these deliberations of key importance. A memorandum of the Abbé de Lionne, written in 1692, does not contradict the account of the two Jesuits, but wraps up the advice given to Desfarges with extensive justifications; the long and the short of it is that he thought the king was dead, and advocated a neutral stance by the French in the expected disturbances which only concerned the Siamese.[50] This explanation did not prevent the director of the MEP seminary in Paris writing to Lionne: "Fr Verjus tells everyone you were the cause of Mr Constance's death and the reversal of the advancement of religion in Siam."[51] Artus de Lionne was to leave Siam suddenly, fleeing a situation for which he was partly responsible, and abandoning Mgr Laneau and his colleagues to their sad fate. This was not the best way to merit the indulgence of posterity.

The shady Véret, in a detailed letter to André Deslandes written on 3 March 1689 in Pondichéry and published by Robert Lingat,[52] explains that he had been assured that the Siamese were taking up arms around Lopburi, "rumour already had it that they wanted to massacre all the French and the other Christians," and it was to put oneself in the lion's mouth to go there. Véret loathed Phaulkon but ought to have understood that to throw the Greek as fodder to his enemies was to cut off the branch on which all the French were perched. The perky tone of his letter to Deslandes proves that Véret did not in the least expect his recall to France and the harsh treatment he would receive there.

Desfarges, whose self-justifying memorandum was seized by the Dutch and published in Amsterdam in 1691,[53] takes up Véret's arguments. He justifies his return to Bangkok, adding that he had learnt that Siamese soldiers were assembling in great numbers to massacre the French, and it was his duty to fly to the succour of his men. These Siamese soldiers, of course, only existed in the imagination of the general.

Vollant des Verquains is very harsh on the vindictive and avaricious clerk Véret ("a self-interested person animated by blind passion who thought he could turn the troubles to his account, thinking of profiting from them")[54] and on Desfarges, presented as stubborn, indecisive, and cowardly. Lanier speaks of "the treason of Desfarges and Véret," accusing the Abbé de Lionne at the same time of having supported a "cabal which was deplorable for French interests," and Mgr Laneau for being involved "at least by his silence."[55]

The Bishop of Metellopolis had indeed spoken much less than his coadjutor Lionne. In the end he had suggested to Desfarges that he send a scout to Lopburi before withdrawing to Bangkok. It was not a bad idea. The general sent off Le Roy with a letter for Phaulkon in which he said that, having learnt in Ayutthaya of the death of the king, he did not wish to add to the upheaval, "but he would lie quiet in the capital for a day or two and, if Constans should elect to withdraw to Bangkok with wife and family, he himself would escort them to the fortress."[56] The officer arrived in Lopburi about midnight; he was very surprised to find the town completely peaceful, and Phaulkon, his wife, and the Jesuits observing a lunar eclipse. Desfarges's letter greatly angered Phaulkon, who wrote to him saying that the king was indeed still alive, that he had earlier warned him not to heed false rumours, and urged him to keep his word and come with his men to Lopburi without delay.

Le Roy carried the letter to Ayutthaya, but Desfarges told him his decision was taken and he was returning to Bangkok with his men. "He never paused to consider," noted Bèze, "whether his desertion of Constans might not imply repudiation of the honour and interests of France, and even its religion."[57] Several days passed with comings and goings between Ayutthaya and Lopburi, but Desfarges remained intractable. He gave Phaulkon to understand that indisposition forced him to return to Bangkok, and that, moreover, "a general should never leave his strong-hold."[58] This idea ought to have struck him rather sooner.

The contemporary Thai historian Dhiravat na Pombejra, noting "Rumours were about that the French were conspiring to take over Siam: even the market women at Ayutthaya knew of this and ran away in fright at the sight of Desfarges," considers that "Desfarges' decision to remain in Bangkok with his troops was therefore the correct one as far as French interests (as opposed to Phaulkon's interests) were concerned. Eighty to a hundred Frenchmen could never have overcome Okphra Phetracha and his followers."[59]

The time lost in these comings and goings between Ayutthaya and Lopburi would be fatal to the Greek. The movements of French troops were to incite Phetracha to bring forward his coup d'état without waiting for the king's death; there would be no time left then to call for assistance from the English in Ayutthaya, who had already helped Phaulkon against the Makassars.

OK-PHRA PHETRACHA'S COUP D'ÉTAT

With the aid of his energetic son Ok-luang Sorasak, who played a leading role according to the *Phongsawadan*, the intendant of the elephants summoned all his supporters. He further increased his numbers by promising important positions to undecided *khunnang*. The prospect of pillaging Phaulkon's residence, which was held to be filled with incalculable treasures, seems to have gained him numerous supporters. Everyone added their slaves and their men subject to the corvée (*phrai som*) to his numbers. Transformed into militias, they were quartered in the temples around Lopburi. Ok-khun Kraisitthisak, Phra Pi's father, armed fourteen thousand men for his son's cause. According to La Touche, Phetracha assembled in a few days an army of seventy to eighty thousand men.

Seeing he no longer controlled the situation, Phaulkon sent provisions to Bangkok, with orders to prepare the stronghold for an eventual assault. He sent off his wife and son Jorge to the Japanese camp in Ayutthaya. Lastly, without revealing what was happening, he implored the king to name one of his half-brothers as his successor, intending to form around him a party capable of neutralizing that of Phetracha. But the antipathy of Phra Narai for his half-brothers was so great, and the fear he had of their mistreating his body so overwhelming, that he merely said he would think about it.

About 10 May, the king assembled his council (including Phaulkon, Phetracha, and Pi), to which he announced his decision, to avoid disturbances after his death, to nominate his daughter, Kromluang Yothathep, regent and trustee of the crown, and place her under the guardianship of Ok-ya Wichayen (Phaulkon), Ok-phra Phetracha, and Phra Pi, and this "until the final offices had been rendered to the royal remains; thereafter she was free to associate whichever prince of the two she preferred to have as a partner with herself upon the throne."[60] Rumour had it that the *kromluang* had a penchant for Chaofa Noi, the younger half-brother; Phra Narai could not have been unaware of it. "The king," Fr Le Blanc explains, "took this disposition because he did not hate the princes sufficiently to remove the crown from them, but neither did he love them enough to place it on their head himself."[61]

This royal decision, intended to maintain civil peace, naturally had the opposite effect. Phetracha immediately sent monks to Ayutthaya to congratulate the *kromluang* and future regent, offering her his services, and requesting her to come at once to Lopburi with Chaofa Noi. Phra Pi, who spent his days in the king's chambers, tried to effect entry into the palace of men loyal to him, but Phetracha's supporters blocked them. The young favourite became angry with Phetracha and reproached him with perfidy; the intendant of the elephants mocked him and his lofty pretensions. He reminded him of his low birth, adding that, "as for him, if he did not have the blood of kings, he had suckled the milk which had nurtured the king."[62]

Phaulkon, sheltering behind the conviction that nothing would happen to him as long as Phra Narai remained alive, sought to exude an air of confidence. He brought back his wife and son from Ayutthaya, and refused to listen to the French in his entourage who advised him to withdraw with his family to Bangkok. Was this blindness on his part, or loyalty to the end for the king who he did not wish to abandon? Whichever, the Greek did not lack nerve. No doubt he trusted the reports given to him by the French priest, Paumard, doctor to both himself and the king, and thought that the king would get better and the conspiracy would collapse of itself.

Phra Pi went to throw himself at the king's feet and told him all he knew about the coup d'état which Ok-phra Phetracha was preparing. Extremely disturbed, the king summoned Phaulkon who confirmed everything. He explained that he had wished to spare the king, seeing he was ill, that the desertion of Desfarges had changed his plans to have Phetracha arrested, that he would return in the morning with a group of Englishmen and Frenchmen to seize the plotter, and that the king should until then pretend to know nothing in order not to provoke the conspirators who controlled the palace. He also told him that his friends had beseeched him to go to a safe place, but nothing could divert him from his duty. According to Le Blanc, he said "If he had to die, it would be at Your Majesty's feet."[63]

But Phra Narai, agitated and unable to control himself, did not stop repeating to all those who had access to his chambers that Phetracha was a traitor whom he would chastise as he deserved. The intendant of the elephants was informed of this immediately and decided to act. He told the chief *sangkharat* that the moment had come. The militias left the temples and the monks roused the people of Lopburi, explaining that they had to take up arms to save the king and the realm, that Ok-phra Phetracha would administer the kingdom in the name of the king, and that Ok-ya Wichayen was a traitor who had wanted to hand the country over to the *farang*.

The people took up their arms and followed the *sangkharat* and his monks who marched in the direction of the palace. Fr Le Blanc, our correspondent on the spot, was caught in the middle of the crowd, and expressed his indignation

> at seeing there was then no one in Louvo to calm this tumult. One hundred resolute men would have scattered this scum of slaves and Indians carrying arms for the first time in their lives. At the head of the troops, carried on the shoulders of six men was the chief *sangkharat* of Louvo . . . This talapoin invited everyone verbally and by his gestures to follow him. He arrived at a small side gate of the palace, which was opened to him by people who had been won over within, and everyone tumbled inside. Barbarians from all sides could be seen, some with the *pras* [knives for cutting wood], others with bamboo stakes with iron or burnt tips, mandarins with sabres and bucklers. They were all in confusion, men, horses, officers and soldiers, mixed haphazardly; the only form of discipline apparent among them was the silence which the leaders imposed on them with a hand gesture.[64]

The same eye witness also indicates that these events took place "at midday on 18 May."

Phaulkon, then discussing events with Fr de Bèze, was informed. "To be rid of me, he begged me to go across to our Fathers in the chapel and pray God for the life of the king which was in great danger," and "went to his wife and took leave of her as though he anticipated never seeing her again."[65] Some French officers of the guards, who were present in his residence, advised him to lock himself up there with all the Europeans in Lopburi, but he declared he was unwilling to abandon the king. La Touche notes: "His fidelity for the King was greater than his fear of death."[66] He ran to the palace followed by the chief of staff Beauchamp, Mr de Fretteville, and the Chevalier Desfarges, the general's younger son.

He entered the palace by a side gate, but

> was arrested by Petratcha and his son who were waiting for him there with a troop of mandarins with drawn sabres. The three French officers were disarmed, and Mr Constance was led into an inner courtyard in the palace. On his way, an executioner appeared, and seizing the opportunity to strike him, raised his scimitar over his

> head, but Mr Constance turned towards Petratcha and, after saying some words to him in Siamese, apparently to ask him for some delay in order to prepare himself for death, the mandarin halted the executioner's blow.[67]

Phaulkon would have ample time to regret this merciful delay.

Shut up with the three French officers, the Greek had no illusions; he had played a cautious game and lost. He sent for some religious books in his residence and passed word to Bèze that he would have liked to have had him at his side to "hear his confession and prepare him for death," but Phetracha was opposed to this. "I would not have scrupled to render an act, such as this, of Christian charity to a man I had such good grounds for liking. But neither his application nor mine were of any avail; nor was it possible ever to see him again before his death, even for a moment."[68]

The first victim of Ok-phra Phetracha, who controlled the palace and thus the whole kingdom, was the blundering and naive Phra or Mom Pi. His father, Ok-khun Kraisitthisak, had fled and his supporters had abandoned him. The king's adopted son had taken refuge in the chamber of the sick king, a prisoner in his own palace, who does not seem to have reacted to events except by uttering powerless imprecations. The royal chamber was sacred, but Phetracha had posted his men close to its door. A Dutch source informs us:

> The following day he asked for a piece of split bamboo (called a tongue scraper) he wanted according to the custom of the Indies, to clean his mouth. When he was offered it and extended his hand to take it, his arm was seized and he was dragged by force from the king's chamber, notwithstanding his terrible cries and the sovereign's protests.[69]

The unfortunate youth was beheaded the following day, 20 May. His head was thrown at Phaulkon's feet with the scornful words: "There is your king!"[70] for Phetracha accused him of having wished to place Phra Pi on the throne. This explains Phaulkon's phrase in the instructions given to Tachard at the end of 1685, and quoted in chapter 18: "I promise and pledge that the successor of the king will be even more disposed to grant everything than his predecessor, and that one will find in him much greater facility, even for religion."[71]

The French and English in Lopburi, including the three French officers arrested with Phaulkon, were not molested. The new ruler of Siam simply sent them to Thale Chupson where Phra Narai had a summer house beside a lake with the same name. At the same time, Phetracha made use of Kosa Pan, who had gone over to his side out of conviction, and Véret, to reassure the gentlemen of the Foreign Missions and invite them to Lopburi.

Mgr Laneau pleaded sickness and sent the Abbé de Lionne. On 25 May the abbé had a meeting with Phetracha (from this point now styled "the Great Mandarin" by the French), who told him he only acted on the king's orders, and charged him with making Desfarges come to Lopburi. He thought that, "as [the missionaries] had sufficient credit with the French general to make him return to Bangkok, they would have even more to make him leave it."[72] Lionne should have understood that Phetracha was indeed obliged to take the French and the Christians into account as long as Desfarges controlled Bangkok. The Jesuits in Lopburi tried to undeceive him and gave him letters for Desfarges, but the abbé tore them up as soon as he left Lopburi.[73]

The abbé's behaviour is all the less comprehensible as Phetracha had treated him harshly, warning him that if he did not make Desfarges come to Lopburi, "he would be offended with him and all the French Fathers; that he would tie them to the mouths of cannons."[74] Such propositions hardly confirm the benevolence which the Great Mandarin pretended to have for the French. Mr Véret wrote this note from Ayutthaya to the Chevalier Desfarges:

> My dear Chevalier, while waiting for the orders of your father you would like me to advise you that at present Ok-phra Phetracha rules, and it is he whom you should obey. So take care not to be surprised by orders which could come to you from another source. We are in safety as if we were in the middle of Paris, and will here-after take some part in these affairs.[75]

One would think one was dreaming.

The Great Mandarin, who had removed the king's entourage apart from a few valets, paid visits to him from time to time, to give the impression he was going to take his orders. His first concern was to secure the royal family. Chaofa Noi had already come to the Lopburi palace; the paralyzed Chaofa Aphaitot was seized in Ayutthaya, placed on an elephant, and brought by force to Lopburi. Having obtained control of the candidates to the throne and provisionally neutralized the French, Phetracha, decked out with the titles of administrator of the kingdom, liberator of the nation, and defender of the faith,[76] felt sufficiently master of the situation to concern himself with Phaulkon. He considered that "the rice was cool enough to eat."

THE END OF PHAULKON

As the Greek had been transferred to an inaccessible part of the palace, no European was witness to the agonies he had to endure. It is known that he was tortured with particular cruelty, with the head of his "accomplice" Phra Pi tied round his neck. The torments continued without interruption for two weeks. The testimony of a priest at the Foreign Missions about the way Phetracha later treated forty-eight *khunnang* who had the misfortune to displease him gives an idea of the hell Phaulkon endured. Faithful to the tradition of the torments witnessed by Jacques de Coutre in the reign of Phra Naresuan, Phra Phetracha had their heads cut each day with blows from a sabre, cut morsels of their flesh which they were forced to eat, cut off their fingers, poured molten lead down their mouths, and exposed them for hours on end under the hot sun. Those who had the misfortune to survive this treatment for twelve days were in the end impaled and disembowelled.[77]

Fr Le Blanc relates that a Siamese secretary, sent by Mme Phaulkon to the palace, "had seen his master in an enclosure of stakes, with three chains about his neck, hands, and feet, and that wishing to come near to him to speak to him, Mr Constance had covered his face with a handkerchief."[78]

The same witness summarizes the rumours which abounded about the tortures inflicted on Phaulkon.

> Some said that first of all the soles of his feet were burnt to prevent him fleeing, and having tortured him, his temples were tightened by an iron circle and his whole body was shredded with blows from the rattan. Others believed that his feet and hands had been cut off, and that the head of the unfortunate Mom Pi was left a long time hung around his neck . . . One should not doubt that these barbarians practised on him the greatest cruelties according to their vindictive and sanguinary nature. Such torments among them include burning

them over a low fire, frying men in vats of boiling oil by plunging them in it from time to time, attaching a famished tiger to them in such a way as it can only eat the extremities, making them swallow molten metals and feeding men for a long period with their own flesh which they had cut off and grilled in their presence.[79]

A Dutch text describes in particular the violence inflicted on Phaulkon by the Siamese soldiery:

> He was handed over to the brutalities of the soldiers, their railleries and insults, in such as way as he was roughly handled, pulled about, covered in their spittle, beaten, pulled by the hair, and so violently dragged along the ground that all his clothes were torn to shreds and he only had on his under-breeches. Although he was allowed to put on other clothes, he was covered by this scum with filth and excrement, insults and oaths, which he endured quite patiently.[80]

Finally, on the evening of 5 June, he was declared guilty of lese-majesty and high treason, and condemned to death. He asked for a confessor which was refused him. He was placed on the back of an elephant and carried with a solid escort to the forest of Thale Chupson. According to witnesses, he had a "fairly tranquil appearance" and murmured prayers. On arriving at the execution spot, he knelt down, took off the cross of the order of St Michael which had been placed round his neck, and requested one of the mandarins to keep it for his son Jorge. A "painted arm" executioner moved forward, and "with the back of his sabre split him down the middle of his body. He fell dying on his face with a great sigh. They despatched his life by cutting off his head with several blows."[81]

Thus died the Greek adventurer who had crossed Siamese history like a shooting star, and who played a decisive role in Siamese-European relations. His French friends had implored him to flee, and he had ample time to do this during the month which passed between Desfarges's treason and his own arrest. Since one cannot deny him both lucidity and imagination, one has to conclude that Phaulkon did not wish to abandon his king, and he accepted his destiny, looking death in the face without blanching.

According to Johan Keyts, the director of the Dutch godown in Ayutthaya, the body of Phaulkon, cut into pieces, was thrown into a shallow ditch and covered with a thin layer of earth.[82] Dogs dug it up the same night and ate it.

The fate of the proud and pretty Mme Phaulkon, then twenty-two years old, was not to be envied. Immediately after the arrest of her husband, their residence was attacked by soldiers and totally pillaged. The lady was rudely pushed about and even tortured, because it was thought she knew where Phaulkon had hidden valuables. According to the German traveller Engelbert Kaempfer who two years later visited Siam, where he obtained information from the Dutch, Phaulkon had been taken during his captivity to his residence, no doubt to indicate the hiding places of his diamonds. "His wife was imprisoned in the stables. Instead of saying farewell to him, she spat in his face and did not want him to embrace his only surviving son, aged four years, another son having recently died."[83] This image is markedly different from the edifying scenes of conjugal harmony offered us by the Jesuit chroniclers. This account confirms the quarrels and scenes of jealousy described in the long letter from the English Catholic to Fr d'Orléans.[84]

Mme Phaulkon was transferred to prison at the beginning of June and "flung into a filthy, stinking stable; she had brought nothing with her and nothing was provided but a lattice framework to serve as her bed."[85] Fr de Bèze, authorized to visit her after a certain time, had his breath taken away on seeing her reduced to this state. The brutal assiduities of Ok-luang Sorasak, who wanted to drag her into his bed, added to the misfortunes of the widow Phaulkon, a quasi-virgin and a quasi-martyr, if one is to believe the hagiographic Jesuits. The shattering crash of the house of Phaulkon has a tragic quality worthy of his Greek origins.

THE KING IS DEAD; LONG LIVE THE KING

The Abbé de Lionne had left Lopburi on 26 May for Bangkok, accompanied by Véret, the chief of staff de Beauchamp, the former *ratchathut* Kosa Pan, and an escort of executioners. Summoned to return at once to Lopburi, Desfarges convened his council, but he did not have a free hand, for his younger son, the chevalier, had been kept back as a hostage by the Great Mandarin. Lionne told him that this journey to Lopburi seemed to him to be useful in the interests of the mission. Véret spoke of the new master of Siam with somewhat forced enthusiasm, and Kosa Pan gave him to understand that the king wished to raise him, and his elder son after him, to the high offices filled by Phaulkon. The bait was crude, but Desfarges, forgetting that "a general should never leave his stronghold," decided to go to Lopburi and to take with him his other son, the Marquis Desfarges. Mr de Vertesalle would command the stronghold in his absence.

He arrived on 2 June and was immediately taken to the palace. Phetracha was waiting for him, surrounded by bared sabres and prostrate *khunnang*, to make clear who was in charge. The Great Mandarin treated him insolently, wanting to know why Phaulkon had summoned him in April and why he had returned from where he came. Desfarges replied as best he could, then heard that His Siamese Majesty desired to send the French expeditionary corps against the Lao rebels, and he should summon his troops to Lopburi. The general replied that his men would only obey his word, and promised to return with them if he were allowed to go back to Bangkok. Phetracha agreed to this, indicating that his two sons would have to remain at the court as hostages. The general was also obliged to write a letter to du Bruant in Mergui, ordering him to join him in Lopburi with the two French companies stationed there. But he contrived the letter in such a way that du Bruant understood it had been written under constraint.

The imprisoned king gave him to understand before his return to Bangkok that he had no part in the orders of the Great Mandarin.[86] The general left on 5 June for Bangkok, decided to dig in there with his men, abandoning his sons to their fate. Ok-phra Phetracha, who had remarked that Desfarges said nothing in favour of Phaulkon, understood that the French, with the exception of the Jesuits, had dropped their former protector. The Greek was executed the same evening.

It took several more weeks for Phetracha to impose his will on the capital and over the furthest provinces of the kingdom. His authority was sufficiently established by the beginning of July to move on to the last act of his assumption of power. Having control of the persons of Chaofa Aphaitot and Chaofa Noi, heirs to the throne, he had them put to death in the royal fashion. They were taken in the evening of 9 July to a temple at some distance from Lopburi. The poor princes were tied up in scarlet velvet sacks and beaten with sandalwood clubs, without a drop of blood being spilt.[87] Ok-luang Sorasak was in charge of this execution, applying strictly the *Kot Monthien Ban* (Law of the Palace), issued in the fifteenth century by Phra Borommatrailokanat, which determined the modalities of putting to death members of the royal family.

The news of the double murder perpetrated in his name felled Phra Narai, whose illness had degenerated into dropsy.[88] Fr de Bèze saw him the following day, so downcast, weakened, and emaciated that he hardly recognized him. The Father tried to convince him to accept baptism, but the sovereign's Chinese doctor, who had received his orders, refused to translate the proposition. Prisoner in his own palace, exhausted by his respiratory problems, and powerless witness to the extermination of his dynasty and his favourites, the king died in despair "on 10 July at ten o'clock at night" according to Bèze, 11 July according to Keyts and Vollant des Verquains.

It appears hardly likely, as the rumours related by François Martin in his *Mémoires*[89] had it, that Ok-phra Phetracha had him poisoned; his illness and the misfortunes of the last weeks brought the king to his end. The contrary, suggested by Fr Le Blanc,[90] seems more probable; the imminent death of the king hastened the ritual execution of the two princes by an order purporting to come from him.

Somdet Phra Narai expired at the age of fifty-six in the thirty-second year of his reign. One regrets the passing of this tolerant monarch, so ready to open his kingdom to Western influences, without considering the dangers and the alienations which could result from such a mixing. He sought the friendship of Louis XIV, and was offered a protectorate.

Phetracha gave the body of the late king all the customary honours. The *khunnang* shaved their heads and dressed in the white of mourning, the palace resounded every three hours with concerts of trumpets and other instruments, the monks recited day and night prayers for the liberation of the soul of the sovereign *bodhisattva*, and people rushed through the streets shouting shrill cries. "The ceremony of freeing two elephants which the king normally rode was also performed. One went off into the forest, the other returned to the palace."[91]

The usurper took the royal bier when he returned in great pomp to the palace in Ayutthaya on 1 August. He was proclaimed king there, and crowned the same day, marrying without delay the *kromluang* Yothathep, princess and heiress to the kingdom. The reign of Phra

Phetracha, which had begun with terror and xenophobia, was to last fifteen years. The new king soon renewed ties with the Dutch, who had discreetly advised and aided him. He was to send an ambassador to Batavia bearing presents which his predecessor had received from the French king. The symbolism of the gesture could not have escaped the Dutch.

The French found parallels between Phra Phetracha and another anti-French usurper who led the "glorious revolution" in the same year and removed James II from the throne: William of Orange, stadtholder of the United Provinces and, by marriage, the King of England. Vollant des Verquains wrote: "The same spirit which led the perfidious mandarin to dethrone the legitimate king of the Siamese only repeated in the Indies what we had seen . . . carried out by the Prince of Orange. And I find this difference between the two usurpers lies in their name, the similarity of their crime and their intentions being exact."[92] He could have added that the two princes had each married the daughter of their dethroned predecessor.

But before profiting from his sceptre, the new king had to resolve the "French question," for it was clear that Desfarges and his garrison would not willingly hand over the fortress of Bangkok.

THE SIEGE OF BANGKOK

The situation was difficult for everyone. La Loubère remarked that the Siamese would not vigorously attack a place "so little fortified," but would only employ "treachery, in which they are very cunning," or reduce it "by famine."[93] As for the French, totally isolated in a country at the other end of the world which had suddenly become hostile, they had to survive in an unfinished and mediocre stronghold. The inventory of their munitions at first sight is rather impressive: 70 cannons, 7,400 cannon balls, 300 barrels of powder, 700 muskets, 600 sabres, 900 lances and pikes, 1,000 grenades, 6,000 rounds of ammunition, 50,000 musket cartridges, etc.[94] But the victuals for 250 officers and men were not inexhaustible, and barges full of armed Siamese which began to encircle the fort made reprovisioning very difficult.

On his return, Desfarges called together a council of war which decided not to hand over the stronghold, especially when they learnt that seven French guards officers, who had tried to escape from Thale

Chupson, had been tied by the neck with ropes to the tails of their horses and flung into prison. The members of the council were unanimous that "they wished to defend themselves in the fort, and rather be killed there with their arms in their hands, than exposed to being massacred like rabble."[95] Immediately a series of practical decisions was made. The hundred cows sent by Phaulkon before his arrest were killed and their meat salted. The small western fort, facing the main fort on the other side of the river, was abandoned, its munitions and portable arms removed, and what was left was more or less destroyed. The remaining cannons were split or spiked.

The Siamese assembled armies of corvée soldiers who built a dozen redoubts around the fort on the left bank of the river on a bend in the Chao Phraya. The estuary of the river was closed and several batteries of cannons (the best were supplied by the willing Dutch) were set up downstream. "In this way," explains Vollant des Verquains, "the hopes of the French to escape or receive assistance were dashed, and they were reduced to the sad necessity of waiting some time, and in the end of seeking an assured death at the hands of their enemies."[96] The prospects were not thrilling, but Desfarges kept up the morale of his troops by having a few Siamese caught in skirmishes hanged from time to time on the walls. The enemy had to understand that they were not fooling around.

Phra Phetracha realized too late that he was wrong to have let the general return. His two sons were forced to write to their father saying that their heads would be cut off if he did not keep his word to bring the Bangkok garrison to Lopburi. This letter was tied to the end of a bamboo pole stuck during the night on the edge of the moat around the fort. Desfarges, a living illustration of the maxim by which "we all have enough strength to sustain the ills of others,"[97] replied to them by the same means "that he felt for their misfortune more than they could imagine, and if he could give his life for theirs, he would do so without difficulty; he exhorted them to follow his example and align their feelings to their duty; if they were ill-used they would have had the honour of suffering for God and the king, and they should be assured that their death would be fully avenged."[98]

This is how fathers of the age wrote to their sons threatened with a terrible death. The tone is doubtless pompous, but it has to be admitted it was effective. Phra Phetracha, who sought a settlement rather than armed conflict, released Desfarges's two sons, who returned to Bangkok where they arrived on 24 June. The moderation of Phetracha was due, according to Engelbert Kaempfer, to the advice of the head of the VOC godown in Ayutthaya who only wanted one thing: the departure of the French.[99]

The blockade of the fortress of Bangkok began to be felt. Several dozen French were killed or seriously wounded in the skirmishes which gave the Siamese to understand that the *farang* were, after all, not invulnerable. Victuals ran low and necessity reduced the besieged to dreary food. "The sick only received bouillons of crows that were shot in the fort, and the whole garrison was close to being reduced to rice and water. Moreover, wood was lacking, and they had to burn the soldiers' barracks and the officers' houses to cook rice and meat."[100]

Two Siamese vessels commanded by French captains were cruising in the Gulf of Siam. Considering these ships might be useful to him, Desfarges sent a capacious longboat in search of them, with a dozen soldiers from Brittany to defend it. The command was given to Lieutenant Saint-Cry (or Saint-Christ). On approaching the bar, the longboat was surrounded by dozens of vessels with hundreds of Siamese crowded on board. The second in command jumped in the water and went over to the enemy. To add to Saint-Cry's woes, the Breton soldiers were too drunk to defend themselves. In this desperate situation, Saint-Cry ordered a general flight. Remaining alone on board, he set fire to the powder the moment a host of attackers came on board. The explosion killed five hundred Siamese. A young Frenchman, although wounded, was able to return to the Bangkok fort where he related the heroic action of Saint-Cry.

Both sides wished to negotiate. To this end, Phra Phetracha sent Mgr Laneau to Bangkok, but the venerable prelate was arrested by the Siamese surrounding the fort. They seized his pectoral cross, his episcopal ring, and his hat, stole the silver and holy vessels belonging to the mission which he wished to place in safety in the fort, and made him stand on the walls of the small western fort in order to get the French to stop firing at them.

This misunderstanding did not improve matters. But the monsoon rains and widespread desertion among the Siamese troops limited hostilities. Negotiations began in earnest. The Bishop of Metellopolis and Mr Véret went backwards and forwards between Bangkok and the capital. Kosa Pan, now *Phra Khlang* to the new king, came to take up quarters in the western fort to direct the blockade and the negotiations.

The days when he said to everyone willing to listen "France big good, Siam little good" were over.

An honourable retreat of the French garrison, on two vessels to be provided against payment by the Siamese, was agreed in principle but the discussions dragged on. The arrival of the *Oriflamme* at the bar of Siam on 9 September[101] broke the logjam. It will be recalled that this vessel left Brest at the beginning of February 1688, commanded by de l'Estrille. Its journey was not easy. When it anchored on 18 May at the Cape, it had already lost fifty soldiers and sailors. The Dutch provided victuals at Batavia which it left on 11 August, but refused to supply a pilot and said nothing about the disturbances in Siam.

The arrival of this powerful ship of 750 tons burden armed with sixty-four cannons clearly impressed the Siamese, who said they "had never seen such a big vessel, and it made them agree to everything sought by the French."[102] The *Phra Khlang* Kosa Pan, after having in vain tried to conceal the revolution and its sequels from the new arrivals, proposed that the king reach a settlement with the French. After a further round of negotiations, "the relation of the details of which would be tedious,"[103] the two sides concluded at the end of September an honourable capitulation drawn up in nine articles.

The King of Siam would place at the disposition of the French two frigates whose quality would be inspected by French carpenters. The Bishop of Metellopolis, the Chevalier Desfarges, and Mr Véret would remain in Siam as hostages until the return of the said frigates. The garrison would leave with drums beating and its arms and baggage, taking the artillery and munitions belonging to the King of France. The Siamese would supply victuals for one year against payment. The missions would retain their privileges and the Jesuits were free to remain or leave. The CIO would keep its godowns and privileges. Desfarges would return the fortress in the state in which he found it.[104]

AN INGLORIOUS DEPARTURE

The arrival at the Bangkok fort of Mme Phaulkon, who came with her son to seek the French king's protection, risked compromising everything. Sainte-Marie, the officer sent to Ayutthaya to arrange the details of the treaty, had taken pity on the lady whose fate had made her a slave and who was still persecuted by the lubricious Ok-luang Sorasak. A chivalrous man, he had helped her flee to Bangkok where she landed on 4 October. Sainte-Marie expected to be congratulated by Desfarges for this gallant gesture, but the general was furious, not wishing to irritate the Siamese. Instead of getting her discreetly on board the *Oriflamme* where she would have been in complete safety, he informed the *Phra Khlang* Kosa Pan of the arrival of the fugitive.

The episode which follows, and which Vollant des Verquains, de Bèze, and Le Blanc have related with a wealth of details, is particularly shameful for Desfarges. He did everything he could to get rid of the tiresome widow, while the officers of his general staff expressed the view that the shame of refusing to shelter her would reflect on the entire French nation. The general drew the influenceable Bishop of Metellopolis and the wretched Véret into his game, cashiered Sainte-Marie, swore at his officers, profited by the occasion to pocket a thousand *pistoles* which Phaulkon was said to owe him, and in vain tried to get the refugee to depart voluntarily.

Desfarges drew up a rather vague document which he had the *Phra Khlang* sign, which was supposed to protect Phaulkon's widow from persecution after the departure of the French. He then sent the chief of staff Beauchamp to the lady to inform her that "not having been able to obtain from the King of Siam permission to take her with him, the present conjuncture of affairs did not permit him to keep her any more, and she had to be resolved to leave at once, unless she wished to be constrained by force to do so."[105] This is how some generals of the time addressed tearful widows who sought their protection.

Mme Phaulkon left the fortress on 18 October "with a proud look on her face, which showed less fear of death than scorn of the French."[106] The Siamese placed her in a barge before the scandalized eyes of the garrison. One officer said: "They set off, and we all remained dismayed looking at each other, unable to say anything."[107] She was condemned to perpetual slavery which was to be rigorously maintained until Phra Phetracha's death in 1703. A month after this shameful expulsion, Fr Maldonado informed Fr de La Chaize: "Mme Constance, together with her mother, her aunts and her grandmother, have been thrown into the princess's kitchen."[108]

With this obstacle removed, nothing more prevented the departure of the French in Bangkok. They left the fortress on 2 November to the beating of drums and embarked on barges "in so much confusion that their departure from Siam resembled an undignified flight."[109] The three hostages who were to remain in Siam to guarantee the treaty accompanied the garrison as far as the bar where the reprovisioned *Oriflamme* was waiting, together with the two frigates promised by the Siamese, the *Siam* and the *Louvo*. When they arrived at the ships, Véret and the younger Desfarges son gaily went on board the *Oriflamme*, without the general lifting his little finger to stop them.

Fathers de Bèze and Le Blanc, safely on board the *Oriflamme*, accused Mgr Laneau of intending to flee as well in spite of his sworn oath. But the Siamese, furious at this perfidy, threw themselves on the frail bishop "who could not put a pistol in his hand like the others."[110] He was going to be made to pay for the treachery of the rest. The treatment inflicted on the prelate by the furious Siamese suggests that they too were convinced he intended to flee.

The Siamese had profited by the confusion of the departure to retain several barges filled with provisions for the French artillery. Envoys were sent on both sides loudly complaining of the inadmissible conduct of the other side. The Siamese finished by releasing a few barges, keeping some, and Desfarges returned two of the five hostages he was retaining. Vollant des Verquains concludes: "In this way disagreement was renewed at the moment of their separation."[111] It must be pointed out that the fine tale of Franco-Siamese relations closed with a complete break, and both sides considered themselves wronged. The Siamese were furious at the bad faith of the French, and the French complained of the perfidy of these idolatrous infidels. A study of the documents suggests that both were right.

The *Oriflamme*, the *Siam*, and the *Louvo* set sail on 13 November. "We distanced ourselves from a land in which so many fortunes had been reversed in one year, at the beginning of which we were at the peak of glorious prosperity, which was then nullified by the most humiliating disgrace. The future will have difficulty in believing this when it contemplates this event."[112] This was the conclusion of the honest Jean Vollant des Verquains.

THE BISHOP IN THE "FIVE PRISONS"

Whilst the French garrison from Bangkok, most of the Jesuits, and a few apostolic missionaries (including the Abbé de Lionne) were sailing towards Pondichéry, the Siamese vented their anger on the French who remained in Siam, principally on the Bishop of Metellopolis and Fr de La Breuille, the only French Jesuit who had chosen not to leave.

Mgr Laneau was chiefly to pity. Hardly had he left his barge than the furious Siamese threw themselves on him, seizing his pectoral cross, his clothes, and a supposed relic of the true cross he wore around his neck. A heavy blow on the head with a stick almost left him for dead on the spot. A rope was put around his neck, his hands were tied, and he was thrown to the ground and dragged through the mud. His attackers left him two hours in the bushes where he was eaten alive by mosquitoes, whilst the "five prisons" were being prepared for him; these were heavy cangues and wooden shackles for the neck, hands, and feet. The mob meanwhile kicked, spat on, and heaped insults on the unfortunate man. Some pulled out the hairs of his beard. He was finally placed in the "five prisons" which caused him to utter terrible cries of pain. Taken in this device to Ayutthaya, he was tied down at a street corner and subjected to the insults of passers-by under a burning sun. A charitable soul built a small thatched bamboo hut for him. The bishop trembled with fever and suffered terribly from the blows he had received, from the "prisons," and from diarrhoea which exhausted him.

He remained three months in this condition, guarded by "painted arms." Fr Paumard, the only one of the priests allowed to move around because he was a doctor, brought him rice, fish, and bananas, and cared for him as best he could.[113]

The poor prelate had ample occasion to meditate on the passion of Christ, and apply this phrase which begins many of his letters: "May Jesus Christ be the sole object of our thoughts." Still imprisoned a year later but taken out of the "five prisons," he wrote to the directors of the MEP: "It is God who, by his infinite love, had chased us from our house, removed all that we had, placed us in prison and made us suffer things which, howsoever clever one might be, one could not conceive in Europe . . ."[114]

The affronts inflicted on the other priests and Frenchmen were hardly less terrible. Imprisoned with thieves and murderers, weighed down by the "five prisons," chained up, mistreated, led by a rope through the streets, employed in the hardest corvée work, they only survived by the charity which Paumard brought them. Fr Maldonado, considered to be Portuguese, was not disturbed in his house in the

Portuguese camp. The seminary of the Foreign Missions was pillaged and abandoned to Chinese who used it as a shop. The church was converted into a temple, replete with Buddha statues and monks. The goods of the French godown were removed into the king's repository, and the buildings given to the Moors.

Fr Maldonado informed Rome that the recently converted Peguans and Siamese almost all apostatized,[115] but Fr Le Blanc praises the Christian mothers "who were sufficiently generous" to disfigure their daughters with strips of burning iron rather than hand them over to the "infidels."[116] The seminarians and many Christians were molested and imprisoned. Fr Pocquet of the MEP, who continued to teach his Cochin-Chinese and Tonkinese seminarians in prison, was subjected every night to particularly humiliating treatment, according to Robert Challe.[117]

A *Catalogue of ecclesiastical and lay prisoners* kept in the archives of the MEP cites the names of ten priests and of Fr de La Breuille, fourteen officers and soldiers, six agents of the CIO, and fourteen other Frenchmen. Among the latter were three captains of Siamese vessels, three mounters of mirrors who had come to install those ordered from France, Mr de Billy, who was Chaumont's maître d'hôtel before being promoted to governor of Joncelang (Phuket), a certain Lapie, "carpenter to the Jesuits," and finally "the young Delaunay, musician."[118]

Here then were the missionaries, the military men, the commercial agents, and artisans sent by Louis XIV in chains and decried. All that had been achieved since 1662 was destroyed in a few weeks twenty-six years later.

Unaware of the consequences of their precipitous departure, the *Oriflamme* and the two Siamese frigates sailed towards the tip of the Malay peninsula. On 24 December, the ships dropped anchor in the roadstead of Malacca, where the Dutch did not allow the Jesuits to land. One of their number, Saint-Martin, died at the beginning of the journey. They set sail on 6 January 1689 to arrive without incident on the Coromandel Coast before Pondichéry at the beginning of February. There the passengers of the three vessels were pleased to find du Bruant and the survivors of the garrison at Mergui, who had arrived a fortnight earlier.

"IN THIS WAY THE FRENCH WITHDREW FROM MERGUI"

Mr du Bruant had set off mid-February 1688 with a detachment of one hundred in three companies, to take possession of the stronghold of Mergui and the island of Pulao Tavoy, ceded to the CIO. They took barges as far at Phetchaburi, and crossed the isthmus on foot, followed by carts taking baggage and munitions. They had only praise for the Siamese during this long six-week march. On arriving at Mergui, the governor of the province of Tenasserim handed over the small star-shaped fort which protected the port.

The governor supplied materials and three thousand *phrai luang*, men subject to the corvée, and they began without delay to make the place "safe from any insult," as the phrase of the time goes. But after one month the *phrai luang* abandoned the worksite by hundreds, and the governor's zeal visibly evaporated. Du Bruant sent an officer carrying a letter of complaint to Phaulkon, but he was intercepted and forced to retrace his steps. The arrival after that of Desfarges's bizarrely compiled letter, ordering him to go to Lopburi with his men to attack the Lao, gave the commander to understand that something strange was occurring at court. The news of the coup d'état only arrived in driblets, but du Bruant finished by understanding why the willingness of the governor had changed to malevolence, and then to open hostility.

The attitude of the Siamese became such that du Bruant took the decision to abandon the incomplete fort where drinking water was almost completely lacking since a newly constructed well had fallen in. A small boat belonging to an Englishman from Madras had anchored in the port, as well as the *Mergui*, a frigate of the King of Siam carrying twenty-four cannons. Du Bruant succeeded in discreetly arming and rigging them, and then had them anchor below the fort so as to permit a rapid evacuation in case of necessity.

At the beginning of June, large numbers of armed Siamese began to concentrate around Mergui, and the supply of victuals to the garrison stopped completely. The stronghold was invested a few days later, and several Frenchmen were killed or made prisoner. One morning the besieged saw a troop of armed Siamese assemble in a temple on a hill near the fort. "Talapoins gave them characters which they thought would make them invulnerable, and opium which makes them bold. They all left the pagoda with barbaric cries and came to line up for the attack."[119] But these Siamese were not Makassars and the French cannons dispersed them without difficulty. They then decided to reduce the stronghold by famine. There were still enough provisions to last some time, but water had to be fetched with sword in hand, which made the situation untenable.

On 24 June, the garrison left its retrenchments without thinking of spiking the cannons. The soldiers, weighed down with arms, munitions, and victuals, tried to go down to the two ships anchored below the fort in good order, but the slope was so steep that they slipped and stumbled on top of each other. The confusion was soon total, in spite of the efforts of the commander and his officers to regroup their men. The Siamese inspired fear by shouting their usual "barbaric" cries, and attacked them with spears and sabres. The French only thought of getting on board in safety, tumbling over each other and abandoning some of their baggage.

The embarkation was so disordered that a longboat sank to the bottom and several officers and soldiers drowned. The Siamese trained the fort's battery on the vessels and killed another dozen men. Du Bruant had the cables of the *Mergui* cut, and the English ship followed his example. The Siamese followed them in rowing boats but dared not approach them. Twenty French died in the embarkation. Le Blanc concludes: "In this way the French withdrew from Mergui, badly equipped, with few victuals, just one anchor, and sorry local sails, at an unfavourable time of the year, taking with them only the consolation . . . of having done their duty in their defence."[120]

A substantial chapter would be needed to relate their wanderings, from their departure from Mergui to their arrival at Pondichéry six months later. Chased by pirates, opposed by the winds, unable to manoeuvre properly for want of sails and anchors (a cannon tied to rope was used), lacking victuals, wood, and water, their voyage among the uninhabited islands off the Burmese coast was a nightmare. They dropped anchor in August before Martaban in the kingdom of Pegu, desperately in need of provisions. Mr de Beauregard, the Jesuit d'Espagnac, and four soldiers went up the Salween River in a longboat. They were arrested by the Peguans as soon as they landed, and the *Mergui* had to abandon them to their fate.

Fr d'Espagnac was reduced to slavery like the rest. Tachard, writing in 1700, said:

> After a thousand cruel torments which he endured in the kingdom of

> Pegu, he was sent to Ava, capital of a kingdom of the same name far inland. Although he was a slave, he had begun to convert a few Christians, when the idolaters accused him before the magistrates of conspiring against the state and training supporters. On this accusation, he was shamefully chased from the town and all nearby habitations. Thus he was obliged to retreat to the forests, exposed to hunger, thirst, snakes and tigers. It was never known for sure in what way he had ended his life after so much suffering.[121]

In the meantime, Fr Duchatz had tried in vain to locate him to buy his freedom.[122] Poor man.

At the end of September, the accidental encounter with *Notre Dame de Lorette*, a CIO vessel, saved the floating Mergui garrison from starvation. Du Bruant set sail again and dropped anchor on the northwest coast of Burma in the kingdom of Arakan. A local Phaulkon, a French minister of the kingdom, supplied them all the victuals they asked for and refused payment, saying he had been sufficiently compensated by the honour he had in serving King Louis. The voyage continued across the Gulf of Bengal to Balassor, where the English seized the Siamese frigate on the pretext that it belonged to a king who was at war with them.

Du Bruant protested in vain; he was put with his men on board an English vessel which took them to Madras, from where they reached Pondichéry. On 15 January 1689, François Martin welcomed the thirty or so who survived Mergui at the French outpost. The *Siam* and the *Louvo* anchored before Pondichéry on 1 February, and the *Oriflamme* on the fourth. The remnants of the French military expedition to Siam were finally reunited, but in a piteous condition. Of 800 troops sent to Siam with the Vaudricourt squadron, and on the *Oriflamme*, only 350 survived.

THE END OF A MILITARY ADVENTURE

There could be no question of leaving so many armed men in Pondichéry. The godown could not feed them, and the local kinglets would have objected. On 6 February, Desfarges summoned a council of war which included Martin and Véret, and Mr d'Estrille, captain of the *Oriflamme*. They had three possibilities: returning to Europe; retaking Mergui; or occupying the Siamese island of Joncelang, also called Junk Ceylon (modern Phuket). François Martin, who resumes the discussion in his *Mémoires*, spoke in favour of Mergui, but was opposed by Véret who favoured Joncelang, the centre of the tin trade. Desfarges, who had no desire to return to France without some armed exploit which would restore his fortunes somewhat, followed Véret. "In the end," Martin sighs, "everyone was for the island of Joncelang, one had to swim with the stream."[123] He assembled rice, vegetables, and salted buffalo meat.

The expedition left on 10 April on the *Oriflamme*, the *Siam*, and the *Louvo*, arriving three months later before Phuket on the west coast of Siam, only to find flooded terrain which was barely inhabited. Not knowing what to do, they fished and hunted, and Desfarges sent back one of the three Siamese hostages with a letter to Ayutthaya, proposing a settlement: the freeing of French prisoners and the restoration of the trading activities of the CIO. He received a reply after a long delay that he first of all had to send back the other two Siamese hostages, and the prisoners would then be released. Desfarges gave in; the two hostages arrived in Ayutthaya at the beginning of December, after which the treatment of the imprisoned Frenchmen in Ayutthaya was somewhat relaxed. Seeing that he was wasting his time in Phuket, Desfarges returned at the beginning of 1690 to Pondichéry, where he found his letters of recall to France.

A year earlier, on 16 February 1689, two frigates of the CIO, the *Normande* and the *Coche*, had left Pondichéry to take to France the news and details of the revolution in Siam. Among the passengers were our leading witnesses: Jean Vollant des Verquains, and Fr Marcel Le Blanc. A dispute between the two captains separated the frigates at the beginning of April. Mr de Courcelles, in command of the *Normande*, had sent a longboat to Mr d'Armagnan, captain of the *Coche*, to ask him to lend him Fr Le Blanc in the afternoons of the Holy Week which was then beginning. His Jesuit, Fr Jean Collusson, was ill. Mr d'Armagnan loftily refused, the two crews booed each other, and Mr de Courcelles, very annoyed, changed his route contrary to the formal orders given by François Martin. Mr d'Armagnan was wrong to refuse his colleague this charitable service. Le Blanc relates in all modesty that the sailors on the *Coche* wept floods of tears on hearing the account of the passion of Christ "on these seas by the barbarous coasts of Africa."[124]

But this stupid quarrel had incomparably more serious consequences. The two frigates dropped anchor at the Cape a week apart (26 April and 4 May), unaware that the War of the League of Augsburg had broken out in Europe, and the United Provinces were at war with France. The Dutch seized without difficulty the two richly laden merchant ships which had come to put themselves in the tiger's lair. The obliging Governor van der Stel told them in consolation, in Portuguese: *"Fortuna de guerra, Senhores!"* Captain d'Armagnan of the *Coche*, the second to arrive, was killed in the Dutch attack on his ship "from a cannon shot which cut his body across the middle," as he was giving the order: "Men, open fire!"[125]

The prisoners were searched "to the innermost recesses of their clothes, and in the most private parts of their bodies," and all the possessions, papers, and letters they were carrying were confiscated. They are now in the Rijksarchief in The Hague. Generous in their way, the Dutch offered each of them a pound of tobacco to smoke. After two months in captivity at the Cape, the French were taken on four Dutch vessels to Zeeland and cast into the prisons of Middelburg. They passed the time there writing their accounts of the revolution in Siam and the sieges of Bangkok and Mergui,[126] waiting for the prisoner exchange which would return them to their country.

Fathers Le Blanc and Collusson were not the only Jesuits to fall into the hands of the Dutch. Fathers de Bèze and Comilh, who had tried to reach China from Pondichéry, were detained by the Dutch in Malacca, and sent via Batavia to Holland. They remained prisoners there until January 1691.

Desfarges, his officers, and two hundred soldiers embarked in March 1690 on the *Oriflamme* which set sail for France, escorting two company merchant vessels, the *Lonray* and the *Saint-Nicholas*. The return journey was terrible. Sickness decimated those on board and they knew they could not stop over at the Cape. The ships were obliged to reach Martinique before returning to France. Half the troops and the sailors died during the crossing or in the West Indies. Everyone is equal in the face of death, but among the important victims were Mr de l'Estrille and Desfarges. Fate was kind to the general who was disgraced in Siam; he died without having to give an account of his treason to two crowns, his abandoning Phaulkon, and the interests of the missions and the CIO.

His two sons each spent fifty thousand crowns in festivities and love affairs during the stopover of two months made by the *Oriflamme* in Martinique. When they were told "that it was ungracious of them to give themselves over to their pleasures so soon after the death of their father," the two brothers replied "that they could not rejoice more at the death of a man . . . who, for all the king's indulgence could not have been spared the rope in France, if his cowardice became known there."[127]

The Desfarges sons were bringing back to France a considerable fortune which their father had amassed in Siam, and which had been formed in part by a very large deposit entrusted to him by Phaulkon. But this fortune, no more than the two prodigal sons transporting it, could not escape fate. On 27 February 1691, the *Oriflamme* was assailed by a terrible storm off the coasts of Brittany, and was lost with all hands. This was the just end of a deplorable military enterprise, the only result of which had been the total ruin of the most ambitious colonial enterprise under Louis XIV.

EPILOGUE

THE BONFIRE OF THE VANITIES

NINETEEN MONTHS after the death of Somdet Phra Narai Maharat, on 19 February 1690, the funeral rites and cremation of his remains took place. The day had been selected by the court soothsayers after lengthy calculations. The dead sovereign whose soul was to be released attached great importance to these ceremonies. The idea that he would be denied them had plagued his final weeks. Whilst preparations for the funeral were made, the bier had been placed on a platform in a room in the palace at Ayutthaya, surrounded by incense burners, candles, and monks reciting prayers.

A great number of temporary stupas, made of heavy beams covered with bamboo and painted and gilded paper had been constructed. These pyramids were lined up symmetrically around a central stupa, some seventy metres high. Inside a large chamber had been created, and in the middle of this the funeral pyre of sandalwood had been prepared; on this the body of the late king was placed. The whole ensemble was to be consumed with purifying and liberating flames.

A member of the Foreign Missions present wrote:

> We were not a little affected to learn that, out of hatred and categoric contempt, the finest pictures of our holy religion had been placed, between images of Our crucified Lord, in order to expose them to the mockery of people of different nations who came in crowds every day to see this great structure which appeared marvellous to them. They did not fail to place there, too, for the same reasons, the portrait of our good king and those of the great nobles of his court.[1]

On 19 February 1690, a fine dream of mutual understanding went up in smoke. An oriental prince had opened his kingdom to a prestigious Western nation motivated somewhat naively by friendship and admiration, expecting in return respect and economic cooperation profitable to both countries. The search for a common language had begun, beyond radical differences, and despite a very different concept of religious tolerance and the unity or plurality of truth. Young mandarins had been sent to France to be raised there among the sons of nobles, and the Jesuits went to learn court Siamese with monks in a royal temple.

It seemed for a moment that everything was possible, and that the kingdom of Louis XIV would be capable of the breadth of mind which Phra Narai expected of him in his distant palace of Lopburi. In a *Mémoire sur les études des missions orientales* (Memorandum of the study of Oriental missions) sent to Mgr Laneau, Claude Fleury, the learned preceptor of the Duke of Burgundy, had dared to write: "All religions are good. There is an appearance of equity in not condemning anyone, and leaving to each individual the freedom of his views."[2] These propositions, affected, it is true, by the development which followed, would have gone right to the heart of Phra Narai. Much ground still had to be covered, but it seemed possible to explore it, in spite of prejudices, dogmatism, and the revocation of the Edict of Nantes.

The complex reasons for the collapse of this dream are found in the events which occurred between 1662 and 1688. Let us give the last word to Turpin, writing eighty years after the end of relations between the two countries. Comparing, in the first few pages of his *Histoire du royaume de Siam* (History of the kingdom of Siam) the fate of different European nations which had entered the Siamese maze, he came to his compatriots:

> The French, who always start well, found temporary prosperity there. But incapable of behaving themselves, they succumbed to the desire of wishing to govern, and censorious of foreign practices, were ridiculous enough to offer themselves as models. This national vice humiliated the proud Siamese, who clung stubbornly to all their customs. And the fortune of the French was as inconsistent as their character.[3]

One has to admit, two centuries after Turpin, that this judgment is not without perspicacity, and that vanity is a powerful historical agent.

But vanity does not like setbacks. The sudden silence about Siam, after the avalanche of accounts in the preceding years, is striking. The official chroniclers of the reign of Louis XIV hardly mention the revolution in Siam. Some things left unsaid tell us more than a wordy testimony. Dangeau, Sourches, and the *Mercure Galant* seem to forget, from one day to the next, the very existence of Siam and the great Siamese projects drawn up by Louis XIV. In the eight thousand pages of the *Mémoires* of Saint-Simon, who began his account in 1691, Siam is only mentioned three times, and that in passing. The great French historian Ernest Lavisse, who died in 1922, and who hardly mentions Siam in the thousand pages he devoted to the reign of Louis XIV, explains: "In France we do not like matters which do not go well right away."[4] Another war between France and the United Provinces and Great Britain, the two European powers most firmly established in Asia, definitively ruined French hopes of having, like them, a lasting Asian policy and interests.

But the catastrophe of 1688 did not cause the complete disappearance of Siam from the conscience of Louis XIV and his subjects absorbed in yet another European war. The King of Siam and his favourite might be trapped by history, and the great favour enjoyed by the missionaries and French merchants might have degenerated into cruel persecution or shameful expulsion, but there was still, as if nothing had happened, the incredible Fr Tachard with his inexhaustible wheezes. Not in the least disconcerted by events, and never ceasing to run around and scheme, this Jesuit prevents us from drawing the curtain on a colourful exotic drama which ended badly.

AND FR TACHARD?

In November 1689 in Saumur, the Jesuit had learnt the news of the revolution in Siam which filtered out of the prison of Middelburg. He informed his mandarins who followed him everywhere, and whom he had meanwhile baptized in the chapel of the Jesuit college in Brest. According to a letter he wrote on 24 November from Brest,[5] Ok-khun Phiphit, Ok-khun Chamnan, and Ok-khun Wiset were not in the least worried. One of them had a sister married to Phra

Phetracha's nephew, and another sang the praises of Ok-luang Sorasak, the heir to the throne, as "having much intelligence, vivacity, and courage, liking mathematics and esteeming the Jesuits." To read the good Father, everything was going along fine. He shed a few crocodile tears for Phra Narai and "that poor Mr Constance," considering the revolution as an "unfortunate contingency," and insinuated that "some Frenchmen could, because of their poor conduct and some misunderstandings, have given occasion to the [new] King of Siam to attack them and chase them from his realm."

Having decided to re-establish good relations with Siam, he cajoled his mandarins, said he was consoled to learn that the *khunnang* and the people of Siam had submitted to "a wise ruler full of good intentions for his subjects," and only sought to serve the new king, "knowing that nothing is possible except with God's will, who especially presides over the raising of monarchs to the throne." Desfarges should have offered his services and those of his men to the new king without hesitation. Finally, those responsible for the troubles could only be the gentlemen at the Foreign Missions, whose "jealousy, resentment and other passions equally unworthy of men devoted to God" he stigmatized, and who "preferred that everyone should die rather than cede their authority."[6] He almost goes as far as to say these gentlemen had sought the misfortunes which overcame them.

Without any official title, he embarked on the *Gaillard*, the flagship of the Duquesne-Guiton squadron, for his third journey to the Indies at the beginning of March 1690. This voyage is well known thanks to the superb *Journal d'un voyage fait aux Indes orientales* (Journal of a voyage to the East Indies) by Robert Challe.[7] Challe does not disguise the antipathy he felt for the self-important airs of the Jesuit who always wanted to be in first place. The same reaction is found in the account of another member of the expedition, the marine guardsman Pouchot de Chantassin.[8] There also exists a little-known manuscript with the title *Relation du voyage aux Indes (1690–1699)* (Account of a journey to the Indies, 1690–1699) which is in fact the journal of the third and fourth voyages to the East Indies of Fr Tachard.[9] Another book would be needed to relate these two voyages. We shall content ourselves with summarizing here the Siamese schemes of this Father who had still not understood that a missionary is supposed to convert the heathen, not undertake diplomatic initiatives which no one had entrusted to him.

At the beginning of the voyage, Guy Tachard had the misfortune to lose Ok-khun Phiphit, who was cast to the waves with honours which shocked Challe. "Six gunshots for a mandarin! What would they do for a general? Two would have been enough, and it is thought that the presence of Fr Tachard accounted for the other four."[10] The two surviving *khunnang* were still more coddled by Tachard, because he hoped to obtain through them an invitation to the court of Siam. Ok-khun Chamnan and Ok-khun Wiset embarked at Balassor for Mergui in November 1690, carrying a grovelling letter to the *Phra Khlang* Kosa Pan, in which the Father notably wrote: "I shall wait either here, or in Pondichéry, for the king's orders and your reply to return at once." Having received no reply, he sent from Pondichéry another letter addressed to the same person in July 1691: "I shall only say that I am waiting here for the orders of the King of Siam to travel to his kingdom."[11]

But the *Phra Khlang* remained silent, and Tachard bit his nails in Pondichéry. He passed the time, not in preaching to the idolatrous Hindus about the crucified Christ, but in setting up vast commercial schemes. In January 1691 François Martin confided to Robert Challe that Tachard owed close to a half a million livres to the CIO without any guarantee on his part. Two years later, the Jesuit profited by the news of the freeing of the Frenchmen imprisoned in Siam to send a letter to Ok-ya Phiphit, Kosa Pan's deputy: "I think day and night of the means of reuniting the hearts of the two great kings, and reestablishing friendship between the two nations, which would bring so many advantages to them . . . Your singular prudence will enable me to procure the means for my rapid return to Siam, and to make my presence useful for starting a dialogue . . . Please grant me the honour of a reply."[12]

This letter was taken to Ayutthaya by the interpreter Vicente Pinheiro, titled Ok-luang Worowathi. The Father had given him instructions insisting on an official invitation from the King of Siam "to show to the king and his ministers in France (who have perhaps not the same viewpoints as me, who will no doubt blame me after the orders they have given me) that I have not rashly committed myself." [13] This proves that Tachard was essentially acting according to his own ends, and had been forbidden by Versailles to meddle further in Siamese affairs.

But fate opposed him. The Dutch seized Pondichéry in September 1693, at the very moment the Siamese court seemed ready to tolerate his presence. All the French at Pondichéry were sent off to Europe, via Batavia and Ceylon. Tachard thus had occasion to see once more the capital of the Dutch Indies, where he was placed at the end of December on the returning fleet. On arrival in Holland, in July 1684, he was allowed to leave for Dunkirk.

Tachard is very discreet about his frequentations in France during the six months preceding his fourth voyage to the Indies, but he seems to have succeeded in convincing Louis XIV to use him in an effort to become reconciled with Siam. He embarked on 27 March 1695 on a squadron of six vessels sent by the king and the CIO to the Indies. On 16 January 1696, the squadron entered the roadstead of Surat, from where the Father travelled to Bengal. He met there, he says, a mandarin who assured him he would be welcome in Siam. In October 1696, he sent another letter to the *Phra Khlang*: "The enemies of the two kingdoms have thwarted my plans. However, the refusal to receive me, far from rebuffing me, only further served to inflame my zeal and my affection for the great King of Siam."[14] This letter says nothing at all about the missionaries, but is concerned with the re-establishment of the CIO in Siam.

This time, Tachard was invited by Phra Phetracha to come to Ayutthaya as the envoy of Louis XIV. He went via Chandernagor where the captain of a French ship is said to have given him a letter from Louis XIV to the King of Siam, but this was a ten-year-old letter which the king had written to Phra Narai in 1687.[15] So what! Preceded by a flood of letters to the gentlemen at the Foreign Missions who were asked to give all honours to the royal letter, and accompanied by Fr de La Breuille, he went on board the *Castricum*, a French ship, to Mergui and thence to Ayutthaya. He tells us that an elephant carried the royal letter and he was very well received everywhere. The *Phra Khlang* seems to have done everything to make the audience in January 1699 as indifferent as possible, perhaps because the envoy brought no presents and the royal letter contained nothing but impersonal compliments.

Fr Tachard spent three weeks in Ayutthaya. He no longer recognized the Siamese capital, where the missionaries had regained possession of their seminary and church in April 1691, and where Mgr Laneau had died in March 1696. "I found the city of Siam much changed: it had become a desert. There were no merchants, and no trading; the Christians, the Moors and other foreigners have almost all gone. The seminary of the gentlemen of the Foreign Missions is open again, and the church complete."[16] He went to see Mme Phaulkon, still a slave, who related her woes and those of her family. The Father held back a few tears, slipped her some money, and left for Mergui.

He carried a letter of Phra Petratcha to Louis XIV, dated 28 January 1699, which was a mass of empty compliments and stereotyped praise, but said nothing about past, present, or future relations between the two crowns.[17] France was no longer interested in Siam, and Siam, which had moved closer to the Dutch, expected nothing of France. The only French still present in Siam were the gentlemen of the Foreign Missions who were slowly recovering from the persecution which had severely affected them.

On 14 September 1699 at Pondichéry, Guy Tachard embarked on the *Zélande* for France, where he arrived at the end of May 1700. He appeared at Versailles on 12 June in the evening. Dangeau, who usually noted the least trifle, does not mention him, and Sourches only grants him a few distracted words, as if he were speaking of a ghost.[18] He was right. Franco-Siamese relations, and the grand designs of the court of Versailles on Siam, henceforth belonged to history. Fr Tachard handed over his letter, engraved on a sheet of gold but insignificant, and returned for the fifth time to Asia. It is to be hoped that this time it was above all to carry the Gospels to the heathen. He died in Chandernagor in Bengal in October 1712.

THE END OF KOSA PAN

No one better embodied the dream of the impossible unity of France and Siam than Kosa Pan, foster brother of Phra Narai and *Phra Khlang* to Phra Petratcha. *Ratchathut* or first ambassador to France in 1686, he had charmed the court and the town with his witty compliments and his sincere admiration for the France of Louis XIV. Readers of the *Mercure Galant* had read and reread his least remarks with delight. With a man like Kosa Pan, one had the feeling that the Franco-Siamese edifice was built on solid rock.

But he could not accept the occupation of Bangkok and Mergui, the two key Siamese strongholds, by a French expeditionary force. Silently disapproving Phra Narai's over-confident policy concerning France, he came closer to the nationalist faction which formed around Ok-phra Phetracha, his half-brother according to the *Phongsawadan*.

It was therefore normal that the new king granted the *Khlang* department to him, and that Kosa Pan loyally served him. The bad faith of Desfarges and Véret at the moment of the negotiated departure of the garrison from Bangkok, seems to have profoundly shocked him.

As soon as he made sure of his power and the French were expelled or imprisoned, Phra Phetracha, like many other usurpers, instituted a reign of terror. Kosa Pan had to endure his cruelties like everyone else. He died in 1700 soon after the atrocious execution of forty-eight *khunnang*, fed for twelve days with their own flesh before being impaled and disembowelled. We owe Mr Bruant of the Foreign Missions the account of his death, dated August 1700.

> He died two months ago, from whiplashes as much as from distress at being continually mistreated. For since royal anger cut off the end of his nose with a blow of a sabre, four years previously, he only suffered persecution on the part of the court for which he was, one believes, somewhat suspect. An older daughter of his, and two or three sons, with his wives and concubines, were all arrested and tortured. His effects were seized two or three days before his death, and rumour at the court had it that out of despair, to end things, he plunged a knife into his chest . . . The body of the Barcalon was taken at night to a pagoda to be interred without ceremony, and deprived of the honour of their ordinary rites, which is to burn the body . . . on a magnificent pyre. This was the sad end of the famous ambassador to France, and chief minister of the great King of Siam now reigning.[19]

Such was the end of Kosa Pan, torn between the French model which had clearly attracted and then abused him, and the harsh Siamese model which finished by crushing him. Some think him the ancestor of the Chakri dynasty which has reigned for more than two centuries in Siam now styled Thailand.

He was the victim of an impossible mirage, and deserves a furtive tear.

NOTES

PREFACE

1. Etienne Gallois, *L'ambassade de Siam au XVIe siècle* (Paris: E. Panckoucke, 1862). Lucien Lanier, *Etude historique sur les relations de la France et du royaume de Siam de 1662 a 1702* (Versailles: E. Aubert,1883).

2. Claude de Bèze, *Memoire sur la vie de Constance Phaulkon, premier ministre du roi de Siam Phra Narai, et sa triste fin,* ed. Jean Drans and Henri Bernard (Tokyo: Presses salésiennes, 1947); English translation by E. W. Hutchinson, *1688: Revolution in Siam* (Hong Kong: Hong Kong University Press, 1968). Joachim Bouvet, *Voyage de Siam,* ed. J. C. Gatty (Leiden: E. J. Brill, 1963).

3. Simon de La Loubère, *Du royaume de Siam,* ed. Michel Jacq-Hergoualc'h (Paris: Editions Recherche sur les Civilisations, 1987); *A New Historical Relation of the Kingdom of Siam* (London, 1693; Singapore: Oxford University Press, 1969; Bangkok: White Lotus, 1986).

4. Claude de Forbin, *Le voyage du comte de Forbin au Siam* (Cadeilhan: Zulma, 1991); The Siamese Memoirs of Count Claude de Forbin, ed. Michael Smithies (Chiang Mai: Silkworm Books, 1996).

5. Michel Jacq-Hergoualc'h, *Etude historique et critique du Journal du voyage de Siam de Claude Céberet, envoyé extraordinaire du Roi en 1687 et 1688* (Paris: L'Harmattan, 1992).

6. Abbé de Choisy, *Journal of a Voyage to Siam 1685–1686,* ed. Michael Smithies (Kuala Lumpur: Oxford University Press, 1993); François-Timoléon de Choisy, *Journal du Voyage de Siam,* ed. Dirk Van der Cruysse (Paris: Fayard, 1995).

7. Chevalier de Chaumont and the Abbé de Choisy, *Aspects of the Embassy to Siam 1685,* ed. Michael Smithies (Chiang Mai: Silkworm Books, 1997).

8. Michael Smithies, *A Resounding Failure: Martin and the French in Siam 1672–1693* (Chiang Mai: Silkworm Books, 1998).

9. Michael Smithies, ed., *The Discourses at Versailles of the First Siamese Ambassadors to France* (Bangkok: Siam Society, 1986).

10. George A. Sioris, *Phaulkon, the Greek First Counsellor at the Court of Siam, an Appraisal* (Bangkok: Siam Society, 1998).

11. La Touche, "Relation de ce qui est arrivé dans le Royaume de Siam en 1688," in Robert Challe, *Journal du Voyage des Indes Orientales,* ed. J. Popin and F. Deloffre (Geneva: Droz, 1998).

12. Michael Smithies, ed., *Three Military Accounts of Events in Siam in 1688: Desfarges, de La Touche, and Vollant des Verquain,* in press.

13. La Loubère, *Kingdom of Siam* (1693), 36; (1987), 207.

14. Georges Coedès, "Siamese Documents of the Seventeenth Century," *Journal of the Siam Society* 14/2 (1921), 7–39.

15. La Loubère, *Kingdom of Siam* (1693) 8; (1987), 137.

16. Muhammad Ibrahim Muhammad Rabi, Ibn, *The Ship of Sulaiman,* trans. John O'Kane (London: Routledge & Kegan Paul, 1972).

17. Jules Michelet, *Histoire de France,* vol. 10.

CHAPTER 1: PORTUGAL'S GOLDEN AGE AND SIAM (1510–1580)

1. Gianfrancesco Poggio Bracciolini, *De Varietate Fortunae libri quatuor* (1447) (Paris: Oliva, 1723). The voyage of Nicolo di Conti is summarized in the *Primo Volume delle Navigationi e Viaggi* of Giambattista Ramusio (Venice, 1550), ff. 364–371.

2. The Latin account of the voyage of Brother William and his companions to the centre of the Tartar empire was translated by William Woodville Rockhill *(The Journey of William of Rubruck to the Eastern Parts of the World)* and published by the Hakluyt Society, 1900.

3. Jaime Cortesão, *História dos descobrimentos portugueses,* new ed., 3 vols., (1979); Charles R. Boxer, *The Portuguese Seaborne Empire* (London: Hutchinson, 1969).

4. The Portuguese cartographic and nautical effort is related in R. Hooykaas, *Humanism and the Voyages of Discovery in 16th century Portuguese Science and Letters* (1979); and Luis de Albuquerque, *Ciência e experiência nos descobrimentos portugueses* (Lisbon: Instituto de Cultura portuguesa, 1983).

5. See Jean Guennou, *Missions étrangères de Paris* (Paris: Fayard, 1986), 13–14.

6. Cortesão, *História,* vol. 3, 47.

7. See Rong Syamananda, *A History of Thailand* (Bangkok: Thai Watana Panich, 1988), 42–43.

8. J. de Barros, *Década terceira da Ásia,* bk. 2, vol. 5, 160. See the commentary of Sir John Bowring, *The Kingdom and People of Siam* (London: John W. Parker, 1857), vol. 2, 60–61.

9. *"Vêm samear de Christo a ley,/ E dar novo costume, e novo Rei." Os Lusíadas,* 7:15.

10. Cited by Joaquim Veríssimo Serrão, *História de Portugal,* vol. 3, (Lisbon: Editorial Verbo, 1980), 154.

11. André-Marie Meynard, *Missions dominicaines dans l'Extrême-Orient,* 2 vols., 1865; Benno Biermann, "Die Missionen der portugiesischen Dominikaner in Hinterindien," in *Zeitschrift für Missionswissenschaften* 21 (1931), 305–327.

12. Leon Lemmens O.F.M., *Geschichte der Franziskanermissionen* (Munster, 1929), 109.

13. Meynard, *Missions dominicaines,* vol. 1, 120–121. See also Biermann, "Die Missionen der portugiesischen Dominikaner in Hinterindien," 322–323.

14. Henri Chappoulie, *Aux origines d'une Eglise, Rome et les missions d'Indochine au XVIIe siècle,* vol. 1 (Paris: Bloud & Gay, 1943), 136.

15. Meynard, *Missions dominicaines,* vol. 1, 121–122.

16. Quoted by Joaquim de Campos, "Early Portuguese Accounts of Thailand," in *Journal of the Siam Society* 32/1 (1940), 17. Campos defends Mendes Pinto with specific and convincing arguments.

17. On the origin and possible meaning of the old name Sornau, Xarnauz, Shahr-i-nao, or Suvarna, see the article by Joaquim de Campos, "Early Portuguese Accounts of Thailand," 13–15.

18. *The Travels of Mendes Pinto,* ed. and trans. Rebecca Catz (Chicago and London: Chicago University Press, 1989), 420.

19. F. Mendes Pinto, *Peregrinação,* ch. 189; Catz, op. cit., idem.

20. See Rebecca Catz, *Fernão Mendes Pinto—Sátira e anticruzada na "Peregrinação"* (1981). The general works of Georges Le Gentil, *Fernão Mendes Pinto. Un précurseur de l'exotisme au XVIe siècle* (1947); and Maurice Collis, *The Great Peregrination, being the Life and Adventures of Fernão Mendes Pinto* (London: Faber & Faber, 1949, 1990) are also relevant.

21. Letter of 5 December 1554 to the Fathers of the Company of Jesus in Portugal, in Maria Teresa Vale, ed., *Fernão Mendes Pinto. O outro lado do mito* (Lisbon: Terra livre, 1985), 148–149.

CHAPTER 2: NORTHERN EUROPE DISCOVERS SIAM (1580–1600)

1. Jaime Cortesão, *L'Expansion des Portugais dans l'histoire de la civilisation* (1930, 1983), 59–60. The quote is condensed.

2. J. Mocquet, *Voyage à Mozambique et Goa (1607–1610)* (Paris: Chandeigne, 1996).

3. *Aziatische Omzwervingen. Het leven van Jaques de Coutre, een Brugs diamanthandelaar, 1591–1627,* ed. Johan Verberckmoes and Eddy Stols (Berchem-Antwerp: EPO, 1988). Stols's introduction admirably summarizes the relationship between Portugal and the Low Countries in the sixteenth century. The new Spanish edition of Jacques de Coutre, *Andanzas Asiáticas,* edited by Eddy Stols, B. Teensma, and J. Verberckmoes, was published as Historia 16 in the series Crónicas de America 61 (Madrid: Información y Revistas, 1990).

4. On the reign of Phra Naresuan, see R. Syamananda, *A History of Thailand,* 53–61, and David K. Wyatt, *Thailand: A Short History* (New Haven/London: Yale University Press, 1984), 100–105.

5. Jacques de Coutre, bk. 1, chs. 7–14 (Dutch ed., 63–90; Spanish ed., 106–142).

6. See B. P. Groslier, *Angkor et le Cambodge au XVIe siècle d'après les sources portugaises et espagnoles* (Paris, 1958), 27–62; D. G. E. Hall, *A History of South-East Asia,* 4th ed. (London: Macmillan, 1987), 146–149, 279–281.

7. Jeremias Van Vliet, *Beschryving van het Koningryk Siam* (Leiden, Fr. Haaring, 1692), 100.

8. Nicolas Gervaise, *Histoire naturelle et politique du royaume de Siam,* vol. 1 (Paris: C. Barbin, 1688), ch. 10.

9. Simon de La Loubère, *Du royaume de Siam,* vol. 1 (Paris: Coignard, 1691), 172; vol. 2 (1693), ch. 6, 45.

10. See Jean Boisselier, *La Sculpture en Thaïlande* (Fribourg: Office du Livre, 1974), 177–178.

11. Wat Chai Mongkhon is also called Wat Chedi Chao Phya Thai. See the reproduction of the chedi of Phra Naresuan in Louis Frédéric, *Sud-est asiatique. Ses temples, ses sculptures* (Paris: Arts et Métiers graphiques, 1964), illus. 406.

12. See the examples in Frédéric, ibid., illus. 292, and Madelaine Giteau, *Angkor. Un peuple - Un Art* (Paris: Bibliothèque des Arts, 1976), illus. 38.

13. Scc D. G. E. Hall, *A History of South-East Asia,* 149.

14. J. Mocquet, *Voyage à Mozambique,* 128–129.

CHAPTER 3: THE DUTCH SET UP SHOP IN SIAM (1601–1608)

1. Guillaume-Thomas Raynal, *Histoire philosophique et politique des établissements et du commerce des Européens dans les deux Indes,* vol. 1 (Geneva: Jean Léonard Pellet, 1780), 151.

2. Cited by Charles R. Boxer at the beginning of chapter 5 in his work, *The Portuguese Seaborne Empire* (1969).

3. See the new edition of the original Latin text with a Portuguese translation, and historic and juridical introduction by Marcello Caetano, *Frei Serafim de Freitas, Do justo império asiático dos Portugueses,* 2 vols. (Lisbon: Instituto Nacional de Investigação Científica, 1983).

4. Cited by Charles R. Boxer, *The Portuguese Seaborne Empire,* 129–130.

5. Van Noort's *Beschryvinghe vande voyagie om den geheelen wereldcloot* was published in vols. 27 and 28 of the Linschoten Vereniging in 1926.

6. See in particular Alfredo Botelho da Sousa, *Subsídios para a história militar marítima da ändia,* 1585–1650, vol. 1 (Lisbon, 1930), 485 et seq.

7. See Marcello Caetano's introduction to the new edition of Freitas, *Do justo império asiático dos Portugueses,* vol. 1, 22.

8. See Boxer, *The Portuguese Seaborne Empire,* 417.

9. *Relação anual das coisas que fizeram os padres da Companhia de Jesus nas suas missões,* cited by M. Caetano in Freitas, *Do justos império asiático dos Portugueses,* vol. 1, 7.

10. The historical circumstances and legal consequences of the Santa

Catarina affair and the intervention of Grotius are developed in the important introduction written by Robert Fruin for the first complete edition of *De Iure Praedae Commentarius* (Amsterdam, 1868).

11. Matthew 11:12 King James Version.

12. Raynal, *Histoire philosophique et politique,* vol. 1, 191.

13. François-Henri Turpin, *Histoire civile et naturelle du royaume de Siam, et des révolutions qui ont bouleversé cet Empire jusqu'en 1770,* vol. 1 (Paris: Costard, 1771), 9–11.

14. On Siamese-Dutch relations in the seventeenth century, the unsigned article by J. A. Van der Chys, "Overzicht der betrekkingen van de Nederlandse Oost-Indische Compagnie met Siam" in *Tijdschrift voor Indische taal-, land- en volken-kunde,* 12 (1864): 416–456, is most important, as is the article by W. Blankwaardt, "Notes upon the Relations between Holland and Siam" in *Journal of the Siam Society* 20 (1926–27): 241–258. Two monographs are devoted to this subject: George Vinal Smith, *The Dutch in Seventeenth Century Thailand* (Dekalb: Northern Illinois University Press, 1977) and Han ten Brummelhuis, *Merchant, Courtier and Diplomat. A History of the Contacts between the Netherlands and Thailand* (Lochem: De Tijdstroom, 1987).

15. Two brief articles about this embassy were published in the same issue of *T'oung Pao*: Paul Pelliot, "Les relations du Siam et de la Hollande en 1608," and J. J. L. Duyvendak, "The First Siamese Embassy to Holland," *T'oung Pao* 32 (1936): 223–229; 285–292.

16. Cited by Pelliot, "Les relations," 227–228.

17. Cited by Pelliot, "Les relations," 223–226.

18. Cited by Duyvendak, "The first Siamese Embassy to Holland," 289.

19. This document, and that before it, are cited in English and Dutch in the article by Duyvendak, "The First Siamese Embassy to Holland."

CHAPTER 4: THE DUTCH AND ENGLISH GODOWNS IN AYUTTHAYA (1609–1664)

1. Cornelis van Neijenrode's *Vertoog* was only published in 1871 in the *Kroniek van het Historisch Genootschap gevestigd te Utrecht,* vol. 27, 279–318.

2. The details of the complicated struggle by which Prasat Thong gained the throne are found in the important thesis by Dhiravat na Pombejra, "A Political History of Siam under the Prasatthong Dynasty (1629–1688)" (London University, 1984), 121–152. This thesis is based on the VOC archives in The Hague and on the Phra Ratcha Phongsawadan or Royal Chronicles.

3. The essential study on the relations between England and Siam in the seventeenth century is the book by John Anderson, *English Intercourse with Siam in the Seventeenth Century* (London: Kegan Paul, 1890).

4. *Macbeth* I.3.

5. See E. W. Hutchinson, *Adventurers in Siam in the Seventeenth Century* (London: The Royal Asiatic Society, 1940), 24–25. The account of the voyages of Ralph Fitch was published in 1599 by Richard Hakluyt, *Principal Navigations, Voyages, Traffiques & Discoveries of the English Nation,* vol. 2, 1, 245–271. *The Voyages of Sir James Lancaster to Brazil and the East Indies, 1591–1603,* ed. Sir William Foster, was published by the Hakluyt Society in 1940.

6. W. Keeling, *A Journall of the Third Voyage to the East Indies, set out by the Company of the Merchants, trading in those parts. In which Voyage were imployed three ships, viz. the Dragon, the Hector and the Consent, and in them the number of three hundred and ten persons, or thereabouts: written by Captain William Keeling, Chief Commander,* in Samuel Purchas, *Hakluytus Posthumus or Purchas His Pilgrimes,* vol. 1 (1625), 195.

7. See Anderson, *English Intercourse with Siam,* 46.

8. See the contributions of J. M. James and, above all, Sir E. M. Satow on the relations between Siam and Japan in the seventeenth century, published in the *Transactions of the Asiatic Society of Japan* 7 (1879): 191–204 and 13 (1885): 139–210.

9. Adams was the pilot of the *Liefde,* the only one of the ships which reached Japan. The *Liefde* was, in fact, the *Erasmus* with a new name. It was shipwrecked off Kyushu; the figure on the prow, representing Erasmus holding in his hand a scroll on which one can read "Erasmus, Rotterdam, 1598" is preserved in the Imperial Museum in Tokyo.

10. The character inspired James Clavell's blockbuster, *Shogun.*

11. See Anderson, *English Intercourse with Siam,* 74–77.

12. Cited by Anderson, *English Intercourse with Siam,* 84–85.

13. See Prince Dhani Nivat and Major Erik Seidenfaden, "Early Trade Relations between Denmark and Siam," *Journal of the Siam Society* 30/1 (1939): 1–15.

14. See Raynal, *Histoire philosophique et politique,* vol. 1, (1780), 554–555.

15. See Brummelhuis, *Merchant, Courtier and Diplomat,* 19–21.

16. Gijsbrecht Heeck, "Derde Voyagie van Gijsbrecht Heeck naer Oost-Indien," *Marineblad* 25 (1910–1911), 422–450.

17. Joost Schouten, *A Description of the Government, Might, Religion, Customes, Traffick and other remarkable Affairs in the Kingdom of Siam,* trans. Roger Manley (London, 1671; facsimile ed., Bangkok: The Siam Society, 1986).

18. See Syamananda, *A History of Thailand,* 70.

19. The full title is longer. The book was published in Leiden in 1692. An English translation by L. F. van Ravenswaay was published in the *Journal of the Siam Society* 7/1, 5–105.

20. Published in a bilingual edition (Dutch and English) presented by David K. Wyatt with the title, *The Short History of the Kings of Siam* (Bangkok, 1975).

21. This appeared in English by W. H. Mundie, *Historical Account of Siam in the Seventeenth Century* (Bangkok, 1904). An extract was published by J.

Bowring, *The Kingdom and People of Siam* (London, 1857, vol. 1, 93–97) but under the incorrect name Van Scheuten.

22. Van Vliet, *Beschryving van het Koningryk Siam,* 98–100.

23. Ibid., 78.

24. Ibid., 97–98.

25. Anna Hariette Leonowens, *The English Governess at the Siamese Court. Recollections of Six Years in the Royal Palace at Bangkok* (1870) (Singapore: Oxford University Press, 1988), 82.

26. Cited by Brummelhuis, *Merchant, Courtier and Diplomat,* 38.

27. Details of the return of the EIC to Ayutthaya appear in Anderson, *English Intercourse with Siam,* 90–111, and E. W. Hutchinson, *Adventurers in Siam,* 24.

CHAPTER 5: SOMDET PHRA NARAI MAHARAT

1. See Jeremy Kemp, *Aspects of Siamese Kingship in the Seventeenth Century* (Bangkok: Social Science Association Press, 1969), 4.

2. See Syamananda, *A History of Thailand* (1988 ed.), 70–71.

3. Dhiravat, "A Political History of Siam under the Prasatthong Dynasty," 196–200.

4. I follow here the chronology suggested by David Wyatt and confirmed by Dhiravat na Pombejra (ibid., 461). Rong Syamananda has Prasat Thong dying in 1655, and prolongs the reign of Chaofa Chai from one day to a whole year, which completely contradicts the correspondence of those in charge of the VOC godown in Ayutthaya.

5. Guy Tachard, *A Relation of the Voyage to Siam performed by Six Jesuits* (London, 1688), 274; original French ed. (Paris, 1686), 282.

6. See Dhiravat, "A Political History of Siam," 132, on the succession in Siam.

7. Dhiravat, "A Political History of Siam," 249–250.

8. See Dhiravat, "A Political History of Siam," 258, and G. V. Smith, *The Dutch in Seventeenth Century Thailand,* 35.

9. Muhammad Ibrahim Muhammad Rabi, *The Ship of Sulaiman,* 97. See later in chapter 15.

10. Prince Damrong, preface to Wannakam Phraya Trang, cited by Gilles Delouche, *Contribution à une hypothèse de datation d'un poème thaï: le "Kamsuam Siprat"* (Paris: La Sorbonne Nouvelle, 1982), 7.

11. See the discussions of a seminar on the history of Lopburi organized in 1979, "La recherche historique sur Phra Narai: points de controverse et idées nouvelles," summarized by Phuthorn Bhudamon in *Phra Narai, roi de Siam, et Louis XIV* (Paris: Musée Guimet, 1986), 31–33.

12. Dhiravat, "A Political History of Siam," 9.

13. M.L. Manich Jumsai, *The Story of King Narai and his Ambassador to France in 1686, Kosaparn* (Bangkok: Chalermnit, 1988), 217.

14. La Loubère, *Kingdom of Siam* (1693), 100.

15. Delouche, *Contribution,* 27

16. See Delouche, *Contribution,* 17, n. 22.

17. See the interview granted by the princess to the *Bangkok Post,* 20 Nov. 1990, 27.

18. Jit-Kasem Sibunruang, "L'âge d'or de la poésie thaïlandaise: la littérature à l'époque de Phra Narai," in *Phra Narai, roi de Siam, et Louis XIV,* ed. Michel Jacq-Hergoualc'h (Paris, 1986), 38.

19. "Rapport de Boureau-Deslandes," in *Histoire de la mission de Siam. Documents historiques,* vol. 1, ed. Adrien Launay (Paris: Société des Missions étrangères, 1920), 106, n. 1.

20. Nicolas Gervaise, *Histoire naturelle et politique du royaume de Siam* (Paris: C. Barbin, 1688), 246. Translated by John Villiers under the title *The Natural and Political History of the Kingdom of Siam* (Bangkok: White Lotus, 1989).

21. Ibid., 242.

22. La Loubère, *Kingdom of Siam* (1693), 101.

23. Machiavelli, *The Prince,* ch. 17.

24. Turpin, *Histoire civile et naturelle du royaume de Siam* (1771), vol. 2, 58.

25. Dhiravat, "A Political History of Siam," 91.

26. Gervaise, *Natural and Political History,* 190–1. The same story, with some minor variations, appears in Turpin, *Histoire civile et naturelle,* vol. 2, 58–60, whose source was almost certainly Gervaise.

27. On Phra Narai's wars in the early 1660s, see D. G. E. Hall, *A History of South-East Asia* (1987), 385; Wyatt, *Thailand: A Short History* (1984), 111; Syamananda, *A History of Thailand* (1988), 71–72; M.L. Manich Jumsai, "Le grand roi Narai," in *Phra Narai, roi de Siam, et Louis XIV,* ed. Michel Jacq-Hergoualc'h (Paris: Musée Guimet, 1986), 28–29.

28. André-François Deslandes-Boureau, *Histoire de M. Constance, Premier Ministre du Roi de Siam* (Amsterdam: Duchesne, 1756), 14.

29. Dhiravat na Pombejra, "Crown Trade and Court Politics in Ayutthaya During the Reign of King Narai (1656–1688)," in *The South-East Asian Port and Polity,* ed. J. Kathirithamby-Wells and J. Villiers (Singapore: Singapore University Press, 1990), 127.

30. La Loubère, *Kingdom of Siam* (1693), 93.

31. Visantanee Pothisoonthorn, *Phra Narai Ratchanivet* (Bangkok: Fine Arts Department, 1988), 21.

32. Cited by Phuthorn Bhudamon, "La recherche historique de Phra Narai: points de controverse et idées nouvelles – Travaux du Séminaire sur l'histoire de Lopburi, 1979," in *Phra Narai, roi de Siam, et Louis XIV,* ed. Michel Jacq-Hergoualc'h (Paris: Musée Guimet, 1986), 31.

33. "For a long time after the treaty of 1664, the Dutch maintained a low profile in Siam." Brummelhuis, *Merchant, Courtier and Diplomat,* 40.

34. Gervaise, *Natural and Political History,* 49.

35. Ibid., 50.

36. This detail is found in La Loubère, *Kingdom of Siam* (1693), 21.
37. Arch. MEP, vol. 856, 11.

CHAPTER 6: THE FRENCH ROYAL EAST INDIES COMPANY

1. See Meynard, *Missions dominicaines,* vol. 1, 58.
2. Michaud, *Biographie universelle,* article on Parmentier.
3. Pierre Grignon, *Journal du voyage de Jean Parmentier de Dieppe à l'île de Sumatra en l'année 1529* (Paris, A. Pinard [1832]).
4. Ibid., 22.
5. Consider for example the description of Brazil by André Thevet, (*Les singularités de la France Antarctique, autrement nommée Amérique, et de plusieurs terres et isles découvertes de notre temps,* 1557) which inspired Montaigne when writing about the cannibals (*Essais,* vol. 1, 31) or the Canadian accounts of Jacques Cartier (1545) and Samuel Champlain (1603).
6. François Cauche, *Relation du voyage . . . à Madagascar, isles adjacantes et reste d'Afrique* (Paris: A. Courbe, 1651). Etienne de Flacourt, *Histoire de la grande isle de Madagascar* ([Paris: P. Lamy, 1658]; ed. Cl. Allibert. [Paris: Inalco-Karthala, 1995]).
7. See Guennou, *Missions étrangères de Paris,* 86–88.
8. Ernest Lavisse, *Louis XIV,* vol. 1 (Paris: Tallandier, 1978), 237.
9. Ibid., 242.
10. Cited by Lavisse, ibid., 243.
11. Paul Kaeppelin, *La Compagnie des Indes orientales et François Martin. Etude sur l'histoire du commerce et des établissements français dans l'Inde sous Louis XIV (1664–1719)* (Paris: Challamel, 1908), 5. I follow closely this fundamental study, chiefly based on the Archives of the Ministry of Colonies and on the four volumes of documents concerning the CIO published by Dernis in 1755–1756. Also to be consulted are *Louis XIV et la Compagnie des Indes orientales de 1664,* by Louis Pauliat (Paris: Calmann-Lévy, 1886), the *Histoire de la Compagnie royale des Indes orientales 1664–1719,* by Jules Sottas (Paris: Plon, 1905), volumes 5 and 6 of the monumental *Histoire de la Marine française,* by Charles de La Roncière (Paris: Plon, 1930–1932), as well as the thesis by Philippe Haudrère, "La Compagnie française des Indes au XVIIIe siècle d'après les sources portugaises et espagnoles," (2 vols., Paris, 1989) on the ultimate evolution of the CIO from 1719–1795.
12. Cited by Kaeppelin, *La Compagnie,* 9.
13. Details are found in Urbain Souchu de Rennefort, *Relation du premier voyage de la Compagnie des Indes orientales en l'île de Madagascar* (Paris, P. Auboüin, 1668), and his *Mémoires pour servir à l'histoire des Indes orientales* (Paris: A. Seneuze, 1688).
14. Cited by Chappoulie, *Aux origines d'une Eglise, Rome et les missions d'Indochine au XVIIe siècle* (1943), vol. 1, 280.

15. Kaeppelin, *La Compagnie,* 15.
16. Ibid., 17.
17. Cited by Kaeppelin, *La Compagnie,* 18–19.
18. Cited by Lavisse, *Louis XIV,* vol. 1, 245.
19. Cited by Kaeppelin, *La Compagnie,* 24.
20. Cited by Lavisse, *Louis XIV,* vol. 1, 248.
21. Ibid., 246.
22. Cited by Kaeppelin, *La Compagnie,* 26.
23. Ibid.
24. Cited by Lavisse, *Louis XIV,* vol. 1, 246.
25. Robert Knox, *An Historical Relation of the Island Ceylon in the East-Indies, together with an Account of the Detaining in Captivity the Author and divers other Englishmen now Living there, and of the Author's Miraculous Escape* (London, R. Chiswell 1681). The account of the unfortunate French embassy fills pt. 4, ch. 14.
26. L. Pauliat, *Louis XIV et la Compagnie des Indes orientales de 1664,* 355.
27. Knox, *An Historical Relation of the Island Ceylon,* 184.
28. Ibid.
29. Pauliat, *Louis XIV,* 357.
30. Cited by Lavisse, *Louis XIV,* vol. 1, 246–247.
31. Pauliat, *Louis XIV,* 364.
32. Ibid., preface xxii.
33. Cited by Kaeppelin, *La Compagnie,* 35.

CHAPTER 7: THE JESUITS IN SIAM, FOLLOWED BY THE FRENCH MISSIONARIES

1. Attention is drawn to the very well-documented article by Fr J. Burnay, "Notes chronologiques sur les missions jésuites du Siam au XVIIe siècle," *Archivum Historicum Societatis Jesu,* 22 (1953), 170–202.
2. See Matteo Ricci and Nicholas Trigault, *Histoire de l'expedition chrétienne au royaume de la Chine, 1582–1610,* new ed. of French trans. of 1617, (Paris, Desclée de Brouwer, 1978).
3. See Chappoulie, *Aux origines d'une Eglise. Rome et les missions d'Indochine au XVIIe siècle,* vol. 1, (1943), 135.
4. See Dhiravat na Pombejra, "A Political History of Siam," 129–130.
5. See Burnay, "Notes chronologiques," 186.
6. *Descriptio regni [Siami] et morum gentis: quid sperandum sit.,* ARSJ, Jap. Sin. 76, ff. 1–6.
7. For an overall view of the missions in the seventeenth century, see chapter 2 ("Grandeurs et tristesses des Missions") in Daniel-Rops, *L'Eglise des temps classiques,* vol. 2: *L'ère des grands craquements* (Paris: Fayard, 1958), 97–183, and Guillaume de Vaumas, *L'éveil missionnaire de la France au XVIIe siècle* (Paris: Bloud et Gay, 1959).

8. Cited by Daniel-Rops, *L'Eglise des temps classiques,* vol. 2: *L'ère des grands craquements,* 108.

9. This is the most common form for his name, which is sometimes spelt La Motte-Lambert.

10. Guennou, *Missions étrangères de Paris,* 34–35.

11. Ibid., 19.

12. Jacques de Bourges, *Relation du voyage de Monseigneur l'Evêque de Béryte, vicaire apostolique du royaume de la Cochinchine, par la Turquie, la Perse, les Indes, etc. jusqu'au royaume de Siam et autres lieux, par M. de Bourges, prêtre, missionnaire apostolique* (Paris: D. Bechet, 1666), 11–12.

13. A. Forest, "Principes, fondements, et aspects de l'action des missionnaires français (Missions étrangères de Paris) au Siam dans la 2e moitié du XVIIe siècle" in *Catholicisme et Société asiatiques* (1988), 110.

14. Cited by Daniel-Rops, *L'Eglise,* 116. The complete text of *Instructio Vicariorum Apostolicorum ad regna Sinarum, Tonchini et Cocincinae proficiscentium* (1659) is reproduced by Chappoulie as an appendix in *Aux origines d'une Eglise, Rome et les missions d'Indochine au XVIIe siècle,* vol. 1 (1943) 392–402. The commentary and French translation of this text are the subject of an article by B. Jacqueline, "L'esprit missionnaire de la S. C. *De Propaganda Fide* d'après les Instructions aux vicaires apostoliques . . . ," *Documents Omnis Terra,* 81:5 (May 1971), 330–345.

15. Forest, "Principes, fondements," 111.

16. Bourges, *Relation du voyage de Mgr de Beryte,* 243–244.

CHAPTER 8: THE DISCOVERY OF BUDDHIST TOLERANCE

1. Translation from Jacqueline, "L'esprit missionnaire de la S.C. *De Propaganda Fide,*" 337.

2. Bourges, *Relation du voyage de Mgr Beryte* (1666), 24.

3. Bourges, *Relation du voyage de Mgr Beryte,* (Paris, 1666; new eds. 1668, 1683). These quotations are translations from the original edition.

4. Ibid., 3.

5. Ibid., 31.

6. Ibid., 35.

7. Ibid., 40–41.

8. In the Vulgate, the Miserere was Psalm 50, now numbered as Psalm 51.

9. Bourges, *Relation du voyage de Mgr Beryt,* 77.

10. Ibid., 85.

11. Ibid., 93.

12. Ibid., 97.

13. Ibid., 98.

14. Matthew 22:21; Mark 12:17; Luke 20:25 KJV.

15. Bourges, *Relation du voyage de Mgr Beryt,* 98–99.
16. Ibid., 99.
17. Ibid., 102–103.
18. Ibid., 117.
19. See M. Jacq-Hergoualc'h's critical edition of La Loubère, *Du royaume de Siam* (1987), 128, 220.
20. Ibid., 129–130. For an account in English of Jacques de Bourges in Siam, see Michael Smithies, "Jacques de Bourges (c. 1630–1714) and Siam," *Journal of the Siam Society* 81/2 (1993), 113–129.
21. Ibid., 171–172. This passage was taken up and summarized by Donneau de Visé in the *Mercure Galant* of July 1686, vol. 2, 37–39.
22. Spinoza, Letter to Albert Burgh, quoted by G. Atkinson, *Les relations de voyages au XVIIe siècle et l'évolution des idées* (Paris: Champion, 1924), 15.
23. Mark 16:15–16 KJV.
24. Quoted by Narada Maha Thera, *The Buddha and His Teachings* (Colombo: Vajirârâma, 1973), 305.
25. On the doubtful authenticity of the miracles attributed to the Buddha, see Jean Naudou, *Le Bouddha* (Paris: Somogy, 1973), 167–268.
26. See a portrait in Guennou, *Missions étrangères de Paris* (Paris, 1986), 8.
27. *The Siamese Memoirs of Count Claude de Forbin, 1685–1688,* ed. Michael. Smithies (Chiang Mai: Silkworm, 1996), 171.
28. Bowring, *The Kingdom and People of Siam* (1857), vol. 1, 337.
29. *L'Etat present de l'Eglise de la Chine,* quoted by Chappoulie, *Aux origines d'une Eglise, Rome et les missions d'Indochine au XVIIe siècle,* vol. 1, 136.
30. Bowring, *The Kingdom and People of Siam,* vol. 1, 349.
31. Bourges, *Relation* (1666), 131.
32. Ibid., 133.
33. Ibid., 135 136.
34. Ibid., 139.
35. Ibid., 140–185.
36. La Loubère, *Kingdom of Siam* (1693), 64.
37. John 14:2 KJV.
38. Boisselier, *La sculpture en Thaïlande,* 30.
39. Cited by Piriya Krairiksh in *The Sacred Image. Sculptures from Thailand* (Cologne, 1979), 15.

CHAPTER 9: THE FRENCH MISSION IN AYUTTHAYA (1662–1670)

1. Bourges, *Relation du voyage de Mgr de Béryte* (1666), 141.
2. See Forest, "Principes, fondements," 114.
3. See Patipat Pumpongphet, "Les fouilles archéologiques dans Mu Ban

Portuget sur le site de São Pedro" in *Phra Naraï roi de Siam et Louis XIV,* ed. M. Jacq-Hergoualc'h (Paris: Musée Guimet, 1986), 23–26.

4. François Pallu, *Relation abrégée des Missions et des Voyages des évêques français envoyés aux royaumes de la Chine, Cochinchine, Tonquin et Siam* (Paris: D. Bechet, 1668), 22.

5. "*Fateor consilium illud extremum esse, sed extremus est morbus christianitatis,*" Paris, Arch. MEP, vol. 876, 101.

6. Adrien Launay, *Siam et les missionnaires français* (Tours: Mame, 1896), 67.

7. Bourges, *Relation*, 221.

8. Ibid., 222–223.

9. Ibid., 224

10. Ibid., 235.

11. Cited by Chappoulie, *Aux origines d'une Eglise, Rome et les missions d'Indochine au XVIIe siècle*, vol. 1, 248.

12. Launay, *Siam—Documents historiques*, vol. 1, 11.

13. Forest, "Principes, fondements," 121.

14. Quoted by Chappoulie, *Aux origines*, vol. 1, 149.

15. Launay, *Siam—Documents historiques*, vol. 1, 12.

16. J. Thévenot, *Voyages aux Indes orientales* (Paris: Charles Angot, 1689), vol. 3, 220.

17. Bourges, *Relation*, 236.

18. Letter of 17 April 1668 to the Duke of Chaulnes, French ambassador in Rome, Arch. MEP, vol. 102, 21.

19. Paris, Arch. MEP, vol. 858, f. 127. This letter is reproduced in Pallu, *Relation abrégée*, 131.

20. Letter of 5 March 1667, written off Crete. Cited by Chappoulie, *Aux origines*, vol. 1, 265.

21. Chappoulie, *Aux origines*, vol. 1, 154.

22. Quoted by Chappoulie, *Aux origines*, vol. 1, 268.

23. Chappoulie, *Aux origines*, vol. 1, 155.

24. ARSJ, Jap. Sin. 76, f. 48.

25. 2 Timothy 2:9 KJV.

26. See two copies, ARSJ, Jap. Sin. 76, ff. 73–74 and 76–79.

27. Chappoulie, *Aux origines*, vol. 1, 157.

28. Details are found in Chappoulie, *Aux origines*, vol. 1, 158.

29. See ARSJ, Jap. Sin. 91–94 ("*Controversiae cum Vicariis Apostolicis*") and especially 94, ff. 11–14 ("*Cartas de alguns senhores clêricos franceses missionários que se chamão apostólicos*"). This is a Portuguese summary of letters intercepted by the Jesuits.

30. ARSJ, Jap. Sin. 93, ff. 187–188.

31. ARSJ, Jap. Sin. 76, f.92.

32. ARSJ, Jap. Sin. 76, 125.

33. Paris, Arch. MEP, vol. 857, 237.

34. Letter of 17 November 1670, quoted by Chappoulie, *Aux origines*, vol. 1, 160.

CHAPTER 10: PHRA NARAI AND THE FRENCH (1665–1679)

1. Concerning the monks' plot, see Turpin, *Histoire civile et naturelle du royaume de Siam* (1771), vol. 2, 60–62, and Pinya, "A History of the French Missions to Siam," *The Imperial and Asiatic Quarterly Review*, series 3, vol. 11 (1901), 334–335.

2. Quoted by Launay, *Siam—Documents historiques*, vol. 1, 15.

3. Launay, *Siam—Documents historiques*, vol. 1, 16 and idem, *Siam et les missionnaires français*, 71–72.

4. Letter of 17 October 1666. Launay, *Siam—Documents historiques*, vol. 1, 17.

5. Launay, *Siam—Documents historiques*, vol. 1, 18–19.

6. Ibid., 19.

7. Gervaise, *Natural and Political History*, 180.

8. Launay, *Siam—Documents historiques*, vol. 1, 20.

9. On the stay in Tonkin of Mgr Lambert in 1669–1670, see Chappoulie, *Aux origines,* vol. 1, 228–237.

10. Quoted by Chappoulie, *Aux origines*, vol. 1, 278–279 and 282.

11. Bénigne Vachet, *Vie de Mgr Laneau* (Arch. MEP, vol. 120). Quoted by Launay, *Siam—Documents historiques*, vol. 1, 41.

12. Louis Laneau, *Salut des infidèles et baptême* (Paris: Centre de Recherche théologique missionnaire, 1988), 23.

13. *Relation des missions et voyages des évêques vicaires apostoliques et de leurs ecclésiastiques ès années 1676 et 1677* (Paris: Charles Angot, 1680), 60.

14. Launay, *Siam—Documents historiques*, vol. 1, 42.

15. Letter of 19 October 1667 to Pallu, then in Europe. See Launay, *Siam—Documents historiques*, vol. 1, 103.

16. Launay, *Siam—Documents historiques*, vol. 1, 43. The quotations which follow without a reference are also taken from the detailed account of the presentation of the letters and public audience, 43–46. Other manuscript sources, slightly different, are mentioned in the following note.

17. AN, Col.C/1/22, ff. 11–15 "Ce qui s'est passé en la présentation des lettres que Sa Sainteté et Sa Majesté Très Chrétienne ont écrites au roi de Siam." Other copies: BN, NAF 7491, ff. 347–349, and ARSJ, Jap. Sin. 76, ff. 388–389.

18. BN, Ms NAF 7491, f. 347 v.

19. Ibid.

20. The Latin text is found in Launay, *Documents historiques*, vol. 1, 45–46, and a very approximate translation into French in idem, *Siam et les missionnaires français*, 83–84.

21. Launay, *Siam—Documents historiques*, vol. 1, 46.

22. See Turpin, *Histoire civile et naturelle*, vol. 2, 75–76.

23. Kemp, *Aspects of Siamese Kingship in the Seventeenth Century*, 20.

24. *Relation des missions et des voyages*, 130.

25. See Kun Chang, *A Comparative Study of the Kathinavastu* (1957).

26. Launay, *Siam—Documents historiques*, I, 76.

27. Quoted by Chappoulie, *Aux origines*, vol. 1, 318.

28. See Launay, *Siam—Documents historiques*, vol. 1, 50–51.

29. Ibid., 47. The detailed account of the stay in Lopburi of the apostolic vicars fills pages 46–50.

30. Dhiravat, "Political History," 323.

31. Ibid., 324.

32. Journal de la mission 9 February 1674, in Launay, *Siam—Documents historiques*, vol. 1, 53.

33. On the first journey of Mgr Lambert to Cochin-China, see Chappoulie, *Aux origines*, vol. 1, 325–329.

34. On the second stay, see Chappoulie, *Aux origines*, vol. 1, 339–343.

35. *Relation des missions et des voyages*, 214.

36. Kemp, *Aspects of Siamese Kingship*, 31.

37. Choisy, *Journal de voyage au Siam*, 15 October 1685.

38. La Loubère, *Kingdom of Siam* (1693), 43.

39. *Relation des missions et des voyages*, 215.

40. Choisy, *Journal de voyage au Siam*, 22 April 1685.

41. Quoted by Chappoulie, *Aux origines*, vol. 1, 369.

42. Chappoulie, *Aux origines*, vol. 1, 371.

43. Letter in Latin of 15–16 November 1682. See Bosmans, ed., "Correspondance de Jean-Baptiste Maldonado de Mons," in *Analectes pour servir à l'histoire ecclésiastique de Belgique*, vol. 36 (1920), 187.

44. See Burnay, "Notes chronologiques sur les missions jésuites du Siam au XVIIe siècle," in *Archivum Romanum Societatis Jesu*, vol. 22 (1953), 193–194.

45. The Latin text of the act of submission signed by Fathers Soares, Maldonado, Thomas, and Alcarez, with the initials of Mgr Laneau, is found in Bosmans, op. cit., 45–46.

46. Launay, *Siam—Documents historiques*, vol. 1, 103–104.

47. Letter of 9 October 1677. Launay, *Siam—Documents historiques*, vol. 1, 104.

48. Letter of 4 September 1678. Launay, *Siam—Documents historiques*, vol. 1, 104.

49. Chappoulie, *Aux origines*, vol. 1, 374.

50. Letter of 27 October 1679. Launay, *Siam—Documents historiques*, vol. 1, 72.

51. Letter of 2 November 1679 to the directors of the seminary of the MEP. Launay, *Siam—Documents historiques*, vol. 1, 73–74.

52. Ibid.
53. Lanier, *Etude historique*, 18.

CHAPTER 11: PHAULKON, THE GREEK FAVOURITE

1. Pierre-Joseph d'Orléans, *Histoire de M. Constance premier ministre du roi de Siam, et de la dernière révolution de cet Etat.* (Paris: D. Horthemels, 1690); "Remarques sur l'Histoire de M. Constance composée par le P. d'Orléans Jésuite," Paris, Arch. MEP, Siam 853, 107–144; "Lettre d'un Anglais catholique au R. P. Pierre d'Orléans Jésuite sur l'Histoire qu'il a écrite de M. Constance," followed by the "Abrégé de la vie et des moeurs de M. Constance," ibid., Siam 854, 887–942.
2. Arch. MEP, Siam 854, 889–890.
3. Deslandes-Boureau, *Histoire de M. Constance* (1756), vi, 10.
4. Arch. MEP, Siam 854, 899–942. Some extracts were published in English by Hutchinson, *Adventurers in Siam in the Seventeenth Century*, 247–255.
5. Arch. MEP, Siam 854, 892–893.
6. Bèze says he was forty at the time of his death (p. 134), Orléans forty-one (p. 110).
7. Turpin, *Histoire civile et naturelle*, vol. 2, 64.
8. *The Siamese Memoirs of Count Claude de Forbin*, 65.
9. Guy Tachard, *Voyage de Siam des Pères Jésuites envoyés par le Roi aux Indes et à la Chine* (Amsterdam: P. Mortier, 1687), 160.
10. Claude de Bèze, *Mémoire sur la vie de Constance Phaulkon, premier ministre du roi de Siam Phra Narai, et sa triste fin*, ed. J. Drans and H. Bernard (Tokyo: Presses Salésiennes, 1947), 4.
11. "Abrégé de la vie et des moeurs de M. Constance," Arch. MEP, Siam 854, 900.
12. Turpin, *Histoire civile et naturelle*, vol. 2, 65.
13. *A Full and True Relation of the Great and Wonderful Revolution that happened lately in the Kingdom of Siam in the East-Indies* (London: R. Taylor, 1690), 2.
14. "Abrégé," 900, 901.
15. Bèze, *Mémoire*, 6.
16. *Het Leven en Daden van d'Heer Constantyn Phaulcon* (1692), 3.
17. Letter of 29 October 1696 to William Gyfford. Quoted by Hutchinson, *Adventurers in Siam*, 59.
18. Bèze, *Mémoire*, 4.
19. "Abrégé ," 901.
20. Claude de Bèze, *1688, Revolution in Siam: The Memoir of Father de Bèze, S.J.*, ed. E. W. Huchinson (Hong Kong: Hong Kong University Press, 1968), 8.
21. "Abrégé," 901.

22. Jean-Baptiste Pallegoix, *Description du royaume Thaï ou Siam, comprenant la topographie, histoire naturelle, moeurs et coutumes, législation, commerce, langue, etc.* (Paris, 1854), vol. 1, 95.

23. Engelbert Kaempfer, *A Description of the Kingdom of Siam (1690)* (Bangkok: White Orchid Press, 1987), 30.

24. Bowring, *The Kingdom and People of Siam*, vol. 2, 345–346.

25. For details about these three persons consult Anderson, *English Intercourse with Siam in the Seventeenth Century* (1890), and Hutchinson, *Adventurers in Siam* (1940). On the White brothers, more particularly Samuel, see Maurice Collis, *Siamese White* (London: Faber & Faber, 1936).

26. Anderson, *English Intercourse with Siam*, 166.

27. *Het Leven en Daden*, 3.

28. Quoted by Collis, *Siamese White*, 49–50.

29. "Abrégé," 902–903.

30. Bèze, *Mémoire*, 8–9.

31. Orléans, *Histoire de M. Constance*, 5–10, and Tachard, *Voyage de Siam des Pères Jésuites*, 161–163.

32. "Abrégé," 903–904.

33. Arch. MEP, Siam 853, 110.

34. Bèze, *Mémoire*, 10–11.

CHAPTER 12: THE DRAMA OF THE FIRST SIAMESE EMBASSY (1680–1681)

1. "Rapport de Boureau-Deslandes," Arch. MEP 856, 10. Launay, *Siam—Documents historiques*, vol. 1, 104–108.

2. Quoted by Kaeppelin, *La Compagnie*, 125.

3. Lanier, *Etude historique sur les relations de la France et du royaume de Siam*, 23, and Kaeppelin, op. cit., 169–170.

4. BN, Ms NAF 9380, f. 84 r.: "Nouvelles écrites de Siam par les missionnaires français en décembre 1680 aux Directeurs du Séminaire des Missions étrangères de Paris. L'arrivée d'un vaisseau français à Siam."

5. Ibid.

6. François Martin, *Mémoires, 1665–1696.* (Paris: Société de l'Histoire des Colonies françaises, 1932), vol. 2, 206.

7. BN, Ms NAF 9380, f. 85 r.

8. Arch. MEP, 856, 13. Launay, *Siam—Documents historiques*, vol. 1, 106 (note).

9. BN, Ms NAF 9380, f. 82 r.

10. Launay, *Siam—Documents historiques*, vol. 1, 106.

11. BN, Ms NAF 9380, ibid.

12. Hutchinson, *Adventurers in Siam*, 64.

13. I have combined the extracts from two sources (BN Ms NAF 9380 and Arch. MEP 856) quoted above.

14. See Hutchinson, *Adventurers in Siam*, 64. Deslandes called the ambassadors Opra Pipatracha Maytri, Luang Vissan Senton, and Cun Nacella Vichay (Launay, *Siam—Documents historiques*, vol. 1, 107).

15. Launay, ibid., and 1 Kings 10:6–7.

16. Arch. MEP, 858, 465 (letter to Louis XIV) and 467 (letter to the pope). Launay, *Siam—Documents historiques*, vol. 1, 110–112.

17. BN, Ms NAF 9380, f. 82 v.

18. Letter of 16 November 1680 to François de Harlay-Champvallon, Arch. MEP, 859, 446.

19. Letter of 18 November 1680. Arch. MEP, 858, 446.

20. Old copy of a letter from Claude Gayme, without addressee or date, BN Ms NAF 9380, f. 150 r.

21. Etienne Gallois, *L'ambassade de Siam au XVIIe siècle* (Paris: E. Panckoucke, 1862), 11.

22. Letter from Claude Gayme to the Directors of the Seminary of the MEP, 18 January 1681 at Bantam. Arch. MEP, 858, 449. Launay, op. cit., vol. 1, 112.

23. Letter of 29 January 1681, from Bantam. BN Ms NAF 9380, f. 87–91.

24. Letter of 25 July 1681 from Bantam to the Directors of the Seminary of the MEP. Arch. MEP, 858. Launay, op. cit., vol. 1, 112.

25. See Lanier, *Etude historique*, 26; Hutchinson, *Adventurers in Siam*, 66; Chappoulie, *Aux origines*, vol. 2, 101.

26. *Mercure Galant*, July 1686, 175–182.

27. "Journal de la Mission," Arch. MEP, 878, 520 et seq. Launay, op. cit., vol. 1, 119.

28. Martin, *Mémoires*, vol. 2, 345.

29. Gallois, *L'ambassade de Siam*, 12.

30. January 1684. Arch. MEP 859, 282. Launay, op. cit., vol. 1, 125–126.

31. Letter in Latin of 16 March 1696 from Ayutthaya, Arch. MEP 863, 413.

CHAPTER 13: BETWEEN TWO EMBASSIES (1682–1684)

1. Kaeppelin, *La Compagnie*, 188.

2. Martin, *Mémoires*, II, 382–383.

3. Arch. MEP, vol. 858, 473. Launay, *Siam—Documents historiques*, vol. 1, 110.

4. Dhiravat, "Political History," 330.

5. "Mémoires en forme de Lettre d'un Anglais catholique au R. P. d'Orléans, Jesuite, sur *l'Histoire de M. Constance . . .* écrite par ce père," Arch. MEP, vol. 854, 904–905.

6. Tachard, *Voyage de Siam des Pères Jésuites* (Amsterdam: P. Mortier, 1687), 164.

7. Bèze, *1688, Revolution in Siam*, 11.

8. Ibid., 11.

9. Ibid., 12.

10. "Note sur C. Phaulkon," Arch. MEP, vol. 880, 15. Launay, op. cit., vol. 1, 124–125.

11. In Launay, op. cit., vol. 1, 53, one reads with the date of 8 February 1674, "Mr Constance returned to the court" with the note at the bottom of the page "Constance Phaulkon"; this is four years before the Greek arrived in Siam. The text in fact reads: "Mr de Constantin returned to the court." (Arch. MEP, vol. 876, 898); it concerns a French trader who had dealings with the *Phra Khlang*.

12. Dhiravat, "Political History," 331; "Lettre d'un Anglais catholique," Arch. MEP, vol. 854, 908.

13. Dhiravat, "Political History," 331–332.

14. Letter of 26 December 1682, Arch. MEP, vol. 859, 190. Launay, op. cit., vol. 1, 123.

15. Ibid., 909.

16. Bèze, *1688, Revolution*, 12–13.

17. Tachard, *Voyage de Siam*, 165.

18. Bèze, *1688, Revolution*, 23.

19. Orléans, *Histoire de M. Constance*, 21.

20. Bèze, *1688, Revolution*, 25.

21. "Lettre d'un Anglais catholique," Arch. MEP, vol. 854, 914.

22. Ibid., 889.

23. Yves de Thomaz de Bossière, *Un Belge mandarin de la Cour de Chine aux XVIIe et XVIIIe siècles. Antoine Thomas (1644–1709), Ngan To P'ing-che* (Paris: Les Belles Lettres/Cathasia, 1977), 20.

24. Bèze, *1688, Revolution*, 26.

25. "Lettre d'un Anglais catholique," 912.

26. Duchesne to the Directors of the Seminary of the Foreign Missions, 13 November 1682. Arch. MEP, vol. 878, 194 et seq. Launay, op. cit., vol. 1, 115.

27. *Lettres de Monseigneur Pallu,* ed. Adrien Launay (n.d.), vol. 2, 274.

28. On the arrest, journey to Madrid, and trial of Pallu, see BN Ms NAF 9380, ff. 92–96; *Relation des missions et des voyages des évêques,* 358 et seq.; Chappoulie, *Aux origines*, vol. 2, 1–5.

29. Quoted by Chappoulie, op. cit., 76.

30. See Chappoulie, op. cit., 77.

31. See Kaeppelin, *La Compagnie*, 175, 189.

32. Duchesne to the Directors of the Seminary of the Foreign Missions, 13 November 1682, Arch. MEP, vol. 878, 194 et seq.; Launay, op. cit., I, 114.

33. "Lettre d'un Anglais catholique," 909–910.

34. Launay, op. cit., I, 114, and Kaeppelin, *La Compagnie*, 189.

35. Kaeppelin, *La Compagnie*, 190.

36. Joachim Bouvet, *Voyage de Siam,* ed. J. C. Gatty (Leiden: E. J. Brill, 1963), 136.

37. Launay, op. cit., vol. 1, 119.

38. "Note sur C. Phaulkon," Arch. MEP, vol. 880, 15; Launay, op. cit., vol. 1, 125.

39. "Lettre d'un Anglais catholique," 906.

40. Hutchinson, *Adventurers in Siam,* 13–14.

41. Ibid., 17.

42. See Dhiravat, "Political History," 357.

43. Bèze, *1688, Revolution,* 17.

44. "Lettre d'un Anglais catholique," 907.

45. Bèze, *1688, Revolution,* 19.

46. See Muhammad, *The Ship of Sulaiman,* 145.

47. Bouvet, *Voyage de Siam,* 103.

CHAPTER 14: THE SECOND SIAMESE EMBASSY (1684–1685)

1. Letter of 7 January 1684. Arch. MEP, vol. 862; 21. Launay, *Siam—Documents historiques,* vol. 1, 126.

2. In addition to the manuscript volumes 110–113 in the archives of the MEP, there is a volume of extracts published in a limited edition in 1865 by Groupy and Co., and some pages are reproduced in *Siam—Documents historiques,* by Adrien Launay.

3. Letter quoted in Launay, op. cit., vol. 1, 127.

4. B. Vachet, *Mémoires,* in Launay, op. cit., vol. 1, 130.

5. Ibid.

6. Letter of 18 January 1684. Arch. MEP, vol. 859, 345; Launay, op. cit., vol. 1, 127.

7. See Hutchinson, *Adventurers in Siam,* 122

8. B. Vachet, *Mémoires,* in Launay, op. cit., vol. 1, 133. The quotations which follow are taken from pages 131–153.

9. J. Evelyn, *Diary,* ed. E. S. de Beer (Oxford: Clarendon Press, 1955), vol. 4, 388.

10. London, Public Record Office, State Papers Domestic 44/56, 129. My thanks go to Mr Anthony Farrington, Deputy Director of the India Office collection in the British Library, for indicating this document.

11. Charles-Gabriel Porée, *La Mandarinade ou Histoire comique du mandarinat de M. l'abbé de Saint-Martin, marquis de Miskou* (The Hague: P. Paupic, 1738). The text is reproduced in *Temps* of 14 October 1932. See also H. Cordier, *Bibliotheca Indosinica,* vol. 1, col. 935–940.

12. B. Vachet, *Mémoires,* in Launay, op. cit., vol. 1, 138.

13. These *Mémoires* were published in an appendix to Choisy, *Mémoires pour*

servir à l'histoire de Louis XIV (Paris: Mercure de France, 1983) by the same author, pp. 287–360.

14. (Paris, Sébastien Mabre-Cramoisy, 1684). Modern edition by Richard Parrish, Editions universitaires de Fribourg, 1981.

15. See the list of Choisy's works in Dirk Van der Cruysse, *L'abbé de Choisy, androgyne et mandarin* (Paris: Fayard, 1995), 457–461.

16. Choisy, *Mémoires*, 142.

17. Charles-Augustin Sainte-Beuve, *Causeries du lundi,* vol. 3, 3 March 1851.

18. Choisy, *Mémoires*, 143.

19. B. Vachet, *Mémoires,* in Launay, op. cit., vol. 1, 138–139.

20. Dangeau, *Journal*, vol. 1, 59 (October 1684).

21. " . . . Como Mr Vachet, clérigo missionário, tinha facilitado em Paris, asseverando que com huma embaixada se faria cristão o Rey de Sião, ao que não quis faltar Sua Majestade Cristianíssima . . ." (Letter of 9 October 1688). ARSJ, Jap. Sin. 76, f. 341 r.

22. "Mémoire pour être présenté à MM. les ministres d'Etat de France, sur toutes les choses qui regardent les envoyés du roi de Siam, par B Vachet (1685)." Arch. MEP, vol. 856, 29 et seq.; Launay, op. cit., vol. 1, 155.

23. Arch. MEP, vol. 854, 923–924.

24. Dangeau, *Journal*, vol. 1, 76 (1 December 1684).

25. Letter in Latin written from Peking on 15 August 1687. *Correspondance de Ferdinand Verbiest*, ed. H. Josson and L. Willaert (Brussels, 1939), 237.

26. Letter of 26 October 1682. ARSJ, Jap. Sin. 76, f. 252 v.

27. Letter in Portuguese of 9 January 1684. ARSJ, Jap. Sin. 76, ff. 261–263 (two copies with autographed signatures).

28. See Chappoulie, *Aux origines*, vol. 2, 103 (n. 5) and 104 (n. 2).

29. ARSJ, Gal. 72, f.139.

30. Letters in Latin of 10 and 20 February 1685 to Fr de La Chaize. ARSJ, Gal. 42, ff. 141a-b, 142, and 143.

31. Letter of 14 March 1685. ARSJ, Gal. 72, ff. 142–143.

32. Vachet, *Mémoires,* in Launay, op. cit., vol. 1, 150.

33. Forbin, *Mémoires* (1839), 469.

34. Chevalier de Chaumont and Abbé de Choisy, *Aspects of the Embassy to Siam, 1685,* trans. and ed. Michael Smithies (Chiang Mai, Silkworm, 1997), 188–189.

35. AN. Colonies, C/1/22. ff. 84–86. This memorandum was published as annex 2 in Dirk Van der Cruysse's annotated edition of Choisy's *Journal du voyage de Siam* (Paris: Fayard, 1995), 380–384.

36. Choisy, *Voyage de Siam* (1995), 41. Translation by Michael Smithies, *Journal of a Voyage to Siam 1685–1686* (Kuala Lumpur: Oxford University Press, 1993), 42.

37. Critical edition of the *Du royaume de Siam* by La Loubère (1987), 20.

38. Tachard, *Voyage to Siam* (English translation, London, 1688), 9–10.

39. Letter of Fr de Fontaney to Fr de La Chaize (Ningpo, 15 February, 1703) quoted in Henri Bernard, *Le Voyage du P. de Fontaney au Siam et à la Chine, 1685–1687* (Tientsin/Shangai: Cathasia, 1942), 8.
40. Bouvet, *Voyage de Siam*, 9.
41. Tachard, op. cit., 11–13.
42. Vachet, *Mémoires*, in Launay, op. cit., vol. 1, 150.
43. *Mercure Galant*, February 1685, 295.
44. Dangeau, *Journal*, vol. 1, 116 (31 January 1685).
45. *Registre des ordres du Roi concernant la Marine. Année 1685*. AN. Marine, B2.52, ff. 45–50. Quoted by Jal, *Dictionnaire de biographie et d'histoire*, art. "Ambassadeurs siamois," 37, and Lanier, *Etude historique*, 49–50.
46. Vachet, *Mémoires*, in Launay, op. cit., vol. 1, 153.
47. Tachard, op. cit., 22.

CHAPTER 15: THE SHIP OF SULAIMAN (1685–1688)

1. See Dhiravat, "Political History," 376–377.
2. Muhammad Ibrahim Muhammad Rabi, *The Ship of Sulaiman*, trans. John O'Kane (London, Routledge & Kegan Paul, Persian Heritage Series, no. 11, 1972), 20.
3. Ibid., 21.
4. See note 2.
5. Ibid., 19.
6. Ibid., 32.
7. Ibid., 32–33.
8. Ibid., 36.
9. Ibid., 37–38.
10. Ibid., 49.
11. Ibid., 54.
12. Ibid., 56.
13. Ibid., 59.
14. Ibid., 61.
15. Ibid., 64.
16. Ibid., 68.
17. La Loubère, *Kingdom of Siam*, 35, 36.
18. Muhammad, *The Ship of Sulaiman*, 83.
19. Ibid., 84–85.
20. Ibid., 87.
21. Ibid., 94–97.
22. Ibid., 98–99.
23. Ibid., 121.
24. Tachard, *Voyage de Siam* (1686), 308.

CHAPTER 16: "THESE POOR PEOPLE WHO ARE GOING SO FAR" (MARCH–SEPTEMBER 1685)

1. Tachard, *Voyage de Siam* (Amsterdam, 1687), 27.
2. Bouvet, *Voyage de Siam*, 22.
3. Choisy, *Journal of a Voyage to Siam 1685–1686*, trans. Michael Smithies (Kuala Lumpur: Oxford University Press, 1993), 43 (7 March).
4. Bouvet, op. cit., 23.
5. Tachard, op. cit., 24–25.
6. *Mercure Galant*, July 1686, vol. 1, 187.
7. Choisy, op. cit., 50 (18 March).
8. Op. cit., 65 (11 March).
9. Op. cit., 65 (23 April).
10. Op. cit., 64–65 (22 April).
11. Op. cit., 69 (1 May).
12. Vachet, *Mémoires*, in Launay, *Siam—Documents historiques*, vol. 1, 156.
13. Sainte-Beuve, *Causeries du lundi*, vol. 3, 3 March 1851.
14. Choisy, *Journal of a Voyage to Siam*, 76 (21 May).
15. Ibid., 44 (7 March).
16. Ibid., 70 (5 May).
17. Ibid., 43 (5 March) and 71 (8 May).
18. Ibid., 47 (13 March).
19. Ibid., 54–55 (24 March).
20. Ibid., 62 (12 April).
21. Ibid., 54 (24 March).
22. Ibid., 72 (10 May).
23. Bouvet, *Voyage de Siam*, 40–41 and Tachard, *Voyage de Siam*, 46.
24. Choisy, *Journal of a Voyage to Siam*, 73 (30 May).
25. Forbin, *The Siamese Memoirs of Count Claude de Forbin, 1685–1688*, ed. Michael Smithies (Chiang Mai: Silkworm Books, 1996), 33. This edition reproduces the 1731 London translation.
26. Choisy, *Journal of a Voyage to Siam*, 79 (30 May).
27. *Mercure Galant*, July 1686, vol. 1, 191–192.
28. Tachard, *Voyage de Siam*, 62.
29. Choisy, *Journal of a Voyage to Siam*, 80 (2 June).
30. Ibid., 81 (2 June).
31. Ibid., 81 (3 June).
32. Bouvet, *Voyage de Siam*, 47.
33. Choisy, *Journal of a Voyage to Siam*, 82 (4 June).
34. Forbin, *Siamese Memoirs*, 35.
35. *Mercure Galant*, July 1686, vol. 1, 195–196.
36. Alexandre de Chaumont, *Relation de l'ambassade de Mr le Chevalier de Chaumont à la cour du roi de Siam, et ce qui s'est passé de plus remarquable durant son voyage* (Paris: Seneuze & Horthemels, 1686), 11.

37. Choisy, *Journal of a Voyage to Siam*, 81 (3 June).
38. Ibid., 83 (6 June).
39. Ibid., 89 (15 June).
40. Ibid., 89 (16 June).
41. Ibid., 95 (3 July).
42. Ibid., 96 (6 July).
43. Ibid., 94 (29 June) and 98 (8 July).
44. Bouvet, *Voyage de Siam*, 60.
45. Choisy, *Journal of a Voyage to Siam*, 102 (15 July).
46. Ibid.
47. Ibid., 104–105 (19 July).
48. Chaumont and Choisy, *Aspects of the Embassy to Siam, 1685*, 190–191.
49. Ibid., 191–194.
50. Choisy, *Journal of a Voyage to Siam*, 111 (4 August).
51. Forbin, *Siamese Memoirs*, 39.
52. Choisy, op. cit., 116 (13 August).
53. Forbin, op. cit., 41.
54. Bouvet, *Voyage de Siam*, 71; Tachard, *Voyage de Siam*, 128; Choisy, *Journal of a Voyage to Siam*, 119 (18 August).
55. Forbin, *Siamese Memoirs*, 41.
56. Ibid., 40.
57. Tachard, *Voyage de Siam*, 143.
58. On the recall of Fr Fuciti, see Chappoulie, *Aux origines*, vol. 2, 45.
59. The expression is from Saint-Simon, concerning the *Histoire de France* of Fr Gabriel Daniel (*Mémoires*, Pléiade, vol. 4, 658).
60. Tachard, *Voyage de Siam*, 149–150; Bouvet, *Voyage de Siam*, 84–85.
61. Choisy, *Journal of a Voyage to Siam*, 125 (24 August).
62. Bouvet, *Voyage de Siam*, 88.
63. Choisy, op. cit., 132–133 (27 August).
64. Bouvet, op. cit., 88.
65. *Mercure Galant*, July 1686, vol. 1, 222–223.
66. Choisy, op. cit., 139 (12 September).
67. Vachet, *Mémoires*, in Launay, *Siam—Documents historiques*, vol. 1, 158.
68. Tachard, *Voyage de Siam*, 158.
69. Choisy, *Journal of a Voyage to Siam*, 142 (23 September).
70. Forbin, *Siamese Memoirs*, 45–46.
71. Bouvet, *Voyage de Siam*, 92.
72. Ibid.
73. Tachard, op. cit., 210.
74. Choisy, op. cit., 143 (26 September).

CHAPTER 17: "A BRILLIANT EMBASSY" (OCTOBER–DECEMBER 1685)

1. Choisy, *Journal of a Voyage to Siam*, 147 (1 October).
2. Vachet, *Mémoires*, in Launay, *Siam—Documents historiques*, vol. 1, 158–159.
3. Letter to Mr Maigrot, 22 June 1686. Arch. MEP, vol. 879, 353.
4. Relation *de la négociation de M. de Chaumont à Siam*, BN, NAF 9380 f. 160 r, Another copy is in AN, Colonies, C/1/22, ff. 94–116.
5. Choisy, op. cit., 144 (29 September).
6. Tachard, *Voyage de Siam* (Amsterdam: P. Mortier, 1686), 168.
7. *Mémoire de Monsieur Constance, premier ministre du roi de Siam, sur l'ambassade que le Roi a envoyée pour l'inviter à se faire chrétien,* AN, Col. C/1/22, f. 117 r. This text of twenty pages, well documented and very favourable to Phaulkon, is by Fr Tachard.
8. Bouvet, *Voyage de Siam* (1963), 98.
9. Ibid., 99–100.
10. Ibid., 100.
11. Tachard, op. cit., 106.
12. Bouvet, op. cit., 106.
13. Italian translation of a letter in Portuguese from Fr Manuel Soares to Fr de Noyelle, 15 December 1685. ARSJ, Jap. Sin. 76, ff. 293–295.
14. Letter from Fr Michel Bellanger, 21 June 1686. ARSJ, Jap. Sin. 76, f. 303 r.
15. See Chappoulie, *Aux origines*, vol. 2, 109.
16. *The Siamese Memoirs of Count Claude de Forbin, 1686–1688*, ed. Michael Smithies (1996), 48.
17. Bouvet, *Voyage de Siam*, 107.
18. Ibid., 108.
19. Ibid., 108.
20. Tachard, op. cit., 175.
21. Choisy, *Journal of a Voyage to Siam*, 149 (7 October).
22. Tachard, *Voyage de Siam* (Amsterdam: P. Mortier, 1686), 177.
23. Choisy, op. cit., 150 (8 October).
24. Forbin, *Siamese Memoirs*, 50.
25. Choisy, op. cit., 151 (10 October).
26. Ibid., 151–152 (10 October).
27. Chaumont and Choisy, *Aspects of the Embassy to Siam,* 41–42. This uses the 1687 English translation.
28. Tachard, op. cit., 176.
29. Choisy, *Journal of a Voyage to Siam*, 154 (13 October)
30. Tachard, *Voyage de Siam*, 187–188.
31. Chaumont and Choisy, *Aspects of the Embassy to Siam*, 43.
32. Choisy, op. cit.,156 (15 October).

33. Ibid., 154 (13 October).

34. Ibid., 157 (15 October).

35. Forbin, *Siamese Memoirs*, 50.

36. Choisy, *Journal of a Voyage to Siam*, 156 (14 October).

37. Arch. MEP, vol. 126, 128 (Launay, *Siam—Documents historiques*, vol. 1, 178).

38. Choisy, op. cit., 157–158 (15 and 17 October).

39. Arch. MEP, vol. 854, 931–932.

40. Tachard, op. cit., 190.

41. Choisy, op. cit., 160 (18 October)

42. Tachard, *Voyage de Siam* (Amsterdam: P. Mortier, 1686), 192.

43. *Mercure Galant*, July 1686, I, 256.

44. Choisy, *Journal of a Voyage to Siam*, 160 (18 October).

45. Ibid., 160, 166 (18 and 19 October).

46. On the "painted arms," see Forbin, *Siamese Memoirs*, 52; Tachard, *Voyage de Siam*, 196; La Loubère, *Kingdom of Siam* (London, 1693) 83, 96.

47. Choisy, op. cit., 161 (18 October).

48. Bouvet, *Voyage de Siam*, 118.

49. Choisy, op. cit., 161 (18 October).

50. Forbin, *Siamese Memoirs*, 53.

51. Ibid.

52. Choisy, *Mémoire sur l'ambassade au Siam, rédigé à bord de l'Oiseau le 1er janvier, 1686.* Arch. MEP, vol. 8, 1 et seq. (Dirk Van der Cruysse, ed., annex 3 in Choisy, *Journal du voyage de Siam* [Paris: Fayard, 1995], 385–397).

53. Forbin, op. cit.,53.

54. Chaumont and Choisy, *Aspects of the Embassy to Siam*, 48–49; Tachard, *Voyage de Siam* (Amsterdam: P. Mortier, 1686), 199–201; AN Col. C/1/22, f. 127; Arch. MEP, vol. 859, 397, in Launay, *Siam—Documents historiques*, vol. 1, 161). The last three versions appear more accurate than Smithies's.

55. *Mémoire de M. Constance . . . sur l'ambassade que le Roi a envoyée . . .* AN, Col. C/1/22, f. 119 v.

56. Tachard, *Voyage de Siam* (Amsterdam: P. Mortier, 1686), 202.

57. Choisy, *Journal of a Voyage to Siam*, 163 (18 October).

58. Ibid., 164 (18 October).

59. *Relation de la négociation de M. de Chaumont à Siam*, BN, NAF 9380, f. 161 v.

60. Tachard, op. cit., 203.

61. La Loubère, *Kingdom of Siam*, 89.

62. Bowring, *The Kingdom and People of Siam*, vol. 2, 259, 286, 308.

63. Choisy, op. cit., 165 (18 October). See also Bouvet, *Voyage de Siam*, 120.

64. Choisy, op. cit., 166 (19 October).

65. Arch. MEP, vol. 862, 153 (Launay, *Siam—Documents historiques*, vol. 1, 159–160); *Mercure Galant*, July 1686, vol. 1, 287–291; Tachard, *Voyage de*

Siam (Amsterdam: P. Mortier, 1686), 204–205. The last version is slightly different.

66. Choisy, *Journal of a Voyage to Siam*, 168 (21 October).

67. *Mémoire de l'abbé de Choisy,* Arch. MEP, vol. 8, 1 et seq. (Launay, op. cit., vol. 1, 162–168).

68. *Relation de la négociation de M. de Chaumont à Siam,* BN, NAF, 9380, f. 160 v.

69. *Mémoire de M. Constance . . . sur l'ambassade que le Roi a envoyée . . .*; AN Col. C/1/22, f. 119 r.

70. Bouvet, *Voyage de Siam*, 122–123.

71. Choisy, *Journal of a Voyage to Siam,* 169 (23 October).

72. Ibid., 180 (4 November).

73. This figure of 2,229 years, also mentioned in the *Relation de la négociation* . . . (BN, NAF, 9380, f. 164 r) goes back to 544 years B.C., the possible date of the birth of the Sakyamuni Buddha (the present Thai Buddhist calendar places this in 543 B.C.).

74. AN Col, C/1/22 ff. 124–125. This dialogue is found virtually unchanged in Tachard's *Voyage de Siam*, proving that he was indeed the author of this memorandum.

75. Choisy, *Journal of a Voyage to Siam*, 179 (4 November). The *kathin nam* observed by the French embassy took place on Sunday 4 November, according to Chaumont and Choisy (ed. Smithies), and the *Mercure Galant*. Bouvet, copied by Tachard, places it a week earlier, on 28 October.

76. *Mémoire de l'abbé de Choisy*, ed. D. Van der Cruysse, 394.

77. See Brummelhuis, *Merchant, Courtier and Diplomat*, 40.

78. *Relation de la négociation* . . . BN, NAF 9380, ff. 161–168.

79. Dhiravat, "Political History," 386.

80. Chaumont and Choisy, *Aspects,* 166–167.

81. Bouvet, *Voyage de Siam*, 133–134.

82. Cited by J. C. Gatty in the introduction to Bouvet, *Voyage de Siam du P. Bouvet* (1963), lxxxviii, n. 2.

83. See E.W. Hutchinson, "Phaulkon's House in Lopburi," in *Journal of the Siam Society* 27 (1934), 38–41; V. Pothisoonthorn et al., *Phra Narai Ratchanivet* (Bangkok: Department of Fine Arts, 1988), 38–41.

84. Choisy, *Journal of a Voyage to Siam,* 191–196 (19 November).

85. Ibid., 194 (19 November).

86. Chaumont and Choisy, *Aspects*, 59.

87. Choisy, op. cit., 198 (23 November).

88. Ibid., 196 (20 November).

89. Ibid., 214 (10 December).

90. Chaumont and Choisy, *Aspects*, 195–196.

91. *Relation de la négociation*. . . BN, NAF, 9280, f. 163 r.

92. Chaumont and Choisy, *Aspects*, 197.

93. Ibid., 196.

94. Tachard, *Voyage de Siam*, 233.

95. Louis Le Comte, *Nouveaux mémoires sur l'état présent de la Chine*, ed. Touboul-Bouyeure (Paris: Phébus, 1990), 30.

96. Bouvet, *Voyage de Siam*, 140–141.

97. Tachard, *Voyage de Siam*, 239.

98. ARSJ, Jap. Sin. 76, ff. 287–288. Phaulkon's letter is followed by another to Innocent XI (ff. 289–290) written the same day and repeating more or less the same things.

99. Ibid., ff. 291–292.

100. Letter of 18 November 1686, cited by Chappoulie, *Aux origines,* vol. 2, 111.

101. See Choisy, *Journal*, 206–208, and Arch. MEP, vol. 879, 117 et seq. (Launay, op. cit., vol. 1, 169–170). Choisy dates the text of the treaty on religion as 10 December; the copy in the MEP is dated 2 December.

102. Arch. MEP vol. 850, 91 (Launay, op. cit., vol. 1, 173–174).

103. Lanier, *Etude historique*, 67. The text of the commercial treaty dated 11 December 1685, is found in BN, NAF, 9380, ff. 169–172. See also the long report of Véret to the directors of the CIO, AN, Col. C/1/22, ff. 151–164.

104. Forbin, *Siamese Memoirs*, 70.

105. *Relation de la négociation*, BN, NAF, 9380, ff. 172–173.

106. For the terms *krob, tiab, bosseta*, and *bossette*, see La Loubère *Kingdom of Siam* (1693), 165–168.

107. Choisy, *Journal of a Voyage to Siam,* 217 (12 December).

108. Ibid., 218 (14 December).

109. Forbin, op. cit., 61.

110. Ibid., 221 (17 December).

CHAPTER 18: THE SIAMESE EMBASSY TO FRANCE (JANUARY 1686–FEBRUARY 1687)

1. *Mercure Galant*, July 1686, vol. 2, 279.

2. Choisy, *Journal of a Voyage to Siam*, 228 (6 January 1686).

3. Robert Challe, *Journal d'un voyage fait aux Indes orientales, 1690–1691*, ed. Deloffre and Menemencioglu (Paris: Mercure de France 1983), vol. 1, 199–201.

4. Chaumont and Choisy, *Aspects of the Embassy to Siam*, 126.

5. See Michael Smithies, ed., *A Siamese Embassy Lost in Africa, 1686: The Odyssey of Ok-khun Chamnan* (Chiang Mai: Silkworm Books, 1999).

6. See the beginning of chapter 15.

7. Chaumont and Choisy, *Aspects of the Embassy to Siam*, 126.

8. Choisy, *Journal of a Voyage to Siam*, 272 (9 May).

9. *Mercure Galant*, September 1686, vol. 2, 27–28 and 92–93.

10. Tachard, *Voyage de Siam* (Amsterdam: P. Mortier, 1687), 170. There is though an error in pagination in this edition, 1–274 being following by a sequence numbered 133–227. The reference is to the second sequence, and should be numbered p. 302.

11. Choisy, *Journal of a Voyage to Siam*, 262 (14 March).

12. Ibid., 270 (25 April).

13. See Georges Coedès, "Siamese Documents of the Seventeenth Century," *Journal of the Siam Society* 14/2 (1921), 12, and M.L. Manich Jumsai, *The Story of King Narai and his Ambassador to France in 1686, Kosaparn* (Bangkok: Chalermnit, 1987), 89–91.

14. Choisy, op. cit., 280 (14 June).

15. Letter from Fr M. Bellanger of 21 June 1686. ARSJ, Jap. Sin. 76, f. 303.

16. Vachet, *Mémoires*, Arch. MEP, vol. 113, 228 (Launay, *Siam—Documents historiques*, I, 180).

17. Brest, Archives of the Maritime District. Cited by Jacq-Hergoualc'h in the introduction to his edition of La Loubère's *Du Royaume de Siam* (1987), 25.

18. Tachard, op. cit., 163 (second sequence).

19. The *Mercure Galant* inserted an engraving of the "machine" in the special volume of September 1686 between pp. 168 and 169.

20. Brest, 21 June 1686. A.N., Col. C/1/23, f. 12 v.; BN, NAF, 9380, ff. 197–198.

21. Michael Smithies, *The Siamese Embassy to the Sun King: The Personal Memorials of Kosa Pan* (Bangkok, Duang Kamol, 1990).

22. Vachet, *Mémoires*, 181.

23. *Mercure Galant*, September 1686, vol. 2, 27–28.

24. The account of Chaumont's embassy in effect fills the second half of the ordinary volume of July (185–325) and the whole of the special volume (1–296). See Dirk Van der Cruysse, "Donneau de Visé et l'ambassade siamoise: entre l'histoire et la littérature," in *Biblio 17—Papers on French Seventeenth Century Literature*, v. 59 (Acts of Columbus, 1990), 199–208.

25. *Mercure Galant*, September 1686, vol. 2, 2–3, 5.

26. *Mémoire de M. de Chaumont de ce qu'il faut faire pour rendre les mêmes honneurs aux ambassadeurs de Siam, que le roi de Siam en a faits à son égard*, AN, Col. C/1/23, f. 12; BN, NAF, 9380, f. 197.

27. Merseburg, *Zentrales Staatsarchiv*, Frankreich, Rep. XI no. 89, fasc. 46, ff. 164–165.

28. *Mercure Galant*, September 1686, vol. 2, 46–47.

29. Ibid., 54.

30. "They were not so pleased when they arrived in Paris, because during their journey there were some places where they were not too well treated, especially at Orléans." Dangeau, *Journal*, vol. 1, 395–396 (2 October 1686).

31. *Mercure Galant*, September 1686, vol. 2, 82–83.

32. Vachet, *Mémoires*, loc. cit., 183.

33. Ibid.

34. *Registre du secrétariat. Année 1686*, AN, O/1/30, f. 289 v.

35. M. de Lionne to M. Martineau, Arch. MEP, vol. 850, 97 (Launay, *Siam—Documents historiques*, vol. 1, 184).

36. M. de Lionne to M. Vachet, 19 August 1686. Arch. MEP, vol. 879, 398 (Launay, op. cit., vol. 1, 185).

37. *Mercure Galant*, September 1686, vol. 2, 173.

38. Marquis de Sourches, *Mémoires*, ed. J. de Cosnac (Paris: Hachette, 1882–1893), vol. 1, 436.

39. Chaumont and Choisy, *Aspects of the Embassy to Siam*, 46.

40. Sourches, *Mémoires*, vol. 1, 436.

41. *Mercure Galant*, September 1686, vol. 2, 197.

42. Sourches, *Mémoires*, vol. 1, 437, n. 3.

43. *Mercure Galant*, January 1687, vol. 2, conclusion.

44. Michael Smithies, ed. and trans., *The Discourses at Versailles of the First Siamese Ambassadors to France 1686–7* (Bangkok, The Siam Society, 1986), 28–30.

45. AN, Col. C/1/23, f. 132.

46. See Gallois, *L'ambassade de Siam*, 102–103; Michel Jacq-Hergoualc'h, "Les ambassadeurs siamois à Versailles, le 1er Septembre 1686, dans un bas-relief en bronze d'A. Coysevox," *Journal of the Siam Society* 72 (1984): 19–36, illus.; Michael Smithies, "The Ladies at Versailles on 1st September 1686. A Note on the Coysevox Bronze," *The Siam Society Newsletter* 2/2 (June 1986): 3–7, illus.

47. Smithies, ed. and trans., *Discourses at Versailles*, 32.

48. Ibid., 40.

49. *Mercure Galant*, September 1686, vol. 2, 223.

50. *Mémoire des présents que le roi de Siam a faits au Roi . . .* , AN, Col. C/1/23, ff. 260–264. This list is reproduced in the editions of Chaumont (Paris, 1687; London, 1687; Chiang Mai, 1997), Choisy (Amsterdam, 1687), and Smithies, ed. and trans., *Discourses at Versailles* (Bangkok, 1986).

51. Choisy, *Voyage de Siam*, 205 (30 October 1685).

52. Chaumont and Choisy, *Aspects*, 201.

53. Sourches, *Mémoires*, vol. 1, 438. Sourches writes "tombac."

54. Dangeau, *Journal*, vol. 1, 378 (2 September 1686).

55. See Michel Jacq-Hergoualc'h, "A propos des canons siamois offerts à Louis XIV qui participèrent à la prise de la Bastille," *Annales historiques de la Révolution Française*, 261 (1985), 317–334, and S. Schama, *Citizens. A Chronicle of the French Revolution* (New York, Knopf, 1989), 388 and 403.

56. *Mercure Galant*, September 1686, vol. 2, 230–231.

57. Letter of 10 October 1686, Bodemann (1891), vol. 1, 76–77.

58. Letter to the Princess Amelise of 23 September 1705, ed. Holand (1867), vol. 1, 492–493. See also the letter to Sophie of Hanover of 16 November 1704, ed. Bodemann, vol. 2, 94.

59. La Bruyère, *Caracteres:* Des esprits forts, no. 29.

60. *Mercure Galant*, September 1686, vol. 2, 325–327.

61. *Mémoire de Phaulkon pour le P. Tachard*, December 1685. Arch. MEP, vol. 879, 151. (Launay, *Siam—Documents historiques*, vol. 1, 179–180).

62. M. de Lionne to M. Martineau, n.d., Arch. MEP, vol. 850, 97 (Launay, op. cit., 184).

63. *Lettres de la cour à l'intendant de la marine.* Brest, Arch. of the Naval District. Cited by Jacq-Hegoualc'h, introduction to La Loubère's *Du Royaume de Siam* (1987), 49. Extracts from the same correspondence quoted subsequently are taken from the same source, pp. 50–53.

64. Ibid., 52.

65. Sourches, *Mémoires*, vol. 1, 466 (2 October).

66. Dangeau, *Journal*, vol. 1, 395–396 (2 October).

67. *Régistre du secrétariat—Année 1686*, AN, O/1/30, f. 330.

68. Mr Storf to Seignelay, St Omer, 4 November. Cited by Gallois, *L'ambassade de Siam*, 112–113. These letters formed in the nineteenth century part of the family archives of the Duchess Decazes. A résumé is found in BN, NAF, 9380, f. 201.

69. *Mercure Galant*, January 1687, vol. 2.

70. Letter of 25 December 1712 from Monteleón to the Marshal de Tessé, cited in Dangeau's *Journal*, vol. 14, 287–289.

71. *Présents du Roi, de Monseigneur, et de Mme la Dauphine pour la cour de Siam*, AN, Col. C/1/23, ff. 47–50.

72. See Gallois, *L'ambassade de Siam*, 118–121.

73. Lanier, *Etude historique*, 89.

74. Fénelon, *Oeuvres*, Pléiade, vol. 1, 832–833. See also H. Sy, "Le sermon de Fénelon sur la vocation des gentils," *Revue d'histoire des missions,* September 1955, 321–338.

75. Dangeau, *Journal*, vol. 2, 7 (14 January 1687).

76. Chaumont and Choisy, *Aspects*, 203.

77. Smithies, ed. and trans., *Discourses at Versailles*, 52–54, and AN, Col. C/1/23, f. 29.

78. *Mercure Galant,* January 1687, vol. 2.

79. Dangeau, *Journal*, vol. 1, 412 (9 November 1686).

80. See Lanier, *Etude historique*, 89–91, and especially Jacq-Hergoualc'h, *Du royaume de Siam,* 26–44.

81. Challe, *Journal d'un voyage fait aux Indes orientales* (1983), vol. 1, 77.

82. *Instructions au sieur de La Loubère, envoyé extraordinaire auprès du roi de Siam* (18 January 1687) Arch. AE, Division historique, *Mémoires et Documents*, Asie, vol. 2 (1636–1734), ff. 93–102.

83. BN, NAF, 9380, f. 206.

84. *Instruction que le Roi veut être mise entre les mains des sieurs de La Loubère et Céberet que S.M. a nommés pour ses envoyés extraordinaires auprès du roi de*

Siam (25 January 1687), AN, Col. C/1/27, ff. 6–15. More extensive extracts of the instructions to the envoys are found in Jacq-Hergoualc'h, *Du royaume de Siam*, 46–48.

85. Turpin, *Histoire civile et naturelle du royaume de Siam* (1771), vol. 2, 88.

86. See Dhiravat, "Political History," 393–394.

87. Bèze, *Mémoire*, 46–47.

88. M. de Lionne to M. Martineau, Arch. MEP, vol. 850, 99 (Launay, op. cit., 199).

89. Lanier, *Etude historique*, 92.

90. Cited by Lanier, ibid., 92–94.

91. ARSJ, Jap. Sin. 76, f. 343.

92. The same details are found in Jacq-Hergoualc'h, *Du royaume de Siam*, 56–57.

93. *Vaisseaux du Roi composant l'escadre commandée par M. de Vaudricourt dans la campagne de Siam de 1687 et 1688.* BN, NAF 9380, f. 205.

94. *Histoire de la Musique*, Pléiade, vol. 1, 1646. See also the dialogue of Voltaire, *André Destouches à Siam (Mélanges*, Pléiade, 931–937) and M-H. Cotoni, "Dépaysement, dissonances, diatribe: André Destouches à Siam," in *Le siècle de Voltaire: Hommage à René Pomeau* (1987), I, 291–303.

95. *Histoire de la Musique*, Pléiade, I, 1589.

CHAPTER 19: THE LA LOUBÈRE–CÉBERET EMBASSY MARCH–DECEMBER 1687)

1. Guy Tachard, *Second voyage du Père Tachard et des Jésuites envoyés par le Roi au royaume de Siam* (Paris: Daniel Horthemels, 1689)—this edition has serious pagination errors; Amsterdam: Pierre Mortier, 1689.

2. AN, Col. C/1/24, ff. 172–211.

3. AN, Col. C/1/24, ff. 4–88. Copy in BN, NAF, 9380, ff. 216–267. Michel Jacq-Hergoualc'h, *Etude historique et critique du Journal du Voyage de Siam de Claude Céberet, envoyé extraordinaire du Roi en 1687 et 1688* (Paris, L'Harmattan, 1992) follows the AN manuscript.

4. Tachard, *Second voyage* (Amsterdam: P. Mortier, 1689), 16–17.

5. Ibid., 23.

6. Ibid., 27–28.

7. Ibid., 33.

8. Quoted by Tachard, ibid., 45.

9. Ibid., 57.

10. *Voyage ou Relation du P. Tachard à Siam*, AN, Col. C/1/24, f. 172.

11. Tachard, *Second voyage* (Amsterdam), 79.

12. Ibid., 117.

13. Abbé de Lionne to Mr Martineau, Arch. MEP, vol. 850, 99 (Launay, *Siam—Documents Historiques*, vol. 1, 199).

14. Account in Portuguese of 9 October 1688, addressed to his superior, ARSJ, Jap. Sin. 76, f. 341 r.

15. Forbin, *The Siamese Memoirs of Count Claude de Forbin*, 1685–1688, ed. Michael Smithies (1996), 77. This uses the 1731 London translation.

16. Ibid., 85

17. On the Makassar revolt, see Forbin, Ibid., 97–119; Turpin, *Histoire civile et naturelle*, vol. 2, 99–121; Anderson, *English Intercourse with Siam*, 285–296; Collis, *Siamese White*, 128–136; Dhiravat, "Political History," 405–410.

18. Forbin, *Siamese Memoirs*, 105.

19. Ibid., 112–113.

20. *Journal de la mission*, Arch. MEP, vol. 879, 520 et seq. (Launay, op. cit., vol. 1, 195).

21. This account is cited in extenso in Anderson, *English Intercourse with Siam*, 289–296.

22. See *Mercure Galant*, March 1688, 239; Sourches, *Mémores*, vol. 2, 133; Dangeau, *Journal*, vol. 2, 103–104.

23. Letter from Véret to the company directors (5 November 1696), AN, Col. C/1/23, f. 94.

24. Deslandes-Boureau, *Histoire de M. Constance*, 29–30.

25. Bèze, *1688, Revolution in Siam*, 56.

26. Ibid.

27. Letters of sixteen pages from Phaulkon to Fr de La Chaize of 20 November 1686, published with others as an appendix in Bèze's *Mémoire*.

28. Forbin, *Siamese Memoirs*, 143.

29. These three letters are dated 24 June 1687. The letters to Seignelay (AN, Col. C/1/23, f. 75 and BN, NAF, 9380, f. 207) and to Lagny (AN, Col. C/1/23, f. 157) were published in Siamese, French, and English by Coedès, "Siamese Documents of the Seventeenth Century," 14–21. The letter to Fr de La Chaize is quoted in Tachard, *Second voyage*, 58–59.

30. AN, Col. C/1/24, f. 173.

31. Bèze, *Mémoire*, 63.

32. Tachard, *Relation*, AN, Col. C/1/24, f. 175.

33. Céberet, *Journal*, AN, Col. C/1/24, f. 9.

34. Jacq-Hergoualc'h, introduction to the edition of La Loubère (1987), 61. Chapter 3 of this introduction (45–74) has interesting comments on the La Loubère/Céberet embassy based on documents in the Archives of the Arrondissement Maritime in Brest, and in AN, Col. C/1/23, 24, and 27.

35. *Copie de l'instruction secrète pour le P. Tachard*, AN, Col. C/1/23, f. 176.

36. Forbin, *Mémoire* (Michaud-Poujoulat, 1839), 499.

37. Tachard, *Second voyage*, 127–165, 230–247.

38. L. Le Comte, *Un Jésuite à Pékin* . . . (1990), 31–61.

39. Tachard, *Second voyage*, 168.

40. Bèze, *Mémoire*, 67–68.

41. Letter from Véret to the company directors (5 November 1696), AN, Col. C/1/23, f. 78.
42. Ibid., f. 93.
43. Ibid., f. 78.
44. Tachard, *Second voyage*, 184.
45. Céberet, *Journal,* f. 13.
46. Tachard, *Second voyage*, 187–188.
47. *Articles passés entre La Loubère et Céberet, et Tachard représentant Constance*, AN, Col. C/1/23, f. 194 (Portuguese and French texts; emphasis added).
48. Céberet, *Journal,* f. 17.
49. Tachard, *Second voyage*, 185.
50. Céberet, *Journal,* f. 18.
51. Ibid., f. 21.
52. Ibid., f. 35.
53. Jacq-Hergoualc'h, introduction to La Loubère, *Du royaume de Siam,* 65.
54. Tachard, *Second voyage*, 198.
55. Abbé de Lionne to Mr Martineau, Arch. MEP, vol. 850, 351 (Launay, *Siam—Documents Historiques*, vol. 1, 200).
56. Phaulkon to Mr Brisacier, Arch. MEP, vol. 882, 351 (Launay, *Siam—Documents historiques*, vol. 1, 193).
57. Lanier, *Etude historique*, 117.
58. Matthew 10:16 KJV.
59. Céberet, *Journal,* f. 54.
60. *Mémoire de M. Constance au Roi au sujet de la religion* (2 January 1688), AN, Col. C/1/24, ff. 110–125.
61. Tachard, *Second voyage*, 223.
62. Lanier, *Etude historique*, 120.
63. Jacq-Hergoualc'h, introduction to La Loubère, *Du royaume de Siam,* 66.
64. Tachard, *Second voyage*, 242–243.
65. Tachard, *Voyage au Siam*, 148–149 (second paginated sequence).
66. *Mémoires en forme de lettre d'un Anglais catholique au R. P. d'Orléans sur l'Histoire de M. Constance,* Arch. MEP, vol. 854, 925.
67. Deslandes-Boureau, *Histoire de M. Constance*, 32–33.
68. Lanier, *Etude historique*, 122.
69. Anderson, *English Intercourse with Siam*, 335–363; Collis, *Siamese White*, chs. 35–40; Smithies, *A Resounding Failure: Martin and the French in Siam, 1672–1693* (Chiang Mai, Silkworm Books), 56–63; Ian Morson, *Four Hundred Years – The British and the Thais* (Bangkok, Nai Suk, 1999), 78–92.
70. AN has the originals of the treaty in French, Siamese, and Portuguese (AN, Col. C/1/23, ff. 222–239). Coedès published the Siamese and French texts with English translation in "Siamese documents of the Seventeenth Century" in *Journal of the Siam Society* 14/2 (1921), 21–38.

71. AN, Col. C/1/22, ff. 199–204.

72. *Convention entre Constantin Phaulkon . . . et Céberet*, AN, Col. C/1/23, f. 212.

73. Céberet, *Journal*, f. 78; Tachard, *Second voyage*, 255–257.

74. Céberet, *Journal*, f. 81.

75. Forbin, *Mémoire*, 503.

76. Lanier, *Etude historique*, 124.

77. See Jacq-Hergoualc'h, introduction to La Loubère, *Du royaume de Siam*, 69.

78. Lanier, *Etude historique*, 124,

79. La Loubére, *Du royaume de Siam* (1691), vol. 1, 108; English ed. (1693), 29.

80. *Déclaration de La Loubère et Céberet à Desfarges*, 12 December 1687. AN, Col. C/1/23, f. 205.

81. AN, Col. C/1/24, ff. 98–100.

82. Tachard, *Second voyage*, 257.

83. Tachard, *Relation*, ff. 204–205.

84. Tachard, *Second voyage*, 271.

85. Ibid., 272.

86. Tachard, *Voyage au Siam*, 266–267.

87. Letter of Vaudricourt to Seignelay, written from the Cape, 22 April 1688. AN, Col. C/1/24, ff. 223–224.

88. La Loubére, *Du royaume de Siam* (1691), vol. 1, 173–174; English ed. (1693), 46.

89. *Mémoire général de tout ce que le roi de Siam a ordonné à son ambassadeur de lui faire faire* [sic] *ou acheter en France*. AN, Col. C/1/23, ff. 249–258.

90. Their names are given in the manuscript account of the third and fourth voyages in Asia of Fr Tachard, BN, Ms Fr. 19030, Ier cahier, 2.

91. Tachard, *Second voyage*, 274.

92. Bèze, *1688, Revolution in Siam*, 70.

93. Tachard, *Second voyage*, 279–333. See also Smithies, *A Siamese Embassy Lost in Africa*.

94. Tachard, *Relation*, AN, Col. C/1/24, ff. 207–211.

95. Lanier, *Etude historique*, 142–143.

96. Forbin, *Siamese Memoirs* (1996), 157–158.

97. Letter of Desclouzeaux to Seignelay, 26 July 1688, cited by Jacq-Hergoualc'h, introduction to La Loubère, *Du royaume de Siam*, 73.

98. Letter of Desclouzeaux to Seignelay, 30 July 1688, cited ibid., 74.

99. See especially AN, Col. C/1/24, ff. 95–128, 220–288.

CHAPTER 20: THE REVOLUTION IN SIAM (1688)

1. AN, Marine, Registre des expéditions de Siam. See L. Lanier, *Etude historique sur les relations de la France et du royaume de Siam* (1883), 147–148.

2. Tachard, *Second voyage au royaume de Siam* (Amsterdam: P. Mortier, 1689), Epître du Roi.

3. Dangeau, *Journal*, vol. 2, 155. The Soulié edition has *Le Bret*, but it is clearly an error; the same edition has *Sebret* when Céberet is mentioned for the first time on 9 November 1686 (vol. 1, 412).

4. Mme Phaulkon was to receive after 1717 a pension of three thousand *livres*. Documents of the lawsuit are in AN, Col. C/1/26; see Lanier, *Etude historique*, 196–197.

5. Mme de Sévigné, letter of 12 August 1689 to Mme de Grignan, *Correspondance*, Pléiade, vol. 3, 666.

6. Sourches, *Mémoires*, vol. 2, 190 (24 July 1688).

7. Forbin, *Siamese Memoirs*, 166–167.

8. Quoted in Lanier, *Etude historique*, 145.

9. Ibid., 506–507.

10. Dangeau, *Journal*, vol. 2, 212 and 187–188 (17 November and 14 October 1688).

11. Tachard, *Second voyage*, 363–367.

12. A study of this visit to Rome is given in Michael Smithies, "Siamese mandarins on the Grand Tour, 1688–1690," in *Journal of the Siam Society* 86 (1998), 107–118.

13. See AN, Col. C/1/25, ff. 13–14 (*Projet de traité pour le Siam*); ff. 18–38 (*Articles du traité franco-siamois*, 28 February 1689); ff. 39–41 (*Traité signé pour le Siam par le P. Tachard*, 15 March 1689).

14. Dangeau, *Journal*, vol. 2, 346 (5 March 1689).

15. AN, Col. C/1/25, ff. 43–46.

16. Lanier, *Etude historique*, 151.

17. Sourches, *Mémoires*, vol. 3, 161. See also Dangeau, *Journal*, vol. 2, 392 (12 May 1689).

18. Dangeau, *Journal*, vol. 3, 18 (5 November 1689); Sourches, *Mémoires*, vol. 3, 171–172 (6 November 1689).

19. See the *Relation des principales circonstances qui sont arrivées dans la révolution du royaume de Siam en l'année 1688*, BN, Ms Fr. 6105 (70 ff.) or the collection of letters of several French officers held prisoner by the Dutch in Middelburg (November 1689) AN, Col. C/1/25, ff. 73–124.

20. Jean Vollant des Verquains, *Histoire de la révolution de Siam arrivée en l'année 1688* (Lille: Jean Chrysostome Malte, 1691).

21. Bèze, *Mémoire du P. de Bèze sur la vie de Constance Phaulkon et sa triste fin*, ed. J. Drans and H. Bernard, (Tokyo: Presses Salésiennes, 1947). The English translation by E. W. Hutchinson, *1688, Revolution in Siam,* was

published in 1968 by Hong Kong University Press (repr. Bangkok: White Lotus, 1980).

22. ARSJ, Jap. Sin. 76, ff. 20–203. There is another manuscript copy in the Municipal Library in Dijon.

23. Marcel Le Blanc, *Histoire de la révolution de Siam arrivée en 1688 et de l'état présent des Indes,* 2 vols. (Lyons: Horace Molin, 1692).

24. Pierre-Joseph d'Orléans, *Histoire de M. Constance premier ministre du roi de Siam, et de la dernière révolution de cet Etat* (Paris: D. Horthemels, 1690).

25. *A Full and True Relation of the Great and Wonderful Revolution that hapned lately in the Kingdom of Siam in the East Indies . . .* (London: R. Taylor, 1690); *Het Leven en Daden van d'Heer Constantyn Phaulcon, eerste geheyme Raad van het Koningrijk Siam, zynde een nader verhaal van 't gene in 't jaar 1688 in 't Koningrijk Siam is voorgevallen* (Leiden: Frederik Haaring, 1692).

26. ARSJ, Jap. Sin. 76, f. 341 et seq. and f. 383 et seq.

27. La Touche, "Relation de ce qui est arrivé dans le royaume de Siam en 1688," in Challe, *Journal du Voyage des Indes Orientales,* ed. J. Popin and F. Deloffre (Geneva: Droz, 1998), 301–337.

28. Bèze, *1688, Revolution in Siam,* 72.

29. Céberet, *Journal de Voyage de Siam*, AN, Col. C/1/24, f. 24.

30. See Dhiravat, "Political History," 422–423.

31. Ibid., 426.

32. Bèze, *1688, Revolution in Siam,* 57–58.

33. Ibid., 59–60.

34. La Loubère, *Du royaume de Siam* (1691), vol. 1, 343–344; (1693), 89.

35. Vollant des Verquains, *Histoire de la révolution de Siam,* 11.

36. Le Blanc, *Mémoires secrets de ce qui s'est passé à Siam,* ARSJ, Jap. Sin. 78, ff. 27, 28–29.

37. Bèze, *1688, Revolution in Siam,* 78.

38. Le Blanc, *Mémoires secrets*, f. 29.

39. Bèze, op. cit., 79

40. Le Blanc, op. cit., f. 31, Bèze op. cit., 94.

41. Le Blanc, op. cit., ff. 23–24.

42. Ibid., f. 24.

43. Ibid., ff. 25, 27.

44. See Dhiravat, "Political History," 430, who quotes Dutch sources.

45. Deslandes-Boureau, *Histoire de Monsieur Constance,* 35.

46. Ibid., ff. 29–30.

47. Bèze, *1688, Revolution in Siam,* 97–98.

48. Vollant des Verquains, *Histoire de la révolution*, 24.

49. Bèze, *1688, Revolution in Siam,* 83. Le Blanc, *Mémoires secrets*, 35–36, more detailed, is identical.

50. *Mémoire de M. de Lionne* (4 January 1692), Arch. MEP, vol. 853 (Launay, *Siam—Documents historiques*, vol. 1, 208–214).

51. Mr de Brisacier to Mr de Lionne (11 February 1692). Arch. MEP, vol. 11, 488 (Launay, *Siam—Documents historiques*, vol. 1, 208).

52. Robert Lingat, "Une lettre de Véret sur la révolution siamoise de 1688," *T'oung Pao* 31 (1935): 330–362.

53. Desfarges, *Relation des révolutions arrivées à Siam dans l'année 1688* (Amsterdam, P. Brunet, 1691). A Dutch translation appeared in 1692 by Frederik Haaring. The memorandum of Desfarges was published in the *Cabinet Historique*, vol. 7 (1861). The original is in the national archives in The Hague.

54. Vollant des Verquains, *Histoire de la révolution*, 28.

55. Lanier, *Etude historique*, 154, 157.

56. E. W. Hutchinson, op. cit., 84.

57. Ibid.

58. Le Blanc, *Mémoires secrets*, ff. 39–40.

59. Dhiravat, *Political History*, 439.

60. Bèze, *1688, Revolution in Siam,* 86.

61. Le Blanc, *Mémoires secrets*, f. 48.

62. Ibid., f. 49.

63. Ibid., f. 51.

64. Ibid., f. 54. See the published version, *Histoire de la révolution* (Lyons: Horace Molin, 1692), vol. 1, 143–145.

65. Bèze, *1688, Revolution in Siam,* 88.

66. La Touche, *Relation*, 313.

67. Le Blanc, *Mémoires secrets*, f. 55.

68. Bèze, *1688, Revolution in Siam,* 90 (slightly modified).

69. *Het Leven en Daden van d'Heer Constantyn Phaulcon*, 10–11.

70. Coolhaas, *Generale Missiven van Gouverneurs-Generaal en Raden aan Heren XVII der Verenigde Oostindische Compagnie*, vol. 5: 1686–1697 (1975), 265; Vollant des Verquains, *Histoire de la révolution*, 59.

71. *Instructions de Phaulkon au P. Tachard*, December 1685. Arch. MEP, vol. 879, 151 (Launay, *Siam—Documents historiques*, vol. 1, 180). The gentlemen at the Foreign Missions interpreted this proposition in the same sense; see Le Blanc, *Mémoires secrets*, ff. 61–62.

72. Le Blanc, *Mémoires secrets*, f. 59.

73. Bèze, op. cit., 122–123; Le Blanc, op. cit., ff. 60–63.

74. Mr Martineau to the directors of the seminary of MEP in Paris, 12 July 1689. Arch. MEP, vol. 859, 498 et seq. (Launay, *Siam—Documents historiques*, vol. 1, 205).

75. Quoted by Le Blanc, *Mémoires secrets*, f. 60.

76. Ibid., f. 59.

77. Mr Braud to the directors of the seminary of MEP in Paris, August 1700. Arch. MEP, vol. 864, 309 (Launay, *Siam—Documents historiques*, vol. 2, 44).

78. Le Blanc, *Mémoires secrets*, f .68.

79. Ibid., f. 77. See published version, *Histoire de la révolution*, vol. 1, 226–228.

80. *Het Leven en Daden*, 11.

81. Le Blanc, *Mémoires secrets*, f. 78.

82. Letter from Johan Keyts to Governor-General Johan Camphuys of 5 December 1688. See Coolhaas, *Generale Missiven*, 265.

83. Kaempfer, *A Description of the Kingdom of Siam, 1690*, 33.

84. Arch. MEP, vol. 854, 887–942.

85. Bèze, *1688, Revolution in Siam*, 95.

86. Ibid., 96–97.

87. Coolhaas, *Generale Missiven*, 266. See also Smithies, *A Resounding Failure: Martin and the French in Siam, 1672–1693* on the death of Phra Narai, 96–97.

88. Vollant des Verquains, *Histoire de la révolution*, 94.

89. Martin wrote: "The king died at the same time . . . It is also held . . . that poison was added to a potion given to the king, which greatly hastened his death." Smithies, *A Resounding Failure*, 96 (Martin, *Mémoires*, [1934], vol. 3, 15). Martin was in Pondichéry at the time.

90. Le Blanc, *Mémoires secrets*, f. 108.

91. Ibid., f. 112.

92. Vollant des Verquains, *Histoire de la révolution*, dedication.

93. La Loubère, *Du royaume de Siam*, (1691), vol. 1, 355; (1693), 92.

94. See *Etat et inventaire de l'arsenal du fort de Bangkok, 1687*, in Gallois, *L'ambassade de Siam au XVIIe siècle*, 130–121.

95. Mr Martineau to the directors of the seminary of MEP, 12 July 1689. Arch. MEP, vol. 859, 498 et seq. (Launay, *Siam—Documents historiques*, vol. 1, 206).

96. Vollant des Verquains, *Histoire de la révolution*, 87.

97. La Rochefoucauld, *Maximes*, no. 19 (1678).

98. Le Blanc, *Mémoires secrets*, f. 82.

99. Kaempfer, *A Description of the Kingdom of Siam*, 34.

100. Vollant des Verquains, *Histoire de la révolution*, 107.

101. According to letters of the VOC, the *Oriflamme* left Batavia on 11 August and arrived 9 September at the bar (Coolhaas, *Generale Missiven*, 218, 266). Le Blanc places the arrival "about 15 August" (*Mémoires secrets*, 116), and is certainly wrong.

102. Le Blanc, *Mémoires secrets*, f. 116.

103. Ibid., f. 117.

104. See the text of the agreement in Vollant des Verquains, *Histoire de la révolution*, 110–113, and Launay, *Siam—Documents historiques*, vol. 1, 217–218.

105. Vollant des Verquains, *Histoire de la révolution*, 142.

106. Deslandes-Boureau, *Histoire de M. Constance*, 48.

107. AN, Col. C/1/25. Quoted by Lanier, *Etude historique*, 168.

108. Letter of 26 November 1688 to Fr de La Chaize, ARSJ, Jap. Sin. 76, ff. 353–354.

109. Deslandes-Boureau, *Histoire de M. Constance*, 51.

110. Le Blanc, *Mémoires secrets*, f. 135. See also Bèze, *1688, Revolution in Siam,* 163.

111. Vollant des Verquains, *Histoire de la révolution*, 147.

112. Ibid., 149.

113. See the detailed descriptions of the sufferings of Mgr Laneau in vols. 854 and 880 of Arch. MEP (Launay, *Siam—Documents historiques*, vol. 1, 220–221).

114. Letter of 24 November 1689. Arch. MEP, vol. 862, 379 et seq. (Launay, *Siam—Documents historiques*, vol. 1, 263–265).

115. Account in Portuguese of Fr Maldonado, ARSJ, Jap. Sin. 76, f. 342.

116. Le Blanc, *Mémoires secrets*, f. 101.

117. Challe, *Journal d'un voyage fait aux Indes orientales*, vol. 2, 11. The fact is confirmed in a document in the Foreign Missions. See Launay, *Siam—Documents historiques*, vol. 1, 224.

118. Arch. MEP, vol. 880, 311 (Launay, *Siam—Documents historiques*, vol. 1, 247–248) where "Launay, musicien," is indicated. Elsewhere (p. 224) he is called "le petit Delaunay, musicien." He must be one of the "three musicians of Mr Constance" who embarked on the *Gaillard* at the beginning of 1687 with André Cardinal-Destouches.

119. Le Blanc, *Mémoires secrets*, f. 150.

120. Ibid., f. 153.

121. Tachard, *Relation de voyage aux Indes (1690–1699)*. BN, Ms Fr. 19030, cahier 1, 24. I return to this manuscript in the Epilogue.

122. "P. Giacomo Duchat, della Provincia di Campagna, fu dalla costa al Pegù per liberare della schiavitudine il P. Despagnac," *Nomi de 15 Padri nostri Francesi che arrivarono a Siam . . . ,* ARSJ, Jap. Sin. 76, f. 343.

123. Martin, *Mémoires*, vol. 3, 28.

124. Le Blanc, *Mémoires secrets*, ff. 178–179. See also Vollant des Verquains, *Histoire de la révolution*, 163–164.

125. Vollant des Verquains, *Histoire de la révolution*, 173 and Le Blanc, *Mémoires secrets*, f. 188.

126. See a series of letters from officers held prisoner in Middelburg, dated November 1689, AN, Col. C/1/25, ff. 73–120.

127. Challe, *Journal* (1983), vol. 2, 238–239.

EPILOGUE: THE BONFIRE OF THE VANITIES

1. *Journal de la Mission,* Arch. MEP, vol. 854, 540 (Launay, *Siam—Documents historiques*, vol. 1, 204).

2. Claude Fleury, "Mémoire sur les études des missions orientales, dédié à Mgr Laneau, évêque de Métellopolis (3 mars 1689)," in *Oeuvres de l'abbé de Fleury* (Paris: Desrez, 1837), 74.

3. Turpin, *Histoire civile et naturelle*, vol. 1, 10–11.

4. Lavisse, *Louis XIV*, vol. 1, 246.

5. AN, Col. C/1/25, ff. 69–71.

6. See a résumé of this letter in Lanier, *Etude historique*, 178–181.

7. Robert Challe, *Journal d'un voyage fait aux Indes orientales,* 2 vols. edited and annotated by F. Deloffre and M. Menemencioglu (Paris: Mercure de France, 1983). The original edition, without the author's name, dates from 1721.

8. Claude-Michel Pouchot de Chantassin, *Relation du voyage et retour des Indes orientales pendant les années 1690 et 1691* (Paris, 1692). See p. 266 concerning the relief of the crew of the *Gaillard* when Tachard disembarked at Pondichéry.

9. BN, Ms Fr. 19030. The text of 114 pages is divided into three books; crossings out and corrections by another hand suggest that at one moment publishing this journal had been considered.

10. Challe, *Journal*, vol. 1, 110.

11. Letters of 27 November 1690 and 11 July 1691. Arch. MEP, vol. 880, 380, and vol. 862, 573 (Launay, *Siam—Documents historiques*, vol. 1, 305–306, 307).

12. Letter of 5 May 1693. Arch. MEP, vol. 881, 17 (Launay, *Siam—Documents historiques* , vol. 1, 308).

13. *Instructions du P. Tachard pour Okluang Vorovathi quand il sera arrivé a Siam*, Pondichéry, 7 May 1693. Arch. MEP, vol. 854, 673 (Launay, *Siam—Documents historiques*, vol. 1, 308–309).

14. Letter of 19 October 1696 "to the Magnificent Barcalon." AN, Col. C/1/25. Cited by Lanier, *Etude historique,* 186.

15. Lanier, *Etude historique,* 187.

16. Tachard, *Relation,* BN, Ms Fr. 19030. Bk. 3, 36–37.

17. See this letter reproduced in Lanier, *Etude historique*, 189.

18. "We also saw arrive that evening at the court Fr Tachard, Jesuit, who was returning from Siam." Sourches, *Mémoires*, vol. 6, 265 (12 June 1700).

19. Fr Braud to the directors of the seminary of MEP, Paris, August 1700. Arch. MEP, vol. 864, 309 (Launay, *Siam—Documents historiques*, vol. 2, 45).

CHRONOLOGY

1511	Autumn	The Portuguese viceroy Afonso de Albuquerque sends an ambassador to Siam.
1516		Embassy of Duarte de Coelho to Ayutthaya: signing of a Portuguese-Siamese treaty.
1567		Two Portuguese Dominicans, Frs Jerónimo da Cruz and Sebastião do Canto, arrive in Ayutthaya.
1569	11 Feb.	Three Dominicans massacred in Siam.
1580	31 Jan.	Death in Portugal of the Cardinal-King D. Henrique; Philip II of Spain annexes Portugal in the same year.
1586		Ralph Fitch is the first Englishman to visit the north of Siam.
1590	June	Accession of Phra Naresuan in Ayutthaya.
1593	18 Jan.	Battle of Nong Sarai; restoration of Siamese independence.
1595		Jacques de Coutre spends eight months in Siam.
1596		Publication of the *Itinerario* of van Linschoten.
1598		Spanish-Siamese treaty signed.
1600	31 Dec.	Creation of the East India Company (EIC) in London.
1601	7 Nov.	Two Dutch vessels, the *Amsterdam* and the *Gouda*, anchor in Pattani in the Gulf of Siam.
1602		Accession of Phra Chao Songtham.
	20 Mar.	Creation of the Verenigde Oostindische Compagnie (VOC).
1603		The first VOC representatives arrive from Pattani in Ayutthaya.
	25 Feb.	Jacob van Heemskerk seizes the *Santa Catarina* in the Singapore Straits.
1604		Henri IV of France grants the monopoly of the French trade in the Indies to a company of merchants from Dieppe, St Malo, and Rouen.
	9 Sep.	The Admiralty in Amsterdam approves the seizure of the *Santa Catarina*.

1605	25 Apr.	Death of Phra Naresuan and accession of his brother Phra Ekathotsarot.
1607		The first Portuguese Jesuit, Fr Baltasar Sequeira, arrives in Ayutthaya.
1608	28 Jan.	Departure from Bantam of a Siamese embassy for Holland.
	Feb.	Opening of a Dutch godown in Ayutthaya.
	10 Sep.	The Prince of Orange receives the Siamese envoys in The Hague.
1609	Nov.	Death of Sequeira in Phetchaburi.
1610	30 Jan.	The Siamese ambassadors leave Holland on the fleet commanded by Pieter Both, first VOC governor-general.
1612	23 June	The EIC opens a godown in Pattani.
	17 Sep.	EIC envoys present in Ayutthaya a letter from James I to the King of Siam, and open a godown in the capital.
1614		Posthumous publication of Fernão Mendes Pinto's *Peregrinação.*
1615		The French company of 1604 is reorganized under the name of the Company of the Moluccas.
1616		Formation in Copenhagen of the Dansk Ostindisk Kompagni (Danish East Indies Company).
1619	4 Apr.	Fr Alexander de Rhodes embarks at Lisbon for Asia.
	17 July	In Pattani, three VOC vessels attack and seize two EIC ships.
1621		Cornelis van Neijenrode writes his *Vertoog* . . ., the first Dutch description of Siam.
1622	6 Jan.	Gregory XV creates the Congregation *De Propaganda Fide.*
1624	28 Jan.	Birth of Pierre Lambert de La Motte, future Bishop of Berythus and vicar-apostolic in Siam.
	Aug.	Diplomatic incident over the seizure by the Spanish of the yacht *Cleen Zeelandt* on the Chao Phraya.
1625	Jan.	Fr de Rhodes arrives in Cochin-China.
1628	13 Dec.	Death of Phra Chao Songtham; accession of Phra Chettharacha.
1629	Aug.	Assassination of Phra Chettharacha; accession of Phra Athittayawong.
	Sep.	Assassination of Phra Athittayawong; accession of Prasat Thong.
1630	End year	Death in prison of Fr Margico, superior of the Jesuits in Ayutthaya.

1632		Birth of Prince Narai, son of Prasat Thong.
1633	May	Joost Schouten obtains in Ayutthaya a monopoly and a plot of land on which the VOC will build a new godown.
1636	10 Dec.	The picnic incident, compromising VOC-Siamese relations.
1637	31 May	Birth of Louis Laneau, future Bishop of Metellopolis and vicar-apostolic of Siam.
1638		Publication of the *Notitie . . . des Coningkrijcks Siams* of Joost Schouten.
	5 Sep.	Birth of Louis XIV at Saint-Germain.
1640	1 Dec.	Duke of Braganza acclaimed King of Portugal, the independence of which is restored.
1641	Jan.	The VOC evicts the Portuguese from Malacca.
	Mid-Oct.	Chulakantamangala (tonsure) ceremony of Prince Narai.
1642		Richelieu forms the first French Indies Company.
1643	14 May	Death of Louis XIII.
1644		Joost Schouten executed at Batavia for sodomy.
1647 or 1648		Birth of Constantine Phaulkon in Cephalonia (Greece).
1650	Feb.	An incident during the cremation of a daughter of Prasat Thong leads to the execution of nearly 3,000 *khunnang* (mandarins).
1651	7 Apr.	Birth of Guy Tachard.
1656	7 Aug.	Death of Prasat Thong, accession of Chao Fa Chai.
	8 Aug.	Chao Fa Chai removed by his brother Narai who installs his uncle Sri Suthammaracha on the throne.
	27 Oct.	Assassination of Sri Suthammaracha; accession of Phra Narai.
1657	Jan.	Failed coup d'état of Prince Trai Phuwanathityawong, half-brother of Phra Narai.
	17 July	Pope Alexander VII receives in audience Vincent de Meur and François Pallu who plead the cause of vicars-apostolic to go to South-East Asia.
1658	Summer	The Holy See nominates F. Pallu, P. Lambert de La Motte, and I. Cotolendi bishops *in partibus* of Heliopolis, Berythus, and Metellopolis.
1659		Creation in Paris of the Society of Foreign Missions (MEP), which only received its definitive statutes in 1700.
1660	11 June	Mgr Lambert de La Motte consecrated bishop in Paris.

1660	27 Nov.	Lambert and two MEP priests embark at Marseilles to take the land route to Siam.
	19 Dec.	The *Saint-Louis*, due to take apostolic missionaries to Asia, sinks near Texel.
1662		Mgr Pallu, Mgr Cotolendi, and Laneau embark at Marseilles.
	19 May	Lambert and his companions arrive in Tenasserim.
	22 Aug.	Lambert arrives in Ayutthaya.
	Autumn	The Persian *Phra Khlang* of Siam proclaims a royal monopoly on all exports.
1663	11 July	Lambert in a letter to the pope proposes the recall of all missionaries in the Indies.
	14 Oct.	Jacques de Bourges returns to Europe.
	Oct.	Dutch blockade of the Chao Phraya, until Feb. 1664.
1664	27 Jan.	Pallu and his companions arrive in Ayutthaya.
	1 Apr.	Publication of *Discours touchant l'établissement d'une Compagnie française* written on the orders of Colbert.
	27 July	Jacques de Bourges in London.
	22 Aug.	Signing of a new VOC-Siamese treaty.
1665	17 Jan.	Pallu leaves Ayutthaya for Europe.
	7 Mar.	The first French Compagnie des Indes Orientales (CIO) fleet leaves Brest.
	29 May	Lambert requests Phra Narai to grant land and materials for building a church.
1666	Jan.	Publication of Jacques de Bourges's *Relation du voyage de Mgr de Béryte au royaume de Siam.*
1667	15 Oct.	Lambert publishes in Ayutthaya a vehement pastoral letter against trading by priests.
	19 Oct.	A letter from Lambert to Pallu discusses the establishment of diplomatic relations between Louis XIV and Phra Narai.
1668	13 Feb.	François Caron arrives in Surat to direct the activities of the godown of the CIO.
	14 Nov.	New treaty between the VOC and Siam.
1669	Feb.	Arrival in Siam of Jacques de Bourges and four other missionaries who had left on the Montdevergue squadron.
	June	Clement IX extends the jurisdiction of the vicars-apostolic to Siam.
	24 Aug.	Clement IX signs a letter in Latin to Phra Narai.
	17 Sep.	Pallu leaves Rome for France and Siam.
1670	31 Jan.	Louis XIV signs a letter to Phra Narai.

1671	July	Arrival in Siam of Bénigne Vachet of the MEP.
1672	6 Apr.	Louis XIV declares war on the United Provinces.
	Oct.	The Jesuits and Dominicans at Ayutthaya refuse to accept the papal brief *Speculatores* which Laneau sends them.
1673	27 May	Pallu returns to Siam after an absence of more than eight years.
	End Sep.	Laneau elected Bishop of Metellopolis and vicar-apostolic in Siam.
	18 Oct.	Phra Narai receives in solemn audience the letters of Clement IX and Louis XIV.
	End Oct.	Annual procession on the Chao Phraya (*kathin nam*); Phra Narai orders a detour to observe the French mission.
	8 Nov.	The three MEP bishops announce to Louis XIV the imminent departure of a Siamese embassy.
	End Nov.	The three bishops are invited to Lopburi.
1674	13 Jan.	François Martin sets up the CIO in Pondichéry.
	End Jan.	Fr Oliva, general of the Society of Jesus, undertakes to have respected the pontifical briefs submitting religious missionaries to the vicars-apostolic.
	25 Mar.	Laneau enthroned as bishop in Ayutthaya.
	20 Aug.	Pallu leaves Siam.
1675	1 June	Pallu, arrested by the Spanish, leaves Manila for Madrid, passing through Mexico.
	6 Nov.	*Phra Khlang* Kosathibodi and the EIC sign a new commercial treaty.
1676	Dec.	Surprised by rain, Phra Narai decides to abandon the annual ceremony ordering the waters to withdraw.
1678	1 Sep.	Phra Narai orders his *khunnang* to select two ambassadors for France.
	Sep.	Arrival in Siam of Constantine Phaulkon.
1679	15 June	Death in Ayutthaya of Lambert de La Motte.
	End summer?	Shipwreck on the Malay coast of Phaulkon supplying arms to rebels in Songkhla.
	End year?	Phaulkon enters the service of the *Phra Khlang*.
1680	Early Oct.	A. Deslandes presents the *Phra Khlang* a letter and gifts from the CIO director in Surat, Baron.
1681		The *Vautour*, carrying Siamese ambassadors to the French king and the pope, anchors at Bantam.
	End Aug.	The three Siamese ambassadors leave Bantam on the *Soleil d'Orient*.
	Dec. (or Jan 1682)	Shipwreck of the *Soleil d'Orient*.

1682	2 May	Phaulkon abjures Protestantism in the Jesuit church in Ayutthaya.
	Mid-May	Phaulkon marries Maria Guyomar.
	4 July	Pallu arrives in Ayutthaya with presents from the pope and Louis XIV.
	Dec.	Conflagration, probably deliberate, of the EIC godown in Ayutthaya.
1683	End June	Pallu leaves Siam for China.
	July	Death of *Phra Khlang* Kosathibodi. Phaulkon in effect succeeds him.
	6 Sep.	Death of Colbert; his son Seignelay is made head of the department of the navy.
	Mid-Sep.	Laneau informs Phra Narai of the shipwreck of the *Soleil d'Orient.*
	Nov.	Phra Narai decides to send two *khunnang* to the court in France.
1684	Jan.	The EIC decides to withdraw from Ayutthaya.
	Sep.	Vachet and Pascot and two Siamese *khunnang* arrive in London.
	Mid-Oct.	The Siamese arrive in Paris.
	29 Oct.	Death of Pallu in Fukien province.
	20 Nov.	Louis XIV receives Vachet in private audience.
	27 Nov.	The Siamese envoys pay their respects to Louis XIV in Versailles.
	16 Dec.	The *Gazette* announces that the Chevalier de Chaumont is named ambassador extraordinary to Siam.
1685	28 Jan.	Louis XIV signs letters patent for the six Jesuit mathematicians due to go to Siam and China.
	3 Mar.	Departure from Brest of the Chaumont/Choisy embassy on the *Oiseau* and the *Maligne.*
	27 June	An embassy from Shah Sulaiman of Persia sets sail for Siam from Bandar Abbas.
	24 Sep.	The French embassy arrives at the bar of Siam.
	18 Oct.	Solemn audience in Ayutthaya of the Chaumont/Choisy embassy: the same day Louis XIV signs the revocation of the Edict of Nantes.
	22 Nov.	Phra Narai receives the six Jesuit astronomers.
	10 Dec.	The Abbé de Choisy is ordained priest in Lopburi by Laneau; his short retreat prior to this allows Tachard to take in hand French Siamese affairs, becoming the confident of Phaulkon.
	22 Dec.	The French embassy sets sail, with Tachard and the Siamese embassy to France on board.

1686	April	Shipwreck near Agulhas Point of the Portuguese vessel *Nossa Senhora dos Milagros* taking three Siamese ambassadors from Goa to Lisbon.
	18 June	Return to Brest of the *Oiseau* and the *Maligne.*
	9 July	The Siamese ambassadors leave Brest.
	Mid-July	Discovery of the Makassar plot in Siam.
	12 Aug.	Solemn entry of the Siamese ambassadors in Paris.
	1 Sep.	Solemn audience of the Siamese ambassadors at Versailles.
	14 Sep.	With the aid of European and Siamese forces, Phaulkon crushes the Makassar revolt in Ayutthaya.
	14 Oct.	The Siamese ambassadors begin their tour of Flanders.
1687	14 Jan.	Farewell audience of the Siamese ambassadors.
	18 Jan.	La Loubère, nominated early November as envoy extraordinary to Siam, along with Céberet, receives his first instructions.
	18 Jan.	The embassy sent by Shah Sulaiman to Siam embarks to return to Persia.
	22 Jan.	Seignelay signs a letter to Phaulkon requesting him to "place complete faith" in Tachard.
	1 Mar.	The Vaudricourt squadron leaves Brest for Siam, taking envoys, troops, Jesuits, and missionaries.
	14 July.	The massacre by the Siamese of about one hundred Englishmen at Mergui.
	25 Aug.	The Abbé de Choisy is elected to the Académie Française.
	26 Sep.	The *Oiseau,* with Tachard on board, arrives at the bar of Siam; Tachard confers with Phaulkon.
	6 Oct.	Arrival at the bar of Siam of the *Gaillard,* the *Loire,* and the *Dromadaire.*
	18 Oct.	Disembarkation of French troops in Bangkok.
	26 Oct.	La Loubère and Céberet arrive in Ayutthaya.
	2 Nov.	Solemn audience of the two French envoys.
	10 Nov.	The envoys follow the king to Lopburi.
	25 Oct.	The *Oiseau* leaves for Pondichéry.
	11 Dec.	Signing of a new Franco-Siamese trade treaty.
	13 Dec.	Céberet leaves Lopburi for Mergui.
	23 Dec.	Farewell audience of La Loubère.
	25 Dec.	Farewell audience of Tachard, now ambassador of His Siamese Majesty to Pope Innocent XI and Louis XIV.
1688	1 Jan.	Céberet arrives at Mergui.
	3 Jan.	The *Gaillard,* the *Loire,* and the *Dromadaire* leave the bar of Siam.
	Early Feb.	The *Oriflamme* leaves Brest taking two hundred troops to Siam. Phra Narai falls seriously ill.
	2 Feb.	Céberet and Forbin leave Pondichéry on the *Oiseau.*

	17 Feb.	Du Bruant leaves Bangkok with three companies to take possession of the fort of Mergui.
	31 Mar.	Summoned to Lopburi, the French General Desfarges discusses with Phaulkon the means of crushing the plot of Ok-phra Petratcha.
	15 Apr.	Desfarges allows himself to be persuaded by Véret and the Abbé de Lionne to abandon Phaulkon.
	18 May	Coup d'état in Lopburi: Ok-phra Petratcha is master of the palace and the king's person; Phaulkon is arrested.
	20 May	Beheading of Phra Pi, Phra Narai's adopted son.
	25 May	Petratcha orders Lionne to ensure Desfarges returns to Lopburi.
	2 June	Desfarges arrives in Lopburi.
	Early June	The Siamese invest the fort at Mergui.
	5 June	Execution of Phaulkon in the forest of Thale Chupson.
	24 June	The French garrison evacuates Mergui.
	Late June	The siege of the fort of Bangkok begins.
	9 July	Murder of Phra Narai's two half-brothers.
	10 or 11 July	Death of Phra Narai.
	18 July	Return to Brest of the *Oiseau.*
	25 July	Return to Brest of the *Gaillard,* the *Loire,* and the *Dromadaire.*
	1 Aug.	Coronation of Phra Phetracha in Ayutthaya.
	9 Sep.	The *Oriflamme* arrives at the bar of Siam.
	4 Oct.	Mme Phaulkon comes to Bangkok to seek French protection.
	18 Oct.	Desfarges hands Mme Phaulkon back to the Siamese.
	2 Nov.	The French garrison leaves the fortress of Bangkok.
	5 Nov.	Tachard leaves Paris for Rome, with three Siamese mandarins.
	13 Nov.	The *Oriflamme*, the *Siam*, and the *Louvo* set sail for Pondichéry.
	23 Dec.	Innocent XI receives Tachard and his mandarins in audience.
1689	15 Jan.	Du Bruant and the survivors of Mergui reach Pondichéry.
	1–4 Feb.	The *Oriflamme*, the *Siam*, and the *Louvo* drop anchor before Pondichéry.
	16 Feb.	The *Normande* and the *Coche* leave Pondichéry for France.
	15 Mar.	Signing of a new Franco-Siamese treaty at Versailles, with Tachard representing Siam.
	10 Apr.	Desfarges's squadron leaves Pondichéry for Joncelang (Junk Ceylon, modern Phuket).
	26 Apr.–4 May	The *Normande* and the *Coche* are seized by the Dutch at the Cape.
	End June	The French held prisoners at the Cape leave on Dutch vessels for the prison of Middelburg.
	5 Nov.	The court of France hears the first news of the revolution in Siam and the sieges of Bangkok and Mergui.

1690	19 Feb.	Funeral ceremonies and cremation of Phra Narai.
	Mar.	Desfarges, recalled to France, embarks with his men on the *Oriflamme*.
	2 Mar.	Tachard starts his third voyage to Asia, embarking with the Duquesne-Guiton squadron.
	7 June	Engelbert Kaempfer arrives in Siam.
	3 Nov.	Death of the Marquis de Seignelay.
1691		Publication of *Du Royaume de Siam* of La Loubère (Paris), and the *Histoire de la Révolution de Siam* of Vollant des Verquains (Lille).
	27 Feb.	The *Oriflamme* sinks with all hands in a storm off Brittany.
	Apr.	Laneau and his priests are released from prison; their seminary and church are restored to them.
1692		Publication of the *Histoire de la Révolution du Royaume de Siam* of Fr Le Blanc (Lyon), and the *Beschryving van het Koningryk Siam* of Jeremias van Vliet (Leiden).
1693	Sep.	The Dutch seize Pondichéry; Tachard is among those deported to Europe.
1694	July.	Tachard returns to France.
1695	27 Mar.	Tachard leaves Port-Louis for his fourth voyage to Asia.
1696	16 Mar.	Death in Ayutthaya of Louis Laneau.
1698	Nov.	Tachard disembarks at Mergui, to travel to Ayutthaya.
1699	Jan.	Phra Phetracha receives Tachard in audience.
	14 Sep.	Tachard embarks at Pondichéry for France.
1700	Spring	Death (suicide?) of Kosa Pan, former first ambassador to France and later *Phra Khlang* of Phra Phetracha.
	12 June	Tachard arrives at Versailles.

KINGS OF AYUTTHAYA

1.	Ramathibodi I	1351–1369
2.	Ramesuan	1369–1370
3.	Borommaracha I	1370–1388
4.	Thong Chan	1388
5.	Ramesuan (second reign)	1388–1395
6.	Ramracha	1395–1409
7.	Intharacha I	1409–1424
8.	Borommaracha II	1424–1448
9.	Borommatrailokanat, ruling in Ayutthaya	1448–1463
	Idem, ruling in Phitsanulok	1463–1488
10.	Borommaracha III, in Ayutthaya	1463–1488
11.	Intharacha II	1488–1491
	(nos. 10 and 11 are the same)	
12.	Ramathibodi II	1491–1529
13.	Borommaracha IV	1529–1533
14.	Ratsada	1533–1534
15.	Chairacha	1534–1547
16.	Yot Fa	1547–1548
17.	Khun Worawongsa	1548
18.	Chakkraphat	1548–1569
19.	Mahin	1569
20.	Maha Thammaracha	1569–1590
21.	Naresuan	1590–1605
22.	Ekathotsarot	1605–1610 (or 1611?)
23.	(Si Saowaphak)	(1610–1611?)

24. Song Tham (Intharacha)	1610/11–1628
25. Chettha	1628–1629
26. Athittayawong	1629
27. Prasat Thong	1629–1656
28. Chai	1656
29. Suthammaracha	1656
30. Narai	1656–1688
31. Phetracha	1688–1703
32. Sua (Sorasak)	1703–1709
33. Phumintharacha (Thai Sa)	1709–1733
34. Borommakot	1733–1758
35. Uthumphon	1758
36. Suriyamarin (Borommaracha)	1758–1767

The seizure and destruction of Ayutthaya by the Burmese on 7 April 1767 and the death of King Suriyamarin a few days later ended the kingdom of Ayutthaya. After the reign of King Taksin of Thonburi (1767–1782), the Chakri dynasty was established in Bangkok, the new capital of the kingdom.

(Source: David J. Wyatt, *Thailand. A Short History*, Yale University Press, 1984, pp. 312–313. For the uncertainties surrounding the end of the reign of Ekathotsarot and the accession of Song Tham, see Wyatt, p. 106.)

BIBLIOGRAPHY

MANUSCRIPT SOURCES

1. PARIS, ARCHIVES NATIONALES (AN)
K/1374 (no. 55–58).
K/1368 (no. 58).
0/1/30. Maison du Roi, registre du secrétariat. Year 1686.
Colonies C/1/22. Siam: 1669–1685.
Colonies C/1/23. Siam: 1686–1687.
Colonies C/1/24. Siam: 1687–1688.
Colonies C/1/25. Siam: 1689–1703.
Colonies C/1/26. Siam: 1689–1717 (Proceedings of the lawsuit of Phaulkon's heirs against the CIO).
Colonies C/1/27. Siam: Tables des expéditions. Years 1687–1689.

2. PARIS, BIBLIOTHÈQUE NATIONALE DE FRANCE (BN)
Fr. 6105: Relation des principales circonstances qui sont arrivées dans la révolution du royaume de Siam, 1687–1688.
Fr. 8210: Pinsonneau (in fact Beauchamp), Relation des révolutions de la cour de Siam, 1693.
Fr. 15476: Mission du P. Tachard.
Fr. 15647, f. 70 sq.: Letter from the bishop of Métellopolis, 24 Nov. 1689.
Fr. 17239, f. 98 sq.: J. Richaud (?), Relation de voyage au Siam fait en 1687.
Fr. 19030: G. Tachard, Relation de voyage aux Indes (1690–1699).
NAF 7485, f. 35: Copy of a letter from Siam (14 Dec. 1675).
NAF 7491, f. 346: "Ce qui s'est passé en la présentation des lettres . . ." (18 Oct. 1673)
NAF 9380: Fonds Margry.

3. PARIS, ARCHIVES DES AFFAIRES ÉTRANGÈRES (ARCH. AÉ)
Fonds "Mémoires et Documents," Série Asie.
Vol. 2 (1636–1734).
Vol. 3 (1664–1733).
Vol. 4 (1687–1810).
See the contents of these three volumes in Kennon Breazeale, "Inventaire des documents sur le Siam conservés aux archives de Paris," in *Journal of the Siam Society*, LXII (1974), 159.

4. PARIS, ARCHIVES DES MISSIONS ÉTRANGÈRES DE PARIS (ARCH. MEP)

In addition to the documents published by A. Launay, *Histoire de la Mission de Siam–Documents historiques* (2 vols., 1920, see *infra*, Printed Sources):

Siam 853, 107–144: Remarques sur l'*Histoire de M. Constance* composée par le P. d'Orléans Jésuite.

Siam 854, 887–942: Mémoires en forme de lettre d'un Anglais catholique au R. P. Pierre d'Orléans Jésuite sur l'*Histoire de M. Constance et des révolutions arrivées à Siam en 1688* écrite par ce Père.

Vol. 1081: the *Brest Journal* of Kosa Pan, in Siamese.

5. THE HAGUE, ALGEMEEN RIJKSARCHIEF (ARA)

In addition to the *Generale Missiven aan Heren XVII der VOC* published by W. Ph. Coolhaas (5 vols., see *infra*, Printed Sources):

VOC 1098–1456: *Overgekomen Brieven. Inkomend Briefboek* (1630–1689).

VOC 855–916: *Bataviaasch uitgaand Briefboek* (1630–1689).

VOC 4025 I, 4026, 4029: Documents seized by the Dutch when capturing the *Normande* and the *Coche* at the Cape, 26 April and 4 May 1689.

VOC 4863: Desfarges, Relation de la révolution de 1688 (published in 1691, see *infra*).

6. ROME, ARCHIVUM ROMANUM SOCIETATIS JESU (ARSJ)

Jap.Sin 76: Siam-Camboja. Relationes Controversiarum. Documenta (1658–1727).

Jap.Sin. 78, ff. 20–203: [M. Le Blanc], *Mémoires secrets de ce qui s'est passé à Siam dans les années 1687 et 1688.*

Jap.Sin. 91–94: Controversiae cum Vicariis Apostolicis.

Gal. 42: Letters from the superiors general of the Society of Jesus to the French Jesuit provinces, 1670–1699.

Gal. 72: Letters from Father de La Chaize.

7. MERSEBURG, ZENTRALES STAATSARCHIV

Frankreich, Rep. XI no. 89, Fasc. 46–47: Ezechiel Spanheim, Dispatches from Paris to the Elector of Brandenburg, June 1686–January 1687.

8. LONDON, PUBLIC RECORD OFFICE

State Papers, Domestic 44/56.

PRINTED SOURCES

Aanmerklijk en Naaukeurig Verhaal der Staatsomkeringen nu laatst in 't jaar 1688 in Siam voorgevallen. Leiden: Fr. Haaring, 1692. English translation by O. Frankfurter, "Siam in 1688: Translation of an early Narrative," *Journal of the Siam Society*, 5/4 (1909): 1–50.

Albuquerque, Luis de. *Ciência e experiência nos descobrimentos portugueses*. Lisbon: Instituto de Cultura portuguesa, 1983.

Alexander Hamilton, a Scottish Sea Captain in Southeast Asia 1689–1723. Edited by Michael Smithies. Chiang Mai, Silkworm Books, 1997.

Ambassade du Roy de Siam envoyée à l'Excellence du Prince Maurice, arrivée à La Haye le 10 septembre 1608. Leiden, 1608.

Anderson, John. *English Intercourse with Siam in the Seventeenth Century*. London: Kegan Paul, 1890.

Atkinson, Geoffroy. *Les relations de voyages du XVIIe siècle et l'évolution des idées*. Paris: Champion, 1924.

Aubin, Jean. "Les Persans au Siam sous le règne de Naraï (1656–1688)." *Mare Luso-Indicum* 4 (1980): 95–126.

Baudiment, L. François Pallu, principal fondateur de la Société des Missions étrangères (1626–1684). Paris: Beauchesne, 1934.

Bayle, Pierre. "Sommona-Codom." In *Dictionnaire historique et critique*, vol. 3, 594–596. Rotterdam, 1715.

Beaulieu, Augustin de. *Mémoires d'un voyage aux Indes orientales, 1619–1622*. Edited by D. Lombard. Paris: Maisonneuve & Larose, 1996.

Bernard, Henri. *Le voyage du Père de Fontaney au Siam et à la Chine (1685–1687)*. Tientsin/Shangai: Cathasia, 1942.

Berval, René, ed. *Présence du Bouddhisme*. Paris: Gallimard, 1987.

Bèze, Claude de. *Mémoire sur la vie de Constance Phaulkon, premier ministre du roi de Siam, Phra Narai, et sa triste fin*. Edited by J. Drans & H. Bernard. Tokyo: Presses Salésiennes, 1947.

———. *1688, Revolution in Siam, the Memoir of Father de Bèze*. Translated into English with introduction, commentary, appendices, and notes by E. W. Hutchinson. Hong Kong: Hong Kong University Press, 1968; Bangkok: White Lotus, 1990.

°Biermann, Benno. "Die Missionen der portugiesischen Dominikaner in Hinterindien." *Zeitschrift für Missionswissenschaften* 21 (1931): 305–327.

Blankwaardt, W. "De Factorij der Oostindische Compagnie te Ayuthia." *Neerlandia* 25 (1921).

———. "Notes upon Relations between Holland and Siam." *Journal of the Siam Society* 20 (1926–27): 241–258.

Bluche, François. *Louis XIV*. Paris: Fayard, 1986.

Boisselier, Jean. *La sculpture en Thaïlande*: Fribourg: Office du Livre, 1974.

———. *La peinture en Thaïlande*. Fribourg: Office du Livre, 1976.

Boonyakanchana, Chaveelak. *Thai Reference Books and their History.* Bangkok: Library Science Papers, 1987.

Bosmans, Henri, ed., "Correspondance de Jean-Baptiste Maldonado de Mons, missionnaire belge au Siam et en Chine au XVIIe siècle." In *Annalectes pour servir à l'histoire ecclésiastique de Belgique*, 36 (1910), 39–86; 187–239.

Bourges, Jacques de. *Relation du voyage de Monseigneur l'Evêque de Béryte, vicaire apostolique du royaume de la Cochinchine, par la Turquie, la Perse, les Indes, etc. jusqu'au royaume de Siam et autres lieux, par M. de Bourges, prêtre, missionnaire apostolique.* Paris: D. Bechet, 1666.

Bouvet, Joachim. *Voyage de Siam.* Edited by J. C. Gatty. Leiden: E. J. Brill, 1963.

Bowring, Sir John. *The Kingdom and People of Siam.* 2 vols. London: John W. Parker, 1857.

Boxer, Charles Ralph. *The Dutch Seaborne Empire (1600–1800).* London: Hutchinson, 1965.

———. *The Portuguese Seaborne Empire (1415–1825).* London: Hutchinson, 1969.

———. *Jan Compagnie in Oorlog en Vrede. Beknopte geschiedenis van de VOC.* Bussum: De Boer Maritiem, 1977.

Breazeale, Kennon. "Inventaire des documents sur le Siam conservés aux archives de Paris." *Journal of the Siam Society* 62 (1974): 149–206.

Bracciolini, Gianfrancesco Poggio. *De Varietate Fortunae libri quattuor* (1447). Paris: Oliva, 1723.

Bruijn, J. R., F. S. Gaastra, and I. Schöffer. *Dutch-Asiatic Shipping in the 17th and 18th Centuries.* 3 vols. The Hague: M. Nijhoff, 1979–1987.

Brummelhuis, Han ten. *Merchant, Courtier and Diplomat: A History of the Contacts between the Netherlands and Thailand.* Lochem: De Tijdstroom, 1987.

Burnay, Jean. "Notes chronologiques sur les missions jésuites du Siam au XVIIe siècle." *Archivum Historicum Societatis Jesu* 22 (1953): 170–202.

Campos, Joaquim de. "Early Portuguese Accounts of Thailand." *Journal of the Siam Society* 32/1 (1940): 1–27.

Carré, Barthélemy. *Voyage des Indes orientales, mêlé de plusieurs histoires curieuses.* 2 vols. Paris: C. Barbin, 1699.

———. *The Travels of the Abbé Carré in India and the Near East, 1672 to 1674.* Translated from the manuscript journal by Lady Fawcett and edited by Sir Charles Fawcett. 3 vols. London: Hakluyt Society, 1947–1948.

Catz, Rebecca. *Fernão Mendes Pinto. Sátira e anti-cruzada na Peregrinação.* Lisbon: Instituto de Cultura portuguesa, 1981.

Cauche, François. *Relation du voyage . . . à Madagascar, isles adjacantes et reste d'Afrique.* Paris: A. Courbe, 1651.

Céberet, Claude. *Journal du voyage de Siam.* Edited by M. Jacq-Hergoualc'h. Paris: L'Harmattan, 1992.

Challe, Robert. *Journal d'un voyage fait aux Indes orientales 1690–1691.* Edited by F. Deloffre and M. Menemencioglu. 2 vols. Paris: Mercure de France, 1983.

———. *Journal du voyage des Indes orientales.* Edited by J. Popin and F. Deloffre. Geneva: Droz, 1998. [First hitherto unknown version of Challe's Journal, containing the *Relation* of La Touche (see infra).]

Chandler, David. *A History of Cambodia.* Chiang Mai: Silkworm Books, 1996.

Chang, Kun. *A Comparative Study of the Kathinavastu.* The Hague: Mouton, 1957.

Chappoulie, Henri. *Aux origines d'une Église. Rome et les Missions d'Indochine au XVIIe siècle.* 2 vols. Paris: Bloud & Gay, 1943, 1948.

Charpentier, François. *Discours d'un fidèle sujet du Roi touchant l'établissement d'une Compagnie française pour le commerce des Indes orientales, adressé à tous les Français.* Paris, 1664.

Chaumont, Alexandre de. *Relation de l'ambassade de Mr le Chevalier de Chaumont à la cour du roi de Siam, et ce qui s'est passé de plus remarquable durant son voyage.* Paris: Seneuze & Horthemels, 1686.

Chaumont, Alexandre de, and François-Timoléon de Choisy. *Aspects of the Embassy to Siam 1685.* Translated and edited by Michael Smithies. Chiang Mai: Silkworm Books, 1997.

Choisy, François-Timoléon de. *Journal du voyage de Siam fait en 1685 et 1686.* Paris: Mabre-Cramoisy, 1687; Amsterdam: P. Mortier, 1687. [Modern ed. presented and annotated by D. Van der Cruysse. Paris: Fayard, 1995.]

———. *Journal of a Voyage to Siam 1685–1686.* Translated and introduced by Michael Smithies. Kuala Lumpur: Oxford University Press, 1993.

———. *Mémoires pour servir à l'histoire de Louis XIV.* Utrecht: Van de Water, 1727. [Modern ed. presented and annotated by G. Mongrédien. Paris: Mercure de France, 1983.]

Coedès, Georges, ed. "Siamese Documents of the Seventeenth Century." *Journal of the Siam Society* 14/2 (1921): 7–39.

Collis, Maurice. *Siamese White.* London: Faber & Faber, 1936.

———. *The Grand Peregrination, being the Life and Adventures of Fernão Mendes Pinto.* London: Faber & Faber, 1949.

Coolhaas, W. Ph., ed. *Generale Missiven van Gouverneurs-Generaal en Raden aan Heren XVII der Verenigde Oostindische Compagnie.* Vols. 1–5. The Hague: M. Nijhoff, 1960–1975.

Cornu, Philippe. *Dictionnaire encyclopedique du Bouddhisme.* Paris: Le Seuil, 2001.

Cortesão, Jaime. *L'Expansion des Portugais dans l'histoire de la civilisation.* Lisbon: Imprensa Nacional, 1983.

———. *História dos Descobrimentos portugueses.* Lisbon: Livros Horizonte, 1979.

Cotoni, Marie-Hélène. "Dépaysement, dissonances, diatribe: André Destouches à Siam." In *Le siècle de Voltaire: Hommage à René Pomeau* (1987), I, 291–303.

Coutre, Jacques de. *Aziatische Omzwervingen. Het leven van Jaques de Coutre, een Brugs diamanthandelaar, 1591–1627.* Edited by Johan Verberckmoes and Eddy Stols. Berchem-Antwerp: EPO, 1988.

———. *Andanzas asiáticas.* Edited by E. Stols, B. Teensma, and J. Verberckmoes. Crónicas de America 61 series, Historia 16. Madrid: Información y Revistas, 1990.

Coward, Barry. *The Stuart Age: England, 1603–1714.* London/New York: Longman, 1994.

Dangeau, Marquis de. *Journal.* Edited by Soulié. 18+1 vols. Paris: Firmin Didot, 1854–1860.

Daniel-Rops, *L'Eglise des temps classiques,* vol. 2: *L'ère des grands craquements.* Paris: Fayard, 1958.

Davis, Bonnie. *The Siam Society under Five Reigns.* Bangkok: The Siam Society, 1989.

Delouche, Gilles. *Contribution à une hypothèse de datation d'un poème thaï: le 'Kansuan Siprat.'* Paris: La Sorbonne Nouvelle, 1982.

Desfarges. *Relation des révolutions arrivées à Siam dans l'année 1688.* Amsterdam: P. Brunet, 1691.

Deslandes-Boureau, André-François. *Histoire de M. Constance, Premier Ministre du roi de Siam.* Amsterdam: Duchesne, 1756.

Dessert, Daniel, La Royale. *Vaisseaux et marins du Roi-Soleil.* Paris: Fayard, 1996.

Dhani Nivat, Prince, and Erik Seidenfaden. "Early Trade Relations between Denmark and Siam." *Journal of the Siam Society* 31/1 (1939): 1–15.

Dhani Nivat, Prince. *A History of Buddhism in Siam.* Bangkok: The Siam Society, 1965.

Dhiradhamrong, Sathon Prayoon. "A la découverte de la Thaïlande sur les traces du P. Guy Tachard (1686–1689)." Ph. D. thesis, University of Caen, 1965.

Dhiravat na Pombejra. "Researching Thai Institutional History of the 17th Century at the *Algemeen Rijksarchief.*" *Itinerario* 4/2 (1980).

———. "A Political History of Siam under the Prasatthong Dynasty (1629–1688)." Ph. D. thesis, London University, 1984.

———. "Crown Trade and Court Politics in Ayutthaya during the Reign of King Narai (1656–1688)." In *The Southeast Asian Port and Polity,* edited by J. Kathirithamby-Wells and J. Villiers, 127–142. Singapore: Singapore University Press, 1990.

Duyvendak, J. J. L. "The First Siamese Embassy to Holland." *T'oung Pao* 32 (1936): 285–292.

Eade, J. C. *South East Asian Ephemeris.* Ithaca: Cornell University Press, 1989.

Evelyn, John. *Diary.* Edited by E. S. de Beer. Oxford: Clarendon Press, 1985.

Fénelon, François de Salignac de La Mothe-. "Sermon pour la fete de l'Epiphanie, sur la vocation des gentils." *Oeuvres,* Pléiade, I, 827–844.

Flacourt, Etienne de. *Histoire de la grande isle de Madagascar.* Paris: P. Lamy, 1658; Edited by Cl. Allibert. Paris: Inalco-Karthala, 1995.

Fleury, Claude. "Mémoire sur les études des missions orientales, dédié à Mgr Laneau, évêque de Métellopolis (3 mars 1689)." In *Oeuvres de l'abbé de Fleury,* 63–87. Paris: Desrez, 1837.

Forbin, Claude de. *Le voyage du comte de Forbin au Siam.* Cadeilhan: Zulma, 1991.

———. *Mémoires.* Michaud-Poujoulat, Paris, 1839. [New edition edited by M. Cuénin. Paris: Mercure de France, 1993].

———. *The Siamese Memoirs of Count Claude de Forbin.* Introduced and edited by Michael Smithies. Chiang Mai: Silkworm Books, 1996.

Forest, Alain. "Principes, fondements, et aspects de l'action des missionnaires français (Missions étrangères de Paris) au Siam dans la 2e moitié du XVIIe siècle." In *Catholicisme et Société asiatiques,* edited by Alain Forest and Yoshiharu Tsuboi, 105–132. Paris: L'Harmattan, 1988; Tokyo: Sophia University, 1988.

———. *Les missionnaires français au Tonkin et au Siam (XVIIe–XVIIIe siècles). Analyse comparée d'un relatif succès et d'un total échec.* Vol. 1, *Histoires du Siam.* Paris: L'Harmattan, 1998.

Frédéric, Louis. *Sud-est asiatique. Ses temples, ses sculptures.* Paris: Arts et Métiers graphiques, 1964.

Freitas, Frei Serafim de. *Do justo império asiático dos Portugueses.* 2 vols. Translated by Marcello Caetano. Lisbon: Instituto Nacional de Investigação Científica, 1983.

A Full and True Relation of the Great and Wonderful Revolution that happened lately in the Kingdom of Siam in the East-Indies. London: R. Taylor, 1690.

Gaastra, F.S. *Bewind en beleid bij de VOC 1672–1702.* Zutphen: Walburg Pers, 1989.

———. *De geschiedenis van de VOC.* Zutphen: De Walburg Pers, 1991.

Gabaude, L. *Le Bouddhisme en Thaïlande.* Paris: Présence du Bouddhisme, 1986.

Gallois, Etienne, *L'ambassade de Siam au XVIIe siècle.* Paris, E. Panckoucke, 1862.

Gatty, Janette. "Le *Voyage de Siam* du P. Bouvet." *Cahiers de l'Association Internationale des Études Françaises* 27 (1975): 123–141.

Gervaise, Nicolas. *Histoire naturelle et politique du royaume de Siam.* Paris: C. Barbin, 1688.

———. *The Natural and Political History of the Kingdom of Siam.* Translated and edited with an introduction and notes by John Villiers. Bangkok: White Lotus, 1989.

Giblin, R. W. "The Abbé de Choisy, Libertine, Missionary, Academician." *Journal of the Siam Society* 8/3 (1911): 1–16.

Giteau, Madelaine. *Angkor. Un peuple - Un Art.* Paris: Bibliothèque des Arts, 1976.

Grignon, Pierre. *Journal du voyage de Jean Parmentier de Dieppe à l'île de Sumatra en l'année 1529.* Paris, A. Pinard [1832].

Groslier, B. P. *Angkor et le Cambodge au XVIe siècle d'après les sources portugaises et espagnoles.* Paris, 1958.

Guennou, Jean. *Missions étrangères de Paris.* Paris: Fayard, 1986.

Hakluyt, Richard. *The Principal Navigations, Voyages, Traffiques & Discoveries of the English Nation.* 8 vols. London: J. M. Dent & Sons, 1927.

———. *The Voyages, Traffiques & Discoveries of Foreign Voyagers.* 2 vols. London: J. M. Dent & Sons, 1928.

Hall, D. G. E. *A History of South-East Asia.* 4th ed. London: Macmillan, 1987.

Haudrère, Philippe. "La Compagnie française des Indes au XVIIIe siècle d'après les sources portugaises et espagnoles." Thesis. 2 vols. Paris, 1989.

Heeck, Gijsbrecht. "Derde Voyagie van Gijsbrecht Heeck naer Oost-Indien." Edited by S. P. L'Honore Naber. *Marineblad 25* (1910–1911), 422–450.

Het Leven en Daden van d'Heer Constantyn Phaulcon, Eerste geheyme Raad van het Koningrijk Siam, zynde een nader verhaal van 't gene in 't jaar 1688 in 't Koningrijk Siam is voorgevallen. Leiden: Fr. Haaring, 1692.

Hooykaas, R. *Humanism and the Voyages of Discovery in 16th century Portuguese Science and Letters.* 1979.

Hutchinson, E. W. "The French Foreign Mission in Siam during the XVIIth Century." *Journal of the Siam Society* 26 (1933): 1–71.

———. "Phaulkon's House at Lopburi." *Journal of the Siam Society* 27 (1934): 1–7.

———. "Four French State Manuscripts relating to Embassies between France and Siam in the XVIIth Century." *Journal of the Siam Society* 27 (1934): 183–244.

———. "The Retirement of the French Garrison from Bangkok in the year 1688." *Journal of the Siam Society* 28 (1935): 37–77.

———. "A French Garrison at Bangkok in 1687–1688." *Journal of the Siam Society* 31 (1939): 119–135.

———. *Adventurers in Siam in the Seventeenth Century.* London: The Royal Asiatic Society, 1940.

Isle, Claude de l'. *Relation historique du royaume de Siam.* Paris: G. de Luyne, 1684.

Israel, Jonathan. *Dutch Primacy in World Trade (1585–1740).* Oxford: Clarendon Press, 1989.

Jacq-Hergoualc'h, Michel. "Les ambassadeurs siamois à Versailles le 1er septembre 1686, dans un bas-relief en bronze d'Antoine Coysevox." *Journal of the Siam Society* 72 (1984): 19–36.

———. "A propos des canons siamois, offerts à Louis XIV, qui participèrent à la prise de la Bastille." *Annales historiques de la Révolution française* 261 (July–Sept. 1985): 317–334.

———. *Etude historique et critique du Journal du voyage de Siam de Claude Céberet, envoyé extraordinaire du Roi en 1687 et 1688.* Paris: L'Harmattan, 1992.

———. *L'Europe et le Siam du XVIe au XVIIIe siècle: Apports culturels.* Paris: L'Harmattan, 1993.

———, ed. *Phra Naraï, roi de Siam, et Louis XIV.* 2 vols. Paris: Musée Guimet, 1986 (exhibition catalogue).

Jacqueline, B. "L'esprit missionnaire de la S. C. *De Propaganda Fide* d'après les Instructions aux vicaires apostoliques . . . " *Documents Omnis Terra,* 81:5 (May 1971), 330–345.

Jit-Kasem Sibunruang, "L'âge d'or de la poésie thaïlandaise: la littérature à l'époque de Phra Narai." In *Phra Narai, roi de Siam, et Louis XIV,* edited by Michel Jacq-Hergoualc'h. Paris: Musée Guimet, 1986.

Johnson, Donald Clay. A Guide to Reference Materials on Southeast Asia based on the Collections in the Yale and Cornell University Libraries. New Haven/London: Yale University Press, 1970.

The Journey of William of Rubruck to the Eastern Parts of the World. Translated by William Woodville Rockhill. London: Hakluyt Society, 1900.

Kaempfer, Engelbert. *A Description of the Kingdom of Siam (1690).* Bangkok: White Orchid Press, 1987.

Kaeppelin, Paul. *Les origines de l'Inde française. La Compagnie des Indes orientales et François Martin.* Paris: Challamel, 1908.

———. *Les escales françaises sur la route de l'Inde. 1638–1931.* Paris: Challamel, 1908.

Keay, John. *The Honourable Company. A History of the English East India* Company. London: HarperCollins, 1993.

Keeling, W. "A Journall of the Third Voyage to the East Indies, set out by the Company of the Merchants, trading in those parts. In which Voyage were imployed three ships, viz. the *Dragon,* the *Hector* and the *Consent,* and in them the number of three hundred and ten persons, or thereabouts: written by Captain William Keeling, Chief Commander." In *Hakluytus Posthumus or Purchas His Pilgrimes,* ed. Samuel Purchas, vol. 1. 1625.

Keijts, Johan. *Beknopt Verhael van de wonderlijke veranderingen voorgevallen in 't koningrijck van Siam in 't jaer 1688.* Amsterdam, 1689.

Kemp, Jeremy. *Aspects of Siamese Kingship in the Seventeenth Century.* Bangkok: Social Science Association Press, 1969.

Knox, Robert. *An Historical Relation of the Island Ceylon in the East-Indies, together with an Account of the Detaining in Captivity the Author and divers other Englishmen now Living there, and of the Author's Miraculous Escape.* London: R. Chiswell, 1681.

[La Haye & Caron]. *Journal du voyage des Grandes Indes, contenant tout ce qui s'y est fait par l'Escadre de Sa Majesté envoyée sous le commandement de M. de La Haye, depuis son départ de La Rochelle de mars 1670.* 2 vols. Paris: Pepie, 1698.

La Loubère, Simon de. *Du royaume de Siam.* 2 vols. Paris: Coignard, 1691. [Modern ed. introduced and annotated by M. Jacq-Hergoualc'h. Paris: Éditions Recherche sur les Civilisations, 1987.]

———. *A New Historical Relation of the Kingdom of Siam.* London, 1693. [Facsimile ed. with an introduction by David Wyatt. Singapore: Oxford University Press, 1986.]

La Roncière, Charles de. *Histoire de la Marine française. IV: Le crépuscule du Grand Règne.* Paris: Plon, 1932.

La Touche. "Relation de ce qui est arrivé dans le royaume de Siam en 1688." In R. Challe, *Journal du voyage des Indes orientales,* edited by J. Popin and F. Deloffre, 301–337. Geneva: Droz, 1998.

Lacouture, Jean. *Jésuites: une multibiographie.* 2 vols. Paris: Le Seuil, 1991.

Lancaster, Sir James. *The Voyages of Sir James Lancaster to Brazil and the East Indies, 1591–1603.* Edited by Sir William Foster. London: Hakluyt Society, 1940.

Laneau, Louis. *Salut des infidèles et baptême.* Paris: Centre de Recherche théologique missionnaire, 1988.

Lanier, Lucien. *Etude historique sur les relations de la France et du royaume de Siam de 1662 à 1703.* Versailles: Aubert, 1883.

Launay, Adrien. *Siam et les missionnaires français.* Tours: Mame, 1896.

———, ed. *Histoire de la mission de Siam. Documents historiques.* 2 vols. Paris: Société des Missions étrangères, 1920.

Lavisse, Ernest. *Louis XIV.* 2 vols. Paris: Tallandier, 1978.

Lawson, Philip. *The East India Company: A History.* London/New York: Longman, 1993.

Le Blanc, Marcel. *Histoire de la révolution de Siam arrivée en 1688 et de l'état présent des Indes.* 2 vols. Lyons: Horace Molin, 1692.

Le Comte, Louis. *Nouveaux mémoires sur l'état présent de la Chine, 1687–1692.* Edited by Fr. Touboul-Bouyeure. Paris: Phébus, 1990.

Le Gentil, Georges. *Fernão Mendes Pinto. Un précurseur de l'exotisme au XVIe siècle.* Paris: Herman et Cie, 1947.

Lemmens, Leon. *Geschichte der Franziskanermissionen,* Munster: 1929.

Leonowens, Anna Hariette. *The English Governess at the Siamese Court. Recollections of Six Years in the Royal Palace at Bangkok* (1870). Singapore: Oxford University Press, 1988.

Lettres de Monseigneur Pallu. Edited by Adrien Launay. n.d., n.p.

Lingat, Robert. "Une lettre de Véret sur la révolution siamoise de 1688." *T'oung Pa* 31 (1935): 330–362.

Manich Jumsai, M.L. "Le grand roi Narai." In *Phra Narai, roi de Siam, et Louis XIV,* edited by Michel Jacq-Hergoualc'h. Paris: Musée Guimet, 1986.

———. *The Story of King Narai and his Ambassador to France in 1686, Kosaparn*. Bangkok: Chalermnit, 1987.

Martin, François. *Mémoires, 1665–1696*. 3 vols. Paris: Société de l'Histoire des Colonies françaises, 1931–1934.

Mendes da Luz, Francisco, ed. *Regimento da Casa da ändia*. Lisbon: Ministério da Educação e Cultura, 1992.

Mendes Pinto, Fernão. *Peregrinação*. Lisbon: Imprensa Nacional-Casa da Moeda, 1998.

Merrien, Jean. *La vie quotidienne des marins au temps du Roi Soleil*. Paris: Hachette, 1964.

Meynard, André-Marie. *Missions dominicaines dans l'Extrême-Orient*. 2 vols. Lyon and Paris: Bauchu et Cie, 1865.

Moquet, Jean. *Voyage à Mozambique et Goa (1607–1610)*. Paris: Chandeigne, 1996.

Morais, Carlos Alexandre de. *Cronologia geral da ändia Portuguesa*. Lisbon: Editorial Estampa, 1997.

Morson, Ian. *Four Hundred Years - The British and the Thais*. Bangkok: Nai Suk, 1999.

Muhammad Ibrahim Muhammad Rabi, Ibn, *The Ship of Sulaiman*. Translated from the Persian by John O'Kane. Persian Heritage Series, no. 11. London: Routledge & Kegan Paul, 1972.

Narada Maha Thera. *The Buddha and His Teachings*. Colombo: Vajirârâma, 1973.

Naudou, Jean. *Le Bouddha*, Paris: Somogy, 1973.

Noguette, Robert. *Relation du voyage et des missions du royaume de Siam ès années 1681 et 1683*. Chartres: E. Massot, 1683.

Orléans, Pierre-Joseph d'. *Histoire de M. Constance premier ministre du roi de Siam, et de la dernière révolution de cet État*. Paris: D. Horthemels, 1690.

Pallegoix, Jean-Baptiste. *Description du royaume Thaï ou Siam, comprenant la topographie, histoire naturelle, moeurs et coutumes, législation, commerce, langue, etc*. 2 vols. Paris, 1854.

Pallu, François. *Relation abrégée des missions et des voyages des évêques français aux royaumes de la Chine, Cochinchine, Tonquin et Siam*. Paris: D. Bechet, 1668.

Parry, John H. *Trade and Dominion: The European Oversea Empires in the Eighteenth Century*. London: Weidenfeld & Nicholson, 1971.

Patipat Pumpongphet. "Les fouilles archéologiques dans Mu Ban Portuget sur le site de São Pedro." In *Phra Naraï roi de Siam et Louis XIV*, edited by M. Jacq-Hergoualc'h. Paris: Musée Guimet, 1986.

Pauliat, Louis. *Louis XIV et la Compagnie des Indes orientales de 1664*. Paris: Calmann-Lévy, 1886.

Pelliot, Paul. "Les relations du Siam et de la Hollande en 1608." *T'oung Pao* 32 (1936): 223–229.

Phuthorn Bhudamon. "La recherche historique sur Phra Naraï: points de controverse et idées nouvelles." In *Phra Naraï, roi de Siam, et Louis XIV*, edited by Michel Jacq-Hergoualc'h. Paris: Musée Guimet, 1986, 31–33.

Pinya. "A History of the French Missions to Siam." *The Imperial and Asiatic Quarterly Review*, series 3, vol. 11 (1901), 331–343.

Piriya Krairiksh. *The Sacred Image. Sculptures from Thailand.* Cologne, 1979 (exhibition catalogue.)

Porée, Charles-Gabriel. *La Mandarinade, ou Histoire comique du mandarinat de M. l'abbé de Saint-Martin, marquis de Miskou.* The Hague: P. Paupic, 1738.

Pothisoonthorn, Visantanee, et al. *Phra Narai Ratchanivet.* Bangkok: Department of Fine Arts, 1988.

Pouchot de Chantassin, Claude-Michel. *Relation du voyage et retour des Indes orientales pendant les années 1690 et 1691.* Paris, 1692.

Primo Volume delle Navigationi e Viaggi of Giambattista Ramusio. Venice, 1550.

Pyrard de Laval, François. *Voyage aux Indes orientales (1601–1611).* 2 vols. Paris: Chandeigne, 1998.

Quaritch-Wales, H. G. *Siamese State Ceremonies.* London: B. Quaritch, 1931.

Raben, Remco, and Dhiravat na Pombejra, eds. *In the King's Trail. An 18th Century Dutch Journey to the Buddha's Footprint. Theodorus Jacobus van den Heuvel's account of his voyage to Phra Phuttabat in 1737.* Bangkok: The Royal Netherlands Embassy, 1997.

Ramusio, Giovanni Battista. *Primo volume delle Navigationi e Viaggi.* Venice: L. Giunti, 1550.

Raynal, Guillaume-Thomas. *Histoire philosophique et politique des établissements et du commerce des Européens dans les deux Indes.* 4 vols. Geneva: Jean Léonard Pellet, 1780.

Records of the Relations between Siam and Foreign Countries in the 17th Century, copied from Papers Preserved at the India Office. 5 vols. Bangkok: Vajirañana National Library, 1915–1921.

Reid, Anthony. *Southeast Asia in the Age of Commerce 1450–1680.* 2 vols. Chiang Mai: Silkworm Books, 1988, 1993.

Relation des missions et voyages des évêques vicaires apostoliques et de leurs ecclésiastiques ès années 1676 et 1677. Paris: Charles Angot, 1680.

Ricci Matteo, and Nicholas Trigault. *Histoire de l'expédition chrétienne au royaume de la Chine, 1582–1610.* New ed. of French trans. of 1617. Paris, Desclée de Brouwer, 1978.

Roques, Georges. *La manière de négocier aux Indes, 1676–1691.* Edited by V. Bérinstain. Paris: Maisonneuve & Larose, 1996.

Satow, E. M. "Notes on the Intercourse between Japan and Siam in the Seventeenth Century." *Transactions of the Asiatic Society of Japan* 13/2 (1885): 139–210.

Schama, S. *Citizens. A Chronicle of the French Revolution.* New York: Knopf, 1989.

Schouten, Joost. *A Description of the Government, Might, Religion, Customes, Traffick and other remarkable Affairs in the Kingdom of Siam.* Translated by Roger Manley. London, 1671. [Facsimile ed., Bangkok: The Siam Society, 1986.]

Serrão, Joaquim Veríssimo. *História de Portugal. vols. 2–4: 1415–1640.* Lisbon: Editorial Verbo, 1979–1980.

Shearer, Alistair. *Thailand, the Lotus Kingdom.* London: John Murray, 1989.

Sioris, George A. *Phaulkon, the Greek First Counsellor at the Court of Siam: an Appraisal.* Bangkok: The Siam Society, 1998.

Sitsayamkan, Luang. *The Greek Favourite of the King of Siam.* Singapore: Donald Moore Press, 1967.

Smith, George Vinal. *The Dutch in Seventeenth-Century Thailand.* Dekalb: Northern Illinois University Press, 1977.

Smithies, Michael. "The Ladies at Versailles on 1st September 1686. A Note on the Coysevox Bronze." *The Siam Society Newsletter* 2/2 (June 1986): 3–7.

———. *The Siamese Embassy to the Sun King. The Personal Memorials of Kosa Pan.* Bangkok: Duang Kamol, 1990.

———. "Robert Challe and Siam." *Journal of the Siam Society* 81/1 (1993): 91–102.

———. "Jacques de Bourges (c.1630–1714) and Siam." *Journal of the Siam Society* 81/2 (1993), 113–129.

———. *Descriptions of Old Siam.* Kuala Lumpur: Oxford University Press, 1995.

———. *A Resounding Failure: Martin and the French in Siam 1672–1693.* Chiang Mai: Silkworm Books, 1998.

———. "Siamese mandarins on the Grand Tour, 1688–1690." *Journal of the Siam Society* 86 (1998): 107–118.

———. *A Siamese Embassy lost in Africa, 1686: The Odyssey of Ok-khun Chamnan.* Chiang Mai: Silkworm Books, 1999.

———, ed. and trans. *The Discourses at Versailles of the first Siamese Ambassadors to France 1686–7, together with the list of their Presents to the Court, in the original French together with a translation into English.* Bangkok: The Siam Society, 1986.

———, ed. *Three Military Accounts of Events in Siam in 1688: Desfarges, de La Touche, and Vollant des Verquain.* In press.

Snellgrove, David L. *The Image of the Buddha.* Unesco: Serindia Publications, 1978.

Sousa, Alfredo Botelho da. *Subsídios para a história militar marítima da ändia, 1585–1650.* Vol. 1. Lisbon, 1930.

Sottas, Jules. *Histoire de la Compagnie royale des Indes orientales 1664–1719.* Paris: Plon, 1905.

Souchu de Rennefort, Urbain. *Relation du premier voyage de la Compagnie des Indes orientales en l'île de Madagascar ou Dauphine.* Paris: P. Auboüin, 1668.

———. *Mémoires pour servir à l'histoire des Indes orientales.* Paris: A. Seneuze, 1688.

Sourches, Marquis de. *Mémoires.* 13 vols. Edited by J. de Cosnac. Paris: Hachette, 1882–1893.

State Papers of the Kingdom of Siam, 1664–1886. London: Ridgeway, 1886.

Subrahmanyam, Sanjay. *L'empire portugais d'Asie 1500–1700. Histoire politique et économique.* Paris: Maisonneuve & Larose, 1999.

Sy, H. "Le sermon de Fénelon sur la vocation des gentils." *Revue d'histoire des missions* September 1955, 321–338.

Syamananda, Rong. *A History of Thailand.* Bangkok: Thai Watana Panich, 1988.

———. *Histoire des Indes orientales.* Paris: A. Seneuze, 1688.

Tachard, Guy. *Voyage de Siam des Pères Jésuites envoyés par le Roi aux Indes et à la Chine.* Paris: Seneuze & Horthemels, 1686; Amsterdam: P. Mortier, 1687; London, 1688.

———. *Second voyage du Père Tachard et des Jésuites envoyés par le Roi au royaume de Siam.* Paris: Horthemels, 1689; Amsterdam: P. Mortier, 1689.

Tambiah, S. J. *World Conqueror and World Renouncer. A Study of Buddhism and Polity in Thailand against a Historical Background.* Cambridge: Cambridge University Press, 1976.

Tarling, Nicholas, ed. The Cambridge History of Southeast Asia. 2 vols. Cambridge: Cambridge University Press, 1999.

Terpstra, H. *De Factorij der Oostindische Compagnie te Patani.* The Hague: Nijhoff, 1938.

The Travels of Mendes Pinto. Edited and translated by Rebecca Catz. Chicago and London: Chicago University Press, 1989.

Thévenot, J. *Voyages aux Indes orientales.* Vol. 3. Paris: Charles Angot, 1689.

Thevet, André. *Les singularités de la France Antarctique, autrement nommée Amérique, et de plusieurs terres et isles découvertes de notre temps.* Paris: La Porte, 1557.

Thomaz de Bossière, Yves de. *Un Belge mandarin de la Cour de Chine aux XVIIe et XVIIIe siècle. Antoine Thomas (1644–1709), Ngan To P'ing-che.* Paris: Les Belles Lettres/Cathasia, 1977.

Turpin, François-Henri. *Histoire civile et naturelle du royaume de Siam, et des révolutions qui ont bouleversé cet Empire jusqu'en 1770.* 2 vols. Paris: Costard, 1771.

Vachet, Bénigne. *Mémoires* (extracts). Paris: Groupy, 1865.

Vale, Maria Teresa, ed., *Fernão Mendes Pinto. O outro lado do mito.* Lisbon: Terra livre, 1985.

Valentyn, François. *Description of the Cape of Good Hope with the matters concerning it.* 2 vols. Cape Town: Van Riebeeck Society, 1971, 1973. Bilingual ed. (Dutch/English), with introduction and annotation in Afrikaans.

Van der Chys, J. A. "Overzicht der betrekkingen van de Nederlandse Oostindische Compagnie met Siam." *Tijdschrift voor Indische taal-, land- en volkenkunde* 12 (1864): 417–456.

Van der Cruysse, Dirk. "Donneau de Visé et l'ambassade siamoise (1686): entre l'histoire et la littérature." *Papers on French Seventeenth Century Literature* 59 (1990): 199–208.

———."Lodewijk XIV en Siam: een hoofdstuk contrastieve mentaliteits-geschiedenis." In *Cultuurwetenschappen in beweging 1980–1990*, edited by Th. Venckeleer and W. Verbeke, 163–177. Louvain/Antwerp: Vlaamse Vereniging voor Cultuurwetenschappen, 1992.

———. "Jacques de Bourges au Siam (1662): splendeur et misères du discours exotique missionnaire." In *Mélanges offerts à Roger Duchêne*, 335–344. Tübingen: Gunther Narr, 1992.

———. "Aspects of Siamese-French Relations during the Seventeenth Century." *Journal of the Siam Society* 80/1 (1992): 63–69.

———. *L'abbé de Choisy, androgyne et mandarin*. Paris: Fayard, 1995.

———. "Connaissance ou méconnaissance de l'Orient? Images du Siam dans la littérature louis-quatorzienne." *French Literature Series* 23 (1996): 67–82.

———. "Choisy, historien du Siam et de l'Asie du Sud-Est." *Aséanie* 1 (1998): 107–122.

———. *Franse Aziëreizigers in de 17de eeuw*. Brussels: Academiae Analecta, 2000.

Van Linschoten, Jan Huyghen. *Reys-geschrift vande navigatiën der Portugaloysers in Orienten*. Amsterdam: Cornelis Claesz., 1595.

———. *Itinerario, voyage ofte schipvaert naer Oost ofte Portugaels Indien*. Amsterdam: Cornelis Claesz., 1596.

Van Neijenrode, Cornelis, *Vertoog van de Gelegenheid des Koninkrijks Siam (1621)*. In *Kroniek van het Historisch Genootschap gevestigd te Utrecht*, vol. 27 (1871): 279–318.

Van Vliet, Jeremias. *Historical Account of Siam in the Seventeenth Century*. Translated by W. H. Mundie. Bangkok, 1904.

———. *Beschryving van het Koningryk Siam, mitsgaders het verhaal van den oorsprong, onderscheyd, polityke regering, d'ecclesiastique en costuymelijke huyshoudinge van d'edelen en borgerlijke lieden, alsmede den loop der negotie, en andere remarquable saaken des Koningryks Siam*. Leiden: Fr. Haaring, 1692. An English translation by L. F. van Ravenswaay was published in the *Journal of the Siam Society* 7/1, 5–105.

———. *The Short History of the Kings of Siam*. Bangkok: The Siam Society, 1975. Bilingual ed. in Dutch/English, presented by David Wyatt.

Vaumas, Guillaume de. *L'éveil missionnaire de la France au XVIIe siècle*. Paris: Bloud et Gay, 1959.

Verbiest, Ferdinand. *Correspondance de Ferdinand Verbiest*. Edited by H. Josson and L. Willaert. Brussels, 1939.

Vollant des Verquains, Jean. *Histoire de la révolution de Siam arrivée en l'année 1688*. Lille: J. Chr. Malte, 1691.

Wood, W. A. R. *A History of Siam from the Earliest Times to the Year 1781 with a Supplement Dealing with More Recent Events*. London, 1926.

Woodward, Hiram W. *The Sacred Sculpture of Thailand—The Alexander Griswold Collection*. Bangkok: River Books, 1997.

Wyatt, David K. "A Persian Mission to Siam in the Reign of King Narai." *Journal of the Siam Society* 62/2 (1974): 151–157.

———. *Thailand. A Short History*. New Haven/London: Yale University Press, 1984.

INDEX OF PERSONS

GEOGRAPHICAL INDEX

INDEX OF SHIPS